Privatization
A Systems Perspective

by
Walter Sobkiw

Published by

C~B
CassBeth

Published by Cassbeth, Egg Harbor Township, New Jersey, USA

First Edition

Library of Congress Control Number 2019954305

ISBN: 978-0-9832530-6-8 (hardcover)

This book is dedicated to our children, their children, and all the future generations.

It is for them, their families, and their world.

Preface

In 2008 I was requested to support universities to help bring back systems thinking and systems engineering as practiced in our industrial base and government from approximately 1945 to 1995. This led me to write two university textbooks on systems engineering, develop course material, teach, and help to establish and shape the direction of university systems engineering curriculum and master's degrees.

Many times, I was asked if this knowledge should be offered outside traditional engineering programs. Each time my response was no because I wanted roots to be established within the engineering education programs. I now realize that systems knowledge needs to be embedded in all forms of education at all levels.

I grew up in a very different world where systems knowledge and thinking were a way of life. It was everywhere. I first learned about it in elementary school when we were taught that we had a system of government, how the system was structured, how it operated, and why we had this system of government.

Just like systems thinking, knowledge, and engineering has disappeared in most companies and government, it has also disappeared from our social fabric. This has resulted in many negative consequences as we struggle to figure out what is happening and how to correct course for a better future.

My previous books were about teaching systems engineering, systems design and systems thinking. This book is about applying this very powerful approach to understanding and solving problems associated with the fundamental system change that is Privatization.

This book provides some privatization history, offers a system view of the situation, identifies unintended consequences, makes comparisons between pre and post privatization time frames, and offers recommendations for moving forward in this new century. The book is divided into multiple sections:

- Introduction
- Privatization Recent History
- Industrial Base
- Universities and Colleges
- Air Transportation
- Federal Aviation Administration
- Privatized Workers
- Federal Government
- Systems Perspectives
- Supporting Information
- Privatization System Conclusions

I considered adding significant content from my previous textbooks to try and offer insight into systems thinking, design, and engineering but I realized the key message in this book would be lost. I encourage readers to seek out my textbooks if they are interested in systems. There is a systems perspectives section that some may view as large, but it is small compared to the full knowledge base.

This book started as standalone papers beginning in 2017 on the effects of privatization. They were offered to colleagues, anyone that was interested, and to elected representatives.

Why did I decide to write this book?

I attended a faculty meeting in 2019 where the topic of discussion was declining undergraduate and graduate education enrollments across the country. They had the data trends and understood the cyclic demographics but there was bewilderment because of the sharp declines. I could see that they were all educators and that they did not understand how our society could be walking away from education especially when we had become such a technologically complex society. As the discussion proceeded, I realized that I stumbled across key data while working on a paper on the unintended consequences of government shutdowns.

A few days after the faculty meeting, I added this key data to an existing paper and passed it to the University. This eventually went to the University government liaison group. It had a huge impact because they were unaware of this data. They were operating at a much higher level when interacting with other universities, companies, and the government. They were thankful for the data and the associated analysis. It was at that point that I decided to capture the work on privatization in this book.

My areas of study are systems engineering and systems application to complex technical and social challenges. I hope that you consider following the same studies.

This book like all my other books could use a great editor. It is filled with bad grammar, bad spelling, poor sentence structure, and just hard to read. All I can say is if you make it through this book you may enjoy the adventure. It may help add some positive value to your adventures. It may even help policy makers moving forward to make more informed decisions.

Enjoy the rest of the book.

Our focus is on privatization from a systems perspective.

Table of Contents

Figures

Tables

Systems Perspectives Privatization Observations

1 Introduction

Privatization is the shifting of government functions into the private sector. The government either joins with private sector companies or shifts all responsibility to the private sector companies to provide services previously performed by the government. The forms of privatization are:

- **Contract Labor, Outsourcing or Contracting Out:** A private company supplies a service to the government using taxpayer money.
- **Contracting Out:** This is an award of monopoly privilege to a private company to supply a service, with price regulation by a government agency.
- **Grants:** The government provides financial assistance to a private company to perform a service using taxpayer money.
- **Vouchers:** Consumers are subsidized by taxpayers and can spend the funds for a service provided by a private company.
- **Franchise Agreements:** The government grants monopoly rights to a private company to produce a given function or provide a service.

Beginning in 2017 I started writing papers on key topics of the day. They all had the same theme of privatization and how things went wrong. So, I decided to repackage and expand on the original papers. The papers are:

- **FAA Privatization:** In 2017 there was significant pressure to fully privatize the FAA. The question of full privatization was analyzed from a systems perspective and a report was prepared for consideration and provided to multiple stakeholders in and out of government.

- **Privatization Effects during Government Shutdowns:** In 2018-2019 the United States Government went into another shutdown due to budget issues directly related to the role of government. A systems perspective was used to perform the analysis and it became clear that a key stakeholder was left out of the entire shutdown and recovery activities, the new privatized workforce.

- **The Current State of US Air Travel:** The current state of US Air Travel is not good. Everyone knows this yet nothing is happening to correct the situation. The decline in US Air Travel has taken decades but now it has reached a point where the system is in serious trouble. This analysis used a systems perspective and reported on the condition of the US Air Travel Transportation System, how it may have arrived at this point and then offered potential suggestions for moving forward in a positive direction.

- **US Government Privatization Unintended Consequences**: Empirical data suggests that privatization has led to systemic government shutdowns and other negative unintended consequences. This analysis provided history, offered a system view of the situation, identified unintended consequences, made comparisons between pre and post privatization time frames, and offered recommendations for moving forward.

This book expands on the original content of these papers and includes new analysis, government documents, and other information like the systems perspectives section. The systems perspectives section is about systems engineering and thinking.

Some may ask what does systems engineering and thinking have to do with public policy like government privatization?

The USA is a new experiment in a system of government that was different form all previous forms of government. It is a system created by people who engaged in systematic thinking. We do not rely on warlords, dictators, monarchs or other approaches based on magic or blind faith. Instead we use common sense and science to try to understand the failures of humanity to then provide an effective system of governance based on checks and balances, transparency, and engaged citizens using laws and regulations to keep the system in balance. This system is found at the Federal, State, and Local levels of government in what may be called a hierarchical distributed architecture. So, not only do the Executive, Legislative, and Judicial branches check each other's power at all the government levels but also the Federal, State, and Local Governments check each other in a complex system architecture to ensure that Liberty and Freedom are preserved.

So, policy decisions should not be based on random requests from narrow vested interests. They need to be based on the roots of the country and those roots are common sense and science using systematic thinking and approaches.

The reality is systems are always in existence and systems always self-correct. The issue is when systems come out of balance it may take years, decades, a lifetime, or multiple lifetimes to self-correct. Our lifetimes are very short and that is why we must engage to correct our systems when they go out of balance and become bad or even toxic to our lives.

2 Privatization Recent History

The effort to privatize United States Government assets and functions started with President Reagans Executive Order 12607 President's Commission on Privatization. It resulted in the 1988 report, Privatization Toward More Effective Government. In 1992 Executive Order 12803 Infrastructure Privatization provided additional guidance on privatizing United States Government assets and functions.

This contrasts with the policy that existed from 1945 to 1987. As World War II was ending, President Roosevelt requested the Office of Scientific Research and Development to identify what the United States should do moving forward after the war. A report was produced called Science the Endless Frontier. This report set the tone and policy of the United States from 1945 to 1987.

This book focuses on the US Air Transportation System and the Federal Aviation Administration (FAA). It goes beyond those examples and what is clear is that there is now evidence to show that privatization has led to systemic government shutdowns and other negative unintended consequences including serious damage to the industrial base, colleges, universities, and the US Citizens.

2.1 Executive Orders

There are two key Presidential Executive Orders and a report that allowed for the privatization of a large portion of the Federal Civil Service.

- Executive Order 12607 President's Commission on Privatization 1987
- President's Commission on Privatization 1988
- Executive Order 12803 Infrastructure Privatization 1992

On September 2, 1987 President Reagan signed Executive Order 12607 President's Commission on Privatization. Its purpose was to investigate privatization of government functions and it included the creation of the President's Commission on Privatization[1]. This executive order is a key document because it clearly outlines the plan to privatize major portions of the US Federal Government and it started everything that was to follow in the coming decades.

Approximately 6 months later, on March 18, 1988, the President's Commission on Privatization published a 287-page report: Privatization Toward More Effective Government[2]. This was a plan to privatize existing government functions and assets.

---

[1] See section 10.1.1 EO-12607 President's Commission on Privatization.

[2] See section 10.1.2 Report of the President's Commission on Privatization.

On April 30, 1992 President Bush signed Executive Order 12803 Infrastructure Privatization. Its purpose was to have each executive department and agency identify assets for privatization.[3]

It was not until the President Clinton administration, when the Federal Activities Inventory Reform Act of 1998 became Public Law 105–2704, that serious action was taken towards privatizing the federal government. The FAIR Act was enacted to create a process for identifying the functions of the Federal Government that are not inherently governmental functions. The Act requires that each year Federal agencies produce a list of activities performed by Federal Government sources for the agency that, in the judgment of the agency head, are not inherently governmental in nature. As policy the Office of Management and Budget provides Circular A-76 Performance of Commercial Activities[5].

As of 2018 we see a major portion of the report Privatization Toward More Effective Government has been executed. In the 1980s many were sensitive to the needs of employees. At that time, it was important to ensure that second class workers were not created with lower salaries and benefits. This was part of the perception that the Federal Government, as the largest employer in the US, should set an example and not facilitate downward spirals. Ensuring and encouraging commerce and upward economic growth and mobility were part of the social fabric when this report was produced. The reports executive summary has the following words:

In addition, any recommendation supporting increased contracting out should be implemented only after full consideration has been given to employee interests.

This government policy was justified and coincident with policy attributed to game theory as described in the BBC television documentary by Adam Curtis The Trap What Happened to Our Dream of Freedom[6]. It originally aired in the United Kingdom on BBC in March 2007. Details of the privatization executive orders, reports, and the BBC television documentary are provided in section 10.1 Government Policy 1987 to Present.

This contrasts with the policies set after 1945. President Franklin D. Roosevelt requested a report from the Office of Scientific Research and Development on what can be done using the lessons learned during World War II. The request resulted in the report Science the Endless Frontier[7]. This report set the policy and tone of the

---

[3] See section 10.1.3 EO-12803 Infrastructure Privatization.

[4] See section 10.1.4 Federal Activities Inventory Reform Act of 1998.

[5] See section 10.1.5 Circular A-76 Performance of Commercial Activities.

[6] See section 10.1.6 The Trap What Happened to Our Dream of Freedom

[7] See section 10.2.1 Science the Endless Frontier

United States up until 1987 when it was abandoned, and the President's Commission on Privatization set the policy and tone of the United States. Details of the policy drivers are provided in section 10.2 Government Policy 1945 – 1981.

2.2 President's Commission on Privatization

The words in President Reagan's Executive Order 12607 the President's Commission on Privatization are interesting but what is more interesting are the words that are missing. The missing words are what criteria should be used when considering a government organization for privatization. For example, should defense and security be part of the criteria. What about stability? Which institutions should be used to take over the previous functions of the newly privatized organization? The questions continue.

Our society consists of many institution types. Each of these institutions have characteristics that allow them to thrive and provide the valuable services that someone somewhere thinks are needed. For example, expecting for profit companies to invest in going to the Moon is foolish. They expect to show profits typically on a short-term basis. Going to the Moon could be a rich person's folly but it is not a viable business. Yet a nation state via its government may conclude that it makes perfect sense to go to the Moon and is willing to make the investment.

Table 1 Institution Types

• Government	• Co-Operatives	• Religious
• Public Education	• For Profit Companies	• Charitable
• Utilities	• Non-Profits	

A fundamental question is: What is the purpose in privatizing a government organization? If the purpose of privatizing government is to reduce costs and or increase efficiency, that is not an appropriate answer because the government organization needs to be fixed to reduce costs and increase efficiency. If on the other hand the purpose of privatizing a government organization is to unleash a sustainable industrial base with many companies able to make immediate profits, then it is appropriate. This of course is in a setting where the taxpayer is properly reimbursed for this government organization that has assets that will be transferred to an entity or entities that the taxpayer does not own; although they could become shareholders. So, the criteria for determining which government organizations to privatize are critical to the implementation of Executive Order 12607.

2.3 Science the Endless Frontier

In 1945 the values of the country were such that the government was viewed as the only entity that could solve previously unsolvable problems. In this setting the report Science the Endless Frontier was produced, and it set the policy of the country for decades. The following are some key points found in the report.

Scientific Progress Is Essential
War Against Disease
National Security
Our Scientific Talent
Scientific Progress Is Essential
Science Is A Proper Concern of Government
Freedom of Inquiry Must Be Preserved
Broad and Basic Studies Needed
Science and The Public Welfare
Science and Jobs
The Importance of Basic Research
Research Within Government
Industrial Research
The Special Need for Federal Support
Renewal of Scientific Talent
Improve Quality Remove Barriers
Generation Must Not Be Lost
A Problem of Scientific Reconversion
Need for Coordination
Publication Should Be Encouraged
New Responsibilities for Government
Centers of Basic Research

Section 10.2.1 Science the Endless Frontier has the full report. This report is also maintained on the National Science Foundation Website.

2.4 Privatization Source[8]

The term "privatization" appeared in a book, Cutting Back City Hall in 1980 by Robert Poole. He co-founded the Reason Foundation, a libertarian organization, in 1978. The book provided support for Margaret Thatcher's privatization efforts in the United Kingdom. He advised the administrations of Ronald Reagan, George H.W. Bush, Bill Clinton, and George W. Bush on privatization and transportation policy. The Reason Foundation publishes the Annual Privatization Report (APR). The APR came from Reason Foundation Trustee David Koch[9].

The roots of privatization appear to come from the libertarian movement. From an elected representative perspective, the libertarians are far from the mainstream electorate as suggested by election results. Yet the idea of privatization has had a huge impact on the makeup of US government.

Privatization is an international trend impacting the entire planet. However, it is important to realize that privatization in another country may be very different than privatization in the US. For example, a country or system with no free market will experience the introduction of a free market commercial and industrial base with privatization. Privatization in a country or system with a free market commercial industrial base, like the US, will experience fundamental changes in its government functions and performance. Both US and international government privatization comes from the same source and its advocates appear to treat both systems the same way - privatize all government functions even in the US.

---

[8] See section 8.7 How Did This Happen for more information.

[9] David Hamilton Koch (May 3, 1940 – August 23, 2019). Koch was a libertarian. He was the 1980 Libertarian candidate for Vice President of the United States and helped finance the campaign. He became president of the subsidiary Koch Engineering in 1979 and became a co-owner of Koch Industries (along with elder brother Charles) in 1983.

3 Industrial Base

Since 1987 the policies associated with privatization have established a whole new set of companies with characteristics that previously never existed. Basically, these companies derive most if not all their revenues directly from federal tax dollars for services. They are essentially in competition with the costs of civil servants. As part of privatization a cost benefit analysis is performed, and the analysis must yield lower costs if a privatized workforce is to be established. All organizations have the same cost categories regardless of their nature – government, for profit, nonprofit, etc. The cost categories are:

- **Labor** includes all labor categories including management and executive personnel. Since the 1980's there has been a trend to bury senior management and executive compensation into overhead. This obscures the overhead costs and their items.
- **Material** includes whatever material is needed to develop and maintain the deliverable. The deliverable can be a product, products, system or technology.
- **General and Administrative** costs are associated with running the operation. This is administrative staff, office supplies, office space, labs, etc.
- **Overhead** includes employee costs above the basic salary or benefits, research and development, and organizational improvements. The additional employee costs are vacation, sick days, holidays, healthcare, retirement[10], education, training, etc. Research and development are for product and technology development. Organizational improvements are for process improvements, organizational assessment, new equipment and tools. When employees are not working on a project then they are working on Research and Development and or Organizational improvements until they are called to support a new project. This cycle guarantees that they are not immediately terminated once project funds stop. This also provides for organization survival growth, and stability.
- **Fee** is the profit an organization attaches to a project bid. The profit can be accumulated and paid to employees as bonuses, shareholders as dividends, or put back into the organization to pursue new markets, products, or technologies. Because of tax law changes in the 1980's the profits can be

---

[10] "This is the first time ever that five different generations are in America's workforce at the same time, from Gen Zers up to baby boomers," Source: Millennials, Gen Xers to baby boomers: Can you retire so I can get a job promotion, Paul Davidson, USA TODAY, November 7, 2019.

accumulated to eventually buy the competition and establish a monopoly or oligopoly.

- **Cost of money** is based on the inflation rate and is the cost associated with going to the markets to borrow money for short term or long-term needs during the project.

In many proposals the money categories get mixed and it is difficult to see where the money is going in a project. However, there are clear categories that can be used to compare different organizations and see how they can justify their bids. The following table shows the difference between a traditional company, a service only company, and a civil service organization.

Table 2 Cost Categories

Overhead	**Traditional Company**	**Service Company**	**Civil Service**
	Benefits		
Vacation	Same	**Less**	Same
Sick Days	Same	**Less**	Same
Holidays	More	Same	Same
Healthcare	Same	**Less**	Same
Retirement	Same	None	Same
Education	Same	**Less**	Same
Training	Less	**None**	More
	Research & Development		
Product	Yes	**None**	Support
Technology	Yes	**None**	Support
	Organization Improvements		
Process Improvements	Yes	**None**	Yes
Organizational Assessment	Yes	**None**	Yes
New Equipment and Tools	Yes	**None**	Yes
	Funds Interruption		
Government Shutdown	No Impact	**Lost Wages**	Reimbursed

The traditional company provides products, technologies, and services. The new privatized worker company only provides services. A civil service organization typically provides services but after World War II was engaged in significant technology development and new product support to industry however, this stopped with the movement into privatization.

What the table clearly shows is that the new privatized worker is a second-class worker that receives fewer benefits and is subject to termination once project funds end. This is because these companies have no activity in the general economy providing commercial or industrial products and services. They have no additional money from the overhead accounts to carry the workers between the projects.

This severely dysfunctional company environment is a direct result of policy of the United States of America since the introduction of privatization. Rather than encourage the development of new companies and industries able to operate in commercial or industrial markets the Federal government has syphoned off hundreds of billions of dollars to feed economically questionable entities to justify a political goal of the appearance of smaller government. This policy has had a serious negative effect on the economic base.

Previously there were companies that provided exclusive services to the Federal government, but these companies were few and far between and the workers numbered in the tens of thousands not millions. They were very special companies staffed primarily with end of career highly accomplished specialists. To have 4 million privatized workers in a setting where they do the same thing as 800,000 civil servants is a disaster and hides the true size of the government workforce which is closer to 4,800,000 rather than 800,000[11]. This is a deception to the taxpayers and a misuse of taxpayer funds and the human resources of the country.

3.1 How Did This Happen

In the late 70's early 80's there was a push to help start new companies especially small disadvantaged businesses. The idea was that they would start with services then grow to eventually provide products, technologies, and services to the entire economy of government, commercial, and industrial markets. Those that would stay in the services space would follow the model of small firms where career growth would include junior and senior partners and distribution of profits to the remaining employees. None of this happened.

So here we sit with millions of people needing these jobs in bad environments with poor benefits and loss of income at the slightest interruption of project funds. This does not happen in commercial markets. Commercial markets may decline quickly, and bad management may hide the facts, but there is time to react and look for a new job or career. Also, these environments do not allow the employees to express themselves and their capabilities because they do not develop new products, technologies, and or markets. They just sit and punch out the requested services.

3.2 Architecture Analysis

Is there a way to capture the architecture of the government and industrial base before and after privatization so that models can be developed to make comparisons? Would this be two architectures or one generic architecture that uses different parameters for two scenarios? This is an attempt to answer these questions.

---

[11] Source Not Expecting Back Pay, Government Contractors Collect Unemployment, Dip into Savings, NPR, January 7, 2019. There is no national database tracking the number of contract employees. Dr. Paul Light a federal workforce expert at New York University provided the estimates. Why is there no national database on this key metric?

The government performs many different functions. It currently exists and an architecture block diagram can be developed. We can begin with a functional block diagram then allocate the functions to subsystems and name the subsystems.

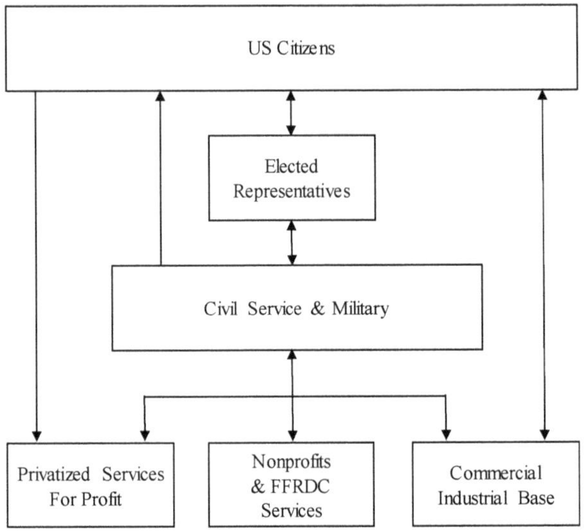

Figure 1 US Government Functional Block Diagram

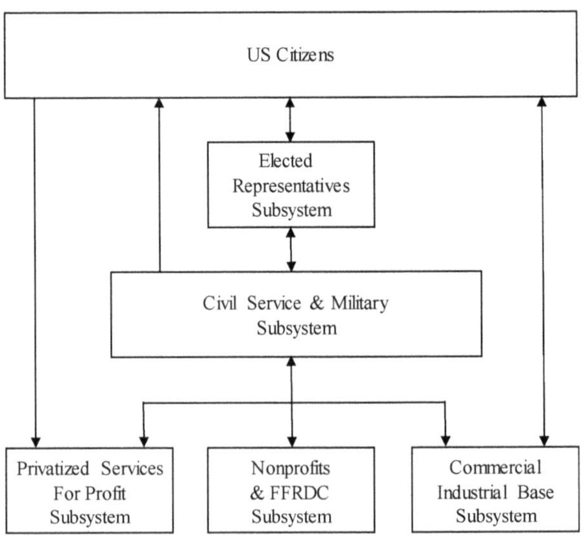

Figure 2 US Government Physical Architecture

We can then connect the subsystems together to show the subsystem interfaces.

We can then identify some of the key items flowing between the subsystem interfaces. The suggested architecture based on this approach is shown below.

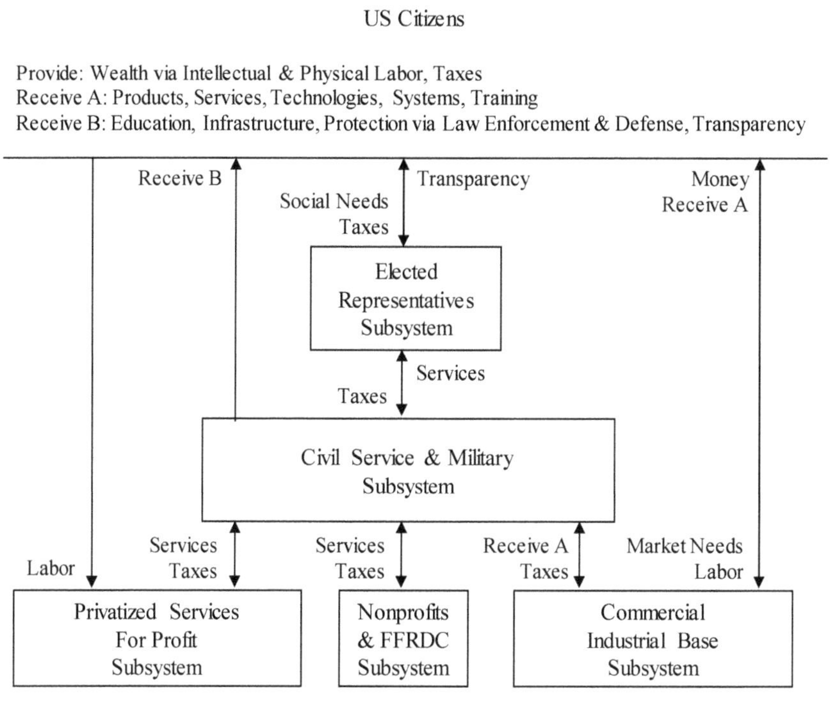

Figure 3 Generic Architecture – US Government as a System

The generic architecture of the US Government is independent of the functions found in each subsystem. It has some form of a topology that is driven by the interfaces. This is a hierarchical architecture with the people shown at the top. The people supply labor and intellectual resources and receive goods and services.

The next step is to determine what is the nature of each of the subsystems. For our analysis the key top-level subsystems are:

- Civil Service & Military Subsystem
- Nonprofits & FFRDC[12] Subsystem
- Commercial Industrial Base Subsystem
- Privatized Services for Profit Subsystem

Each subsystem has its own set of functions and architecture with subsystems that perform the functions. The details may vary but there are a common set of lower level functions that apply to all the subsystems. These are the lower level

[12] Federally Funded Research and Development Centers (FFRDC)

functions for each subsystem:

- Contracts
- Vendor Monitoring
- Administration
- Human Resources
- Operations
- Engineering
- Support
- Maintenance
- Research and Development

It is interesting that all the functions are starting to look like what may be found in an organizational chart. They are also starting to look like cost centers in an organization. So, this begs the question, can mental models be developed in terms of staffing level and or money flows for the architecture circa 1987 versus the architecture circa 2019.

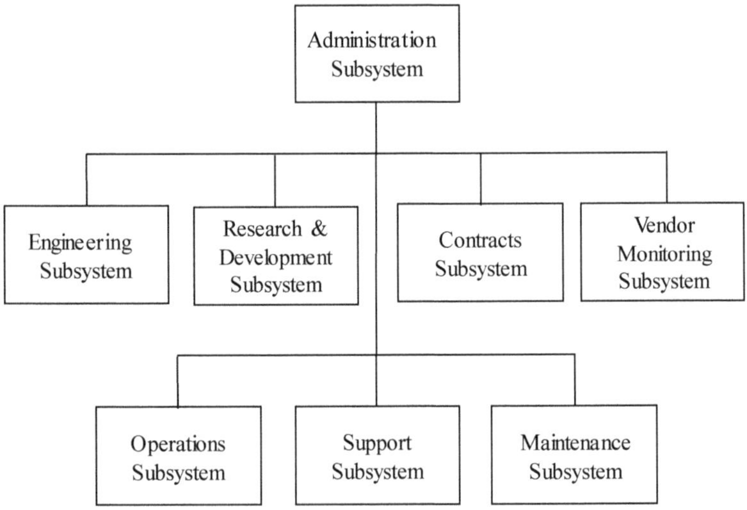

Figure 4 Government and Company Key Subsystems

The following is a mental model of government services developed in a spreadsheet for an un-privatized system and a privatized system. Each subsystem is identified and then each function is itemized for each subsystem. An assumption is then made for the staffing levels in each area for each system approach. This is performed for both the un-privatized system of 1987 and the privatized system of 2019. This represents one of many possible mental models.

In this mental model there is still a privatized services subsystem in 1987 however in 1987 there is only 1 contract for 1 company and in 2019 there are 10 contracts for 10 privatized services companies. To allow this to happen in 2019 the commercial industrial base subsystem loses its services piece of the overall available funds and resulting staff levels.

Table 3 Model of Government Services 1987 vs 2019

Core Big Engineering & Big Science Activities	**Un-privatized 1987 (Staff Levels)**	**Privatized 2019 (Staff Levels)**
Civil Service		
Contracts	10	100
Vendor Monitoring	20	200
Administration	10	10
Human Resources	10	10
Operations	500	500
Engineering	100	75
Support	0	0
Maintenance	30	1
R&D	30	1
Subtotal	710	897
Non-Profit / FFRDC		
Contracts	2	1
Vendor Monitoring	2	1
Administration	2	1
Human Resources	2	1
Operations	1	1
Engineering	10	5
Support	2	1
Maintenance	1	1
R&D	10	5
Subtotal	32	17
Privatized Services for Profit		
Contracts	1	10
Vendor Monitoring	1	20
Administration	1	10
Human Resources	1	10
Operations	1	1
Engineering (non-R&D)	1	**500**
Support	5	**500**
Maintenance	5	**5000**
R&D	1	1
Subtotal	17	6052

Table 3 Model of Government Services 1987 vs 2019

Core Big Engineering & Big Science Activities	**Un-privatized 1987 (Staff Levels)**	**Privatized 2019 (Staff Levels)**
Commercial Industrial Base		
Contracts	100	100
Vendor Monitoring	200	200
Administration	100	100
Human Resources	50	50
Operations	0	0
Engineering	1000	1000
Support	**500**	5
Maintenance	**5000**	10
R&D	**300**	30
Subtotal	7250	1495

We see that R&D goes from 300 in 1987 to 30 in 2019 and those engineers move over to support the privatized services that are not involved in R&D and the level is increased to 500. A summary is offered with some additional analysis.

Table 4 Privatization Industrial Base Damage Unexpected Consequence

Core Big Engineering & Big Science Activities	**Un-privatized 1987 (Staff Levels)**	**Privatized 2019 (Staff Levels)**
Civil Service	710	897
Non-Profit / FFRDC	32	17
Privatized Services for Profit	17	6052
Commercial Industrial Base	7250	1495
Total	**8009**	**8461**
Privatization Overhead (8461/8009)		**5.64%**
Industrial Base Damage (1495/7250)		**-79.38%**

The un-privatized system uses companies that engage in R&D, produce technologies, products, systems and provide services[13]. They are the traditional companies of 1987. The privatized system uses the new companies that only provide services. This summary suggests that:

[13] R&D Productivity Second Edition; Hughes Aircraft, June 1978, AD Number A075387, Ranftl, R.M., Carver City, CA Hughes Aircraft Co., Second Edition, 1978, OCLC Number 4224641 or 16945892. ASIN B000716B96.

1. The overhead associated with privatization is 5.64% (8461/8009). This number was less than expected.
2. Meanwhile the Industrial Base Damage is significantly more than expected at -79.38% (1495/7250).

This unfortunately does show reality when we examine the number of companies that provided technology, products, and services in the past versus today. The consolidations and closures of extremely powerful and competent companies in the last decade of the last century is huge and may be the result of the government policy on privatization.

Everyone that lived through this transition knows that services money was syphoned from companies that produced technologies, products, and systems into the new services companies and that this money was traditionally associated with support, maintenance, and R&D. The support and maintenance staffs were not just punching out the services, but they were also feeding back to the company R&D pipeline for the next generation technologies, products, and systems. The feedback was severed when the employees found themselves in the new privatized companies that only provide services. The traditional companies were cut off from this enormous source of information, creativity, and funding.

Again, both results were unexpected. The expectation was large overhead with little impact or damage to the industrial base. The opposite happened once the mental model was executed.

When the major policy decision was made to move towards privatization it is unclear if various economic models were run to try and understand the system ramifications. Other modeling and analysis can be performed to try and understand if we are better off now with privatization or if we need to change direction and transition into a new system. Some of the suggested models to run today are:

- This system architecture analysis
- An agent-based model
- Various economic models

3.3 Available Systems

There is enough historical evidence to compare what happened to the industrial base and the systems they produced before and after privatization. The time epochs are 1900 to 1945, 1945 to 1987, and 1987 to 2019. The time epoch 1900 to 1945 establishes a baseline. The time epoch 1945 to 1987 represents what happened as part of the New Deal, where government was viewed as the only alternative to address additional needs outside of just Defense. The time epoch 1987 to 2019 represents the age of privatization, where the New Deal was rejected, and the private sector was viewed as the source to address additional needs previously performed by the government.

The following text has multiple tables. These table are difficult to review. Start by just scanning the systems. Then examine the entries in the columns. Some readers will agree, others will disagree with the detailed entries. However, there is a big picture that starts to surface that will be offered after these tables are presented. The following table is a list of systems that surfaced between 1900 and 1945.

Table 5 Systems Established 1900 to 1945

Systems Services 1900 - 1945	Primary Enabler Facilitator	Initiator Companies
Food	Agriculture	Consumer
Clothing	Commerce	Consumer
Housing		Consumer
Oven	Market	Consumer, Industrial
Refrigerator	Market	Consumer, Industrial
Urban Public Transit	Local Government	Monopolies
Train Transportation	Commerce Dept	Monopolies
Local Distribution	Commerce Dept	Consumer, Industrial
Regional Distribution	Commerce Dept	Consumer, Industrial
National Distribution	Commerce Dept	Consumer, Industrial
International Distribution	Commerce Dept	Consumer, Industrial
Family Retail Stores	Market	Consumer, Industrial
Department Stores	Market	Consumer, Industrial
Grocery Store	Market	Consumer, Industrial
Limited Higher Education	Land Grant Colleges	
Books		Consumer, Industrial
Newspapers		Consumer
Magazines		Consumer, Industrial
Film		Consumer
Theatres	Local Government	Consumer
Local Bars	Local Government	Consumer
Parks	Local Government	Consumer
City Electricity	Local Government	Utilities
City Water	Local Government	Utilities
City Sewage	Local Government	Utilities
Broadcast Radio Free	FCC	Consumer, Industrial
Home Records & Players		RCA, Industrial
Storage Media 75 RPM Records		RCA, Industrial
Telegraph		Western Union

Table 5 Systems Established 1900 to 1945

Systems Services 1900 - 1945	Primary Enabler Facilitator	Initiator Companies
Telephones	FCC	Consumer, Industrial
Air Conditioning Industrial		Industrial

You are probably saying to yourself that this is useless information and that it is wrong. Yet someone somewhere was compelled to produce this type of data. If you ask them why they did this, they can't give you an answer. This is an example of complex systems engineering at its finest - looking at useless irrelevant data. This is a form of saturation on the problem space. Before computers this data would be spread on a table or pinned on a wall. People would immerse themselves in a 3D space of the data. This is serious saturation and involves looking at relevant and irrelevant incomprehensible data.

At some point synthesis begins. The data is refined to try and make sense of what surfaced. Again no one knows why they are doing it, they are compelled to work with it much like an artist works with their creation. Eventually patterns start to surface[14]. It is at this point that everyone on the systems team gets engaged. So, keep reading and try to let the creativity process takeover.

The following is a list of systems that surfaced between 1945 and 1987.

Table 6 Systems Established 1945 to 1987

Systems Services 1945-1987	Primary Enabler Facilitator	Initiator Companies
See pre 1945 systems services. In general, they all expanded during this time. Then new systems services surfaced.		
Ubiquitous Electricity	Rural Electrification Act of 1936	Utilities
Ubiquitous Water	Local Government	Utilities
Ubiquitous Sewage	Local Government	Utilities
Ubiquitous Oven	Market	Consumer, Industrial
Ubiquitous Refrigerator	Market	Consumer, Industrial
Washers	Defense conversion	Consumer, Industrial
Dryers	Defense conversion	Consumer, Industrial
Garbage Disposals	Defense conversion	Consumer, Industrial
Rural Electrification	Rural Electrification Act of 1936	Utilities
Rural Telephones	Rural Electrification Act of 1936	Utilities
Rural Hospitals	Dept of Health & Human Services	Nonprofits

[14] See section 9.2.8 Creativity and Innovation Process.

Table 6 Systems Established 1945 to 1987

Systems Services 1945-1987	Primary Enabler Facilitator	Initiator Companies
Rural Education	GI Bill, PLATO	Control Data Corp
Rural Air Transport	FAA	Consumer, Industrial
Ubiquitous Higher Education	GI Bill, NSF, DOD, NASA, FAA	Industrial
New Housing Concepts	Department of Transportation	Consumer, Industrial
New Office Buildings	Department of Transportation	Consumer, Industrial
New Retail Buildings	Department of Transportation	Consumer, Industrial
New City Concepts	Department of Transportation	Consumer, Industrial
Automobiles	Department of Transportation	Consumer
Freeways	Department of Transportation	Industrial
New Cities (suburbs)	Local	Industrial
Local Distribution	Commerce Dept	Consumer, Industrial
Regional Distribution	Commerce Dept	Consumer, Industrial
National Distribution	Commerce Dept	Consumer, Industrial
International Distribution	Commerce Dept	Consumer, Industrial
Family Retail Stores	Market	Consumer, Industrial
Ubiquitous Retail Stores	Market	Consumer, Industrial
Ubiquitous Department Stores	Market	Consumer, Industrial
Ubiquitous Malls	Market	Consumer, Industrial
Strip Shopping Centers	Market	Consumer, Industrial
Grocery Store	Market	Consumer, Industrial
Supermarkets	Market	Consumer, Industrial
Convenience Store	Market	Consumer, Industrial
Ubiquitous Telephones	FCC	Consumer, Industrial
Broadcast Television Free	FCC	Consumer, Industrial
Broadcast Radio Free	FCC	Consumer, Industrial
Broadcast FM Radio Free	Market	Consumer, Industrial
Home Hi-Fi Records & Players	Market	Consumer, Industrial
Audio Tape Recorders	Market	Consumer, Bing Crosby
Home Hi-Fi Tape Recorders	Market	Consumer, Bing Crosby
Video Recorders	Market	Consumer, Industrial
Storage media Microfilm	Fed Government	Consumer, Industrial
Storage media 33 LP	Market	Consumer, Industrial
Storage media 45 Record	Market	Consumer, Industrial
Storage media 8 Track	Market	Consumer, Industrial
Storage media Reel to Reel	Market	Consumer, Industrial
Storage media Cassette	Market	Consumer, Industrial
Storage media VHS	Market	Consumer, Industrial

Table 6 Systems Established 1945 to 1987

Systems Services 1945-1987	Primary Enabler Facilitator	Initiator Companies
Storage media Betamax	Market	Consumer, Industrial
Storage media Laser Disc	Market	Consumer, Industrial
Storage media Drum	DOD, NASA, FAA	Consumer, Industrial
Storage media Tape Drive	DOD, NASA, FAA	Consumer, Industrial
Storage media Disc Drive	DOD, NASA, FAA	Consumer, Industrial
Storage media CD Audio	Market	Consumer, Industrial
Storage media CD Computer	Market	Consumer, Industrial
Scientific Computers	DOD, NASA, FAA	Industrial High Tech
Industrial Computers	DOD, NASA, FAA	Industrial High Tech
Small Business Computers	DOD, NASA, FAA	Industrial High Tech
Office Computers	DOD, NASA	Industrial High Tech
Fail Safe Computing	NASA, DOD, FAA	Industrial
Software	DOD, NASA, FAA	Industrial
Government Internet	NSF, NASA, DOD, FAA	Industrial
Nuclear Power	DOE	Industrial
Jet Air Transportation	FAA, Commerce Dept, DOD	Industrial
Satellites communications	NASA	Hughes, High Tech
Satellites weather	NASA, NOAA	Hughes, High Tech
Satellites navigation	DOD, NASA	Hughes, High Tech
Satellites earth study	NASA	Hughes, High Tech
Satellites universe study	NASA	Hughes, High Tech
Space Probes Planetary	NASA	Hughes, High Tech
Space Probes Interstellar	NASA	Hughes, High Tech
Manned Space Flight	NASA, DOD	High Tech
Moon Landing	NASA	High Tech
Space Shuttle	NASA	High Tech
Frozen Food	Agriculture	Consumer
Packaged Food	Agriculture, NASA	Consumer
Dry Foods	NASA	Industrial
New Foods	Agriculture, NASA	Consumer
Food Additives	Agriculture	Consumer
New Clothing Materials	NASA	Consumer, Industrial
Plastics	NASA	Consumer, Industrial
Fiberglass	NASA	Consumer, Industrial
Composites	NASA	Consumer, Industrial
Air Conditioning Home	NASA	Consumer, Industrial
Air Conditioning Auto	NASA	Consumer, Industrial
Electronics Severe Environment	NASA	Hughes, RCA, Industrial
Electronics Auto Environment	NASA	Hughes, RCA, Industrial

Table 6 Systems Established 1945 to 1987

Systems Services 1945-1987	Primary Enabler Facilitator	Initiator Companies
Transistors	DOD	Bell Labs
Semiconductor Heat Pumps	DOD	High Tech
Lasers	DOD	Hughes
Solar Cells	NASA	Bell Labs, Hughes
Liquid Crystals	DOD	RCA
Light Valves	DOD	Hughes
Light Emitting Diodes	DOD	High tech
Ion Propulsion	NASA	Hughes
Robotics	DOD, NASA	Hughes
Autonomous Vehicle AI	DOD	Hughes

The following is a list of systems that surfaced between 1987 and 2019.

Table 7 Systems Established 1987 to 2019

Systems Services 1987-2019	Primary Enabler Facilitator	Initiator Companies
See pre 1945 systems services. In general, they all expanded during this time. Then new systems services surfaced.		
Ubiquitous Electricity	Rural Electrification Act of 1936	Utilities
Ubiquitous Water	Local Government	Utilities
Ubiquitous Sewage	Local Government	Utilities
Ubiquitous Oven	Market	Consumer, Industrial
Ubiquitous Refrigerator	Market	Consumer, Industrial
Washers	Defense conversion	Consumer, Industrial
Dryers	Defense conversion	Consumer, Industrial
Garbage Disposals	Defense conversion	Consumer, Industrial
Rural Electrification	Rural Electrification Act of 1936	Utilities
Rural Telephones	Rural Electrification Act of 1936	Utilities
Rural Hospitals	Market	**Disappearing**
Rural Education	Market	Community Colleges
Rural Air Transport	Market	**Disappearing**
Ubiquitous Higher Education	Market	**Disappearing**
New Housing Concepts	Department of Transportation	Consumer, Industrial
New Office Buildings	Department of Transportation	Consumer, Industrial

Table 7 Systems Established 1987 to 2019

Systems Services 1987-2019	**Primary Enabler Facilitator**	**Initiator Companies**
New Retail Buildings	Department of Transportation	Consumer, Industrial
New City Concepts	Department of Transportation	Consumer, Industrial
Automobiles	Department of Transportation	Consumer
Freeways	Department of Transportation	Industrial
New Cities (suburbs)	Local	Industrial
Local Distribution	Market	**Disappearing**
Regional Distribution	Market	**Disappearing**
National Distribution	Market	**Disappearing**
International Distribution	Market	Consumer, Industrial
Family Retail Stores	Market	**Gone**
Ubiquitous Retail Stores	Market	**Disappearing**
Ubiquitous Department Stores	Market	**Disappearing**
Ubiquitous Malls	Market	**Disappearing**
Strip Shopping Centers	Market	**Disappearing**
Grocery Store	Market	**Gone**
Supermarkets	Market	Consumer, Industrial
Convenience Store	Market	Consumer, Industrial
E-commerce	HPCC Act 1991 (Gore Bill)	Consumer, Industrial
Ubiquitous Telephones	FCC	Consumer, Industrial
Broadcast Television Free	FCC	Consumer, Industrial
Broadcast Radio Free	FCC	Consumer, Industrial
Broadcast FM Radio Free	Market	Consumer
Home Hi-Fi Records & Players	Market	**Gone**
Audio Tape Recorders	Market	**Gone**
Home Hi-Fi Tape Recorders	Market	**Gone**
Video Recorders	Market	**Gone**
Smart Phone	Market	Consumer, Industrial
CD Players	Market	Consumer
DVD Players	Market	Consumer
Cell Phones	Market	Consumer
MP3 Recorders & Players	Market	Consumer
MP4 Recorders & Players	Market	Consumer
Cable TV Pay	Market	Consumer
Storage media Microfilm	Fed Government	**Gone**
Storage media 33 LP	Market	**Gone**
Storage media 45 Record	Market	**Gone**
Storage media 8 Track	Market	**Gone**

Table 7 Systems Established 1987 to 2019

Systems Services 1987-2019	**Primary Enabler Facilitator**	**Initiator Companies**
Storage media Reel to Reel	Market	**Gone**
Storage media Cassette	Market	**Gone**
Storage media VHS	Market	**Gone**
Storage media Betamax	Market	**Gone**
Storage media Laser Disc	Market	**Gone**
Storage media Drum	DOD, NASA, FAA	**Gone**
Storage media Tape Drive	DOD, NASA, FAA	**Gone**
Storage media Disc Drive	DOD, NASA, FAA	Consumer, Industrial
Storage media CD Audio	Market	Consumer, Industrial
Storage media CD Computer	Market	Consumer, Industrial
Storage media DVD Video	Market	Consumer, Industrial
Storage media DVD Computer	Market	Consumer, Industrial
Scientific Computers	Market	**Gone**
Industrial Computers	Market	**Gone**
Small Business Computers	Market	**Gone**
Office Computers	Market	Industrial High Tech
Fail Safe Computing	Market	Industrial
Software	Market	Industrial
Government Internet	Market	**Gone**
Personal Computers	Market	Consumer, Industrial
Internet	Market	Consumer, Industrial
Nuclear Power	DOE	Shutting Down
Solar Power	Market	Consumer, Industrial
Wind Power	Market	Consumer, Industrial
Jet Air Transportation	FAA, Commerce Dept, DOD	Industrial
Satellites communications	NASA	High Tech
Satellites weather	NASA, NOAA	High Tech
Satellites navigation	DOD, NASA	High Tech
Satellites earth study	NASA	High Tech
Satellites universe study	NASA	High Tech
Space Probes Planetary	NASA	High Tech
Space Probes Interstellar	NASA	**Gone**
Manned Space Flight	NASA, DOD	**Gone**
Moon Landing	NASA	**Gone**
Space Shuttle	NASA	**Gone**
Frozen Food	Agriculture	Consumer
Packaged Food	Agriculture, NASA	Consumer

Table 7 Systems Established 1987 to 2019

Systems Services 1987-2019	Primary Enabler Facilitator	Initiator Companies
Dry Foods	NASA	Industrial
New Foods	Agriculture, NASA	Consumer
Food Additives	Agriculture	Consumer
New Clothing Materials	Market	Consumer, Industrial
Plastics	Market	Consumer, Industrial
Fiberglass	Market	Consumer, Industrial
Composites	Market	Consumer, Industrial
Air Conditioning Home	Market	Consumer, Industrial
Air Conditioning Auto	Market	Consumer, Industrial
Electronics Severe Environment	Market	Industrial
Electronics Auto Environment	Market	Industrial
Transistors	DOD	**Gone**
Semiconductor Heat Pumps	Market	Consumer, Industrial
Lasers	Market	Consumer, Industrial
Solar Cells	Market	Consumer, Industrial
Liquid Crystals	Market	Consumer, Industrial
Light Valves	Market	Consumer, Industrial
Light Emitting Diodes	Market	Consumer, Industrial
Ion Propulsion	NASA	High Tech
Robotics	Market	High Tech
Autonomous Vehicle AI	DOD, Market	High Tech

It is difficult to visualize the trends. The following table offers one potential visualization. A 1 indicates the system exists, 0 the system does not exist, 2 or more indicates the system is better for that time than other times. You can scan the tables and then jump to the findings at the end of the table.

Table 8 Systems Lost after Privatization

Systems Services	1945	1987	2019	Primary Enabler Facilitator	Initiator Companies
1900 to 1945					
Food	1	1	1	Agriculture	Consumer
Clothing	1	1	1	Commerce	Consumer
Housing	1	1	1	Market	Consumer
Oven	1	1	1	Market	Consumer, Industrial
Toaster	0	1	1	Market	

Table 8 Systems Lost after Privatization

Systems Services	1945	1987	2019	Primary Enabler Facilitator	Initiator Companies
Refrigerator	1	2	2	Market	Consumer, Industrial
Urban Public Transit	1	1	1	Local Government	Monopolies
Train Transportation	1	1	1	Commerce Dept	Monopolies
Automobile	1	2	3	Market	Consumer
Ship Transport	1	2	2	Commerce Dept	Consumer, Industrial
Blimp Transport	1	0	0	Market	Consumer
Prop Airplane Transport	1	2	1	Commerce Dept	Consumer, Industrial
Limited Higher Education	1	2	1	Land Grant Colleges	Citizens
City Universities	1	1	0	Benefactors	Citizens
Public School Education	1	2	1	Government	Citizens
Physical Libraries	1	2	1	Government	Citizens
Books	1	2	1	Market	Consumer, Industrial
Newspapers	2	2	1	Market	Consumer
Magazines	2	2	1	Market	Consumer, Industrial
Film	1	1	1	Market	Consumer
Theatres	1	1	1	Market	Consumer
Local Bars	3	2	1	Market	Consumer
Parks	1	2	1	Local Government	Consumer
City Electricity	1	1	1	Local Government	Utilities
City Water	1	1	1	Local Government	Utilities
City Sewage	1	1	1	Local Government	Utilities
Air Conditioning Industrial	1	1	1	Market	Industrial
Broadcast Radio Free	2	3	1	FCC	Consumer, Industrial
Home Records & Players	1	2	0	Market	RCA, Industrial
Storage Media 75 RPM Records	1	0	0	Market	RCA, Industrial
Telegraph	1	1	1	Market	Western Union
Telephones	2	3	1	FCC	Consumer, Industrial

Table 8 Systems Lost after Privatization

Systems Services	1945	1987	2019	Primary Enabler Facilitator	Initiator Companies
			1945 to 1987		
Ubiquitous Electricity	1	2	2	Rural Electrification Act of 1936	Utilities
Ubiquitous Water	1	2	2	Local Government	Utilities
Ubiquitous Sewage	1	2	2	Local Government	Utilities
Ubiquitous Oven	1	2	2	Market	Consumer, Industrial
Ubiquitous Refrigerator	1	2	2	Market	Consumer, Industrial
Washers	0	1	1	Defense conversion	Consumer, Industrial
Dryers	0	1	1	Defense conversion	Consumer, Industrial
Garbage Disposals	0	1	1	Defense conversion	Consumer, Industrial
Microwave Oven	0	1	1		
Rural Electrification	0	1	1	Rural Electrification Act of 1936	Utilities
Rural Telephones	0	1	1	Rural Electrification Act of 1936	Utilities
Rural Hospitals	0	1	0	Market	Disappearing
Rural Education	0	2	1	Market	Community Colleges
Rural Air Transport	0	1	0	Market	Disappearing
Ubiquitous Higher Education	1	2	0	GI Bill	Disappearing
PLATO Computer Education	0	1	0	GI Bill, PLATO	Control Data Corp
Computer Based Training	0	1	1	Government	DOD
New Housing Concepts	0	2	1	Department of Transportation	Consumer, Industrial
New Office Buildings	0	2	1	Department of Transportation	Consumer, Industrial
New Retail Buildings	0	2	1	Department of Transportation	Consumer, Industrial

Table 8 Systems Lost after Privatization

Systems Services	**1945**	**1987**	**2019**	**Primary Enabler Facilitator**	**Initiator Companies**
New City Concepts	0	2	1	Department of Transportation	Consumer, Industrial
New Cities (suburbs)	0	2	1	Local	Industrial
Safe Automobiles	0	1	1	Department of Transportation	Consumer
Freeways	0	2	1	Department of Transportation	Industrial
Jet Air Transportation	0	1	1	FAA, Commerce Dept, DOD	Industrial
Local Distribution	1	1	0	Market	Disappearing
Regional Distribution	1	1	0	Market	Disappearing
National Distribution	1	1	1	Market	Disappearing
International Distribution	1	1	2	Market	Consumer, Industrial
Family Retail	1	1	0	Market	Consumer, Industrial
Ubiquitous Retail Stores	1	2	1	Market	Disappearing
Ubiquitous Department Stores	1	2	1	Market	Disappearing
Ubiquitous Malls	0	2	1	Market	Disappearing
Strip Shopping Centers	0	1	1	Market	Disappearing
Grocery Store	1	0	0	Market	Gone
Supermarkets	0	1	1	Market	Consumer, Industrial
Convenience Store	0	1	1	Market	Consumer, Industrial
Ubiquitous Telephones	1	2	1	FCC	Consumer, Industrial
Broadcast Television Free	0	2	1	FCC	Consumer, Industrial
Broadcast Radio Free	1	1	1	FCC	Consumer, Industrial
Broadcast FM Radio Free	0	1	1	Market	Consumer
Home Hi-Fi Records & Players	0	2	0	Market	Gone
Audio Tape Recorders	0	2	0	Market	Gone
Home Hi-Fi Tape Recorders	0	2	0	Market	Gone
Video Recorders	0	2	0	Market	Gone
CD Players	0	1	0	Market	Consumer

Table 8 Systems Lost after Privatization

Systems Services	1945	1987	2019	Primary Enabler Facilitator	Initiator Companies
Storage media Microfilm	0	1	0	Fed Government	Gone
Storage media 33 LP	0	1	0	Market	Gone
Storage media 45 Record	0	1	0	Market	Gone
Storage media 8 Track	0	1	0	Market	Gone
Storage media Reel to Reel	0	1	0	Market	Gone
Storage media Cassette	0	1	0	Market	Gone
Storage media VHS	0	1	0	Market	Gone
Storage media Betamax	0	1	0	Market	Gone
Storage media Laser Disc	0	1	0	Market	Gone
Storage media Drum	0	1	0	DOD, NASA, FAA	Gone
Storage media Tape Drive	0	1	0	DOD, NASA, FAA	Gone
Storage media Disc Drive	0	1	1	DOD, NASA, FAA	Consumer, Industrial
Storage media CD Audio	0	0	0	Market	Consumer, Industrial
Storage media CD Computer	0	0	0	Market	Consumer, Industrial
Scientific Computers	0	1	0	Government	Gone
Industrial Computers	0	1	0	Government	Gone
Small Business Computers	0	1	0	Market	Gone
Office Computers	0	1	1	Market	Industrial High Tech
Fail Safe Computing	0	1	1	Government	Industrial
Software	0	1	1	Government, Market	Industrial
Government Internet	0	1	1	Government	Industrial High Tech
Nuclear Power	0	2	1	DOE	Shutting Down
Solar Power	0	1	2	Market	Consumer, Industrial
Wind Power	1	1	2	Market	Consumer, Industrial
Satellites communications	0	1	1	NASA	High Tech

Table 8 Systems Lost after Privatization

Systems Services	1945	1987	2019	Primary Enabler Facilitator	Initiator Companies
Satellites weather	0	1	1	NASA, NOAA	High Tech
Satellites navigation	0	1	1	DOD, NASA	High Tech
Satellites earth study	0	1	1	NASA	High Tech
Satellites universe study	0	1	1	NASA	High Tech
Space Probes Planetary	0	1	1	NASA	High Tech
Space Probes Interstellar	0	1	0	NASA	Gone
Manned Space Flight	0	1	0	NASA, DOD	Gone
Moon Landing	0	1	0	NASA	Gone
Space Shuttle	0	1	0	NASA	Gone
Genetics	0	1	1	HHMI	Non-Profit
Disease Control	0	1	1	CDC	Government
Pharmacy	0	1	1	FDA	High Tech
Life Saving Procedures	0	1	1	DOD, Market	High Tech
Frozen Food	0	1	1	Agriculture	Consumer
Packaged Food	0	1	1	Agriculture, NASA	Consumer
Dry Foods	0	1	1	NASA	Industrial
New Foods	0	1	1	Agriculture, NASA	Consumer
Food Additives	0	1	1	Agriculture	Consumer
Genetic Applications	0	1	1	Market	Consumer, Industrial
New Clothing Materials	0	1	1	Market	Consumer, Industrial
Plastics	0	1	1	Market	Consumer, Industrial
Fiberglass	0	1	1	Market	Consumer, Industrial
Composites	0	1	1	Market	Consumer, Industrial
Air Conditioning Home	0	1	1	Market	Consumer, Industrial
Air Conditioning Auto	0	1	1	Market	Consumer, Industrial
Electronics Severe Environment	0	1	1	Market	Industrial
Electronics Auto Environment	0	0	1	Market	Industrial

Table 8 Systems Lost after Privatization

Systems Services	1945	1987	2019	Primary Enabler Facilitator	Initiator Companies
Transistors	0	1	0	DOD	Gone
Semiconductor Heat Pumps	0	1	1	Market	Consumer, Industrial
Lasers	0	1	1	Market	Consumer, Industrial
Solar Cells	0	1	1	Market	Consumer, Industrial
Liquid Crystals	0	1	1	Market	Consumer, Industrial
Light Valves	0	1	1	Market	Consumer, Industrial
Light Emitting Diodes	0	1	1	Market	Consumer, Industrial
Ion Propulsion	0	1	1	NASA	High Tech
Robotics	0	1	1	Market	High Tech
Autonomous Vehicle AI	0	0	1	DOD, Market	High Tech
1987 to 2019					
Cell Phones	0	2	1	Market	Consumer
Smart Phone	0	1	2	Market	Consumer, Industrial
DVD Players	0	2	1	Market	Consumer
MP3 Recorders & Players	0	2	1	Market	Consumer
MP4 Recorders & Players	0	0	1	Market	Consumer
Cable TV Pay	0	1	1	Market	Consumer
Digital TV	0	0	1	Market	Consumer
Storage media DVD Video	0	0	1	Market	Consumer, Industrial
Storage media DVD Computer	0	0	1	Market	Consumer, Industrial
USB Flash Drives	0	0	1	Market	Consumer, Industrial
USB Hard Disk	0	0	1	Market	Consumer, Industrial
Personal Computers	0	1	1	Market	Consumer, Industrial
Internet	0	1	1	Market	Consumer, Industrial
E-commerce	0	1	2	HPCC Act 1991 (Gore Bill)	Consumer, Industrial

Table 8 Systems Lost after Privatization

Systems Services	1945	1987	2019	Primary Enabler Facilitator	Initiator Companies
Totals	**54**	**184**	**130**	This shows the number of systems available for each time frame. The numbers significantly increase after 1945. Then the number of systems decline by 2019.	
Systems	**New**	**Lost**		This shows the number of new systems that surfaced and the number of systems that have disappeared.	
1900 to 1945	**32**	**NA**			
1945 to 1987	**108**	**-3**			
1987 to 2019	**14**	**-64**			

As we examine the details in these tables, we see that prior to 1945 the US was in survival mode establishing basic necessities. After 1945 the US was in the mode of improving the quality of life with many new systems. After 1987 we see many systems associated with a higher quality of life replaced by other systems. We also see some systems disappear. The big question is are things getting better, worse, or staying the same from a basic necessities and quality of life perspective, also is there potential evidence of important systems disappearing with no replacement.

The Totals row represents the number of systems available for each time frame. The numbers significantly increase after 1945 from 54 to 184. Then the number of systems decline by 2019 from 184 to 130.

The next series of rows show the number of new systems that surfaced and the number of systems that have disappeared. By 1987 there were 108 new systems but by 2019 there were only 14 new systems. Meanwhile by 1987 there were 3 systems lost but by 2019 there were 64 systems lost. The numbers may change as new information is accessed and added but a serious trend has been detected. The trend suggests that the number of available systems is declining.

3.4 Recommendations for the Short Term

The short-term recommendations include policy changes that can happen immediately. They include changes to government service contract requirements and then broader topics that require government attention and actions.

Service Contract Recommendations

The service contracts are constantly expiring, being renewed or replaced. In addition, new service contracts are constantly being developed. This is a key area where some of the suggested policy goals can start to be addressed.

Beginning immediately all new and renewed services contracts especially engineering and science services contracts need to include product and technology development requirements as follows:

1. The new service companies must engage in new product and or technology development related to the work performed.
2. The new service companies must provide a semiannual report on product and or technology development. It is recognized that most will be failures. Previous history suggests a 10% success rate, but companies must not be penalized for failures.
3. All services contracts must allocate reasonable funding to support product and technology development that starts at a minimum of 3% of the contract value.
4. The government must maintain a database of the products and or technologies developed so that they can move into the broader industrial base as part of a market clearing house.
5. In no instance shall these overhead items be used to discriminate between different vendor cost proposals.
6. The government must maintain a database on the number of privatized workers and number of privatized services companies by year beginning in 1980 and make this data easily accessible by the people.

Broad Policy Recommendations

1. Science the Endless Frontier set the policy and tone of the United States from 1945 to 1981. This document needs to be reviewed by everyone that is in a position charting a course for the future. The US is a system of government based on fundamental scientific principles. We need to rediscover that simple fact.
2. Industrial policy is tightly coupled to basic engineering principles. The Engineers especially the Systems Engineers need to be at the front of the table during future policy discussions and decisions. Locking them out of the conversation has been devastating to the industrial base. The product and systems oriented industrial base have been and will continue to be Engineering based.
3. There was a huge shift away from basic systems thinking as focus was placed entirely on finance and self-interest where the belief surfaced that the greatest profits and self-interest would lead to the greatest good. We once again know that is a fantasy and a path that eventually leads to disaster.
4. When President Johnson was interviewed by Walter Cronkite during the Apollo 11 Moon Landing Walter Cronkite specifically asked President Johnson his thoughts on the new Management Techniques and Systems Engineering that were developed and how they might be applied broader to industry. Having lived through that time I know that they were adopted and

used across the spectrum of industry up until approximately the mid 1990's when they were replaced by the new MBA generation ideas and techniques. Systems engineering and the new management techniques that are now old need to be reinvigorated. There are systems engineering programs growing at the University level but once again government policy is needed to ensure that this investment is not lost.

5. It is critical that the government not accept practices of faster better cheaper for the sole purpose of hiding the true costs of systems development, maintenance, and operations. This can only happen if the government relies on the foundation of education coming from engineering and science-based Universities and companies. The age of snake oil salespeople selling a quick fix tool and or process never goes away and the government must always be vigilant and ensure that those seeds never sprout. At the same time the government should encourage innovation. This is difficult with so much of the industrial base centered on services contract staff with no connection to product development, manufacturing, or technology development. Somehow service staff employees need to be bought back into the reality loop via effective government policy mechanisms.

Product and Technology Stimulation Recommendations

All intellectual property belongs to the people that originate the intellectual property. They assign the rights to external entities such as their employers. In the past there were unwritten contracts where employees would enjoy the fruits of their efforts via immediate compensation using bonuses or better salary and retirement. Retirement was essentially the collection of residual income from their work. This relationship no longer exits so there needs to be a mechanism to encourage product and technology development. The product and technology stimulation requirements suggestions are:

1. All service contracts need to include requirements to encourage and reward service contract employees that contribute to and or develop new products and or technology.
2. All product and or technology developed during the execution of a services contract is jointly owned by the originating employee or employees and the company. The ownership split is determined by the service contract requirements. It is recognized that no one will participate unless the split is in the favor of the originators. The company can reduce their split, if they desire, as it competes for talent.
3. The product, products, technology, technologies may be sold or licensed to other entities and markets outside the government. This translates to government investment that is then spun off to the non-government commercial industrial base and economy.

3.5 Recommendations for Privatization Transformation

It is clear from empirical data that the USA has wasted 30 years of funds spent on millions of people in entities that are not performing in the market. This needs to stop as soon as possible. The issue is how to make an effective transition. This will require significant analysis, but these are some guidelines. They all fall under the simple concept of De-Privatizing the US Government and reapplying resources and tax dollars more effectively.

De-Privatizing only applies to service companies that were exclusively established to provide government services as a result of privatization and could not survive in the commercial industrial economy without government funding. These are the entities that are a huge drain on the economy as extremely talented staff is drained from the general economy and constrained by what they can provide especially once it comes to new innovative ideas and applications.

1. Having thousands of service contracts that are constantly expiring is a great employment mechanism for contract administrators but a complete disaster for employees and companies that want to produce products and technologies. Unfortunately, significant organizational knowledge has been lost on how to avoid this grossly inefficient system on the way to privatization. There needs to be research into the past to determine how government previously operated especially in civilian high technology areas such as the FAA, NASA, etc.
2. The Federal Government must stop the practice of lowest bidder to justify lowest costs at the cost of the worker. Money must be put back into the Overhead items. Yes, the costs will be higher than the costs of a civil service organization because there is management overhead associated with administration and control on both ends and there is a fee (profit) that must be paid. However, we now have to fix the damage and move forward with a new system.
3. There should be no large service companies deriving more than 50% of their revenues from government services. They need to figure it out - merge, invest, do something to engage in the economy and grow it. No one will do this voluntarily so legislation may be needed for companies to wean themselves off government funds. Legislation must be passed so that after 5 years no entity can derive more than 50% of its earnings from the government unless it is less than 200 employees where 50% are highly experienced or end of career workers or 100% employee owned.
4. Money and compensation are much simpler to manage today than 30 years ago when entities were conceived where their only purpose was to print pay checks. The Government must establish a mechanism that cannot be compromised where people can directly bill the government for services they provide. The system must ensure that nepotism and conflicts of interest are detected and properly addressed.

5. The US Government needs to be De-Privatized. President Reagan called for smaller and less intrusive government. Instead it has been privatized with trillions of taxpayer dollars wasted as vested interests just enabled the flow of money into a select few with little regard for any serious investments in the economy. As a result, the industrial base has been severely damaged with symptoms throughout the population of economic hardships.
6. The last time the government was reorganized was in the late 1950's and early 1960's. As the path to De-Privatization is set the government needs to be reorganized to meet the needs of the 21st century. This will not happen overnight and will take time to correct the path that took decades to get us to this point of severe dysfunction and lost opportunities.
7. As the economy has struggled and new threats have surfaced a new security state apparatus has surfaced that is privatized. History teaches that such trends are very dangerous as accountability gets lost and freedoms disappear in the name of security but are actually driven by revenues and profits. The security apparatus should be the first to be De-Privatized. The responsibility for protecting citizens clearly rests with the government and not private companies with no other revenue streams other than taxpayer dollars[15].
8. NASA was able to send humans to the Moon in 1969. To accomplish this 400,000 people worked on the program and 20,000 companies were involved in the effort. This effort involved developing new technologies and engineering systems that transformed our world using new materials, machines, management techniques, new systems and space age products. This was an example of a balance between government, industry, and academia – a magic mixture. That mixture does not exist today because of the privatization efforts of the past few decades. When examining the De-Privatization of the government, this history needs to be studied to find a reasonable path forward.

[15] See section 8.6 Privatized Security Clearances.

4 Universities and Colleges

Tuition costs for higher education are extremely high and the financial impact to the post 1980 generation has been devastating. Paying upwards of $300,000 for an undergraduate education such as an engineering degree that may result in a first-year job starting salary of $70,000 per year is not sustainable. Others who pursue other life education choices are in even more dire financial conditions.

Congress has decided to pass legislation that essentially will not allow students to write off their education debt in bankruptcy. Prior to 1976, student loans could be cancelled in bankruptcy like other types of debt. Less than 1% of it actually was canceled. In the late 1970s lawmakers added a condition that student loan borrowers would have to wait at least five years after they began repayment to file for bankruptcy. In 1990, that waiting period was increased to seven years. By 2000 the rules changed and now people with federal or private student loans cannot cancel their debt in bankruptcy unless they can prove their loans pose an undue hardship. Congress never spelled out what undue hardship means, and this leads to unfairness in the courts. For the same case one judge may rule an undue hardship while another judge in the same building may reject the hardship request. Federal Reserve chairman Jerome Powell said that he is "at a loss to explain" why student loans are treated differently than other types of debt in bankruptcy.

The bottom line is that many students have essentially become indentured servants with no hope of a reasonable financial future, and some have decided to leave the country. This is clearly documented in the popular media as of 2019. This is not unlike when the United States was young and many were fleeing indentured servitude in their countries of origin to find freedom and a new way of life in the new land, now the United States. This is now a very sad part of the recent history of the United States, establishing policies and laws that caused this tragic condition.

Bankruptcy protection should have never been taken away from student loans in the first place. It was an important mechanism to check and balance the system. Too many bankruptcies would have focused attention on the root cause of the problem. Now there is the massive negative unintended consequences of this fundamental systemic change.

4.1 How Did This Happen

Student debt has gone from just under $400 billion in 2004 to $1.4 trillion in 2018. Prior to 1980 higher education would result in a higher paying career where any education debt could be easily repaid and not be a burden. Today because of the high cost of tuition the higher paying career does not allow for the debt to be reasonably serviced. What has changed in the cost of higher education since 1980 when costs were relatively reasonable?

It was always known that tuition could never fund the costs associated with higher education and so gifts from large and small donors were a large component to the financial bottom line. There were land grant colleges established to address special needs that allowed for many to get a higher education. However, the cost of higher education was too high from most colleges and universities for most families to afford prior to World War II. After World War II the GI Bill provided huge funding to colleges and universities at the undergraduate level with service men and woman deciding to get a higher education. At the same time the policies as set out in Science the Endless Frontier resulted in contracts with enough overhead to fund Maters Degrees for employees in Government and major Companies.

The GI Bill fundamentally is still in place and young men and woman that leave the military can pursue their undergraduate degrees. However, the numbers are less than in the past.

Privatization has made a huge negative impact on the number of students able to pursue both undergraduate and graduate level education. During the 2018-2019 government shutdown the media identified that 800,000 civil servants and 4.1 million privatized workers were impacted by the shutdown[16]. The new privatized service companies do not have the overhead funds to provide for tuition reimbursement and if they do it is very small at the graduate level. In the past the funding was not limited, and students would commit to completing a graduate level degree in 18 to 24 months. Because of funding limitations, students must spread their education across 5 years or more discouraging any desire to pursue a master's degree. Meanwhile there is no funding for someone to start or complete their undergraduate degree while working in a lower level position at a service company providing privatized government workers.

4.2 Architecture Analysis

In the Industrial Base discussion, a model was shown for government and company operations. The analysis showed that overhead was shifted away from traditional companies to the new service companies and that the overhead budget was slashed in the new service companies to justify their role of replacing civil servants. What is not shown in the model is a critical function and overhead item – Personnel or Human Resources.

Personnel had extremely important functions prior to 1987 one of which was training and education. The shift happened with the rise of privatization and

---

[16] There is no national database tracking the number of contract employees. Dr. Paul Light a federal workforce expert at New York University provided the estimates. Not Expecting Back Pay, Government Contractors Collect Unemployment, Dip into Savings, NPR, January 7, 2019.

massive company consolidations as sources of overhead were targeted and eliminated. This allowed for a new set of rules to be applied to the new service companies.

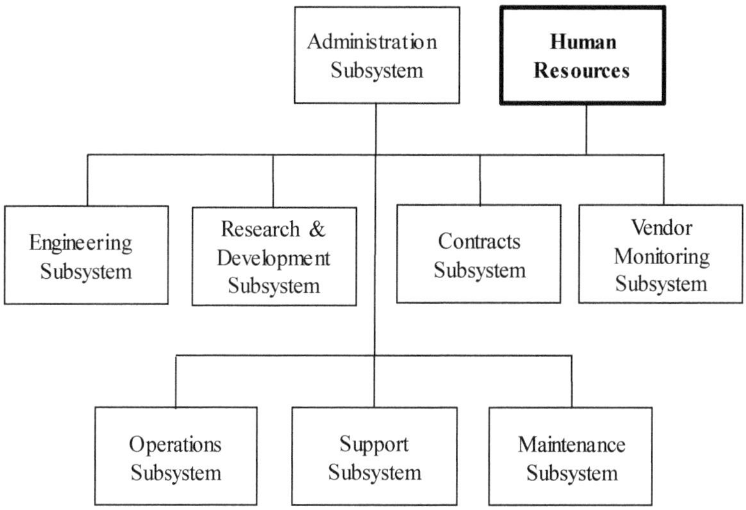

Figure 5 Government and Company Model Missing Human Resources

The service companies providing privatized government workers never included the traditional Human Resources overhead items of training and education. The new service company model was based on temporary work placement companies that existed prior to 1987. Their functions were limited to screening resumes and providing employee exit paperwork upon termination of a service contract. This was not unlike what exists in a temporary work placement company.

Table 9 Human Resources Functions

Personnel Functions	**Traditional Company Pre 1987**	**Service Company**	**Traditional Company Post 1987**	**Civil Service Post 1987**
Employee Screening	Yes	**Limited**	Partial	Partial
Promotion Screening	Yes	**None**	Partial	Partial
Review Systems	Yes	Yes	Yes	Yes
Employee Records	Yes	Yes	Yes	Yes
Training	Yes	**None**	None	Yes
Education	Yes	**None**	Limited / None	Limited
Health Benefits	Yes	**Limited**	Yes	Yes
Employee Assistance	No	**None**	Yes	Yes
Retirement Processing	Yes	**None**	Limited	Yes
Employee Exit	Yes	Yes	Yes	Yes
Lawsuit Mitigation	None	Yes	Yes	Yes

Removing 4.1 million people that are part of the new services companies replacing traditional civil servants from the higher education pipeline is a huge impact. Many of these people are professionals needing the best education resource available and yet they have been cut off from that resource. In order to remain competitive with the new service company model, traditional companies still attempting to engage in product, technology, and system development have been forced to reduce their Human Resources overheads and provide limited or no education reimbursement.

A horrifying trend has recently surface where the new Internet based companies offer no education reimbursement. They have walked away from what many considered a social responsibility that surfaced after 1945 and started to end in 1987.

This impact can be quantified using the ratio of civil servants and privatized workers. There are two system alternatives. The first is the current system and the second is the system that existed prior to 1987 where all employees were properly reimbursed for education. The results are bad and show an 84% loss in university participation at the government worker level. It is unclear if this number is similar from the traditional company level. However, we know that the new Internet based companies are not paying for any higher education costs.

Table 10 University Impact

People	System A (Today)	System B (pre 1987)
Education Reimbursement	0800,000	4,900,000
No Education Reimbursement	4,100,000	0
University Participation	16% (800,000 / 4,900,000)	100%

4.3 PLATO

I pulled this topic out of the Systems Perspectives section. It may seem out of place and distract from the key issue of lost funding. However, it shows the commitment to higher education that no longer exists and clearly treats money as irrelevant as serious problems just need to be solved as effectively as possible.

Prior to World War II education was limited to the few who could afford to attend. In 1944 the GI Bill provided free education to World War II veterans. This was a very different time, where humanity had witnessed incredible horrors and was ready for a new way. This was also the time when Science the Endless Frontier was provided at the request of the president of the United States[17]. The USSR launched the Sputnik I satellite in 1957, and this energized the US Government into spending more on science and engineering education.

[17] Science The Endless Frontier, A Report to the President by Vannevar Bush, Director of the Office of Scientific Research and Development, July 1945.

So, there was a great need to offer higher education to a much larger segment of the population. However, there were two challenges that needed to be overcome. The first was capacity and the other was location. Not only was capacity insufficient for all the new students but also many students were located in areas where there were no colleges or universities.

Chalmers Sherwin a physicist at the University of Illinois realized the need and suggested a computer-based learning system to William Everett the engineering college dean. William Everett recommended that Daniel Alpert, another physicist, convene a meeting with engineers, administrators, mathematicians, and psychologists. After several meetings they were unable to agree on a single design. Rather than accept failure Alpert mentioned the challenge to a laboratory assistant, Donald Bitzer. Donald had been thinking about the problem, suggesting he could build a demonstration system.

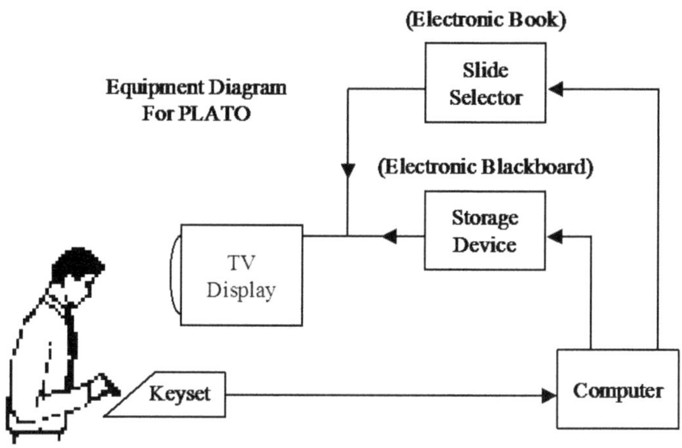

Figure 6 PLATO Bock Diagram 1960

Donald Bitzer is regarded as the Father of Programmed Logic for Automatic Teaching Operations (PLATO). He realized that good graphics were critical to a learning environment. In that time there were only text-based displays. He developed the PLASMA display specifically for PLATO. Notice that his Human Capital level would have been rated zero. Also, his KSA level once compared to all the experts would have been embarrassingly low, again zero. However, because humans have infinite potential Donald transformed our world[18].

Many modern concepts in multi-user computing were developed on PLATO, including forums, message boards, online testing, e-mail, chat rooms, picture languages, instant messaging, remote screen sharing, and multi-player games. It was

---

[18] Hughes Aircraft told everyone that their credentials were irrelevant beyond the basic engineering levels. They clearly stated that you with their infinite potential would have the equivalent of several PhDs very soon. This is a sign of a learning organization.

the precursor to the Internet and the Internet would not exist without PLATO.

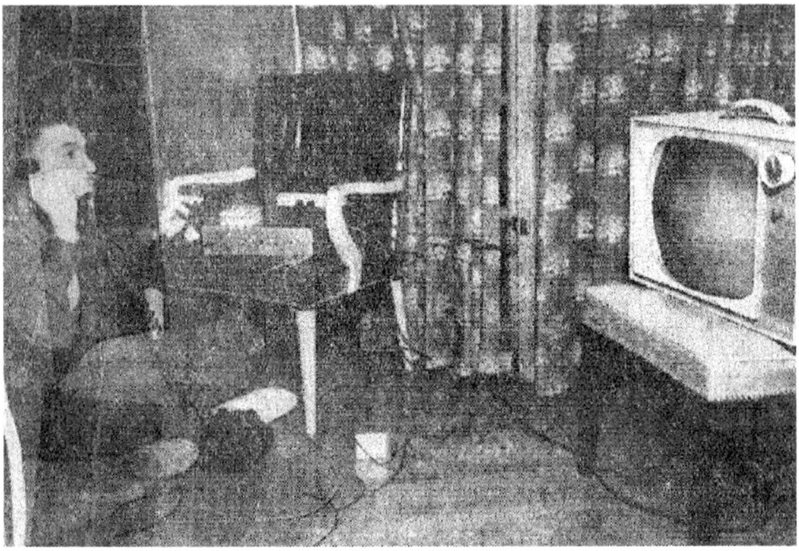

Figure 7 First PLATO Demonstration[19]

Don Bitzer conceived PLATO as a system as shown in a block diagram. The first system was demonstrated March 10, 1960. It used a Television, connected to a graphics generator, keyboard, and dialup modem connected to a computer via long distance telephone wire. Today the concept and equipment are straightforward however in 1960 most of the hardware did not exist. Also, there were many challenges such as the display and response time.

The display was a big challenge in 1960 because of cost and the ability to offer fast response time. Storage tube displays were expensive and didn't have the response time characteristics needed for an interactive teaching system. Raster graphic displays were expensive and large because they used memory and memory was very expensive and large. The solution was to invent and commercialize the gas plasma display panel.

The responsiveness of the system was a serious challenge. For a student to be properly engaged in a lesson, the computer response had to feel instantaneous. In technical terms, this meant that the system response had to appear in less than 100 milliseconds. We know this today as the user preview area response time. This was when batch processing was the norm and programs would run over night, not instantaneously.

---

[19] Don Bitzer Friday March 10, 1961 demonstrates the system at Allerton House. The student indicates their response to a learning exercise by pressing buttons on the keyboard, which is connected to an Illiac computer by long distance telephone wire.

4.4 Recommendations for the Short Term

The short-term recommendations include policy changes that can happen immediately. They include changes to government service contract requirements and then broader topics that require government attention and actions.

Beginning immediately all new and renewed services contracts especially engineering and science services contracts need to include education reimbursement requirements as follows:

1. All services contracts must allocate reasonable funding to support education reimbursement.
2. The reimbursement level must be such that a student can complete a degree in the minimum amount of time and not be limited because of funding constraints.
3. Life is complex and even more complex when employees work and go to school. All service contract must allocate reasonable funding to support an effective employee assistance program.
4. In no instance shall these overhead items be used to discriminate between different vendor cost proposals.

<u>Broad Policy Recommendations</u>

1. There was a huge shift away from basic systems thinking as focus was placed entirely on finance and self-interest where the belief surfaced that the greatest profits and self-interest would lead to the greatest good. We once again know that is a fantasy and a path that eventually leads to disaster.
2. It has been acknowledged within many academic circles that the huge movement of MBA staff into board rooms as a result of the massive number of MBA degrees in the 1980's has caused serious damage. While MBA staffs are great at executing business activities, they have no vision. The vision comes from the engineers and they need to return back to the board rooms. As a result, many Universities have introduced entrepreneur programs specifically to get engineers into the board rooms of major companies. However, they are acting alone, and it is unclear how this can happen without major policy from the government. The government needs to investigate how to help shift away from the previous model to the new model the universities have adopted.
3. It is critical that the government not accept practices of faster better cheaper for the sole purpose of hiding the true costs of systems development, maintenance, and operations. This can only happen if the government relies on the foundation of education coming from engineering and science-based Universities and companies. The age of snake oil salespeople selling a quick fix tool and or process never goes away and the government must always be vigilant and ensure that those seeds never sprout. At the same time the

government should encourage innovation. This is difficult with so much of the industrial base centered on services contract staff with no connection to product development, manufacturing, or technology development. Somehow service staff employees need to be bought back into the reality loop via effective government policy mechanisms.

4.5 Recommendations for Privatization Transformation

1. Everyone needs to understand that there is a huge difference between a Government Organization and a Private Company. Basic civics education needs to be made part of all levels of the educational system from elementary school to the college and university levels. It is outrageous to have adults with significant educational backgrounds not know and understand the difference between government and industry or know that government can accomplish certain things that are impossible for industry to accomplish alone and that industry should not even be given those burdens.
2. NASA was able to send humans to the Moon in 1969. To accomplish this 400,000 people worked on the program and 20,000 companies were involved in the effort. This effort involved developing new technologies and engineering systems that transformed our world using new materials, machines, management techniques, new systems and space age products. This was an example of a balance between government, industry, and academia – a magic mixture. That mixture does not exist today because of the privatization efforts of the past few decades. When examining the De-Privatization of the government, this history needs to be studied to find a reasonable path forward.

5 Air Transportation

The U.S. Air Transportation System consists of two extremely large systems:

1. Air Travel Transportation System
2. Air Traffic Control (ATC) System

Many view the Air Travel Transportation System from the perspective of the ATC system suggesting that it somehow impacts the Travel portion of the system. However, the Travel portion of the system is separate and distinct from the ATC portion of the system.

Figure 8 Air Travel Transportation circa 1943[20]

This analysis will take a systems perspective and report on the condition of the

[20] Source US Government. A DC-3 flies over Oklahoma City.

US Air Travel Transportation system. It will identify some history, suggest how we may have arrived at this point, and then offer potential suggestions for moving forward in a positive direction.

Figure 9 Air Traffic Control – ATC circa 1935[21]

5.1 Recent User Experience

We begin with my recent user experience. We decided to go to Disney World for Spring Break in 2019. This is what we experienced.

Shock and Abuse

- We arrived early at ACY International and quickly went through TSA pre-check.
- Once we found the gate, we decided to go to get a bite to eat. As we sat down the waitress asked if we were sure we wanted to sit down and eat. We said, why what is wrong. She proceeded to say all flights were canceled.
- We did not hear any announcement of cancellation over the airport PA system.
- None of the airport screens showed any flights were canceled. Our flight was green and still showed on time.

[21] Source US Government. Newark tower.

- I had multiple emails through the day showing on time, on time, delayed 1 hour, on time.
- We proceeded down to the ticket area, there was a large number of people. We asked those in line about cancellations, and they said yes, the flights were canceled.
- Still no public announcement, no employees making statements to the crowds.
- As we wait in line, I get an email the flight is canceled. The email time stamp says 3:50 PM but the time is 4:30 for a 6:05 PM flight. Header time stamps do not match any of the times.
- Children are crying, parents are frantic, one ticketing agent was visibly shaken and appeared to be previously crying. Insufficient number of ticketing agents.
- One ticking agent tells everyone to go to one area.
- Half hour later after the line grows ticketing agents tells everyone to go back to the previous area so that new passengers could be handled. People from the back of the line now are part of the front of the line in new area. People rebel get vocal and do not move.
- Not sure why they did not just open a new line for new passengers trying to fly out. How can these people not have this basic crowd control concept - common sense?
- We finally get to the ticket agent. There is no greeting. We wait about 30 seconds for the agent to say something like "hello", "sorry", "we will get you there", instead there is nothing just silence. I eventually hand the agent our hard copy tickets and say help.
- The agent proceeds to type at lightning speed and starts to very quickly speak things we can't understand.
- We start over and ask, when can you get us to Orlando? More lightning speed typing - Thursday night. But this is Saturday, is there anything else you can do - NO. What if we fly to a nearby city? More feverish typing - Tampa Tuesday night. Is that all you can do - yes. Ok let's do it - Tuesday Tampa. There is an up charge of $500. Can we cancel, yes within 24 hours? Ok, let's do it.

Help from Normal People

- Meanwhile our daughter in Orlando at Disney World finds a 7:00 AM American flight out of Philly for $1000. We book that flight.
- The ACY garage has an attendant and lets us drive away for free rather than pay for the time parked. We thanked them for being human. They told us they have horror stories of what happens at the ACY airport.
- We go back home and try to sleep because we need to wake up at 2:00 AM to catch the 7:00 AM Philly flight.

Loss of the Dream That Once Was Real

- We get to Philly I drop off my wife at terminal B and I go park in long term parking past terminal F.
- It's late and the buses are not visible, so I proceed to walk. Terminal F is not far and as I recalled from days past Philly had people movers.
- I go into Terminal F but cannot enter because security has blocked access to the people movers. I go back down and proceed to walk outside in the rain and cold to Terminal B. My wife would have never made the walk with her 3 hip replacements. I periodically look up at the walkways with the people movers wondering if they are still running but with no people.
- We go through TSA pre-check. The containers holding our personal items are filthy. It has been 18 years since the systems were established. I guess they never replaced or cleaned anything.
- We get on the plane. The seats are sized for elementary school children, they are violating MIL-STD-1472 ergonomic safety standards. I take a breath and I can't breathe. In about half an hour I feel that I am going into a coma because of no life support. They are violating MIL-STD-1472 ventilation safety standards. The noise is outrageous, way beyond MIL-STD-1472, they are violating noise safety standards.
- The airplane bounces around and rocks like a Cessna 172 that I used to Pilot. Once again, the design is very poor.
- We arrive in Orlando Airport. That Airport is an Architectural Marvel - Beautiful - At least that is the way it was.
- Today TSA has converted it into an architectural disaster.
- They had 18 years to figure out how to move it from an architectural disaster and restore the architectural beauty of this nation state wonder.
- They did nothing in 18 years.

<u>Outrageous Corporate Behavior</u>

- At Disney World our daughter tells us the airline is refusing to cancel our reservation without a fee even though it was done before the 24-hour time limit.
- The next day she spends most of the morning dealing with the airline. Eventually I get an email suggesting they made the refund.
- The second day she spends most of the morning dealing with the travel insurance to pay for the $1000 American Airlines ticket.
- Not sure about the cost of 1 day lost for the room.

<u>Horrible Flight is Now Normal</u>

- Time to leave Disney World.
- We cannot change our flight from ACY to Philly without significant costs, so we fly back to ACY international. The car is in Philly.

- We get on the plane. The seats are sized for elementary school children, they are violating MIL-STD-1472 ergonomic safety standards. I take a breath and I can't breathe. In about half an hour I feel that I am going into a coma because of no life support. They are violating MIL-STD-1472 ventilation safety standards. The noise is outrageous, way beyond MIL-STD-1472, they are violating noise safety standards.
- The airplane bounces around and rocks like a Cessna 172 that I used to Pilot. Once again, the design is very poor.
- We pay $35+$5 to Lyft to get us back to our house 5 miles away. The Lyft driver says it was a good decision I reserved the time otherwise we would spend the night in the empty ACY airport.

Public Transportation

- The next morning, we proceed to the Absecon Train station and I catch the Bus. I was thinking that maybe I am old, and I am over reacting.

Major Awakening with Public Transportation

- So, I ride the Bus to PATCO, to the Philly subway, to the Train, to Philly Airport.
- I get on the Bus. It is clean, the seats are sized for normal people, I take a breath and I can breathe. They have a sufficient number of buses running so that they are not overloaded with people. The system is sized to handle peak and unanticipated peak loads. It bounces, it's a bus, but it is smoother than the airplanes I just experienced. It does make noise but is well within MIL-STD-1472 standards for normal conversation. I am able to easily converse with a passenger across the aisle. What happened to the stable smooth quiet whisper jets from my youth! Wow this is 2-3 times better than airplane travel.
- I get on the PATCO. It is clean, the seats are sized for normal people, I take a breath and I can breathe. They have a sufficient number of trains running so that they are not overloaded with people. The system is sized to handle peak and unanticipated peak loads. It is very smooth and very quiet, no noise. What happened to the stable smooth quiet whisper jets from my youth! Wow this is 3-5 times better than airplane travel.
- I get on the Philly Subway. Everyone knows the Philly Subway is horrible. But you only spend 5 - 10 minutes on the subway not 2 - 6 hours like on a plane. The Philly Subway matches my airline travel experience. It is actually better because I only spend a few minutes in the torture chamber.
- I get on the SEPTA Train. It is clean, the seats are sized for normal people, I take a breath and I can breathe. They have a sufficient number of trains running so that they are not overloaded with people. The system is sized to handle peak and unanticipated peak loads. It is very smooth and very quiet, no noise. What happened to the stable smooth quiet whisper jets from my youth! Wow this is 3-5 times better than airplane travel.

- I pick up my car and drive home.

I am sure we can pull from 10-20 years' worth of complaints to the FAA, Airline Companies, and Airports and find this same experience. There are many articles in the popular media which provide the same information. Disney was great as always.

There has been no responsibility or action from anyone to address these complaints. The system just gets worse with each passing year. Every time I have traveled by air since 2001 my experience has only become worse. This time it nearly killed me. I am 63 years old and on multiple occasions I nearly collapsed. I am surprised I did not have a heart attack or a stroke.

When I was flying as a young man my view of air transportation was spectacular. Way beyond public transportation in every way, 10 times better.

- Everything was extremely high tech, today they do not even use PA systems at gates to board passengers - they scream at the mob
- The people were very smart, polite, and very helpful
- There were always glitches (weather, mechanical issues, and people sick) but they always tried to get you to your final destination even if it meant bus rides and other airlines
- I flew about once every 2 months for 20 years, never did I ever get treated like an animal, herded into a cage, or delayed more than 1-4 hours

It is obvious that people have complained, the media has written about the bad system, and yet nothing has been done on the way down to this rock bottom place where the next system state is total collapse. The following article is an interview with United Airlines CEO David Oliver[22]:

United Airlines CEO Oscar Munoz acknowledged key pain points customers face when traveling today, including airlines' ***increasingly shrinking seat sizes.***

"I think we are nearing a point certainly that we can't do that anymore," *Munoz told ABC News. The interview was conducted prior to the U.S. grounding of the Boeing 737 Max.*

He said that air travel used to be a thrilling experience but has turned into a laborious process.

"It's become so stressful," he told the outlet, "from when you leave, wherever you live, to get into traffic, to find a parking spot, to get through security."

---

[22] United Airlines CEO: By the time you sit on our planes, 'you're just pissed at the world' David Oliver, USA TODAY Published 9:18 a.m. ET April 25, 2019.

Munoz added ***"By the time you sit on one of our aircraft ... you're just pissed at the world."*** *He also said that the experience won't be improved by something like coffee or a cookie.*

This appears to be a request for help. There are many different types of business cultures, some take the high road and others take the low road. It is wonderful when industry leaders can match business success with taking the high road. What happens when businesses take the low road and become the leaders in an industry? How can this toxic cycle be broken?

5.2 Cities without Air Transportation Services

Unfortunately, the problem is worse than what is happening to the individual traveler. Today we have a system where cities have lost effective air transportation services because airlines have decided to eliminate routes based on their individual business needs regardless of the broader impacts on the economy and quality of life.

Atlantic City is one of the metro areas impacted by the shutting down of unprofitable air routes. This leaves airports like Atlantic City with little or no air transportation services. By the 1980s, rural and remote areas lost airline service. Many state capitals have lost airline services completely and are only accessible by automobile or private plane. Even medium-sized airports have been severely impacted with the loss of airline services. This is extremely disruptive to the local and national economy, as important centers of commerce are now isolated. This is a small sampling of cities that have been severely impacted:

- Pittsburg
- Cincinnati
- Memphis
- Albany
- Little Rock
- Sacramento
- Buffalo

This was all fully documented in the popular media and yet no one took the desperately needed corrective actions.

5.2.1 Loss of Air Transportation Services

The loss of transportation services across the country[23] has been documented for years. Taxpayers made major investments in air transportation infrastructure that the airline companies squandered. This is not a good story and hits at the heart of major systemic breakdown that must be addressed.

St Louis

St. Louis made a major commitment to its airport infrastructure and by 2006

[23] Washington Monthly, Terminal Sickness, by Phillip Longman and Lina Khan, March / April 2012.

local taxpayers invested a billion dollars to build a third runway at Lambert International Airport. This involved disrupting communities and removing hundreds of homes.

By 2012 available seat miles are one third of the 2000 level. Two of Lambert's five concourses are now empty. The one that serviced the TWA hub is only partially used. The third runway is now redundant. This happened after American Airlines took over TWA and Lambert International Airport was downgraded from International status to a mid-continental hub.

St. Louis's loss of service happened even though the population of the metropolitan area is the eighteenth largest in the U.S. It also experienced growth between 2000 and 2010. The city is home to eight Fortune 500 companies and is a major center for international companies like Anheuser-Busch InBev, Monsanto, Boeing, Emerson Electric, Express Scripts, and Nestlé Purina. It also has a research base with institutions like Washington University and a fast-growing medical sciences sector. The GDP of the metro area rivals that of oil-rich Qatar.

The taxpayers made a major investment to support the airline companies that then walked away from that investment because it was not their money. They had zero risk exposure. This scenario is like states building highways and then having automobile companies tell their drivers that they cannot use the highways.

Like most other midsize American cities, St. Louis's economy and quality of life has been severely damaged by a handful of airline executives. There is no accountability. All the risk was pushed to the taxpayer. This is a classic case of cost shifting to an unsuspecting stakeholder[24].

Memphis

Memphis International was designated a hub by Northwest in 1986. The airport undertook record-breaking expansion projects to house the airline and its regional carrier, Northwest Airlink. There is no competition at the airport and so the airport has extremely high airfares. Even though the airfares are high the service levels are dropping. Delta purchased Northwest and the executives reduced the airport's hub status. In 2011 the airline cut 25 percent of its flights from the city. Once again there is significant damage to the local economy and quality of life.

Pittsburg

During the 1990s Pittsburgh invested heavily in its airport infrastructure. It had more than 600 daily nonstop flights. When U.S. Airways merged with America West and concentrated its hub operations in Philadelphia and Charlotte, Pittsburgh service crashed. U.S. Airways daily flights fell from 542 to 68. Half the gates and two concourses are closed. Pittsburgh International airport is mostly empty.

Flying in and out of Pittsburgh has become too much trouble and companies are now hosting meetings near New York City and Washington, D.C. The University of

---

[24] See section 9 Systems Perspectives where cost shifting is discussed in multiple areas of the section.

Pittsburgh Medical Center, the biggest employer in the region, staff, researchers, and physicians are choosing to drive to professional conferences whenever they can. Flying between Pittsburgh and New York or Washington now takes a whole day because flights go through Philadelphia or Charlotte. Once again there is significant damage to the local economy and quality of life.

5.2.2 Ignoring System Performance Realities

When deregulation was proposed it was within the context of the existing system of the day. It was an attempt to improve the system by allowing new companies with new ideas to enter the system. Shutting down transportation routes to various cities was never envisioned or desired. Yet when the empirical data started to surface of this extremely negative consequence, there was no attempt to correct the system and move it back into an effective performance level while also allowing for new companies and ideas to participate. Instead everyone ignored the declining system performance.

Table 11 Leading Population Centers

Rank	Core City	Metro Population	Metropolitan Statistical Area	Region
1	New York	19,979,477	New York, Newark, Jersey City, NY, NJ, PA MSA	Northeast
2	Los Angeles	13,291,486	Los Angeles, Long Beach, Anaheim, CA MSA	West
3	Chicago	9,498,716	Chicago, Joliet, Naperville, IL, IN, WI MSA	Midwest
4	Dallas Fort Worth	7,539,711	Dallas, Fort Worth, Arlington, TX MSA	South
5	Houston	6,997,384	Houston, The Woodlands-Sugar Land MSA	South
6	Washington, D.C.	6,249,950	Washington, D.C., VA, MD, WV MSA	South
7	Miami	6,198,782	Miami, Fort Lauderdale, West Palm Beach, FL MSA	South
8	Philadelphia	6,096,372	Philadelphia, Camden, Wilmington, PA, NJ, DE, MD MSA	Northeast
9	Atlanta	5,949,951	Atlanta, Sandy Springs, Roswell, GA MSA	South
10	Boston	4,875,390	Boston, Cambridge, Quincy, MA, NH MSA	Northeast
11	Phoenix	4,857,962	Phoenix, Mesa, Chandler, AZ MSA	West
12	San Francisco	4,729,484	San Francisco, Oakland, Fremont, CA MSA	West
13	Riverside / San Bernardino	4,662,361	Riverside, San Bernardino, Ontario, CA MSA	West

Table 11 Leading Population Centers

Rank	Core City	Metro Population	Metropolitan Statistical Area	Region
14	Detroit	4,326,442	Detroit, Warren, Dearborn, MI MSA	Midwest
15	Seattle	3,939,363	Seattle, Tacoma, Bellevue, WA MSA	West
16	Minneapolis–St. Paul	3,629,190	Minneapolis, St. Paul, Bloomington, MN, WI MSA	Midwest
17	San Diego	3,343,364	San Diego, Carlsbad, San Marcos, CA MSA	West
18	Tampa / St. Petersburg	3,142,663	Tampa, St. Petersburg, Clearwater, FL MSA	South
19	Denver	2,932,415	Denver, Aurora, Lakewood, CO MSA	West
20	St. Louis	2,805,465	St. Louis, MO-IL MSA	Midwest

Source Based on 2018 MSA population estimates from the U.S. Census Bureau

Although we have leading population centers the country is much bigger than suggested by major population center data. Yet the air transportation system ignores this simple fact as it struggles to maintain services.

There have been massive consolidations, steep cuts in wages and benefits, rising fares, huge direct and indirect subsidies. Yet the industry is unable to service its debt and provide reasonable levels of service. Its executives see no way out except to continue to merge, cut capacity, and reduce services to the point of making air travel horrible and only used as a last resort by the people.

The industry's problems are structural and deepening. This is negatively impacting cities, industries, and people that depend on effective and affordable air service. The fundamental problem is that the airline business model doesn't work.

The cost to the airlines of short-haul service is always going to be much higher than that of long-haul service, regardless of how the industry is organized or how much money can be squeezed from the employees or extracted from the customers via snake oil sales methods. A tremendous amount of resources is used to get a plane in the air. If the plane lands a short time later, it is hard to earn the fares necessary to cover the cost.

Along with short-haul long-haul service system characteristics, there are the system characteristics of low and high passenger counts. It costs the same to maintain an air traffic control tower, a runway, ticketing and baggage-handling facilities regardless if an airport serves five or fifty flights a day, or whether each plane carries five or fifty passengers. The fixed costs on low-volume routes are the same as high-volume routes. However, airline service to the public and the economy needs to provide routes to as many places as possible with a reasonable level of service and cost to the passengers.

Unless something is done fewer people will be flying to fewer places. This will devastate the economy. The high fixed cost of the remaining routes may be spread among a diminished number of passengers. Cross-subsidization between short-haul and long-haul routes is the only answer.

The Founders of the USA understood that companies alone could not provide broadly distributed postal service because of the high cost of delivering mail to smaller towns and far-flung cities. They wrote into the Constitution Section 8 Clause 7: To establish Post Offices and post Roads. Thus, government would take on the challenge of providing the necessary cross-subsidization to ensure everyone would get the mail regardless of location. In the same section is Clause 3: To regulate Commerce.

5.3 How Did We Get Here

On May 20, 1926 President Calvin Coolidge signed the Air Commerce Act of 1926 into law. The act instructed the Secretary of Commerce to:

- Foster air commerce
- Designate and establish airways
- Establish, operate, and maintain aids to air navigation (but not airports)
- Issue and enforce air traffic rules
- Arrange for research and development to improve such aids
- License pilots
- Issue airworthiness certificates for aircraft and major aircraft components
- And investigate accidents

The new Aeronautics Branch, operating under the Department of Commerce assumed primary responsibility for aviation oversight. This legislation was passed at the urging of the aviation industry who believed the airplane could not reach its full commercial potential without federal action to improve and maintain safety standards.

In 1938, the Civil Aeronautics Act transferred the federal civil aviation responsibilities from the Commerce Department to the Civil Aeronautics Authority, a new independent agency. The legislation expanded the government's role by giving the CAA the authority and the power to regulate airline fares and to determine the routes that air carriers would serve.

In 1940 President Franklin D. Roosevelt split the Civil Aeronautics Authority (old CAA) into two agencies:

1. Civil Aeronautics Administration (CAA)
2. Civil Aeronautics Board (CAB).

The new CAA now part of the Department of Commerce and was responsible for:

- Air Traffic Control (ATC)
- Airman and aircraft certification
- Safety enforcement
- Airway development

The new CAB was an independent federal agency and was entrusted with:

- Safety regulation
- Accident investigation
- Economic regulation of the airlines (regulation of commercial airline routes and fares)

In 1958 Federal Aviation Act was passed. This legislation gave the CAA's functions to a new independent body, the Federal Aviation Agency. The act transferred air safety regulation from the CAB to the new FAA, and also gave the FAA sole responsibility for a common civil-military system of air navigation and air traffic control. The CAB remained to perform its economic and regulation functions of the airlines. So, the new functional allocation in the system became:

<u>FAA Functions</u>

- Air Traffic Control (ATC),
- Airman and aircraft certification
- Safety enforcement
- Airway development
- Safety regulation
- Common civil-military system of air navigation and air traffic control

<u>CAB Functions</u>

- Accident investigation
- Economic regulation of the airlines (regulation of commercial airline routes and fares)

On Mar 2, 1966 President Johnson recommended to Congress the creation of a Cabinet-level Department of Transportation (DOT). The President noted that the United States lacked a coordinated transportation system permitting travelers and goods to move conveniently from one means of transportation to another, using the best characteristics of each. The responsibility for transportation within the Federal government, he observed, was fragmented among many agencies resulting in a series of uncoordinated modal policies. What was needed was a single department to develop and carry out comprehensive policies and programs for transportation in its totality. The President proposed that the following agencies and functions be consolidated in the new department the Office of the Under Secretary of Commerce for Transportation; the Bureau of Public Roads; the Federal Aviation Agency; the

U.S. Coast Guard; the Maritime Administration; the safety functions of the Civil Aeronautics Board (CAB); the safety functions and car service functions of the Interstate Commerce Commission (ICC); the Great Lakes Pilotage Administration; the St. Lawrence Seaway Development Corporation; the Alaska Railroad; and certain minor transportation-related activities of other agencies. The President also recommended the creation within the new DOT of a National Transportation Safety Board (NTSB), which would absorb the safety functions transferred from the CAB and ICC.

The new DOT combined major federal responsibilities for air and surface transport. The Federal Aviation Agency's name changed to the Federal Aviation Administration (FAA) and it became one of several agencies within DOT (e.g., Federal Highway Administration, Federal Railroad Administration, the Coast Guard, and the Saint Lawrence Seaway Commission).

The new NTSB took over the CABs role of investigating and determining the causes of transportation accidents and making recommendations to the secretary of transportation.

The CAB still had the role of regulation of commercial airline routes and fares. The CAB was merged into DOT with its responsibilities limited to the regulation of commercial airline routes and fares.

The new system function allocation became:

<u>FAA Functions</u>

- Air Traffic Control (ATC)
- Airman and Aircraft Certification
- Safety Enforcement
- Airway Development
- Safety Regulation
- Common Civil-Military System of Air Navigation and Air Traffic Control

<u>NTSB Functions</u>

- Accident Investigation

<u>CAB Functions</u>

- Economic Regulation of The Airlines (regulation of commercial airline routes and fares)

5.4 Disaster in the Making

In 1978 the U.S. Airline Deregulation Act was passed and deregulated the airline industry. It removed government control over fares, routes, and market entry of new airlines. It introduced a free market into the commercial airline industry. It phased out the CAB regulation authority.

The legislation removed various restrictions on airline operations over a four-year period, with complete elimination of restrictions on domestic routes and new services by December 31, 1981, and the end of all domestic fare regulation by January 1, 1983. In practice, changes came sooner. The act did the following:

- **CAB's authority to set fares was gradually eliminated;**
- CAB was required to expedite processing of various requests;
- Standards were liberalized for the establishment of new airlines;
- Airlines were allowed to take over service on routes underutilized by competitors or on which the competitor received a local service subsidy;
- American-owned international carriers were allowed to offer domestic service;
- Burden was placed on the CAB to block a route as inconsistent with "public convenience";
- CAB was prohibited from introducing new regulation of charter trips;
- Certain subsidies for carrying mail were terminated effective January 1, 1986, and Essential Air Service subsidies effective 10 years from enactment;
- **Existing mutual aid agreements were terminated between air carriers;**
- **CAB was allowed to grant antitrust immunity to carriers;**
- FAA was directed to develop safety standards for commuter airlines;
- Intrastate carriers were allowed to enter into through service and joint fare agreements with interstate air carriers;
- Air carriers, in hiring employees, were required to give preference to terminated or furloughed employees of another carrier for 10 years after enactment;

The Remaining regulatory authority was transferred to the United States Department of Transportation (DOT) and the CAB itself was dissolved in 1984 and closed January 1, 1985. Safety inspections and air traffic control remained in the hands of the FAA. The act also required the Secretary of Transportation to report to Congress about air safety and any deregulation impacts.

The CAB functions started in 1938 and then moved into other agencies with time. Its last function of regulating aviation services including scheduled passenger airline service ended when the CAB was formally abolished in 1984 as part of the 1978 U.S. Airline Deregulation Act.

When the CAB was abolished its one remaining key function was not moved into another agency as was the approach since 1938. Instead the function of **Economic Regulation of the Airlines** was removed; no one was overseeing the airline routes or fares. This function was left to the Oligopoly Airline Providers.

Coincident with this time the Reagan Administration took power in Washington and antitrust laws were not favored and enforcing existing antitrust laws stopped. The key function of supporting effective commerce and a reasonable air travel experience was removed from government oversight and left to the unchecked free market, the Oligopoly Airline Providers, to make choices as the system evolved.

However, the airspace belongs to the people and the companies are effectively given a license to use and profit from that airspace based on the needs of the people[25].

5.5 Unintended System Consequences

Prior to 1978, the United States policy treated airline service as a public convenience and necessity. It used the CAB to assign routes and set fares. The U.S. government ensured that comparably sized cities received service equal in quality and price. It also made sure that the smaller cities maintained routes including connections to the large cities as part of a national air transportation system. It was an air transportation systems network where all cities were considered important and equal stakeholders in the national system infrastructure. The architecture of the system was different prior to 1978.

Access to computers was limited prior to 1978. They were probably used but not to the full extent possible given today's computer capabilities. Today computer access is a non-issue and using computers to optimize the air transportation network will likely lead to a significantly more efficient system than using random decisions within company oligopolies each maximizing their own interests at the expense of a national transportation system network. In 1978 the concept of a network did not even exist for the most part; it was foreign and exotic. Today networks are the fabric of society.

In 1978, Ted Kennedy, Stephen Breyer (Kennedy's Senate aide), economist Alfred Kahn (selected by President Carter to run the CAB), and Ralph Nader developed a plan to lower the cost of airline fares by increasing airline price competition. It was called deregulation but the unintended consequences of eliminating the CAB, coupled with multiple administrations lack of antitrust enforcement, shifted control of the airline industry from experts answerable to the public, to corporate boardrooms and Wall Street. Their needs did and do not match the needs of public convenience and necessity or of maintaining an effective air transportation systems network.

Regulating airline fares and determining routes were important new functions in the system architecture of 1938. So, how did we get here? The subtle change in the system architecture by closing the CAB and not moving its key function to another subsystem transformed the system in ways many did not imagine, and they would not have allowed had they known the unintended consequences.

---

[25] See section 1 Privatization Recent History for Franchise Agreements, Grants, and Contracting Out for the possible privatization approaches.

Department Of Commerce 1926
1. Foster air commerce
2. Designate and establish airways
3. Establish, operate, and maintain aids to air navigation (but not airports)
4. Issue and enforce air traffic rules
5. Arrange for research and development to improve such aids
6. License pilots
7. Issue airworthiness certificates for aircraft and major aircraft components
8. Investigate accidents

Civil Aeronautics Authority 1938
1. Foster air commerce
2. Designate and establish airways
3. Establish, operate, and maintain aids to air navigation (but not airports)
4. Issue and enforce air traffic rules
5. Arrange for research and development to improve such aids
6. License pilots
7. Issue airworthiness certificates for aircraft and major aircraft components
8. Investigate accidents
9. Regulate airline fares
10. Determine the routes

Figure 10 System Architecture Transition State 1 (1926 - 1938)

The system functions remained intact between 1926 and 1938. In 1938 new functions were added: (9) regulate airline fares and (10) determine the routes.

Civil Aeronautics Administration (CAA) 1940
1. Air Traffic Control (ATC)
2. Airman and aircraft certification
3. Safety enforcement
4. Airway development

Civil Aeronautics Board (CAB) 1940
1. Safety regulation
2. Accident investigation
3. Economic regulation of the airlines

Federal Aviation Agency (FAA) 1958
1. Air Traffic Control (ATC)
2. Airman and aircraft certification
3. Safety enforcement
4. Airway development
5. Safety regulation
6. Common civil-military system of air navigation and air traffic control

Civil Aeronautics Board (CAB) 1958
1. Accident investigation
2. Economic regulation of the airlines

Figure 11 System Architecture Transition State 2 (1940 - 1958)

In1958 the functions increased to include a common civil military system for air navigation and air traffic control. The key functions of regulating the airline routes and fares still existed and was part of the CAB.

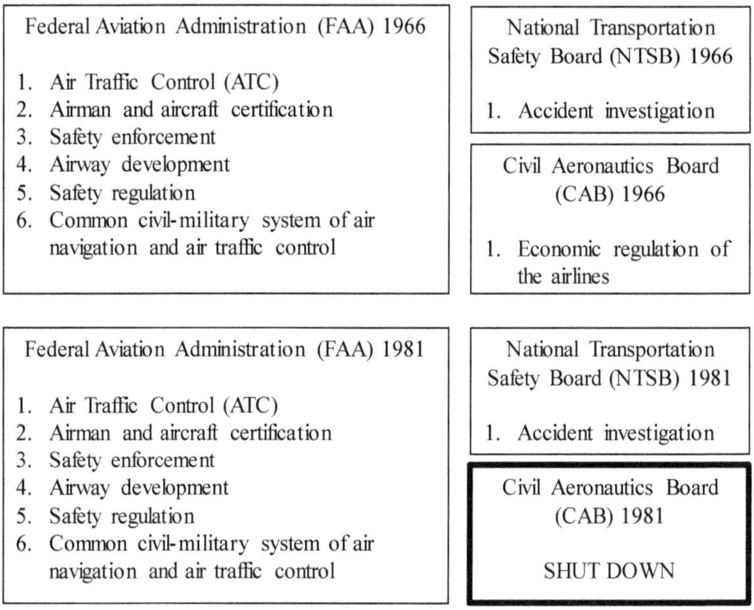

Figure 12 System Architecture Transition State 3 (1966 - 1981 - present)

In 1981 the CAB was shut down but unlike in previous decades when the government was reorganized and yet preserved key functionality, in this case the key functionality of regulation of the airline routes and fares was discontinued.

5.6 Railroads and Airlines

The challenges associated with effective air transportation are not new and date back a few thousand years when various civilizations addressed the problem of roads to ensure effective commerce between ports, villages, and cities. In modern times the USA addressed this same challenge with:

- Postal Service
- Water Way Canals
- Road Transportation
- Train Transportation
- Telegraph Services
- Electric Services
- Telephone Services
- Water Services

In all cases the people recognized the need to service the smallest of populations and that those services could never be financially sustainable. It was always recognized that funding needed to come from external sources. The problem was well understood with the founding of the USA and the Constitution included words associated with postal services.

Over 100 years ago people struggled with how to maintain a fair efficient railroad transportation system. Railroads were built across the country, much like start-up airlines in the 1980s. Over time, the high fixed cost of railroad transportation and the economics of an unchecked transportation system left all routes unprofitable except for a few key routes.

5.6.1 Railroad Transportation History

The air transportation history begins with a history of the US railroads. The railroads experienced the same issues as the airlines when the industry was deregulated. Unfortunately, we ignored our history and relied on anti-trust legislation to prevent the same plight that the early railroad system experienced. That did not work.

How to maintain an equitable and efficient railroad network was challenging. In the 1800s railroad lines were built to the farthest corners of the US. The high fixed cost of railroading and economics of different routes left all but the core of the system unprofitable. Even though railroads maintained a monopoly more than 30 percent of domestic mileage failed by the 1870s.

High fixed costs and cutthroat competition led to consolidation and downsizing. Consolidation led to even more monopoly power first over small and midsize towns and cities and then over large cities. By the 1880s, the economies of major cities like Philadelphia, Baltimore, St. Louis, and Cincinnati were impacted based on how railroad financiers (robber barons) would fix rates. Americans faced price discrimination when traveling or shipping to places dominated by a single railroad trust or pool.

Secretary of Transportation Brock Adams noted: "While the result of other ordinary competition was to reduce and equalize prices, that of railroad competition was to produce local inequalities and to arbitrarily raise and depress prices. The teachings of political economy were at fault."

5.6.2 Interstate Commerce Commission

The response was the creation of the Interstate Commerce Commission (ICC) in 1887. It evened out the prices between different regions, classes of passengers, and shippers so that the railroads could earn enough money to cover their costs, improve their infrastructure, and give their investors a fair reward. The profits earned on highly trafficked long-haul routes were rechanneled by government policy to cover the cost of providing balanced and affordable service throughout the country. It required what might be called an industrial policy and details, such as setting the relative prices of shipping hogs verses hams from point A to B.

Government regulation of railroad pricing and routes worked well as evidenced by the country emerging as an industrial powerhouse during this system. Managing the structure and pricing of railroads was critical to maintaining small-scale entrepreneurs and of midsize manufacturing cities like Cincinnati or St. Louis. The government did not pick winners or losers. Rather it prevented narrow interests from gaming the system in their favor at the cost of the country.

This model was eventually used to regulate the future telephone, power, and airline companies. Natural monopolies could remain in private hands and earn a profit, but not at the cost of skewing the overall efficiency, balance, and fairness of the American economy.

5.6.3 Civil Aeronautics Board

The U.S. used the ICC system approach for the new airline industry and established the Civil Aeronautics Board (CAB) in 1938. The legislation was based on the system concept of a "public right of transit". The citizens needed a reliable aviation system designed to meet their business and safety requirements and the previous history of the railroads that yielded the knowledge that unregulated competition would be unable to satisfy that need.

During the time when the CAB was in place the airline industry matured and grew. With the introduction of the DC-8 and other jets, fares fell, and a mass market tourist industry developed with destinations such as Disney World and the Caribbean.

5.6.4 Deregulation – We Forgot Our History

So why did the Carter administration decide to stop the government's regulation of airlines? There were several reasons for this fundamental change in the system. The old regulatory system had become litigious and rule bound. It became impossible to start a new airline company unless the CAB was somehow bypassed. Southwest Airlines became an example which started in 1971 by flying only within Texas allowing it to avoid regulation by the CAB. Southwest's success with discount fares were significant because inflation became a serious economic problem and consumers focused on low prices everywhere.

Many started suggesting that the New Deal regulatory state had been compromised by established companies and industries leading to corporate socialism. For example, no new major airlines emerged since the 1930s. The general perception was that protected from competition, both airline management and unions were overpaid at the expense of the consumer.

The Carter administration accepted the perception that the New Deal regulation system stopped working and used it to justify deregulating airlines, railroads, trucking, and natural gas industries. They also took steps toward rolling back banking regulation. Many believed that any monopolies that may surface would be checked by rigorous antitrust enforcement. The incoming Reagan administration continued with this policy shift but then included anti-trust laws in the same category as deregulation. Enforcement of anti-trust laws stopped.

With airline deregulation and no enforcement of anti-trust laws many communities instantly lost air service as the route structure quickly moved into the hub-and-spoke system. This eliminated many direct flights. During this time period there were price declines and expansion of short haul routes, but they were the result of declines in the price of oil because of a world oil glut. These benefits would have surfaced without deregulation and perhaps consumer prices may have even been lower.

The Economic Policy Institute performed a study in 1990 and factored in the price of energy. The study concluded that airline fares fell more rapidly during the ten years before 1978 than they did during the ten years after 1978. The Journal of the Transportation Research Forum in 2007 confirmed the energy cost connection continued throughout the years. This is an obvious finding and easily seen when examining the costs in the system. The only time when fares declined because of market forces was the period after 9/11 when the public stopped flying.

Inflation adjusted air prices fell more slowly after the elimination of the CAB. They are attributed to the continuous decline in service quality. There are more overbooked planes flying to fewer places, long waits in hub airports, the inability to make last-minute changes in itineraries without paying exorbitant fares, and the loss of heartland city routes that don't happen to be hubs. Most of the post-deregulation system price declines cannot be repeated; The loss of airline unions with resulting reduction in salaries and benefits, termination of pension plans, delayed replacement of aging aircraft, elimination of complimentary meals, elimination of checked baggage, the reduction of seat sizes and legroom to a point approaching the limits of human endurance.

5.6.5 Prospects

All industry forecasts call for further consolidation and rising consumer costs obfuscated by various fees and promotions to confuse the actual fare cost. This will be accompanied by declining service on all but the most heavily trafficked routes.

Short-term fare wars may break out on some routes if foolish investors bring a start-up airline to town. Periodic dips in energy prices may bring some temporary reduced costs. Over time, empirical evidence has shown that nearly all start-ups are eventually shutdown by incumbent airlines. The incumbent airlines despite increasing consolidation, heavy public subsidies, and reductions in vital service to major cities, will remain unable to earn enough to be stable.

This result would not surprise those who struggled in the late nineteenth and early twentieth centuries with the railroads, telephones, electrical power, and other natural monopolies that provide public services. They'd recognize the boom-and-bust cycle of new entrants in the early period of airline deregulation and the subsequent trend toward consolidation, deteriorating service, and increasing price discrimination. This is the economic history of a natural monopoly that lacks the benefits of government regulation.

A regulatory system can degenerate and start to do harm such as stifling competition. The CAB in late 1970s did become too cumbersome. Some suggested that using private lawyers rather than technocrats was the root problem. Regardless the system like all systems needs to be modified as needed to optimize results and prevent negative consequences. In hindsight the CAB as a system should have been modified not eliminated and abandoned to the magic hand of the market.

Further the country should not have stopped enforcing antitrust laws after the Reagan administration. However, some suggest strong antitrust enforcement wouldn't have helped, because airlines like railroads, waterworks, electrical utilities, and large public services systems require concentration both to achieve economies of scale and to enable the cross-subsidization between low and high cost service necessary to preserve their value.

When it comes to natural monopolies that are essential to the public, there is no equitable or efficient alternative to having the government regulate or coordinate entry, prices, and service levels. This is proven by history and a bit of systems common sense. For example, it would be inefficient if each city had many waterworks and sewers. Millions of Americans would still be waiting for indoor plumbing, just as millions had to wait decades for telephone and electrical service. When the government stepped in with systemic interventions like the New Deal's rural electrification program, telephone and electrical service became ubiquitous.

Road transportation in all its forms is not much different from air transportation. For example, if there was a deregulated private interstate system, there would be toll roads running straight and fast between the largest population centers. Occasionally, exuberant investors might try to make a profit by constructing a new artery road. But the high fixed cost of building roads would mean that most smaller cities would be left out of the system with dirt roads or would have to pay unsustainably high tolls. Owners of major highways, seeking to avoid competition, would gradually buy up owners of lesser highways, and then each other, until everyone pays outrageous tolls and the whole economy and quality of life is negatively impacted. This is easily shown via system common sense and validated with empirical data, mental models, and agent-based models.

There is always a system. The system may be good or bad. The problem is when people must live with a bad system because there is no ability to modify or change it for the better. The previous generations changed their systems. They learned from the initial railroad system. They eventually applied those lessons to new systems like telephones, electrical power, initial air transportation, and the interstate freeway system. The current generation must learn that again and change the failed deregulated air transportation system.

The previous generations did not have the luxury of computers, systems practices like modeling and even the luxury of people to think about things from systems perspectives. They had to live through it and then make changes along the way. The current generation has these tools and should never have to live through these systemic blunders again. They must learn to modify their systems at the first sign of negative unintended consequences.

5.6.6 Air Transportation Today

Other approaches have been tried in the past like the current deregulation approach. They failed to provide for what was needed, which is effective services for everyone including the smallest of communities. Now we find ourselves where the promise of airline deregulation has proven to be false and the system is failing and causing harm to commerce and the general public.

The aviation industry can trace its roots to the Department of Commerce. It is about commerce, not heavily subsidized business making false claims of profit over the needs of the people that the aviation system serves. The lesson of the railroads was clear in the minds of the people of that time. In 1978 and in 2019 it is distant academic history.

Table 12 Airline Financial Data

Airline	Net Income	Profit	Revenue	Fares	Expenses	Fuel	Labor
American	7,895	6,189	41,084	29,173	34,895	6,189	10,066
Delta	4,539	7,845	40,816	28,437	32,971	6,503	10,445
United	7,301	5,167	37,864	26,333	32,697	6,345	10,014
Southwest	2,181	4,117	19,820	18,347	15,704	3,616	6,689
JetBlue	677	1,198	6,416	5,907	5,218	1,348	1,628
Alaska	829	1,291	5,594	3,961	4,303	808	1,233
Hawaiian	193	431	2,313	2,015	1,882	416	526
Spirit	331	509	2,142	1,267	1,632	461	378
SkyWest	113	216	1,932	1,876	1,716	115	732
Frontier	146	276	1,604	1,277	1,328	346	313
Total	24,204	27,239	159,585	118,592	132,346	26,148	42,023
All	25,596	27,993	168,874	126,880	140,881	26,977	45,385

Source Bureau of Transportation Statistics May 2, 2016, 4th Q 2015 Airline Financial Data
Amounts are in millions of dollars

Sadly, we lost the idea of new companies offering new and better services, the original promise of deregulation. Instead there have been massive mergers that concentrated control in the hands of a few giant carriers and the heavily subsidized industry is providing extremely poor-quality services. Basing a business model on baggage fees and change fees is an extremely poor choice. The system is huge the costs are enormous. Dealing with minutia and noise fees is a waste of time and energy. It distorts critical data needed to effectively manage the system.

There were a significant number of mergers that took place after deregulation. The system went from 27 major airlines to 8 in a very short period. This does not include many of the small commuter airlines that offered routes such as Newark / Atlantic City allowing for flights to major destinations.

Table 13 Airline Mergers circa 1987 and 1989

<table>
<tr><td>American</td><td></td><td rowspan="2">American</td></tr>
<tr><td>Air Cal</td><td></td></tr>
<tr><td>United</td><td></td><td rowspan="2">United</td></tr>
<tr><td>Pan Am (transpacific routes)</td><td></td></tr>
<tr><td>Texas International</td><td></td><td rowspan="8">Texas Air</td></tr>
<tr><td>Continental</td><td></td></tr>
<tr><td>New York Air</td><td></td></tr>
<tr><td>Frontier</td><td rowspan="4">Peoples Express</td></tr>
<tr><td>Britt</td></tr>
<tr><td>PBA</td></tr>
<tr><td>Braniff (Latin America)
Eastern</td></tr>
<tr><td>Rocky Mountain</td><td></td></tr>
<tr><td>Delta</td><td></td><td rowspan="2">Delta</td></tr>
<tr><td>Western</td><td></td></tr>
<tr><td>Northwest</td><td></td><td rowspan="4">Northwest</td></tr>
<tr><td>North Central</td><td rowspan="3">Republic</td></tr>
<tr><td>Southern</td></tr>
<tr><td>Hughes Airwest</td></tr>
<tr><td>TWA</td><td></td><td rowspan="2">TWA</td></tr>
<tr><td>Ozark</td><td></td></tr>
<tr><td>USAIR</td><td></td><td rowspan="4">USAIR</td></tr>
<tr><td>PSA</td><td></td></tr>
<tr><td>Empire</td><td rowspan="2">Piedmont</td></tr>
<tr><td>Henson</td></tr>
<tr><td>PAN AM</td><td></td><td rowspan="3">PAN AM</td></tr>
<tr><td>National</td><td></td></tr>
<tr><td>Ransome</td><td></td></tr>
</table>

Sources Business Week, October 5, 1987 and Wall Street Journal, Mar 10, 1989

The airline mergers and shutdowns continue and the lineup of airlines in 2019 does not clearly translate to the lineup of airlines in 1989. The bottom line is the industry has been unstable at best since deregulation. It is also unclear what happened to the small commuter airlines connecting cities like Atlantic City to major airports with major air routes that citizens previously enjoyed.

Table 14 Major Airlines 1989 and 2019

Circa 1989	**2019**
American	American
Delta	Delta
United	United
Texas Air	Southwest

Table 14 Major Airlines 1989 and 2019

Circa 1989	2019
Northwest	JetBlue
TWA	Alaska
USAIR	Hawaiian
PAN AM	Spirit
	SkyWest
	Frontier

Meanwhile the industry has instituted pricing practices that distort the true cost of flying with the addition of fees normally associated with travel. While these fees are very disruptive to the travelling stakeholders, they are of negligible value to the overall bottom line.

Table 15 Aggregate Airline Financial Data ($ millions)

Year	Revenue	Fares	Bag Fees	Change Fees	Expense	Fuel	Labor	Profit	Income
11	153,294	114,299	3,393	2,390	148,048	43,755	35,377	5,246	490
12	156,470	115,975	3,450	2,538	150,467	44,902	37,195	6,003	98
13	161,597	121,333	3,350	2,814	150,286	42,629	38,043	11,311	12,169
14	169,277	127,455	3,530	2,981	154,677	43,431	40,771	14,600	7,447
15	168,874	126,880	3,814	3,012	140,881	26,977	45,385	27,993	25,596

Source Bureau of Transportation Statistics May 2, 2016, 4th Q 2015 Airline Financial Data

The FAA in 2009 found that commercial aviation accounts for approximately 5% of U.S. gross domestic product and contributes $1.3 trillion in annual economic activity as well as helps generate and support 10 million jobs annually. The data shows that it is about commerce $168 billion versus $1.3 Trillion. The system decisions impacting the $1.3 Trillion dollar number are what matter.

5.7 System Observations

The current state of air travel is not good. Everyone knows this yet nothing is happening to correct the situation. The performance decline in the system has taken decades but now we have reached a point where the system is in total chaos and perhaps near collapse. The system is extremely large and its downward spiral in performance is decades in the making. Recovery will be painful and take years, but recovery must begin immediately before the system collapses completely. At this point some are suggesting the current collapsing system is severely harming cities, people, and companies across the United States.

There are multiple systems elements that have been ignored in the Air Travel Transportation system. Moving away from a systems perspective and not engaging in systems thinking is a problem. There are many aspects to systems thinking but the following elements are offered as being completely ignored with the result that the Air Travel Transpiration system performance dropped to extremely poor levels.

Stakeholders

A stakeholder analysis is critical to any system. The stakeholders need to be identified along with their needs. Not all stakeholders are relevant in a system and it is important to identify the key system stakeholders.

The key stakeholders in the Air Travel Transportation system are the passengers and taxpayers. Airline executives, managers, and stockholders are irrelevant in this system because it is so heavily subsidized and has such a huge impact on the economy and well-being for the USA.

Passengers and taxpayers have been completely ignored as everyone assumed that Air Travel Transportation operates in a free market. Unfortunately, Air Travel Transportation is not a free market. The passengers and taxpayer cannot use their dollars to select which companies should go out of business because of outrageous schemes and poor performance. Instead the most egregious company with the worst idea that translates to some small increment of revenue dictates how all the other companies behave. The only choice left for the passengers is to use an alternative mode of transportation.

The reality is that people are using automobiles to support business and non-business travel. In this authors case I drive to Boston for business rather than fly because there are no flights to Boston from Atlantic City International Airport; the nearest flight is 50 miles away in Philadelphia. I am actually located 8 miles away from Atlantic City International Airport. This is pathetic especially since these flights previously existed. My daughters' family chooses to drive to Disney World Florida from New Jersey rather than fly because of the nightmare and outrageous inconveniences of flying. So, people are choosing with their dollars, they are choosing NOT to fly. They use automobiles and clog major roadways with traffic.

The taxpayer continues to subsidize this poorly performing system via dollars spent on DOD and NASA activities that the commercial aviation industry uses without a second thought. The new materials, electronics, engines, air frames, software, ground ATC systems, and space-based systems for communications and GPS all move for free to the airline companies. This is hundreds of billions of dollars of taxpayer funds. Meanwhile passengers are forced to tradeoff travel by air versus other forms of transportation like the automobile.

Table 16 Air Versus Car Transportation

Item	**Air**	**Car**
Travel Time (NJ to Florida)	2h 15m	48h 2 days stop sleep over
Motel	NA	$150
On / off plane	1h	NA
Airport Security plus 1h buffer	3h	NA
Airport Travel plus 1h buffer	3h	NA
Finding lowest price ticket	14h	NA
Cost searching for ticket ($30/hr)	$420	NA
Distance	120 miles	1070 miles
Travel + Parking Fee 10 days	$300	NA
Ticket Cost	$157	$535 (.50/mile)
Baggage fee	$80	NA
Change fee	$100	NA
Family group	4	4
Ticket Cost per group	$1248 - $1648	$535
Total Travel Time	9h – 1 day	48h – 2 days
Travel Prep Time	14h – 2 to 5 days	NA
Total Time	**23h – 3 working days**	**48h – 2 working days**
Total Cost	**$1,668**	**$685**

The table shows that a simple 2-hour flight is converted into a 9-hour journey. This means that an entire day is lost. This is important because a 2-hour flight and a reasonable overhead of an additional 1 hour saves the day and allows work or pleasure to be part of the same travel day, rather than lost. Also spending 14 hours to find the lowest priced ticket is a clear example of cost shifting to an unsuspecting stakeholder, the passenger. This is a huge cost to the overall economy as the airlines effectively institutionalized a casino for purchasing tickets. The massive waste of time is inexcusable and in stressful times like War might be considered an act of sabotage, draining critical resources from the people.

So, what are the needs of the Passenger and Taxpayer stakeholder?

- Minimal overhead time when traveling, a 2-hour flight should only have 1 additional hour to get to the airport, board the plane, and takeoff. Yes, this existed when I traveled as a young engineer everywhere, for decades.
- Minimal costs that rival automobile transportation even for a family of 4.
- Do not waste the time of the traveling public to arrange for travel. One price for everyone, 15-minute travel research and completed order.

- Taxpayers are provided with reasonable air transportation service regardless of where they live. Air routes must be re-established between medium and small cities.
- New air transportation craft must be investigated and offered for rural settings.
- Proper passenger cabins based on human factors analysis designs must be provided that are safe, comfortable, enjoyable and uplifting.

System Boundary and Key System Functions

One of the dangers of systems analysis is that the analysis is compromised by external forces. A way to compromise the system analysis is to draw the system boundary too small so that all the serious challenges are removed. The system boundary for the U.S. Air Travel Transportation system must include the industrial base, passengers, taxpayers, and yes, the U.S. government. Claiming that the system boundary is just the airline companies and revenue from the passengers is a compromised system boundary.

We now have empirical data that shows when the CAB was removed and its critical functions of economic regulation of the airlines (regulation of commercial airline routes and fares) stopped, the system started on a path of poor performance. Terminating existing mutual aid agreements between air carriers and granting antitrust immunity to carriers was irresponsible. The knowledge was there, history was there, yet both knowledge and history were rejected and the irresponsible were permitted to enter positions of authority and impact the system.

The system boundary needs to be expanded to include the U.S. government. Previous functions from the last century and new functions from this century need to be added to the system to stabilize it and move it into a positive performance path.

Performance Tracking

The FAA has used systems engineering to support its planning. Much of this work impacted the new National Airspace System Plan (NAS Plan) in 1981. The NAS Plan Chapter II – Demand on the System had key system performance data. It was replaced by the Capital Investment Plan.

Who is tracking the performance of the Air Transportation System? Some suggest the free market tracks the performance of the system, but we know this is NOT a free market system. It is an oligopoly with very powerful influences in Washington D.C.

There is always an ideal system. The difficulty is to find the ideal system and then bring it into reality. Sometimes the ideal system surfaces quickly and everyone on the team agrees that it is the ideal system, but they do not know how to get to the ideal system.

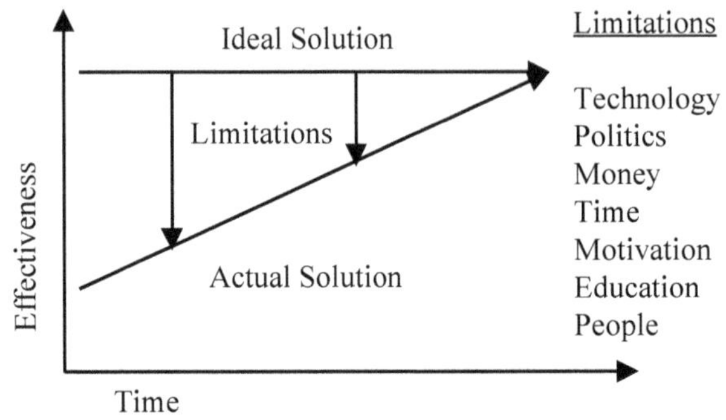

Figure 13 Ideal Air Transportation System Convergence

There could be many limitations that need to be addressed. These limitations include technology, politics, money, time, motivation, education, people, etc. There should be no tolerance for politics or money. In both cases these are external forces that can destroy any system.

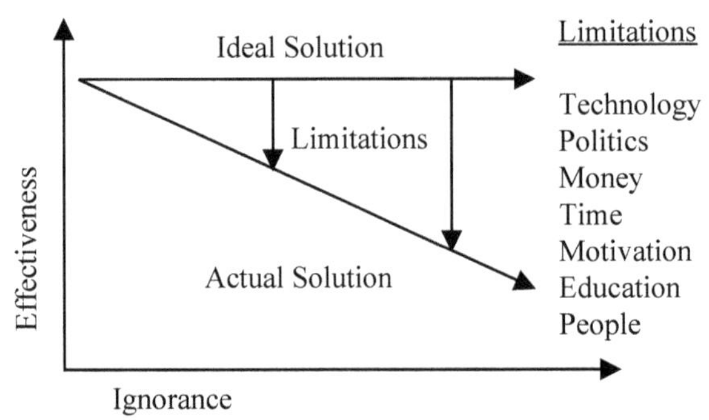

Figure 14 Ideal Air Transportation System Loss

Sometimes the ideal system is in clear sight and the approach for developing the ideal system is clearly visible. The system even may be in place but not necessarily available for this set of stakeholders. However, the ideal system and its availability fade as ignorance grips the stakeholders.

The possible scenarios associated with the ideal system and the actual solution can be identified. Realizing these possible scenarios exist will help system practitioners understand their roles in the organization. It will also act as a gage to measure the organizations' ability to actually engage in systems engineering, systems thinking, and systems practices.

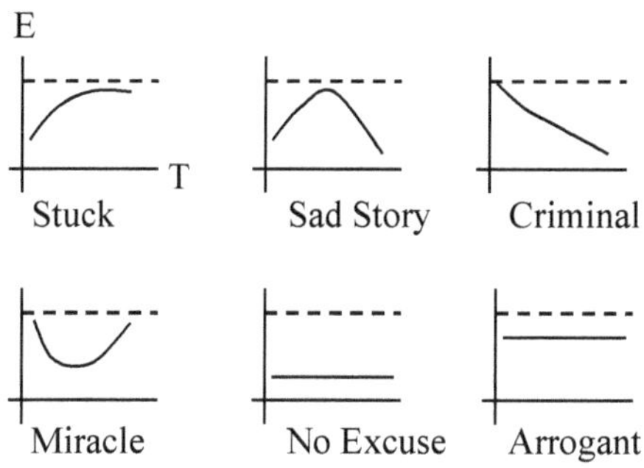

Figure 15 Air Transportation System Failure Scenarios Over Time

The reality is organizations that get lost are compromised by politics and then excuses such as money and schedule are offered. Alternatively, they are compromised by politics and then excuses of technology, people, education, and motivation are offered. There is not much system practitioners can do once an organization is compromised other than attempt to point out the condition and the ramifications of the condition or leave the organization.

It is clear that the US Air Transportation System is following the curve called Criminal. It is also clear that systems practitioners cannot leave, they must stay and help to fix the system.

5.8 System Recommendations

The recommendations cover four separate areas.

1. The first is to provide an air transportation system that serves the entire USA from commerce and citizen needs perspectives.
2. The second is to ensure not only safe but comfortable transportation in the passenger cabin.
3. The third is to address the negative effects of TSA on the traveling public and the airport infrastructure.
4. The fourth is to start doing some real systems engineering to maximize the performance of the system.

The people of the USA own the airspace and allow that airspace to be used as a privilege by companies who provide proper and effective services.

Effective Ubiquitous Air Transportation

This is not a business problem. This is not a social economic problem. This is a systems engineering problem. Various conceptual systems can be developed and modeled using the vast computer processing capabilities we have today. The models can help to optimize the system to ensure that commerce is maximized.

The FAA should be given a new role like the CAB role of regulating the air transportation routes. Key to this recommendation is for the FAA to re-establish previously shutdown routes and investigate the development of new routes as the population of the USA has significantly grown since 1983. We now have new small cities with the addition of 100 million people since 1980 when deregulation started.

Table 17 USA Population Growth

Year	USA Population	Growth
1950	151,325,798	14.5%
1960	179,323,175	18.5%
1970	203,211,926	13.3%
1980	226,545,805	11.5%
1990	248,709,873	9.8%
2000	281,421,906	13.2%
2010	308,745,538	9.7%
2019	328,915,700 estimated	6.5%

Source US Census Bureau

Why would anyone provide antitrust immunity if the point of deregulation was to allow new companies to form and enter the market? Yet that is exactly what happened when the CAB was shut down as part of deregulation - the **CAB was allowed to grant antitrust immunity to carriers.** The United State government should start enforcing anti-trust violations again, suggesting the breakup of major carriers and the encouragement of establishing new air carriers. This suggests some of the former CAB functions need to be re-established as part of the FAA.

The sad part is that we lost many great air transportation companies. Few realize that a company consists of a culture, values, policies, procedures, practices, and tools that determine how a company operates and provides services. When a company shuts down or is merged all of that is lost. It is found in the former employees, but few can transfer the good parts to their new employers.

Unfortunately, when a great company is destroyed via external forces, it can never be replaced. The adage of humpty dumpty being pushed off the wall and no one ever being able to fix humpty dumpty applies.

This new generation will need to stumble through and throw out the bad and bring in the new. It is a huge challenge because the history is truly gone from what once was spectacular; they are on their own to forge a new future in the sky and on the ground. The goal that must never be compromised is to provide effective ubiquitous air transportation in the whole of the USA.

Passenger Cabin Safety and Comfort

The FAA was created with 1958 Federal Aviation Act (Public Law 85-726). A key set of words from the act are related to safety, human factors, and research and development:

The Administrator shall develop, modify, test, and evaluate systems, procedures, facilities, and devices, as well as define the performance characteristics thereof, to meet the needs for safe and efficient navigation and traffic control of all civil and military aviation except for those needs of military agencies which are peculiar to air warfare and primarily of military concern, and select such systems, procedures, facilities, and devices as will best serve such need and will promote maximum coordination of air traffic control and air defense systems. The Administrator shall undertake or supervise research to develop a better understanding of the relationship between human factors and aviation accidents and between human factors and air safety, to enhance air traffic controller and mechanic and flight crew performance, to develop a human-factor analysis of the hazards associated with new technologies to be used by air traffic controllers, mechanics, and flight crews, and to identify innovative and effective corrective measures for human errors which adversely affect air safety. The Administrator shall undertake or supervise a research program to develop dynamic simulation models of the air traffic control system and airport design and operating procedures which will provide analytical technology for predicting airport and air traffic control safety and capacity problems, for evaluating planned research projects, and for testing proposed revisions in airport and air traffic control operations programs. The Administrator shall undertake or supervise research programs concerning airspace and airport planning and design, airport capacity enhancement techniques, human performance in the air transportation environment, aviation safety and security, the supply of trained air transportation personnel including pilots and mechanics, and other aviation issues pertinent to developing and maintaining a safe and efficient air transportation system.

Never did the people in 1958 anticipate that anyone would push negative human factors elements on the passengers in the cabin of an aircraft. Instead the opposite was true, how to make the passenger more comfortable. Aircraft flying at 30,000 feet will instantly kill a human without proper life support which includes proper pressure, temperature, oxygen, and yes ergonomics that includes proper seating and isolation from noise, shock, and vibration. The actions today to maximize revenue at the expense of the passenger would be considered totally unacceptable in 1958. Today civil aviation violates the human factors studies performed by the Department of Defense (DOD) captured in various standards like MIL-STD-1472 and by the FAA in conjunction with the DOD.

The FAA must be given the charter, if it does not exist, to regulate what happens in the aircraft cabin where passengers are located. This includes ergonomics and passenger cabin loading.

For ergonomics, this means seat sizes must expand and rows of seats must be removed for proper leg room. There are also issues associated with the ability of passengers to safely exit the aircraft in an emergency. This may impact isle width and other elements of the cabin. The standards exist, they need to be enforced.

The recent trend of 100% passenger capacity must not be permitted except in the case of unexpected events like weather, maintenance, or crew issues. The numbers exist; they must be properly analyzed and not distorted. Proper capacity loading must be established and enforced. Currently there is clear evidence that the industry routinely runs 100% capacity flights with its overbooking policies. The passenger capacity issue is serious and subtle. There are impacts on the cabin air quality and on the system as a whole to deal with rare but expected events. For example:

- When the system experiences grounded aircraft there is no ability to handle the increased passenger load if the passenger load is always at 100%.
- As the numbers of passengers increase the cabin air quality drops. The life support systems are incapable of providing proper ventilation when the cabin is filled to capacity.

Passenger cabin capacity is based on calculations normally performed on any system capacity analysis when the models of a system are developed. Having one carrier optimize their revenue by ensuring 100% capacity de-optimizes the overall system performance. This is a classic example of having an unbalanced architecture where one element is optimized at the expense of all other elements.

This knowledge dates back to the mid 1960's when complex systems were being analyzed and developed. The numbers are clear, never load a subsystem beyond 80% capacity or system thrashing will occur. Good systems engineering limits capacity between 50% and 75%. It is also critical that the numbers not be cooked. The numbers that matter are the capacity loads of the typical flights when the system is fully loaded and stressed.

To be clear, the industry reports that passenger capacity is in the 80% range. This number is an aggregate across the system. There are low capacity routes that distort the numbers and actual system performance. The problem is that certain flights are constantly at 100% capacity. The capacity should never exceed 80% on any flight except in extreme situations and then this must be accounted for in the system to minimize abuse.

TSA Effects

The first hijacking in the US occurred on May 1, 1961 when a passenger on a flight to Key West Florida forced the pilot to fly to Cuba. On Sep 5, President Kennedy signed Public Law 87-197, an amendment to the Federal Aviation Act of 1958. The law prescribed death or imprisonment for not less than 20 years for interference with aircrew members or flight attendants in the performance of their duties. Pertinent parts of the US Code were made applicable to certain other crimes aboard aircraft in flight. To help enforce the act, a special corps of FAA safety inspectors was trained for duty aboard airline flights.

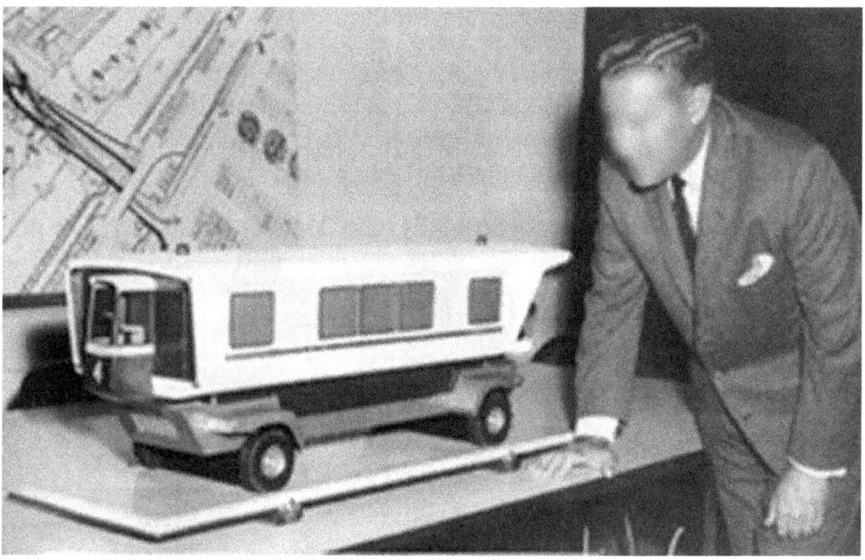

Figure 16 Mobile Lounge circa 1958[26]

We lost sight of who we are. A picture is worth a thousand words. FAA Administrator Elwood Quesada examines a mobile lounge model, a new concept for speeding the flow of boarding and deplaning passengers at the new Dulles International Airport.

Previously airports were secured at the terminal level with entry to a subset of gates associated with a physical element of the airport containing groups of gates. Today airports are secured at a multiple set of terminals level. This means that massive numbers of people must pass through a single checkpoint. This may allow for faster flight transfers, but it hampers the flow of all other passengers. It leads to excessive wait times (2 hours) to just enter the airport. Some travelers experience missed flights (sometimes the process takes more than 2 hours especially on holidays). TSA pre-check is a band aide on a bad and unequal system.

Is this decision based on security or cost? Would more TSA staff be needed if the airports were secured at the terminal level as in the past?

[26] Source US Government.

No one wants to touch this issue with a ten-foot pole. However, it needs to be examined and addressed. Security was always an issue but at what point do we move from a safe secure environment to a toxic ugly environment in a system that still may be compromised by those wanting to do harm.

Systems Engineering for the Air Travel Transportation System

It's time for people to start thinking and dreaming again. Models need to be developed, system analysis performed, systems thinking and systems engineering findings need to be rolled into a new Air Travel Transportation system for a new generation. Part of this involves not only gathering system data but making sense of the data to maximize the systems performance. Data visualization is key to this effort. Some suggested metrics for this new century are:

Table 18 Air Travel Transportation System Metrics for the 21st Century

System Performance Metrics	2019	1982	1978
Each airport per year for the last 40 years			
Number of airlines			
Number of destinations			
Total max cost of ticket per destination 1	Note 1	Note 1	Note 1
Total min cost of ticket per destination 1	Note 1	Note 1	Note 1
Total max cost of ticket per destination n	Note 1	Note 1	Note 1
Total min cost of ticket per destination n	Note 1	Note 1	Note 1
Tot max cost of ticket per mile per destination 1	Note 1	Note 1	Note 1
Tot min cost of ticket per mile per destination 1	Note 1	Note 1	Note 1
Tot max cost of ticket per mile per destination n	Note 1	Note 1	Note 1
Tot min cost of ticket per mile per destination n	Note 1	Note 1	Note 1
Total max cost of ticket per mile airport	Note 1	Note 1	Note 1
Total min cost of ticket per mile airport	Note 1	Note 1	Note 1
Airport Government Subsidy			
Entire system per year for the last 40 years			
Number of airlines	10		27
Number of destinations			
Total max cost of ticket	Note 1	Note 1	Note 1
Total min cost of ticket	Note 1	Note 1	Note 1
Total max cost of ticket per mile	Note 1	Note 1	Note 1
Total min cost of ticket per mile	Note 1	Note 1	Note 1

Table 18 Air Travel Transportation System Metrics for the 21st Century

System Performance Metrics	2019	1982	1978
Total Government Subsidy			
Passenger Cabin			
Seat Size Width (inches) note 2	16	20	20
Leg Room – Pitch (inches) note 2	28	36	36
Seat Padding note 2			
Isle Width			
Window Size			
Passenger Capacity Normal Operations (%)	100%	70%	70%
Passenger Capacity Stressed Operations (%)	Unable	95%	95%
Free Food and Drinks	No	Yes	Yes
Free Checked Bags	No	Yes	Yes
Free Carry on Bags	Some	Yes	Yes
Shock	High	Low	Low
Vibration	High	Low	Low
Noise	High	Low	Low
Note 1 Today airlines quote a price that is misleading. Travelers rarely get the low prices, even with no checked bag. This is price deception or obfuscation so it looks like tickets are cheap, but reality is different when travelers must fly on their dates and not airline dates. This significantly distorts the data when comparing prices with the past. Any comparisons must consider this distortion. Total includes ticket, carry on and checked bag fees, food, Internet booking fees, taxes, no deception, obfuscation, confusion in the systems analysis. Note 2 The FAA currently does not regulate the size or design of seats.			

The data for this table is available from the FAA. It just needs to be accessed and published for review. It will clearly show the cities that have been hurt as time progressed and the true cost of flying. With this data analysis serious systems planning, and engineering can then be restarted. Section 10.3 FAA NAS Plan 1989 has system metrics data that the FAA gathered in the 1980s to try and understand system performance. The data should be accessed and studied to establish the system performance metrics for this new century.

The recommendations are based on previous system observations with decades of empirical data for reference. If these recommendations are not followed, then the people of the USA must be prepared to see:

1. Air transportation collapse for the general population.
2. Air transportation available only to elites as costs continue to rise.
3. Air transportation available only between major metropolitan regions.

4. Unsafe conditions as people are physically and emotionally harmed.
5. Cancellations continue at great expense to the travelers.
6. More subsidies to a bad random system not based on sound engineering.
7. Severe negative impact on the economy.

This is not a business. Never was and never will be. It was and still is about the country's commerce. Air transportation is either effective or not. The data is starting to show that it's very ineffective today. The question is what the future will bring. Unfortunately, history suggests no one will do anything and the system may collapse at the national level just like it did for people in Pittsburgh, Cincinnati, Atlantic City, etc.

5.9 Legislation Recommendations

The only way to fix the US Air Transportation System is through effective legislation. That legislation must be based on serious analysis and not pop culture opinions or talking points from industry. The following is offered to help develop this critically needed legislation.

The FAA role must be expanded to include some old functions performed by the defunct CAB and some new functions to deal with the unintended consequences of deregulation and recent security challenges:

1. Regulate air transportation routes and ensure reasonable prices for unprofitable routes.
2. Ensure community requested routes are provided to all commercial airports.
3. Prohibit unequal pricing based on gambling concepts (random unequal pricing).
4. Prohibit hidden fees that are part of normal travel (baggage, cancelations, changes, etc.).
5. Require mutual aid agreements between all air carriers.
6. Remove antitrust immunity on all air carriers.
7. Encourage establishment of new airlines.
8. Always expedite processing of various requests.
9. Ensure passenger cabin safety and comfort.
10. Provide guidelines to TSA to re-establish normal airport operations.
11. Remove prison camp mentality re-establish architectural travel wonders of our airports.
12. Assume a new role of Systems Engineering for the Air Travel Transportation system.

6 Federal Aviation Administration

6.1 Introduction

Each year the FAA releases its Capital Investment Plan (CIP). This is a 5-year plan that identifies and describes the capital investments needed to sustain and modernize the infrastructure, systems, services, and procedures for safe and efficient operation of the National Airspace System. The FAA 2018–2022 CIP included the following significant statement on FAA privatization:

"The Administration has proposed to shift FAA's air traffic control function to a non-governmental, non-profit organization in 2021. Under this proposal, the non-governmental, non-profit organization would manage and invest in those capital programs that support air traffic control starting in 2021."

Legislation to privatize the FAA includes H.R.4441 Aviation Innovation, Reform, and Reauthorization Act of 2016[27] and H.R.2997 21st Century Aviation Innovation, Reform, and Reauthorization Act[28].

6.2 Stakeholders

All systems analysis begins with identifying the system stakeholders and their needs. There are many reports on privatizing the FAA, but they all fall short of identifying the actual relevant stakeholders in the system. Typically, privatization advocates consider the following stakeholders:

1. Congress
2. Commercial Airlines
3. General Aviation and Business Aviation
4. Labor
5. Airports

Upon examination this stakeholder list is almost irrelevant. The stakeholders that matter and must be addressed in a systems analysis of privatizing the FAA are:

1. Taxpayers

---

[27] H.R.4441 - Aviation Innovation, Reform, and Reauthorization Act of 2016, 114th Congress (2015-2016).

[28] H.R.2997 - 21st Century Aviation Innovation, Reform, and Reauthorization Act or 21st Century AIRR Act, 115th Congress (2017-2018).

2. Military
3. ATC Industrial Base
4. Flying Public
5. Mail and Goods Transport Users
6. Small Cities and Rural Areas
7. Universities
8. High Technology Industries
9. Aerospace Industries
10. Future Generations

Two major stakeholders are discussed below Taxpayers and Military.

6.2.1 Taxpayers

The most important stakeholder of all is the people of the United States. When this stakeholder is included the analysis must address the content of Public Law 86-726 - Federal Aviation Act of 1958. It also must include a full financial analysis of all the assets of the FAA. This financial analysis should not only include physical and intellectual property assets, but it should include the current and future resulting benefits from the research, development, services, and other activities performed by the FAA.

If the FAA is privatized, then Public Law 86-726 - Federal Aviation Act of 1958 must be removed and replaced. That replacement might follow the lead of NASA where currently NASA must determine how to indemnify any damages that might result from the activities of privatized entities engaged in rocket systems. So, the precedent is set where the taxpayer would be held responsible for increasing costs of damages that may surface if a privatized entity proceeds to mismanage the air traffic control system. Further the taxpayer would be unable to correct the situation because of loss of visibility and control of a private entity. Essentially the people of the United States will have all their FAA assets taken from them and then they will be left with all future air travel liabilities.

It is not only a legal obligation but also a moral obligation to pay back the taxpayer for the decades of support they provided to the FAA. The taxpayer will not own, have visibility into, or control this new entity. It is unclear how the FAA assets will be disbursed through the decades. What is clear is that the taxpayer should be reimbursed for this asset. The payments can be distributed to match the investments made since 1927 using inflation adjusted dollars over the next 90 years. As suggested in section 10.4 FAA Taxpayer Investment, this is over $8 billion dollars per year in 2017 dollars for 90 years.

Today we have evidence that a privatized FAA in the future could become an asset of a for-profit-company and the assets would never make it back to the taxpayer. The following is from the FAA history[29]:

- Dec 2, 1929 Fifteen air carriers pooled $100,000 to set up the not-for-profit organization, Aeronautical Radio, Inc. (ARINC), to serve as the single coordinator of aeronautical communications for the air transport industry, using a common network of ground stations.
- August 11, 2013 Rockwell Collins announced it had agreed to purchase ARINC, Inc., for $1.39 billion. The purchase, when completed, would expand Rockwell Collins' aerospace business by combining its avionics and cabin technologies with ARINC's ground-based navigational networks. (See December 2, 1929.)

6.2.2 Military

A systems analysis of privatizing the FAA includes the defense needs of the United States. The military is responsible for defending the United States and part of that defense is air defense. The fundamentals of air defense are Surveillance, Identification, Threat Assessment, Engagement, and Final Assessment. The Surveillance function is critical to this capability and the FAA is a major and critical element of the Surveillance function because of the large numbers of FAA eyes on the airspace. Pop ups and Visual Flight Rules (VFR) aircraft that intrude on controlled airspace are an everyday occurrence and must be addressed by some system element. It is not inconceivable to imagine if those eyes are lost then those that would do harm would take advantage of the situation and cause massive damage. Mining of the FAA history for DOD and Defense yields 145 references starting in the 1930's and continuing into the 2000s[30].

6.3 System Architecture Alternatives

All systems analysis efforts identify the full set of reasonable architecture alternatives. All reports that follow the privatization directive only consider the set of architecture alternatives once privatization is performed such as:

1. Government Corporation
2. Non-Profit, Independent Organization
3. For-Profit, Private Corporation
4. Funding Reform within the Current Structure

Because privatization is considered a given in the architecture alternative shown above, the obvious and proven options are omitted. The first option is to keep the

---

[29] The following is from the FAA history available on the FAA website. These events were found using a document mining tool. Additional FAA history events are captured in the body of this text and section 10.5 FAA History.

[30] See sections: 10.5.1 SAGE History, 10.5.3 ADIZ, and 10.5.4 Hijack and Terrorists.

current system in place with no change and the second option is to transfer the FAA function into the Department of Defense (DOD). A third option is to split the air traffic control operations out of the FAA. The expanded architecture alternatives list includes:

1. Keep FAA Intact
2. Move FAA into DOD
3. Split out Air Traffic Control Operations and Move into New Entity

Further, a systems analysis considers tradeoff criteria that are critical to the selection of large complex systems architectures. Most analysis driven by privatization ignore the critical tradeoff criteria.

6.3.1 Architecture A - Keep FAA Intact

The first option of keeping the current system, the FAA, is an obvious potential approach. The privatization reports fail to address why the current system, the FAA, must be shut down and replaced with a new system, a privatized entity, other than to state that the current system is slow to adopt new technologies. Adoption of new technologies is an important system tradeoff criterion however, there are other system tradeoff criteria that must be considered. These tradeoff criteria of very large systems are well known and always part of the architecture analysis, but they are not included in the privatization reports.

Since privatization reports do not review the FAA history an important pattern is missed. The pattern is that the FAA always engaged in new technology and system evolution. That pattern changed in the 1980's coincident with the push for privatization and rejection of non-DOD related government functions. It is reasonable to conclude the FAA was operating in a more hostile environment after 1980 than before 1980[31].

6.3.2 Architecture B - Move FAA into DOD

None of the reports suggesting privatization address that most air traffic control in other countries is performed by the military. Also, countries that privatized their systems have airspace characteristics where the military surveillance function is less critical because of small size, large areas of undeveloped land, or massive existing military surveillance operations.

In the previous century when countries where attempting to modernize, the airspace would always be analyzed to determine the nature and place of air defense and air traffic control sensors and systems. This was a normal practice performed by US DOD companies engaged in these very large system projects. Understanding the airspace is critical to understanding the automation systems to be developed to

[31] See section 10.5.6 Startup Shutdown.

manage, control, and defend the airspace of a nation state.

Transferring the FAA into the DOD might seem like an absurd idea to those in the FAA, but it does have benefits. The political reality is that a very powerful faction in the US government believes that the only role of government is defense. They reject the New Deal from the previous century and are actively trying to shut down all non-DOD related government activities. Moving the FAA into the DOD would remove it from this massive political disagreement that manifests itself as budget battles. This is a decade's long battle at this point in our history. With movement into DOD the FAA would gain budget stability. It also would be able to tap into the vast DOD R&D resources. The current civilian employees would remain civilian employees.

A very vocal stakeholder that might question this action is the large commercial airline companies who have a distant memory of forming ARINC in the previous century. However, ARINC is now gone and the world is much more complex than 1929 when ARINC was formed as a nonprofit to serve the air transport industry communications needs.

There is one other relatively silent stakeholder that would question this action and that is the taxpayer faction who believes that a nation state must provide for more than the common defense. They believe there is a proper role for government that no other institutions can provide. Examples include going to the Moon or building an air traffic control system. There is a large history suggesting this role for air traffic control that should be reviewed and understood as represented by the following excerpts from the FAA history:

- May 20, 1926 President Calvin Coolidge signed the Air Commerce Act of 1926 into law. The act instructed the Secretary of Commerce to foster air commerce; designate and establish airways; establish, operate, and maintain aids to air navigation (but not airports); arrange for research and development to improve such aids; license pilots; issue airworthiness certificates for aircraft and major aircraft components; and investigate accidents.
- Sep 11, 1961 The Project Beacon task force on Air Traffic Control (see Mar 8, 1961) submitted its report to the FAA Administrator. While finding that the air traffic control system was "being expertly operated by a highly skilled organization," the report concluded that substantial improvements were needed to meet the future challenge of aviation's projected growth. FAA urgently needed an overall systems plan. In effect, the recommended improvement involved a major reorientation of the modernization effort that had been launched in 1957 following the Curtis report. Keyed to the use of an air traffic control radar beacon system (ATCRBS) as a primary means of providing controllers with aircraft position information, the new concept found little promise in ground-based altitude measuring devices such as the 3-D radar under test as part of the earlier program (see Apr 7, 1961, and Dec 27, 1963). The report also urged expanded use of general-purpose computers rather than

special computer systems formerly under development for air traffic control. **Rejecting the idea of fully merging air traffic control with the SAGE air defense system**, the report urged that only radar elements of SAGE be used for the air traffic control system (see Apr 17, 1960, Feb 21, 1962, and Dec 1, 1963).

- Mar 2, 1966 President Johnson recommended to Congress the creation of a Cabinet-level Department of Transportation. The President noted that the United States lacked a coordinated transportation system permitting travelers and goods to move conveniently from one means of transportation to another, using the best characteristics of each. The responsibility for transportation within the Federal government, he observed, was fragmented among many agencies resulting in a series of uncoordinated modal policies. What was needed was a single department to develop and carry out comprehensive policies and programs for transportation in its totality. The President proposed that the following agencies and functions be consolidated in the new department the Office of the Under Secretary of Commerce for Transportation; the Bureau of Public Roads; the Federal Aviation Agency; the U.S. Coast Guard; the Maritime Administration; the safety functions of the Civil Aeronautics Board (CAB); the safety functions and car service functions of the Interstate Commerce Commission (ICC); the Great Lakes Pilotage Administration; the St. Lawrence Seaway Development Corporation; the Alaska Railroad; and certain minor transportation-related activities of other agencies. The President also recommended the creation within the Department of a National Transportation Safety Board, which would absorb the safety functions transferred from CAB and ICC. (See Oct 15, 1966.).

The above references suggest that moving the FAA into DOD would be a betrayal of the vision from the previous generations. As shown in the history record this was a topic of significant discussion and the goal was to view air traffic control as part of an integrated transportation system that would add significant value to the economy via emergent system benefits. They may not have been able to predict those benefits, but they clearly understood, respected, and believed those benefits would surface – history clearly shows that they were correct.

6.3.3 Architecture C - Split out Air Traffic Control Operations

There is a third option to consider. This would involve splitting the FAA functions into Operations and Non-Operations. The Non-Operations portion would continue to engage in research and development and the safety missions. The Operations portion would engage in daily air traffic control. The Operations portion would be privatized. Unlike the other options just described, this is an unproven approach. This would also be a cause of concern for system elements related to Defense and protecting the Nation State airspace as previously discussed.

6.3.4 New Tradeoff Criteria

Some privatization reports include a tradeoff matrix with criteria. Unfortunately, the criteria are not associated with measuring the goodness of each architecture approach. Instead the criteria are associated with the narrow view of privatization:

1. Governance
2. Funding
3. Bonding authority
4. Safety regulation separated from provision
5. Transition issues
6. Congressional influence
7. Political feasibility
8. Other

Finding and working with the tradeoff criteria is critical to making an informed decision. Excluding key criteria results in a gamed solution where the full systems perspective is not offered. It can be viewed as a form of propaganda in the extreme.

The tradeoff criteria should include a traditional architecture tradeoff. Although the following criteria may be incomplete, they are an example from which to identify the proper and complete set of architecture selection tradeoff criteria.

Table 19 Architecture Traditional Tradeoff Criteria

Resilience	Transition	Testability
Robustness	**Interoperability**	Reliability
Ruggedness	Usability	Maintainability
Survivability	Availability	Training
Brittleness	Fault tolerance	**Supportability**
Flexibility	Graceful degradation	Survivability
Reconfigureability	**Performance**	Comfort
Scalability	**Capacity**	Sustainability
Stability	**Growth**	**Effectiveness**
Controllability	**Technology insertion**	**Safety**
Elegance	**Ability to meet**	**Security**
Symmetry	**requirements**	**Vulnerability**
Beauty	**Performance**	Deployment
Simplicity	User acceptability	Shutdown
Reasonableness	Produceability	Disposal

Table 20 Architecture Sustainability Tradeoff Criteria

Carbon Pollution	Visual Pollution	Internal Sustainability	Social Mobility
Water Pollution	Fuel Sustainability	External Sustainability	**Freedom and Liberty**
Land Pollution	Regeneration	Survivability	**Quality of Life**
Air Pollution	**Progress**	Population Growth	**Happiness**
Noise Pollution	Model Results	**Standard Of Living**	

6.4 FAA Privatization Considerations

Most reports appear to be part architecture tradeoff and part position paper. Although they may have many references, they are narrowly focused and do not capture the broad systems perspective. Simple Internet searches related to Air Traffic Control yield a broader perspective on the situation. This all suggests superficial and confusing analysis by those seeking FAA privatization.

These reports claim that the FAA is too slow to modernize the air traffic control system. However, they offer no recent evidence to suggest that is the case.

If the FAA is too slow to modernize these privatization reports do not perform a root cause analysis. Part of the root cause analysis of problems in a complex system is history. Both relevant and what may appear to be irrelevant history of the system under study and similar systems must be performed. Although the privatization reports may provide historical references, they are incomplete and again focused on privatization and not the system. They do did not address the following key historical events:

- The Semi-automatic Ground Environment (SAGE)
- Air Traffic Controller Strike of 1981
- Executive Order 12607 President's Commission on Privatization
- Advanced Automation System
- Mandated Use of Commercial-Off-The-Shelf (COTS) Equipment
- FAA Automation History by Decade and Impacts

6.4.1 The Semi-automatic Ground Environment (SAGE)

The SAGE system was developed after World War II to defend against the new nuclear threat. It was the first computer-based system for tracking and intercepting enemy bomber aircraft. By 1963 the system consisted of 22 Sector Direction Centers and three similar Combat Centers linked to North American Aerospace Defense Command (NORAD) and another site at the Canadian Forces Base (CFB) North Bay in Canada.

The engineering effort was huge, and it gave birth to our modern computers. Prior to this time computers were viewed only as calculators. SAGE introduced the concept of situational awareness and presented alphanumeric data and graphics to operators sitting at display consoles. The consoles had keyboards for entering data and pointing devices to select objects on a screen. The command centers included large screen displays. This technology eventually transferred to air traffic control. It is because of SAGE that IBM was able to develop the FAA En Route System and Burroughs and Univac were able to develop the Terminal systems.

SAGE was one of the most advanced and successful large computer systems ever developed. From it flowed our modern air traffic control and air defense systems. Computers, displays, keyboards, pointing devices, software, intercomputer connections, and packet switching; everything that we use in our computing and communications activities have roots in SAGE and the work that followed in future air traffic control and air defense systems.

SAGE is important to this discussion because it represents massive automation for airspace management systems. These systems have a long history of breaking new ground and pushing the practical limits of technology. It is because of this push that we enjoy a worldwide air traffic system that allows for almost anyone to fly anywhere, something not possible when SAGE was first conceived. Automation and its challenges are a recurring theme in the history of the FAA.

6.4.2 Air Traffic Controller Strike of 1981

Privatization of the FAA did not surface until the air traffic controller strike in 1981 when President Reagan fired 11,345 striking controllers. What is not generally known, is that President Reagan called Hughes Aircraft to see if they could help to address the crisis. Hughes Aircraft was responsible for developing the Joint Surveillance System which replaced the SAGE system. Hughes also developed air defense and international air traffic control systems for most of the non-communist world. The result was that Hughes Aircraft became involved in the FAA programs. Hughes was unable to help with the crisis and it is obvious that this event was so profound that it clearly resulted in Executive Order 12607, 1987.

Meanwhile various companies were interested in the FAA trust fund that was growing and becoming sizable. Within the halls of Hughes Aircraft, the topic of taking over the FAA surfaced as part of the privatization discussions. This was quickly dismissed by Hughes management. The first issue was liability and the example of a midair over Manhattan was used in discussions[32]. The second was the nature of the company. They clearly stated that they are a technology company solving problems and developing systems no one would touch with a ten-foot pole.

So why are these Hughes antidotes appropriate to this discussion? It is because they capture the conversations of the day in this complex systems challenge. There were other discussions also having to do with why very well-paid people, the air traffic controllers, destroyed their careers. They were not a minority but a majority of the workforce. What was really wrong with the system? There was no desire for a root cause analysis, only reaction and then crisis.

- Jan 17, 1962 President John F. Kennedy issued Executive Order 10988, which guaranteed the right of Federal employees to join organizations--i.e., any lawful association, labor union, federation, council, or brotherhood "having as

---

[32] The liability issue did not bother the Hughes staff. They felt that they were the only organization outside the government that could handle the liability. They just thought that it was wrong and stupid as they shook their heads and laughed in disbelief. How do I know? I was there smiling, being silent, listening in awe but with no fear of the brilliant people that surrounded me. Talk about being confident that the world was in good hands, wow.

a primary purpose the improvement of working conditions among Federal employees"--and engage in collective bargaining. The order also made provision for Federal agencies to accord informal, formal or exclusive recognition to employee organizations. FAA Administrator Halaby argued unsuccessfully before Kennedy Administration councils that air traffic controllers, because they served a national defense function, should be excluded from the provisions of the order. (See Jan, 1968.)

- Jan 19, 1968 FAA Administrator McKee approved the realignment of the functions of the Associate Administrator for Personnel and Training (see Oct 1, 1965). Under the new organizational structure, the agency established a separate Office of Personnel and a separate Office of Training, as well as a Manpower and Planning Staff and an Executive and Military Personnel Staff. This realignment provided a closer grouping among traditional personnel and training functions and permitted a quicker response to agency needs. The new office became operational on Feb 1, 1968. Jan, 1968 A group of dissatisfied air traffic controllers in the New York area formed the Professional Air Traffic Controllers Organization (PATCO). By the end of Jun 1968, PATCO had a national membership of well over 5,000 FAA employees. (See Jan 17, 1962, and Jul 3, 1968.).

6.4.3 Executive Order 12607 President's Commission on Privatization

In 1987 Executive Order 12607 President's Commission on Privatization was issued by President Reagan. There is no question that this executive order was a reaction to the Air Traffic Controllers Strike. The resulting report on privatization specifically mentioned the FAA as a target for being privatized.

What was the purpose in privatizing the FAA? Was it to reduce costs and or increase efficiency? That is not an appropriate answer because if that was the case the FAA needed to be fixed to reduce costs and increase efficiency. If on the other hand the purpose of privatizing the FAA was to unleash a sustainable industrial base with many companies able to make immediate profits, then it was appropriate.

Privatizing the FAA would not lead to a new industrial base that is part of the general economy. Instead it would only exist at the pleasure of the taxpayer. The alternative, if that was the case, was to fix the FAA. Unfortunately, no one approached the question of privatization from a systems perspective and no systems analysis was performed. The discussion in this text is the first attempt to start a systems analysis of the FAA and the implications of privatization.

6.4.4 Advanced Automation System

Section 10.5.7 Advanced Automation System (AAS) has a discussion of an important FAA program from the 1980's. This is a critical read for anyone reviewing this analysis. This excerpt is from a section addressing Technology Assessment and Maturity. It is offered to illustrate the complexity that is inherent in a system like the ATC system. It should not be invalidated because of disagreements on the content. Instead the message should be – this is big and complex, be very careful when proceeding.

This is a small preview of the section. It is offered because it suggests that powerful organizations do have an impact and if they are following a narrow agenda there will be massive negative consequences:

Hindsight is always 20/20. That was a common saying in the ATC community circa 1980. However, the GAO report, which rejected the AERA concept because it was too risky, was the wrong answer. It is interesting they did not give a history of air traffic control and reference the SAGE system. Without that context no one would realize that air traffic control advances were always driven with new and innovative technologies.

Few realize the AAS was just a continuation of the approaches used in the previous systems – technology and automation. The systems evolved from what can be termed a manual system to an automated system. AAS was just the next logical step in automation. For more information see sections:

10.5.2 Replacing the Manual System
10.5.2.1 Project Beacon
10.5.2.2 NAS Stage A and Project Beacon Evolution
10.5.2.3 Advanced Automation System and NAS Stage A Evolution

AAS is now part of the FAA history. The FAA has moved on and new automation is now being implemented as the system continues to evolve. Although the above text is tightly focused on the FAA and AAS, what should not be lost in that history is the extreme pressure the FAA and its industrial base faced as privatization was constantly looming on the horizon. There is no question that this caused many companies to shy away from doing business with the FAA because this politically charged environment was just too unstable. Rather than stop the attacks on the FAA they just continued to increase as the push for privatization continued. From more information see section 10.5.6 Startup Shutdown.

6.4.5 Mandated Use of Commercial-Off-The-Shelf (COTS) Equipment

Coincident with the FAA push for new technologies in the 1980's and 1990's Washington was considering other policies that eventually led to a major push to use Commercial-Off-The-Shelf (COTS) solutions for future government systems. At the time this strategy seemed reasonable because of the massive high technology base that was available. However, as time moved on it became clear that COTS was eventually leading to many companies stopping their research and development investments and eventually impacting the system solutions available for systems like air traffic control and air defense. This also led to a shift away from developing research and development prototypes at the FAA. This activity was the life blood that fed the previous automation efforts.

This COTS policy was attributed to controlling the costs of government, which were viewed at the time as being out of control. It was believed that the commercial industrial base could produce anything that the government would need. This was in a setting where the government previously invested in research and development because the industrial base could not produce what it needed. For example, it needed SAGE, it wanted to go to the Moon, and it needed a new air traffic control system. Many within the high technology industrial base viewed the COTS policy as devastating.

6.4.6 FAA Automation History by Decade and Impacts

The FAA maintains a history of its and its predecessor government organizations. The history captures key FAA events by year and is in excess of 700 pages. Reviewing this history is critical to understanding its operations. In this analysis a document mining tool was used to start to understand this history and some example reports are in section 10.5 FAA History. The following is one interpretation of the FAA history.

- **1950's:** This was the decade of SAGE. The FAA was established via public law and within that law was embedded the concept of performing research and development. This makes sense because of the massive success and transformation that SAGE represented. The ATC system was manual using broadband technologies. It needed to change.
- **1960's:** This was the decade of moving the manual system to an automated system with the use of beacon RADAR, computers, communications, and other technologies.
- **1970':** This was the decade of NAS Stage A. Automation of the manual activities of the air traffic controller was a clear success. Towards the end of the decade dreams of new levels of automation beyond the manual activities were being captured in labs at NAFEC, MITRE, Hughes, Sanders, and a plethora of companies that were starting to form an ATC industrial base.
- **1980's:** The 1980's was supposed to follow the successful model of the 1960's and 1970's. Instead political upheaval in Washington that is now clear to the most uninitiated started to negatively impact the FAA. A large portion of the workforce was fired, and the FAA was targeted for privatization.
- **1990's:** The effects of government downsizing and the massive political infighting take their toll on the FAA and its shrinking industrial base. The Berlin Wall comes down and hopes of a new economic age are lost as Norm

Augustine sets the policy that defense companies should downsize and merge rather than seek and develop new industrial and commercial markets. There is no leadership in Washington on this serious issue as government continues to move away from the New Deal policies. This further disrupts and shrinks the FAA industrial base as IBM sheds Federal Systems group, RCA, Hughes Aircraft, Burroughs, Univac, E-Systems, Martin Marietta, Lockheed, and dozens of other companies go through multiple mergers and downsizing events.

- **2000's:** A time for recovery. The FAA using its diminished and fragile industrial base regroups and starts to build new levels of automation as part of the ERAM, STARS, ADS, TSAS, TBFM and other programs. Significant portions of the previous AAS work at Hughes is captured and merged into the ATC system via Raytheon while Lockheed takes on the previous AAS[33] work from IBM Federal Systems Group.
- **Future:** The future is uncertain. What is certain is that today's policies and actions will affect future generations. Rather than supporting the FAA there is a massive disruptive element as the push for privatization continues. What is clear from the past is that the FAA was able to provide a system that has transformed the United States and the world with air travel that is available to billions of people. For more information see sections: 10.5.5 Super Sonic Transport (SST) and 10.5.6 Startup Shutdown.

6.5 B737 MAX Disaster

Boeing produced the B737 MAX and it became in one of the worst engineering disasters in recent times. To reduce costs Boeing focused on reduction of fuel costs and the result was the introduction of the B737 MAX with the more efficient CFM International LEAP-1B engines[34]. After two fatal crashes of the Boeing 737 MAX, regulatory authorities around the world grounded the 737 MAX until further notice. The accidents occurred with Lion Air Flight 610 on October 29, 2018 and Ethiopian Airlines Flight 302 on March 10, 2019.

On March 10, 2019 Ethiopian Airlines was first to ground its MAX fleet, effective the day of its accident, and one day later, March 11, China's Civil Aviation Administration ordered the first regulatory grounding. Most other agencies and airlines followed suit over the next two days. The US Federal Aviation Administration (FAA) initially reaffirmed airworthiness of the MAX on March 11 but grounded it on March 13. The groundings affected 387 MAX aircraft serving

---

[33] Some in the FAA may cringe at the use of the term AAS and Advanced Automation System, but that is exactly what is happening. The ATC system is continuing to evolve, and new levels of advanced automation are being added to the system. Words are important, they have real meaning and not the meaning that someone attaches as part of what they consider damage control.

[34] Must Reads: How a 50-year-old design came back to haunt Boeing with its troubled 737 Max jet, Los Angeles Times, Ralph Vartabedian, March 15, 2019.

8,600 weekly flights for 59 airlines.

After the first crash, evidence was mounting in the public media that there was a problem with the B737 MAX[35] and many were questioning why the FAA was not taking action that may have even included grounding the aircraft. The excuse was that not all the facts were available to ground the aircraft. Even after the second aircraft crashed the FAA was referring to insufficient facts to warrant grounding of the aircraft[36]. Meanwhile after the second crash on March 11, 2019 the rest of the world grounded the aircraft and would not allow it to enter their airspace. Eventually the FAA on March 13, 2019 also grounded the aircraft[37]. This is the first time the FAA did not lead the world in such a critical situation.

The United States Department of Transportation on March 19, 2019 ordered an audit of the regulatory process that led to the aircraft's certification in 2017. In August 2019, Forbes estimated that the 737 MAX would not resume service before 2020. As of December 2019, the B737 MAX is still grounded[38].

6.5.1 FAA Review

On June l, 2019, the FAA chartered the Boeing 737 MAX Flight Control System Joint Authorities Technical Review (JATR), consisting of technical representatives from the FAA, National Aeronautics and Space Administration (NASA), and civil aviation authorities from Australia, Brazil, Canada, China, Europe, Indonesia, Japan, Singapore, and the United Arab Emirates[39]. The body of the report and the executive summary are in this text[40].

The details of the report represent traditional certification, engineering, and systems engineering perspectives. The report suggests that traditional certification, engineering, and systems engineering perspectives were missed and thus could have contributed to the B737 MAX disasters. The letter accompanying the report does not reflect the content of the report. It has words that are irrelevant but support the existing political agenda to outsource and privatize the FAA safety and certification roles. It is clear from the report that the FAA has lost its ability to support these services. This is clearly stated in the public media and on October 28, 2019 the

---

[35] Flawed analysis, failed oversight: How Boeing, FAA certified the suspect 737 MAX flight control system, Seattle Times, Dominic Gates aerospace reporter, March 17, 2019.

[36] We now know this was coming from incompetent and dangerous management. The facts were that the mission critical system was not fault tolerant and fail-safe.

[37] Flying the Boeing 737 Max 8: A pilot's view from inside the cockpit, Washington Post, Todd C. Frankel, March 17, 2019.

[38] How the Boeing 737 Max safety system differs from others, USA TODAY, George Petras, March 11, 2019.

[39] Joint Authorities Technical Review Observations, Findings, and Recommendations, Submitted to the Associate Administrator for Aviation Safety, U.S. Federal Aviation Administration October 11, 2019.

[40] See section 10.6 B737 MAX JATR Findings.

following was offered[41]:

- The Federal Aviation Administration's industry-friendly approach to oversight allowed Boeing to submit documentation that obscured the dangers of the B737 MAX, according to documents, interviews and the findings of investigations.
- Instead of trying to reclaim its oversight powers after the deaths of 346 people over the past year, the FAA has been pressing with plans to further reduce its hands-on oversight of aviation safety, according to current and former officials.
- The FAA has been pushing for changes to speed approval on critical safety questions and remake regulations using voluntary consensus standards, according to interviews and documents. This could result in outsourcing policymaking on airplane safety to industry groups outside the public's view, according to industry experts.

Having developers certify their own products is viewed as irresponsible and dangerous by seasoned engineering professionals and engineering managers[42]. This is not a technology issue. It is a social issue that is not understood by financially educated and driven management. They don't know how people will compromise systems as the engineering challenges surface each day.

Many have questioned how Boeing, a company renowned for engineering, made basic mistakes leading to a pair of deadly crashes. Longtime Boeing engineers say the effort was complicated by a push to outsource work to lower-paid contractors.

- Boeing and its subcontractors relied on temporary workers making as little as $9 an hour to develop and test software from countries lacking a deep background in aerospace[43]. It was controversial because it was less efficient than Boeing engineers just writing the code. It took many rounds going back and forth because the code was not done correctly.
- Engineers complained of pressure from managers to limit changes that might introduce extra time or cost.
- Boeing was intent on reducing costs, including moving work from Puget Sound, because it's very expensive. Slowly over time it eroded the ability for Puget Sound engineers to design.

---

[41] FAA's lax oversight played part in Boeing 737 Max crashes, but agency is pushing to become more industry-friendly, Washington Post, Michael Laris, Ian Duncan Lori Aratani, Oct. 28, 2019.

[42] Boeing Had Too Much Sway in Vetting Own Jets, FAA Was Told, Bloomberg, Peter Robison, and Alan Levin, March 17, 2019.

[43] Boeing's 737 Max Software Outsourced to $9-an-Hour Engineers, Bloomberg, Peter Robison, June 28, 2019.

- A former software engineer recalled a manager saying at an all-hands meeting that Boeing didn't need senior engineers because its products were mature. This was in a room full of a couple of hundred mostly senior engineers. They were being told that they weren't needed.

The FAA said nothing about this technology at a critical time when pilots were learning how to fly the plane. How much did the FAA know about the technology, especially given its history of delegating to industry?

- In practice, one Boeing engineer would conduct a test of a particular system, while another Boeing engineer would act as the FAA's representative, signing on behalf of the U.S. government that the technology complied with federal safety regulations. Hundreds of Boeing engineers did this as the company sought to verify the performance of mechanical systems, hardware installations and massive amounts of computer code, say former FAA officials, engineers and aeronautics experts. This is a self-licking ice cream cone.[44]
- This was happening during a period when the Transportation Department's Office of Inspector General (IG) was warning the FAA that its oversight of manufacturers' work was insufficient.
- Between the design in 2011 and the first plane in 2016, the IG criticized the FAA's handling of the self-certification system in three successive reports. The IG said in 2011 that the FAA's system for deciding which technologies carried the highest safety risks was not effective. Investigators also said the FAA did not adequately train company employees to spot noncompliance with safety requirements.
- The IG singled out the government's oversight of the Seattle-area FAA office that supervised Boeing's certifications. The IG reported the FAA does not know whether it has adequate staffing levels needed to meet workload requirements.
- Responding to the IG, the FAA agreed with much of the criticism and vowed to keep working to improve oversight of its self-certification programs. It defended the outsourcing of certification, writing to the IG in 2015 that the expanding magnitude of the U.S. aerospace industry requires that the agency delegate an increasing number of oversight functions to the companies it regulates.

After September 11, the FAA was spread thin and manufacturers complained to Congress about delays in certification. The Republican-controlled Congress in 2003 ordered the FAA to delegate more nuts-and-bolts compliance work to the plane manufacturers. This is privatization of certification.

---

[44] How the FAA allows jetmakers to 'self certify' that planes meet U.S. safety requirements, Washington Post, Aaron C. Davis, Marina Lopes, March 15, 2019.

- FAA engineers were swamped with an unmanageable oversight role and the FAA did not push back to correct the situation. In 2009, the FAA delegated authority to Boeing the first of what would become more than 80 aviation companies that were allowed to certify the safety of their own products.
- The FAA saw the approach as an improvement. Previously government contractors inspected airplane systems, usually without adequate staff, technical training or time to evaluate increasingly complex new technology.
- From an FAA employee: I had 45 contract inspectors reporting to me. I couldn't spend much time with any one of them, or on any one issue. I thought this really helped. Companies were held accountable, and it increased the number of people inspecting.
- The number of inspectors at Boeing jumped from about 300 contractors reporting to the FAA to 500 in-house Boeing employees.
- From an Industry employee: Conceptually it makes sense because FAA can't be everywhere, but the reality is it is flawed, you have the fox watching the henhouse.

Notice there was no desire to increase the FAA budget and rebuild FAA capability. Instead unstable contracts employing privatized workers with no longevity or deep career expertise were given this critical work. This is in a setting where public law establishes the FAA to ensure the safety of air transportation. This begs the question, is the law that established the FAA being violated in the name of privatization?

The bottom line is that Boeing and the FAA have management issues. They marginalized and pushed the engineers, technicians, operators, and all those competent to work in the area out of the decision authority loop. This is exactly what happened with the Space Shuttle Challenger[45] disaster in 1987.

This disaster is worse than the Challenger disaster not only because more people died but the USA may have lost its commercial aviation industrial base[46]. This is a direct result of industry consolidation into Boeing and because of the loss of capability and competence in Boeing.

In the end the FAA should have protected Boeing from itself. They had final veto on the certification of the aircraft. Because of this failed oversight, Boeing as a business will suffer. The US aviation industrial base has been severely damaged.

What could the FAA have done? The FAA must respond to the political appointees and congress. The direction was clear, get out of the way. However, they could have formally communicated the dangers to congress and included line

---

[45] On January 28, 1986, the NASA Space Shuttle broke apart killing all seven crew members: five NASA astronauts, one payload specialist, and a civilian schoolteacher.

[46] See section 10.7 Jet Airliners for a list of worldwide manufacturers.

items in the budget to perform proper certification. They did not do that[47].

What could Boeing have done? They could have rejected the self-licking ice cream cone and lobbied for more money for the FAA to do its job correctly.

6.5.2 The Engineering

The Maneuvering Characteristics Augmentation System (MCAS) on the B737 MAX caused the aircraft to violently nosedive and crash into the earth. The MCAS was triggered by a single sensor that fed a single computer an erroneously high value for the jet's angle of attack.

MCAS activated for up to 10 seconds, swiveling the horizontal tail, known as the stabilizer, to aggressively pitch the nose of the aircraft down. When countered by the pilots, the system stopped, then kicked in again with a new activation 5 seconds later. The pilots struggled against repeated nose down movements on each flight, the first 12 minutes and the second 6 minutes, but the planes catastrophically lost control and crashed in a high-speed nosedive[48].

The original MCAS architecture was not fault tolerant and fail-safe. The new design is a standard fault tolerant fail-safe architecture that is always used in all mission critical systems where loss of life is possible.

- The fault tolerant approach is to use redundancy and compare values before the system acts on the airplane flight profile. This is standard practice.
- The fail-safe approach is to let the pilots have control of the plane, not the automation system, if the automation system is unable to make a fully checked decision. Letting humans have control when an automation system is unable to make a confirmed decision is standard automation practice.
- Two flight control computers will be used, rather than just one as in the previous system. Both computers will process readings from the sensors on both sides of the airplane. They will cross-check and compare values. If they disagree, the system will be shut down.
- Two angle of attack sensors will be used instead of just one as in the previous system.
- If the sensors disagree by more than a nominal amount, the system assumes a false signal and will not activate.
- The system will not activate, unless the angle moves suddenly from below a threshold to a new high value. This will mitigate the condition if both sensors get stuck at the same wrong high value.

---

[47] FAA misled Congress on inspector training for Boeing 737 Max, investigators say, Washington Post, Michael Laris, September 23, 2019.

[48] Boeing's fix tames the 'tiger' in the 737 MAX flight controls, say experts and critics, Dominic Gates, Seattle Times, Nov. 17, 2019.

- If both sensors together register a sudden movement to a high angle of attack, the system will activate once only, not repeatedly, as in the accident flights. The pilots will then have full control.
- The movement of the horizontal stabilizer to pitch the jet nose down will be limited. The pilot will always be able to counter it by pulling back on the control column.

The MCAS architecture was completely flawed because it was not a fault tolerant architecture with fail-safe mechanisms. No certification board with reasonable engineering background would allow this system to move forward[49]. Certification would be instantly stopped. That did not happen. The question is, why were the engineers cut out of the loop.

For example, your automobile brake system is fault tolerant and has a fail-safe mechanism. Automobile brakes have a primary and secondary hydraulic cylinder. If a hose should fail to the breaks located on any wheel the primary or secondary hydraulic fluid may be lost causing either the front or back brakes to fail but not both at the same time. If there should be a catastrophic failure of the primary and secondary hydraulic system you have a fail-safe parking brake that you can activate that uses a mechanical linkage to the brakes. This is common knowledge to all engineers and most people whole drive and maintain automobiles.

There is no justification for the original Boeing design or its approval by the FAA. This is all common knowledge for people who work on mission critical systems. The concepts go back decades. There is also no justification for the talking points issued by Boeing and the FAA suggesting that this was just a software problem. How they thought this could be hidden with damage control is beyond me. I have no words except outrage and disgust.

6.5.3 Further Investigations

The investigations continue as of January 2020. The aircraft is still grounded. The Boeing CEO was fired in December 2019 and he will leave with more than $60 million dollars. Documents were released by Boeing to congressional investigators and the internal communications are being made public. This is a sample of the internal communications.

2015 August: this is what these regulators get when they try and get in the way. They impede progress.

2017: this airplane is designed by clowns, who in turn are supervised by monkeys.

---

[49] This is criminal negligence. It is obvious that incompetent management was overriding engineering. This is a classic example of why only engineering managers up through the executive levels should be involved in these types of systems.

2017 March: stress the importance of holding firm that there will not be any type of simulator training required. ... Boeing will not allow that to happen, ... We'll go face to face with any regulator who tries to make that a requirement.

2017June: Airline was persuaded not to require simulator training. Looks like my jedi mind trick worked again! ... These are not the droids you're looking for.

These are summaries from Internet message boards associated with the media articles on the Boeing 737 MAX engineering management disaster:

This is a broken culture and an executive and board failure. The current executives and board are clearly incapable of creating and supporting a safety culture, and they all need to be replaced.

I work for a federal agency, and management has repeatedly retaliated against me for raising concerns that could result in grave catastrophic events. It has severely impacted my health as I face hostility without a realistic path forward. This is a cultural problem.

Boeing was allowed to self-certify. Government deregulation and oversight withdrawal has put citizens in danger.

These communications show a picture of a catastrophically failed corporate culture and the lengths the severely dysfunctional and compromised Boeing executives and management were willing to go to in order to evade scrutiny from regulators, flight crews, and the flying public. The rot begins at the top and once it is established it is difficult to remove.

6.6 *It's Not Just The FAA*

Unfortunately, the problem is not isolated to the FAA. The Food and Drug Administration (FDA) is suffering from the same issues[50].

In 2019 a small start-up pharmacy with 14 employees found that Zantac and its generic form, ranitidine, contained a chemical thought to cause cancer. More than 40 countries have either stopped sales or launched investigations. In the US, the FDA confirmed unacceptable levels of N-nitrosodimethylamine (NDMA), in some ranitidine products including in syrups taken by babies.

The company checks the chemical makeup of drugs before shipment to consumers. It rejects more than 10 percent of the batches because tests detect

[50] A tiny pharmacy is identifying big problems with common drugs, including Zantac, The Washington Post, Carolyn Y. Johnson, November 8, 2019.

contaminants, medicines that don't dissolve properly, pills that contain the wrong dose, and other problems. Occasionally they find a problem so urgent they play the role of watchdog.

This is a pharmacy company, buying drugs from wholesalers, and then selling to consumers. As of 2019 it is the only company that chemically tests the medicines it dispenses. The company was started when the founder refilled a prescription only to find that the new identical drug didn't work. The doctor suggested trying another pharmacy because it was probably a bad batch. The founder searched for a lab to verify the chemical contents of medications and could not find any.

In 2012, hip replacement manufacturer Stryker announced it was issuing a voluntary recall on the Rejuvenate ABG II modular neck stems. The main problem was corrosion and release of cobalt and chromium into the blood stream. Stryker announced it would settle the lawsuits, paying upwards of $1.4 billion to patients.

The root cause of the failure was the hip was fast tracked through the FDA. Certification was based on the one-piece hip system. The Rejuvenate ABG II system broke the hip into two pieces allowing surgeons to perform a better fit and perhaps more procedures per day.

The problem is that any engineer or machinist could immediately detect that the dissimilar metals between the two pieces would cause electrolysis and lead to breakdown and release of cobalt chromium into the blood stream. This is a classic case of extreme arrogance and ignoring key stakeholders.

The FDA like the FAA appears to have been missing proper staff with the correct education, experience, skills, and access to information.

6.7 FAA Budget And Economic Impact

The FAA budget consists of funds that come from the Airport and Airway Trust Fund (AATF) and the General fund. The Airport and Airway Revenue Act of 1970 created a Trust Fund that comes from aviation excise taxes. It provides a dedicated source of funding for the aviation system and is independent from the General fund which comes from all the taxpayers.

The authority to collect aviation excise taxes and to spend from the Aviation Trust Fund must be periodically reauthorized by congress. If the FAA's authorization expires without an extension, then it is unable to spend any revenues allocated from the Trust Fund.

The Trust Fund provides the primary source of funding for the FAA and receives revenues from a variety of excise taxes paid by users of the national airspace system. The excise taxes are imposed on domestic passenger tickets, domestic flight segments, international passenger arrivals and departures, and on purchases of air travel miles for frequent flyer and similar programs. Taxes are also imposed on air cargo waybills and aviation fuel purchases. The largest sources of excise tax revenues are related to transportation of passengers.

Table 21 FAA Budget

ACCOUNT NAME	Mandatory Discretionary	2017 ($000)	2018 ($000)	2019 ($000)
Operations	**D**	**$10,025,852**	**$9,957,766**	**$9,931,312**
General		$852,852	$847,060	$1,298,591
AATF		$9,173,000	$9,110,706	$8,632,721
Facilities & Equipment (AATF)	**D**	**$2,855,000**	**$2,835,612**	**$2,766,572**
Research, Engineering & Development (AATF)	**D**	**$176,500**	**$175,301**	**$74,406**
Grants in Aid for Airports (AATF)	**M**	**$3,350,000**	**$3,350,000**	**$3,350,000**
Aviation User Fees	M	$137,778	$140,257	$140,176
Aviation User Fees (transfer to EAS)	M	($130,828)	($140,257)	($140,176)
TOTAL:		**$16,414,302**	**$16,318,679**	**$16,122,290**
Mandatory		$3,356,950	$3,350,000	$3,350,000
Discretionary		$13,057,352	$12,968,679	$12,772,290
General		$852,852	$847,060	$1,298,591
AATF		$15,554,500	$15,471,619	$14,823,699
Source: Budget Estimates Fiscal Year 2019, Federal Aviation Administration, Exhibit II-4.				

Revenues deposited in the Trust Fund are subject to congressional appropriations and included in the federal budget. At the end of 2018 the Airport and Airway Trust Fund had a cash balance of $17.0 billion. The 2019 Trust Fund excise tax revenues is forecast to be $16.3 billion. The Trust Fund provides funds for four major FAA accounts.

- **Operations:** The Operations account funds the administration, operation, repair, and maintenance of the National Airspace System (NAS) and aviation safety oversight.
- **Facilities & Equipment (F&E):** The F&E account provides for current infrastructure, and the advancement of NextGen air Traffic Control (ATC) systems.
- **Research, Engineering and Development (RE&D):** The RE&D account funds the research and services that ensure a safe, efficient, and environmentally compatible air transportation system.

- **Grants-in-Aid for Airports:** The Grants-in-Aid for Airports account funds the FAA's Airport Improvement Program (AIP), which supports the development of a nationwide system of public-use airports to meet the current needs and the projected growth of civil aviation.

The Trust Fund may cover both capital and operating costs. In 2018, it provided all of the funding for two of FAA's four accounts, the F&E and the RE&D accounts.

The Airport Improvement Program provides grants for construction and safety projects at airports and is often funded entirely by the Airport & Airway Trust Fund. In 2018 the Airport Improvement Program received an additional 1 billion dollars in discretionary funding for airport grants from the General Fund. In 2019, the Airport Improvement Program received an additional $500 million from the General Fund.

The Trust Fund provided about 86.7 percent in 2018 and 94.4 percent in 2019 of the funding for the Operations Account. The remainder of the Operations Account is funded by the General Fund revenues.

When we examine the numbers in the FAA budget, we see that the R&D allocation does not align with any reasonable levels expected from a high technology organization like the FAA. It also does not align with the FAA public law that clearly states the FAA must engage in R&D activities.

The DOD can be used as a model to determine the potential FAA R&D budget. The DOD R&D portion of its budget is 15.93%. If this was used as a basis to determine the FAA R&D allocation, this would increase the FAA R&D budget from $74 million to $2.57 billion. Even if the level dropped to 10% or 5%, we see the FAA R&D budget is completely irresponsible and suggests that an external force like privatization has seriously harmed the FAA R&D activities, the FAA organization and its ability to serve the taxpayers.

Table 22 FAA R&D versus DOD R&D Budget

2019	Budget (000)	R&D (000)	R&D %	R&D at 15.9% (000)
FAA	$16,122,290	$74,406	0.46%	$2,568,892
DOD	$693,058,000	$95,253,000	15.93%	NA

The FAA in 2009 found that commercial aviation accounts for approximately 5% of U.S. gross domestic product and contributes $1.3 trillion in annual economic activity as well as helps generate and support 10 million jobs annually. The $16 billion dollars for the FAA show that the country has lost sight of its priorities. The FAA needs to be properly funded in this next century. The R&D budget alone needs to go from essentially zero ($74 million) to $2.5 billion dollars. The assets built up from the previous century are almost all gone. The clock is ticking, and the outcome will not be good when it expires.

6.8 FAA Privatization Observations

The ATC system is critical to the future stability of the United States. What is required, before any privatization attempts, is a full system engineering analysis of the FAA as an organization driven by system thinking not narrow interests, select ideologies, or political forces. This means multiple analysis perspectives must be offered and properly communicated from multiple institutions. The final analysis must be rock solid so that no one can invalidate it regardless of time and resources. Until such analysis is performed it would be reckless to dismantle a government agency that has transformed the United States and the world. It is undeniable that because of the FAAs massive success almost anyone can engage in air travel, a priceless element in our new world that we cannot risk losing.

Several years ago, a professor from Princeton became interested in why so many of our institutions are failing. This led to the book "On Bullshit"[51]. His observation is that there are people engaged in pushing an agenda by either lying or engaging in Bullshit. Further he suggests that liars are redeemable because they know they are lying but Bullshit artists are not redeemable because they don't care if they are lying or telling the truth. They are only pushing their agenda. This author prefers to refer to this as propaganda. Its only purpose is to push an agenda and not seek truth.

This humble author suggests we came to this sad state of affairs because we lost our roots in systems thinking and systems engineering. This is a complex subject and outside the realm of this FAA privatization analysis other than to clearly state there must be a return to systems thinking and systems engineering. The FAA is only one institution that is being challenged because of this **critical loss in our national capability**.

In keeping with a systems thinking and systems engineering perspective, whenever an architecture is proposed it should include the existing approach, dream approach, and then other approaches. Each architecture must be taken to its point of perfection. Then the approaches should be subjected to a fully transparent and easily understood tradeoff. At the end of the tradeoff journey the answer becomes clear to all the stakeholders who are seeking truth rather than an agenda. So, who will take the current architecture of the FAA as a government organization to its point of perfection in this critical tradeoff?

If privatization does not happen then it is clear that a recovery plan needs to be put in place to remove the negative impacts of the decade's long battle between the two factions. This recovery plan not only needs to include the FAA but also the industrial base which has been severely damaged as companies sought other markets, merged, or closed. In this are the workers who have paid a dear price from job loss, stalled careers, and lost careers. It is too late for the striking controllers of the early 80s but it's not too late for the current generation keeping the FAA ATC

---

[51] On Bullshit, Harry G. Frankfurt, Princeton University Press, January 2005, ISBN 9780691122946.

system up and running while planning and implementing its future. Finally, the air traveling public has paid a huge price. Air travel today unlike in the past is a **very ugly experience** and it is a direct result of damage done to the FAA during this historic period of political upheaval.

Since these ideas were developed the B737 MAX disaster happened. This is a clear symptom that the FAA privatization efforts have been devastating. The question of trying to find a different system architecture to perform the functions of the FAA outside of accountable government is no longer an option. Instead what is now the key issue is how will the US rebuild its capability within the FAA and undo the damage of privatization and choked off budgets that were used to justify the possibility of full privatization. As a reminder the FAA has a very long history:

- May 20, 1926: President Calvin Coolidge signed the Air Commerce Act of 1926 into law. The act instructed the Secretary of Commerce to foster air commerce; designate and establish airways; establish, operate, and maintain aids to air navigation (but not airports); arrange for research and development to improve such aids; license pilots; issue airworthiness certificates for aircraft and major aircraft components; and investigate accidents.
- Dec 2, 1929: Fifteen air carriers pooled $100,000 to set up the not-for-profit organization, Aeronautical Radio, Inc. (ARINC), to serve as the single coordinator of aeronautical communications for the air transport industry, using a common network of ground stations.
- August 11, 2013: Rockwell Collins announced it had agreed to purchase ARINC, Inc., for $1.39 billion. The purchase, when completed, would expand Rockwell Collins' aerospace business by combining its avionics and cabin technologies with ARINC's ground-based navigational networks. (See December 2, 1929.)

6.9 Reality Check

The FAA and its government predecessors have a long historical record beginning on May 20, 1926 when President Calvin Coolidge signed the Air Commerce Act of 1926 into law. The act instructed the Secretary of Commerce to foster air commerce; designate and establish airways; establish, operate, and maintain aids to air navigation (but not airports); arrange for research and development to improve such aids; license pilots; issue airworthiness certificates for aircraft and major aircraft components; and investigate accidents.

Nothing has changed since that time. The need for enhanced and protected Commerce via Infrastructure, Research and Development, and Regulation still exists. The technologies are just different, and the scale is beyond anyone's imagination in 1926.

In this new century once again the technologies and scale will be beyond anyone's current imagination. Thinking the system is old and can be handled by a single private enterprise with a business mindset is not only naive but very dangerous. It will very likely lead to the collapse of air travel as simple and useless business practices are incapable of addressing the true challenges that will surface.

What is needed is proper legislation so that the FAA can be freed from its current problems and do what it needs to do for the people of the United States. The days of political infighting must come to an end and the realization that business cannot and should not solve all problems must be acknowledged.

1. It's not about jobs it's about ensuring the stability and effectiveness of the Air Traffic Control and Commercial Aviation industrial base in the United States.
2. It's not about taxpayer costs it's about ensuring the existing transportation system does not collapse and continues to grow in this new century.
3. It's not about inefficient government versus efficient business it's about business incapable of doing what only government can do.
4. It's not about the unfunded FAA it's about stopping political infighting so that a critical part of United States infrastructure is not sabotaged.
5. It's not about the inefficient FAA it's about ensuring all organizations public and private are as efficient as our technologies, processes, and practices allow.
6. Imagine the ability to fly almost anywhere at any time at reasonable costs going away and becoming cost prohibitive, some of us know what existed just 60 years ago before the FAA.
7. Imagine the current ugly travel experience that surfaced coincident with deregulation continuing to become even more ugly, some of us know the beauty in travel that existed before.
8. Imagine the disconnect from the DOD infrastructure leading to security and safety issues that are just to horrific to imagine. Yes, the FAA and DOD interact very closely every day and always did.
9. Imagine a tightly held cartel doing whatever they want whenever they want in a collapsed Air Traffic Control and Commercial Aviation industrial base as a total unchecked monopoly.
10. Imagine missing the application of all the new technologies that will surface in the next 100 years because the FAA is gone. Yes, they consumed technology.
11. Imagine missing the development of all the new technologies in the next 100 years because the FAA is gone. Yes, they created technology.
12. Can you imagine walking where you need to go 20 years from now because it's all gone, yes it can wink out, it's all only less than 60 years old, it's all very fragile, think sustainability.

6.10 Recommendations

The following recommendations are associated with budget legislation. The next budget year the FAA should be working with this corrective legislation. It will take years to rebuild the FAA so legislation must happen immediately. There is no more time left as evidenced by the B737 MAX disaster.

1. Fix the FAA R&D program so that the FAA can do what it needs to do for all the future programs in the next 100 years.
2. Provide proper FAA R&D funds normally associated with such organizations.
3. Provide proper funds to rebuild the FAA certification capability. This includes hiring career industry international resources with proper education and experience backgrounds.
4. Fix the human resources organization by removing elements that attempted to allow for FAA privatization but instead severely damaged the workforce and industrial base.
5. Retitle all employees directly paid by the government to remove any business implications such as COO, Vice Presidents, etc. This is not a company; it is a nation state government organization.
6. Fix the systems engineering elements within the FAA with a proper education and training program.
7. Refocus the FAA away from just operations and safety to also ensuring a proper high-quality Air Traffic Control system, Industrial Base, and Air Transportation system, it's about commerce.

To deal with any future attempts to harm the FAA with privatization schemes the next budget cycle legislation should include the following:

1. If the FAA is privatized, the trust fund tax ceases immediately and its balance transfers to the taxpayer.
2. If the FAA is privatized, the taxpayers are reimbursed for all tangible and intangible assets as identified in the analysis in this text.
3. If the FAA is privatized, the taxpayers are reimbursed for all costs since 1926. Reimburse the trillion dollars to the taxpayer, period.

The following recommendations are offered to the people. What Can You Do?

Act fast and don't assume someone will save the day. Unless you act it will happen regardless of what happens in Washington DC and the big current events.

1. Contact your elected representatives.
2. Spread the word on social media.
3. Demand news organizations do serious investigative reports on this topic.
4. Do your own research and write your own papers.
5. Talk to everyone about this.
6. Understand this is probably the single most important thing that will happen in this century and help others to understand this simple fact, it's that big.

7 Privatized Workers

A systems approach was used to start an analysis of United States federal government shutdown impacts and it became clear that a key stakeholder has been left out of the entire shutdown and recovery activities, the new privatized worker. This issue has been fully ignored by all parties as narrow self-interests are addressed rather than attempting to fully understand the problem from a systems perspective.

On December 22, 2018 the United States Government entered another shutdown because of the inability to pass a new budget. Each time the government has shutdown it has impacted a new workforce that surfaced as a result of privatization - the privatized government workforce. Previously once the budget is passed and government operations resume, new legislation compensates the civil servants who were furloughed during the shutdown. However, the privatized workers that work side by side with the civil servants in various offices, labs, and government bases are not compensated in future legislation.

7.1 Systems Perspective

During the 2018-2019 government shutdown the media focused on the civil servants where 420,000 must work without pay and 380,000 were sent home in the furlough. However, 4.1 million government contractors were laid off and will collect unemployment and dip into savings. There is no national database tracking the number of contract employees. Dr. Paul Light a federal workforce expert at New York University provided the estimates. Not Expecting Back Pay, Government Contractors Collect Unemployment, Dip into Savings, NPR, January 7, 2019.

If there were a clear systems perspective the discussion would include the system boundary, stakeholders, history, impacts, and critical analysis.

- What is the systems boundary? Why is the system boundary being drawn too small so that the entire system is not considered (privatized workers)?
- Who are all the system stakeholders? Why are some left out of the discussion? Why do some stakeholders have no voice?
- What is the system history? Why are there constant shutdowns? Is there more to the shutdown events than the immediate claims?
- What are the total system impacts? Are people being harmed? Are critical projects disrupted or severely damaged?

- What are the critical analysis results? Have stakeholders impacted by shutdown layoff committed suicide, lost marriages, walked away from careers? What are the impacts to their children?

This leads to the broader question, what are the unintended consequences of privatization.

7.2 Privatization Effects during Government Shutdowns

Today government functions are performed by traditional civil servants and privatized workers. They work side by side in various government offices, labs, and military bases supporting the same operations and basically performing the same functions with the same educational and skill levels.

During the past few decades the budget has been delayed and multiple government shutdowns have occurred. Both civil servants and their privatized counterparts are not permitted to work during a government shutdown. In all cases after the shutdown is resolved legislation has been passed to reimburse the civil servants. However, their privatized counter parts working side by side are not reimbursed. In addition, there is evidence suggesting that the privatized workers are discouraged from claiming unemployment with their respective states.

The problem was further exacerbated in 2018 when President Trump closed government offices for President Bush's funeral and for Christmas Eve in 2018 and 2019. Once again, the civil servants were compensated while the privatized workers lost pay for each of the days the government offices were closed.

The shutdowns and random holiday declarations unfairly and severely impact the privatized workforce with loss of income. The privatized employees' only mistake is working in the government privatized workforce alongside their civil servant counterparts rather than for a traditional government contractor with its own offices, operations, and contracts.

Treating the privatized workforce in this way is obviously a gross injustice and severely out of character for the United States of America. The Commission on Privatization was aware of the potential abuse of power that may surface and clearly stated in the executive summary:

"In addition, any recommendation supporting increased contracting out should be implemented only after full consideration has been given to employee interests."[52]

It is clear, that employee interests have been ignored and severely compromised.

The US Federal Government has experienced multiple years when it was unable

---

[52] President's Commission on Privatization published a 287-page report, Privatization Toward More Effective Government, March 18, 1988.

to pass a new budget in time for the next year - US Federal Funding Gaps. However, until 1980 the government did not stop its functions or fail to pay its bills on time and in full, unlike today. It was obvious that the US Federal Government would eventually pass a budget and pay its bills. This changed in 1980 with a reinterpretation of the Antideficiency Act of 1884. It is unclear why this bad law has remained when it is obvious that it has caused serious harm to the USA. Sabotage is defined as to deliberately destroy, damage, or obstruct (something), especially for political or military advantage.

Since 1980 the US Federal Government has experienced multiple shutdown events because of its inability to agree on a new federal budget. The following table shows that the shutdown events have become more severe as time has moved on. Also because of the privatization of the government there are severe impacts to large numbers of workers that now form the new privatized contractor workforce.

Table 23 Shutdown History

Shutdown	Days	Civil Servants Furloughed	Privatized Contractors Not Paid
1980	1	1,600	
1981	1	241,000	
1984	1	500,000	
1986	1	500,000	NOT reimbursed number unknown
1990	3	2,800	NOT reimbursed number unknown
Nov 1995	5	800,000	NOT reimbursed number unknown
1995–1996	21	284,000	NOT reimbursed number unknown
2013	16	800,000	NOT reimbursed number unknown
Jan 2018	3	692,900	NOT reimbursed number unknown
2018–19	35	reimbursed 380,000	NOT reimbursed 4.1 Million

7.3 Legislation

Senate - Compensate Civil Servants (800,000)

On January 17, 2019 President Trump signed S.24 Government Employee Fair Treatment Act of 2019 into law. This followed the precedent set with previous shutdowns. However, the privatized workforce as contractors were not reimbursed. This is an unfair treatment under the law and breach of thousands of contracts situation. Further the civil servants that were required to work without pay were not reimbursed for the extra workload and extremely stressful work settings. The major problems with this law are:

1. Breach of Contract
2. Unequal Treatment Under the Law
3. Does not discourage future shutdowns

The only alternative left for the privatized contractors was for someone to bring a lawsuit against the Federal Government and claim that this law must be expanded to include everyone using the same arguments used by Ruth Bader Ginsburg in Charles E. Morito vs. IRS care giver deduction 10th Circuit 1972 to extend protections of the Equal Protection Clause of the Fourteenth Amendment to contractors.

There were attempts to pass legislation for some of the privatized workers but once again not all of the 4.1 million privatized workers were included.

- H.R.339 Low-Wage Federal Contractor Employee Back Pay Act of 2019
- S.162 Fair Compensation for Low-Wage Contractor Employees Act of 2019

The house introduced H.R.339 Low-Wage Federal Contractor Employee Back Pay Act of 2019. But Sec 750 had the following discriminatory text that did not include all the privatized workers: "Sec. 750. If a Federal contractor that provides retail, food, custodial, or security services to the Federal Government places the employees of such contractor on unpaid leave as a result of any lapse in appropriations which begins in fiscal year 2019, the Government shall provide compensation to such employees at their standard rate of compensation for the period of such lapse." If the text deleted "retail, food, custodial, or security" then the proposed legislation would have treated everyone equally. Once again, even though this legislation failed it was fundamentally flawed because of:

1. Breach of Contract
2. Unequal Treatment Under the Law
3. Did not preserve the rule of law
4. Violated precedent set by Ruth Bader Ginsburg in Charles E. Morito vs IRS care giver deduction 10th Circuit 1972
5. Did not include financial pain to discourage future shutdowns

The senate introduced S.162 Fair Compensation for Low-Wage Contractor Employees Act of 2019. It did not include all the Federal Contractor Employees and limited weekly compensation to $965. The text for this bill only addressed non-professional contractors in the Definitions section - The term "employee" means the following and once the references are traced not all contractors are included. Hiding this by using references is not good. The privatized contract employees include large numbers of professionals that are not included in this definition of employee. A related bill from the house HR824 Low-Wage Federal Contractor Employee Back Pay Act of 2019, increased the weekly compensation to $1,400. If the text was modified to include ALL Federal Contractor Employees, then the proposed legislation would have treated everyone equally. Once again, even though this legislation failed it was fundamentally flawed because of:

1. Breach of Contract

2. Unequal Treatment Under the Law
3. Did not preserve the rule of law
4. Violated precedent set by Ruth Bader Ginsburg in Charles E. Morito vs IRS care giver deduction 10th Circuit 1972
5. Did not include financial pain to discourage future shutdowns

The House and Senate were not listening. This is extremely serious because it is obvious that all privatized workers must be reimbursed. The essence of any new legislation should include everyone. The legislation proposed text should have been clear and short:

1. Each excepted employee of the United States Government or of a District of Columbia public employer who is required to perform work during a covered lapse in appropriations shall be paid for such work, at the employee's standard rate of pay plus 10%, at the earliest date possible after the lapse in appropriations ends, regardless of scheduled pay dates.
2. Each contract employee of the United States Government or of a District of Columbia public contract employee not permitted to work and has lost wages due to layoff or other actions as a result of a covered lapse in appropriations shall be paid via their existing contracts for the period of the lapse in appropriations, at the contract employee's standard rate of pay, at the earliest date possible after the lapse in appropriations ends, regardless of scheduled billing dates.

The rational is simple. Excepted government employees forced to work during the shutdown experienced significant increased workload and work stress. This is like a war zone where 25% is the expected pay rate increase. However, since loss of life is not expected, the standard night rate 10% differential is suggested. Privatized contractor employees were victims of Breach of Contract and Unequal Treatment Under the Law. This must be done to preserve the rule of law and follow the clear precedent set by Ruth Bader Ginsburg in Charles E. Morito vs IRS care giver deduction 10th Circuit 1972.

7.4 Litigation

There does not appear to be any litigation from the shutdown events. Since 1980 there have been a total of 85 days of lost compensation due to shutdowns. It is unclear why no companies or their employees have challenged the Federal Government using the following as a basis:

- **Breach of Contract** The (1) contractors performed as expected, (2) the agencies performed as expected, and (3) there was no change in direction on the part of the contracting agencies. This is a clear breach of contract where an external element causes the failure of payment. In such cases the injured parties are to be reimbursed the original contract amounts even if the services are not performed. There is even the possibility of damages due to this third-party interference in the performance of a contract.

- **Equal Treatment Under the Law** Even though clear precedent was set by Ruth Bader Ginsburg in Charles E. Morito vs IRS care giver deduction 10th Circuit 1972 the legislation to reimburse civil servants has not been extended by the courts to include everyone not just a narrow select privileged group.
- **Violation of Public Law 105–270** The current contracts and shutdown actions violate The Federal Activities Inventory Reform Act of 1998 Public Law 105–270 Section 2 item (e) REALISTIC AND FAIR COST COMPARISONS. This is a provision for realistic and fair cost comparisons when considering contracting in the private sector. This includes the costs of quality assurance, technical monitoring of the performance of the function, liability insurance, and employee retirement and disability benefits, and all other overhead costs. The other overhead costs should include the cost of shutdowns. Clear precedent was set by 1987 and all future contracts should have included provisions for government shutdowns.
- **Violation of Circular A-76 Performance of Commercial Activities** It is clear that the Government is not following its policies and the intent of the public law Federal Activities Inventory Reform Act of 1998, Public Law 105-270. This policy establishes that the Government should not compete with the commercial industrial base. This suggests what a commercial entity looks like – it engages in commercial business. Unfortunately, as a result of the privatization efforts over the past few decades the Government has established a new entity that has no commercial activity and yet is considered a company that offers privatized contract services exclusively to the Government. The policy states that the business needs to be a commercial business, not one artificially created by the Government.

One can only conclude that there is severe harassment and intimidation to prevent anyone from trying to seek justice.

The government shutdowns have now reached a crisis point because with each shutdown the number of days increases. The latest shutdown of 35 days normally would translate into a collapsed state with a call for a new government and new elections. Yes, it is that serious. Litigation may stop this action instantly. Reimbursing 1 to 4 million workers for 85 days of lost pay would translate into billions of dollars not including the damages that surfaced in breach of contract litigation and impacts of the shutdowns including suicides, lost careers, etc.

7.5 Privatized Worker Unions

So where are the unions to support the new privatized workforce? The privatized workforce is fragmented across hundreds of privatized worker companies. In the case of the FAA SE2020 and SE2025 programs there are approximately 379 companies providing privatized workers. This means that 300+ companies would need to be organized by multiple unions representing very low numbers of employees in each company.

There are about 4 million workers in this category with thousands of companies between the workers and the Federal Government. This is an impossible task. Further organizing 30 people in a company is pointless because they do not have issues with their companies. It is the Federal Government that is doing the damage with shutdowns, bad contracts, and potentially unconstitutional legislation that is hurting the workers.

Unfortunately, it looks like a system has been established to bypass the unions and associated laws that protect workers and their rights. It is difficult to imagine that this is an unintended consequence of privatization especially given the anti-union history of the 1970s and 1980s. It's a new century in the USA.

The only way for the privatized workers to escape this bad situation is to seek employment outside the privatized workforce settings or for certain Federal Government organizations like the FAA to be sold off to a private entity. Once the private entity is established then one or more unions can step in and organize the workforce.

One of the key elements of a union contract is that only a small percentage of the workforce can be contract employees; this is typically less than 10%. The limit of contract employees set to 10% is interesting because there are multiple Federal Government unions and a government facility could be subjected to the 10% contract employee limit. However, that has not happened. It is not unusual to see a government facility with 50%, 60%, and 70% of the workforce as contract employees. Once again, it's a new century in the USA.

7.6 How Did This Happen

It is unclear why legislators sworn to uphold the constitution, the rule of law, and tasked with representing all the citizens as part of their public trust would ignore the situation of 4.1 million privatized contract employees during government shutdowns. The privatized contract employees have no representation in Congress. There is no political action committee, union, or corporate lobbyists to represent their interests. This is extremely cynical and suggests that the system is catastrophically broken. A less cynical view of the budget battles and the role of government is that every part of the budget is squeezed, and this is a convenient way to reduce the cost of government with the least amount of resistance. In other words, Congress is aware of the plight of privatized contract employees, but their needs are sacrificed as part of a bigger more important need to reduce the cost of government.

7.7 Recommendations for The Short Term

After the shutdown is over, legislation has been passed to compensate the civil servants and contracts have been modified to ensure companies providing the privatized workers receive the original contract value, However, the privatized workers are not compensated for lost wages.

The argument is that companies cannot bill the government for work not performed. However, the civil servants are compensated for work not performed. One interpretation of law is used to deny wages to one group out of two groups of workers that are both equally hurt by the shutdown.

Another interpretation can be that the law should treat everyone equally. If the privatized workers are not paid, then the civil servants should not be paid. If the civil servants are retroactively compensated for work not performed, then the privatized workforce should be retroactively compensated for work not performed.

As the shutdown time increases there comes a point where healthcare and other benefits such as retirement, 401K contributions, and other benefits are impacted. The privatized workers may move to more expensive COBRA healthcare and lose time that contributes to their benefits before their civil servant coworkers because of shorter pay cycles.

The recommended remedy to this gross injustice is based on the concept that everyone must be treated equally under the law:

1. All future legislation that allows civil servants to be compensated after a shutdown must include their privatized counterparts who work side by side everyday as part of the United States of America government functions. The reasons include breach of contract, unequal treatment under the law, preserve the rule of law by not violating precedent set by Ruth Bader Ginsburg in Charles E. Morito vs IRS care giver deduction 10th Circuit 1972 and it is the right thing to do.
2. An investigation of previous shutdowns must be performed to determine how previous shutdowns affected the privatized workforce and if needed they must be compensated for their lost income and harm since 1988.
3. Legislation must be provided to ensure that such gross injustice does not occur in the future.
4. This must happen immediately.

It's not that complex. Essentially each contract for privatized workers is automatically updated to include a new payment associated with the shutdown.

7.8 Recommendations for the Future

Automatically reimbursing privatized workers after a government shutdown should be added to the body of law for future shutdowns so that companies providing privatized workers can float the costs of the shutdown using traditional financial mechanisms. The guarantee of government reimbursement will allow this to happen.

It is unfortunate that special legislation is needed to deal with this serious dysfunction of government. This is a symptom of a larger systemic problem associated with privatization and the role of government. Executive Order 12607 President's Commission on Privatization may have been issued with the best of intentions, However, there is now decades of empirical data to suggested that there are serious unintended consequences and that there is significant harm.

The reality is as we pursued the path of privatization beginning in 1987 no one really bothered to investigate the role of government and industry. Basic civics class 101 was never considered. This analysis needs to happen, and future policy needs to be established to correct this serious problem that leads to constant budget standoffs and government shutdowns that penalize one group of workers while preserving another group of workers.

8 Federal Government

The government is not maintaining statistics on the number of privatized workers, so the true size of government is unclear. This has led to budget challenges and government shutdowns. This has become worse with each passing year. This was the initial analysis of the impact of privatization on the US Government. Upon further examination of government privatization, the impacts are massive and extremely serious. Privatization may be compromising the US Democracy.

8.1 Federal Budget

The impacts of privatization are now evident. One of the largest impacts is the inability to fund the government when the budget expires. This has resulted in multiple government shutdowns.

In 1987 President Reagan issued Executive Order 12607 President's Commission on Privatization. The words are interesting but what is more interesting are the words that are missing. The missing words are what criteria should be used when considering a government organization for privatization[53]. For example, should defense and security be part of the criteria. Should analysis be performed to determine the short term and long term social and economic impacts? What should that analysis include and how would the analysis be validated?

There are many different institutions and the following is a small example:

- Government
- Public Education
- Utilities
- Co-Operatives
- For Profit Companies
- Non-Profits
- Religious
- Charitable

Each of these institutions has characteristics that allow them to thrive and provide the valuable services that someone somewhere thinks is needed. For example, expecting For Profit Companies to invest in going to the Moon is foolish. They expect to show profits typically on a short-term basis. Going to the Moon is not a viable business. Yet a nation state via its government may conclude that it makes perfect sense to go to the Moon and is willing to make the investment even if it is not quantified in terms of dollars.

A fundamental question to ask is - what is the purpose in privatizing a

---

[53] See section 9.2.7 Key Requirements Specifications and Traceability. If any of the requirements are not met because of privatization then either the privatization architecture needs to be modified or it must be rejected, and privatization immediately stopped.

government organization. If the purpose of privatization is to reduce costs and or increase efficiency, then that is not an appropriate answer. The broken government organization needs to be fixed to reduce costs and increase efficiency. If on the other hand the purpose of privatizing a government organization is to unleash a sustainable industrial base with many companies able to make immediate profits, then it is appropriate. This of course is in a setting where the taxpayer is properly reimbursed for this government organization that has assets that will be transferred to an entity or entities that the taxpayer does not own; although they could become shareholders. So, the criteria for determining which government organizations to privatize are critical to the implementation of Executive Order 12607 President's Commission on Privatization.

The political reality is that a very powerful faction in the US believes that the only role of government is defense. They reject the New Deal and its key elements outlined in Science the Endless Frontier from the previous century and are actively trying to shut down all non-Department of Defense (DOD) related government activities. This massive political disagreement manifests itself as budget battles and government shutdowns. This is a decade's long battle at this point in our history and is getting worse with time.

8.2 Government Shutdowns

The US Federal Government has experienced multiple years when it was unable to pass a new budget in time for the next year - US Federal Funding Gaps. However, until 1980 the government did not stop its functions or fail to pay its bills on time and in full, unlike today. It was obvious that the US Federal Government would eventually pass a budget and pay its bills. This changed in 1980 with a reinterpretation of the Antideficiency Act of 1884. It is unclear why this bad law has remained when it is obvious that it has caused serious harm to the USA. Sabotage is defined as to deliberately destroy, damage, or obstruct (something), especially for political or military advantage.

Since 1980 the US Federal Government has experienced multiple shutdown events because of its inability to agree on a new federal budget. The following table shows that the shutdown events have become more severe as time has moved on. Also because of the privatization of the government there are severe impacts to large numbers of workers that now form the new privatized contractor workforce.

Table 24 US Government Shutdown Trend

Shutdown	Days	Civil Servants Furloughed	Privatized Contractors Not Paid
1980	1	1,600	
1981	1	241,000	
1984	1	500,000	
1986	1	500,000	NOT reimbursed number unknown
1990	3	2,800	NOT reimbursed number unknown

Table 24 US Government Shutdown Trend

Shutdown	Days	Civil Servants Furloughed	Privatized Contractors Not Paid
Nov 1995	5	800,000	NOT reimbursed number unknown
1995–1996	21	284,000	NOT reimbursed number unknown
2013	16	800,000	NOT reimbursed number unknown
Jan 2018	3	692,900	NOT reimbursed number unknown
2018–19	35	reimbursed 380,000	NOT reimbursed 4.1 Million

8.3 Federal Government Architecture Change

The architecture of the government has changed and with that change the system has been significantly impacted. Tax money is being diverted from the industrial base to the new privatized companies offering services.

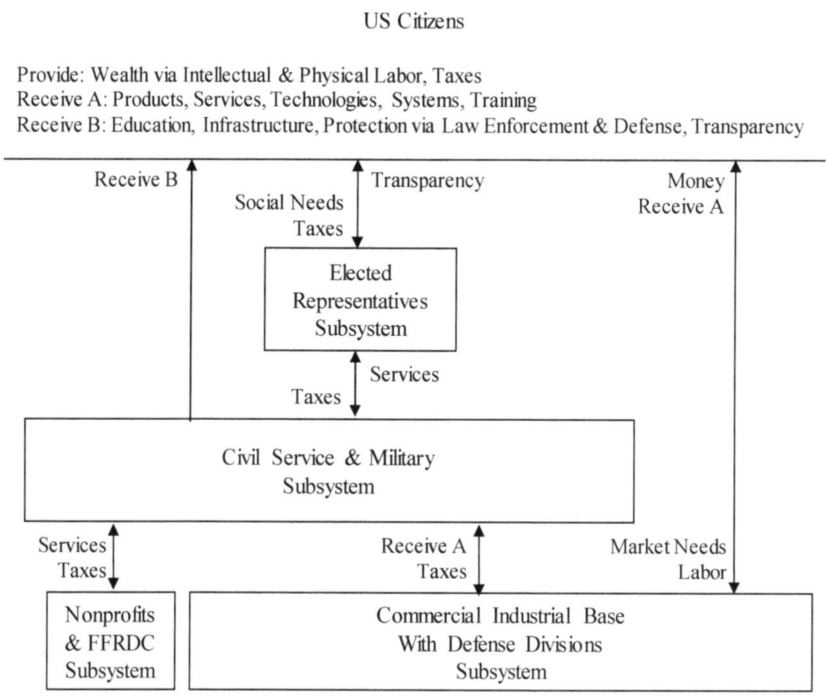

Figure 17 Pre-Privatization System Architecture[54]

As the privatized companies provide services, transparency associated with government is not available from the private enterprises. There is also a severe disconnect between citizen needs that is present not only with the elected service subsystem but also with the commercial industrial base. This is significant and manifested itself as commercial and industrial companies shedding their divisions

[54] See section 9.4.3.6 Nonmarket / Social Needs.

that support the government with products and technologies. For example, RCA in Camden New Jersey at one time was a significant commercial and industrial company that provided consumer products to every household in the US. It also maintained defense divisions[55].

As RCA was divested its commercial and industrial operations went to overseas companies and the defense divisions moved to General Electric, then Martin Marietta, which merged with Lockheed to become Lockheed Martin, then L-3 Communications[56]. These are all defense companies with no real consumer or industrial operations.

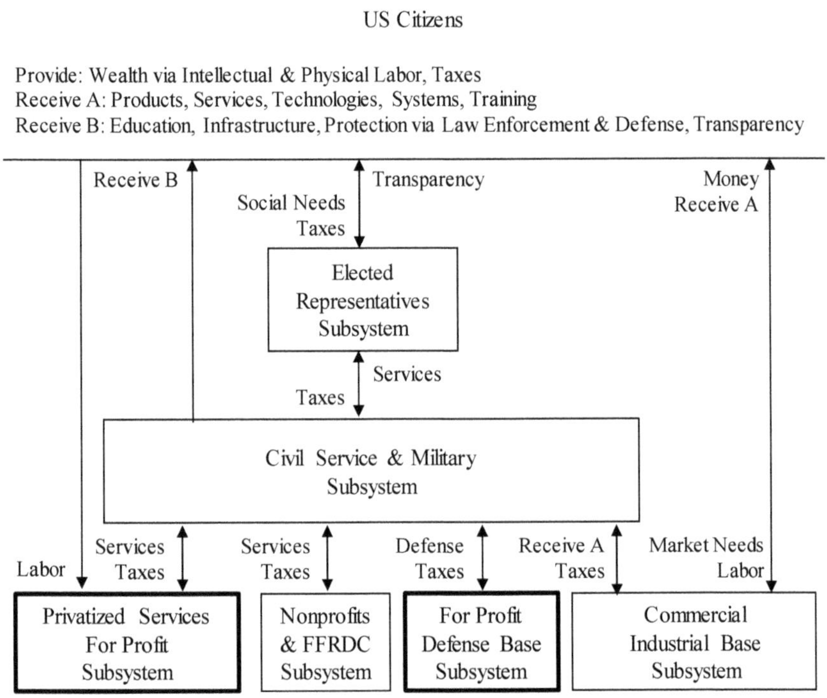

Figure 18 Post Privatization System Architecture

In companies like RCA the commercial and defense divisions would have staff move between the two areas as the cyclic economic conditions changed. There were times when the commercial industrial economy would be down, but government spending would be up. Then the economy would cycle out of the downturn and commercial industrial work would become a priority. Rather than have wholesale

---

[55] Sarnoff stated that RCA never intended to make money on defense. The commercial industrial divisions made money. The defense divisions were the company's patriotic duty.

[56] Consumer electronics went to Thompson Electronics, France, and industrial television systems went to Panasonic, Japan. The broadcasting division, NBC, went to General Electric.

staff reductions the staff moved between the divisions. So commercial industrial engineers responding to the needs of the market would be assigned to the defense divisions and bring their market perspectives, or commercial citizen needs to the government. This was also a significant source of excellent commercial industrial R&D that was made available to the US government for their needs. The staff would eventually move back to the commercial industrial divisions. This no longer exists with the Post Privatization System Architecture.

The Commercial Industrial Base in the Post Privatization System Architecture is misleading. The reality is the companies providing products and systems to the government are former defense divisions that have been shed from their original commercial industrial roots.

In the pre-privatization system architecture, the Nonprofits tended to provide services. However, there was a nonprofit that developed massive technology, products, and systems; that company was Hughes Aircraft. At its peak it employed 85,000 people where two thirds of the staff were engineers or scientists. Hughes Aircraft started as a division of Hughes Tool Company, a significant industrial company that was basically a cash cow for Howard Hughes and all his ventures. In 1953 The Howard Hughes Medical Institute (HHMI) was formed, and Hughes Aircraft reformed as a subsidiary of the foundation. This made Hughes Aircraft a nonprofit corporation.

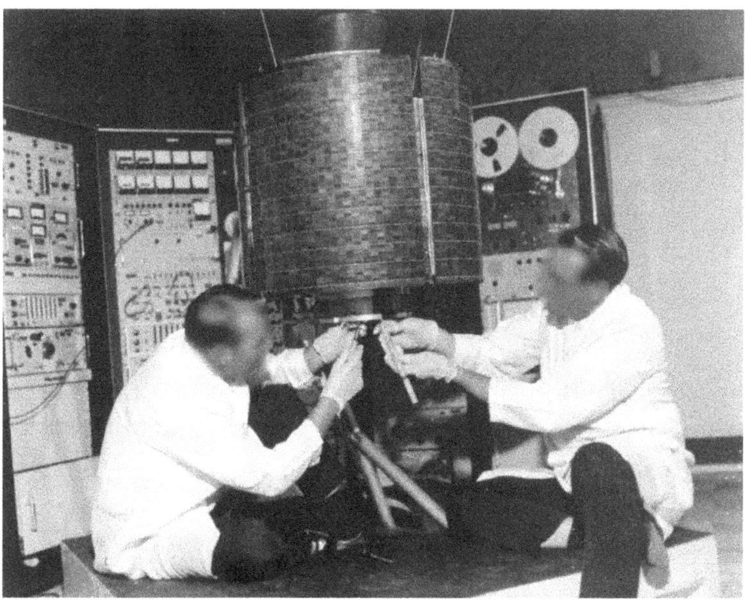

Figure 19 Early Bird - First Communications Satellite[57]

[57] Photo: NASA. Engineers checkout Early Bird-Communication Satellite.

The Early Bird was the world's first communication satellite. NASA launched the satellite built by Hughes Aircraft Corporation on April 6, 1955 at 6:48pm EST from Complex 17a at Cape Kennedy, Florida. Early Bird was built for the Communications Satellite Corporation and weighed about 85 pounds after being placed in a synchronous orbit of 22,300 miles above the Earth. It was positioned over the Atlantic to provide 240 two-way telephone channels or 2-way television between Europe and North America. The outer surface of Early Bird was covered with 6,000 silicon-coated solar cells, which absorbed the sun's rays to provide power to the satellite for its intricate transmitting and receiving equipment.

Figure 20 Intelsat IV Communication satellite[58]

Two beautiful girls standing next to this massive machine. A machine that would bring their worlds together and elevate their understanding and consciousness of the world to such levels that some would have considered it impossible just a few short years ago. Intelsat IV in an anechoic (sound absorbing) chamber. Built by Hughes Aircraft it stood over 17 feet tall with a capacity of about 6,000 voice grade

[58] Photo: NASA. Intelsat IV in an Anechoic chamber

circuits or 13 television channels. Intelsat was an international organization of 65 nations that was established August 20, 1964 out of the growing demand for channels of communication and greatly expanded the commercial communications network. The Intelsat IV was placed in a synchronous orbit over the Atlantic.

8.4 DOD and Defense Companies

When the Berlin Wall came down there was an opportunity to convert some defense companies to commercial industrial enterprises much like what happened after World War II. That did not happen due in large part to privatization. Everyone knew everything changed when IBM shed its IBM Federal Systems Group in the 1990s. Thousands of the best engineers working in these entities as part of business development bought proposal after proposal to their senior executive staffs to provide products and systems to non DOD government organizations, industrial, and commercial markets. All these proposals were rejected, and the focus remained on trying to win the next DOD contract in a market that was severely reduced. Eventually the common talking point was that the DOD companies could not transform. The only approach considered was consolidation or shutdown[59].

The defense industry invented microwave ovens, jet travel, digital computers, software languages, operating systems, space-based communications, scientific probes to other planets, and access to space with the space shuttle. In the 1990s the defense industry had more than 50% of their market disappear.

When the Berlin Wall fell, the U.S. government began chopping major portions out of the defense budget. Defense procurement declined by more than 60% in constant dollars between 1989 and 1997. At the same time, NASA's budget and commercial airline spending on new planes fell.

The impact on the defense industry was devastating, exceeding that of the stock market crash of 1929 when about 29% of the nation's GNP eventually disappeared. Estimates suggest that approximately three-quarters of the 120,000 companies that once supplied the Department of Defense disappeared by 1997. They shut down their defense lines of business or dissolved them altogether. The surviving companies laid off highly skilled, dedicated workers at the rate of one every 45 seconds for several years.

Table 25 Defense Consolidation

1990 Primarily Defense Divisions within Industrial Companies	1997 Defense Companies
Boeing, Rockwell, McDonnel Douglas	Boeing
Lockheed, Martin Marietta, GE Aerospace, RCA Aerospace, Loral, General Dynamics, Sanders, Gould Ocean Systems, Xerox Electro-	Lockheed

[59] Reshaping an Industry: Lockheed Martin's Survival Story, Norman R. Augustine, Harvard Business Review, May–June 1997 Issue.

Table 25 Defense Consolidation

1990 Primarily Defense Divisions within Industrial Companies	1997 Defense Companies
Optical Systems, Goodyear Aerospace, Fairchild Weston, Honeywell Electro-Optics, Ford Aerospace, Librascope, IBM Federal Systems, Unisys Defense, LTV Missiles	Martin Marietta
Hughes Aircraft, E-Systems, Raytheon, Texas Instruments	Raytheon
Northrup, Westinghouse, Grumman	Northrup Grumman

In 2010 DOD spending on contracts was $316 billion. Approximately half of the money was spent on buying services. During the first four years of the Iraq war, the government hired approximately 190,000 contracted personnel (privatized workers) in direct service contracts. This is greater than the total number of troops at the high point of the surge and is roughly 23 times the number of troops provided by our allies. The ratio of uniformed military to contractors in the 1991 Gulf War was approximately 50:1. The contracting presence in Afghanistan reached over 100,000 contractors, resulting in a 1:1 ratio (data from 2010)[60].

The Pentagon (as of 2010) estimates that $10 billion dollars went missing or was misspent by private military contractors in Iraq. Thousands of weapons disappeared in Iraq and Afghanistan and some fell into the hands of local insurgents or transnational terrorist groups. Because of shoddy electrical work performed by contractors, troops died inside US bases. Contractors were involved in many of the most egregious and embarrassing incidents in the war, including Abu Ghraib and the Nisour Square shootings in September 2007.

Contracting services has grown 700 percent in recent years while the Pentagon workforce responsible for this role has shrunk by 25 percent. In 1997 one DOD auditor was responsible for $642 million in private contracts; in 2010 it was one for every $2.02 billion in contracts.

Contracting officers have stated they are too busy signing new contracts to go back and review performance of existing contracts. The result is that contracts turn bad. For example, the tragic electrocutions and Abu Gharib horror had no government contracting officers on site. If they were onsite, they would have been aware of the situations and intervened to prevent the misconduct.

Once again, the key issue is what activities are appropriate to privatize? The DOD never defined what are "inherently governmental" functions and instead were driven by the new political realities to outsource and build a privatized workforce. Private military firms can provide any military service or function, from strategic leadership to piloting jet fighters to cooking. What areas should private firms be

[60] The Regulation of New Warfare, The Brookings Institution, Peter W. Singer, February 27, 2010

used in the ultimate government function of being engaged in war is the key question today[61]. The term "inherently governmental" is used many times in US code and appears in 120+ pages of DOD documents, but remains unclear and is ignored when it comes to actual contracting for privatized workers. This is how the US government had a company with privatized interrogators at Abu Ghraib, using an IT services contract written in 1998 as the point of origin.

In 2010 many suggested the Pentagon could not perform its most basic public responsibilities without privatized services contractors. In the absence of privatized workers there would be extreme difficulty supporting basic operations and tasks like convoy movement, provision of critical supplies (e.g. food, fuel, and ammunition), and running the Office of the Secretary of Defense and the Joint Staff. Various new weapons sectors are becoming exceptionally dependent on privatized workers; examples are cyberwarfare and the Predator/Reaper unmanned aerial systems. Over 60 percent of intelligence operations are outsourced to privatized workers (2010).

Since September 11, 2001 the DOD has been held in special regard. However, the budgets have been enormous, the wars have been long and difficult, and the privatization has been massive with few knowing the extent of the privatization. If the examples of unintended negative consequences of privatization apply to DOD, then this is devastating as lives are lost and massive resources are applied.

8.5 Presidential Impeachment and Ukraine

On December 13, 2019, the House Judiciary Committee voted to pass two articles of impeachment: Abuse of Power and Obstruction of Congress[62]. On December 18, 2019, the House of Representatives voted in favor of impeaching President Trump on both articles.

The Trump administration as part of rebuilding the aging infrastructure has offered proposals that are based on massive privatization of roads and other infrastructure. The privatization policy spans multiple administrations and includes both political parties. The infrastructure privatization policy has not received much push back and had nothing to do with the impeachment. Instead the policy disagreements are over immigration, border security, tax policy, and recently international topics such as tariffs, trade agreements, military operations and NATO. The impeachment also has nothing to do with the policy disagreements.

At the heart of this impeachment is the country of Ukraine and its struggle with the invasion from Russia, loss of its territorial integrity, and a commitment made by the USA.

In 1994 the country of Ukraine had the world's third largest nuclear weapons

---

[61] See section 9.2.7 Key Requirements Specifications and Traceability for guidance. This was clear in the past but somehow, we lost that commonsense knowledge as the privatization political dogma has gripped policy makers in government and industry.

[62] See section 10.9 Presidential Impeachment.

stockpile. They gave up their nuclear weapons between 1994 and 1996 as part of an agreement that would ensure that its territorial integrity would be preserved. The Budapest Memorandum on Security Assurances is an agreement signed at the Organization for Security and Co-operation in Budapest, Hungary on December 5, 1994. The agreement was signed by three nuclear powers, the Russian Federation, the United Kingdom, and the United States of America.

By the start of the new century the US started to make business deals and investments in Russia especially for the development of its oil resources. The same was happening in Ukraine on a smaller scale. The people of Ukraine had a strong distaste of the Russian communists who were brutal to them and they wanted to align themselves more with Western Europe and perhaps become part of NATO[63]. This eventually led to an internal revolution where the Russian friendly Ukraine president was removed from power. Russia panicked and invaded Ukraine[64].

The countries that signed the treaty to protect Ukraine responded with economic sanctions on Russia. This caused all the business deals in Russia to come to a standstill. Meanwhile Russia acting in its own interest wanted to shift the political landscape in the USA so that the sanctions would be removed.

Unexpectedly the US people elected President Trump who himself and his key backers had significant business interests in Russia. These business interests were fully known and disclosed in the popular media before and after the election. When Trump entered office, his policies were friendly towards Russia.

President Trump with little knowledge or respect[65] for the government that he found himself leading made a serious mistake and betrayed his public trust by trying to force the Ukrainian President to make public statements about a political rival, Vice President Biden's son, in exchange for arms previously agreed to be provided to Ukraine to defend themselves against the Russian attack and territorial annexation in Ukraine. It is obvious that President Trump was trying to restart business interests in Russia but he may have given aid and comfort to an enemy country. Aiding the enemy in time of war is the only way someone can be charged for treason under the US constitution[66]. The attack on Ukraine was an attack on the US because of the Budapest Memorandum on Security Assurances and the

---

[63] The North Atlantic Treaty Organization (NATO) is a military alliance between 29 North American and European countries. The Treaty was signed April 4, 1949. Independent member states agree to mutual defense in response to an attack by any external party. Since its founding, the member states have increased from the original 12 countries to 29. The most recent state added to NATO is Montenegro on June 5, 2017. NATO (2019) recognizes Bosnia and Herzegovina, Georgia, North Macedonia and Ukraine as aspiring members.

[64] There are historical reasons for Russia to want Ukraine aligned with them rather than Eastern Europe. Unfortunately cause and effect forced the Ukrainians to want to distance themselves from Russia.

[65] This is documented in the public media by his comments on the government he leads.

[66] See section 10.9 Presidential Impeachment.

enormous sacrifice and trust the Ukrainians had when giving away their nuclear arms.

Lost in all of this is the fact that Ukraine gave up their nuclear missiles and when the time came to protect them nothing happened. The message to powers seeking nuclear capability like North Korea and Iran is clear and the precedent has been set for a generation. As the US struggles with short term impeachment the long-term policy impacts on nuclear weapons are huge and will last decades. The situation is very serious. Cause and effect and balance of power move history[67].

The roots of this tragedy are clearly traceable to government privatization. This book covered privatization only in the US, but privatization is a worldwide trend[68] that included Russia. Unfortunately, Russian defense conversion[69] and privatization was not going well. They did not have 100 years of history to tune the system and protect against extremes as nation state assets were being claimed. This affected their internal policies and ultimately their approach to the country of Ukraine.

I need to go back to the nuclear missiles issue. There was great hope when the Berlin Wall came down and then great joy that the world had one less nuclear annihilation threat on our small blue plant. Below is the document that was supposed to protect the country of Ukraine from invasion in exchange for Ukraine eliminating all its nuclear weapons.

Table 26 Ukraine Memorandum on Security Assurances

Memorandum on Security Assurances in connection with Ukraine's accession to the Treaty on the Non-Proliferation of Nuclear Weapons, December 5, 1994. The United States of America, the Russian Federation, and the United Kingdom of Great Britain and Northern Ireland, Welcoming the accession of Ukraine to the Treaty on the Non-Proliferation of Nuclear Weapons as a non-nuclear-weapon State, Taking into account the commitment of Ukraine to eliminate all nuclear weapons from its territory within a specified period of time, Noting the changes in the world-wide security situation, including the end of the Cold War, which have brought about conditions for deep reductions in nuclear forces.

[67] See section 9.2.6 Cause and Effect and Balance of Power.

[68] Transforming Government Through Privatization, Annual Privatization Report 2006, 20th Anniversary Edition, Reason Foundation.

[69] Report to the Chairman, Committee on National Security, House of Representatives, April 1997 Cooperative Threat Reduction, Status of Defense Conversion Efforts in the Former Soviet Union, GAO/NSIAD-97-101.

Table 26 Ukraine Memorandum on Security Assurances

Confirm the following: 1. The United States of America, the Russian Federation, and the United Kingdom of Great Britain and Northern Ireland, reaffirm their commitment to Ukraine, in accordance with the principles of the CSCE Final Act, to respect the Independence and Sovereignty and the existing borders of Ukraine. 2. The United States of America, the Russian Federation, and the United Kingdom of Great Britain and Northern Ireland, reaffirm their obligation to refrain from the threat or use of force against the territorial integrity or political independence of Ukraine, and that none of their weapons will ever be used against Ukraine except in self-defense or otherwise in accordance with the Charter of the United Nations. 3. The United States of America, the Russian Federation, and the United Kingdom of Great Britain and Northern Ireland, reaffirm their commitment to Ukraine, in accordance with the principles of the CSCE Final Act, to refrain from economic coercion designed to subordinate to their own interest the exercise by Ukraine of the rights inherent in its sovereignty and thus to secure advantages of any kind. 4. The United States of America, the Russian Federation, and the United Kingdom of Great Britain and Northern Ireland, reaffirm their commitment to seek immediate United Nations Security Council action to provide assistance to Ukraine, as a non-nuclear-weapon State Party to the Treaty on the Non-Proliferation of Nuclear Weapons, if Ukraine should become a victim of an act of aggression or an object of a threat of aggression in which nuclear weapons are used. 5. The United States of America, the Russian Federation, and the United Kingdom of Great Britain and Northern Ireland, reaffirm, in the case of the Ukraine, their commitment not to use nuclear weapons against any non-nuclear-weapon State Party to the Treaty on the Non-Proliferation of Nuclear Weapons, except in the case of an attack on themselves, their territories or dependent territories, their armed forces, or their allies, by such a state in association or alliance with a nuclear weapon state. 6. The United States of America, the Russian Federation, and the United Kingdom of Great Britain and Northern Ireland will consult in the event a situation arises which raises a question concerning these commitments. This Memorandum will become applicable upon signature. Signed in four copies having equal validity in the English, Russian and Ukrainian languages.

In 1991 the doomsday clock was set to 17 minutes before midnight. The dream of a nation state sacrificing its nuclear weapons did not set the clock back further in

1994 when the Budapest Memorandum on Security Assurances was signed. Instead by 1998 the clock moved to 14 minutes before midnight. The sacrifice of the Ukrainians was ignored. The clock as of 2018 is at 2 minutes before midnight[70].

8.6 Privatized Security Clearances

The Office of Personnel Management (OPM) is responsible for a large part of the management of security clearances for the United States Government. Except for the Nuclear Regulatory Commission, which maintains its own system, separate programs for each executive department have gradually been merged into a single, government wide clearance system. OPM investigates individuals for Secret and Top-Secret clearances. Sensitive Compartmented Information (SCI) clearances are managed by individual agencies.

In 1996 the security clearance investigation branch of the OPM was privatized, and US Investigations Services Inc (USIS) was formed. This was a direct result of Vice President Al Gores' efforts to reduce the size of civil service[71]. The new privatized entity, USIS initially was an employee-owned company initially made up of the previous civil servants.

The Carlyle Group invested in USIS and in 2003, Welsh, Carson, Anderson & Stowe also invested in USIS. In 2007, Carlyle announced that it would sell USIS to Providence Equity Partners, a private equity firm, for $1.5 billion dollars. In 2012, USIS received a $253 million for contract work at the OPM. This was 67% of OPM's contract spending for the year. The following failures happened:

- In 2007, a privatized OPM contract investigator employed by USIS conducted the field work for the background investigation on Aaron Alexis. He fatally shot twelve people at the Washington Navy Yard on Monday, September 16, 2013.
- In 2011, a privatized OPM contract investigator employed by USIS conducted the field work for the security clearance re-investigation on Edward Snowden[72]. He leaked classified documents beginning on June 5, 2013 and now resides in Russia.

On June 18, 2013, the Subcommittee on Efficiency and Effectiveness of Federal Programs and the Federal Workforce and the Subcommittee on Financial and Contracting Oversight for US Senate Homeland Security and the Governmental Affairs Committee, held a joint hearing[73]. The OPM assistant inspector general for

---

[70] See section 10.9.3 Doomsday Clock.

[71] Al Gore Reinventions Created USIS's Outsourced Vettings, Bloomberg, Nick Taborek, June 24, 2013.

[72] Watchdog faults background check of NSA leaker, Associated Press, Richard Lardner and Kimberly Dozier, June 20, 2013.

[73] Firm that did background check on Snowden is under investigation, The Washington

investigations, testified that USIS was under investigation since late 2011 and that it involved a complicated contract fraud case. The OPM inspector general did not reveal the reason for the investigation of USIS and when asked about Snowden's security clearance re-investigation stated that there may have been some problems[74].

The problem is that the privatized company cut corners to process clearances[75]. It is unclear if this is the cause for the serious security failures just described[76], but this was very bad. It started with a whistle blower[77] and ended with USIS going away. In 2015, USIS's parent company, Altegrity (also known as Corporate Risk Holdings) filed for bankruptcy. It is unclear what happened to the defunct company security clearance databases in the chaos of the last days of operations[78].

There is a big difference between a private company investigating potential employees for a company and the US Government investigating US citizens to grant a clearance in support of nation state activities. Companies have no need to know if someone's fathers family members were tortured and murdered by communists or if their mother was forced to work in a slave labor camp during World War II. To have this type of information in the hands of a private company is a severe compromise of the nation state security apparatus[79]. This is a direct result of following the dogma of privatization with no thoughts from a system perspective or even simple common sense[80].

8.7 How Did This Happen

As previously described, privatization appeared in a book by Robert Poole, Cutting Back City Hall, 1980. He co-founded the Reason Foundation, a libertarian organization, in 1978. The book provided support for Margaret Thatcher's privatization efforts in the United Kingdom. He advised the administrations of Ronald Reagan, George H.W. Bush, Bill Clinton, and George W. Bush on privatization and transportation policy. The Reason Foundation publishes the Annual Privatization Report (APR). The APR came from Reason Foundation

---

Post, Joe Davidson, June 20, 2013.

[74] NSA leaker Snowden's clearance had 'problems'; firm that vetted him under probe, The Washington Times, Shaun Waterman, June 21, 2013.

[75] Justice Department says USIS submitted 665,000 incomplete background checks, The Washington Post, Tom Hamburger and Debbi Wilgoren, January 23, 2014.

[76] Same firm checked background of Navy Yard shooter, Snowden, Reuters, Tabassum Zakaria, September 19, 2013.

[77] The whistleblower who exposed U.S.'s flawed security clearance system finally gets his reward, The Washington Post, Christian Davenport, December 18, 2015.

[78] Major DHS contractor hit by cyberattack, The Hill, Julian Hattem, August 6, 2014.

[79] U.S. Homeland Security contractor reports computer breach, Reuters, Eric Walsh, August 6, 2014.

[80] In times of war this would be viewed as sabotage and a clear example of treason.

Trustee David Koch[81].

The roots of privatization appear to come from the libertarian movement. From an elected representative perspective, the libertarians are far from the mainstream electorate as suggested by election results. Yet the idea of privatization has had a huge impact on the makeup of government.

Modern privatization may have started with President Reagan but there was little movement in that direction. It was not until the Federal Activities Inventory Reform (FAIR) Act[82] under President Clinton's administration that privatization started to transform the government.

The question is how was this accomplished without the full knowledge and approval of the electorate?

As each new president takes office, they can change the political appointees that head each government organization. The policies are set by the Presidents political appointees while the civil servants and military must execute that policy. Taken to the final state, privatization would replace the entire civil service and military with a few contract administrators and monitors. Government would be completely gone. It would be handed over to private companies with no transparency or accountability to the citizens. These companies would be completely outside the commercial industrial base with no connection to the free market system.

History teaches that nature abhors a vacuum. Systems perspectives teaches that there is always a system. The issue is in the absence of conscious effort what will fill the vacuum in the absence of government. Will it be a good system or a bad system? The choices are known by looking at history and they are the following systems:

1. Criminals
2. Warlords
3. Dictators
4. Monarchy
5. Democracy

It would be nice to think that everyone can live in peace with freedom and liberty for all without Democracy but that is not the lesson of history and that is not what even the simplest systems analysis shows.

---

[81] David Hamilton Koch (May 3, 1940 – August 23, 2019). Koch was a libertarian. He was the 1980 Libertarian candidate for Vice President of the United States and helped finance the campaign. He became president of the subsidiary Koch Engineering in 1979 and became a co-owner of Koch Industries (along with elder brother Charles) in 1983.

[82] Public Law 105-270, Federal Activities Inventory Reform (FAIR) Act of 1998, 105th Congress, Oct. 19, 1998.

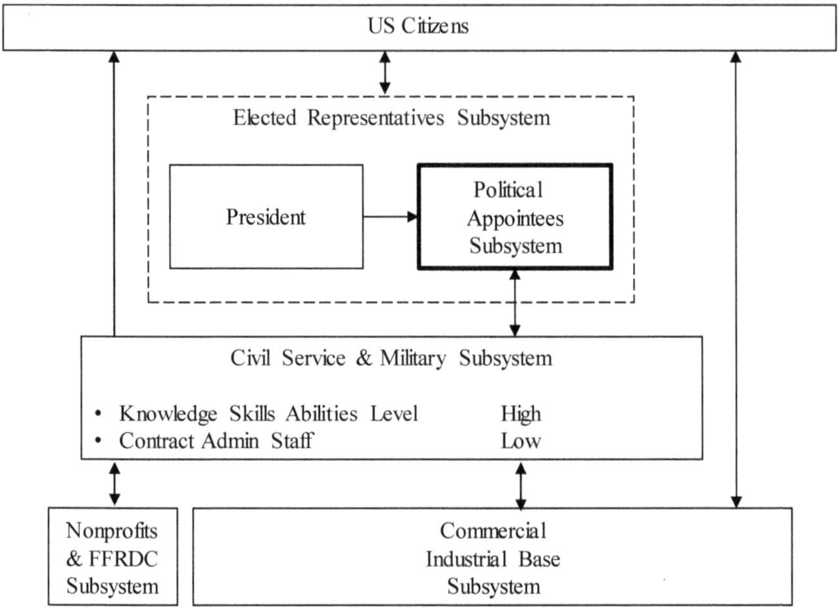

Figure 21 Pre-Privatization Political Appointees Impact

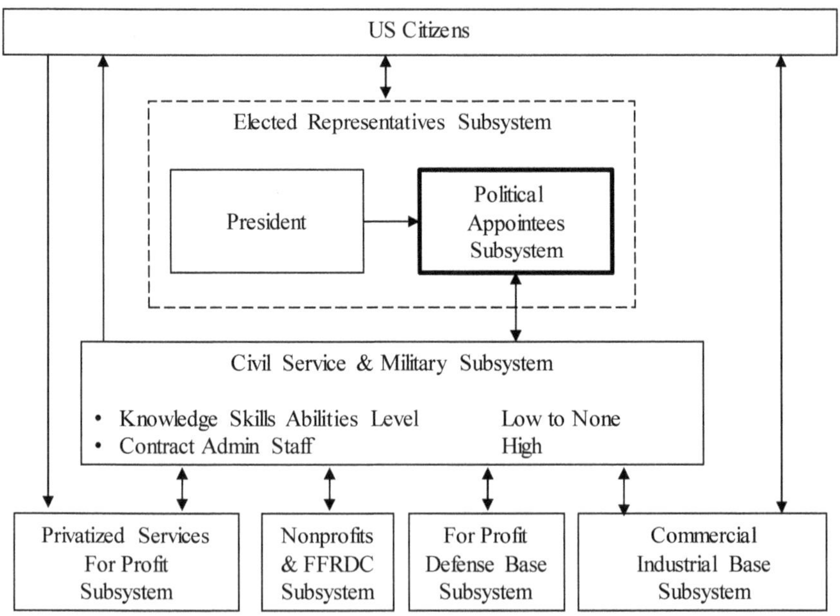

Figure 22 Post Privatization Political Appointees Impact

Today there are towns that have decided to privatize their engineering functions. These engineers ensure that new construction meet codes and is safe and proper for the community. It is not uncommon for developers to hire local engineering firms to design the drainage, road placement, and other aspects of a new community. In privatized government communities the same engineering firms that perform the design then certify the design and final product. The problem happens when residents note grading errors in new properties and the engineering firm that made the mistake certifies that everything is ok. The residents only recourse is to hire an outside engineering firm and take the case to court. This is an example of a very bad system. This is an example of a privatized system. Mistakes are always made; the issue is what happens when they need to be corrected. Who will protect the interests of the taxpayer?

8.8 Observations

When we examine the pre and post privatization system architectures we see that the driver is citizen needs and that the needs fall into two categories: market needs and social needs. The market needs are satisfied by a free and open market engaged in commerce. The social needs are satisfied by our democratic government that balances the needs of all the people. The difference between the two systems is how the social needs are being satisfied.

The approach to meeting the social needs of the citizens has changed significantly as the policy to privatize the government has matured. We see that companies have formed that exclusively derive all or most of their earnings from the taxpayers. The traditional companies that provided market needs shed their government divisions as their services earnings from their military products and systems were diverted to the new services companies. This resulted in the formation of standalone for-profit defense companies.

As the services shifted away from government into the new privatized services and standalone defense companies, transparency and the ability of the citizens to control the size of their tax expenditures has been removed. Lobbyists representing these new entities control the dialog and the approach to meeting the social needs of the citizens. The democratic system of government has been replaced by a non-democratic corporate system of government and these corporations have little or no connection to the reality of market needs and commercial industrial commerce.

The question is how much of the government has been split between the democratic system and the privatized system? Before privatization this was not a concern. The government tapped the commercial industrial base to satisfy the social needs of the citizens. Today that is not the case.

The social needs derive from common sense. They were codified on July 4, 1776 with the Declaration of Independence:

We hold these truths to be self-evident, that all men are created equal, that they are endowed by their Creator with certain unalienable Rights, that among these are Life, Liberty and the pursuit of Happiness.--That to secure these rights, Governments are instituted among Men, deriving their just powers from the consent of the governed, --That whenever any Form of Government becomes destructive of these ends, it is the Right of the People to alter or to abolish it, and to institute new Government, laying its foundation on such principles and organizing its powers in such form, as to them shall seem most likely to effect their Safety and Happiness.

The key system requirements for this government are:

- Life
- Liberty
- Safety
- Happiness

The result was a new system for governance based on democratic principles. The role of that government is stated in the constitution:

We the People of the United States, in Order to form a more perfect Union, establish Justice, insure domestic Tranquility, provide for the common defence, promote the general Welfare, and secure the Blessings of Liberty to ourselves and our Posterity, do ordain and establish this Constitution for the United States of America.

The Bill of Rights and the Constitution are the A-Level requirements for the new system that is the United States Government. These fundamental documents and further discussion of these documents are in section 10.8 Government Constitutions.

All systems development and changes go through the same phases of concept, design, implementation, verification, and validation. The verification phase ensures that the implementation follows the requirements and the validation phase ensures that the system is the correct system. The judicial system is supposed to ensure that the requirements are being followed. However, they are not enforcing some key requirements such as antitrust laws. The citizens check to see that the requirements are being followed and they also have the task of validating the system. The citizens cannot verify and validate the system if they are unaware of how it is being changed by hidden interests that want to keep the electorate in the dark. The following key system process activities are compromised:

- Verification via the judicial system enforcing laws
- Validation via citizens making sure the system is correct and makes sense

8.9 Recommendations

Much like in 1980 when the Reagan revolution was started, we see that the government is broken but now because of privatization. After 35 plus years of privatization policies we see that the system has exhibited many unintended consequences as it was gamed by the new services companies tapping into a new market called taxpayer funds. We also see that the ability of government to function has been diminished and the impacts may even include serious negative international consequences.

1. The recommendations for fixing the government include the same recommendations suggested for fixing the Industrial Base, Colleges and Universities, Air Transportation and the FAA.
2. The most fundamental recommendation is to pass legislation so that no entity can receive more than 50% of their earnings from government unless they are a nonprofit or less than 200 employees. Tapping the taxpayers as a market is irresponsible and outrageous behavior that must be stopped. Companies must operate in the free market that is not rigged by hidden interests. If they cannot make it in the free market, then they go away.
3. It is critical that the process of De-Privatization start immediately. The new privatized companies need to merge with viable consumer and or industrial companies responding to real market needs. These companies need to understand that both commercial, industrial, and government operations should be seamless so that in the future government divisions not become isolated with little or no roots in reality.
4. The citizens need to be told that privatization has been pushed into the government without their full knowledge and that they need to decide what to do moving forward.
5. The congress needs to stop doing what hidden interests want especially because of campaign contributions. This is a democracy where all the people must be represented, or it will collapse. The democracy is key because when someone claims that this is a republic that immediately justifies the actions of hidden interests. This is a form of bribery and tyranny. It is taxation without representation.
6. Everyone needs to understand that there is a huge difference between a Government Organization and a Private Company. Basic civics education needs to be made part of all levels of the educational system from elementary school to the college and university levels. It is outrageous to have adults with significant educational backgrounds not know and understand the difference between government and industry or know that government can accomplish certain things that are impossible for industry to accomplish alone and that industry should not even be given those burdens.

7. A massive education effort needs to show everyone how and why US government was founded, how it operates, the responsibility of the citizens, and the dangers of hidden interests that want to destroy the system of government that is this Democracy implemented as a Republic.
8. NASA was able to send humans to the Moon in 1969. To accomplish this 400,000 people worked on the program and 20,000 companies were involved in the effort. This effort involved developing new technologies and engineering systems that transformed our world using new materials, machines, management techniques, new systems and space age products. This was an example of a balance between government, industry, and academia – a magic mixture. That mixture does not exist today because of the privatization efforts of the past few decades. When examining the De-Privatization of the government, this history needs to be studied to find a reasonable path forward.

9 Systems Perspectives

At this point you are welcomed to skip this section and go to section 11 Privatization System Conclusions and then return to this section. If you decide to proceed you can stop at any point and then return. You can also jump around in this section and review the topics that are of initial interest. Eventually you should go through all the sections so that you are fully immersed in the systems perspective and have a greater appreciation for the key content of this book.

This section has topics from my other books, two of which are textbooks, on systems engineering. It was a challenge to decide which sections to include because each book builds upon the previous books and the content is very large. The first textbook was about systems practices while the second textbook was an attempt to show how systems thinking, engineering, and design are performed. This is a small systems perspectives section. Let us begin.

Systems' engineering has many definitions, but they all point to common overlapping themes. From a dictionary viewpoint the word systems come from the word *systema* circa 1603. The word *systema* is defined as:

A complex of anatomical structures functionally related.

This makes sense given the time frame and the focus people had on trying to understand how the human body works. I prefer this more modern definition of systems engineering:

Discipline that concentrates on the design and application of the whole (system) as distinct from the parts. It involves looking at a problem in its entirety, taking into account all the facets and all the variables and relating the social to the technical aspect[83].

The second part of the definition has been lost to time: **"relating the social to the technical aspect"**.

When given the opportunity I offer my description of systems thinking, engineering and practice as follows:

---

[83] This is from Simon Ramo. He was an Electrical Engineer that started his career with GE in 1936 went to Hughes Aircraft in 1946 and became a founder of TRW in 1953.

Imagine a place where you can create things and make decisions where there are no hidden agendas and all stakeholders are treated equally. How would potential approaches surface, how would they be narrowed and selected, how would decisions be made? What tools and techniques would be used if they were not the greatest moneyed interests, the most politically powerful, or the most dangerous?

How about using logical methods based on reasonable techniques understood by reasonable people in a process that is fully transparent and visible to everyone. Everyone has a view of all the alternatives. Everyone has a view of all the decision paths. Everyone has an opportunity to impact the alternatives and decision paths.

Do not fall for the rhetoric that this is mob rule or design by committee. These are reasonable people using thousands of years of tools, techniques, processes, and methods to make informed decisions. There are no hidden agendas with vested interests or people who just give up and go silent or worse compromise. Everyone is comfortable with the decision because it is intuitively obvious to all. Everyone obviously has responsibility in such an endeavor. No one can ignore that responsibility. That in a nutshell is Systems Practice.

The reality is many of us engage in systems practices in our everyday lives when we reject fate and try to control our destinies. We use whatever tools we have at our disposal to make these decisions everyday of our lives. Everyone engaged in our modern world should have some say in its evolution and that say should be from the system perspective of his or her view. So, we can start at this point by saying that you as a systems practitioner do the following:

1. Always broaden your horizons and perspective. Just when you think you have it, move to a broader view.
2. Reject the status quo. If you find yourself in that mix, step out of it and look for truth. It takes time for a valid solution to solidify.
3. Reject all vested interests including hidden interests.
4. Try to see the forest from the trees but always zoom in onto the leaf of a particular tree and find the cute bug sitting on the edge.
5. Avoid the trap of being set only at one abstraction level, the high level. You must be able to scale all abstraction levels simultaneously. This is hard.

9.1 Systems Approach

Systems are multi dimension. To understand a system, multiple views must be considered. This means there are different kinds of pictures, analysis, and words all grouped into some cohesive set so that all can understand the system. For example, most individuals will attempt to view a system from a financial point of view. But there are also functional and performance points of views in which a system can be optimized.

When designing an audio amplifier for a new sound system for the home do the designers first focus on the financial aspects of an amplifier or do they focus on the power output, frequency response, and amplifier noise? So why do people today immediately drift towards tracking the money when attempting to design or optimize systems like healthcare, transportation, electric power, fuels, villages or cities? Could it be because they lack basic knowledge in representing systems from a functional and performance point of view? Did people in the past focus on function and performance first when designing cars, houses, villages, radios, televisions, stereos, toasters, etc?

The reality is a system with a given set of functional and performance characteristics will be at a given cost. The designers can choose to reduce performance or functionality to reduce costs, but then they run the risk of creating a useless system from the user point of view, those that must rely on the system. In some cases, this reduced functionality and or performance can lead to loss of life. Most focus on examples of airplanes falling from the sky, bridges falling down, or cars killing needlessly. However, we should never forget that people have died from bad water, bad food, bad sanitation, bad drugs, bad health care, and even bad cities that result in crime and destruction of human spirit.

Those that engaged in systems practices in the last century realized that our technologies have become so powerful that we could literally destroy our planet. The start of a nuclear world was the first time this realization surfaced and was unfortunately true. By the 1970's people started to realize the ramifications of our actions on our fragile global environment and future generations. The realization that there is no place to run, there is no hidden valley protected from our actions coupled with our massive technology. Shangri-La does not exist.

So people started to practice this thing called systems engineering. From this flowed various systems practices with vast application potential. Did they invent systems engineering or did it just naturally emerge in a complex space where nothing else would work? Does it matter? The point is systems engineering was studied, practiced, and honed to such a high level of maturity that people could clearly point to systems engineering as the only way to get a job done and deliver working solutions.

Not everyone was or is engaged in systems engineering activities. Those that were touched by the power of our post World War II technologies engaged consistently in systems engineering; for example, those that had seen the nuclear tests and the promise of powerful technologies but at huge risks and costs. For them, systems engineering, or systems practices had become common sense. Some but not all went on to build houses, appliances, roads, satellites, and many of the systems we all enjoy. The dilemma is that not everyone was or is now involved in systems and some outside the peer group erroneously feel it is foreign and complex.

There are many traps that people can fall into when they first enter the systems engineering or practices space. For example, most believe systems engineering will result in the perfect optimized solution, architecture, or design – the system. The reality is that multiple architecture approaches will work, but these architectures must be born from the fire of systems engineering. Each architecture or system will shine in a particular area and be weak in another area. Money can be applied to the weak architecture areas to bring it into the desired performance level. Also, any of these architectures will cost about the same in the end. This realization was born from empirical data at Hughes Aircraft[84], Fullerton, California circa 1982 and communicated to me by a very senior Hughes person. He had worked with Howard Hughes in the early years. His name was also Howard and yes, he was brilliant.

Unfortunately, little work transitioned back to the universities from institutions like Hughes Aircraft. These institutions have disappeared and the senior people who gave birth to modern systems engineering or practices have started to pass on. I am younger and thus just an echo of these people and their work. Everywhere I have gone I have tried to pass on this body of knowledge.

9.2 Fundamentals

The following are key observations about systems. They apply to all systems and should be considered whenever a system is being analyzed, developed, or modified.

9.2.1 Good and Bad Systems

There is always an ideal system. The difficulty is to find the ideal system and then bring it into reality. Sometimes the ideal system surfaces quickly and everyone on the team agrees that it is the ideal system, but they do not know how to get to the ideal system. There could be many limitations that need to be addressed. These limitations include technology, politics, money, time, motivation, education, people, etc. I have no tolerance for politics or money. In both cases these are external forces that can destroy any system.

Sometimes the ideal system is in clear sight and the approach for developing the ideal system is clearly visible. The system even may be in place but not necessarily available for this set of stakeholders. However, the ideal system and its availability fade as ignorance grips the stakeholders.

The possible scenarios associated with the ideal system and the actual solution can be identified. Realizing these possible scenarios exist will help system practitioners understand their roles in the organization. It will also act as a gage to measure the organizations' ability to engage in systems engineering, systems thinking, and systems practices.

---

[84] Hughes Aircraft, See the University of Las Vegas Howard R. Hughes College of Engineering archives.

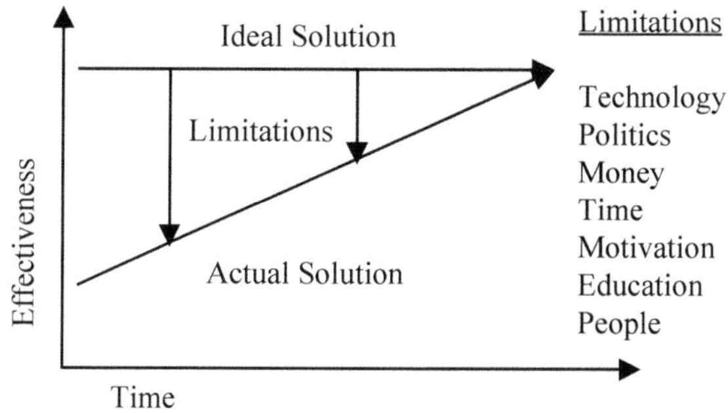

Figure 23 Ideal System Convergence

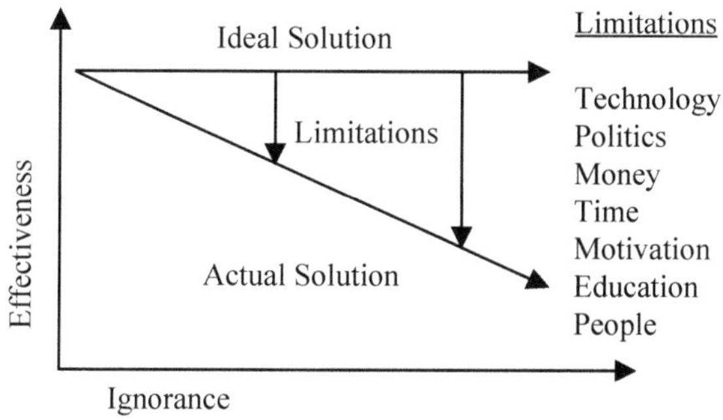

Figure 24 Ideal System Loss

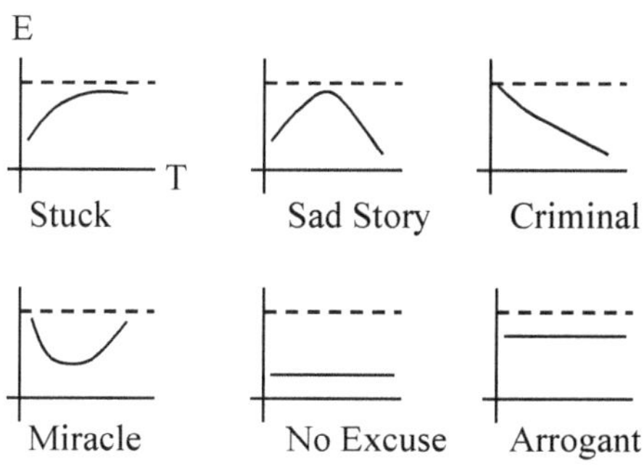

Figure 25 Organizational Failure Scenarios - Effectiveness over Time

The reality is organizations that get lost are compromised by politics and then excuses such as money and schedule are offered. Alternatively, they are compromised by politics and then excuses of technology, people, education, and motivation are offered. There is not much system practitioners can do once an organization is compromised other than attempt to point out the condition and the ramifications of the condition or leave the organization.

9.2.2 Momentum

Momentum is a term found in physics[85] where an object is understood from a speed, direction, and mass point of view. Typically, one would calculate the amount of momentum in an object to determine what it would take to change its speed or direction if an external force were applied. For example, if you had the unfortunate experience of pushing a car you know that it takes a great deal of effort to get the car moving. Once it is moving, keeping the car in motion requires much less effort. Conversely if you ever needed to stop a car you are pushing; you know that it takes a great deal of effort to stop the moving mass.

This concept of momentum can be quantified in physics once applied to objects. However, this same concept applies to organizations and architectures in the abstract. It may not be quantifiable, but it most certainly exists and needs to be realized, respected, and qualitatively understood.

Observation 1 Momentum

Privatization Comments: There is a great deal of momentum built into the privatization system and so changing direction will be difficult and take time. There are many small businesses and minority owned businesses that stand to lose if the privatization contracts disappear. It is unclear what would happen with the employees in these businesses. These businesses lobbied Washington and from their perspectives they won even if their employees and the citizens lost. This is the fundamental issue and why there is so much built up momentum in privatization. It is now the accepted status quo of those in power.

9.2.3 Hysteresis

Hysteresis[86] refers to a condition where application of input is not immediately addressed. There is a time delay. Once the action starts, removing the input does not immediately stop the action.

An example is a heater thermostat. When the temperature is set to 70 the heater will not activate until the temperature falls to 68. Further the heater will run until the temperature reaches 72. This prevents the heater from constantly turning on and off. The delta between the on and off points is set by the heater technician.

In the real world of systems engineering people attempt to track progress using metrics without realizing that different metrics have different Hysteresis characteristics. For example, attempting to track projects solely using Earned Value

---

[85] Fundamentals of Physics, David Halliday and Robert Resnick, John Wiley & Sons Inc; Revised edition (January 1, 1974), ISBN: 0471344311

[86] Physical and Quantum Electronics Series, Demetrius T. Paris, F. Kenneth Hard, McGraw-Hill Book Company, 1969, Library of Congress CCN 68-8775, ISBN 070484708.

Management System (EVMS)[87] techniques is extremely dangerous. By the time EVMS shows a project is in trouble, severe damage has occurred, and recovery will be significantly more challenging. Meaningful non-financial metrics always have less Hysteresis than EVMS but they require a domain expert to understand and appreciate. In the ideal situation both EVMS and design metrics are tracked.

The same can be said of operating a live system, tracking its money flow has very large Hysteresis characteristics once compared with the systems non-financial metrics. The trick is to find the meaningful non-financial metrics, the essence of the system performance.

Observation 2 Hysteresis

Privatization has hysteresis just like any other system change. It takes a while to see all the effects including the unintended consequences. We now have a few decades of data and we can see that the effects of privatization are not good. The question now is how to correct the system and move forward. Should there be small changes or massive changes and how do we measure the results. There are approaches as always when a systems perspective is used:

Privatization

- Accelerate privatization
- Maintain the current rate of privatization
- Slow down privatization
- Stop further privatization

De-Privatization

- Slowly upgrade privatized companies to participate in the industrial base
- Quickly upgrade privatized companies to participate in the industrial base
- Slowly move privatized companies into commercial industrial companies
- Quickly move privatized companies into commercial industrial companies

The hard reality is because the system is so large and complex, all the De-Privatization approaches need to happen as soon as possible. Privatization needs to stop immediately. Taxpayers are not a market to be tapped and drained.

9.2.4 Peak Load and Burnout

Everyone should do the simple experiment of taking an electric light bulb and

---

[87] American National Standards Institute/Electronic Industries Alliance ANSI/EIA-748, Establishes 32 minimum management control guidelines for an EVMS to ensure validity of information used by management. The Unites States Federal government adopted the guidelines in ANSI/EIA-748 for use on government programs and contracts.

burning it out by slowly increasing the supplied voltage. This is an incredible lesson. The same should be done with a mechanism of gears such as a mechanical clock where one of the gears is continuously increased in speed until the gears start to strip their teeth and the mechanism stops.

All systems must be designed to withstand the ravages of a worst-case peak load. However, it needs to be understood that no system can survive continuous operation (100% duty cycle) at its worst-case peak load. Many think that this is inefficient. They do not understand. In complex systems such as a restaurant, the peak load happens at breakfast, lunch, and dinner. In between those times there is preparation, maintenance, and the storage of energy. The energy is stored in the humans who must serve the peak load when it happens.

There are statistical methods that can be used to understand the peak loads. Agner Krarup Erlang[88] studied telephone systems and the result is the Erlang distribution, which is tied to a peak time of day, usually before lunch. The Internet exhibits two peak loads during a normal business day. Other modeling and distributions are Poisson process, Bernoulli process, and Markov processes.

All systems exhibit a peak load. There is a desire, when resources are low or policy makers are ignorant to create systems, which assume an average spread of the load. These systems fail or stop providing critical services when the natural peak arrives. There are various approaches to modeling the peak load. The ideal approach is to derive empirical data and then test the system in live situations prior to taking the system live.

9.2.5 Timing and Sizing

Many people equate timing and sizing with computer systems from the last century. But timing and sizing applies everywhere. A bridge needs to be appropriately sized to handle rush hour traffic in a reasonable way. The same is true for a road. A store needs to have some number of cashiers to process the customers in a reasonable time. The same is true for a restaurant and its count of waiters, tables, and cooks.

This all requires some quantitative understanding of the operation. It can be modeled using a static model implemented in a spreadsheet, but the model must have reasonable worst-case scenarios in addition to the typical and lightly loaded scenario cases. These three scenarios should be understood and appreciated as the system is sized.

9.2.6 Cause and Effect and Balance of Power

Causality or cause and effect is the relationship of an event and a second event

---

[88] Mathematician statistician engineer, Agner Krarup Erlang (January 1, 1878 to February 3, 1929) invented traffic engineering and queuing theory.

which is the result of the first event. Cause and effect in many cases is a chain of events where a causing event is a resulting event of a previous cause.

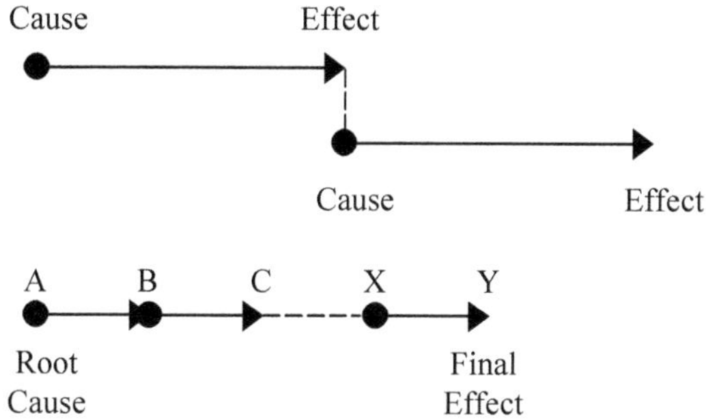

Figure 26 Cause and Effect

One of the biggest issues associated with cause and effect is to find the full chain of events and not be misled to a premature conclusion. There is always the temptation to be superficial and not view a situation from different perspectives. Cause and effect is a fundamental principal found in almost all system practices. Many will point to:

- State transition and mode analysis
- Root cause analysis
- Failure analysis
- Diagnosis troubleshooting debugging
- Sequence Analysis
- Timing sizing and load analysis

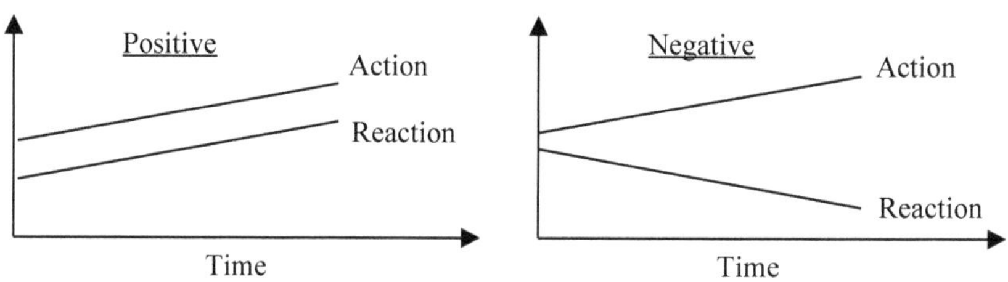

Figure 27 Causal Relationships

Cause and effect also can be used to understand the relationship between different system variables. There can be either a positive or negative effect between these variables, usually referred to as a causal loop.

- In a positive causal loop or link two nodes or variables increase together or decrease together in a linear or non-linear fashion.

- In a negative causal link, the two nodes change in opposite directions. If one node increases the other node decreases.

A causal loop can change from positive to negative or negative to positive. This is usually an unexpected state change.

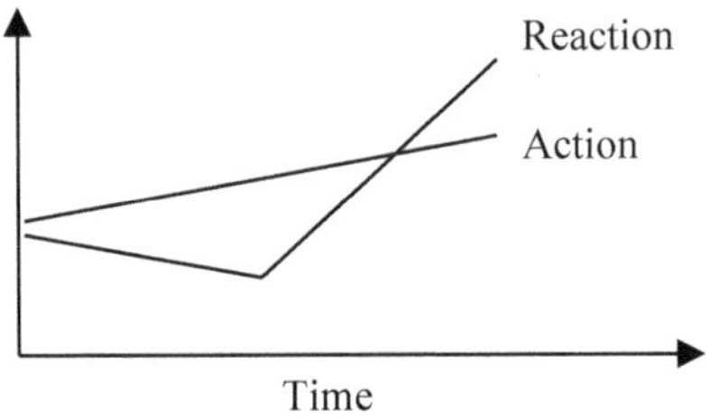

Figure 28 Causal Relationship State Change

It is best illustrated with a social system example. Assume a ruthless dictator applies draconian rules on the population to instill fear. Most of the population complies out of fear, However, there is a very small segment that always rebels. As more draconian tactics are used then eventually most of the population rebels. This is an example of a flip from a negative causal loop where increased draconian tactics reduces the populations desire to rebel, until a state change happens, and then increased draconian pressure leads to increased rebellion.

Balance of power and system stability are synonymous. When there is a shift in the balance of power the system will shift until the balance of power is restored. This is what history teaches for social systems. In social systems the problem is when there is a loss of balance of power the system correction might manifest itself as war, revolution, or total collapse with resulting chaos.

In social systems cause and effect and the balance of power are tightly coupled. They move history. They define history.

Observation 3 Cause and Effect and Balance of Power

Privatization Comments: One of the fundamental questions that must be asked is how privatization has become such a powerful force. One of the possibilities is the change in tax law allowed the accumulations of vast wealth into the hands of the few. This led to incredible power including the power to subvert Democracy. The next question is why anyone would want to subvert Democracy. In order to continue expansion of that wealth, new markets needed to be tapped. The largest and most obvious market to tap is the taxpayers. This is an example of cause and effect.

9.2.7 Key Requirements Specifications and Traceability

Identifying and tracking the requirements and issues in a system may mean the difference between success or failure of a system. The purpose of requirements analysis is to identify the key requirements, perform analysis and capture the requirement details in specifications, and then establish forward and backward traceability of the requirements.

Not all requirements and issues are the same. Some are make or break situations. Key requirements are drivers of the system solutions. They can be technology, performance, cost, schedule, production, maintenance, logistics, support, and other drivers. These drivers may exist because the state-of-the-art is being pushed or previous knowledge shows these requirements and issues are make or break items.

Key requirements and issues come in layers. There are key requirements and issues at the highest level and are parts of the architecture dialog. There are key requirements and issues at the subsystem levels. There are key requirements and issues at the component levels. There are key requirements and issues at the abstract levels like maintenance, training, support, and other areas that do not make up the physical solution but are part of the system solution. In many ways they are the kickoff of an activity for each new layer of the system development.

Specifications are information products that house the requirements. Requirements at the highest abstraction level precisely describe what a system is supposed to do and at the lowest abstraction level describe how the system does it. The lowest level requirements are design and implementation details.

Specifications can take many forms. For example, a flyer can list features that are important to a customer. These features can be any abstraction level that someone thinks separates this system or product from another system or product. They can be blueprints, which show design details of a house under construction. They can be text documents, which describe what the system is supposed to do. Low level specifications can be product brochures or even line items in a table of a book listing hundreds of items like pipe fittings. So, requirements and specifications can take on many forms and capture many levels of abstractions. Ideally the requirements should be grouped by abstraction level.

Traceability is about being able to connect and follow in a forward and backward direction all the documented goals, needs, high medium low level requirements, analysis, design artifacts, system elements and piece parts. Forward traceability is achieved when the highest level, such as a goal or need, can be tracked and followed through to the requirements, design, system elements and piece parts. Backward traceability is achieved when a system element or piece part can trace its existence to all the succeeding higher levels of documented evidence up to the highest level, typically a goal and or system need.

For large complex systems this is accomplished with information stored in a relational database. The database contains all the information and all the parent child links between the information products at each succeeding level of abstraction. The links are the roads that are followed when traceability is examined. All parents should have child links and all child links should have parent links. If there are missing links then, there is a break in traceability, and a problem with the system. Reports formatted as tables are generated from the database and reviewed for missing and bad links. When issues are detected, action is taken to address the issue. This may be a trivial fix where the database is updated with the correct information or it may be a serious fix involving changes to the system.

Very-course-grain traceability is at the document level. This is the simplest form of traceability to implement. It is a connection from a parent specification document to a child specification document. Many times, traceability is also needed to other information products. Since the traceability is very-course-grain, this is not unreasonable.

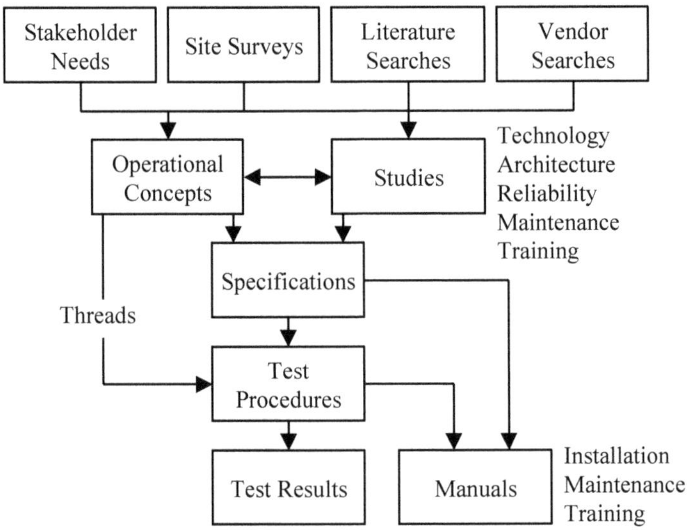

Figure 29 Document Tree

Very-course-grain traceability is used in proposals and plans. It is also used as introductory material to show the context of an information product.

Course-grain traceability is at the paragraph level. It is typically used to show requirement traceability when there are no automated tools. The child document contains a Requirement Traceability Matrix (RTM) as an appendix.

Table 27 Requirement Traceability Matrix (RTM)

Subsystem Specification	System Specification
3.2 Electric Vehicle	NA
3.2.1 Engine	3.7
3.2.2 Transmission	3.7
3.2.3 Suspension	3.3, 3.4, 3.5
3.2.4 Interior	3.1
3.2.5 Body	3.2

The RTM lists the current document paragraph numbers and headings in the left most column of a table. Each paragraph is a separate row. An additional column lists the paragraph number and optionally the heading of the parent document.

Writing requirements destined for the database use a slightly different style. The document headings stay the same, however the content at the paragraph level is parsed into stand-alone lines rather than clumped as one or more paragraphs clustered below a heading. When the document is imported into the database then each line becomes a separate row in the database with its own project unique identified (PUI) number. The PUI items then are marked for traceability to other PUI items in upper or lower level specifications.

Specifications using a database include a parent child report in the appendix. The parent child report shows the PUI and text of both the parent and child requirements. Just like in the RTM the parent is the left column and the child is the right column. This obviously significantly increases the size of the specification and so the parent child report is typically delivered under a separate cover. The specification then has a matrix with just the PUI numbers of both the parent and child or the PUI and text of the parent and just the PUI for the child.

Table 28 Parent Child Report

PUI	System Text	Subsystem PUI and Text
SSS-14	Requirement A	SRS-77 Requirement SRS-23 Requirement
SSS-16	Requirement B	SRS-79 Requirement
SSS-17	Requirement C	Missing child

Unlike course-grain traceability, fine-grain traceability includes a report showing that all the parent requirements trace to one or more child requirements. That means the parent document remains alive until the child document is complete. This process ensures that requirements are complete and consistent between levels. This is a critical step that significantly improves the quality of the requirements and attempts to surface all the requirements. A missing child link is a sign of a problem that must be corrected.

Table 29 Child Parent Report

PUI	Subsystem Text	System PUI and Text
SRS-77	Requirement	SSS-14 Requirement SSS-15 Requirement
SRS-78	Requirement	SSS-15 Requirement
SRS-79	Requirement	Missing parent

Traceability reviews are needed to ensure that all the requirements have been captured. Parent child reports are produced for each specification. If there are holes, this is an indication of missing requirements or requirements not needed for the system. This cannot be done with a single parent or child report. Both perspectives and views are needed for closure.

The first report lists the parent requirements in the left-hand column and the child requirements in the right-hand column. If a right-hand column is blank, this is an indication of missing children. This represents forward traceability.

The second report lists the child requirements in the left-hand column and the parent requirements in the right-hand column. If a right-hand column is blank, this is an indication of a missing parent. This represents backward traceability.

Observation 4 Key Requirements and Specifications

Privatization Comments: The System Specification contains the requirements for a system at the highest level. All other lower level specifications flow from and trace to the System Specification. It comes from the system needs. When examining a social system like a government, its founding document or documents form the information product or products that are the needs analysis[89] and resulting System Specification[90] for the system that is the government.

The system requirements are not just the stated requirements but also the intent of the requirements. Not all the details can be stated or anticipated until the system starts to unfold and eventually operate. Common sense and reasonable logical extrapolation are used when addressing the intent of the original requirements.

The following is a potential list of privatization related system requirements for the US Government that can be derived from the Declaration of Independence and Constitution. Whenever the question of privatization arises each of these requirements should be examined to see if they are not met because of privatization. If one of the requirements are not met because of privatization then either the privatization architecture needs to be modified or it must be rejected, and privatization immediately stopped.

Declaration of Independence Derived Requirements

DIR-1	The system acknowledging that all people are created equal shall ensure that all people are treated equally and that special interests do not have unique access and control of the legislature and other government bodies.	GN-3[91]
DIR-2	The system acknowledging that all people have unalienable Rights shall protect and enhance Life, Liberty, and the pursuit of Happiness.	GN-3

[89] See section 10.8.1 Declaration of Independence.

[90] See section 10.8.2 Constitution and Amendments.

[91] See section 10.8 Government Constitutions for parent requirement.

DIR-3	The system acknowledging that to secure these unalienable Rights, the Government is instituted.	GN-3
DIR-4	The Government derives it's just powers from the consent of all the governed and not special interests.	GN-3
DIR-5	The system acknowledging that the Right of the People to institute Government, laying its foundation, organizing its powers, shall seem most likely to enhance their Safety and Happiness.	GN-3
DIR-6	The system shall allow for Laws, the most wholesome and necessary for the public good ensuring that special interests are not harming the people.	GN-5
DIR-7	The system shall allow for Laws of immediate and pressing importance ensuring that special interests are not harming the people.	GN-6
DIR-8	The system shall allow for Laws for the accommodation of large districts of people ensuring that special interests are not harming the people.	GN-7
DIR-9	The system shall ensure that legislative bodies are at places of normal access, comfortable, and close to the depository of public Records that are accessible by all, for the sole purpose of not fatiguing them or the people into compliance by those attempting to subvert the system.	GN-8
DIR-10	The system shall ensure that Taxes are spent with the full Consent of the governed, with full accounting, and are not channeled into hidden stakeholders and special interests.	GN-23
DIR-11	The system shall ensure that special interests do not abolish our most valuable Laws and alter fundamentally the Form of our Government.	GN-26

The single requirement DIR-4, "The Government shall derive its powers from the consent of the governed" invalidates all privatization of any government function because the people transferred their power to the government for this function not some entity outside of government. Either the function is removed from the Government and no tax money used to provide that function or the function must be performed by the government and not any privatized entity.

<u>US Constitution Derived Requirements</u>

UCR-1	The system shall ensure that a more perfect Union is not compromised.	C-2
UCR-2	The system shall ensure that Justice is not compromised.	C-2
UCR-3	The system shall ensure that domestic Tranquility is not compromised.	C-2

UCR-4	The system shall provide for the common defense.	C-2
UCR-5	The system shall ensure that the general Welfare is not compromised.	C-2
UCR-6	The system shall ensure and secure Liberty to ourselves and our Posterity.	C-2
UCR-7	The system shall treat all people equally and ensure that special interests do not have unique access and control.	C-2
UCR-8	The system shall ensure that it is not compromised by special interests or hidden stakeholders.	C-4, C-5
UCR-9	The system shall establish Post Offices and post Roads.	C-34
UCR-10	The system shall promote the Progress of Science and useful Arts.	C-35
UCR-11	The system shall collect Taxes, Duties, Imposts and Excises.	C-28
UCR-11	The system shall pay Debts and provide for the common Defense and general Welfare of the United States.	C-28
UCR-12	The system shall ensure that all Duties, Imposts and Excises are uniform throughout the United States.	C-28

Bill of Derived Rights

BOR-1	The system shall ensure that no person is deprived of life, liberty, or property without due process of law.	R-16
BOR-2	The system shall not deny any person equal protection of the laws.	R-48
BOR-3	The system shall ensure that the citizen votes are not be nullified, denied, or abridged by anyone, special interests, or hidden stakeholders.	R-55, R-72, R-103, R-114

The general intent of all the requirements are:

- The Government shall derive its powers from the consent of the governed.
- The Government shall be transparent and accountable to the people.
- The Government shall listen to the will of all the people.
- The Government shall serve all the people.
- The Government shall perform for the benefit of all the people.
- If the Government fails to meet its requirements, it shall be replaced via voting in an un-compromised election process.

In a free market the people get rid of bad companies by not buying their products and services. In a Democracy the people get rid of bad government by voting representatives out of office.

In a privatized system the people cannot get rid of the bad actors by not purchasing their services or by voting them out. They are captive in a system of taxation without representation where tyranny can flourish, and horrible acts can be committed in the people's name using their tax dollars.

9.2.8 Creativity and Innovation Process

There is a simple formula that can be applied by anyone to spur creativity and innovation. Herman Helmholtz (1821 to 1894) studied creativity and introduced the idea that there are 3 stages to creativity: saturation, incubation, and illumination. Graham Wallas expanded on these ideas and offered them in his work, Art of Thought, 1926. The Wallas stage model, creative insights and illuminations, has 4 or 5 stages. The additional stage is called Intimation and may be viewed as part of Incubation or Illumination.

1. **Preparation:** initial work on problem, focusing mind on problem, exploring problem space
2. **Incubation:** problem is internalized, unconscious mind, nothing externally is happening, 2a. Intimation: sub-stage, person gets feeling solution close
3. **Illumination:** insight or idea bursts into conscious awareness
4. **Verification:** idea is verified, elaborated, and applied

For this text the formula for personal creativity and innovation is Saturate, Incubate, Synthesize, Optimize, and Select[92].

1. **Saturate**: Exactly as the word implies. Immerse yourself in the material, no matter how mundane or irrelevant it may seem in the beginning. Talk to everyone about the material and dialog if possible.
2. **Incubate**: Exactly as the word implies. Sleep on it and let the miracle of the human mind go to work on the problem.
3. **Synthesis**: Happens after incubation. You can't stop it; it is human. Eventually approaches will start to surface. Mature these approaches as you continue to saturate and incubate.
4. **Optimize**: As the word implies, take each viable approach and move it to its most elegant limit.
5. **Select**: You guessed it, pick your best approach.

This process of personal creativity dovetails in and out of the systems process. It is hard to say if they are separate or one and the same, but I like to think I practice

---

[92] This author was exposed to these ideas in elementary school and has practiced them since that time. These ideas were periodically reintroduced in middle and high school.

both at the same time. The personal creativity model can be expanded to teams engaged in systems engineering design.

1. **Saturate**: Immerse the team in the material, no matter how mundane or irrelevant it may seem in the beginning. The entire team is engaged and meets regularly to exchange findings. Humans are left and right brain creatures. To fully understand a situation, words and pictures are needed. The words backed up with mathematics, logic, set theory and a picture born of true inspiration are the heart of communicating our visions. Essentially these all represent different perspectives of a problem and are associated with saturating our minds with the problem.
2. **Incubate**: Exactly as the word implies where the team sleeps on it and we let the miracle of the human minds go to work on the problem. A team of people needs time to incubate a problem. It is at this point that a gestalt surfaces and the team starts to become more than the sum of its individual minds. You will not know when incubation will start but you will detect it as the team members start to offer parts of a solution. Gradually more solution parts emerge then someone or some members start to put the whole picture together. These people are typically the systems architects. They emerge with the system solution; you cannot appoint the system architects.
3. **Synthesis**: Just like for the personal case, this happens after team incubation. You can't stop it; it is human. Eventually various approaches start to surface from within the team. Mature these approaches as you continue to saturate and incubate. In many ways systems engineering is purely about synthesis rather than reduction. Throw all kinds of things on the table and start to put them together. Putting together the non-obvious pieces can lead to major breakthroughs. It is at this point that the natural systems architects that emerged start to inspire the team. The rest of the team starts to find their comfort zones in various specialization areas.
4. **Optimize**: Just like for the personal case and is as the word implies where the team takes each viable approach and moves it to its most elegant limit. The specialists really start to take on the load at this time as the system architects maintain the vision and adjust the vision based on the specialists' findings.
5. **Select**: Just like for the personal case the team picks the best approach. The selection is born from intense tradeoff analysis using the Measure of Effectiveness (MOE) equation. The selection is fully transparent and understood by all the stakeholders. It is born of reason and common sense.

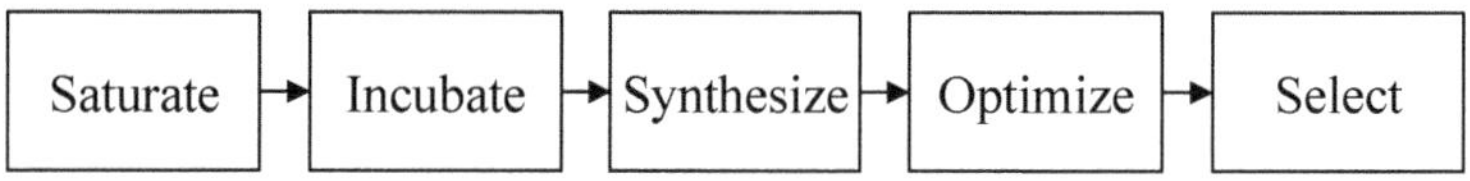

Figure 30 Creativity Innovation Event

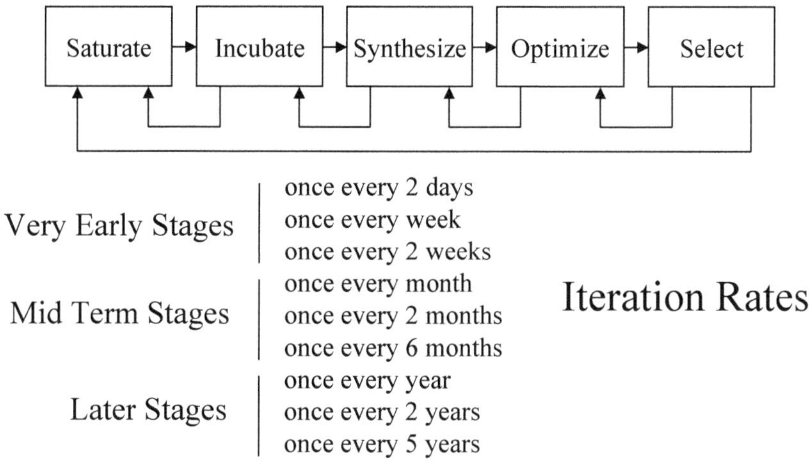

Figure 31 Creativity Innovation Iteration

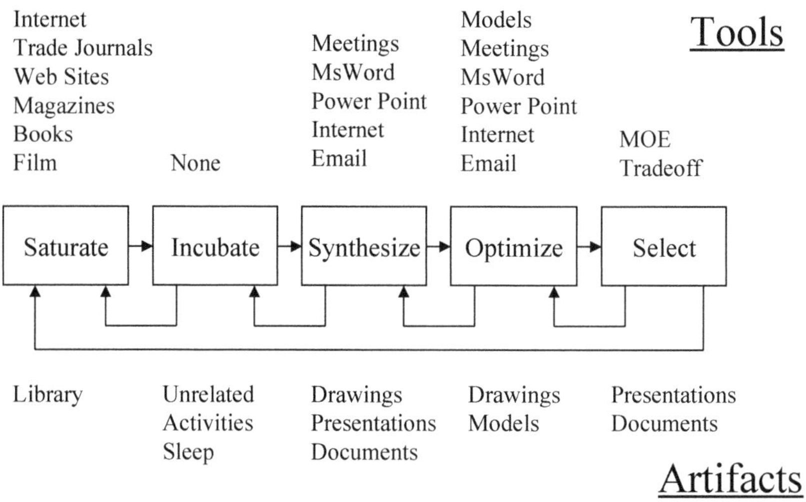

Figure 32 Creativity and Innovation Process

Obviously this needs to be a process not a series of events that just translate into an event. There should be feedback loops with iteration and iteration rates.

As this creativity innovation process is executed tools and artifacts should be identified and used to support the process.

When this model is applied to a team, different team members progress through the model stages at different times. Some move very quickly through the stages and they try to pull everyone along with their ideas. Others lag behind. Both these two groups, the leaders and laggards, are important because they challenge the team.

So, how does the team know it is done? Does everyone need to come to the same ending conclusion? One approach to determining closure is to measure the point of diminishing returns. For example, have there been no new additions to the ideas or arguments and have the open issues become relatively benign. However, care needs to be taken because the team just may not be effective. Adding new team members and determining if new insights surface can check if the process has reached a natural conclusion and was not artificially shutdown.

9.2.9 Maslow's Hierarchy of Needs

Maslow's Hierarchy of Needs suggests different levels of needs and that the lower needs must be satisfied before people will seek the next higher-level need[93]. For example, a person lacking food, safety, love, and esteem would probably first try to satisfy the need for food than safety. The needs are typically represented in a pyramid called Maslow's Pyramid where the lowest level needs are at the bottom and the highest-level needs are at the top. The needs from lowest to highest are:

1. **Physical**: This is the most basic need for air, water, food, clothing, and shelter. This also includes the instinctive need for sex.
2. **Safety**: If there is physical stability then safety surfaces, as the next need. This includes physical safety and security of the body such as personal security, health and wellbeing, avoiding accidents, illness, and their adverse impacts. There is also an element of stability that suggests justice, fairness, consistency, reliability, predictability manifested in elements such as employment, personal finances / savings / investments, resources, family, health, property, morality or laws.
3. **Love**: If there is a safe environment then love and belonging surfaces as the next need. This is a social need and includes feelings of belonging. There is a strong desire for friendship, intimacy, and family leading to friends, boy or girl friend, wife, children. This also includes social groups such as clubs, office clicks, religious affiliations, professional organizations, sports teams, mentors, close colleagues, and confidants.
4. **Esteem**: If there is an environment of love then esteem surfaces as the next need. This is an interesting gate because the musical rock group the Beatles[94]

---

[93] Abraham Maslow proposed this in a paper in 1943. A.H. Maslow, A Theory of Human Motivation, Psychological Review 50(4), 1943.

[94] "All You Need Is Love" by John Lennon credited to Lennon and McCartney. Performed by The Beatles on the first live global television broadcast via satellite on June 25

had a song, which clearly stated that "all you need is love". This need includes self-esteem, confidence, achievement, respect of others, self-respect, reputation, prestige, self-confidence, worth, strength, usefulness, to be needed in the world. There were many themes in movies and music of the 1950's and 1960's where the pursuit of esteem led to disastrous consequences as egotistical characters would cross moral boundaries and lose their souls. Terms such as saving face, damage control and, what will the neighbors think are examples of severely misplaced esteem.

5. **Self-Actualization**: Even if all the other needs are satisfied, there may still be discontent and restlessness. Musicians need to make music, artists need to paint, and poets need to write for ultimate happiness. What a person can be, he must be, this need is called self-actualization[95]. It refers to the desire for self-fulfillment.

Maslow's view of self-actualization is further refined and based on his approach of studying extremely healthy accomplished people which he viewed as self-actualized. This was contrary to previous approaches of studying people with impairments. From these studies using his qualitative biographical analysis approach key characteristics started to surface:

- Morality, lack of prejudice, ends don't justify the means
- Creativity, spontaneity, acceptance of facts
- Differentiate fake and dishonest from real and genuine
- Problem solving rather than surrender or avoidance
- Nonconformity, humility, respect

He identified a way of thinking and called it Being-cognition or B-cognition. The B-values are:

- **Truth**, rather than dishonesty
- **Goodness**, rather than evil
- **Beauty**, not ugliness or vulgarity
- **Unity**, wholeness, transcendence of opposites, rejection of arbitrary or forced choices
- **Aliveness**, not deadness or mechanization of life
- **Uniqueness**, not bland uniformity
- **Perfection and necessity**, not sloppiness, inconsistency, or accident
- **Completion**, rather than incompleteness
- **Justice and order**, not injustice and lawlessness

1967, Our World, seen by 400 million in 26 countries.

[95] Kurt Goldstein, originated idea of self-actualization in his book: The Organism 1934.

- **Simplicity**, not unnecessary complexity
- **Richness**, not environmental impoverishment
- **Effortlessness**, not strain
- **Playfulness**, not grim, humorless, drudgery
- **Self-sufficiency**, not dependency
- **Meaningfulness**, rather than senselessness

The final takeaway from Maslow's pyramid is the idea of maturity and progressing to a mature state. It is common sense and easily seen in nature where babies grow into children, teenagers, young adults, adults, middle age, and old age. The same holds true for companies and organizations. The progression might be as follows from least mature to most mature:

- **Level 1**: Collection of bodies, temporaries or consultants, working a project
- **Level 2**: Full time employees, rented facilities equipment, a few projects
- **Level 3**: Employees, owned facilities and equipment, some programs
- **Level 5**: See level 3 plus a product
- **Level 6**: See level 3 plus multiple product lines
- **Level 7**: See level 3 plus multiple product lines and a technology
- **Level 8**: See level 3 plus multiple product lines and multiple technologies

Observation 5 Maslow's Hierarchy of Needs

Privatization Comments: Privatization and policies unleashed on the citizens coincident with privatization have pushed most everyone down on the hierarchy of needs. This is extremely dangerous to a Democracy which requires an electorate that is high on the hierarchy of needs.

Table 30 Maslow's Hierarchy of Needs and Democracy Stability

Citizen Stability[96]	Democracy Stability	Privatization Level
5. Self-Actualization	5. Very Strong Democracy	**5. No Privatization**
4. Esteem	4. Healthy Democracy	**4. No Privatization**
3. Love	3. Maturing Democracy	**3. No Privatization**
2. Safety	2. Struggling Democracy	2. Partially Privatized
1. Physical	1. Collapsing Democracy	1. Fully Privatized

9.2.10 Ethics

Ethical considerations while developing and managing systems should be part of

[96] What Becomes Of The Broken Hearted, Jimmy Ruffin, June 3, 1966. "As I walk this land with broken dreams, I have visions of many things, But happiness is just an illusion, Filled with sadness and confusion, What becomes of the broken-hearted…"

all the information products. This is especially true for the information products at the higher levels such as system architecture documents, operational concepts, and sustainability analysis. The following are guidelines that can be used to stimulate ethical discussions in the system and management of the activity:

- Is there a conflict of interest?
- Is a stakeholder getting a hidden benefit?
- Is a stakeholder being harmed?
- Is there a hidden stakeholder?
- Is information being suppressed?
- Is there evidence of abuse of power?
- Is the environment totalitarian dictatorial intimidating harassing?
- Is the environment secretive where there is no reason to be secretive?
- Is the team not solving the obvious problems that others seem to ignore?
- Is the team ignoring obvious problems others seem to solve?
- Are checks and balances being removed or made ineffective?
- Is a stakeholder being marginalized?
- Is staff being marginalized?
- Is there a misuse of technology?
- Do the needs of the one out weight the needs of the many and do the needs of the many out weight the needs of the one[97]
- Is physical harm being permitted
- Is loss of life being permitted
- Is physical harm being permitted because it makes financial sense?
- Is physical loss of life being permitted because it makes financial sense?

Observation 6 Ethics

Privatization Comments: Are the privatization advocates behaving ethically and disclosing all the facts to the electorate so that they can make a fully informed decision?

9.3 Organizational Capabilities

Vendor product evaluation and selection is a key element in system solutions. If the wrong vendor or product is selected the system can fail. To avoid the potential for failure an organization's capability can be examined and assessed. This becomes very apparent when an organization is subjected to a proposal or vendor selection

[97] An interesting take away from a popular movie: Star Trek II: The Wrath of Khan, Writers: Gene Roddenberry, Harve Bennett, Jack B. Sowards, Samuel A. Peeples (uncredited), Jack B. Sowards (screenplay) and Nicholas Meyer (screenplay uncredited), 1982.

process. Typically, the selection process includes the technical approach, company assessment, and cost. The company assessment includes items such as:

- Years in business
- Size of company and project size relative to company
- Company financial stability
- Company employee turnover rate and layoff history

When a company is viewed from its technical ability to take on a particular job with a particular set of needs, its capabilities are reviewed. This obviously includes listing the unique products and technologies the company offers and its match with the need. There is However, a generic approach to view a company's capabilities. The following are ordered lists of company capabilities from the most capable to the least capable:

- Develops and owns successful significant technologies
- Develops and owns successful product lines
- Develops and owns successful products
- Delivers successful projects
- Provides Services

- Has the top 3 workforce in the industry
- Has an extremely capable and proven workforce
- Has a collection of existing people willing to work
- Has a vessel that can employ a collection of people

- Owns its land buildings and equipment
- Leases its buildings owns its equipment
- Leases its buildings leases its equipment
- Uses a client's buildings and equipment

Observation 7 Organizational Capabilities

Privatization Comments: The new privatized entities have no inherent internal capabilities. They are basically temporary employment agencies that have captured extremely skilled and competent workers in a system that is rigged. The workers are unable to escape their plight unless they move to other parts of the country with a strong commercial and industrial economy. Some employees with very strong backgrounds that can only be used in the most complex settings like government systems have no choice but to be employed by a privatized entity. The commercial industrial base no longer participates in the areas requiring these very high skill levels. Examples are engineers and scientists but there are others in this category.

As privatization has expanded the capabilities of the government have been severely diminished because the primary function has become distributing tax money in an unchecked system. It does not even have contract administration capabilities because there is insufficient and unqualified staff to determine if the contracts are being effectively executed.

The commercial industrial base has lost capability because it has been locked out of the traditional system support roles. The Integrated Logistics Support (ILS) organizations in these companies have been moved to the privatized services companies.

What needs to happen is that the privatized companies need to grow up through effective policy. Their capabilities need to drastically increase, or they need to merge with real companies that have internal capabilities outside of the resumes that they collect on any given day.

9.4 Stakeholders and Needs

The term stakeholder is relatively new and comes from the project management world[98]. The idea is that project success is based on the acceptability of all that have a vested interest in the project. The traditional systems engineering viewpoint was to consider all those who will interact with the system. This is a subtle but important distinction. For example, what is the role of a company president in the operation of an infrastructure system like Air Traffic Control. Yet the roles of air traffic controllers, pilots, maintainers, and system managers immediately start to become apparent. The old terms were system users, maintainers, and operational managers.

So, the dilemma is to make sure that at the start of a project the stakeholders in the system are identified and separated. There are stakeholders that may have the ability to kill a project, but they will never interact with the system. The system engineering team should not get lost in the noise of project management issues and instead must focus on identifying the true stakeholders in the system. One way to do this is to identify all the system external interfaces. Most individuals normally identify people interacting with a system as an external interface. As the system evolves, it becomes apparent that many of these people interacting with the system are a part of the system and they get moved back into the system boundary to become internal interfaces interacting with a machine subsystem or other people.

9.4.1 Possible Stakeholders

The following is a generic list of stakeholders. It can be used to stimulate discussion and identify stakeholders for the system being developed. Each system is unique, and it is critical that the system stakeholders be identified.

---

[98] Strategic Management: A stakeholder approach, Freeman, R. Edward, Pitman Publishing, 1984, ISBN 0273019139.

Table 31 Generic List of Stakeholders

• Customers	• Policy Makers
• Competitors	• Operators
• Markets	• Users
• Sponsors	• Maintainers
• Visionaries	• Administrators
• Prototypes	• Regulators
• Previous Systems	• Producers
• Interfacing Systems	• Providers
• Investors	• System Opponents

Once the stakeholders are identified, the needs for each stakeholder are understood and clearly stated. The needs are then converted to key requirements. This is the start of the top-level requirements for the system.

One way to begin the process of identifying the stakeholders is to list the high-level system requirements and associate them with a stakeholder. As the stakeholder list starts to unfold, other stakeholders start to surface. The requirements of the new stakeholders are then identified. This is a chicken and egg sequence and is not complete until the analysts exhaust their list of stakeholders and their requirements.

A stakeholder diagram looks similar to a system context diagram, but it shows stakeholders as external interfaces to system. This diagram can exist in parallel with the system context diagram, or if the stakeholders are external interfaces, they can be shown grouped together on the context diagram.

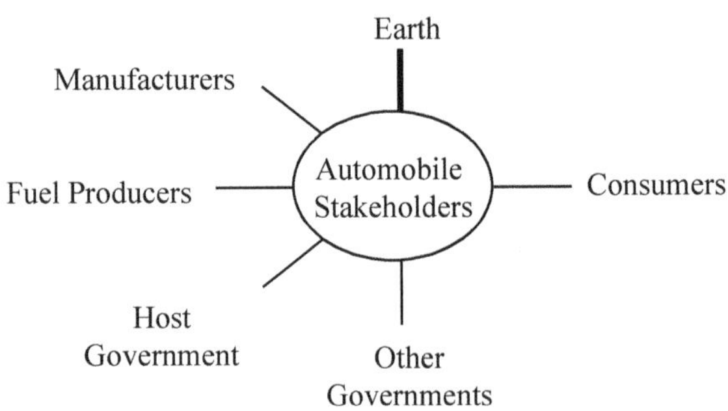

Figure 33 Less Obvious Stakeholders

It is easy to consider people as stakeholders in a system. But are there other stakeholders and do they matter? In early 1970's people became aware of their impact on the planet[99].

[99] United States Senator Gaylord Nelson (Democrat) started Earth Day on April 22, 1970 to raise awareness and appreciation for the Earth's natural environment. President Richard

When identifying the stakeholders care should be taken to use precise words to represent a group of stakeholders. This can be a topic of significant debate.

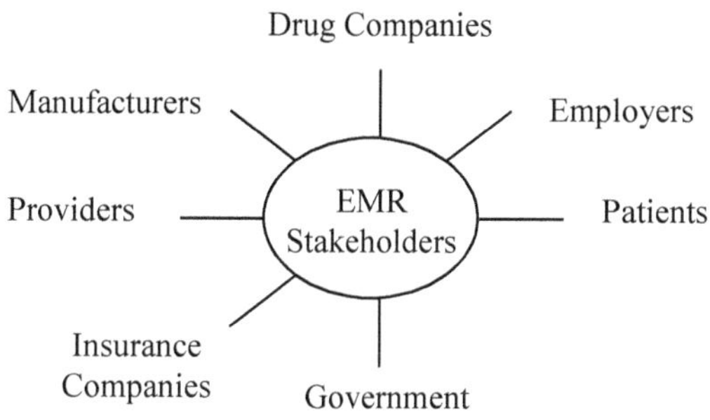

Figure 34 Precisely Defined Stakeholders

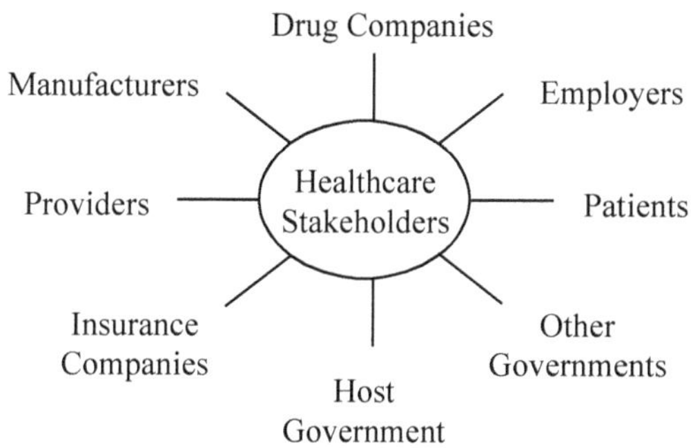

Figure 35 Groups and Benefiting Stakeholders

The stakeholders and their needs must be identified and clearly communicated. This can be done using a set of tables, presentation slides, or via text with supporting graphics in a document. It should include the following key items:

- Stakeholder category by specific clear name
- Brief description of stakeholder job, role, activities
- Number in that stakeholder category
- Specific needs of the stakeholder category
- Key requirements of the stakeholder category
- Key issues associated with the stakeholder category
- Conflicts with other stakeholders

9.4.2 Divergent Stakeholders

Sometimes it is easy to group the stakeholders because they share similar

Nixon (Republican) proposed the EPA, which began operation on December 2, 1970.

interests. Sometimes some stakeholders do something to benefit other stakeholders. Placing these stakeholders strategically on a diagram may help to aid the discussion. Initially those relationships may be unclear. However, as the stakeholders are identified and understood there may be benefits to show a left right relationship or other special representations of the stakeholder groups in the diagram.

Many times, some stakeholders have divergent requirements. For example, health insurance companies have the primary requirements of increasing earnings and profits while the policyholders have the primary requirements for good health and long life. These are divergent requirements. Some will attempt to argue that maximizing earnings and profits in a health insurance company will result in maximum health and long life to the customers, but there is no analysis that can show this linkage.

Observation 8 Divergent Stakeholder Needs

Privatization Comments: The average citizen, the largest stakeholder has been left out of the privatized system. Only the vested interests are considered and the original goals of less taxes and less government intrusion on the average citizen is totally lost. Instead the average citizen is unprotected as government has walked away from its responsibilities and they are not represented despite their taxes as privatization expanded and huge entities control the dialog and system results.

9.4.3 Needs Analysis

The Needs Analysis changes with different organizations trying to satisfy the need. For example, NASA uses a codified process to provide a needs assessment. Companies that pursue projects using a business development organization to scout for opportunities engage in pre-proposal then proposal activities to address the need. Companies that offer products engage in significant market analysis. Technology organizations also may engage in market analysis but are focused more on the technology for its own sake, pushing it to new levels, thus satisfying their own need to pursue and break new ground.

Recently many have started to address the topic of needs. Terms such as needs assessment, statement of needs, and needs analysis have entered the discussion when developing a new solution, system, design, architecture, etc. However, there are older words that address the same space and it is worth considering them and the approaches and ideas they considered.

Problem solving is a very generic phrase that was used in the 1970's, 80's, and even 90's for identifying and addressing a problem. Many viewed the ability to solve problems as the most important skill someone could possess. Many engineering schools base their education concept around the ability of a student to solve a complex problem. Engineers are thus considered extremely valuable because of their powerful problem solving skills. How does problem solving work?

9.4.3.1 Problem Solving in Mathematics and Engineering

Problem solving has several steps in mathematics and engineering. It begins by stating the problem. This seems simple but that is not the case. There is enormous complexity in detecting the problem and then properly stating it for closure. The problem statement needs to be clear so that when a solution is offered it is obvious that the problem is solved. Further it must be the correct problem and not a different problem.

The next step is the identification of the given or known conditions. These are precisely stated. Although this seems like a simple task yet many fail to identify the relevant given conditions. Many times, some known elements are missed while others are irrelevant and just add noise or distraction to the problem solving space.

Next come the assumptions. Many times, the problem has unknowns and assumptions need to be made to address the unknowns. Again, the trick is to find all the possible assumptions and pick the relevant assumptions.

Finally, with the problem clearly stated with the givens and assumptions, different techniques, methods, practices can be applied to try and solve the problem.

9.4.3.2 Problem Solving in a Body of Knowledge

Within the problem space there is also the act of solving a problem in a body of knowledge and publishing a paper on the work. This can be part of a technical conference or as part of a product development. In this case a simple set of questions is used to frame the content of the paper. They are:

1. What problem is being potentially solved?
2. What are the current approaches to dealing with the problem?
3. What is wrong with the current approaches?
4. What are the alternatives to consider?
5. What is the proposed solution?
6. Why is the proposed solution better than the current approaches and the other possible alternative approaches?

So, the techniques and methods, and practices used for problem solving are as varied as the entire body of knowledge we have at our disposal. They can be quantitative using complex mathematics and logic or qualitative using analogies and the soft sciences.

9.4.3.3 Filling a Market Void

Viewing the market and addressing a market void is paramount when starting a new company or developing a new product. The methods, techniques, and practices are to perform a market analysis and use elements such as:

- Surveys and Focus groups
- Market research and testing

It becomes interesting when a new product, system, or solution, is offered for which there is no market. For example, early introductions of the automobile, telephone, radio, television, and electricity fall into this category. A market needed to be created for each of these new technology solutions. These solutions anticipate a need rather than determine the need from existing stakeholders. So what tools, techniques, strategies can be used to create a market:

- Great marketing campaign, but what does that mean? Use the Veblen effect[100]; appeal to the ego and exclusivity of the less enlightened.
- Establish small example and point to the exceptional advantages. Niagara Falls provided AC electric power for the first time on a large scale[101]. This was used to show the benefits of AC electricity.
- Educate the stakeholders. This was a technique used to successfully introduce computers in the last century.
- Broadcast the new breakthrough design promising a new way far and wide.
- Use the Socratic method of discourse where questions and answers stimulate critical thinking and illuminate ideas. The goal is to lead to the obvious conclusions.

9.4.3.4 Fulfilling the Market Need

This now takes us back to needs, identifying the need, and satisfying the need. It is complex and buried within this is solving a perceived problem and filling a market void even if no one acknowledges the problem initially and a market void does not initially exist.

Identifying the need becomes easier if there is a sponsor that suspects there may be a void that must be addressed. For example, there is sufficient data from stakeholders or other systems to suggest there is a need. To offer a more specific example, there may be consumers of automobiles and electric power who may want the energy sources to be more sustainable. So, a need starts to emerge for cleaner personal transportation and energy production.

These are possible steps that can be taken to identify and bound the need. These steps are similar to and overlap requirement elicitation:

---

[100] The Veblen effect is described in this text.

[101] The Electrical World, A weekly Review of Current Progress in Electricity and Its Practical Applications, Volume 29, WJJC (The W.J. Johnston Company), Library of Princeton University, January 2 to June 26 1897.

- Research
- Clear problem statement
- Understand the market
- Site surveys and visits of similar systems
- Understand the current approaches
- Interviews, questionnaires, user observations
- Workshops, working groups, prototyping
- Brainstorming, role playing, operational examples

9.4.3.5 Assessing Market Need Value

There may be a clearly defined need and there may be broad statements that suggest the size of the consumers wanting the need to be satisfied. However, without knowing the value of the need it is difficult to justify the costs associated with fulfilling the need. The value can be either financial or non-financial. For example, some value a day at the beach more than a day at the mountains.

Non financial value can be captured with the Measure of Effectiveness (MOE). The MOE is a critical measure used in the last century to evaluate systems and make major decisions associated with extremely large projects. It is a measure of goodness for each dollar spent. Measure of Effectiveness (MOE) = sum of tradeoff criteria / total cost. This will be discussed further in selecting architectures.

9.4.4 Nonmarket Social Needs

Needs have traditionally been categorized into market and nonmarket needs. With privatization the nonmarket and market needs have become confusing. I have decided to take the social needs terminology used by psychologists and expand it to include more than what is found in areas such as Maslow's Hierarchy of Needs. For this text it embodies everything that is suggested in the Bill of Rights[102] and the US Constitution[103] that is part of the US Democracy, implemented as a republic. This system called the US government provides services that free market business cannot provide and still be a free market and still implement a democracy.

Observation 9 Nonmarket Social Needs

Privatization Comments: Privatization has thrown a monkey wrench into the traditional term of Nonmarket Needs. We now see that privatized companies are providing Nonmarket Needs such as military troops, prison guards, and security clearance investigations. The issue is that the function needs to be separated from the implementation. While looking for a more meaningful and descriptive term for this need category I considered:

---

[102] See section 10.8.1 Declaration of Independence.

[103] See section 10.8.2 Constitution and Amendments.

- Society needs
- Social needs
- Community needs
- Citizen needs
- Human needs
- Staying with nonmarket needs

The use of Nonmarket needs was first introduced in the late 1940's when the implementation of key government functions were not confused with nation state organizations and private enterprises. Now that there is this confusion because of privatization, I have taken social needs used by psychologists to communicate what used to be referred to as Nonmarket needs.

Social Needs: When identifying the Social Needs, all areas of human activity are considered and satisfied with implementations that do not compromise a free and transparent Democracy, and the free market cannot support and still be a free market. -- walt

Today nonmarket needs are being satisfied by the new privatized companies. They cannot survive in the free market and exist because of taxpayer funds. These companies compromise the Democracy because they are private enterprises with liberal use of non-disclosure documents and proprietary restrictions.

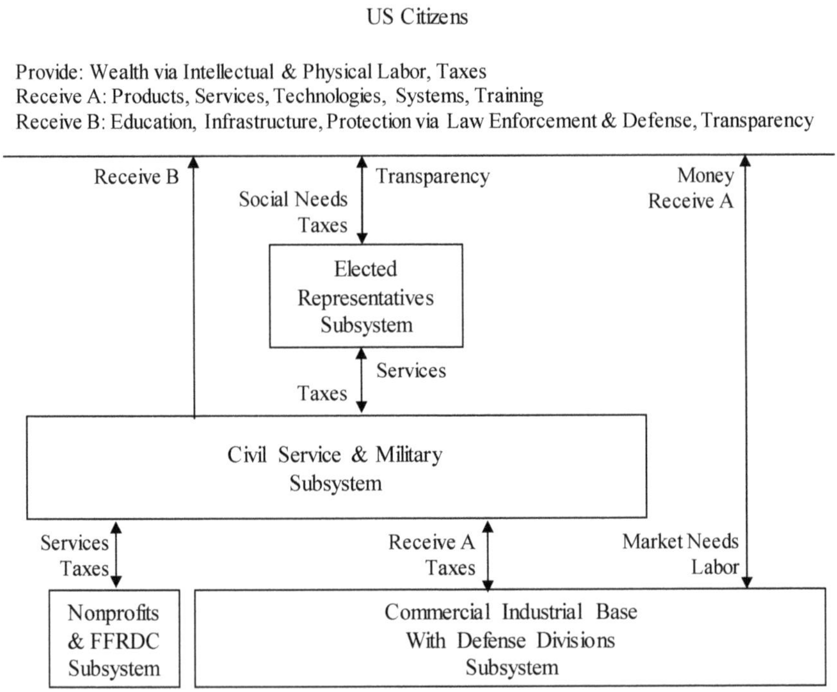

Figure 36 Social and Market Needs in a Democracy

The social needs are captured by the elected representatives and deliberated for reasonableness. If the decision is made to satisfy the social needs, then taxes are used to enable the implementation of the needs. The social needs are then delivered back to the US Citizens as Receive B systems and services.

9.5 System Boundary

The start of all systems engineering efforts is to identify the system boundary. The system boundary can be shown with a context diagram. Without a context diagram you will never know what you are building. More importantly, no one else will know what you are trying to build. There is no common frame of reference from which to start communicating with other system designers. So, it is critical to establish the system context. This is the boundary that defines the system.

9.5.1 Context Diagram

Draw a square or a circle on a piece of paper. Put the name of the system in the circle. Label the inputs and outputs of your system. Explain why the system boundary is the system boundary. If you are given a system boundary, a context diagram, convince yourselves the system boundary is valid. If it is not the correct system boundary, then fix it. Always include the system boundary and its rationale with all discussions and presentations of the system architecture. It is the highest-level view of a system.

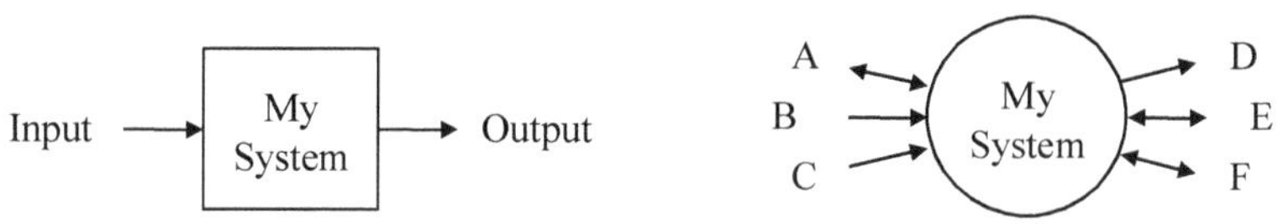

Figure 37 Generic Context Diagram

Your system is shown surrounded by external systems that interface to your system. These systems are not part of your system, but they interact with your system via its external interfaces. The external systems can impact your system, and your system does impact the external systems. They play a major role in establishing the requirements for your system. Systems further removed are those in your system's context that can impact your system but cannot be impacted by your system. These systems in your system's context are responsible for some of your system's requirements.

Your context diagram changes significantly during the early stages of a project as participants attempt to bound the system. At some point stability is achieved. That stability is based on various arguments. Those arguments must be captured and presented each time the context diagram is shown, and the system boundary presented. At some point near the implementation phase someone eventually starts to think about a marketing flyer for the system. The context diagram always appears in some form in a good marketing flyer. Just as project participants needed to understand the boundary of the system, so do the clients who will buy, use, and maintain the system. So, the context diagram never goes away.

Suppose you are building a vacation house. What would the system boundary of the vacation house show? Would the house use city sewer, cesspool, or an outhouse? Who would be interested in the decision? What about heating, will it be oil based? Will food be stored in the house or will everyday be an adventure to the local restaurants? Is the land an external interface? Will the house be built on flat dry land, a hillside, swampland, or on water?

Suppose you are building your everyday house. How long will it take you to get to its final form? Is transition strategy important?

Do you need backup mechanisms for some services? For example, is cell phone communications your only source of traditional voice communications or do you also need a telephone landline? Should the traditional telephone be self-powered via the telephone line or rely on external power? That question is interesting because the argument may be associated with the internal functionality of the telephone system rather than the context diagram. However, if the telephone within the house needs power from the landline then the telephone external interface needs to provide that power source.

Is this all common sense and so a context diagram is not needed? Is an artist rendering of the house and land more appropriate with a mini spec sheet listing the rooms and their sizes better? Are both needed when trying to understand the house system boundary?

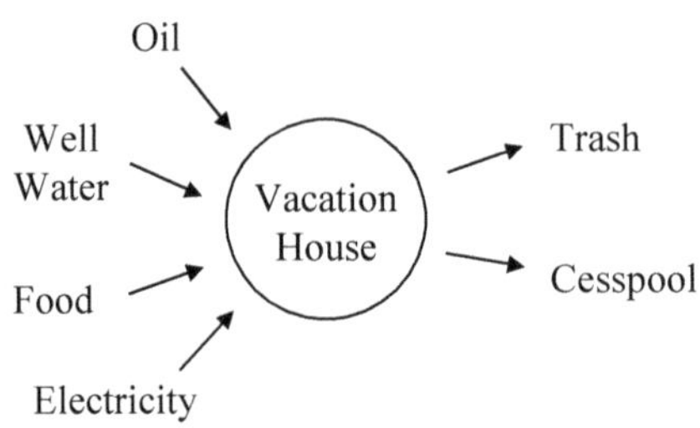

Figure 38 Context Diagram - Vacation House

What if the house is on a cruise ship, on a space station, on Mars, or in a poor country? What if the house is an office building, industrial park, shopping mall, condominium complex, apartment buildings, or a Planned Urban Development (PUD) community?

The previous house context diagrams are potentially at a view that is lower than we may need at this time. For example, what is the house context in reference to the community? Is the house in a city, suburb, or rural area? What are the community elements that you in the house will interface with and interact? These elements might be schools, shopping, health care providers, hospitals, employment, houses of worship, restaurants, malls, industrial parks, air quality, water quality, crime, community involvement, etc. What are the walking distances, driving times, and driving distances? Is the community flat, hilly, wooded, or sandy? Where is the nearest mountain, lake, or ocean? What are the weather and the seasonal variations?

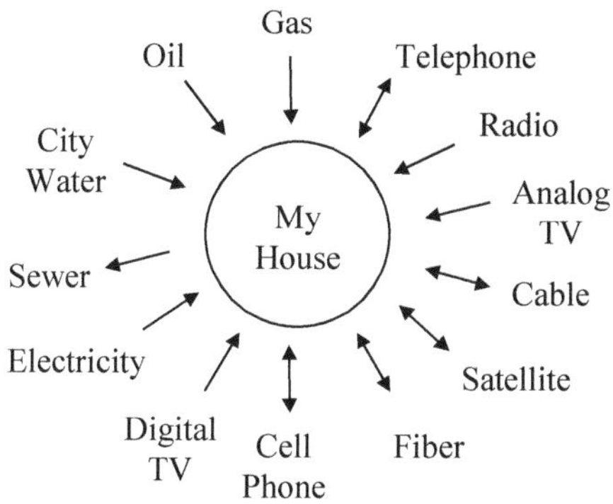

Figure 39 Context Diagram - My House

What is the style of house and is that really part of the house context? For example, is the house a colonial, split level, bi-level, rancher, or other style? Is the house attached and is the attachment just another house in a twin arrangement or is it a row of townhouses? If the house is attached is there a firewall and is that part of the external interface or do you own the firewall? Is the house a collection of rooms in a shared building and is it on the 50th floor of a building?

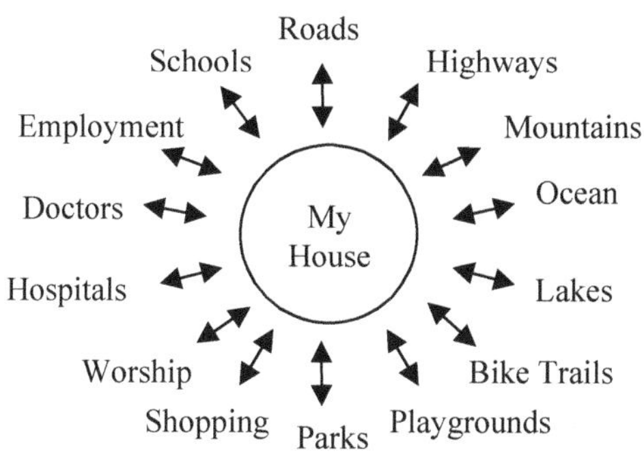

Figure 40 Context Diagram - My House in the Community

In many ways these elements are the connections that the house inhabitants share with the community. Does the community really facilitate these connections or make them difficult? So, the house is affected by the community interface. Do you need to live near an airport? If so, add it to your context diagram.

Does it make sense to build houses where there are no schools, shopping, or industry? What is the impact on surrounding communities? Does it make sense for a community to not have a master plan or architecture vision if houses are being built with no supporting community elements? Is it ethical to operate in that fashion and do ethics and morals enter into systems solutions?

9.5.2 Concept Diagram

The system boundary also can be shown with a concept diagram. The system concept diagram contains pictorials, or icons, of the system and its interfaces. A simple picture readily recognizable by the team can represent each interface.

One suggestion is to draw a system concept diagram by hand and scan the image. As the concept matures and is accepted someone within the organization will eventually clean up the picture. Another suggestion is to find a similar image in a library and modify it to support your needs. However, you may find yourself compromising on your vision, as your try to modify the picture and the modification is difficult and not exactly in line with your original vision. Do not compromise. Your vision is key and must be captured for all to see and understand.

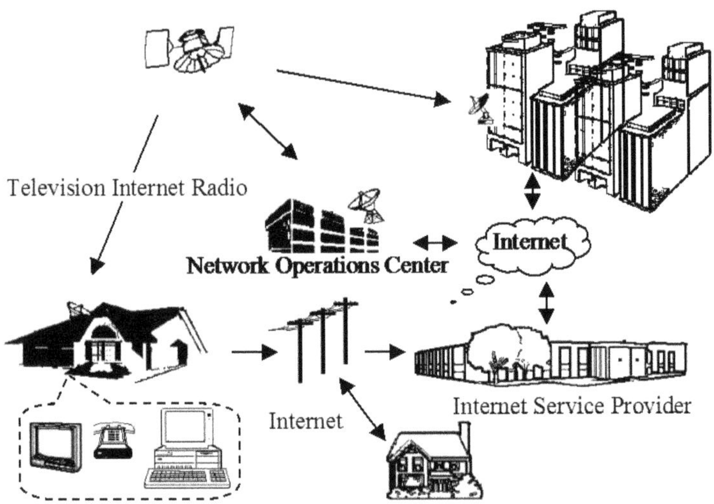

Figure 41 Satellite System Concept Diagram

In many ways this simple issue of being able to create a free form concept diagram, an artist's rendering, is at the heart of many engineering issues today. Since so much has been created in the past 50 years, reuse has become common practice. However, as these systems have aged and become stressed new visions and concepts are needed to fill the void. This means someone somewhere must create the first picture. Are you working with artists that are trying to understand the vision?

Observation 10 System Boundary

Privatization Comments: The system boundary did not include the entire system when privatization was considered. Not only were the privatized workers not included but also the US citizens were not in the system boundary. As a result, key system functions were removed from the system. These system functions traced directly to the Declaration of Independence, Constitution, and Bill of Rights.

9.6 Functions Performance and Subsystems

What does a reductionism[104] thing like functions have to do with systems? Interesting question and its answer is in the way humans solve problems. Before any problem solving can begin saturation needs to happen. Saturation is a process where information is accessed and digested by people. The information can be directly or indirectly related to the problem. Functions are a way for humans to saturate themselves with the system under study. It is a hub from which many paths can be followed and considered.

Once a preliminary system boundary is drawn, the system functions and performance need to be identified. A function is not attached to any physical element. It is abstract and tends to be defined with a noun and an action verb. Many times, a single word can represent a noun and action verb phrase. System functions can be listed, or they can be represented in block diagrams. Performance is stated in quantitative terms and can be measured.

For an existing system the functions and performance are characteristics of the system. The performance is also equated with the metrics from the system. For new non-existing systems, function and performance become requirements that the team tries to implement. There are also characteristics for new non-existing systems that are requirements, such as identifying a color that must be used. So, context is important when referring to characteristics.

For example, a health care system exists in many countries. It has functions and performance, which can be identified, understood, and potentially adjusted to make it more effective. Operational managers gather metrics, which are the performance measurements from the system, and they use those metrics to track conscious changes in the system. If the operational managers are not tracking the functional and performance characteristics of their system, then the system is very low on its capability maturity curve.

Some feel that only the money flow through a system needs to be tracked to optimize a system, However, that does not yield an engineering or scientific understanding of the system. Further, such a limited view may actually break the system and make it dangerous or of no value to the stakeholders.

The key issue is that a system must have a certain level of function and

---

[104] Reductionism is a method or theory of reducing complex things to elements that are less complex, However, systems are more than the sum of their parts.

performance and the level of function and performance will be at a cost. The cost may be excessive because the system may be inefficient. But implementation efficiency should not be tied to function level and performance. Poor efficiency can be the result of excessive system overhead or poor technology, which a good system functional and performance analysis should surface. For complex systems with limited or no competition there is no relationship between functional performance and maximizing financial results.

Observation 11 Functions Performance and Subsystems

Privatization Comments: Identifying and understanding the system functions is critical before they are allocated to a subsystem. Not identifying all the system functions and or making the wrong allocations in the system will lead to a poor system or worse a system that causes harm or loss of life.

When deciding if a government function should be privatized the Declaration of Independence, Constitution, and Bill of Rights should be parsed and two columns added to each item: privatized and government. The rows should then be marked for each alternative using better, worse, same for all citizens not just the vested interests lobbying for the privatization. Additional criteria can be added like:

- Loss of life - security
- Loss of health - security
- Liberty for all citizens
- Freedom for all citizens
- Happiness for all citizens
- Transparency for all citizens
- Accountability to all citizens
- Democracy

If the function allocation is bad, then Democracy is lost, and the result is Fascism, Communism, Feudalism, Dictatorship, or another horrible system where the people suffer.

Because of privatization, major functions were removed from government that protected all citizens and encouraged healthy competition in the commercial industrial base. As a result, people have died, and the commercial industrial base has been hurt. As previously described the FAA and FDA certification failures have resulted in loss of life and damage to the aviation and health industrial base.

9.6.1 Functional Decomposition

Functional decomposition takes the top-level system functions and finds the lower level functions within each of those top-level functions. The decomposition typically continues until no more lower level functions can be identified.

There are tools available to perform this activity, However, there is nothing like taking 100 pictures and posting them on the walls in a room. The first sheet contains the Context diagram or the level 0. The next sheet contains the Level 1 diagram. The next series of sheets contain the Level 2. The next series of sheets contain the Level 3. The decomposition continues until all the leaves are reached. As the process unfolds functions are moved across boundaries and across levels.

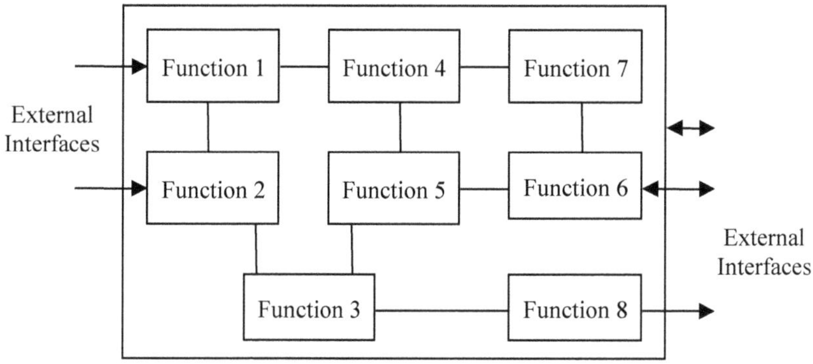

Figure 42 Functional Block Diagram Level 1

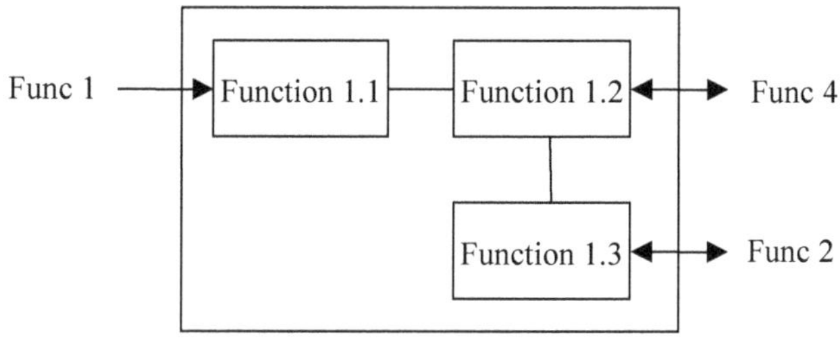

Figure 43 Functional Decomposition Level 2

9.6.2 Allocations

Allocation takes the system functions and places them into an element that will implement the function. Depending on the function and its allocation the system will exhibit a certain performance. Changing the allocations will change the system performance.

Allocations and decomposition are closely related. Allocations are multi-dimensional and address various aspects of the systems view. We can start the allocation process from any perspective. Once the functions are allocated to possible physical entities, analysis can be performed to test the effectiveness of the decomposition. The following is a list of possible allocation targets:

- **System**: This is the highest level of the system and an allocation to this level suggests that the process, function, and resulting requirements apply to all the system elements. An example is a maintenance philosophy that dictates user manuals be developed. Other examples include safety, fault tolerance, security, etc.
- **Segment**: A system segment is a physical location in a system that has multiple physical locations. The segments will share common subsystems and lower

level functions and their implementations.

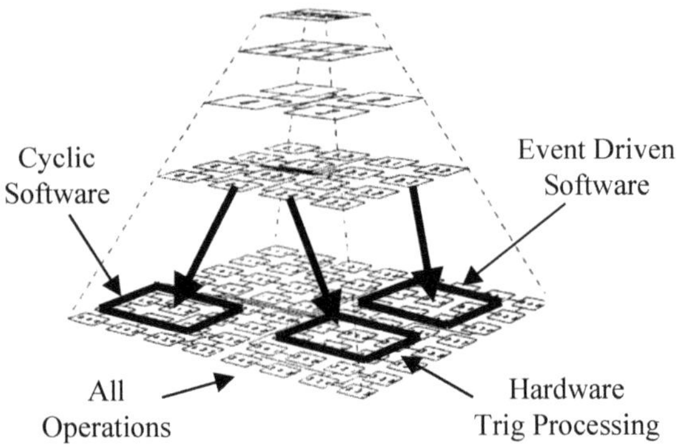

Figure 44 Decomposition and Allocations

- **Subsystem**: A subsystem is a physical entity that executes the functions. In computer automation it is a computer with software that supports the functions. Subsystems can also decompose into lower level subsystems.

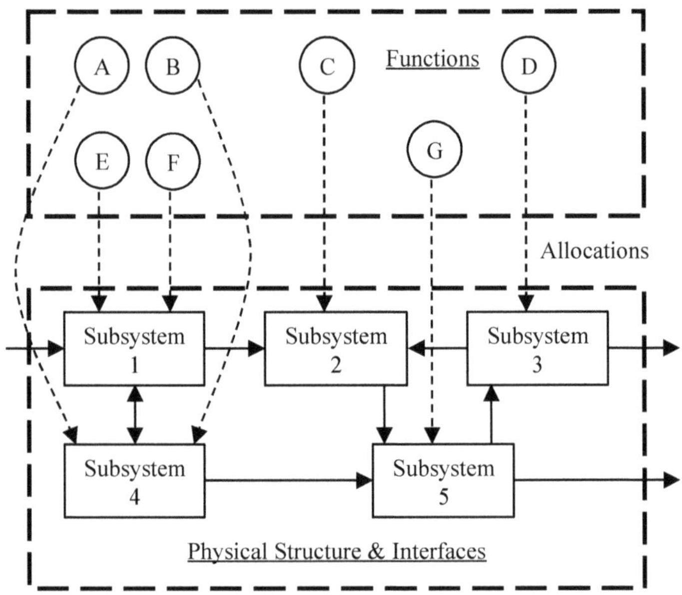

Figure 45 Functional Allocations

- **Operations**: Operations are functions performed by humans. Prior to computer automation, people in large organizational entities performed many functions. Today people tend to be in maintenance roles and augment automation implemented on computer-based systems. When systems are studied, automation tends to be the first approach to making a system better. However, not all system problems can be solved with technology. The system solutions might come from the social political economic sciences. For example, replacing teachers with a computer screen may not yield an effective educational system.

9.6.3 Balance and Performance Levels

The physical architecture surfaces when functions are allocated to subsystems. Functions allocated to physical elements become subsystems.

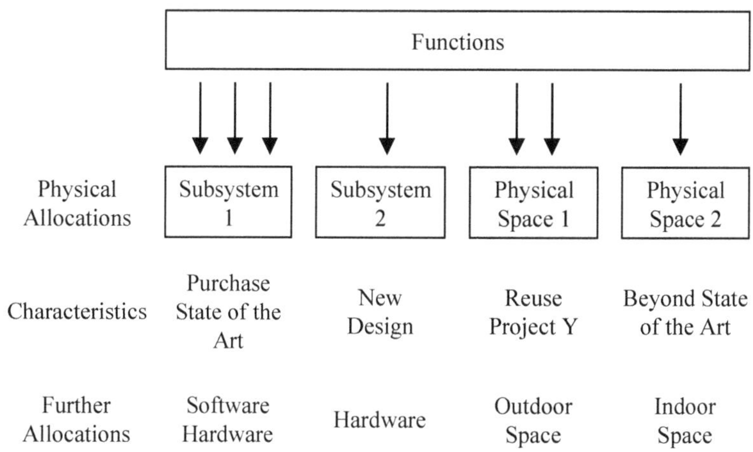

Figure 46 Functions Allocated to Physical Elements Become Subsystems

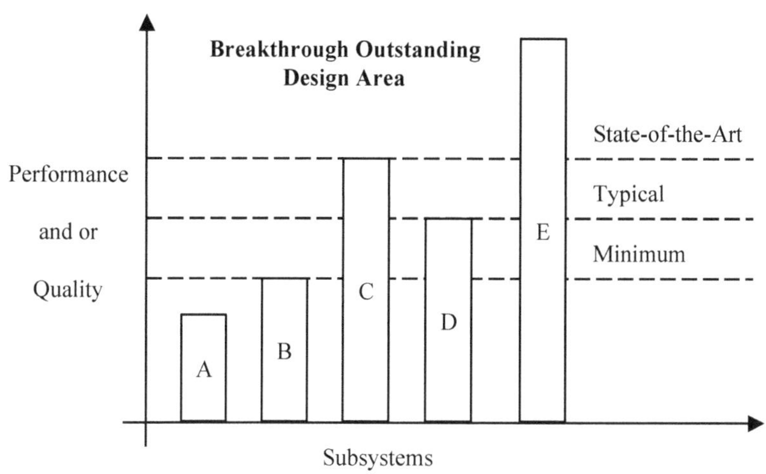

Figure 47 Unbalanced Architecture

The allocations affect the subsystem interfaces and the subsystem performance needs. This drives the choice of subsystem technologies, characteristics, and detailed design choices. This also drives system performance.

Functional allocation and the design choices will affect the architecture balance. Architecture balance suggests that all subsystems and or physical spaces in the architecture are matched from a performance view. If there is a subsystem that limits the maximum performance of other subsystems, then it should be examined for improvement. This may mean a different design for the deficient subsystem.

From a processing point of view this is a processing bottleneck and is called an architecture bottleneck. The physical architecture design should minimize the architecture bottlenecks.

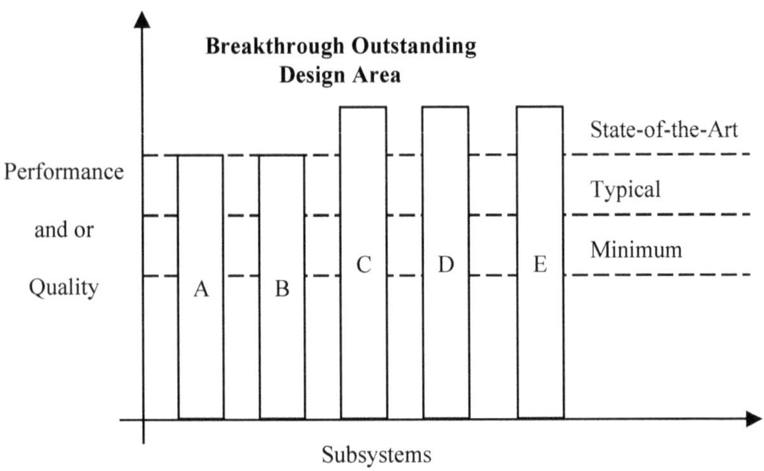

Figure 48 Balanced Outstanding Physical Architecture Design

Similar arguments can be made for other characteristics of the design. For example, one subsystem should not be pushed to a beyond state-of-the-art condition by other subsystems because of a poor functional or detailed design allocation. For example, on a system that is weight constrained, a subsystem should not be given a severe weight budget because of the convenience of other subsystems. The following are some of the items to consider when examining architecture balance:

- Performance levels and bottlenecks
- Quality levels
- Technology levels
- Number of new designs
- Number of interfaces
- Complexity of interfaces

9.6.4 Performance Allocation

At some point in the design there needs to be a performance allocation to the subsystems in the design. Typically, the subsystems will contribute to the loss of overall performance.

For example, each subsystem may introduce errors. The overall system error would be the sum of errors from each subsystem. In other cases, a subsystem may act as the weakest link in a chain and drive the performance down of the system to its individual performance level. For example, connecting a low performance loudspeaker to a high-performance sound system will not make the speaker sound better. Instead all the benefits of the high-quality sound system are lost, and the overall quality is a provided by the low performance loudspeaker.

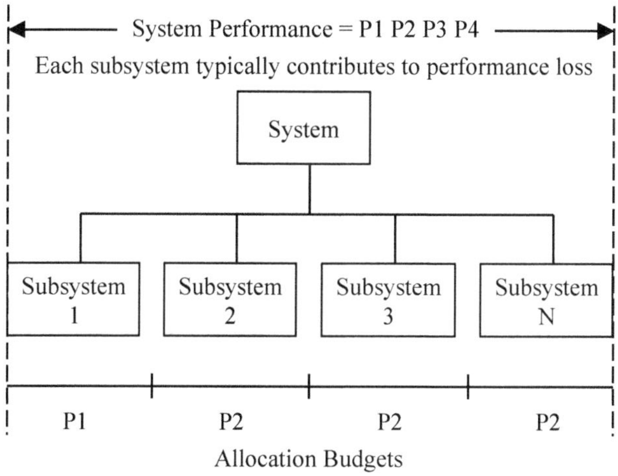

Figure 49 End to End System Performance Degradation

The search for the key performance parameters in a design is part of the system engineering and design process. Examples of similar designs in the same and other domains should be investigated. Usually a design is trying to push the envelope of existing designs so this hunt for the key performance measures should not be as difficult as some might suggest.

9.6.5 Performance Critical Functions and Requirements

All systems have functions and performance. Performance is stated in quantitative terms and can be measured. The performance is associated with a function and how the function is implemented. Many times, the function is implemented with technology, which then bounds the upper and lower limits of the resulting performance.

Performance is analyzed within the context of a subsystem technology and its selected size. Performance numbers are typically timing, but they can be failure rates, reliability, error introductions, noise, frequency response loss, power loss, energy loss, death rate, cure rate, lines of code, processing load, cost of operations or any performance number needing to be allocated for some important insight into the system.

A system must have a certain level of function and performance and the level of function and performance will be at a cost. The cost may be excessive because the system may be inefficient. But implementation efficiency should not be tied to function level and performance. Poor efficiency can be the result of excessive system overhead or poor technology, which a good system functional and performance analysis should surface. For complex systems with limited or no competition there is no relationship between functional performance and maximizing financial results.

Performance can be identified for one or more functions; however, the performance may exceed the state-of-the-art for the subsystem or subsystems that will support the functions. Yet the desired performance may be critical to the system. For example, a serious automobile accident on a highway may block traffic for miles. Yet people are critically injured. The introduction of a helicopter into the health care system seems like common sense today but it was a major breakthrough for the previous generation. Only 60 years ago there was no solution. It was beyond the state-of-the-art.

New systems push the state-of-the-art in one or more areas. The challenge is to identify these areas and apply resources so that the system can become a reality.

Finding the quantitative measures of a system is not a simple task. Pioneers in previous centuries showed us how to extract and analyze performance numbers for electrical circuits and mechanical structures. Today we have a plethora of legacy systems and knowing the key performance numbers is critical so that various alternatives can be understood, compared, and form the foundation for new systems.

All systems start relatively small and evolve. The focus changes and things that were once impossible are added to the system as the decades unfold. In the beginning the story of the automobile was about speed, then durability, then suspension, aesthetics in form versus function arguments, safety like lights and brakes, comfort like windows, then wipers, heat, air conditioning, radio, FM radio, stereo, power windows, power seats, cruise control, and now GPS. In many ways this is like a pyramid model. You start with a base and build upon each layer until a pinnacle of perfection is reached both in terms of function and performance.

It is always sad when progress is lost, and things go back in terms of function or performance. Buried in the concept of performance is quality. A high-quality solution is a solution that does everything exceptionally well.

The strategy for dealing with performance critical functions is similar to the strategy used to deal with all critical functions. The first steps are to tag the performance critical functions and the performance critical requirements in the using well-understood and accepted criteria. Performance is a function of the design approaches. The performance should be tracked for each design approach even if they all meet the accepted performance expectations. The reason for this is to always try to push the envelope of performance and quality.

At some point functional requirements and performance budgets need to be allocated to the various system elements. These allocations need to be based on sound analysis. It makes no sense to allocate a budget such as weight to an element if that allocation exceeds the known available products or worse the technologies for that element, and that portion of the weight budget can be easily accommodated by another element.

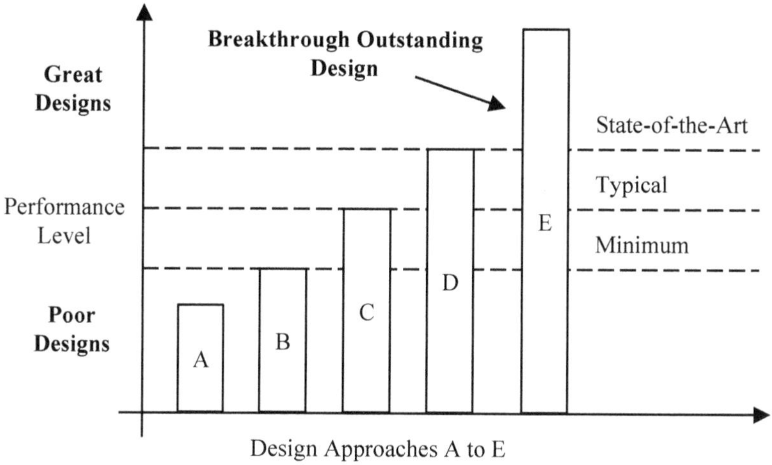

Figure 50 Breakthrough Outstanding Design Performance

So, technology impact is a key issue that needs to be considered when decomposing and allocating function and performance. This means that someone must always be cognizant of the technology impacts throughout the system engineering effort especially during the physical architecture design. A physical architecture design based on an imbalance of technology maturity or worse needlessly excessive technology immaturity must be avoided

9.7 System Architecture

System architecture development or design follows a model that can be shown as a process. The model includes needs, requirements, alternatives, respect for all stakeholders, key understanding of the past, anticipations of the future and studies.

As there is movement down the decomposition tree the lower abstraction level architecture designs may impact the upper level architecture designs. As there is movement down the architecture design tree there is more reliance on existing components that are commercially available. Some of the components, assemblies, subsystems, and systems may not offer sufficient performance even at the state-of-the-art level and so new technologies may need to be developed.

So how is this really done, this thing called system architecture design? When that question is asked many will jump into a process description. Others will fixate on one, two, or a few analysis techniques. All these views are incomplete and when new teams are formed and they are given a vetted process description along with descriptions of how to execute some of the analysis, they fail unless there are designers in the team who have done design in the past.

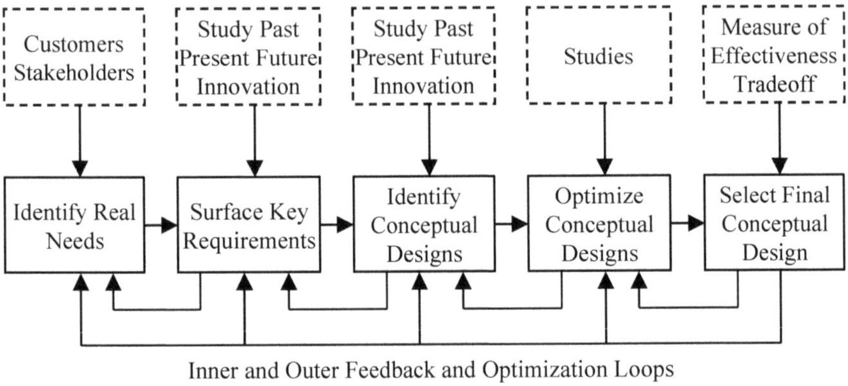

Figure 51 System Architecture Development

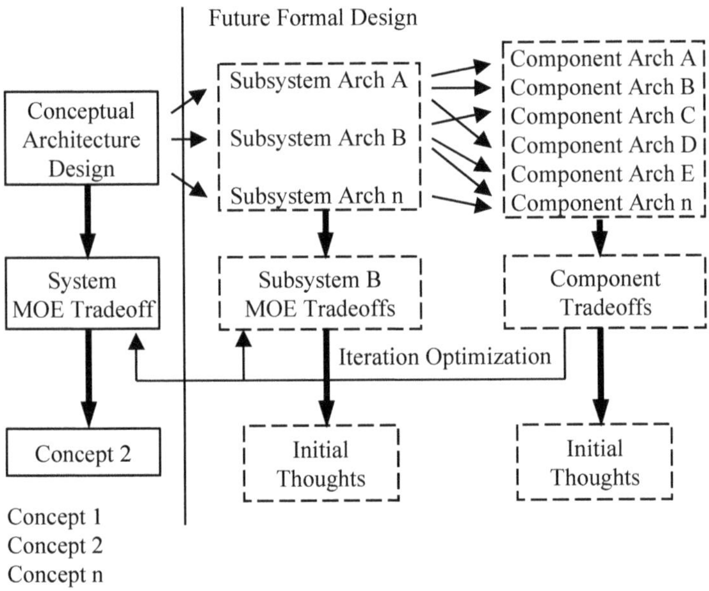

Figure 52 System Architecture Abstraction Levels

The designer experience can come at any time in the life of the designer. It does not magically happen to someone after they have completed a formal education as an adult. For example, the designs from an individual can be simple designs developed by someone at the young age of 10 or more complex designs developed as professionals in an industry.

Designers rely on previous works that are designs. Sometimes others develop the designs and the new designers study these previous bodies of work while at other times the previous designs are works developed by the designer that forms their experience base. Designers may surface as they support other aspects of the project. For example, they may be engaged in one of the analysis practices or they may be apprentices assigned to existing designers.

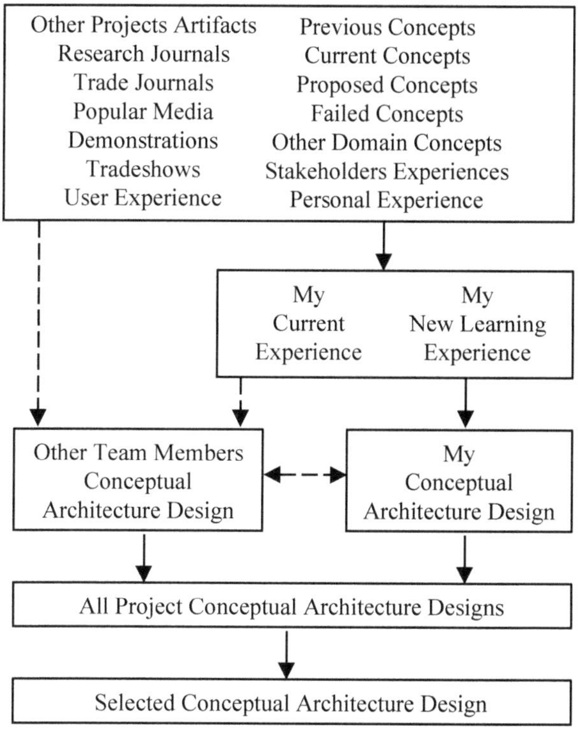

Figure 53 System Architecture Development Sources

The act of taking the system functions and allocating them to a physical structure leads to different interfaces and performance characteristics. Optimizing the architecture is accomplished by formal and informal trade studies. The steps are actually simple but executing the steps and ensuring the result is effective is not so simple. The following is a sample of possible steps to follow:

- Draw an architecture design block diagram
- Allocate functions to the block diagram elements
- Identify the interfaces
- Perform analysis to determine the performance of the architecture

- Repeat this process for 3 to 5 architecture alternatives
- Perform an architecture tradeoff using a Measure of Effectiveness (MOE)
- Document the architecture trade study
- Document the selected architecture
- Using all the analysis capture all the requirements in the specifications
- Stay vendor and product independent

We all have patterns that we naturally gravitate towards and we will incorporate them into the architecture. Allow that to happen and capture the result. Then proceed to remove vendor and product dependencies. In some cases that may not be possible, there may be only one vendor and or product.

Observation 12 Architecture Drawings

Privatization Comments: A key element of architecture is to draw a diagram of the architecture alternatives. A picture is worth a thousand words and the pre and post privatization architectures are very telling. These high-level architecture diagrams can be used as a starting point for specific privatization questions for each government organization. Draw the pictures, look at them, add notations, and decompose the lower levels to see the sub architectures.

9.8 Architecture and Value Systems

At some point the system architecture must be selected. Architecture selection is the most important activity on any systems effort. Pick the wrong architecture and people may spend decades implementing it only to find it has emergent properties that are catastrophic. Pick the wrong architecture and no one may be able to successfully implement it. Pick the wrong architecture and billions of dollars may be spent yet quickly displaced by another better architecture solution at a fraction of the cost. Pick the wrong architecture and everyone may get sick or die. For example, some believe the fall of Roman Empire can be traced to the use of lead[105]. Pick the wrong architecture and your system is a failure.

Observation 13 Architecture Tradeoff Criteria

Privatization Comments: The traditional architecture tradeoff criteria were discussed in the Federal Aviation Administration system architecture alternatives[106].

Part of the answer to selecting the right architecture is to engage in systems

---

[105] Ancient Rome lined their pipes and water tanks with lead, used lead plates and eating utensils, wine makers sweetened sour wine by adding lead powdered syrup. Some modern historians have suggested the fall of the Roman Empire may have been partially due to lead.

[106] See section 6.3 System Architecture Alternatives.

analysis. The other part is to make an impartial selection immune to any external influences. The selection needs to be based on evidence traceable to all the formal and informal studies. Buried in this challenge is the concept of value is - Which architecture has the greatest value?

As previously discussed, there is no guidance given on what to privatize in the government. Depending on the political winds' privatization happens. However, a system architecture analysis using traditional architecture tradeoff criteria should be performed. The tradeoff criteria in this case should also include the Declaration of Independence, Constitution, and Bill of Rights specific line items[107]. They can then be aggregated for a higher-level picture. Then other criteria must be added like:

- Loss of life - security
- Loss of health - security
- Liberty for all citizens
- Freedom for all citizens
- Happiness for all citizens
- Transparency for all citizens
- Accountability to all citizens
- Democracy

Normally in an architecture tradeoff and selection all the alternatives must meet the requirements and the intent of the requirements to make the cut into the tradeoff analysis. The problem is that a strong argument exists that privatization in most instances does not satisfy the system requirements as embodied in the Declaration of Independence, Constitution, and Bill of Rights. So, the tradeoff must include the requirements by each line item in each of these top-level system requirements that established the US as a nation state. There should be 3 tradeoff tables:

1. Ability to meet requirements
2. Traditional architecture tradeoff criteria
3. Citizen tradeoff criteria (Life, Liberty, Happiness, Democracy preservation)

9.8.1 Financial Metrics and Value

Financial metrics fall under the broad area of economics. They are based on two important economic principles: (1) Fixed and Variable Costs, and (2) Supply Versus Demand. Everyone is familiar with financial metrics and many erroneously believe all decisions should be based exclusively on one or more of these financial metrics. Examples of financial metrics are:

- Lowest Cost
- Economic Value Added (EVA)

---

[107] See section 9.2.7 Key Requirements Specifications and Traceability.

- Highest Profit
- Return on Investment (ROI)
- Total Cost of Ownership (TCO)
- Internal Rate of Return (IRR)
- Real Option Value (ROV)
- Return on Assets (ROA)
- Return on Infrastructure Employed (ROIE)

There are limitations to financial metrics. Let's look at Total Cost of Ownership (TCO). It is a financial metric that attempts to capture all costs from the perspective of the owner. It typically includes purchase, operation and maintenance. The problem with TCO is that it is from the perspective of the owner. It does not take into account cost shifting or indirect costs, which must be paid by other stakeholders or even non-stakeholders.

For example, airline companies are commercial companies and certainly have costs, However, the indirect costs of the air traffic control system which includes airports, air traffic control centers, navigational aids, voice communications, satellites, etc. are paid for by the taxpayer. In addition, the indirect costs associated with aircraft include research, development, and technology transfer from military aircraft to the commercial sector. Building and creating maintenance and support mechanisms for something that does not fall from the sky has huge indirect costs.

There are other indirect costs such as pollution that are borne by other elements of society. Noise pollution results in large tracts of land being reserved for special use around airports. Carbon pollution recently has started to enter the dialog and it is a cost that someone must bear.

In a perfect world the financial analysis results would match the system analysis results. However, in an imperfect world with artificial markets and indirect cost shifting we see our current state of affairs. The system analysts can build the models, perform the analysis and show the inefficiency in the markets and its impacts. It is then up to policy makers to determine how to proceed.

If we step back, we see that value is not only financial but also non-financial. For example, some value a day at the beach more than a day at the mountains. How do you capture the value of a bridge that connects two cities? How do you capture the value of a road that heads into a wilderness? These are interesting questions and they were addressed in the last century.

There is a technique that is based on a simple concept - value is more than apparent financial results; Apparent because it is all relative to your context or view. For example, it might make sense to do something because it can translate into thousands of jobs or it can cause people to view a physical land area as attractive so they will move there and buy houses and or open businesses. These can be reduced to dollar numbers, but it is more complex. It uses the following elements:

- Life Cycle Costs (LCC)
- Measure of Effectiveness (MOE)

9.8.2 Economics 101

The first chapter in economics 101 books is about the free market and all its benefits. All the remaining chapters are all the conditions where the free market fails because of externalities. A classic example is water pollution where someone upstream has a great business but pollutes the water and everyone else downstream is now dealing with poisoned water unable to keep their horses, cows, chickens, or families alive.

The only way to deal with these externalities is either through violence where one side takes out the other side or through government using its tools of laws and regulations. This challenge and remedy are as old as civilization. Why occasionally new generations need to relearn this painful history is a sad mystery.

9.8.3 Supply and Demand

Supply and demand is a multidimensional concept that relates price, quantity, consumers, and producers. It offers several financial metrics and is a fundamental element of modern economics. Supply and demand are based on the following assumptions:

- Consumers behave rationally
- Producers behave rationally
- There are many independent consumers
- There are many independent producers

In this ideal environment of rational behavior and a level playing field of many independent consumers and producers the following relationships logically surface:

- Consumers as a group will buy more product items or service units (quantity) as price decreases
- Producers as a group will increase the number of product items or service units (quantity) as price increases

This relationship is shown in a supply and demand graph. A demand curve represents consumers and shows what price they are willing to pay for an item. As price decreases more consumers enter the market and so more items are sold. The supply curve represents the producers. As prices rise, they are motivated as a group to find ways to offer more items. This may be with the introduction of new producers or new processes and or technologies that allow for more items to be made available. In both cases the quantity increases or decreased with price. The intersection of the supply and demand curves is the ideal price where there is no excess quantity or insufficient quantity. It is the point of equilibrium.

The lines in the supply and demand graph can be various shapes and slopes.

Obviously infinite quantity is not possible. Eventually the supply costs start to increase rapidly with each increment in quantity. Eventually as the demand cost becomes very high, sales decrease rapidly with each increment in cost. So, the lines are curved as they approach the limits of the market size and the technology.

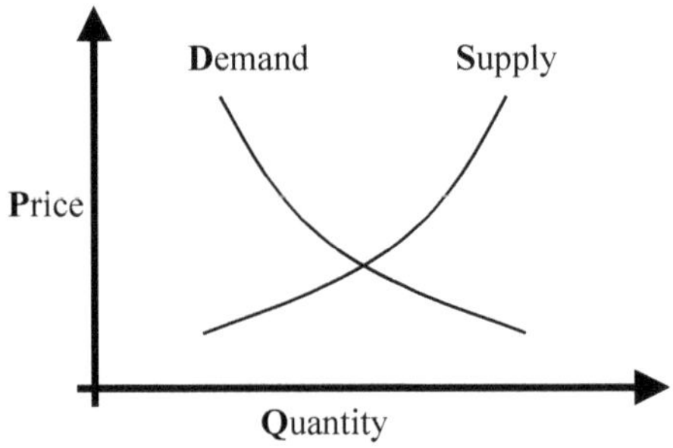

Figure 54 Supply and Demand Graphs

However, the supply and demand model has flaws. Typically, as a teaching example a land analogy is offered and illustrates the concept, but it is wrong in practice. The reality is that there is always more land if one is willing to look outside the current system context or boundary. There are other neighborhoods, towns, cities, regions, etc. There are even alternatives such as artificial islands or landfills and vertical locations such as skyscrapers.

Additionally, consumers and producers do not behave rationally. The tulip mania of the 1630's is an example of a speculative bubble[108]. At the peak of the tulip mania in 1637 some tulip bulbs sold for more than the annual income of a skilled craftsman. There have been many economic bubbles. Time and time again consumers convinced themselves that they should pay a price for an item that far exceeds its rational price point as they rode a speculative bubble and hoped not to be the holders of the items once the bubble burst.

Producers when acting in their own interest always try to increase market share. This eventually leads to buying out the last of the remaining weaker competitors. At some point barriers of entry such as capital, branding, regulations or any combination become so significant that essentially oligopoly or monopoly surfaces. The empirical evidence is everywhere in the USA today.

So, consumers and producers do not behave rationally[109]. Although there are

---

[108] From Mackay, Charles (1841), Memoirs of Extraordinary Popular Delusions and the Madness of Crowds: "In 1634, the rage among the Dutch to possess them was so great that the ordinary industry of the country was neglected, and the population, even to its lowest dregs, embarked in the tulip trade. As the mania increased, prices augmented, until, in the year 1635, many persons were known to invest a fortune of 100,000 florins in the purchase of forty roots."

[109] Irrational human behavior happens in all systems. It needs to be acknowledged and

many consumers in this highly automated age but there are not many producers. Also, in this age of mass media and mass influence the risk of irrational consumer behavior has risen beyond any expectation for consumers to behave rationally. This is not to say that they are stupid. They are just acting on the information they are offered and if that information is overwhelming and tainted, then there is no other expectation other than irrational behavior. The cottage industry model with consumers that have limited information access fits more appropriately with the supply and demand model; this model disappeared a hundred years ago.

Understanding the supply and demand facts of life was key to introducing new products and technologies in the last century. When electricity was first offered the general attitude was why. When the telephone was first offered the same issues surfaced. However, realizing that consumers do not act rationally, strategies surfaced that stimulated interest in new products and services. The concept of Veblen[110] goods was applied to many new products and services in hopes of creating new markets.

Veblen goods and services are associated with high social status and exclusivity. Veblen goods and services have a different demand curve from normal goods. In a Veblen good or service, decreasing the price reduces the consumers desire to buy because it is no longer perceived as exclusive or high status. A price increase will increase the consumers' perception of status and exclusivity making the good or service more desirable. There are limits to the price increases and at some point, demand will drop even in the exclusive high-status market.

Veblen combined sociology with economics in the book "The Theory of the Leisure Class" (1899)[111]. The book suggested that there was a difference between industry, run by engineers, which manufactures goods for the general population, and business, which exists only to make profits for a leisure class. Unlike industry, which is productive, business allows the leisure class to engage in "conspicuous consumption", where the economic contribution is "waste" that contributes nothing to productivity.

So how does this relate to implementation architecture design? System design in the early stages is characterized as groups of ideas and concepts. These ideas and concepts are circulating in what is essentially a small test market with the participating stakeholders. In many ways these stakeholders are an early indication of how the consumers or users will receive the product or system. In this setting many questions can be asked. For example, what is the incremental cost of adding a certain feature that separates one design from another and what is the impact on

---

respected. Users will find ways to misuse the system.

[110] Thorstein Bunde Veblen, (July 30, 1857 – August 3, 1929) an American sociologist and economist was the first to introduce the term "conspicuous consumption" and concept of status seeking.

[111] Thorstein Bunde Veblen (1899) The Theory of the Leisure Class, An Economic Study of Institutions, London: Macmillan Publishers.

stakeholder acceptability? So conceptually each design approach can have a set of supply and demand curves.

If we replace the x-axis Quantity on the supply and demand chart with Features where different approaches can be different design features as viewed by consumers, then some interesting ideas surface. The features are the function, performance, quality, and aesthetic levels of the design. Further there is a continuum from least costly to produce to most costly to produce based on the features. The project stakeholders can be extrapolated to the broader market consumers and or users. They have a price they are willing to pay for each design increment feature block. This is the internal stakeholder demand curve. This demand curve could be augmented with a market study.

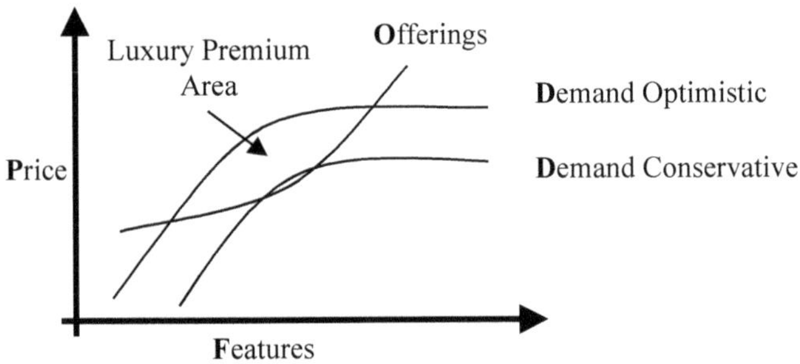

Figure 55 Offerings and Demand

As we examine the demand-offering chart there are several observations. The Offerings curve shows that the cost to produce each design increases with increasing features. It is not linear or smooth. The Demand curve shows that consumers will only pay a certain price for the design regardless of the level of features. It also shows that if the demand intersects the offering at some point, there is an area where a premium price can be charged for some increment of features. These features fall into the luxury category and represent opportunity to increase margins via the offering of luxury features.

Imagine buying and building a house in 1960's suburbia USA. Let's start with the consumer. Here you are living in the city. You have a car and there are new roads to take you into a different world. As you travel these roads you see various farms being sold to developers who are building houses. You stop in, wander through a few sample homes, pick up some brochures, and drive through the new streets. You leave the small development of 50 - 300 houses and drive around the surrounding community. What value system can you use to make your final decision? Are you considering the price with the various features? One developer offers a larger lot at the expense of a smaller house. Another developer offers a large house and large lot but at a different location up the road.

Imagine being a builder. The war is over, and you partnered with a brilliant architect you met in the military. You have dreams of building a new world. What features do you offer to separate you from the competition? How do you attempt to speculate what people might want when they themselves are not sure? The Veblen effect does not work. These are people who just lived through a depression and war, they are looking for a different way. What do you do?

Fortunately, in this scenario everyone got what they wanted except for the people left behind in the cities. It took decades for the Veblen effect to take hold of the new cities being born after the World War II. Housing bubbles that led to whole communities being bulldozed in some insane frenzy of Veblen effect and massive speculation did not surface until the new century.

9.8.4 Cost Shifting and Life Cycle Costs

Unlike traditional financial metrics which are based on artificial system boundaries that attempt to maximize the benefit of one stakeholder at the expense of another stakeholder[112], Life Cycle Costs (LCC) is a broad metric used to capture all the costs from all the stakeholders. It attempts to stop cost shifting to unsuspecting stakeholders.

At the highest level of LCC there are direct costs attributed to a project or program and then there are indirect costs that are attributed to infrastructure[113] or other costs not typically allocated to the project or program. Typically, it is the indirect costs that significantly impact the selection of the architecture. Cost shifting is the practice where the true system costs are shifted to other stakeholders who may be unaware of their newfound responsibility. The traditional Life Cycle Cost (LCC) equation is modified to remove any possibility of cost shifting.

LCC = R+D+P+O+M+S+I+E or PROMISED

Where:

R = Research	S = Shut Down & Disposal
D = Development	
P = Production	I = Infrastructure
O = Operation	E = Environment & Waste
M = Maintenance	

---

112 Essentially the total costs in traditional financial metrics are shifted and the true cost burden is hidden or obfuscated.

113 Executive Order 12803 - Infrastructure Privatization April 30, 1992, (b) "Infrastructure asset" means any asset financed in whole or in part by the Federal Government and needed for the functioning of the economy. Examples of such assets include, but are not limited to: roads, tunnels, bridges, electricity supply facilities, mass transit, rail transportation, airports, ports, waterways, water supply facilities, recycling and wastewater treatment facilities, solid waste disposal facilities, housing, schools, prisons, and hospitals.

Infrastructure (I) represents the cost of establishing the infrastructure so that others can offer system solutions. Examples are government funded research, development, and operations of air traffic control systems and research and development of airplanes for defense that are then transferred to civilian use. In this setting it is absurd to think a commercial airline company is a real business that funds all its costs. It becomes even more absurd when managers of these entities think they should derive revenue by charging for toilet services while in flight. It would be impossible for these companies to exist if the true cost of flying were factored into the business. They could not exist. The same is true of all the businesses that benefit from the rural electrification program, interstate highways, roads, space satellite systems and a plethora of other infrastructure projects that no business could justify in a reasonable business mode. But that does not mean the Infrastructure costs should not be identified for various system solutions. To the contrary they should be clearly identified so that a system does not become a burden on the people[114].

In the USA the direct costs have typically been borne by commercial companies and indirect costs have been borne by the taxpayer. For example, automobiles will not sell unless there is a road infrastructure. Airplanes cannot fly unless there are airports and an air traffic control system. Further airplanes would not exist without defense projects that invested in aircraft. Spaceships carrying satellites that offer commercial services cannot fly without NASA launch and tracking systems.

It is always an interesting moral situation when companies forget that if the true costs of the products and services were passed on to the customer, assuming they could actually implement the infrastructure, they would quickly go out of business. This is a modern political discussion that has resurfaced approximately 40 years after the end of World War II and has not been resolved in the USA at this time.

Recently there has been a massive trend to shift operations and maintenance costs to customers. This translates into massive amount of time taken away from customers as they try to navigate a company's services and or product offering. This started with software where users were given immature products and they were forced to deal with software that would lock up their computers. This eventually moved to help centers where the customer would be unable to get any assistance when problems surfaced. It has moved to the actual purchase of services and products. Consumers spend many hours across multiple days searching for deals and looking for hidden costs before being able to make a final purchase for a service and or product. This is cost shifting. There is a price paid in the system when the system boundary is properly drawn.

9.8.5 Measure of Effectiveness

Minimizing life cycle costs, although extremely beneficial when compared to

[114] What is the Infrastructure cost of a catastrophic Nuclear Power Plant disaster?

other financial metrics, still does not offer a true indicator of the value of one architecture over another architecture.

Value is not only financial but also non-financial. For example, some value a day at the beach more than a day at the mountains.

The Measure of Effectiveness (MOE) is based on the concept that the tradeoff criteria in an architecture tradeoff matrix should not include cost or requirements. It is a given that all solutions will satisfy the known requirements at some cost.

Cost is used at the bottom of the tradeoff matrix where each approach total rating (sum of all the tradeoff criteria) is divided by cost. This essentially identifies the ***goodness of each approach per unit of cost.*** This is called the Measure of Effectiveness or MOE. This is expressed as the following equation:

MOE = Sum of tradeoff criteria/cost to produce approach

The MOE equation is the heart of systems engineering. It is fundamental and drives everything. The tradeoff criteria ratings are the result of analysis, which may take years and involve hundreds of stakeholders.

A word of caution, most institutions do not base their decisions on the MOE or measure of goodness of an approach. So, there is confusion on what the MOE actually represents. For example, some refer to the MOE in terms of what is actually the tradeoff criteria. They state that the MOE is based on operational needs and then are silent on the relationship between the sum of the tradeoff items and cost. So, the idea of MOE is obscured and lost. The following is a description of MOEs from NASA:

"MOEs are the "operational" measures of success that are closely related to the achievement of mission or operational objectives in the intended operational environment. MOEs are intended to focus on how well mission or operational objectives are achieved, not on how they are achieved, i.e., MOEs should be independent of any particular solution. As such, MOEs are the standards against which the "goodness" of each proposed solution may be assessed in trade studies and decision analyses. Measuring or calculating MOEs not only makes it possible to compare alternative solutions quantitatively, but sensitivities to key assumptions regarding operational environments...[115]"

Notice the term MOE has become plural, the plural MOEs usage and the description clearly represent tradeoff criteria. However, in this ontology the criteria are lost, and the MOE is obfuscated. Some practitioners are familiar with the subtle distinction between the singular and plural MOE term and use them appropriately in the process[116]. However, for clarity, especially in highly controversial settings the

[115] NASA Systems Engineering Handbook, NASA/SP-2007-6105 Rev1, National Aeronautics and Space Administration NASA Headquarters Washington, D.C. 20546, December 2007.

[116] At Hughes Aircraft I / we used the single MOE to select architecture approaches. This

MOE term should not be used with the tradeoff criteria for the ontology. Do not use MOE and MOEs together in any process description. Use MOE and tradeoff criteria terminology.

Another potential trap where the MOE could be lost or inappropriately used is if people attempt to equate it to cost benefit analysis. Cost benefit analysis is primarily performed in the financial domain while the MOE with its use of non-financial tradeoff criteria works outside the financial domain. Also cost benefit analysis is typically used to justify an intervention as opposed to picking an architecture approach. The intervention is meant to disrupt the status quo with the intent of reducing future costs.

The MOE is the only value system that uses non-financial variables in the equation. In many ways it is like shifting from the time domain to the frequency domain to perform circuit analysis in electrical engineering. The view that the MOE offers is not possible when using strictly financial variables. Examples of other financial analysis that might be equated with the MOE are:

- Cost-Effectiveness Analysis
- Economic Impact Analysis
- Fiscal Impact Analysis
- Social Return On Investment (SROI) Analysis

9.8.6 Architecture Identification and Tradeoff Selection

At some point architecture alternatives, tradeoffs, and selection need to be addressed. Are there any unique tradeoff criteria to consider when selecting an architecture? How can the architectures be depicted? What process can be reasonably followed to select the architecture especially when sustainability surfaces? The following is a list of possible new sustainable related criteria to consider in architecture development:

- Sustainability
- Short & long-term environmental impact: Air, land, water, sea, space
- Air, water, and land pollution
- Noise[117] and visual pollution
- Cost Shifting
- Technology Maturity, Stability, Growth Potential
- Maintainability, Producibility, Supportability
- Aesthetics, form, user acceptability

---

can be referred to as the architecture MOE.

[117] Noise pollution is a real issue addressed by air traffic control systems for decades.

To start the process, identify the architecture alternatives. The identification includes the name of the architecture, a simple picture and a few words that capture the essence of the architecture approach. This is limited to a single page for each architecture approach.

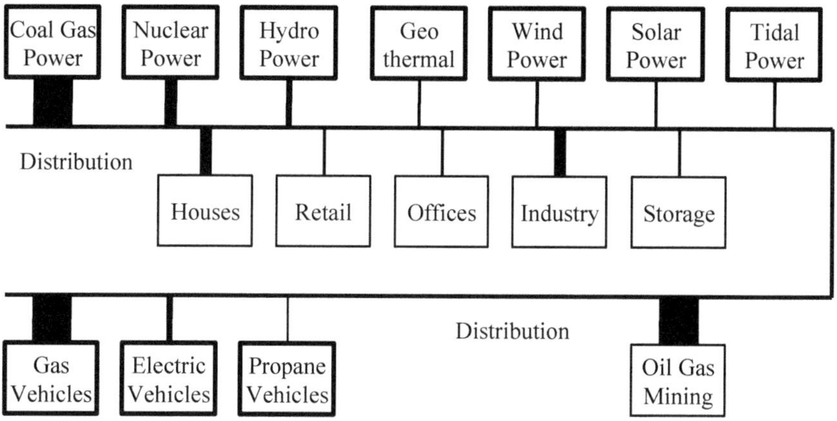

Figure 56 Sustainable Architecture Depiction - Sankey Diagram

What should be considered in the architecture of a power generation system for a community[118]? If the focus is on a new wind farm that will produce power does it make sense to use one type of wind turbine in a homogeneous system or should the system solution use multiple sizes and types of wind turbines in a heterogeneous architecture arrangement? Should the architecture use different energy generation technologies? What are the maintenance and support impacts of heterogeneous architectures and are they mitigated by the advantages?

Identifying the architecture alternatives, surfacing the tradeoff criteria and selecting the most effective architecture is one of the most important practices in systems engineering. It is especially important when questions of sustainability surface.

9.8.7 Architecture Types

When we think of buildings and architecture, images of Greek, Roman, Gothic, Victorian, and other building architectures appear in our minds. There are images and words that we use to describe these building architectures.

Are there architecture types and do we consider them when we start to conceive our architectures? The short answer is yes. We cannot avoid it; our background always comes into play even if we are not fully conscious of the influences.

Architectures have structure, behavior, and internal connectivity. In the last

---

[118] The Rural Electrification Act of 1936 supplied the infrastructure and funding to electrify isolated U.S. farms. May 20, 1936, S. 3483, Public, No. 605.

century those engaged in computer architectures were consciously introduced to different architecture types and their behavior. These architectures were borrowed from observations of nature and human organization. We started to study and try to understand these systems using various techniques. Understanding these computer architectures provides a framework for future system architects irrespective of the system being developed.

9.8.7.1 Centralized Architecture

At one extreme is the concept of a centralized architecture. This is characterized by a very large central element responsible for most if not all the functions. It attaches to lower level entities with little or no processing power that usually are given the function of interfacing to the outside world, the peripherals. A mainframe computer would do all the processing while printers, displays, keyboards, trackballs, switches, indicators, etc. would interface to the outside world. Disk drives, tape drives, paper tape readers / punchers, card readers / punchers, etc. would read and store all the data.

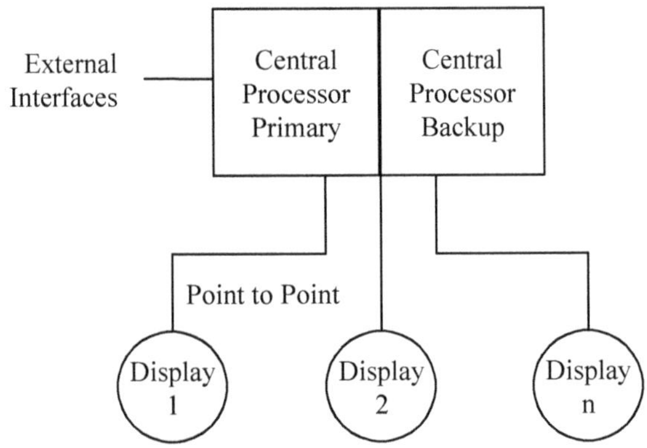

Figure 57 Centralized Architecture

There are reasonable non-computer analogies. For example, in an organizational setting many people would be given a function with little or no decision authority while one individual or a very small group would have all the decision authority. In a structural setting one central element might be given the load bearing weight such as in a single beam in the basement of house.

The advantages of a centralized architecture are:

- Little overhead to coordinate, everything is done in one place
- Consistent processing of all functions
- Least amount of parts to break
- Simple one direction connection control communications

The disadvantages of a centralized architecture are:

- Everything stops and fails when the central element breaks
- Everything stops or fails near maximum capacity limits
- Impact of Failure (IOF) is greatest
- Priorities are needed for running functions on the one element
- Slower response time as load increases
- Requests need to be queued and some requests are always last

9.8.7.2 Fully Distributed Architecture

At the other extreme is the fully distributed architecture. This is characterized by many small-processing elements responsible for all the functions. The functions or data can be split across small processing elements. There can be combinations of split functions and data. An example of this is the personal computer. We can each sit down at our fully distributed element and perform any function using our data. Anyone else can sit down and perform the same functions using their data. We also can log on to our bank computer and perform financial transactions from what we view as a centralized resource[119]. In the fully distributed architecture, there is a maximum level of functional and data distribution. It is an idealized concept with compromise limiting the level of distribution as the system is considered.

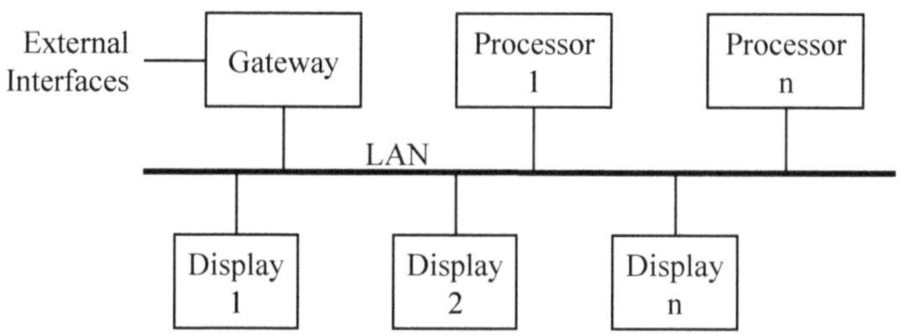

Figure 58 Fully Distributed Architecture

The advantages of a fully distributed architecture are:

- No single point of failure
- Failure is isolated to the failed element
- Impact of Failure (IOF) is completely minimized
- No need to queue requests
- Processing performed on the spot with very fast response time

The disadvantages of a fully distributed architecture are:

[119] A banking computer system is actually highly distributed, but we all connect to it via the Internet in a client server architecture. We perceive it as a central resource.

- Significant overhead if processors need to coordinate
- Complex startup depending on coordination
- Greatest amount of parts
- Difficult to manage and assess status

9.9 Mental Models and Validation

Model validation builds confidence that the model addresses the correct issues, provides accurate representations of the real-world settings, and is used because of its value and correctness in representing some aspect of the system.

A model can be validated using historical data, However, there is no guarantee that history will repeat unless a logical analysis can prove the repetition. For example, a RADAR tracking algorithm is deterministic and various flight patterns can be duplicated to both verify and validate the model.

When a model is non-deterministic then validation using historical data is of limited use. Validation becomes challenging under the following conditions:

- There is no historical data
- Controlled experiments on the live system cannot be performed to gather real world data and compare with the model
- The system does not exist there are no similar systems to compare against
- The model is fundamentally nondeterministic
- The model is nonlinear with many points of inflection and state changes

The approach to validate a model is to use various mental model[120] inputs to break the model. These mental models translate into scenarios and expected outputs. If the model breaks, then it needs to be updated to capture the mental model and its scenario.

The danger is that the scenarios derived from various stakeholder mental models may not capture unexpected and hidden non-linearity's, points of inflection, and state changes. So, initial incorrect model outputs must be clearly explained in a precise accurate unambiguous manner or the mental model must be invalidated using the same approach.

Once the mental model scenarios have been executed then those scenarios for the model have been validated. The model is technically not validated but there is a high degree of confidence that the model will properly execute similar scenarios and the model should be considered validated. The process and logic are similar to a legal case where there is a large body of evidence showing why the model is valid for its intended use.

---

[120] A mental model is a person's intuitive perception or thought process about how something works in the real world.

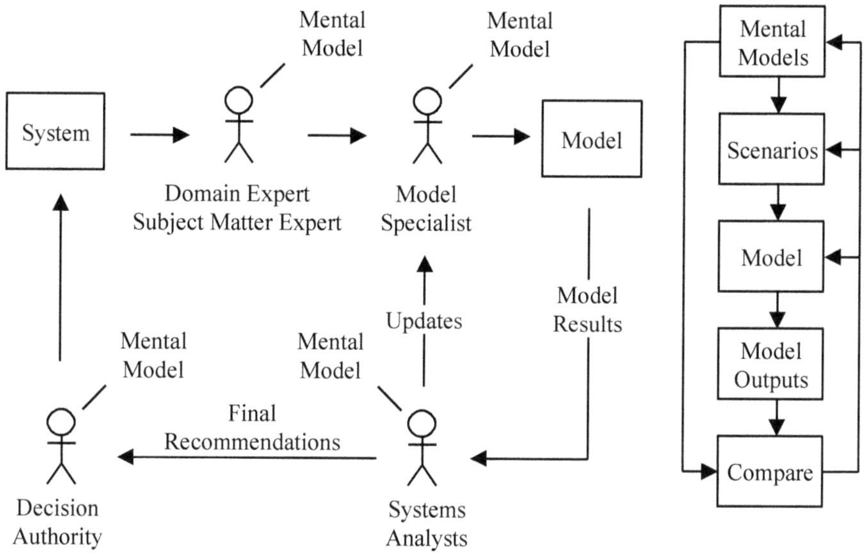

Figure 59 Model Verification and Validation

At the end of the validation process everyone has a better understanding of the system and its behavior. During the iterative validation process of running different mental model scenarios various discussions surface and validation can be stated:

- Assumptions and requirements validation
- Calibration validation
- Process validation
- Face validity
- Data, Theory, and algorithm validation
- Emergent (unexpected) behavior validation

The timeline between model development, verification, and validation quickly blur. This suggests that model implementation should be started early and expanded as new insights surface. It is not unreasonable to spend a majority of the time in model validation as each new scenario results in major changes, minor changes, and then tweaks to the model.

9.10 System Implementation

Eventually a system moves from concept, to functional structure, and then to implementation. The implementation of a complex system draws from the industrial base using existing products and new designs.

This can be extended to include intellectual property in patent databases, work at R&D labs, universities, etc. This is accomplished by being a participant in the industry. Conferences are attended, trade journals are read, industry surveys are performed, requests for quotes and information are solicited, requests for proposals are offered, vendor visits and demonstrations, product brochures are reviewed etc. This is done to gain access to and understand information that can be used in the implementation of the system.

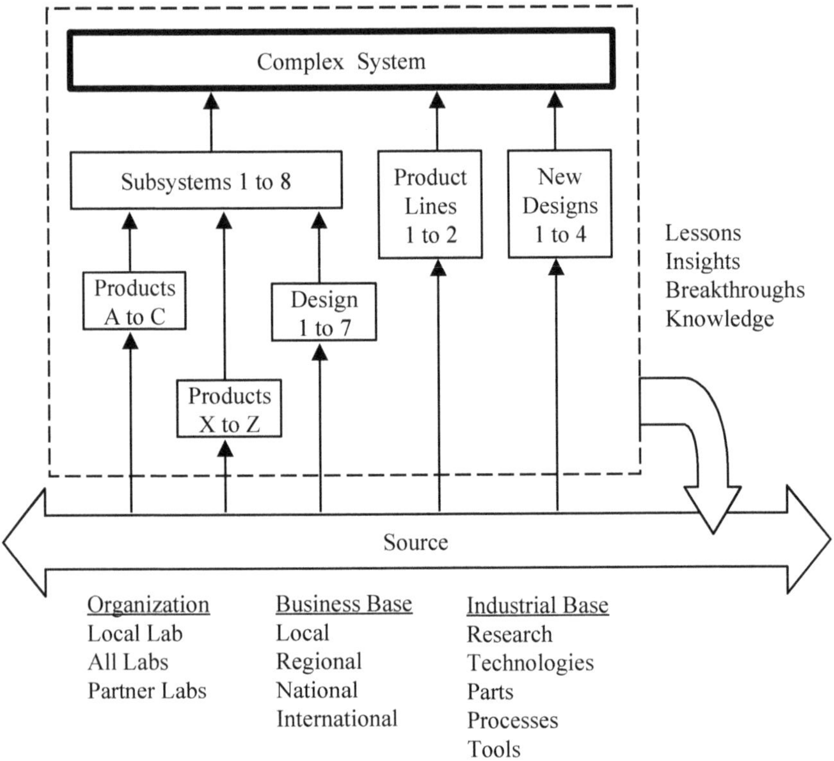

Figure 60 Implementation Architecture Design and Industrial Base

9.11 Previous Century Systems

Today we marvel at the US interstate highway system. However, 45 years ago people drove their automobiles on these new roads for miles and there was nothing. Today cities exist around these roads. What possessed the previous generation to build roads into the middle of nowhere? What did they use as a value method? Were these roads built exclusively for survival from a war or was something else going on in the minds of the people[121]? The goal of building a national network of roads was

[121] Interstate Highway System authorized by Federal-Aid Highway Act of 1956 also known as National Interstate and Defense Highways Act of 1956. In addition to private and commercial transportation, it would offer transport for military supplies and troop

decades in the making. It is interesting to see that one of the primary arguments was funding sources and national defense. The Federal-Aid Highway Act of 1956 was also known as National Interstate and Defense Highways Act of 1956.

There is a bridge connecting NJ with Philadelphia that was built in 1929, the Benjamin Franklin bridge. It is a huge bridge able to support traffic capacity in this new century. Not much was going on in 1929 in southern New Jersey. What possessed the people to build this incredible bridge that still works? What did they use as a value method?

Figure 61 Needs of the Highway Systems 1955-1984

The argument of the role of government and how projects would be funded surfaced time and time again after World War II as the society was moving into a modern post nuclear world. Eventually the concept of Dual Use Technology surfaced. It refers to technology that can be used for both peaceful and military purpose[122].

Today we take satellites for granted. They give us television, position information, personal communications across massive distances, weather information, geological surveys, etc. How did we get here? What were the arguments between some futuristic vision, defense, and business?

---

deployments in emergencies or foreign invasion.

[122] Dual Use Technology, Dual Use Processes, Dual Use Products all refer to Dual Use where peaceful and military use is possible. It became part of the national dialog after World War II. Early references are not easily found. A Survey of Dual-Use Issues, IDA Paper P-3176 Prepared for Defense Advanced Research Projects Agency (DARPA).

Figure 62 Hughes NASA Surveyor Lunar Lander

Hughes Aircraft designed and built the Surveyor spacecraft[123]. Surveyor 1 was the first lunar lander to explore the Moon. The NASA Jet Propulsion Laboratory managed the program. It was launched May 30, 1966 and landed June 2, 1966. Its landing weight was 596 lbs. (270 kg). There were 11,237 images transmitted to Earth.

Syncom stands for synchronous communication satellite. Syncom, a NASA program started in 1961 to build geosynchronous communication satellites. All the Syncom satellites were developed and manufactured by Hughes Space and Communications. Syncom 2, launched in 1963 and was the world's first geosynchronous communications satellite. In the 1980s, the Syncom continued with Syncom IV which were much larger satellites, also manufactured by Hughes. They

[123] A spacecraft system consists of various subsystems, depending on the mission: Life support, attitude control, guidance navigation and control, communications, command and data handling, power, thermal control, propulsion, structures, payload, ground segment, launch vehicle, and a great stereo.

were leased to the United States military under the Leasat program.

Figure 63 Hughes Syncom 2 First Geosynchronous Satellite

Hughes Aircraft built the Galileo spacecraft at its El Segundo, California plant. The Jet Propulsion Laboratory (JPL)[124] managed the Galileo mission for NASA. Germany supplied the propulsion module. NASA's Ames Research Center managed the probe. It was controlled by six RCA 1802 Cosmac[125] microprocessor CPUs. The 1802 CPU had previously been used onboard the Voyager and Viking spacecraft.

Galileo was launched on October 18, 1989 from the Space Shuttle Atlantis on the STS-34 mission. It arrived at Jupiter on December 7, 1995. The spacecraft was the first to perform an asteroid flyby, discover an asteroid moon, orbit Jupiter, and launch a probe into Jupiter's atmosphere. Because of Galileo scientists think that the Europa moon may have a salt-water ocean beneath its frozen surface. So, on September 21, 2003, after 14 years in space and 8 years of service in the Jovian system, Galileo's mission ended by sending it into Jupiter's atmosphere. The goal was to avoid any chance of contaminating local moons with bacteria from Earth.

---

[124] JPL is a federally funded research and development center.

[125] Each microprocessor clocked at about 1.6 MHz was fabricated on sapphire (silicon on sapphire) a radiation static hardened material ideal for spacecraft. It was the first low power CMOS processor. It was previously used onboard the Voyager and Viking spacecraft.

Figure 64 Hughes Galileo Spacecraft

The Galileo spacecraft and its attached Inertial Upper Stage booster are released from the payload bay of Atlantis on October 18, 1989.

Figure 65 JPL Viking Lander and Mars Landscape

Viking 1 and 2 space probes were sent to Mars. Each probe had an orbiter designed to photograph the surface of Mars and a lander designed to study the planet from the surface. The orbiter also provided communication for the lander once it touched down. The landers conducted biological experiments designed to detect life in the Martian soil. Three separate teams designed the experiments. One experiment turned positive for detection of metabolism. However, another test failed to reveal any organic molecules in the soil. Most scientists became convinced that the positive results were likely caused by non-biological chemical reactions from highly oxidizing soil conditions. The total cost of the Viking project was approximately $1 billion US.

Pioneer 10 and Pioneer 11 explored the outer planets and left the solar system. They carry a golden plaque, showing a man and a woman and information about us on Earth. The Pioneer plaque image is engraved into a gold-anodized aluminum plate, 152 by 229 millimeters (6 by 9 inches), attached to the spacecraft's antenna support struts to help shield it from erosion by interstellar dust.

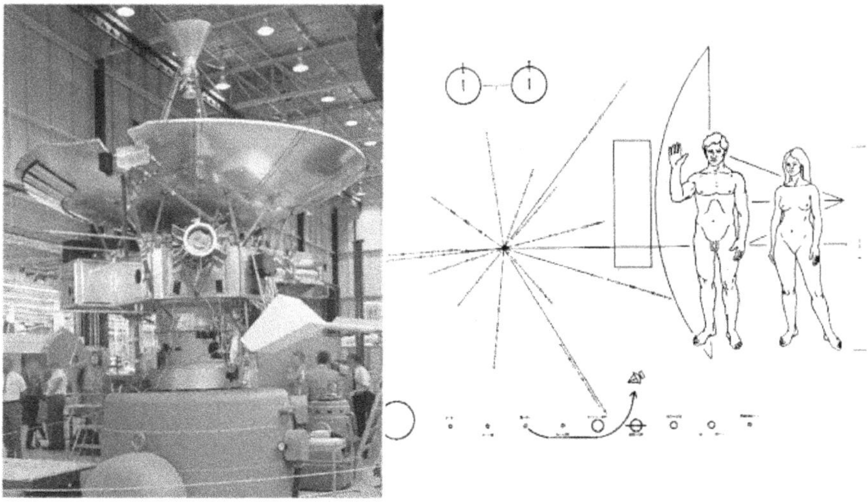

Figure 66 TRW Pioneer 10 Probe and Plaque

Pioneer 10 in the final stage of construction at the TRW[126] plant in Southern California. 20 December 1971 NASA Ames Research Center.

Voyagers 1 and 2 space probes were launched in 1977. The original mission was to study Jupiter and Saturn; however, the probes were able to expand their mission and continue into the outer solar system. They are currently on course to exit the solar system. These probes were built at JPL. Voyager 1 has crossed into the heliosheath, the region where interstellar gas and solar wind start to mix. Voyager 1 is the farthest human made object from Earth.

[126] Simon Ramo and Dean Wooldridge left Hughes Aircraft and formed the Ramo-Wooldridge Corporation with financial support from Thompson Products. The company became TRW Inc in July of 1965. TRW was active in development of missile systems and spacecraft. They were involved in the development of the U.S. ICBM program via the Teapot Committee led by John von Neumann. They pioneered systems engineering and served as the primary source of systems engineering for the U.S. Air Force ballistic missile programs. In 1959 the US Congress issued a report recommending that the companies Space Technology Labs (STL) be converted to a non-profit organization. With nearly half of STL's employees the Aerospace Corporation was formed in June of 1960.

Figure 67 Voyager Space Probe

Many point to technological achievements of NASA. Few point to the approach of phased missions, where each is a steppingstone to the next more challenging mission. Few also point to the simulations used to not only train astronauts and mission personnel but also understand the systems on Earth. This relentless dedication to steppingstones and simulation is an important lesson for all major system practitioners. The irony is that even in that non-reactive systems driven environment Apollo 1[127] was struck with tragedy. At the senate inquiry following the Apollo 1 fire Senator Anderson questioned Astronaut Frank Borman, "What caused the fire?" Frank Bormans' response was:

"**A failure of imagination.** We've always known there was the possibility of fire in a spacecraft. But the fear was that it would happen in space, when you're 180 miles from terra firma and the nearest fire station. That was the worry. No one ever imagined it could happen on the ground. If anyone had thought of it, the test would've been classified as hazardous. But it wasn't. **We just didn't think of it.** Now who's fault is that? Well, it's North American's fault. It's NASA's fault. It's the fault of every person who ever worked on Apollo. It's my fault. I didn't think the test was hazardous. No one did. I wish to God we had."

Could you imagine going to the moon without these fundamental concepts in place? How do you measure the value of phased missions and simulations?

Many stakeholders view the interstate highway system as an example of what went wrong and an unsustainable future with massive suburban sprawl. However, people forget that millions of people were trapped in dirty cities with bad air and no

---

[127] Apollo 1 was to be the first manned mission to the moon. On January 27, 1967 a fatal fire killed all three crewmembers (Command Pilot Virgil "Gus" Grissom, Senior Pilot Edward H. White, and Pilot Roger B. Chaffee). This happened during a pre-launch test of the spacecraft on Launch Pad 34 at Cape Canaveral.

connection to nature. The cities were becoming increasingly unlivable. Although the following message is a broad message about the environment it captured what many people were subjected to in the cities:

"...there are already more rats in New York than people. By 1980, you will need a gas mask and a flashlight to get to the office. There won't be any birds or bees or trees unless we stop what we are doing, we are going to kill ourselves.[128]"

The interstate highway system allowed millions of people to move to a place of clean air, cool nights, grass, trees, and the sound of birds and views of rabbits and squirrels (nice versions of rats). This would never have happened without the interstate highway system. Certainly trains, trolleys, and other public transportation systems existed before the rise of the interstates and automobiles and yet people by the millions were trapped in bad cities.

Were there other alternatives? Was there a failure of imagination? Or was this an example of massive imagination with abandoned emergence that needed to be addressed by the next generation? What if the automobile were to be powered with a perfectly clean energy source, would the view of interstate highways change?

What happens to people who are unable to drive because of health or old age? Do they move back to the cities that are now showing signs of relieved stress and reintroduce the stresses? Many roads in more enlightened communities were built with large grass medians to accommodate future public transportation needs. However, rather than consider light rail or other alternatives the medians were used to add more lanes to the existing road. The argument was always cost as the current generation decided to base the economy on services rather than build infrastructure for the next generation. What would a system of shared ubiquitous public transportation and ubiquitous roads look like and would it be internally and externally sustainable[129]?

Observation 14 Previous Century Systems

Privatization Comments: Was this golden age made possible because of an effective balance of government and industry? Have we lost that balance? Is that why there is no Space Shuttle today? What else is lost besides the Space Shuttle that was the Space Transportation System?

---

[128] Earth Day Public Service Announcement (archival) from the transcript of the documentary, Earth Days, Documentary Film, December 2009, story of growing awareness and understanding of environmental crisis and emergence, during the 1960's and '70's.

[129] See section 9.13 Sustainability and Progress.

Figure 68 Space Shuttle[130]

[130] Source US Government. Space Transportation System operational 1981 to 2011.

9.12 Misuse of Technology

Misuse of technology is an interesting topic. There are different dimensions that should be known to the stakeholders. Most will focus on the simple philosophical case of technology being used for good or bad activities. If it is used for bad activities, then it is a misuse of technology. However, there are other dimensions to misuse of technology. The following are other perspectives on technology misuse. At what point is technology in a system being misused?

- The technology adds no value to a system
- The technology actually hurts the system, but the stakeholders are unaware of the damage
- The technology hurts the system, the stakeholders are aware of the damage, but are powerless to stop using it

- The technology is prematurely abandoned
- The technology is stopped because of status quo
- The technology is viewed as a commodity

- The technology only appeals to the ego
- The technology is poorly understood
- The technology is not sustainable

At what point does misuse of technology translate into deviant design practices? By definition systems practices should prevent deviant design practices and misuse of technology. Some deviant design practices and misuse of technology are:

- Wasting peoples time by forcing useless actions especially for ulterior motives
- Fooling or deceiving people into taking undesired actions especially when the user is harmed
- Manipulating biological systems to mask poor system performance while doing harm to the biological system (e.g. using blue background to fuzz out poor resolution displays causing eye fatigue as it continuously focuses and defocuses)
- Manipulating biological systems to mask poor system performance even though there is no harm
- Consciously reducing performance even though the technology supports much higher levels of performance at no additional cost
- Reducing performance to allow large quantity but undesired low-quality content when performance can match technology with a reasonable quantity level of high-quality content
- Ignoring scientific knowledge and previous experience especially as related to

human factors
- Using technology to compromise inalienable rights

When we look at a system from a functional or requirements point of view, we see that there are root functions and requirements. From the roots other elements are identified via decomposition until we reach a natural limit where no more decomposition is possible. These are the leaves or primitives. We also see that there are core functions and requirements. Without this core, the system does not exist.

If inalienable[131] rights are a core root requirement where does the decomposition lead? The most famous first level decomposition is “life, liberty, and the pursuit of happiness” from the United States Declaration of Independence. Are there other decompositions from the key requirement of technology not compromising inalienable right? The following is a possible list:

- Technology that does not violate people’s inalienable rights to privacy. This is interesting because inalienable or natural rights are not dependent on cultural or government laws, customs, or beliefs.
- Technology that does not knowingly harm people. Knowingly harm is based on some human in some setting knowing the technology can cause harm to the uninformed or misinformed.
- Technology that does not place a significant burden on a people or society. This is where people become slaves to the technology regardless of benefit. It is most egregious if the benefit is small or nonexistent.

Observation 15 Misuse of Technology

Privatization Comments: Has privatization led to a massive and seriously negative misuse of technology? If so, what will put the system back in balance?

9.13 Sustainability and Progress

Sustainable development has become a significant topic of discussion in recent years. Some have argued that it is the next great challenge and that we should focus our energies towards sustainability in this new century. So, what is sustainable development?

The Brundtland Commission[132] defined sustainable development as development that "meets the needs of the present without compromising the ability of future generations to meet their own needs." Sustainable development is usually

[131] Inalienable rights are self-evident and universal.

[132] Brundtland Commission, or the World Commission on Environment and Development, known by its Chair Gro Harlem Brundtland, convened by the United Nations in 1983 published Our Common Future, also known as Brundtland Report, in 1987.

divided into social, economic, environmental and institutional. The social, economic, environmental areas address key principles of sustainability, while the institutional area addresses key policy and capacity issues.

It is obvious that a people should try to live well now and in the future. The issue is the mechanisms they have at their disposal to accommodate that life. One of those mechanisms is systems engineering to develop the most effective solution.

Although it seems obvious to systems engineers that systems practices should be used to address the sustainability challenges of this new century, others not versed in systems practices have other views. For example, product-oriented people feel that their products are a perfect fit in a particular niche of sustainability. Technology people think they have a magic technology that will solve a challenging sustainability issue. Financial people think that tax incentives or virtual markets will spur innovation and let business rise to the occasion of sustainability needs. We as systems practitioners know that none of these will work in isolation. Instead we realize that systems thinking, and engineering is the only way to start to chip away at this problem.

9.13.1 Progress

Is progress and sustainability part of the same goal? That is an interesting question. Progress was used extensively in the last century. It was progress that led to lights in the dark, safe water, sewage, safe abundant food[133], refrigeration, telephones, radio, television, washers, dryers, garbage disposals, automobiles, airplanes, etc. This was extremely difficult, and people made enormous sacrifices to put these systems in place. They significantly benefited the future generation. The question is what progress is this generation making for the future generations?

"Progress is movement in a forward direction. It is a combination of achievement and forward vision, which serves its creator without fear or unforeseen consequence. There can be no progress if these rules are not respected. Technology is not progress unless it is combined in the direction of humanity. Pseudo progress can destroy the natural foundations of human life. It can lead to a society of chaotic beings that can result in global suicide"[134].

Misuse of technology is a serious consideration when addressing progress and sustainability. The Earth has a limited set of resources and one of the most

[133] Many people are still hungry, but most have concluded this is a political problem. This may soon change as the population continues to grow and potentially outstrips our ability to provide safe food even in a perfect political situation.

[134] Paraphrased from an interview with Burkhard Heim (February 9, 1925 - January 14, 2001) a German theoretical physicist. He devoted a large portion of his life to the pursuit of a unified field theory. One of his childhood ambitions was to develop a method of space travel, which contributed to his motivation to find such a theory.

important resources is people. Misusing their abilities and energies is not sustainable. It is critical that we not waste time with useless adventures that may lead to financial fortunes for some in a time of plenty and lose our opportunity to do what must be done before the times get challenging. It was only slightly over 100 years ago that humanity lived in the dark. We should not take our modern world for granted.

9.13.2 Growth

Many equate and discuss growth in terms of economics and finance such as gross domestic product (GDP). However, GDP as a measure of growth is very misleading.

Money is a method of storing wealth so that a simple common element can be used to exchange goods and services. It does not relate to or show the quality or usefulness of the goods and services. The argument is that the goods and services will always follow the need and quality based on the consumer and their choices. This assumes a rational consumer. However, what happens if consumers become irrational either because of their own failings or because of external forces? What happens if the money becomes a means to an end rather than a mechanism to fund useful projects[135]?

If the focus is on the quality of life as a market need that can be targeted and filled with the introduction of washers, dryers, toasters, personal transportation, entertainment[136], etc. then the introduction of useful goods and services is easily explained. However, with massive technology and the ability to produce goods and services anywhere, technology abuse can overcome our sustainable systems, and flood markets with useless products. At this point GDP becomes a useless metric.

9.13.3 Space Program

There never would have been an environmental movement that started in the 1970's without the U.S. space program and its unbelievable mission of going to the moon. The picture of the fragile Earth in a sea of blackness while seen from a dead space body inspired visionaries to take a whole new view of our world and our place in the system. This is a classic example of emergence and justification of technological growth for the sake of growth.

The sad part is the space program was an outgrowth of defense. It only grew to its level of performance because of the concept of Dual use Technology and a presidential initiative. It was not viewed as something that made sense and the next

---

[135] In my humble opinion this is the cause of all depressions. The money gets locked up in the hands of a few and the velocity of money drops to such a low level that all useful work stops. It's not that the few are evil it is just that they cannot duplicate the creativity and innovation of millions of people at the working levels.

[136] Many educational and soul-searching works can be captured on film and in music.

step for humanity to follow. So, even though we depend on satellites for every aspect of our life, few are willing to fund the fundamentals of trying to survive in the ultimate hostile environment even though that knowledge is easy to equate with us being able to effectively manage our resources on Earth.

Figure 69 Earth Rising Seen from Moon and Neil Armstrong on Moon

9.13.4 Internal versus External System Sustainability

Internal system sustainability is the ability of a system to sustain itself. Bad systems should fail and disappear, However, what should a people do if good systems fail and disappear.

Table 32 Internal Sustainability and Maturity Levels

Food 1. None 2. Hunter Gatherers 3. Family Farmers 4. Regional Farms 6. Large Farms 7. Large green houses 8. Vertical Farms	Water 1. Stream 2. River 3. Well 4. Town Square 5. Piped 6. Treated Piped	Waste Management 1. None 2. Raw into River 3. Processed into River except during rain 4. Processed into River 5. Effluent watering system
Health Care 1. None 2. Doctor 3. Clinic 4. Hospital 5. Research Hospital	Construction 1. None 2. Mud Hut 3. Durable Materials 4. Office Buildings 5. Skyscrapers	Employment 1. None 2. Investor 3. Worker 4. Owner
Education 1. None 2. Traditions 3. Verbal Apprentice 4. Elementary 5. High School	Transportation 1. Foot 2. Animal 3. Train 4. Public Transit 5. Automobile	Energy 1. None 2. Individual Intermittent 3. Individual Continuous 4. Group Intermittent 5. Group Continuous

Table 32 Internal Sustainability and Maturity Levels

6. College	6. Plane 7. Spaceship	
Communications 1. Verbal 2. Smoke 3. Print 4. Telegraph 5. Radio 6. Telephone 7. Satellite 8. Cell Phone 9. Internet	Security 1. None 2. Random 3. Random + Police 4. Police 5. Police + Military 6. None Needed	Wealth Exchange Finance Investments 1. Barter 2. Precious items 3. Money 4. Equities - Stocks, Mutual Funds 5. Interest Bearing - Bonds, Banks 6. Trusts - Real-estate Investment Trusts 7. Taxes Bonds - For infrastructure

Who decides the difference between a good and a bad system? For example, what if the clean safe water delivery systems in the U.S. were permitted to fail and go away to be replaced with bottled water? All communities have a maturity level and it should never be assumed that a community can sustain its' current level of existence without serious effort.

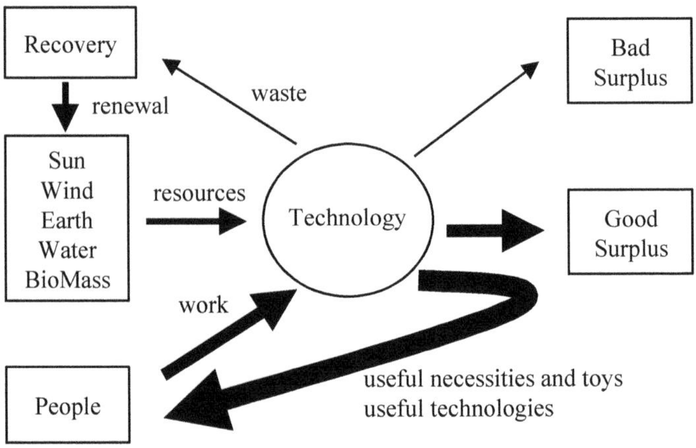

Figure 70 Technology and Sustainability - Sankey Diagram

External sustainability is a measure of a systems impact on its surrounding community. This is the traditional ecological view of sustainability. Some will point to a scale where one balances the other, However, it is not an either-or proposition. The easy way out is totally unacceptable. Somehow internal and external sustainability must be addressed.

It is easy to slip into simple economic views of the problem. However, stepping back and doing things like drawing simple context diagrams and then attempting to go into the context diagrams may yield important insights.

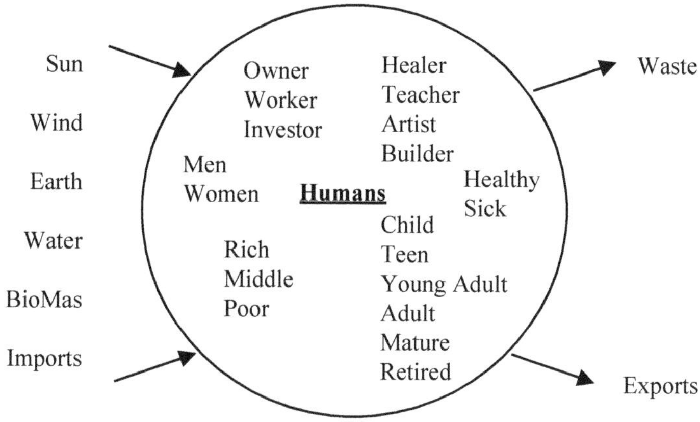

Figure 71 Sustainable Community

9.13.5 Sustainability Push Versus Pull

Things either can be pushed into the mainstream or pulled in by the mainstream. This applies to new ideas, technologies, architectures, processes, methods, products, etc. The problem arises when a new technology that is good surfaces and the mainstream rejects it in favor of the status quo especially if the status quo is less effective and everyone knows it, this displacement technology[137]. There are also cases where new technologies arrive and there is no status quo but the stakeholders still reject the technology. The following are examples of challenges faced by previous generations to establish new technologies that are now the mainstream:

Electricity versus gas
AC versus DC electricity
Automobile versus horse
Telephone versus letter
Radio versus telegraph
Airplane versus railroad
Airplane oceanic versus ship
Television versus movie house
Automobile versus public transit
Airplane cargo carrier versus truck
Cell phone versus land line phone
Internet versus print media versus retail versus sales staff, etc

It is interesting to list home appliances and entertainment:

Indoor water
Indoor sewage
Electricity
Telephone
Radio
Reel to reel tape recorder
Cassette tape recorder
Video tape recorder
Laser video player
Cell phone

[137] The early Internet was an example of a massive displacement technology.

Automobile
Washer
Television
Dryer
Garbage disposal
Dish washer
Stereo record player
Stereo FM radio and record player
Compact disk (CD) player
Digital video disk (DVD) player
Personal computer
Internet
MP3 player
Global Positioning System (GPS)
Internet phone

So what tools, techniques, strategies can be used to convert from push to pull and if the conversion is not happening what can be done to enable that conversion. The following are some possibilities:

- Great marketing campaign, but what does that mean? Use the Veblen effect[138]; appeal to the ego and exclusivity of the less enlightened.
- Broadcast the Measure of Effectiveness (MOE) findings far and wide. This was a technique used for new systems such as satellites.
- Establish small example and point to the exceptional advantages. Niagara Falls provided AC electric power for the first time on a large scale[139]. This was used to show the benefits of AC electricity.
- Educate the stakeholders. This was a technique used to successfully introduce computers in the last century.
- Use the Socratic method of discourse where questions and answers stimulate critical thinking and illuminate ideas. The goal is to lead to the obvious conclusions.

The alternative to converting from a push to a pull scenario is to force the push. Some of the techniques are:

- Convert a waste element to a revenue producer. This is a form of recycling that happens at the production level.
- Legislation which forces the new technology to be adopted or makes the old technology illegal or tightly controlled.
- Tax incentives in the form of reduced taxes or tax credits.
- Create a virtual market. Sulfur dioxide is used as an example to establish other commodity markets for harmful by products such as carbon dioxide.

---

[138] The Veblen effect is described in this text.

[139] The Electrical World, A weekly Review of Current Progress in Electricity and Its Practical Applications, Volume 29, WJJC (The W.J. Johnston Company), Library of Princeton University, January 2 to June 26 1897.

With the introduction of mass media there is information overload so demonstrations of new technology may not move the technology from a push to a pull. A classic example is the manned space program which resulted in humans stepping foot on the moon. Even though that was a spectacular demonstration of technologies, it was soon abandoned. Six Apollo missions landed astronauts on the Moon, the last in December 1972. In these six Apollo space flights, 12 men walked on the Moon. Apollo began after President John F. Kennedy's 1961 address to Congress declaring a national goal of landing a man on the Moon by the end of the decade.

9.13.6 Moving Forward

After World War II the USA fell into the cold war. This led to massive defense spending and the space race. To justify some of this expenditure the people convinced themselves of the concept of dual use[140]. Although inefficient, dual use did lead to practical systems needed for the emerging modern society. Interstate freeways became the backbone of the country as new cities emerged along its corridors. Defense RADAR was applied to civilian air traffic control and weather services. Computers and massive communications from the SAGE system gave birth to our highly automated and interconnected way of life and certainly the space race yielded satellites and other technologies that transformed our world.

The problem is dual use has become a dated concept. There is little flowing into practical applications of everyday life as defense has taken on the concept of using commercial elements and the space program has turned into low level activities[141] that are not pushing any technologies to their limits. So, the dilemma is who will pay for the new technologies and systems needed for our sustainable future?

The argument starting in the 1980's has been that the markets will provide for new technologies and systems, as they are needed. The idea is that the financial sector, which stores capital, would make capital investments available for new ventures. However, capital was not released for investment in new technology, development, and systems. Instead capital was being used to chase other capital via various financial investment products[142].

---

[140] Dual Use Technology, Dual Use Processes, Dual Use Products all refer to Dual Use where peaceful and military use is possible. It became part of the national dialog after World War II. Early references are not easily found. A Survey of Dual-Use Issues, IDA Paper P-3176 Prepared for Defense Advanced Research Projects Agency (DARPA).

[141] The Space Shuttle has been flying since 1981, some suggest NASA has turned into a taxi service for satellites rather than a technology driver and developer.

[142] My Life as a Quant: Reflections on Physics and Finance, Emanuel Derman, Wiley, 2007, SBN 0470192739. How I Became a Quant: Insights from 25 of Wall Street's Elite, Richard R. Lindsey, Wiley, 2009 ISBN 0470452579. The Quants: How a New Breed of Math Whizzes Conquered Wall Street and Nearly Destroyed It, Scott Patterson, Crown Business, 2010, ISBN 0307453375

Infrastructure	**Manufacturing**	**Services**
Housing		
Water	Durable Goods	Value Added
Sewage	Automobiles	Education
Lighting	Computers	Health Care
Power	Televisions	Restaurants
Roads		Intellectual Prop
Trains	Non-Durable Goods	
Automobiles	Toilet paper	Overhead
Planes	Detergent	Insurance
Satellites	Food	Investments
Space Ships		

Figure 72 Infrastructure Manufacturing Services

So where is the intelligent application of capital? Who decides who gets funded and under what conditions?

Outside the free market another approach is to use government funds to support projects people think are needed for their society. An example is government provided healthcare in some countries. As the details are uncovered it becomes more complex and many people immediately point to socialism as the approach with a negative connotation.

So, the argument is socialism versus capitalism when deciding how to apply capital to a problem. Whether it is taxes and a politician deciding where to apply the money or investments and savings with a financial executive deciding where to apply the money the result is the same. Projects that must be funded for sustainability are not funded. The only way out of this intellectual box is to accept the following:

- Dual use technology no longer exits
- It's not about socialism or capitalism
- Someone needs to pay for indirect costs that no business can ever justify

A bold approach is to get government back into the research business and directly fund sustainable projects in much the same way government funded defense and space in the dual use technology days. There even may be resurgence in dual use as defense realizes some of the sustainable projects may directly impact their needs. Also, perhaps NASA should return back to manned space missions. After all, not only is the extremely hostile space environment the ultimate teacher for sustainability but humanities future also may lie in the stars.

9.13.7 Going Backward

The fundamental element of the Earth is dirt. There is nothing wrong with dirt.

There are billions of organisms living on dirt, in dirt, within dirt, between dirt, at one with the dirt. Humans at one time lived in the dirt and they certainly can return back to living in the dirt. The problem is billions of existing people cannot survive on a dirt-based system.

So, what uplifted humanity away from the dirt and allowed 6 billion people to survive? The answer is technology applied in our systems.

The problem is our current technologies in our systems have reached their limits and our technologies and systems are causing long-term problems for our Planet. Some think that we should consciously reduce our population, or the Earth will reduce our population involuntarily. However, who gets to decide whom goes and who stays and under what conditions should all this devolution happen?

It's time to grow up. Asking for a conscious reduction in population is wrong. At what point do we stop our devolution and say everything is now in balance? Perhaps there is a reason for 6 billion people that may not become apparent until a small asteroid hit makes 5.5 billion people go away.

Necessities			Luxuries
	Transportation	Entertainment	
Food	Cars	Movies	Jewelry
Clothing	Trains	Concerts	
Shelter	Planes	Theatre	
Infrastructure			
	Information	Services	
	Computers	Health Care	
	Televisions	Education	
	Radios		

Figure 73 From Necessities to Luxuries

It is obvious that dual use practiced after World War II yielded technologies that allowed 6 billion people to emerge. However, dual use was never very efficient and has been abandoned. So, the issue is who funds the projects needed for our sustainability - survival?

Business does not care about large-scale technology or the long-term survival and growth of humanity. They only care about profits, which tend to be tied to short term needs - and that is perfectly appropriate. There is no relationship between profit and large-scale sustainability projects.

So, the question is who will make the investments needed for a future that not only gracefully supports 6 billion people today but also allows for reasonable growth and a happy healthy future?

Table 33 Our Progress to Date

Tech Level	Waste	Surplus	People
Hunter Gatherers	None	None	0.1 million
Agricultural	None	Food, Clothing	1 million

Table 33 Our Progress to Date

Tech Level	Waste	Surplus	People
Industrial	1 Earth	Food, Clothing, Infrastructure	200 million
Technological	4 Earth's	Food, Clothing, Infrastructure, Information	6000 million

9.13.8 Approaches from Our Civilization

There are many different ways to solve problems. What are those ways - techniques - methods - tools that we humans have used in the past 5000 years to solve problems?

In the early 2000's a tool was created to analyze technical specification text. Its purpose was to help in the authoring of requirement text. As part of its operation, it allowed a user to create analysis rules using concepts based on the Internet search engine. It also allowed a user to profile a document by mining and counting word instances.

One day this tool was applied to a document from the European Union on global warming, "Green Paper a European Strategy for Sustainable, Competitive and Secure Energy". Much to everyone's surprise meaningful insights surfaced from the analysis and new rules were created. The tool was then applied to the "Stern Review: The Economics of Climate Change" from the UK, once again there was meaningful output and new rules were created. It was finally applied to the "Climate Change Technology Program Strategic Plan" from the United States, and something very important happened.

The participants started to create rules that attempted to identify and characterize how humans solve problems. This was based on the knowledge of the team and research on the Internet trying to find techniques for solving problems. This all fell under the umbrella of trying to analyze policy documents.

The first thing that surfaced was the idea of broad approaches to solving problems like:

- Markets
- Technology
- Education
- Science
- Government
- People
- International Efforts
- Engineering
- Systems

The next thing that surfaced was the realization that there were categories of approaches - tools - techniques - methods - processes for solving problems like:

- Institutions
- Societal Approaches
- Organizational Tools

- Nation State Tools
- International Tools

Then it was realized there were other aspects of policy document analysis like:

- Social Warnings
- National Roles
- International Roles
- Special Interests

This is an example of technology running amok and yielding progress in many areas. The first was an attempt to try to quantify and characterize documents that were deemed very political with no redeeming content. It was found that the documents did not have a political agenda and were representations of different levels of maturity on the subject. The second was an attempt to study history and try to identify and categorize how humans solve problems using real approaches.

What is interesting is if someone runs the tool on the three documents, they as tool users change. They are more able to discern rhetoric from real statements of possible solutions in a political speech. In other words, they are able to more easily separate Bullshit[143] from honest attempts to address problems using traditional techniques and tools known throughout history. They become more critical and able to discern higher quality from the incoming signals.

The following is just a list of the rules and some details that are authored in the policy analysis tool:

- <u>Broad Approaches</u>: Markets, Technology, Education, Science, Government, People, International, Engineering, Systems, Alternatives
- <u>Institutions</u>: Academia, Government, Industry, Labs, Think, Tanks, NGO, Non, Profits, Popular, Media, Technical, Media, Associations
- <u>Societal Approaches</u>: Peaceful, Sacrifice, Stressed, Violent
- <u>Organizational Tools</u>: Technical, Process, Management, Gestalts, Implementation
- <u>Nation State Tools</u>: Policy, Legislate, Regulate, Deregulate, Tax, Military, Departments, Resources, Proactive, Transparency
- <u>International Tools</u>: Policy, Resources, Proactive
- <u>Social Warnings</u>: General, Human, Anger, Environment, Health, Economic, Earth
- <u>National Roles</u>: Religion, Defense, Money, Wealth, Education, Agriculture, Health, State, People, Labor
- <u>International Roles</u>: People, Government, Industry, International, Academia,

[143] On Bullshit, Harry G. Frankfurt, Princeton University Press, January 2005, ISBN 9780691122946.

Community, Money, Time

- Special Interests: Defense, Intelligence, Food, Health, Pharmaceuticals, Chemicals, Mining, Energy
- Emotions: Happy, Sad, Love, Hate, Fear
- Overall Reaction: Positive, Negative

Observation 16 Sustainability and Progress

Privatization Comments: It takes more to run our civilization than just privatization and the resulting entities. The world is complex.

The point is that generations upon generations of humans have identified thousands of approaches to solve problems. These approaches should always be revisited and expanded upon with each new challenge. In fact, technology might even help us to determine if we have exhausted our current list of approaches to a challenging problem.

9.13.9 Sustainability Practitioners

Although sustainable development is not new and it is obvious that we practiced some form of sustainable development to get us to this point in our history, it appears that something new has surfaced to cause such interest. Perhaps it is our increasing sensitivity to our technologies and systems and their impact on our world. Perhaps we are detecting that our current systems and technologies have reached their limits and it is time for the next step.

This text has suggested the next step in this quest for sustainability must include systems practices. It offers some suggestions to systems practitioners as they attempt to address sustainability in their system solutions. Although system practices are known in the systems community and the community gets very excited over small details of some aspect of a systems practice, the reality is that many outside the community need basic introduction to the field, especially those attempting to offer sustainable solutions.

9.14 Large Complex Systems

All systems have the potential to exhibit unintended consequences. Large systems in particular exhibit unintended consequences.

Observation 17 Large Complex Systems

Privatization Comments. Our systems that allow for billions of people to now inhabit the earth are complex. If they go bad the negative unintended consequences are massive and may last for generations. Relying on magic to get us through the next 100 years is not a viable option. The only option is the systems perspective based on science and common sense.

The approach to minimize the unintended consequences is to perform various analysis. As the analysis is performed the system architecture is modified until everyone agrees the system is fully understood. These systems analysis practices surfaced with the massive renaissance that occurred after 1945. The following extracts are a small sampling of the analysis practices.

9.14.1 Mission Critical Systems

Mission critical systems are systems where loss of life is possible if they fail. In the past there were few mission critical systems. Today almost every system is mission critical.

For example, a child's toy on the surface may appear to be non-mission critical. However, the toy may be compromised by a bad batch of paint that is poisonous because of an error made by a supplier. The system is not the toy but the entire production and distribution process. The system boundary is critical to ensure that the system is fully considered and not descoped to make the potential unintended consequences go away.

Many times, a system uses a machine to support the users. If the machine fails, there can be serious harm or loss of life. These mission critical systems typically support 3 single points of failure. This implies that there are 3 levels of redundancy. Further one of the redundant elements should be an orthogonal solution to avoid the possibility of a latent design defect appearing in each element simultaneously.

For example, a computer-based system might use 4 voting computers where 1 computer, the orthogonal element, is a different design and implemented by a different development team. An automobile has a brake system that uses 3 redundant elements, 2 of which are separate hydraulic elements, and the third is an orthogonal solution of a cable. This existed before the introduction of computer automation and was clearly adopted for the new computer-based systems.

9.14.2 Technology Readiness Levels

Technology assessment is used to determine the need to develop or inject technological advances into a system. The first step is to determine the current technological maturity of the system in terms of technology Readiness Levels (TRL). The second is to determine the difficulty and strategy for moving a technology from one TRL to the next.

TRL is a gage that measures the state of the art of a technology. There are different TRL scales associated with different organizations. There is overlap between the different scales and some translation may be needed as part of establishing the TRL scale for an organization. The following is a list of different organizations offering TRL scales:

- National Aeronautics and Space Administration (NASA)

- Department of Defense (DOD)
- North Atlantic Treaty Organization (NATO)
- European Space Agency (ESA)
- Federal Aviation Administration (FAA)

Table 34 Technology Readiness Levels - NASA[144]

NASA TRL	Description
1. Basic principles observed and reported.	Lowest level of technology readiness. Scientific research begins to be translated into applied research and development. Examples might include paper studies of a technology's basic properties.
2. Technology concept and / or application formulated.	Invention begins. Once basic principles are observed, practical applications can be invented. The application is speculative, and there is no proof or detailed analysis to support the assumption. Examples are still limited to paper studies.
3. Analytical and experimental critical function and / or characteristic **proof of concept**.	At this step in the maturation process, active research and development (R&D) is initiated. This must include both analytical studies to set the technology into an appropriate context and laboratory-based studies to physically validate that the analytical predictions are correct. These studies and experiments should constitute "proof-of-concept" validation of the applications / concepts formulated at TRL 2.
4. Component and / or **breadboard** validation in **laboratory environment**.	Following successful "proof-of-concept" work, basic technological elements must be integrated to establish that the pieces will work together to achieve concept-enabling levels of performance for a component and / or breadboard. This validation is devised to support the concept that was formulated earlier and also should be consistent with the requirements of potential system applications. The validation is relatively "low-fidelity" compared to the eventual system: it could be composed of ad hoc discrete components in a laboratory.
5. Component and / or **breadboard** validation in **relevant environment**.	At this level, the fidelity of the component and / or breadboard being tested has to increase significantly. The basic technological elements must be integrated with reasonably realistic supporting elements so that the total applications (component-level, subsystem-level, or system-level) can be tested in a "simulated" or somewhat realistic environment. A major step in the level of fidelity of the technology demonstration follows

[144] Generic TRL descriptions found in NPR 7123.1, NASA Systems Engineering Processes and Requirements, Table G-19.

Table 34 Technology Readiness Levels - NASA[144]

NASA TRL	Description
	the completion of TRL 5.
6. System / subsystem model or **prototype** demonstration in an operation environment.	A model or prototype system or system, which would go well beyond ad hoc, "patch-cord," or discrete component level breadboarding, would be tested in a relevant environment. At this level, if the only relevant environment is the environment of space, then the model or prototype must be demonstrated in space.
7. System **prototype** demonstration in an operational environment.	Prototype near or at planned operational system. TRL 7 is a significant step beyond TRL 6, requiring an actual system prototype demonstration in a space environment. The prototype should be near or at the scale of the planned operational system, and the demonstration must take place in space. Examples include testing the prototype in a test bed.
8. Actual system competed and "flight qualified" through test and demonstration.	Technology has been proven to work in its final form and under expected conditions. In almost all cases, this level is the end of true system development for most technology elements. This might include integration of new technology into an existing system.
9. Actual system flight proven through successful mission operations	Actual application of the technology in its final form and under mission conditions, such as those encountered in operational test and evaluation. In almost all cases, this is the end of the last "bug fixing" aspects of true system development. This TRL does not include planned product improvement of ongoing or reusable systems.

Although the TRL descriptions appear to be straightforward it is important to define the terms. Moving the domain from Space to a different domain such as Air Traffic Control will add even more confusion further necessitating clear definitions. Without these definitions trying to assign levels even in the space domain is a challenge. Many will think they can define a breadboard, but not everyone will have the same definition and the alternative definitions may be appropriate. This is a classic communications and perception problem that surfaces when a team starts to work on any problem. A relevant environment in one application may be irrelevant to another. Many of these terms cross engineering fields and had, at one time, very specific meanings to a particular field. The following TRL related definitions and terminology come from NASA[145] and can be used as a starting point:

[145] Lists hardware and software TRLs and offers a description of the terminology: Technology Readiness Levels (TRLs), NPR 7120.8, NASA Procedural Requirements, NASA Research and Technology Program and Project Management Requirements, February 05, 2008.

- **Proof of Concept (TRL 3)**: Analytical and experimental demonstration of hardware / software concepts that may or may not be incorporated into subsequent development and / or operational units.
- **Breadboard Laboratory (TRL 4)**: A low fidelity unit that demonstrates function only, without respect to form or fit in the case of hardware, or platform in the case of software. It often uses commercial and / or ad hoc components and is not intended to provide definitive information regarding operational performance.
- **Breadboard Relevant Environment (TRL 5 - 6)**: Sometimes called a Brassboard, a medium fidelity functional unit that typically tries to make use of as much operational hardware / software as possible and begins to address scaling issues associated with the operational system. It does not have the engineering pedigree in all aspects but is structured to be able to operate in simulated operational environments in order to assess performance of critical functions.
- **Prototype Unit (TRL 6 - 7)**: The prototype unit demonstrates form, fit, and function at a scale deemed to be representative of the final product operating in its operational environment. A subscale test article provides fidelity sufficient to permit validation of analytical models capable of predicting the behavior of full-scale systems in an operational environment.
- **Engineering Unit (TRL 6 - 8)**: A high fidelity unit that demonstrates critical aspects of the engineering processes involved in the development of the operational unit. Engineering test units are intended to closely resemble the final product (hardware / software) to the maximum extent possible and are built and tested so as to establish confidence that the design will function in the expected environments. In some cases, the engineering unit will become the final product, assuming proper traceability has been exercised over the components and hardware handling.
- **Mission Configuration (TRL 9)**: Final architecture / system design of the product that will be used in the operational environment. If the product is a subsystem / component, then it is embedded in the actual system in the actual configuration used in operation.
- **Laboratory Environment (TRL 1 - 4)**: An environment that does not address in any manner the environment to be encountered by the system, subsystem, or component (hardware or software) during its intended operation. Tests in a laboratory environment are solely for the purpose of demonstrating the underlying principles of technical performance (functions), without respect to the impact of environment.
- **Relevant Environment (nominally TRL 5)**: Not all systems, subsystems, and / or components need to be operated in the operational environment in order to

satisfactorily address performance margin requirements. Consequently, the relevant environment is the specific subset of the operational environment that is required to demonstrate critical "at risk" aspects of the final product performance in an operational environment. It is an environment that focuses specifically on "stressing" the technology advance in question.

- **Operational Environment (TRL 6 - 9)**: The environment in which the final product will be operated. In the case of space flight hardware / software, it is space. In the case of ground-based or airborne systems that are not directed toward space flight, it will be the environments defined by the scope of operations. For software, the environment will be defined by the operational platform.

Experience is needed to determine TRL. Even with clear definitions, deciding if a prototype is really a prototype or an engineering breadboard can be challenging. Describing elements in terms of form, fit, and function based on design intent and subsequent performance helps in assessing the TRL.

A team should perform the TRL assessment. Team members can be systems engineers, users, and other stakeholders. They do not have to be discipline experts, but they must understand the current state of the art technology. Some feel it should be well balanced and experienced. I feel the team should include young engineers, mathematicians, or scientists who will challenge the status quo. This will obviously require an open non-threatening environment. The questions, especially the obvious questions will stimulate learning and offer different perspectives.

There will be significant discussion when attempting to assign TRL numbers to the various system elements. Sometimes it helps to view the TRL elements from a different perspective. For example, a series of questions that frame the TRL can be developed with the accepted set of definitions and terms.

9.14.3 Safety

System safety is the hunt for unexpected hazards. If the unexpected can be discovered, then a system mechanism can be provided. The problem is one of finding the unexpected. Fault tree analysis and Failure Mode Effects Analysis (FMEA) are formal techniques for finding the unexpected. However, safety is generally addressed through past experience. These are hard painful lessons learned from history. Each domain has lists of safety hazards that have resulted in unsafe events. These lists need to be accessed and reviewed so that the team can focus on finding and addressing new safety issues related to their system.

Hazards are conditions that can lead to an unsafe situation that can result in or contribute to a mishap or accident. Are there general hazards that can apply to all systems? Can these general hazards be decomposed in the same way functions are decomposed and mitigated in the system? The short answer is yes. We are human biological systems with various subsystems that we can easily relate to and find hazards. The following is a list of our body's subsystems and possible hazards:

- **Light Hazards (Eyes)**: Mixing blue with other colors causes the eyes to constantly refocus thus potentially leading to myopia. Poor contrast ratio such as using gray letters on black buttons leads to eyestrain. Poor ambient light for documents or machine markings leads to eyestrain. Loss of night vision due to on coming bright lights or non-use of red lights in cabin instrumentation. Small letters forcing eye strain. Small objects with close placement forcing excessive crossing of eyes.
- **Noise Hazards (Ears)**: Excessive noise for short periods of time or low-level noise for long periods of time leading to hearing loss. Quick air pressure changes that may burst eardrums. Talking over loud ambient noise leading to strained vocal cords.
- **Physical Hazards (Body)**: Sharp edges that can cut. Poor placement causing frequent bumps and bruising. Excessive physical weight, shock (traumatic movement), or vibration that can pull muscles, damage tendons, or break bones. Repeated motion causing damaged tendons. Loud vocalizations for long periods of time.
- **Environmental Hazards (Body)**: Excessive heat or cold. Exposure to high voltage or radiation. Poor, polluted, or poisoned air. Dangerous substances or poisons ingested or absorbed by the skin. All of these can seriously damage the body.
- **Cognitive Processing Hazards (Brain or Mind)**: Shift changes that do not follow natural circadian cycles. Frequent shift changes with no time to transition internal body clock. Long periods of work without rest. Long periods before sleep cycles. Visual, sound, and or tactile sensory overload. Light and noise hazards, which result in unnecessary cognitive processing to detect images. Trying to detect garbled speech in high noise static settings. Trying to detect objects in high noise low contrast light settings. All of these lead to impaired thinking, judgement, and cognitive abilities.
- **Physical and Emotional Stress Hazards**: Can lead to temporary or permanent physical or cognitive impairment. Sources can be poor machine, social, and economic systems. For example, constant reorganization and workforce churn in a company or industry is a significant stress source with future indirect health care costs not paid by the offending system.

9.14.3.1 Safety Mitigation

There are various safety mitigation approaches. They each have their levels of effectiveness. The approaches for developing the safest system starting with the most effective and ending with the least effective are:

- **Inherently Safe**: Use design selection to make the architecture, design, and implementation inherently safe by eliminating the hazard. If the hazard cannot be removed, try to make the mishap of minimal consequence via an inherently safe approach exclusive of safety mechanisms.
- **Use Safety Devices**: If hazards cannot be eliminated or their risk not reduced through design selection use fixed, automatic, or other protective design features or devices. Consider fault tolerances and make provisions for periodic safety checks of the safety devices.
- **Warning Devices**: When Inherent Safety or Safety Devices are not possible, use devices to detect an unsafe condition and produce an adequate alarm signal to alert personnel of the hazard. The signals are designed to minimize incorrect personnel reaction. Standards when present are followed. Use a warning device for each Safety Device just in case it fails.
- **Procedures and Training**: When Inherent Safety, Safety Devices, or Warning Devices are not possible, use procedures and training to mitigate the risk. Procedures and training can include personal protective equipment, checklists, and two or more people checking each other's actions in a fault tolerant process. Certification or personnel proficiency training is used for safety-critical tasks and activities. For Level 1 and 2 hazards using just warning, caution, or other forms of write advisories is unacceptable. They can be used but the hazard remains, and appropriate approvals are needed as part of the hazard risk acceptance rules. Use procedures and training as a backup mechanism for other mitigation approaches just in case they fail.

9.14.3.2 Levels of Automation and Safety

Within the safety critical boundary there is software that has different characteristics. These characteristics lead to different levels of rigor that should be applied as part of the safety process. The roots go back to very early software-based systems and are based on the concept of levels of automation. The more automation offered by the software with less ability for a human to understand the situation or override the results, the more critical. As the years have passed the levels and definitions have changed but the concept of automation level has been the driver.

Table 35 Software Control Categories – Historical

MIL-STD-882C	RTCA-DO-178B
(I) Software exercises autonomous control over potentially hazardous hardware systems, subsystems or components without the possibility of intervention to preclude the occurrence of a hazard. Failure of the software or a failure to prevent an event leads directly to a hazard occurrence.	(A) Software whose anomalous behavior, as shown by the system safety assessment process, would cause or contribute to a failure of system function resulting in a catastrophic failure condition for the aircraft. (B) Software whose anomalous behavior, as

Table 35 Software Control Categories – Historical

MIL-STD-882C	RTCA-DO-178B
(IIa) Software exercises control over potentially hazardous hardware systems, subsystems, or components allowing time for intervention by independent safety systems to mitigate the hazard. However, these systems by themselves are not considered adequate. (IIb) Software item displays information requiring immediate operator action to mitigate a hazard. Software failure will allow or fail to prevent the hazard's occurrence. (IIIa) Software items issues commands over potentially hazardous hardware systems, subsystem, or components requiring human action to complete the control function. There are several, redundant, independent safety measures for each hazardous event. (IIIb) Software generates information of a safety critical nature used to make safety critical decisions. There are several, redundant, independent safety measures for each hazardous event. (IV) Software does not control safety critical hardware systems, subsystems, or components and does not provide safety critical information.	shown by the System Safety assessment process, would cause or contribute to a failure of system function resulting in a hazardous/severe-major failure condition of the aircraft. (C) Software whose anomalous behavior, as shown by the system safety assessment process, would cause or contribute to a failure of system function resulting in a major failure condition for the aircraft. (D) Software whose anomalous behavior, as shown by the system safety assessment process, would cause or contribute to a failure of system function resulting in a minor failure condition for the aircraft. (E) Software whose anomalous behavior, as shown by the system safety assessment process, would cause or contribute to a failure of function with no effect on aircraft operational capability or pilot workload. Once software has been confirmed as level E by the certification authority, no further guidelines of this document apply.

The latest software control categories clearly mix an implementation approach that helps to address the safety issues associated with software. The implementation approach is fault tolerance and redundancy. The fact that this element is introduced suggests that the software does perform some level of safety critical processing.

Table 36 Software Control Categories - Latest[146]

Level	Name	Description
1	Autonomous (AT)	Software functionality that exercises autonomous control

[146] System Safety, DOD Standard Practice, MIL-STD-882E, 11 May 2012.

Table 36 Software Control Categories - Latest[146]

Level	Name	Description
		authority over potentially safety-significant hardware systems, subsystems, or components without the possibility of predetermined safe detection and intervention by a control entity to preclude the occurrence of a mishap or hazard. (This definition includes complex system/software functionality with multiple subsystems, interacting parallel processors, multiple interfaces, and safety-critical functions that are time critical.)
2	Semi- Autonomous (SAT)	Software functionality that exercises control authority over potentially safety-significant hardware systems, subsystems, or components, allowing time for predetermined safe detection and intervention by independent safety mechanisms to mitigate or control the mishap or hazard. (This definition includes the control of moderately complex system/software functionality, no parallel processing, or few interfaces, but other safety systems/mechanisms can partially mitigate. System and software fault detection and annunciation notifies the control entity of the need for required safety actions.) Software item that displays safety-significant information requiring immediate operator entity to execute a predetermined action for mitigation or control over a mishap or hazard. Software exception, failure, fault, or delay will allow, or fail to prevent, mishap occurrence. (This definition assumes that the safety-critical display information may be time-critical, but the time available does not exceed the time required for adequate control entity response and hazard control.)
3	Redundant Fault Tolerant (RFT)	Software functionality that issues commands over safety-significant hardware systems, subsystems, or components requiring a control entity to complete the command function. The system detection and functional reaction includes redundant, independent fault tolerant mechanisms for each defined hazardous condition. (This definition assumes that there is adequate fault detection, annunciation, tolerance, and system recovery to prevent the hazard occurrence if software fails, malfunctions, or degrades. There are redundant sources of

Table 36 Software Control Categories - Latest[146]

Level	Name	Description
		safety-significant information and mitigating functionality can respond within any time-critical period.) Software that generates information of a safety-critical nature used to make critical decisions. The system includes several redundant, independent fault tolerant mechanisms for each hazardous condition, detection and display.
4	Influential	Software generates information of a safety-related nature used to make decisions by the operator but does not require operator action to avoid a mishap.
5	No Safety Impact (NSI)	Software functionality that does not possess command or control authority over safety-significant hardware systems, subsystems, or components and does not provide safety-significant information. Software does not provide safety-significant or time sensitive data or information that requires control entity interaction. Software does not transport or resolve communication of safety-significant or time sensitive data.

Associating safety critical software functions with control categories allows for the identification and prioritization effort. The safety critical code can receive the appropriate robustness and level of rigor over the lifecycle without wasting resources in other software areas not needing the same levels of robustness and rigor. The software with the highest level of control over safety critical hardware receives more attention or level of rigor than software with less safety risk potential. Autonomous software with functional links to catastrophic hazards demands more coverage than software that influences low severity hazards.

9.14.4 Security

Security is a systems practice that everyone can relate to because it is fundamental like eating, breathing, drinking, being safe, etc. There are instinctive responses that guide us in the area of security. However, there are basic elements of security that have been established and are used to help us develop secure systems.

Security is about protecting something of value from a threat. All things have value and all things have threats. The issues are do the things have sufficient value and are the threats likely to happen such that protection is needed. For example, your life has great value and if you live in a high crime rate area or war zone you have real threats that you acknowledge and try to avoid.

Protecting life and property are physical things that physical security addresses. However, security also applies to non-physical things. There are virtual things, which may manifest in a physical form such as a document, storage media, Internet cloud, etc. Examples include your identity, bank account, personal information, employee performance appraisals, your image (picture), ownership records, court records, etc. This is typically referred to as information security.

There are security techniques and mechanisms that can be used to assess and protect physical and or information items. The initial physical and information security elements to consider are:

- **Threat Assessment**: Identify the things that must be protected or secured and rate their importance or value.
- **Security Perimeter**: Establish security perimeters or boundaries and place the most important or valuable items in the inner most security boundaries.
- **Penetration Analysis**: Identify the threats, determine the changes of each threat associated with an item penetrating the boundary. Once the boundary is penetrated determine the impact (loss of life, physical harm, significant financial harm, etc)

As the security analysis and architecture are further refined additional security techniques and mechanisms need to be considered. Those that tend to be associated more with information security are the need to know, authentication, and non-repudiation. Other security elements to consider are security abuse, simplicity, logging auditing, overhead impacts.

9.14.4.1 Threat Assessment

Threat assessment starts by building a list of items to be protected. The next step is to assign importance or value to each of the items in the list. The items in the list should be grouped and re-grouped based on their relationships to each other and their importance or value. At this time there may be a desire to start to discuss the security boundary or perimeter. Allow the discussions and thoughts to freely flow. For example, a company has many databases. What are the most valuable company databases that need to be protected from a threat?

Financial	Internal Process Documents
Contracts	Payroll
Employee Performance Appraisals	Employee Retirement
Product Documents	Employee 401K
Intellectual Property Documents	Employee Health Selection

It is hard to separate the threat from the list of secured items. For example, some will view the external threat of theft by a competitor. Others view the internal threat of lost data due to broken equipment or operator error. Others may view the internal threat from an employee just given a termination notice. It does not matter on the view, make a full list and place a threat assessment against each item in the list.

Table 37 Security Threat Assessment Levels

Level	Threat Assessment	Description
1	Grave	Loss of life or Physical Harm
2	Financially Catastrophic	Financially destroys an organization or and individual, no chance of recovery
3	Financially Devastating	Financial losses causing reorganization or change in lifestyle
4	Financially Serious	Financial losses leading to setbacks in plans, investments, or savings / profits
5	Financially Insignificant	No impact on organization or individual

It is critical that all stakeholders be considered not just the entity needing security. For example, an organization pushing responsibility to employees to not divulge proprietary information on a company tool that is implemented on an Internet cloud system is irresponsible and violates common sense security. The company should host the tool on its own computer network inside its own security boundary or inspect and validate all information before it is transferred to the Internet cloud computing service.

9.14.4.2 Security Perimeter

A security perimeter is a boundary that prevents possible threats from entering and causing harm.

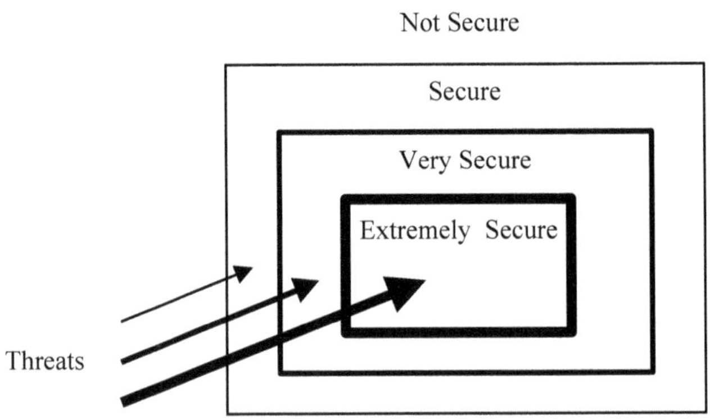

Figure 74 Security Perimeter

For example, a barn for chickens protects them from wolves. There can be multiple security perimeters or layers such that the least secure area is the outside perimeter and the most secure is the inside perimeter. For example, a chicken farm may have a fence around the barn area, a barn, and a room with closing doors in the barn housing new baby chickens. Breaking into the most secure area requires penetrating several security boundaries, each becoming more challenging to penetrate.

9.14.4.3 Inherent Security No Security Perimeters

It there a way to secure a system without having one or more security boundaries. Is such a system more secure than one that does have security boundaries? Such a system is inherently secure. No security mechanisms are needed to offer security. There is no need for a security boundary.

For example, you can implement a software tool on a computer network that is completely isolated. There are no connections anywhere. The application might be to prepare your tax returns and store your financial information using an isolated standalone computer in a locked house. Alternatively, you can implement the tax tool on a computer network connected to the Internet. The data is stored on your computer, but the computer is connected to the Internet. The computer network may be very secure with multiple security boundary levels, but it will always be less secure than the totally isolated computer. Finally, you can prepare your tax return using an Internet cloud computing service where the data is stored on the cloud. Your trust moves from a locked house, to the Internet that will not try to scan your computer, to a vendor that processes and stores your data that will not compromise it even if it goes out of business.

9.14.4.4 Penetration Analysis

Penetration analysis is a study of the effectiveness of the security architecture or approach. The system is subjected to threats and an assessment is made. An approach is to use fault tree analysis to security. The fault in this case is loss of security for a class of items. The basic events represent the threats and the logic gates represent the security architecture. There may or may not be redundancies in the security architecture. For example, a perimeter fence with dogs and cats roaming the barn area to protect the farm animals are examples of redundancy that can be captured in the fault tree analysis.

Once a threat has been shown to penetrate a boundary it needs to be assessed. This assessment was performed as part of threat assessment, but it needs to be transferred or copied to the penetration analysis. The number of security failures then characterizes it. In general, the more serious the threat, the more security elements and backup mechanisms should be broken.

For example, if a grave threat surfaces and three or more backup mechanisms failed then the architecture is considered acceptable[147]. However, if the grave threat

---

[147] Loss of automobile breaks is a threat and can lead to loss of life. There are two hydraulic breaks (primary and secondary) and one manual cable based parking brake.

surfaces with just the breakage of two backup mechanisms then the security architecture needs to be improved until there are a minimum of three failed backup mechanisms to allow the grave threat to penetrate.

Table 38 Penetration Analysis Criteria

Level	Penetration Result	Minimum
1	Grave	Three backup security mechanisms fail.
2	Financially Catastrophic	Two backup security mechanisms fail.
3	Financially Devastating	Multiple security mechanisms fail.
4	Financially Serious	Security mechanism failed.
5	Financially Insignificant	No security mechanisms triggered.

9.14.4.5 Compartmentalization or Need to Know

Compartmentalization or need to know is fundamental in information security and is similar in concept to Impact of Failure (IOF) described in this text. The goal is to reduce the impact of information loss by limiting access to the information. Only the people who need private information to perform their jobs have access to the private information. This is called need to know.

People who have access to private information with no need to know are potential threats just like people who have a need to know, but they increase the size of the threat pool. The concept is that the more people that know about a private information database the greater the threat. So, the approach is to reduce the size of the pool and remove access from those with no need to know the information.

9.14.4.6 Authentication

Security authentication is confirming the identity of an individual or machine. There are four approaches to authenticating an individual:

- **Special Knowledge**: such as a username and password, employee number, social security number, account number, etc.
- **Physical Token**: such as a badge with name a picture, automobile key, house key, electronic device with changing alpha numeric pattern, electronic key stick, etc.
- **Biological Evidence**: such as fingerprint, retinal pattern, hand pattern, signature, face, voice, etc.
- **Third Party**: such as an authenticated employee signing in an employee that forgot their badge, a bouncer at the door of a knight club screening potential customers for entry, etc

Authentication can use one or more authentication approaches. Many times, in very secure computer settings special knowledge in the form of a user name password and a computer security token is offered. When accessing very secure facilities a token such as a badge and either special knowledge in the form of access code or biological evidence such as a signature is offered.

9.14.4.7 Access Control

Access control is a mechanism that allows authorities to control access to physical areas and information. In order to gain access, the entity requesting access needs to be authenticated. If proper authentication is not provided the entity is denied access. This can be in the form of a security guard or guards protecting a perimeter or a machine denying access to a physical location or its services.

9.14.4.8 Privileges

Once access is granted to an area, certain privileges are associated with the access. These privileges for physical security are unlimited. You can walk within the entire security perimeter. However, in the case of information security access may be associated with different privilege attributes. These privilege attributes are a function of the domain. For example, in banking they can be associated with deposit, withdraw, and transaction records privilege access attributes. In the case of a computer they can be read, write, and program execute privilege attributes.

Privileges also exist at different levels. For example, someone can allow their information to be shared with a group. The sharing can be one or more of the privilege attribute settings. There is also the concept of a super authority, which can access everything at any time. Examples of super authorities are government via court actions, potentially internal system maintainers, and potentially trusted internal system operating specialists.

9.14.4.9 Nonrepudiation

Nonrepudiation is a mechanism where the source or recipient cannot deny that the source is not the originating source or that a third party cannot claim that the originating source is not the source. This accomplished using a trusted third-party person, a trust third party machine, or mutually exchanged receipts.

When a contract is signed a third party also can sign the contract stating that they witnessed the signature of one or both parties. A notary public with an official number and stamp is used to witness many contract signatures such as for the transfer of real estate property. The third-party signature is the mechanism that supports non-repudiation in a contract. A notary will check the identity of the individual, maintain a log of the transaction, and complete the signature with a note identifying the type of identity credential checked (e.g. driver license).

Another approach to non-repudiation is to issue a receipt to both parties and have both parties acknowledge the mutual receipt exchange. For example, in a transaction involving the transfer of goods and services in exchange for currency, the exchange is completed only when a receipt is generated and given to both parties. There is also a log generated, which may be in the form of another copy of the paper receipt or it may be an electronic entry in a computer file. The transaction is not complete until both parties acknowledge and receive the receipt. So, a transaction is a mechanism that supports non-repudiation via the receipts. There is no third party, but the source and recipient acknowledge both receipts (copy to buyer and copies to seller).

Nonrepudiation in the digital Internet domain is accomplished with third party electronic certificates coming from trusted electronic certificate authorities. The certificates are used in the public key infrastructure to establish an encrypted trusted communication mechanism on an open network. The certificates attest that the identity and public key belong together in the web of trust. The web servers log the various server requests.

The strongest non-repudiation mechanism is a trusted third-party person and the weakest is the mutual exchange of receipts. Third party witnessing and transaction receipts have an extremely long history. Trusted third party machines is a relatively new development that arose with the proliferation of the Internet and online business transactions.

9.14.4.10 Basic Security Systems

At this point there is sufficient information to discuss the fundamentals of security. This section is a combination of thought experiments or what-ifs and knowledge transfer.

When you go to a bank you open an account and list yourself as the account holder. You are given an account number and you provide your name, personal information, and a handwritten signature. Until the bank tellers get to know you, you need to provide your account number, some form of identification, usually with a picture, and a signature. At that point you deposit or withdraw from your account. You are given a transaction receipt. You can add other people to your account. They may be only authorized to make deposits but no withdraws. Or they may be authorized to make deposits and withdraws but no access to transaction records. These people are now part of your group and you assign appropriate account privilege attributes for your group (deposit or deposit and withdraw). If you break the law and are found guilty the government may gain a court order to access your account. They may decide the entire bank location has a problem and they may request access to multiple accounts. As part of this process they can review the deposit and withdraw records and confiscate the account balances. In this simple bank thought experiment are the fundamentals of security: authentication, access control, privileges, and non-repudiation.

Visualize a time when people thought that one massive computer could provide processing services for thousands of people with very different needs. That time existed in the 1960's. The thought process was that the central computer was extremely expensive and needed to be centralized to keep costs to a minimum. People would use terminals that offered a display screen, keyboard, pointing device, and perhaps voice recognition and synthesis. How would people keep their work separate such that an error from one user would not propagate to thousands of users? How would they ensure their data was private and secure? What was born was the multi-user multi-tasking operating system and one implementation was called UNIX.

A UNIX[148] account is accessed via a user name and a password that is set by the user. The password is encrypted so no one knows its pattern. If forgotten the account needs to be reset with a new temporary password. Once logged in the user is assigned virtual memory for program use and a computer time slice to run programs. The user is also given storage space to house data and programs. The virtual memory is completely private. No one can access it. Further the current users' programs cannot go beyond the users assigned virtual memory. If the user creates a broken program with an endless loop the computer time slice cannot be exceeded so the other users are not impacted. Once logged in the user decides the file and program execution privileges. The privilege attributes are read, write, and execute. The privilege levels are user, group, and everyone. The defaults are set by your account and start with only the user having read, write, and execute privileges. These privileges are clearly shown when listing the directory content using three groups of three letters. From left to right the first three letters are the privileges for all, followed by the next three letters which are the privileges for a group, followed by the last three letters which are the privileges for the user.

- rwx rwx rwx Everyone has read write execute access
- r-- rw- rwx Everyone has read access, group has read write access

When an account is created it is either a user account, a user account associated with one or more groups, or a super user or root account with unlimited privileges.

So, the UNIX security approach follows the manual security approach used for hundreds of years in domains such as banking. The idea is to attach authentication, access control, privileges, and non-repudiation to a person, group of people, or a super account.

Recently security mechanisms have surfaced which attach security attributes and levels to data elements. This obviously translates to enormous complexity, because in the end someone in the form of a person needs to assign the security settings. This becomes interesting because people tend to make mistakes and the more they

---

[148] I had the privilege of using a Systems Engineering Labs (SEL) 3277 with the MPX-32 operating system circa 1980. A few dozen Hazeltine monochrome terminals provided multi-user access and I never used a keypunch again.

have to do, the greater the number of mistakes.

9.14.4.11 Security and Simplicity

Inherent in security is simplicity. It is like fault tolerance. The simpler the mechanisms the more secure. The less people have to do the more secure. When establishing a security boundary simplicity also translates to smaller size. That is why a reasonable threat assessment needs to be performed. If everything in the system is tagged at the same high threat level, then there is high probability nothing will be secure as the system struggles with traditional system load and capacity issues. Simplicity also translates to making sure the things that need protecting are protected and not surrounded by less critical system elements that burden the security-processing core.

9.14.4.12 Security Overhead Impacts

Security always translates to system overhead. The overhead results in reduced response time and more processing needs. This translates to cost. If the system is subjected to excessive security processing because of a poor threat assessment, security effectiveness will decrease.

9.14.4.13 Security Logging and Auditing

Security logging tracks certain security related events. For example, access logs for visitors into a facility can be used which record a visitor's identity, association, contact information, escort name, time in, and time out. A computer can log users attempting to log into a system. Successful and unsuccessful attempts can be logged with information such as user account, time stamp, and number of failed login attempts. A website may have logging enabled, which shows the visiting domain or Internet Protocol (IP) address, what link they went to on the site, what link they came from on the Internet, and their software configuration (operating system and browser).

Once logs are generated, they can be audited to look for security concerns. Repeated attempts to break into user accounts may cause changes to the user account visibility or access to the login screen. Review of web server logs may show repeated attempts to deny service and the decision might be to block one or more IP addresses at the router. Auditing is also a review of the security mechanism and its records. The audit may involve physical inspections of facilities, computer logs, reports, actions taken, etc.

9.14.4.14 Fail Secure

Fail secure acknowledges that if there is any unexpected system failure, the system fails in a secure state. A secure state is achieved if no security compromise is possible. For example, a broken access control mechanism should fail such that access is prevented under all but the most extreme trusted conditions.

9.14.4.15 Security Monitor

A security monitor is a passive mechanism that searches for insecure patterns. A camera in a bank or department store coupled to some form of processing to detect insecure patterns is an example. A separate computer program that scans all inputs, outputs, and process start-ups shutdowns is another example of a security monitor. This is generally referred to as virus detection software. A monitor may or may not act if a security issue is detected. For example, a security monitor may detect three unsuccessful account login attempts and lock the account requiring the user to be re-established in the system. Re-establishing the account is accomplished with a more secure mechanism.

A security monitor takes resources away from the system. It becomes less and less effective as more elements are monitored more often. If everything is monitored, it is not a very effective approach to security. A count of the incorrect number of logins mechanism (three tries and account is locked) is an effective security monitor. It is also better than forcing users to have long obscure passwords that they will just write down. Alternatively scanning every piece of data entering a computer is not an effective security monitor as evidenced by the constant release of virus scanning software and patterns. In fact, this approach always results in some number of users being compromised before the new security (virus) detection pattern and or software is released. A good analogy is that you cannot monitor every blade of grass and then tell each blade of grass which direction it should grow. It eventually becomes silly and futile.

9.14.4.16 Additional Information Security Elements

Information security protects information from unauthorized access, viewing, recording, disclosure, modification, use, disruption, and destruction. Information security uses all traditional security elements discussed thus far and includes new elements of confidentiality, integrity, and availability.

- **Integrity**: Data cannot be modified without detection. There are many mechanisms such as error detection codes and electronic signatures that can be used to ensure the data is not modified.
- **Confidentiality**: Information is not disclosed to unauthorized individuals or systems. This can be accomplished by encrypting the data transmissions, access control, and physical layouts that prevent over the shoulder computer screen views.
- **Availability**: Service is always available when needed. The system can become unavailable because of hardware, software, and operator failures. It also can

become unavailable because of an attack such as denial of service.

9.14.4.17 Secure Architectures

As in all architecture approaches, the best security architecture is the simplest least complex approach. As complexity increases so does the possibility of failure.

Complexity can be measured by the number of functions, interfaces, and items subjected to security. Complexity also can be measured by the number of people in the loop. They are in the loop because of flexibility that does not lend itself well to automation. The problem is that people make mistakes especially under stressful repetitive conditions. As with all architectures there are collections of tricks and lessons learned that should be considered:

- **Changing computer passwords too frequently**. Forcing the use of very obscure passwords. Too many passwords. These will lower security as people violate policy and write them down. A better approach might be to lock the account after three unsuccessful login attempts.
- **Applying the same tight security screening measures equally** to all threat elements even those that are obviously very low security threat levels. This wastes precious resources that can be applied to the real potential threats.
- **Not logging security related events**. Not reviewing the logs. Not using automation techniques to review the logs.
- **Ignoring audit findings**. Not modifying or improving the system when there are security breaches.

9.14.4.18 Security Abuse

Security abuse is an interesting concept. Everyone is familiar with the concept of people given special privileges in the name of security and then abusing these privileges. History is full of horrific events in this regard. Electronic security abuse is new. The following is a sampling of recent security abuses:

- Blocking access to legitimate websites because of security software filters thus infringing or breaking restraint of free trade laws in the U.S.
- Forcing users to frequently change or have obscure passwords rather than unsuccessful login account activity detection and block.
- Allowing computer operating systems that are inherently insecure to proliferate through an infrastructure.
- Forcing automated downloads and installation without user knowledge or understanding.
- In large systems there is the simple concept of freezing a proven stable baseline. Serious damage is done with moving baselines and unstable releases.

9.14.4.19 Sources of Security Failure

There are many sources of security failure. Obviously understanding the domain with a history of known issues and applying Fault Tree Analysis and Failure Mode Effect Analysis (FMEA) can surface security failures. When people think of security they automatically think of threats. However, security can break down in the absence of any threat. Security can break down as part of normal system operations. The following is a list of various security failures:

- **Non-Security Failure**: The system normally breaks, and security information is left vulnerable. This does not mean security is compromised. It is only compromised if a threat can capitalize on the situation.
- **Untested Latent Defect**: Some aspect of the system is untested, and an internal set of conditions results in security information left vulnerable. Again, this does not mean security is compromised. It is only compromised if a threat can capitalize on the situation.
- **Latent Defect Exploit**: Some aspect of the system is untested, and an adversary exploits it to gain access to the system and cause a security failure.
- **Security Failure**: A clever threat breaks through the security mechanisms and can gain access to the system and cause a security failure.
- **Trusted People Mistakes**: Trusted people make undetected human mistakes, which leaves information vulnerable.
- **Trusted People Compromised**: Trusted people are compromised and willingly compromise security either by disrupting security mechanisms and or transferring trusted information to unauthorized users.

9.14.5 Fault Tolerance and Fail-Safe

Fault tolerance and fail-safe systems is a broad subject that branches into all aspects of faults, errors, and failures. The broad approaches to dealing with system failures are fault avoidance, fault removal, and finally fault tolerance. When it is realized that a system needs fault tolerance then all the other approaches to mitigate faults should have been used in the system. It is like a layering approach where the final layer is fault tolerance. Before we can begin discussing fault tolerance, we need to appreciate all aspects of faults, errors, failures and the approaches to dealing with them in a system.

The approach to fault tolerance is to add redundancy to a system through replication. If the main part should break the redundant element can support the function. The redundancy can be inherent in the structure of the system or a special consideration of the system. For example, a wood frame house uses walls made of 2x4 wood studs placed some distance apart from each other. A typical wall will have several 2x4 studs and if one or two studs should break the wall will remain intact. It is inherently fault tolerant and redundant.

In the case of physical structures, replication can only be accomplished with the addition of physical items. The replicated physical items can be of the same type or a different type. The redundant structure can duplicate the main structure or be a completely different structure. For example, a bridge can be replicated by using two side-by-side structures. Alternatively, a bridge can be backed up by another bridge a few miles away using the same materials and structure or different materials and structure. One or more ferries also can back up a bridge.

If the same materials and structure are used for redundancy, then the backup is a replication. If different materials and or structures are used, then the backup is a redundant element but not a replication. Fault tolerance tends to be stronger if replication is not used for redundancy because replication may have an unknown single point of failure. For example, termites or fire can compromise wood studs.

In the case of a process the replication or redundancy can be physical and or time displaced. A physical structure implements the process so the same physical redundancy approaches can be used. However, processes rarely use the physical structure 100% of the time. So, the process can be duplicated in different time slots and compared against previous process runs. The duplicate process can follow the same design and algorithms or use a different design or algorithms. It can be designed and implemented by the same team or a different team.

Fail-safe is acknowledging that if there is any unexpected failure, the system fails in a safe manner. Many times, this means a graceful degradation or loss of functions so that the system can continue to operate but at a significantly reduced performance and or functional level, otherwise the loss of the system might lead to an unsafe condition.

One approach to making a fail-safe system is to use fault tolerance. The system continues to operate in the presence of one or more failures. However, in the most extreme mission critical systems, fault tolerance may not be enough, and the system must fail safely no matter what. Typically, that means the system stops and the human takes over the function.

When developing a fail-safe system, a failure analysis is performed where unsafe events are identified, and fault trees are developed. This is a top down approach that starts early with the architecture and is refined as the design and implementation unfold. There also may be a failure modes and effects analysis. This is a bottom up approach where each component in a system is broken and then the system impact is determined. This uses the final design information and may also use the final production system that is subjected to test as each component is broken. Based on the failure analysis findings the system is then structured and modified to mitigate the unsafe events.

Most safety issues are traceable to human error. It is the job of the automation system or manual process to protect the humans from themselves by making sure they do not make errors. If an airplane falls from the sky normally the airplane is blamed for the failure rather than the pilot (e.g. wing falls off). If an airplane crashes on the ground with no evidence of failure in the sky the pilot is blamed rather than faulting the system. The reality is that automated pilot control surfaced over 60 years ago. To blame a pilot for a system failure that should protect the pilot against human error is no longer appropriate unless criminal activity can be identified where the pilot wants the aircraft to crash.

9.14.6 Human Factors

This section is large. I wanted to pass on some of this information because there is so much disregard for human factors in all our modern systems. The issue is all our systems are about us and helping all of us to live better. Privatization as a system is no different. In theory it should have helped us to live better.

When we think of human factors, we focus our attention on the modern machine age and how humans interact with our modern-day machines. However, human factors are as old as our civilization. You know when you have properly fitting garments. You know when you sit in a comfortable chair. You know when you sit at a nice table of food. How was the decision made for the size of a plate, fork, and knife? How was the decision made for the size of a door, a window, a room size? We can usually detect bad human factors design decisions. However, sometimes we cannot detect subtle human factors design errors. This can result in loss of health such as damaged eyes, ears, vocal cords, muscles, tendons, bones, nerves, etc.

After World War II there was great interest in understanding how we humans interact with our environment. Labs were established and extensive studies were performed in these great labs. Sometimes the studies were trivial and common sense and at other times the studies were significant. In all cases they needed to be reflected in our systems. In 1958 the Public Law 85-726, known as the Federal Aviation Act of 1958, established the Federal Aviation Administration (FAA). The following is an excerpt from the Federal Aviation Act of 1958:

"The Administrator shall develop, modify, test, and evaluate systems, procedures, facilities, and devices, as well as define the performance characteristics thereof, to meet the needs for safe and efficient navigation and traffic control of all civil and military aviation except for those needs of military agencies which are peculiar to air warfare and primarily of military concern, and select such systems, procedures, facilities, and devices as will best serve such need and will promote maximum coordination of air traffic control and air defense systems. The Administrator shall undertake or supervise ***research*** *to develop a better understanding of the relationship between human factors and aviation accidents and between human factors and air safety, to enhance air traffic controller and mechanic and flight crew performance, to develop a human-factor analysis of the hazards associated with new technologies to be used by air traffic controllers, mechanics, and flight crews, and to identify innovative and effective corrective measures for human errors which adversely affect air safety. The Administrator*

shall undertake or supervise a ***research*** *program to develop dynamic simulation models of the air traffic control system and airport design and operating procedures which will provide analytical technology for predicting airport and air traffic control safety and capacity problems, for evaluating planned research projects, and for testing proposed revisions in airport and air traffic control operations programs. The Administrator shall undertake or supervise* ***research*** *programs concerning airspace and airport planning and design, airport capacity enhancement techniques, human performance in the air transportation environment, aviation safety and security, the supply of trained air transportation personnel including pilots and mechanics, and other aviation issues pertinent to developing and maintaining a safe and efficient air transportation system."*

Observation 18 Human Factors

Privatization Comments: It is unlikely that industry would perform any of the research required by the new government organization, the FAA. This is something that industry should not be expected to do or burdened with as they pursue valid commercial industrial commerce. This is a government function and traces to the founding requirements of the US[149].

We all know that we have our five senses of sight, sound, hearing, taste, and feeling[150]. We also know that our physical bodies can only carry so much, reach so far, withstand certain temperatures, take a certain amount of G forces, pressure, and loss of atmosphere. We also know our bodies need a certain amount of water and food and must excrete a certain amount of waste. This is all common sense for the modern industrial human. However, when we think of our systems, this common sense can easily be lost. Further, the details may be unknown to those outside the specialty-engineering role of human factors.

9.14.6.1 Human Factors Basics

When the system boundary is drawn broad enough there is always human interaction. Human factors address physical and cognitive needs of humans. Social behavior and psychological needs are also elements that many tend to ignore. This human interaction or human factors is an extremely important aspect of all systems. Although MIL-STD-1472[151] is broad and deep, it is an excellent starting point for all teams to review. Some of the more important human factor topics include:

---

149 See section 9.2.7 Key Requirements Specifications and Traceability.

150 Human Information Processing, Peter H. Lindsay, Donald A. Norman, Academic Press, 1977.

151 Human Engineering Design Criteria, DOD, MIL-STD-1472C May 1981, MIL-STD-1472D March 1989, MIL-STD-1472E October 1996, MIL-STD-1472F August 1999.

Vision and Displays
Hearing and Audio
Voice and Phraseology
Touch and Tactile Feedback
Ergonomics
Taste and Smell
Sensory Overload
Feed Back
Response Time
Vision Versus Sound
Visual and Sound Noise
Circadian Sleep Cycles
Stress Sources
Ethics

9.14.6.2 Vision and Displays

We can use our basic understanding of system decomposition to identify our bodies' functions and their subsystems. The eye is an example of a subsystem. Understanding this subsystem is key to integrating it into our systems. When we address vision there are key topics that should be considered:

- Night Vision
- Display Flicker
- Field of View
- Color Use
- Contrast
- Display Distance
- Display Surface Area
- Text Size

An image is projected on our retina, which is lined with rod and cone cells. The eye uses rods and cones to detect light. Rod density is greater in the peripheral retina than in the central retina. The rods are more sensitive than the cones but are only able to detect what we perceive as monochrome or black and white images. The cones require more light but are able to detect color and fine detail.

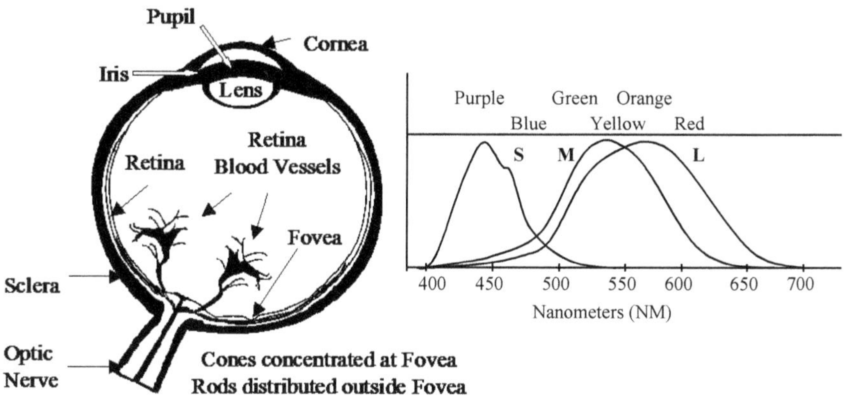

Figure 75 Human Eye Cone Cell Response Curves

The cones are densely concentrated near the fovea. There are few cones present at the sides of the retina. We can detect more details in the center or the fovea region. Images are also most sharply in focus at the fovea, when directly looking at an object. Not far from the fovea, near the center of the retina there are nerve connections, so there is a blind spot in this region. The eye compensates for this blind spot and different detection characteristics by involuntarily movement. If the eye were to become perfectly stationary the rods and cones would stop firing and the image would fade.

There are three types of cone cells that respond to different frequencies of light. There is overlap between the response curves of the cells. The greatest overlap is with the cells that detect red and green. Cone cells that respond mostly to long light wavelengths are designated L for long and peak in the red region. Cone cells that respond mostly to medium light wavelength are designated M for medium and peak at green. Cone cells that respond mostly to short wavelength light are designated S for short and peak in the blue region. The signals received from the three cone cell types let the brain perceive all possible colors. Rod cells have peak sensitivity at 498 nanometers (nm) this is approximately the Blue-Green region.

Table 39 Eye Cone Cells and Color Ranges

Cone Cells	Color (nm)	Range (nm)	Peak wavelength (nm)
S	470 Blue	400–500	430
S + M	493 Blue Green	-	-
M	500 Green	450–630	540
M + L	535 Yellow Green	-	-
M + L	570 Yellow	-	-
M + L	600 Orange	-	-
L	700 Red	500–700	570

9.14.6.2.1 Night Vision and Eye Rods and Cones

As the brightness increases our rods saturate and stop detecting the image while the cones start to activate and begin to detect the image. If the light is suddenly reduced, the rods will not detect any images until they have time to recover. This is referred to as night vision recovery and it can take several minutes for the rods to recover and allow someone see in the low light condition. Light in the red band does not impact rod night vision. So, instrument gages in aircraft use red lighting. In facilities where there is the possibility of the loss of all lighting, emergency lighting is red. Maintaining night vision in such settings may save lives.

Automobiles use red lights on the back to indicate their presence and to show when a driver is stopping. If the lights were "white" then the night vision of the person following the vehicle would be lost. The white lights are needed on the front of a vehicle so that the driver can see the road, but now there is the possibility of damaging night vision of drivers from ongoing vehicles. So, there is a delicate balance where the lights are directed down towards the road. Some light is permitted to go above the road so signs with light reflecting paint can be seen. The light reflecting paint on the signs allows for less light to intrude into the visual space of the ongoing vehicle. People who do not maintain their headlight alignments or use illegal lights where the brightness is beyond the limits of maintaining night vision capability of oncoming vehicles is against the law. It is amazing how something as simple as vehicle lighting results in very complex system interactions that even interface to our system of law.

9.14.6.2.2 Display Flicker and Eye Persistence

Our eyes have image persistence. If an image is flashed very quickly, the image slowly fades. It is this persistence that allows us to see when the eye is moving, viewing film in a theater (that is projecting images at 30 times a second), or viewing Cathode Ray Tube (CRT) images (at some refresh rate). The image persistence for most people is about 1/30 of a second and decays at some rate.

There are two artificial light technologies that are used extensively in our workspaces. The first is incandescent and the second is fluorescent. Incandescent light is a constant light. The brightness does not change or go on or off. Fluorescent light actually flashes, and the flash rate is based on the power source. Our power source in the USA is alternating current with a 60 Hz frequency. As a result, our older fluorescent lights flash at a 120 Hz rate, twice the rate of the power source. We do not see the flash because our eye has image persistence of 1/30 of a second or 30 Hz. If our electric AC frequency were to slow down, then at some point near 30 Hz many people would start to detect flashing lights from fluorescent fixtures.

In our systems when we couple old florescent lights with CRT displays, we will detect display flicker as the two light sources synchronize. Changing the CRT refresh rate reduces the flicker as synchronization is minimized, but not eliminated. Newer fluorescent lamps use high-frequency electronic ballast's that power the light tube at 5 kHz. This is faster than the natural decay rate of the gas in the tube, so the light production becomes continuous.

Display flicker is annoying. Further in multiple human-factors lab studies it has been shown that perceived and unperceived display flicker leads to significant human fatigue. This fatigue in an air traffic controller can lead to an erroneous clearance, which can lead to loss of life. Command and control centers are dark with no florescent lights.

Computer CRTs paint an image across a phosphor screen with some persistence level. The slower the phosphor (more persistence) the more smeared a fast-moving image appears. The faster the phosphor (less persistence) the more "black time" between refreshes and thus greater the chance of perceiving flashing or display flicker. The phosphor and display refresh rates are tuned to match the eye persistence and minimize flashing. The problem is what happens if a light source that also flashes is introduced into the system (fluorescent lighting). This was a massive problem when computers were introduced that used display monitors based on flashing images (CRT technology) into offices with flashing fluorescent lights.

Studies in Air Traffic Control and other systems in the 1970's showed that display flicker introduced massive user fatigue. It increases stress levels and reduces cognitive ability. If the beating frequency between the two light sources approaches certain rates it could induce epileptic seizures[152]. Although various communities knew this in the 1970's it was ignored as personal computers were rolled out in the 1980s. This condition lasted up until approximately 2008[153].

It is unclear what the results were in office settings where people were subjected to fluorescent lights and computer displays. It is also unclear how many users did not know enough to change their display refresh rates to minimize display flicker. Further it is unclear why many computer support departments in these environments did not attempt to deal with this issue that at one time was considered common sense. Simple procedures passed to employees or performed by support staff could have mitigated the display flicker by just changing the CRT display refresh rate. That did not happen, and flickering displays were the norm in most settings. It's unclear what the health care and system error costs were as a result of this destructive arrogance[154]. Today Liquid Crystal Displays (LCD) are used in offices. The LCD technology uses static images; there is no refresh rate or flashing images painting at 30 times a second. However, as technology shifts display flicker may resurface.

9.14.6.2.3 Field of View and Eye Rod Cone Distribution

The visual field of view and what we actually see is determined by the eye rod cone distribution. There are approximately 125 million rods and 6 million cones. The fovea has the highest density of cones and there are no rods at the fovea.

The fovea has the highest cell packing density allowing the highest visual acuity or detail detection. The cone cells in the fovea region have smaller receptive fields, than the periphery cone cells. The smaller receptor fields require more light. There is a tradeoff between light sensitivity and detail detection. Fovea vision is optimized for fine details and peripheral vision is optimized for coarser information. Fovea vision is used to see highly detailed objects while peripheral vision is used for organizing a large scene and for seeing large objects.

The percentage of cones is blue (4%), green (32%), and red (64%). The cones also have a retinal distribution resulting in asymmetrical color detection. The center is primarily green cones (most densely packed for detail), surrounded red cones, with the blue cones on the periphery. The center of the retina has no blue cones. The

---

[152] Photosensitive Epilepsy, suggestions are to avoid screen flicker rates of 2-55Hz.

[153] Many CRT monitors were being replaced by LCD displays by 2008.

[154] It is one thing if a society does not know something, such as display flicker pre 1970's. It is another if it has the data and decides to ignore it and ignore specialists. This is the worst form of ignorance.

rod cone distribution[155] and field of view can be graphically represented.

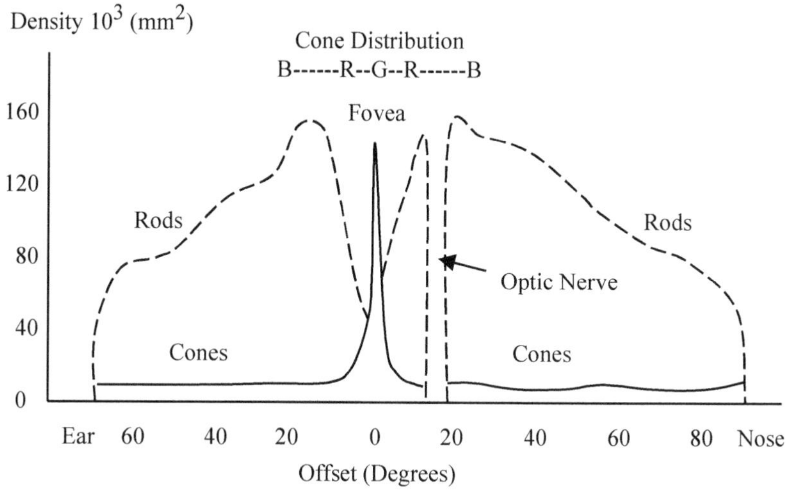

Figure 76 Rod Cone Distribution and Field of View

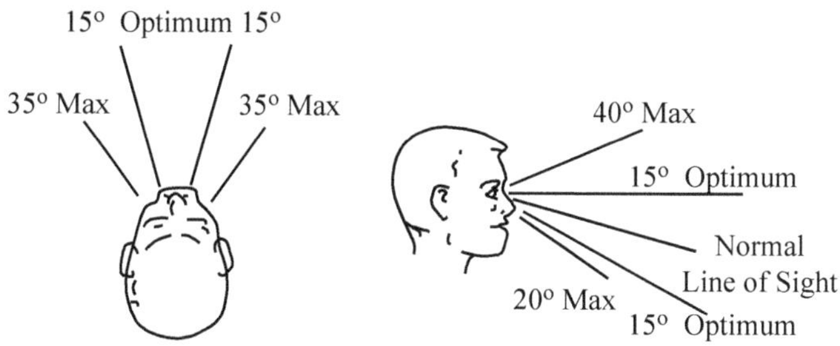

Figure 77 Field of View Eye Rotation

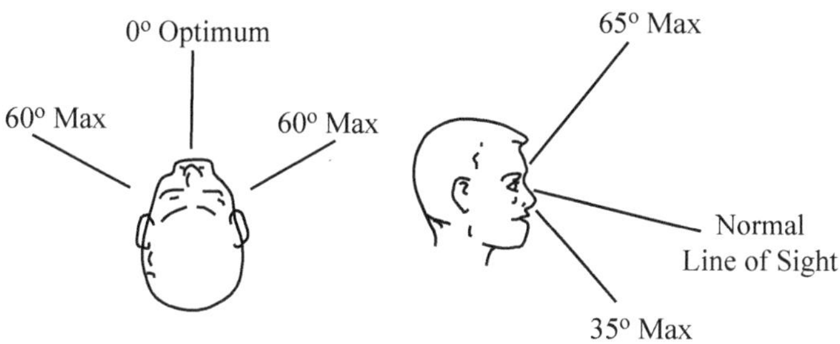

Figure 78 Field of View Head Rotation

[155] Optics, Eugene Hecht, 2nd Ed, Addison Wesley, 1987, ISBN 020111609X.

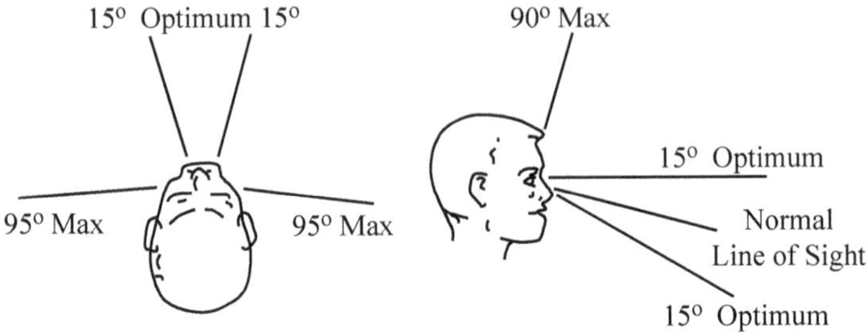

Figure 79 Field of View Eye and Head Rotation

Even though our field of view approaches 180 degrees, what we perceive as images and detailed color images is much smaller. This has enormous implications in photography, film, display layout, and anything where people visually interact with a system.

9.14.6.2.4 Color Selection Eye Focal Points

The eye lens focuses incoming light on the retina. Different wavelengths of light have different focal lengths. The lens must change its shape so that the light is focused correctly.

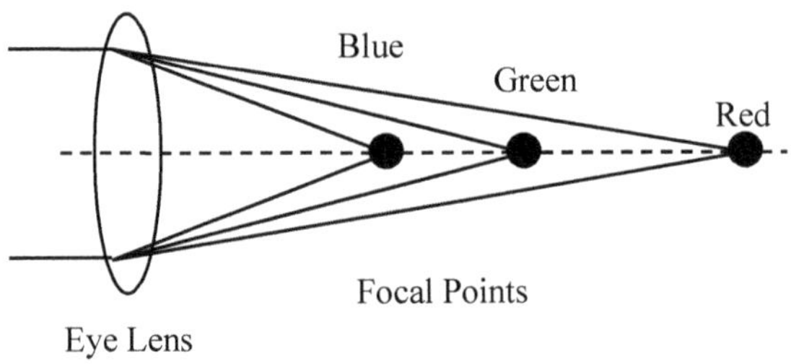

Figure 80 Color and Focal Length

Longer wavelengths have a longer focal length. Red is the longest focal length and blue is the shortest. For an image to focus on the retina, the lens curvature must change with wavelength. Red light needs the greatest curvature and blue light the least curvature. When pure blue and reds are intermixed, the lens is constantly changing shape and the eye becomes fatigued.

The eye lens is like a prism. When the light enters it is bent. If you look at the prism you will see that blue is bent the most. That means when we look at something with blue, the eye will focus on most of the light on the retina, but the blue items will be in front of the retina. If there is enough blue, then the eye will constantly shift focus to place the blue on the retina (everything else is out of focus) then place the other items on the retina (blue is then out of focus).

Notice green is in the center on the prism. Green boards replaced black boards in the 1960's. Studies showed that the green boards led to less eye fatigue, which makes sense based on where the focal length falls relative to white chalk. Also, green activates the color detecting cones and rods rather than just the monochrome rods. As we know from eye function the cones are also able to process more detail than the rods.

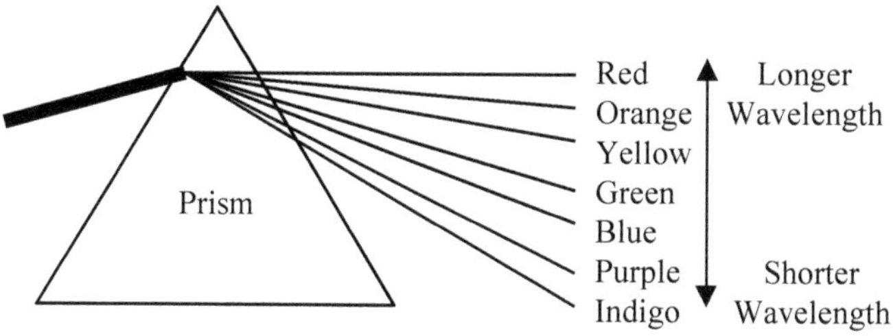

Figure 81 Prism and Light Bending

The lens absorbs about twice as much in the blue region as in the red region. As we age the lens yellows, which means it absorbs more of the shorter wavelengths. So, older people are more sensitive to longer wavelengths (yellows and oranges) than they are to the shorter wavelengths (cyan to blue). The eye fluid also absorbs light and it absorbs more light as we age especially blue. So, older people are less sensitive to light especially blue. Their apparent brightness level decreases especially blue. This translates to important guidelines:

- Avoid the simultaneous display of highly saturated, spectrally extreme colors. This causes the lens to rapidly change shape and tires the eyes. Use colors that are close together in the spectrum. De-saturate colors wide in spectrum but pay attention to contrast. Reducing contrast will reduce perception and cause serious stress. Transparent displays should never be used where operators must safely interact with a system.
- Since there are no blue cones in the center of the retina, Pure blue should not be used for text, thin lines, and small shapes, they are difficult to see. Using blue background color may blur the raster lines on a poor display, but the cost is enormous as the eye constantly tries to focus. This is a serious stress issue and may lead to eye problems.
- Avoid colors adjacent to blue. Blue does not contribute to brightness and creates fuzzy edges.
- As eyes age higher brightness levels are needed to distinguish colors.
- Colors change in appearance as the ambient light level changes.
- The magnitude of a detectable change in color varies across the spectrum.
- Since there are few cones on the periphery of the retina, avoid red and green in the periphery of large displays.

9.14.6.2.5 Contrast

As contrast drops operator fatigue increases. This can lead to system errors. So, it needs to be addressed in the system displays.

Contrast is affected by ambient light conditions. The brighter the ambient light the less contrast in a display, it gets washed out. As display brightness increases in an ambient light setting, its contrast improves. However, there comes a point where the display brightness will overload the operator eyes. This suggests that maximum contrast options should be selected when laying out alphanumeric symbol based (text) display information.

When displaying text, maximum contrast always should be used. Black background should use full brightness green and or red text. Full black (not gray or almost black, but black) text should use full brightness white background. A gray background can use black, red, green, and yellow text.

Transparent windows have very poor contrast and include visual noise (unnecessary visual data) that can lead to fatigue or visual sensory overload. The following are some quantitative contrast suggestions:

- Color options should have a color contrast ratio greater than 1:5.
- Contrast between light characters and a dark screen background should be greater than 6:1 and 10:1 is preferred.
- Contrast between dark characters on a light screen background should be greater than 1:6 and 1:10 is preferred.
- In bright ambient light to attract attention and to sharpen edges contrast ratio should be greater than 7:1.
- In dark ambient light with continuous reading, contrast ratio should be greater than 5:1.
- To hide image or display problems and smooth edges contrast ratio should be less than 3:1.

9.14.6.2.6 Color Use

Color is a good coding approach, but it needs to be used in a way so that if color is lost the information can still be provided. There are color perception differences between people and some users are unable to reliably differentiate color codes in a display. Using another code, such as text redundantly, along with the color is the best way to ensure that all people can detect the information.

To preserve night vision red background lighting (greater than 620 nm) should be used. Adding blue and white lights, especially strobe lights, not only damages night vision but also causes the eye to severely defocus. The defocusing is most severe in nighttime conditions.

For black background displays green text, symbols, and lines provide the highest visual perception. Offering red and variants of red green mixture such as orange and yellow are the most effective use of color in dark ambient light conditions with black or gray display surfaces.

When offering color pure blue must be avoided because the eye will defocus, visual acuity will be lost. Using blue background to defocus the eye so that a defective background, such as poor display resolution or noisy display circuits, is not only unethical but it also degrades system performance as the eye is constantly refocusing. This significant unnecessary stress results in fatigue, eyestrain, headaches, visual perception errors, and impaired cognitive ability, which can lead to system errors.

Blue detecting cone cells are further away from the fovea suggesting blue visual alerts at the visual periphery extremes can be used to attract the attention of an operator. Blue light emitting diodes (LED) use very little power for the relative amount of light they emit. Ideally white light should be used to attract attention to extreme visual peripheries unless the background is bright, and the white alert contrast is poor. However, something as important as an alert always should be placed within the most sensitive field of view area. That is 6 degrees, followed by 60 degrees, and at the worst case 120 degrees of the visual field of view.

If blue is used it should be mixed with red and green. This will reduce some of the focus issues, However, adding mixtures of the other base colors to a primary color moves the color to more of a pastel shade. This is good for an interior room wall but is a problem when high contrast ratios are needed such as when displaying text on a background.

Status indicators need to use consistent color-coding schemes based on Red, Yellow, and Green. These colors are closest in depth of field and are thus in reasonable focus on the retina.

- **FLASHING RED**: Used for critical alerts and failures. Indicates emergency conditions, which require immediate operator action to avert impending personnel injury, equipment damage, or both. Indicates personnel or equipment disaster.
- **RED**: Used for critical alerts and failures. Master summation if there is a no-go, error, failure, or malfunction. It alerts the operator that the system or any portion of the system is inoperative, or that a successful operation is not possible until appropriate corrective or override action is taken.
- **YELLOW**: Used for warnings. Indicates marginal condition, caution, or impending danger. Alerts the operator to situations where caution, recheck, or unexpected delay is necessary.
- **GREEN**: Used for system normal. Indicates a function is activated, equipment is in tolerance, ready, or a condition is satisfactory and that it is all right to proceed. The green indicator should be larger, and preferably brighter, than all other indicators.
- **WHITE**: Used to show system settings. Indicates normal system status

conditions that do not have right, wrong, or failure implications. These normal status conditions are alternative functions (FM selected) or state conditions (on, off, test in progress, function available).

- **BLUE**: Used for advisory. Blue should be avoided because of the focus issues. If blue must be used it should be mixed with red and green (pastel version of blue) minimizing the focus issues.

9.14.6.2.7 Blink or Flash Rates

Blink or flash rate should range from 2-5 Hz. The higher the blink rates the more urgency perceived by the operator. When developing a status indicator blink or flash rate concept, a common blink rate should be used for all the indicators. The number of blink rates should be limited to three blink rates (slow, medium, and fast) although MIL-STD-1472 suggests only two flash rates. The following general practices should be used:

- **Duty cycle**: A measure of the on and off time. A 50% duty cycle is preferred. The percentage of "on" time should be equal to but not less than the percentage of "off" time.
- **Flash rate**: No more than two flash rates should be used according to MIL-STD-1472, However, this text suggests three flash rates may be used in some applications. The flash rates should differ by more than 2 Hz. The higher flash rate reflects more critical information and should be less than 5 Hz (6 Hz with three flash rates). The slower flash rate should be greater than 0.8 Hz. Flashing should be synchronized, or massive cognitive overload may happen, and the operators could freeze.
- **Text**: Characters that must be read should not flash. An adjacent flashing symbol or flashing background can be used on text that must be read.
- **Flash suppression**: Event acknowledgment or flash suppression control needs to be provided.
- **Flashing area**: Only a small area of a display should flash at any time.
- **Flasher device failure**: If the display is energized and the flasher device fails, the light should illuminate and burn steadily preferably at higher brightness.

9.14.6.2.8 Warning and Caution Displays

A warning or caution display should be presented in a location so the operator has a greater probability of detecting the triggering condition than normal observation would provide in the absence of the display. Warning displays are red and caution displays are yellow.

- **Warning Displays**: Warning displays are flashing red. The flash frequency is 3-5 Hz with a 50% duty cycle. The flash rates for all warnings need to be synchronized. If used with caution displays, warning displays should be coded to be easily distinguished from caution displays.

- **Caution Displays**: Caution displays are yellow. A minimum of two different characteristics (text and color) is used for rapid identification and interpretation of caution displays. If used with warning displays, caution displays should be half the intensity of the warning signal. If cautions take the form of flashing text, the text should flash at a rate not greater than 2 Hz with a duty cycle (on off interval) of approximately 70% on.
- **Text Height**: Text height for visual warning and caution displays are 8.7 to 17.4 mrad (30 to 60 minutes of subtended arc) as measured from the longest anticipated viewing distance, with the larger size used where conditions may be adverse.
- **Co-location**: Warning displays and response information m should be grouped in a single location. When text information about warning conditions are listed in a single location, warnings and caution information should be grouped separately and the user should have the option to list warning and caution messages in priority, chronological or last in order.

9.14.6.2.9 Display Distance Placement and Text Size

Display distance impacts the field of view, display size, minimum size of text and symbols, and the eye's degree of adjusting to close up vision. As display distance decreases a point is reached where the eyes start to excessively cross to focus on an object; This is fovea-based vision. This will cause fatigue, eyestrain, and headaches. These all will reduce system performance and impair cognitive abilities. As display distance decreases, display quality issues surface, such as poor display resolution, repeatability, focus, etc.

- **Minimum Viewing Distance**: This is a subject of much controversy, but the bottom line is that the greater the distance from the display surface the less eyestrain for a user[156]. This needs to be balanced with the proper size of display objects and the reach of the controls around the display. The following are various guidelines that exist in the community:
  - ❑ The effective viewing distance to displays, with the exception of cathode ray tube displays and collimated displays, should be more than 330 mm (13 in) and preferably greater than 510 mm (20 in).
  - ❑ Some suggest preferred viewing distance is 20 to 40 inches others suggest 18 to 24 inches. Notice the significant difference.
  - ❑ Computer users should view their display from a safe distance, which is between 21 and 27 inches. Closer distances risk serious eyestrain,

---

[156] It is well known that people who work close-up on objects eventually develop vision problems.

headaches, and other problems that can result from overuse of the eyes.

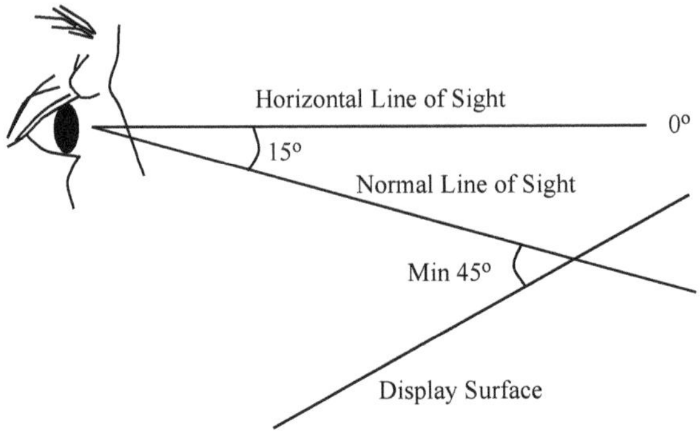

Figure 82 Line of Sight

- A 50 cm (20 in) viewing distance should be provided. When periods of display observation are short, or when dim signals must be detected, the viewing distance may be reduced to 25 cm (10 in). Design should permit the observer to view the display from as close as desired. Displays which must be placed at viewing distances greater than 50 cm (20 in) due to other considerations should allow the user to modify display size, symbol size, brightness ranges, and resolution.
- Air defense and air traffic control consoles in fixed facilities used displays that were approximately 32 inches from the operator eyes to the center of the display. This text recommends this distance. It is proven over decades of safe operations with tens of thousands of personnel spending their entire careers at these displays effectively performing their tasks with minimal side effects.

- **Viewing Angle**: The viewing angle is the normal line of sight of an operator. This is 15 to 20 degrees down.
- **Angle of View**: Displays should be perpendicular to the operator's line of sight (have a 90° viewing angle at screen center) whenever feasible. No part of any display including secondary displays should present a viewing angle of less than 45° from the operator's normal position.
- **Participants Angle of View**: All critical observers need to view the display as perpendicularly as possible. In no case should observers be forced to view displays at an angle of less than 40° from the plane of the screen.
- **Color Object Size**: For accurate color perception the major dimension of isolated large symbols subtends greater than 8.7 mrad (30 min) of visual angle, preferably 13.1 mrad (45 min). The height of small symbols and characters subtend greater 5.8 mrad (20 min) of visual angle, as measured from the longest anticipated viewing distance, and should have a color contrast ratio not less than 1:5. For fovea vision under relatively high levels of illumination use

symbols that subtend greater than 5.8 mrad (20 min) of visual angle.

- **Alphanumeric Size**: Alphanumeric characters should be scaled to subtend at least 15 minutes of arc; other complex shapes should subtend at least 20 minutes of arc.
- **Character Height**: The visual angle subtended by height of black-and-white characters should be greater than 4.6 mrad (16 min) with 5.8 mrad (20 min) preferred. The visual angle subtended by height of color characters should be greater than 6.1 mrad (21 min) with 8.7 mrad (30 min) preferred.
- **Character Stroke Width**: This applies if stroke display technology is used. Stroke line width is greater than 1/12 but less than 1/6 the number of pixels used for character height. This offers a open character while also offering a reasonable line width.
- **Font Characteristics**: Font style should clearly differentiate similar characters (letter L/number 1, letter Z/number 2). A common standard font should be used. Where users must read quickly under adverse conditions (poor lighting), a sans serif style should be used. Text should contain a conventional mix of uppercase and lowercase letters. The use of all capital letters should be limited to abbreviations and acronyms.
- **Grayscale**: There should be a minimum of at least five grayscale levels. For handwriting, resolution of fine detail, or complex image interpretation, a minimum of eight distinguishable grayscale levels should be provided.
- **Geometric Stability (jitter)**: Over a period of one second, the movement of a picture element is less than 0.2 mrad (41 sec) of visual angle.

Character height can be calculated using Tan(theta) = S/D where theta is the visual angle in radians, degrees, minutes and seconds, S is the character height, D is the viewing distance normal to the screen. So, S = (Tan (theta))/D. Character height should never be less than 2.5 mm or 0.098 inches[157].

9.14.6.2.10 Display Technologies

When we develop systems and they use some form of visual interface a display technology or approach is used. There are two approaches to offering a display: continuous and dot based. An example of a continuous display is a painting produced by using brush strokes. An example of a dot-based display is a painting, which uses a paintbrush, but the paintbrush creates an image by using "dots". As the user steps away from the painting the dots are integrated by the eyes and a continuous image is offered. The display resolution of a continuous display is driven by the size of the paintbrush and the ability to steadily hold the brush with minimum pressure. The display resolution of a dot-based display is driven by the

[157] Electronically / Optically Generated Airborne Displays, DOD Handbook, MIL-HDBK-87213A February 2005, MIL-HDBK-87213 December 1996.

size of the dot. So, if a paintbrush and its user have the ability to paint a small dot or line then the continuous display will offer a higher resolution display. The dot-based display resolution is cut off at the level of the size of the dot. If someone can paint smaller than the dot, then information or resolution is lost. That is a very important relationship and needs to be considered at all times.

Displays can be illuminated from the back and front or they can operate from ambient light. A poster uses ambient light in the daytime. During the night artificial front lighting illuminates the poster. In the last century front illuminated labels evolved to back illuminated indicators, to Cathode Ray Tubes (CRT), various forms of Liquid Crystal Displays (LCD), Plasma Displays, Light Emitting Diode Displays (LED), and Digital Micromirror Device (DMD) displays or Digital Light Processing (DLP)[158], Liquid Paper. The following are various display technologies and their fundamental characteristics:

- **CRT Monochrome**: A monochrome CRT uses a continuous phosphor painted on the screen surface. It is a continuous display surface. Its ability to paint progressively smaller lines and symbols is driven by the bandwidth of the deflection electronics. When this technology was developed, and standards established mid last century the deflection electronics were implemented with tube technology. By the turn of the century the tubes were displaced with exotic semiconductors with bandwidth to drive CRT technology to very high levels of resolution.
- **CRT Color**: A color CRT no longer uses a continuous phosphor. Instead phosphor dots are painted on the screen surface that produce red, green, or blue light. Mixing the three colors produce the desired color. This display resolution is limited to the size of the dots. Eventually the dots were replaced with small vertical rectangles. This eliminated the dead space between the dots and offered a brighter picture. It also was less prone to color errors with less bleed across the different colors.
- **CRT Color Projection**: Color projection uses 3 contiguous phosphor CRTs (red, green, and blue) to project an image[159]. The electronics evolved to such a high level of precision and accuracy that it was possible to align the CRT images and offer extremely high-resolution contiguous stunning color displays.
- **Liquid Crystal Light Valve**: This large screen display uses 3 contiguous phosphor CRTs (red, green, and blue) to modulate a liquid crystal light valve illuminated by an arc lamp. This display is used for large audience venues and in command and control centers. In recent years the large venue audience displays have shifted to DLP color displays[160].

---

[158] DLP is a trademark of Texas Instruments.

[159] Hughes Aircraft drove this technology, it eventually moved to home television.

[160] Hughes Aircraft was the primary supplier of liquid crystal light valve large screen

- **LCD Color**: Color LCD technology moved into television and computers by the early part of the new century. They are a dot-based display. The resolution of these displays is limited to the dots per inch. There are also mismatches between image decay, the human eye, and the standards. As a result, fast moving images appear unnatural. This is being addressed in part by increasing the display refresh rates. Their image quality is significantly lower than CRT projection displays but they offer a small package. It is easy to pack three or more LCD units in the same shipping space as a single projection unit
- **Plasma Color**: Plasma displays use small gas tubes that emit light when stimulated. They are a dot-based display. The resolution of these displays is limited to the dots per inch. They are being displaced by LCD displays as LCD display characteristics such as contrast ratio are improving.
- **DLP Color**: This is an interesting mix of dot-based display and an apparent continuous image. It uses mirrors that represent dots to reflect light. The reflection can be modulated and there is light bleed. Dots are not visible with these displays. However, bright scenes tend to throw large amounts of light and distort the brightness of the scene. DLP color displays have started to move into movie theatres. The resolution is less than film, but the image is steadier than an old worn film projector. Contrast ratio is not as good as film and there are issues with bright scenes in the theatre applications.
- **Electronic Paper**: Electronic paper uses ambient light. There is no back lighting. It is ideal for any light conditions including in bright sunlight such as on a beach. They have started to move into electronic book readers. They are monochrome and update too slowly to support moving images.
- **Film Projection**: Film is over 100 years old, but its display characteristics exceed all other display approaches. A 35MM image can be projected on a movie theatre screen 100 feet across and there are no lines, dots, or grain. Film can resolve 5000 lines per inch[161].

It is possible to quantify various display characteristics However, as technology changes the comparisons become tricky and new measures of performance may be needed for effective comparison. Some of the performance characteristics to consider when selecting a display approach are:

- **Spot Distortion**: Spot diameter should not vary by more than a ratio of 3:2, for any two points on the screen. Distortion should not be sufficient to cause obvious non-linearity anywhere on the screen when viewing alphanumeric

---

displays. They were extremely popular in the 1980's.

[161] FUJICHROME Velvia 50 Professional [RVP50] has a resolution of 160 lines/mm or 6299 lines/inch. The 5000 line per inch number was used for film at Hughes circa 1981 as a goal for one day offering electronic displays with the same resolution and color as film.

formats or picture images. Circles should appear as circles across the entire screen and not as ovals or other variants across the screen. The image should be a faithful presentation, circles are circles and not ovals (wrong aspect ratio used).

- **Geometric Distortion**: The combined effects of all geometric distortion should not displace any point on the display from its correct position by more than 5% of the picture height.
- **Brightness Linearity**: Brightness linearity is a measure of the uniformity of the brightness across a display surface. It is also a measure of the faithful reproduction of the bright ranges once compared to the original source. In a digital system this is driven by the number of bits dedicated to the brightness channel and associated analog compression expansion prior to digitization. In analog systems this is driven by the linearity of the analog circuits and the display.
- **Position Linearity**: This is a measure of the ability for the display to reproduce positions of elements once compared to the original source.
- **Contrast Ratio**: Contrast ratio is an example where care needs to be taken to develop an effective metric and test. One reasonable test approach uses alternating white and black squares to determine contrast ratio. However, measurements are affected by ambient light. A display may offer a better contrast ratio under high ambient light conditions than another display with less maximum brightness output, but the lower brightness display may offer a superior contrast ratio in low ambient light conditions. The best displays from best to worst are Film Projection, CRT, Plasma, DLP, and LCD.
- **CRT Safety**: When using Cathode Ray Tubes (CRT) a transparent safety screen, which may be part with the CRT faceplate, is used to prevent implosion injury. Protection is also needed against low-intensity X-radiation.
- **Glare**: Glare management is a large issue in low and high light conditions. This is handled by adding coatings to a display surface or Fresnel lens that not only directs the emitted light but also reduces glare.
- **Bezel**: When using multiple displays a matted surface finish should be used on the bezel to avoid reflection. The reflection adds visual noise.

9.14.6.3 Hearing and Audio

Just as the eye and its ability to see is related to displays, the ear and its ability to hear is related to audio. The ear can hear from 20 to 20,000 Hz. We have two ears with a visible area called the pinna or auricle or auricula. The pinna is one of the mechanisms used to help localize the source of a sound.

A simple experiment anyone can perform is to slide the middle finger across the thumb to make a noise. And sweep it around your head while making the noise.

Starting at the right sweep to the left and notice how the sound location changes.

Sound travels at a fixed speed. So, there is a minor time delay of sound arriving at the farthest ear because it needs to travel further. Most of the location information is associated with the arrival time of the sound at each ear. As the location changes the frequency content also changes ever so slightly. At the extreme sides the signal contains more high frequency sounds. So, localizing sound in front uses not only arrival time of sound at each ear but also the subtle frequency content change and the perceptual template residing in the brain from previous experience.

Continue around your head and sweep from left to right behind your head. Notice how you can determine that the sound is coming from the back. That is because the signal has less high frequency content. The pinna filters the higher frequencies more than the lower frequencies, as it needs to travel through the tissue.

In addition to the pinna there are other elements that affect our perception of sound. These elements are part of the environment and the ear operation. Other elements to consider that are fundamental to audio and hearing:

- **Spatial Separation**: The ear cannot determine direction of low frequency content below approximately 100Hz. Spatial separation increases with increasing high frequency content.
- **Air Attenuation**: The air tends to attenuate higher frequencies more than lower frequencies. It is very good at removing distortion such as clicks, pops, hiss, and even amplifier clipping which introduces square waves into the signal.
- **Voice Optimization**: The ear pinna and ear canal are optimized to the frequencies associated with normal speech frequency response.
- **Ear Damage**: The ear can be damaged by loud noise. It also can be damaged by long exposure to noise, not necessarily very loud, of the same frequency content, such as a room loaded with machinery.

9.14.6.3.1 High Fidelity Recording Playback

When we go to a concert, we hear sound coming from the front of the stage and we hear sound coming from reflections in the auditorium, including the back walls. Music recording engineers understand these issues and try to duplicate the characteristics of world class auditoriums. This is an art of multiple microphone placement and mixing of the various sound sources[162].

If you place two microphones, one at each end of a stage the sound will arrive at different times to each microphone. For example, a guitar signal on the left will arrive at the left microphone first then the right microphone. In addition, echo from the various auditorium structures will arrive at each microphone.

If you mix a portion of the left microphone signal on the right, there is a component that arrives on the left and right channel at the same time. Now here is

---

[162] Some recording studios in the 1950's and 1960's had basements with cinderblock tunnels to try to simulate the effects of auditoriums.

where it gets interesting. You can leave the mix as is, with the very low-level echo or you can combine the left and right channel but flip one of the channels by 180 degrees. This can be accomplished with a transformer or amplifier stage. This will cancel the primary signal coming from the stage of the left guitar and what will be left are all the sounds arriving at different times. This is called ambient sound. This ambient sound can then be sent to the left, right, or both channels.

When played back on a stereo the user can modify the recording engineers' mix of ambient sound by flipping the phase of one of the channels and mixing it into the primary channels. In the past this was easily accomplished with a resister between the negative amplifier terminal and both speakers' negative terminals. Today's amplifiers use dual push pull amplifiers with a floating negative and the technique cannot be used. However, these capabilities have been added in the preamplifier stages of many modern amplifiers. In addition, characteristics of the pinna have been simulated and offered in sound processing systems[163]. So, the user can turn a knob and change their location in the auditorium from the front to the back as desired.

The details of high-quality recording and mixing can only be appreciated when the actual signal is preserved. There are various metrics that evolved with the discipline and they include:

- **Frequency Response**: This is a measure of a system to faithfully reproduce audio frequency ranges. Even though our ears hear between 20 to 20,000 Hz, some suggest there is interaction between higher frequencies and so they should be captured. Also, the frequency response is rarely flat and so a system that has a broader frequency response will have more of a flat response in the hearing range. Typical goal 25 to 33,000 Hz +/-3 dB.
- **Wow and Flutter**: In the past audio was captured on electromechanical devices. They were based on motors and transport mechanisms that had speed variations or vibrations from less than perfect mechanical parts (bumps and not round). Typical goal less than 0.03% WRMS.
- **Signal to Noise Ratio**: Recording media inherently has some level of noise. The noise is increased by electronics. The higher the signal to noise ratio the better. Compressors and expanders can significantly improve signal to noise ratio, but they add non-linearity to the audio level. Typical goal uncompressed better than 65 dB, compressed expanded greater than 128 dB
- **Dynamic Range**: This is the range of loudness available in the system. The higher the dynamic range of the system the better the sound reproduction. Typical goal for dynamic range is 128 dB with compressor expander with 1

[163] The Hughes Aircraft Sound Retrieval System (SRS) used in high fidelity simulator sound systems was commercialized and offered in many consumer products starting in the late 1980's.

kHz peak recording level.

- **Harmonic Distortion**: When a signal is introduced into an audio system the audio system produces artifacts not found in the original signal. This is determined by submitting a signal such as a 1 kHz Sinusoidal wave and measuring the amplitude of other frequencies that are added by the system. The typical goal is less than 0.4%.
- **THD at RMS Power**: Total Harmonic Distortion (THD) at Root Mean Square (RMS) power is a measure of harmonic distortion of a power amplifier. As the power is increased the THD increases. The RMS power is the maximum power before the amplifier begins to produce square waves. Square waves are a sign of massive THD. They contain many frequency components at high amplitude levels. The typical goal is less than 0.7%.
- **Intermodulation Distortion (IMD)**: IMD is a measure of the introduction of unwanted signals when two signals are input into the audio system. Typical goal should be less than 0.1%.
- **Channel Separation**: All systems have cross talk. The level of cross talk increases with modulation techniques and fancy mixing of channels on physical media. Typical goal greater than 65 dB.
- **Quantization Distortion SQNR**: This is associated with converting an analog signal to digital format. It is a result of the number of bits available with each sample. The total number of bits represents the loudness levels in the system. Fewer bits lead to higher quantization distortion[164]. For example, 16 or 24 bits is very bad for quiet passages. An approximate formula is SQNR = 6.02 X number of bits. The problem is the quiet passages have huge levels of quantization distortion (24 dB). Some suggest this poor quality has changed the nature of music and moved it to highly compressed signals with lots of boom-boom. All ambience or ambient sound is lost.

Care is needed when using metrics or specifications when comparing different technologies. These specifications or metrics come with various test approaches that may need to be expanded when a different technology is introduced.

For example, the frequency response of FM radio and television is 30-15 kHz, CD is 20-20 kHz, professional and audiophile audio 20-22 kHz, and AM radio extending up to 5 kHz. However, the CD frequency response is very misleading. The Nyquist[165] sampling rate of 44 kHz drives the CD frequency response. So, the maximum frequency response is 22 kHz, beyond that there is severe noise and so an analog extreme cutoff high-pass filter is used to remove frequencies past 20 kHz. This contrasts with analog systems, which have a gentle roll off of frequency

---

[164] Discrete Time Systems, James A. Cadzow, Prentice Hall, 1973, ISBN 0132159961.

[165] The Nyquist–Shannon sampling theorem establishes that to reproduce a signal the sampling rate needs to be twice the rate of the highest frequency component in the signal.

content. So, in a CD based system there is nothing after 22 kHz. In an analog system there is content well beyond its rated response. An analog system rated at 20-22 kHz will have content at 23 kHz, 25 kHz, 30 kHz albeit at ever lower sound levels.

Another example is that a different technology may call for the introduction of a new metric that just does not apply with other technologies. For example, a digital system uses some number of bits to capture the audio level at an instant in time (a sample at the 44kHz rate). If there are not an infinite number of bits, then the level will not follow the signal smoothly but will jump based on the next bit level. This is referred to as quantization distortion. For very quiet passages the quantization distortion can approach infinity for small bit systems such as 16 and 24 bits. The approach to dealing with this is to use an analog Compressor and Expander, Compander[166], to keep the analog to digital converter full with bits. The problem is this approach introduces non-linearity into the signal and does not fully address the quantization distortion issue. Analog systems have no quantization distortion.

Some suggest that moving to digital media has changed the nature of music. To reduce quantization distortion and file storage size the analog signals are severely compressed prior to digitization. This reduces the quantization distortion but introduces analog compression expansion non-linearity, another form of distortion. So, everything is at the same loudness levels. Also, there is a shift to very low bass content which is has better reproduction because of massive over sampling. Additionally, the severe cutoff of frequencies at the sampling rate to prevent noise from insufficient sampling has shifted the focus away from producing sound with high levels of separation and ambience.

9.14.6.3.2 Voice Grade Application

Voice grade applications include telephones, public announcement (PA) systems, and automated announcement systems. There is less of a need for high fidelity because the human voice tends to be range only up to 8 kHz.

- **Telephony**: The US telephone useable frequency range is 300-3400 Hz. Empirical data before the breakup of AT&T suggested 220-3.3 kHz with 3.2 kHz for short and medium connections and 2.7 kHz in long distance connections. The allocated bandwidth for a single voice channel is usually 4 kHz, including guard bands, allowing a sampling rate of 8 kHz for digital transmission.

---

[166] In a Compander the signal is sent to a non-linear transformation prior to transmission. A reverse of the transformation happens at reception. The transformation boosts the quiet portions and reduces loud portions. Noise is reduced because the quiet signals are louder, compared to the noise in the transmission channel. In this case more bits are used to represent a quiet signal.

- **Voice Frequency**: Voice Frequency (VF) or Very Low Frequency (VLF) is the band in the electromagnetic spectrum allocated to 300-3000Hz.
- **Human Voice Range**: The human voice range is approximately 200-7000 Hz. There are differences that occur with age and gender, 120 Hz for men and 210 Hz for women.
- **Normal Speech Rate**: A normal speech rate is 150 to 180 words per minute. Slow speech rate is approximately 100 and maximum intelligible speech rate is approximately 300 words per minute.
- **Dropouts**: Dropouts are a recent phenomenon associated with cellular phones and early IP phones. The longer the dropout and greater the number of dropouts the less intelligible the signal. With a normal speech rate of 150–160 words per minute a 1-second dropout is significant.
- **Intelligibility**: Speech intelligibility decreases with decreasing bandwidth. For single syllables, 3.3 kHz bandwidth yields an accuracy of only 75 percent, as opposed to over 95 percent with 7 kHz bandwidth

9.14.6.3.3 Noise Response

When exposed to loud sound such as loud music we tend to get used to the loud sound. When we leave the loud sound setting, we notice that normal sounds are very quiet, and our ears may ring. Eventually, if there is no damage to the ears our hearing returns to normal. The basic mechanisms inherent in this ability allow us to filter noise.

When we are exposed to sound with pink noise in the background such as static or hiss, the static or hiss tends to eventually fade, and we just hear the sound. This characteristic is most pronounced when both ears are subjected to the same sound environment. This phenomenon is at the heart of many systems, which use sound for detection, such as early metal detectors and shortwave telegraph tones. If the signal is a pure tone (sinusoid) or a complex tone (combination of sinusoids), the ear can detect it. The ear also efficiently detects periodic modulation in the very low frequency range and responds to variations in intensity or frequency.

9.14.6.3.4 Sidetone

Part of the noise canceling ability of the ears is associated with both ears picking up the same sound signals. Although sidetone was initially introduced to help people talk into telephones, as the systems improved it was found that sidetone had another benefit. It tended to cancel the background noise and allowed the listener to more clearly hear and understand the speaker on the other end of the phone line. The following are sidetone considerations:

- **Speaker Sidetone**: The speaker's verbal input should be in phase with its reproduction as heard on the headset. This sidetone should not be filtered or modified before it is received in the headset.

- **Feedback**: For sound powered telephones[167] in-phase feedback or sidetone level can be used to control talker's vocal effort within limits. Feedback or sidetone is 3 to 6 dB lower than the produced speech. This increases the vocal effort and improves the signal-to-noise ratio.

In elementary school I was introduced to sidetone by using a small phone system in the classroom. We were asked to make conversation with our hands on and off the handset microphone. There was also a switch to enable disable sidetone. When the microphone was covered or the switch used to disable sidetone, the background noise was eliminated, and it was difficult to hear the person at the other end of the phone line. Background noise was coming in the open ear and someone talking was coming in the ear covered by the handset.

This was a simple but effective experiment that introduced us to hearing and perception. The sidetone needs to be sent to someone speaking while only the speakers' voice should be sent to the listener at the other end of the telephone link. It is interesting how cell phone systems ignored the whole sidetone feature - can you hear me now - was a popular cell phone advertising phrase used to target signal dropouts, not sidetone. In a mobile phone setting it is more important to cancel the background noise than offer a side tone. However, a sidetone can easily be added with another microphone.

9.14.6.3.5 Ambient Noise

Ambient noise can be a nuisance needing techniques such as sidetone or it can be a health hazard. Sound is measured in units called decibels. On the decibel scale, an increase of 10 dB means that a sound is 10 times more intense, or powerful. This is perceived as sounding twice as loud. Refrigerator humming is 45 decibels, normal conversation is approximately 60 decibels, and city traffic can reach 85 decibels.

Long or repeated exposure to sounds at or above 85 decibels can cause hearing loss[168]. The louder the sound the shorter the time period before the hearing loss. Sounds of less than 75 decibels, even after long exposure, are unlikely to cause hearing loss. Noise sources that can cause Noise Induced Hearing Loss (NIHL) include motorcycles, firecrackers, and small firearms, all emitting sounds from 120 to 150 decibels. The following are some system considerations:

---

[167] These are telephone systems used in extreme emergency situations and are found on ships and industrial settings. They do not need power; they work exclusively on the electromagnetic characteristics of the transducers.

[168] Noise-Induced Hearing Loss, U.S. Department of Health and Human Services - National Institutes of Health - National Institute on Deafness and Other Communication Disorders, Publication No. 08-4233, December 2008.

- **Noise Danger Signs**: Permanently post noise danger signs in areas with noise levels above 100 dBA or 140 dBP.
- **Noise Hazard Area Signs**: Permanently post on or in equipment noise hazard caution signs if steady-state noise levels are 85 dBA or greater. This posting is regardless of exposure time or duty cycle.
- **Manuals**: Manuals identify and discuss the system noise danger (100 dBA or 140 dBP) and hazards (85 dBA). Manuals include operator, maintenance, observer, field, technical, etc. The discussion topics include hearing protection locations, recommended hearing protection devices, noise levels of equipment and the distance at which the noise is below 85 dBA.

9.14.6.3.6 Audio Signals

Audio signals are machine generated audio signals that provide status, warnings, or alarms to operational, maintenance, or bystander personnel in the system. Audio signals are provided under the following conditions:

- Call attention to imminent or potential danger.
- Short, simple, and transitory information needing an immediate or time-based response.
- Visual display is restricted. Visual sensory overload, excessive ambient light, limited mobility, degraded vision, anticipated operator inattention.
- As part of a redundant notification element for a critical event. The audio signal backs up and reinforces a flashing alarm or warning display.
- Warn, alert, or cue operator for subsequent additional response.
- Custom or usage has created anticipation of an audio display.
- Voice communication is necessary or desirable.

The ear is a good detector of periodic signals in noise. Even when signals are considerably weaker than the background noise, if the signal is a pure tone (sinusoid) or a complex tone (combination of sinusoids), the ear can detect it. The ear also efficiently detects periodic amplitude and frequency modulation in the very low frequency range and responds to variations in intensity or frequency. The following guidelines are offered for audio signals:

- **Signal meaning**: Each audio signal should have only one meaning.
- **Discomfort**. Audio warning signals should not cause discomfort or "ringing" in the ears. Levels should not exceed 115 dB at the ear of the listener. This is especially important if personnel must pass close to the sound emitter such as a fire alarm.
- **Audibility**: A signal-to-noise ratio of at least 10 dB should be provided in at least one octave band between 200-5,000 Hz at the operating position of the

intended receiver. Signal to noise ratios can be greater as long as the levels do not exceed 115 dB at the ear of the listener.

- **Attention and Startle Reaction**: Startle reaction should be minimized. Signals with high alerting capacity should be provided when the system or equipment requires the operator to concentrate attention. Signals should not be so startling that they hinder appropriate responses or interfere with other functions by holding attention away from other critical signals. The increase in sound level during any 0.5 seconds period should be less than 30 dB to minimize startle reactions. The first 0.2 seconds of a signal should not be presented at maximum intensity, use square topped waveforms, or present abruptly rising waveforms.
- **Differentiation**: Audio alarms intended to bring the operator's attention to a malfunction or failure should be different than routine signals, such as bells, buzzers, and normal operation noises.
- **Prohibited Signals**: Signals that may cause confusion with the operational environment should not be used for alarms or warnings. The following are examples:
    - Modulated or interrupted tones that resemble navigation signals or coded radio transmissions.
    - Steady signals that resemble hisses, static or sporadic radio signals.
    - Trains of impulses that resemble electrical interference, whether regularly or irregularly spaced in time.
    - Simple warbles that may be confused with the type made by two carriers when one is being shifted in frequency (beat-frequency-oscillator effect).
    - Scrambled speech effects that may be confused with cross modulation signals from adjacent channels.
    - Signals that resemble random noise, periodic pulses, steady or frequency modulated simple tones.
    - Signals similar to random noise generated by air conditioning or any other equipment.
- **Apparent Urgency**: The attention gaining characteristics of signals should match the relative priority of the signal. They include rapidity of pulse pattern, frequency, and intensity.
- **Frequency Range**: The frequency range should be 200-5,000 Hz. The range of 500-3,000 Hz is preferred. When signals need to travel over 300 m (985 ft), sounds with frequencies below 1,000 Hz should be used. Frequencies below 500 Hz should be used when signals must bend around obstacles or pass through partitions. The selected frequency band should differ from the most intense background frequencies.

9.14.6.4 Video and Audio Compression

Switching from analog to digital has given system managers options in managing the system and this significantly impacts the quality of audio and video. Digital compression reduces file size, which reduces the size of transmission bandwidth and storage. However, compression also reduces the quality of the signal. The problem is there are no accepted metric to measure the effects of compression. Some of the effects of video and audio compression are:

- Severe pixelation with fast moving images, dark nighttime scenes, fog, water, cloud filled skies
- Loss of detail especially facial detail where color becomes uniform and there are no bumps, lumps, pores as found in a normal face
- Artifacts around facial features especially around the eyes
- Chopping of video frames to fit time slots
- Loss of stereo separation as audio is converted to mono
- No dynamic range as all frequency content is compressed to one loud level
- Severely reduced frequency response as sampling rate is severely reduced

9.14.6.5 Voice and Phraseology

Many systems with significant cognitive load and or communications that may have extreme noise use an established phraseology. The phraseology not only uses words that offer less confusion but also phrases that are succinct and minimize communication time. Air traffic control uses phraseology between the pilot and air traffic controller[169].

The idea of using certain pronunciations of numbers and letters surfaced with early radio communications where excessive noise may garble the messages. As the systems evolved and operator cognitive load increased it became obvious that efficient unambiguous communications via an established phraseology would reduce system errors. The following number character pronunciation is an early example and forms the start of the concept of using a phraseology:

0 Zero ZE–RO
1 One WUN
2 Two TOO
3 Three TREE
4 Four FOW–ER
5 Five FIFE
6 Six SIX
7 Seven SEV–EN
8 Eight AIT
9 Nine NIN–ER

A Alfa ALFAH
B Bravo BRAHVOH
C Charlie CHARLEE
D Delta DELLTAH
E Echo ECKOH
F Foxtrot FOKSTROT
G Golf GOLF
K Kilo KEYLOH
L Lima LEEMAH
M Mike MIKE
N November NOVEMBER
O Oscar OSSCAH
P Papa PAHPAH
Q Quebec KEHBECK
T Tango TANGGO
U Uniform YOUNEE FORM
V Victor VIKTAH
W Whiskey WISSKEY
X X–ray ECKSRAY
Y Yankee YANGKEY

---

[169] Air Traffic Control, FAA, 7110.65P February 2004, 7110.65T August 2010.

H Hotel HOHTELL
I India INDEE AH
J Juliett JEWLEE ETT
R Romeo ROWME OH
S Sierra SEEAIRAH
Z Zulu ZOOLOO

9.14.6.6 Touch and Tactile Feedback

Haptics is the sense of touch. Many refer to this as tactile feedback. Tactile feedback is a mechanism offered by a system element to signal a user via the sense of touch. It usually is associated with forces, vibration, and motions offered to a user by a control such as a push button. However, touch can be used to detect temperature, texture, force, vibration, motion, and motion distance. The feedback can be extreme and result in pain that triggers an involuntary user response to remove the pain. The fingertips are the most sensitive to touch feedback and are easily used for system interaction. Tactile feedback can take many forms.

9.14.6.6.1 Vibration

Vibrating the hand controls of an aircraft prior to its stall conditions where wing lift is suddenly lost because of high climb rate and low airspeed is a form of tactile feedback. Once a stall happens all airlift is lost and the airplane nosedives towards the ground. Vibrating the controls is a huge tactile feedback event that matches the huge consequences if the airplane is permitted to stall.

Audible alarms are also used to indicate if an airplane is approaching stall speed. However, the audible alarm may be washed out by sensory and cognitive processing overload of the pilot. Because of the constant physical link between the pilot and the airplane yoke, it is unlikely that vibrating controls will be masked in this scenario.

9.14.6.6.2 Force and Push

Force is used in robotics to signal the user on the level of force being applied by a robotic tool. This first surfaced in the 1950's to signal operators remotely handling radioactive material.

Many systems use switches to interact with the system. In a noisy environment a switch that distinctly needs more pressure and then clicks into position as it is pressed offers an indication that does not need visual or audio feedback that the switch has been pressed. It is a very strong tactile feedback mechanism.

The same concept can be applied to a rotary valve or a lever. The use of increasing the force as in the case of a rotary valve may be unneeded. In fact, defective valves which are stuck because of rust or other conditions may have the opposite force relationship. The force is extensive until the valve is freed. This is an important tactile feedback indication, a stuck valve.

9.14.6.6.3 Snap Action

Snap action is a variant of push tactile feedback. Rather than offer progressively more force as a switch is pressed, the force is relatively the same all the way through the push distance, but there is a distinctive snap or sudden increase in force then decrease and stop when the switch is activated. The snap is reinforced with a mechanical click sound.

9.14.6.6.4 Detents

Detents mechanically resist or arrest the rotation or sliding of a control. The detent positions can easily communicate five positions: 0%, 25%, 50%, 75%, and100% or off, one quarter, half, three quarters, and full. In the case of a push switch there are two positions, depressed (or pressed) and not depressed (or not pressed). Monetary switches are only depressed when the operator is applying pressure. As soon as the pressure is removed the switch returns to the normal position (not pressed). A spring-loaded lever with detents is a variant of a momentary switch but has multiple push states that provide operator feedback via the detents.

9.14.6.6.5 Position Size Shape Texture Movement

As an operator interacts with a system the position of a particular interface is imprinted. Maintaining the position via a fixed console position aids in the imprint. This is reinforced with visual feedback.

Size of a control relative to other controls signals the operator on the control type. This is initially reinforced with visual feedback. As the user continues to interact with the system the position and size work together to offer tactile feedback that is sufficient for the operator to take action with the control.

The shape of a control such as edges, curves, lumps, convex, concave, flat, square, round, button, lever, wheel, vertical pedal, horizontal pedal offers operator feedback. Different shapes and bump use can separate a control from a group of controls on a panel. They can signal the relative position such as when trying to locate the center of a logical collection of buttons. It is easy to identify three-dimensional characteristics in controls.

Texture such as roughness, smoothness, hardness can be used to separate different controls. A variant of this also can include temperature.

The attachment of the control provides further information as it changes position based on its attachment. For example, a foot-peddle attached at the top, bottom, left, right, or center.

9.14.6.6.6 Physically Disparate

Physically disparate tactile feedback is not logically associated with the physical control that is being activated. For example, a touch screen offers no tactile feedback as part of its physical characteristics. However, the touch screen can be coupled to a vibrating device to offer tactile feedback when an operator makes a touch entry. This type of control is extremely versatile because the touch screen can offer an infinite choice of labels, which are used as part of visual feedback that reinforce the tactile vibrating feedback mechanism[170].

9.14.6.6.7 Mission Critical Tactile Feedback

In critical applications all feedback needs a backup mechanism. The backup feedback mechanism for tactile feedback is usually visual, such as enabling a light indicator, offering a response in a display area, or changing some other system visual output such as a dial or an entire display area.

Another backup mechanism is sound. Sound is extremely effective on keyboards, touch telephones, pointing devices such as a mouse. A digital camera uses a prerecorded sound of a mechanical camera shutter to provide feedback that the camera take-picture button has been pressed.

In mission critical systems special care needs to be taken when there is no tactile feedback. Many of these systems approach the human sensory load limit inputs and, in a crisis, the traditional visual and audio feedback mechanism may be lost as information overload sets into the operator. An approach to consider is to couple a vibrating device either on the chair, headset, or some other location on the operator.

9.14.6.7 Ergonomics

Just like our eyes and ears have characteristics that we need to understand before we start to offer system interface approaches, our bodies have characteristics that need to be identified and understood. Ergonomics starts with the physical body, its size, movements and continues with design that addresses the fit between humans and machines in the operating environments. It considers the user's capabilities and limitations to ensure that tasks, equipment, information and the environment are safe and effective. Poor ergonomics design can result in fatigue, which can impair cognitive ability leading to system errors. It also can lead to health issues or even loss of life. This analysis should be used to develop effective design solutions and offer guidelines for system users and maintainers to reduce risk of injury[171].

9.14.6.7.1 Anthropometry

Anthropometry is measurement of the human body to understand human physical variation[172]. Anthropometric data can be grouped and organized in many ways. The following grouping is offered for body physical characteristics and their

---

[170] Cell phones have recently coupled touch entry with vibrating tactile feedback.

[171] The US Department of Labor Occupational Safety and Health Administration (OSHA) offers ergonomic guidelines for different industrial settings.

[172] Anthropometry of US Military Personnel, DOD-HDBK-743A, February 1991; Body size information in the form of anthropometric data.

impact on a system:

- **Foot Size and Ankle Movement**: Affects pedal designs and other foot related controls.
- **Sitting Knee Height and Clearance**: Affects seating and shelf height. Affects objects to the left and right that might bang into knees.
- **Sitting Leg Length**: Affects space offered to stretch legs and feet.
- **Sitting Eye Height**: Affects the placement of displays and controls.
- **Arm Length**: Affects the placement of controls so that they can be reached without stretching.
- **Folded Arm Length**: Affects length of shelves and side arm rests.
- **Arm Length**: Affects reach distance. Stretching and twisting should be avoided.
- **Standing Head Height**: Affects placement of hanging lights, ceiling height, door height, etc.
- **Standing Eye Height**: Affects the placement of displays, wall lighting fixtures, wall art, light switches, etc.
- **Shoulder Height**: Affects the height placement of controls and physical items. Moving arms above shoulder height stresses the shoulder.
- **Floor to Hip Distance**: We tend to use our hips to move objects such as opening push doors and closing doors.
- **Floor to Hanging Hand Distance**: Affects the placement of standing controls such as door openers and light switches.
- **Handgrip Size**: Affects the size of an object that can be gripped by one hand. It is the ability for the fingers to lock onto an object.
- **Fingertip Surface Area**: Affects the size of buttons and other finger-manipulated devices. Many small keypads use some form of tactile and visual feedback to make sure a user presses the desired key even though a finger or thumb tip may cover multiple keys. It is a delicate balance of pressure points and feedback.

Anthropometric data changes with time and population[173]. The recent trend has been for humans to be taller than in the past. To address these differences especially in a workstation or cockpit setting, the positions of various elements can be adjustable. For example, in an automobile the seat position, seat height, seat angle, back angle, lumbar support, and thy supports can be adjustable. The wheel height and length can be adjustable. The foot pedals can adjust to accommodate the leg length of the driver.

---

[173] Ergonomic data can be accessed but it is also appropriate to gather measurements on you and the team members as a starting point. You are part of the ergonomic sample set.

9.14.6.7.2 Ergonomic Risk Factors

Ergonomic risk factors have some probability of causing muscular or skeletal problems. Some of the risk factors are carpal tunnel syndrome, tendentious, rotator cuff injuries (shoulder problem), epicondylitis (elbow problem), trigger finger (repeated use of a single finger) and, muscle strains and back injuries. They are associated with repetitive, forceful, or prolonged exertions of the hands or feet, frequent or heavy lifting, pushing, pulling, carrying, prolonged awkward postures, vibration and cold.

- **Force**: physical effort needed to perform heavy lifting, pushing, pulling or to maintain control of the equipment or tools.
- **Repetition**: performing the same motion or series of motions frequently for an extended period of time.
- **Awkward Prolonged Static Postures**: assuming positions that place stress on the body. Examples include repeated or prolonged reaching above the shoulder height, using a tool with wrists bent, head turned to one side, leaning over, bending forward or to the side, twisting, twisting torso while lifting, kneeling, or squatting.
- **Contact Stress**: using the hand, foot, hip as a hammer. Pressing the body or part of the body such as the hand, foot, and hip against hard or sharp edges.
- **Vibration**: whole body vibration may damage joints of the skeletal system. Vibrating tools such as sanders, chippers, drills, grinders, or reciprocating saws may result in fatigue, pain, numbness, increased sensitivity to cold, and decreased sensitivity to touch in fingers, hands, and arms.

Before departing proven safe standard norms of ergonomic design, anthropometric data needs to be accessed and analyzed so that reasonable justification is offered. Moving from accepted practices in even the most benign looking elements can lead to severe consequences including loss of life.

Shirking seat size on an airplane to get a few more passengers on a flight restricts leg and body movement that then restricts blood flow and circulation. Deep Vein Thromboses (DVT) blood clots form deep inside legs and form with immobility such as after surgery, long plane flight, or car ride. If they dislodge and travel to the lungs a pulmonary embolism develops and is potentially fatal. About 20 to 25 percent suffer sudden death. A human that is unable to stretch and move legs while seated is being abused and may die.

9.14.6.7.3 Ergonomic Design Starting Points

There are many existing systems which can be used as a starting point for the ergonomic design of a new system. The following are starting guidelines that can be used to stimulate the ergonomic considerations of many systems:

- **Weight**: Repetitive lifting should be less than 10 pounds. Rarely lifted items should be less than 40 to 50 pounds.
- **Reach**: The maximum viewing distance to displays located close to their associated controls should not exceed 635 mm (25 inch).
- **Work Surface Height**: Desktops and writing tables are 74 - 79 cm (29 to 31 in) above the floor.
- **Writing Surfaces**: If consistent with operator reach requirements, writing surfaces on equipment consoles are not less than 40 cm (16 in) deep and should be 61 cm (24 in) wide.
- **Seat Pan and Vertical Adjustment**: The seat pan has an adjustable height of 38 to 54 cm (15 to 21 in) in increments of no more than 3 cm (1 in) each. If seat height exceeds 53 cm (21 in), a footrest is provided, and single pedestal seats have a 5-legged base. The seat pan needs a 0 - 7° adjustable tilt rearward, be between 38 - 46 cm (15 - 18 in) wide and should be 40 cm (16 in) deep.
- **Backrest**: A supporting backrest that reclines 100° - 115° should be provided. The backrest engages the lumbar and thoracic regions of the back and supports the torso in such a position that the operator's eyes can be brought to the eye line with no more than 8 cm (3 in) of forward body movement. The backrest width is 30 - 36 cm (12 - 14 in).
- **Cushioning and Upholstery**: Where applicable, both the backrest and seat are cushioned with at least 25 mm (1 inch) of compressible material. Upholstery is durable, nonslip, and porous.
- **Armrests**: Armrests that are integral with chairs are at least 5 cm (2 in) wide and 20 cm (8 in) long. Modified or retractable armrests are provided when necessary to maintain compatibility with an associated console and are adjustable from 19 to 28 cm (7.5 to 11 in) above the compressed sitting surface. Distances between armrests are not less than 46 cm (18 in).
- **Seat Base**: Chairs have at least four supporting legs. Swivel chairs should have five supporting legs. The diameter of the seat base of swivel type chairs should be 46 cm (18 in).
- **Footrests**: Footrests contain nonskid surfaces and are adjustable from 2.5 to 23 cm (1 to 9 in) above the floor, not less than 30 cm (12 in) deep, and 30 - 40 cm (12 - 16 in) wide. Footrest inclination is 25 - 30°.
- **Knee Room**: Knee and foot room is not less than 64 cm (25 in) high, 51 cm (20 in) wide, and 46 cm (18 in) deep beneath work surfaces; however, if a fixed footrest or a foot-operated control is provided, the height dimension is increased.
- **Display Placement, Normal**: Visual displays mounted on vertical panels and used in normal equipment operation are located 15 - 117 cm (6 - 46 in) above the sitting surface.
- **Display Placement, Special**: Displays that must be read precisely and

frequently are located in an area 36 - 89 cm (14 - 35 in) above the sitting surface, and no further than 53 cm (21 in) laterally from the centerline.

- **Warning Displays**: For seated operations, consoles needing horizontal vision over the top, critical visual warning displays are mounted more than 57 cm (22.5 in) above the sitting surface.
- **Control Placement, Normal**. Controls mounted on a vertical surface and used in normal equipment operation are located 20 - 86 cm (8 - 34 in) above the sitting surface.
- **Control Placement, Special**. Controls that need precise or frequent operation are located 20 - 74 cm (8 - 29 in) above the sitting surface.

9.14.6.8 Feedback

When a human is introduced into the system a feedback loop is established. Negative feedback reduces noise in a system. Positive feedback adds noise to a system. This is a critical issue that needs to be understood in the machine human feedback loop of the target system. If at any time the system moves from a stable negative feedback condition to a positive feedback condition the human will eventually be swamped with sensory and or cognitive overload.

9.14.6.9 Response Time

When computers were first introduced in the 1960's there were studies to determine operator stress levels as a function of computer response time. The time was categorized into preview area, transaction response time, and busy time. The preview area echoed the characters typed by the operator. It was found that the preview area should offer a sub second response time. A transaction is a completed entry that is submitted to the computer. If it took more than 3 seconds for the computer to respond a busy light started to flash and it should respond within 6 seconds. If the response time exceeded 10 seconds the busy light should go to a steady on state and stay illuminated until the computer offered the response[174]. If the response time exceeded 60 seconds a countdown display was offered. The following is an updated set of response time suggestions:

- **Key Response**: Key depression until positive response, appears to represent mechanical keyboard tactile feedback, e.g., "click" 0.1 seconds
- **Key Print**: Key depression until appearance of character, appears to be similar to a preview area, 0.2 seconds
- **Page Turn**: End of request until first few lines are visible, 1 seconds
- **Page Scan**: End of request until text begins to scroll, 0.5 seconds

---

[174] The FAA, IBM, and others performed these studies with articles published in trade journals during the 1970's.

- **XY Entry**: From selection of field until visual verification, 0.2 seconds
- **Function**: From selection of command until response, appears to be similar to a transaction response time, 2 seconds
- **Pointing**: From input of point to display point, 0.2 seconds
- **Sketching**: From input of point to display of line, 0.2 seconds
- **Local Update**: Change to image using local database, e.g., new menu list from display buffer, 0.5 seconds
- **Host Update**: Change where data is at host in readily accessible form, e.g., a scale change of existing image, appears to be similar to a transaction response time, 2 seconds
- **File Update**: Image update requires an access to a host file, appears to be similar to a busy condition, 10 seconds
- **Inquiry (Simple)**: From command until display of a commonly used message, appears to be similar to a transaction response time, 2 seconds
- **Inquiry (Complex)**: Response message requires seldom used calculations in graphic form, appears to be similar to a busy condition, 10 seconds
- **Error Feedback**: From entry of input until error message appears, appears to be similar to a transaction response time, 2 seconds
- **Slow Response Time**: If computer response time will exceed 15 seconds, the user should be given a message indicating that the system is processing.
- **Standby**: When system functioning requires the user to stand-by, a WORKING, BUSY, or WAIT message or appropriate icon or indicator should be displayed until user interaction is again possible. If delay is likely to exceed 15 seconds, the user should be informed.
- **Long Delays**: For delays exceeding 60 seconds, a countdown display should show delay time remaining. This is especially important in automated telephone-based interactions.
- **Long Operations**: For long operations a progress indicator should be provided.

9.14.6.10 Vision Versus Sound

There is an old saying that a picture is worth a thousand words[175]. However, pictures can be open to interpretation unless precise symbols are used. Today it is easy for many to relate to download time because of the Internet. There is a download time associated with different sensory inputs. For example, a movie takes significantly less time to download than a book. Although the experience is different each is able to provide the same messages.

When interacting with a system the vision and sound inputs need to be balanced.

---

[175] At Hughes Aircraft when STOP was first introduced, they performed several studies to determine how many words were used to augment a facing graphic in a topic. The number was approximately 500 words.

More information can be consumed via the visual path than the sound path. If the visual path is reinforced with the sound path the input is even faster and less prone to error. The same is true with tactile feedback. A click and force difference with an indicator change are extremely fast and effective.

9.14.6.11 Visual and Audio Noise

When presenting data and information to a user it is important to minimize the visual and audio noise. Noise increases the recognition time and is a source of significant errors.

Display noise can be reduced with user selectable display filters, display offset, and range scaling. Display filters allow the operator to quickly enable disable categories of information. Ideally a single user action such as a button press enables disables a display filter. Display offset allows the information to be moved into the fovea field of view. Range scaling removes extraneous information and allows other relevant information to be provided.

Sound noise can be reduced with sound contouring via an equalizer that changes frequency content, clever noise removal mechanisms during clicks and pops, and squelch circuits that mute audio when then is no sound. In digitized audio systems, dropouts can be minimized with buffering.

Even though display and audio noise are a serious operator load issue, the only alternative may be to subject the operator to the noise environment. Humans are one of the most effective approaches for detecting patterns in a visual smudge or noisy sound. Part of the human cognitive processing mechanism tends to eventually "tune out" the noise so that when a different pattern arrives, it is detected So pink noise in the form of sound static or visual noise in the form of snow and double images tends to fade and only the sound and pictures are detected. Broadband sensor RADAR (Radio Detection and Ranging) and Sonar (Sound Navigation and Ranging), operators use this characteristic.

9.14.6.12 Sensory Cognitive Data Information Overload

It is possible to overload a human with too much system information that may or may not need a reasoned and correct response. The problem is when the human is overloaded, this can lead to serious health consequences and erroneous human responses. Erroneous human responses can lead to increased costs, damage to property, physical harm or death.

There is a distinction between data and information. Information is collections of data that have some reason to be grouped together. This group may result in a conclusion. This is typically referred to as fusion. Many people in the loop systems use humans to perform data fusion. This requires use of the senses and cognitive processing, each of which can be overloaded.

Sensory overload happens when one or more senses reach their load limits. The following are examples of sensory overload. Display too much information in an area that exceeds the normal field of view of the operator, rapidly changing and scrolling displays. Too much audio such that there is no dead time to offer a voice or pointing hand response, the responses just stack up while the audio continues to stream to the recipient. Constantly speaking unable to receive audio input from a half-duplex communications channel. Even if the eyes and ears are not overloaded the limbs may be unable to respond quickly enough with button presses, button pushing, touch entry, mouse moving, joystick movement, trackball spinning, etc.

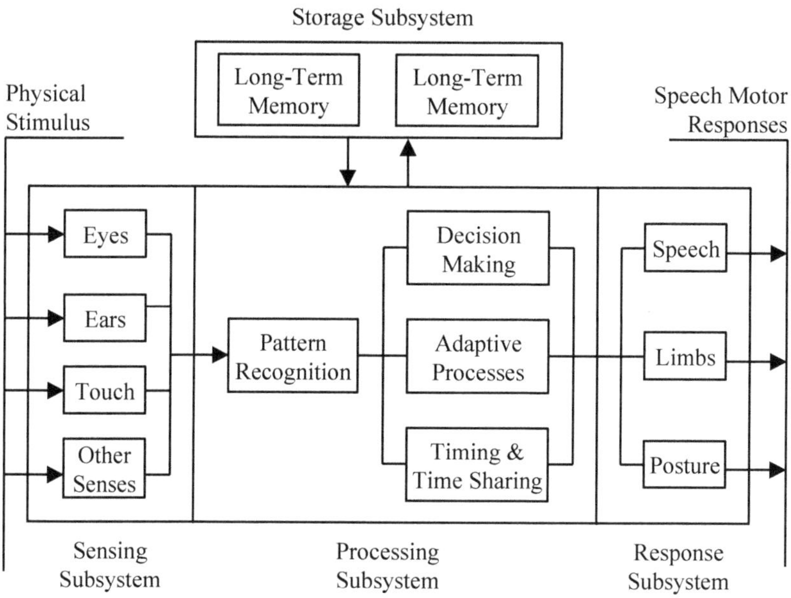

Figure 83 Human Information Processing System

Typically, long before the senses are overloaded the user hits their maximum cognitive processing ability. They are unable to process the individual data elements and offer responses based on internal rules, heuristics, algorithms, experience, and or instinctive response.

Data overload is a condition where the user is unable to form meaningful information. There is no fusion or conclusion. There is too much noise or extraneous data preventing the formation of information or data fusion.

Information overload is a condition where the system presents too much noise and the user is unable to filter and get to the most important information that needs immediate action. Even though the user is presented highly processed and fused information, the effect is the same as with too much raw data. The user is unable to detect what needs detection from what becomes a vast noise pool.

Thrashing is a condition where a processing element starts to process an input but is unable to complete the processing because another input arrives that displaces the processing of the first input. Either the first input or another input then displaces the second input processing. In this trashing condition processing never completes on any input. People just like machines can enter into a thrashing condition.

9.14.6.13 Protecting Humans from Themselves

All systems must protect humans from themselves. It is a given that humans will make mistakes and attempt to do bad things. The systems need to be designed such that when they are misused or abused the humans will be protected. This is extrapolated to all life and even property. For example, the steering radius of an automobile can be made very tight. This is great when trying to parallel park, However, when driving at high speed trying to avoid a deer in the road the human panic might lead to oversteering the vehicle and the vehicle turns over. There is a balance between easy parallel parking and minimizing the effects of oversteering.

Many times, this is confused with safety, but it is more complex and subtle. This is something that needs to be engrained in the team as a key requirement. Mature organizations in the last century had this embedded in their cultures.

9.14.6.14 Circadian Sleep Rest Cycles

Disruption of the circadian rhythm results in fatigue. The effects include degraded judgment, degraded situation awareness, degraded decision-making, memory; slowed reaction time, lack of concentration, fixation, and worsened mood. Other effects are decreased work efficiency, degraded crew coordination, reduced motivation, decreased vigilance, and increased variability of work performance. Fatigue can lead to increased system errors, which can cause physical harm or loss of life. Humans have a biological clock that is approximately 24 hours 11 minutes[176]. It is reset with the presence of light.

Jet lag or circadian rhythm sleep disorders occur when there is a change in work schedules or time zones. Time is needed to transition from a day work shift to a night shift (sleep phase shift). The amount of time depends on the number of hours the schedule is shifted, and the direction of the shift. During this transition, the circadian rhythm disruption or jet lag can produce effects similar to sleep loss. The following guidelines should be used to minimize circadian rhythm sleep disorders.

- Minimize the frequency of shift changes and extend the weeks before changing a person's shift from day to night or vice versa.
- It takes time for the person to adjust to shift changes, from day to night, or

---

[176] Initial studies suggested the clock was closer to 25 hours, However, those studies allowed participants to use incandescent room light. At the time it was believed the room light was not strong enough to affect the cycle. Later studies suggested that ordinary room light can shift the circadian cycle by more than 40 minutes.

midnight to the day.

- A frequent change in schedule disrupts the circadian rhythm and results in chronic fatigue.
- One month or longer in one shift pattern is suggested and results in a lower chance of chronic fatigue.
- Direction of the shift change should rotate ahead. An early day shift should go to a late day or early night shift, and late night shift to an early day shift.
- There should be at least 24 hours off before starting the next shift change.
- Jet lag recovery takes one day for every time zone crossed. The body clock gets out of synchronization with a rapid change in time zones; it encounters daylight or darkness contrary to the normal rhythm.

It is easier to reset the circadian rhythm (recover) from jet lag than from night shift work because the sun follows the person. Artificial methods have been used to try to reset the rhythm of night shift workers. The approach is to use high intensity lights at work and closed thick window curtains in the morning when the person is sleeping. Some suggest that the light intensity should be 10,000 LUX (bright sunlight) while others suggest 1000 LUX (overcast day) may be sufficient to reset the circadian rhythm. Office lighting is typically 300-500 LUX, which is similar to sunrise or sunset on a clear day.

When fatigue does set in due to circadian rhythm disruption and or progressive sleep loss, caffeine provides a temporary benefit. It affects the nervous system in 15 to 20 minutes. The effects include increased heart rate and increased alertness. It lasts for approximately 4 to 5 hours but can last up to 10 hours in especially sensitive individuals.

Table 40 Caffeine Levels[177]

Percolated Coffee	140 mg / 7 oz
Brewed Coffee	80-135 mg / 7 oz
Coca-Cola	34 mg / 12 oz
Tea	70 mg / 6 oz
Chocolate	5-35 mg / 1 oz

Regular caffeine use can lead to caffeine tolerance and undesirable side effects such as elevated blood pressure, stomach problems, insomnia, and disrupted sleep if taken too close to bedtime. Caffeine affects sleep and should not be consumed 4 to 5 hours prior to sleep. It makes falling asleep more difficult, reduces sleep length, and disrupts the quality of sleep. The follow situations are appropriate for caffeine:

---

[177] Commercial Transportation Operator Fatigue Management Reference, Department of Transportation, Human Factors Coordinating Committee, Research and Special Programs Administration, July 2003.

- In the middle of a night shift especially on the first and second day of the work week when circadian disruption is most pronounced and alertness most compromised
- Mid-afternoon when post lunch alertness dips because of insufficient sleep
- Prior to an early morning commute following a night shift, but not within 4 hours of going to sleep because it prevents sleep

Caffeine should not be part of the system. The system should be designed to respect the circadian cycles of humans. Ignoring this information and inducing human stress in the system shifts long-term health costs to other stakeholders and still opens the system to possible circadian cycle fatigue-based disasters[178].

There have been attempts to increase the circadian cycle from 24 hours to 28 hours. This would translate to a six-day week. However, they have been unsuccessful, and this suggests that life on Earth is based on the 24-hour cycle[179].

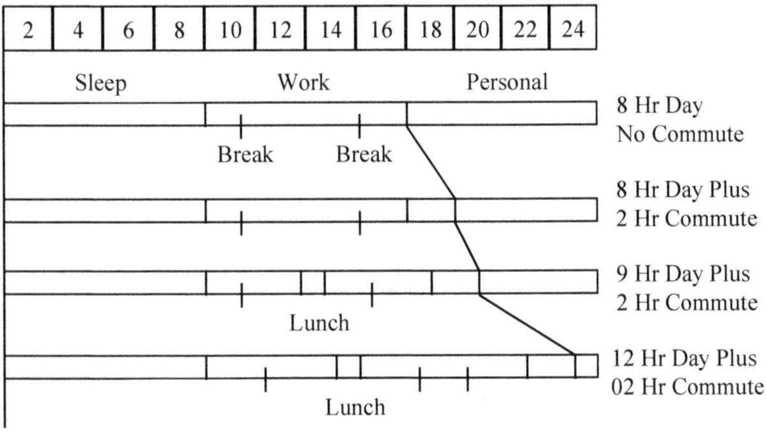

Figure 84 Work Shifts - Daily Time Allocation Alternatives[180]

A big question is do we live to work or do we work to live. Are we slaves to our systems or do our systems serve us? These are profound cultural questions that get to the heart of quality of life.

---

[178] August 18, 1993 in Guantanamo Bay, Cuba involving a DC-8. NTSB report probable cause: "The impaired judgement, decision-making, and flying abilities of the captain and flightcrew due to the effects of fatigue".

[179] Work performed at Harvard University by Charles Czeisler, M.D., Ph.D. and associates. William J. Cromie, Human Biological Clock Set Back an Hour, The Harvard University Gazzette, 1999.

[180] This time budget allocation is no different than allocating timing budgets in systems such as computers, communications, command and control, hospital emergency rooms, call processing centers, maintenance activities, etc.

There are some systems that need people 24/7. Examples are health care, air traffic control, police, fire fighters, etc. The question then arises, which work schedule is the best for maintaining healthy alert people. The 8-hour shift allows for shift changes to happen with minimum disruption to circadian cycles. The 12-hour shift has the worst impact when shifts change. Rather than 8-hour slides, it is a 180-degree flip between sleep and non-sleep time. The rate of shift changes (weekly, monthly, quarterly, semiannually, or random) can minimize the severe negative impacts of 12-hour shifts.

Personal time is a different state of being for a human. It is non-sleep time where people are engaged in other activities rather than the focused needs of work. It is unclear if this additional stimulation offers benefits in the short and long term. Removing this waking decompression time in the 12-hour shift is something to consider in such a system. For example, offering comfortable pleasant lounges with different seating and private space for quick power naps during the 12-hour work shift may reduce fatigue and benefit the system and the people.

9.14.6.15 Stress Sources

Understanding sources of stress and designing the system to minimize stress will not only maintain health of the people in the system but also minimize system errors that can lead to cost shifting to unsuspecting stakeholders, property damage, physical harm, or even loss of life. The sources of stress are:

- Poor display design with excessive field of view, characters and symbols that are tool small, use of blue colors, poor contrast, low brightness, excessive useless data or information
- Excessively loud noise or prolonged exposure to moderately loud settings
- Poor audio with poor frequency response, excessive digital quantization distortion and under sampling, digital dropouts, excessive static clicks pops, insufficient volume control
- Poor ergonomic design leading to repetitive motion disorders, restricted blood flow, excessive force strains or bone breaks, bumps, bruises, and cuts
- Poor environmental conditions of extreme heat, cold humidity, insufficient ventilation that leads to toxic fume exposure or reduced oxygen intake
- Ignoring circadian cycles and need for rest by not having breaks during work periods, excessively long work schedules, shifting work schedules with no time for circadian cycle readjustments
- Poor response time and inconsistent response time from the machines in the system increase stress and lead to fatigue and system errors

9.14.6.16 Ethics in Human Factors

Ethics is a major concern in all areas of a system. All information products should contain a section on ethical issues and considerations. This is especially true in human factors. Poor human factors decisions can lead to damaged eyes, ears, muscles, joints, bones, tendons, lungs, circulation, nerves, glands, skin, etc. The big issues are usually addressed but the small issues such as straining eyes tend to get overlooked except in the most sophisticated system settings. However, these small issues when ignored lead to increased healthcare costs and degraded system performance as users struggle to interact with a bad system.

Even though we know all these human factors issues, new appliances such as televisions, audio, and video devices have recently started offering remote control devices that violate simple ideas of color use, text size, button grouping, button sizes, and tactile feedback. Using gray text over a black button is outrageous. Using buttons so small that multiple key press errors occur for a device that sits on a coffee table is wrong. Not using functional groupings and using same size buttons is a total disrespect of the user. Not standardizing remote controls for multiple home entertainment appliances so that a typical setting has a plethora of separate remote-control devices is a sign of not appreciating technologies impact on the world and the user in particular.

9.14.7 Tests, Verifications and Validations

There is a large endless list of tests, verifications and validations. This is just a small sampling of the kinds of tests that may exist in a domain. It is offered to broaden and deepen the perspective on test, verification, and validation.

9.14.7.1 Verification

Verification testing is used to determine if the system is designed and implemented according to the specifications. The requirements are allocated to different test levels and to different test procedures and cases within the procedures. That allocation represents the bi-directional traceable path between each requirement and each atomic test procedure.

The test procedures can be grouped as needed for the unique system but should respect the concept of unit, subsystem, and system level verification. There may be many unit test procedure books, many subsystem test procedure books, but only a few system test procedure books. Examples for splitting the system procedures into separate books are:

- System Environmental Test Procedures
- System Functional Test Procedures
- System Performance Test Procedures
- System Recovery Test Procedures
- System Interoperability Test Procedures
- System Certification Test Procedures

Specifications are imperfect and changes may be made to the specifications as a result of the tests. However, these changes should be minimal if a good system engineering activity was performed.

As the tests are dry run in preparation for formal test witnessing, defects will surface. These defects and resulting changes need to be formally tracked using a defect-tracking tool. Whenever a defect is detected as much information about the defect should be gathered and documented. This should include an initial assessment of the defect[181].

Table 41 Classifying Defects During Testing

Priority	Applies if a problem could
1 Grave	a. Prevent accomplishment of an operational or mission essential capability b. Jeopardize safety, security, or other requirement designated critical c. Result in loss of life or health
2 Catastrophic	a. Adversely affect the accomplishment of an operational or mission essential capability and no work-around solution is known b. Adversely affect technical, cost, or schedule risks to the project or to life cycle support of the system, and no work-around solution is known
3 Critical	a. Adversely affect the accomplishment of an operational or mission essential capability, but a work-around solution is known b. Adversely affect technical, cost, or schedule risks to the project or to life cycle support of the system, but a work-around solution is known
4 Marginal	a. Result in user operator inconvenience or annoyance but does not affect a required operational or mission essential capability b. Result in inconvenience or annoyance for development or support personnel, but does not prevent the accomplishment of those responsibilities
5 Negligible	Any other effect

9.14.7.2 Validation

Validation is used to determine if the right or correct system was designed and implemented. This comes from the user perspective. At one level the operational concepts are used to test the system. At another level the community revisits the system mission and either the system successfully satisfies the mission or not.

Validation can start at the development facility where the system is staged before delivery. Operators can be bought in and the system can be put through various operational scenarios using simulated inputs. Validation can continue at the development facility using some combination of mixed simulation and live data. At some point the system is delivered.

The first site is a key site and is a significant gate. Unlike the operators that may

---

[181] MIL-STD-498 Category And Priority Classifications For Problem Reporting. There is an overlap with the FMEA categories found in MIL-STD-1629A.

have been used at the development facility, these operators must live with this system. What they say and do is significant. Just like at the development facility, the testing can begin with simulated data, then a combination of simulated and live data, then a session using only live data during an off-peak time, such as midnight.

Once confidence is developed, the key site will decide to take the system live with the ability to go back to the previous system. There may be setbacks at any time during this validation sequence, however, eventually all the bugs are worked out and the site goes live with the new system and one or more other sites are recommended for the new system roll out.

The system is not fully validated until all the sites have been delivered and operating with the new system for a reasonable period of time. This time period may be as long as a year. At some point the old system is phased out as the new system has proven itself. It is validated.

9.14.7.3 Highly Accelerated Life Test

Highly Accelerated Life Test (HALT) is used to identify and resolve design weaknesses. It is typically performed during engineering development. It can be performed at the unit, subsystem, or system level. The approach is to progressively apply more environmental stresses in a methodical measured manner until a failure is detected. Obviously, this should be beyond the design requirements However, surprises do surface when components are integrated into an assembly. There are commercial environmental test chambers available for this type of testing. The environmental stresses are:

- Cold step and Hot step
- Rapid temperature cycles
- Stepped vibration and shock
- Power switch and fluctuation
- Combined stress tests

9.14.7.4 Safety Tests

Safety tests are used to find unsafe elements in a system. Many times standards are invoked for safety requirements. These standards are highly specialized and typically include many tests with a certificate that is issued when the system or product is shown to meet the standard. A good example is a certificate from Underwriters Labs (UL)[182].

---

[182] Found in 1894 Underwriters Labs ® (UL) has been testing products and writing standards for safety for more than a century.

9.14.7.5 Capacity Stress Testing

Capacity Stress Testing takes selected performance requirements and subjects the system to progressively more stringent performance requirements until a failure is detected. This testing can be isolated to a single performance item or a group of performance requirements that represent a scenario of ever-increasing challenge. Examples include:

- Continuously add more load to a physical structure
- Continuously increase the number of transactions into a computer-based system until thrashing[183] occurs
- Continuously increase the speed of a motor until it flies apart
- Continuously increase the number of simulated aircraft in an air traffic control system until tracks are dropped
- Continuously increase the number of simulated aircraft in an air traffic control system until the operators are overloaded and near misses increase and more aircraft are placed into holding patterns

9.14.7.6 Destructive Testing

Tests can be destructive such that the item under test is compromised or destroyed. However, fully verifying a requirement may call for a destructive test. This is best described with an example of an electrical fuse. A non-destructive test for a fuse is to check its continuity. A destructive test for a fuse is to continuously increase the current and measure when and how quickly the fuse blows (i.e. works). However, once the fuse is blown it is of no value. An approach to destructive testing is to sample a production run to verify that an entire batch is working as expected. The implication being that the production run is consistent, and the process is not compromised if a selected sample set behaves as expected.

9.14.7.7 Characterization Tests

Characterization Tests are performed to characterize an existing device, subsystem, system, product, etc. It is used to compare against alternative choices and compare against possible future system upgrades or outright replacement. Informed consumers are aware of tests and associated resulting specifications for audio products and automobiles. Sometimes when characterization tests are performed the original design specifications are exceeded.

---

[183] A resource stops doing useful work because there is contention. Once started, thrashing is typically self-sustaining until something occurs to remove the contention. For example, multiple processes accessing a shared resource repeatedly and neither willing to relinquish control so the resource can complete one of the processes while the other patiently waits.

In the past it was common engineering practice to de-rate components and include extra capacity and room for meeting performance requirements in the design. As design has become more precise with miniaturization, automation, and computers many solutions are offered at the specification limits. So, a bridge built in the 1960's may catastrophically fail[184] while a bridge in the same location built at the start of the previous century is still standing and offering service.

9.14.7.8 Architecture Verification and Validation

This text places great importance on architecture. However, can the selected architecture be tested, verified, and validated before it is designed and implemented? Is the architecture tradeoff analysis sufficient evidence to show that the architecture was tested, verified, and validated?

The case for the selected architecture is embodied in the architecture studies and models. The typical studies and models that test and verify the architecture are against the system key requirements and include:

- Timing, sizing, load studies and models
- Reliability, maintainability, availability studies and models
- Functional decomposition and allocation
- Requirements decomposition allocation and allocation

The studies and models that validate the architecture include:

- Operational sequence diagrams
- Operational simulations
- Operational simulation prototypes, and demonstrations

9.14.7.9 Software Intensive System Verification

Software intensive systems have a challenge because so many logical and arithmetic elements are within the total software set. All of these elements are suspect until verified. The problem is many of these elements are rarely executed at the system level and if they are executed, their limit conditions and internal paths may be unexercised without inserting computer failures. So, software is tested at different abstraction levels and on different environments outside the normal target execution environment.

---

[184] I-35W Mississippi River bridge (Bridge 9340) eight-lane, steel truss arch bridge opened in 1967 collapsed during evening rush hour August 1, 2007. Some have suggested modern precise engineering practices were a factor as the bridge reached its original design life. Older bridges with the same design life included less precise over engineering practices, yielding long life.

- **Unit Testing**: This is the smallest atomic test performed. The test might be something as simple as to perform a compile and link. Depending on the application, the testing may include developing unit stubs and drivers to stimulate the inputs and observe the outputs. It may go further and exceed the input limits and or stimulate all possible values in all possible conditions. These exhaustive unit level tests are associated with extremely critical software units.
- **Configuration Item Testing**: Once multiple units are grouped into a configuration item such as a standalone application, it can be tested. The goal is to surface the unexpected emergent behavior associated with multiple unit interactions and their interfaces. This testing may or may not be in the target environment. It also may or may not include a debugger, which can provide white box testing services such as inserting faults and examining internal intermediate values.
- **Integration Testing**: Once all the software configuration items are available, they are typically loaded on the final target environment and subjected to integration testing. This may be as simple as verifying that the software executes on the hardware to verifying all the software requirements as specified in the software requirement specification(s).

9.14.7.10 Interoperability Tests

Interoperability tests are a difficult subject because initially everyone assumes some gold standard test fixture is developed to support interoperability tests of devices and systems from various vendors. However, no one wants the responsibility for validating the gold standard or even paying for its development. So, there tends to be a mad rush to be the first out of the gate so that they become the gold standard that everyone else needs to meet. Other will need to make the changes, if needed, not the one who first made it to the gate.

9.14.8 Quality

There are four broad areas to consider when addressing quality from a systems perspective. They are quality perceptions, quality assurance, quality control, and quality improvement. What may not be apparent is that making the fundamental decision to be systems driven will force many of the elements associated with quality to be practiced. So, there is a direct relationship between using systems practices and movement into high quality.

9.14.8.1 Quality Perceptions and Attributes

From a systems practices point of view quality is about doing everything well. The implication of that statement is that function and performance is pushed to the limits in a balanced reasonable solution.

Quality perception is best illustrated by examples. In these examples it becomes apparent that there is some connection between quality perceptions and the Measure of Effectiveness (MOE).

An automobile can accelerate form 0-60 miles per hour in 6 seconds. However, it may idle roughly, not start in all temperatures, poorly handle turns and road bumps, consume large amounts of oil and gas, and have the paint fade in 1 year. Alternatively another automobile also may go from 0-60 miles per hour in 6 seconds, run smoothly, start all the time, handle really well, consume very small amounts of gas, have a paint job that allows you to see your eyelashes 10 years later, and have a great sound system. Obviously the second automobile is higher quality[185].

As we look deeper into this comparison, we clearly see the second automobile has a higher MOE. So, there is a relationship between MOE and quality. However, quality includes more attributes[186] than the MOE criteria in an architecture study. These attributes become apparent as different solutions are compared. These comparisons should include all stakeholders including consumers of the systems[187].

It is easier to compare the quality of two approaches that use the same basic architectures (e.g. comparing gas engine automobiles) than two approaches with different architectures. (e.g. gas versus electric automobiles). What if we tried to compare a reel-to-reel tape recorder with a cassette tape recorder, CD player, or MP3 recorder player? The problem becomes even more interesting if the stakeholders are different such as an audio aficionado and a casual music listener.

The reel-to-reel tape recorder may have spectacular sound quality with frequency response, harmonic distortion, and signal to noise ratios that bring tears of joy to an audio aficionado. It also uses storage media that has been shown to last a lifetime.

Meanwhile an MP3 player is not even measured for frequency response, harmonic distortion, or a new distortion associated with digitization called quantization distortion because the numbers are so poor. Music is lost as files disappear and music sound quality changes as files of different compression and sampling ratios are recorded.

The casual music listener will prefer the MP3 player to the reel-to-reel because

---

185 This was the difference between a muscle car and a high-end luxury car circa 1969. Many luxury cars were very fast with standard positraction rear ends or front wheel drive and large block engines with massive carburetors. Rather than sit and burn rubber they would chirp and just fly like bats out of hell (e.g. Riviera, Toronado, Eldorado, Imperial, etc).

186 The 1960's were noted for publications that always compared meaningful attributes of various products. In many cases the consumer was educated on the engineering specifications or the science prior to the comparison. In recent years critical assessment has been overcome by hype and uneducated consumers are unable to easily make informed choices.

187 Sample publications are / were Consumer Reports, Stereo Review first published in 1958 by Ziff-Davis, Popular Mechanics first published 1902.

of portability. For the music aficionado the reel-to-reel is higher quality compared to the MP3 player. For the casual listener the MP3 player is higher quality than the reel-to-reel until of course they hear a reel-to-reel sound system play their favorite songs. Then they start their quest for higher quality sound. They become educated.

This is an interesting scenario because this can result in a downward trend of quality for an entire class of systems. The MP3 player audio quality was compromised for cost and portability. However, as time marches on, the reel-to-reel systems disappear from the market because there is more money to be made with MP3 players. A new generation is never exposed to what once existed; they do not know any different. So, there is no desire to improve the audio quality of the MP3 player. It is good enough; not realizing what is being missed and what was lost. The end result is devolution in quality.

Quality attributes are sometimes referred to as the "ilities". They are non-functional and are very similar to tradeoff criteria when selecting architecture alternatives. They are:

- Accessibility, Autonomy, Accountability, Credibility
- Accuracy, Precision, Correctness, Integrity
- Adaptability, Customizability, Composability, Configurability, Tailorability
- Availability, Dependability, Reliability, Durability
- Deployability, Distributability, Discoverability
- Efficiency, Effectiveness, Affordability
- Elegance, Simplicity, Demonstrability
- Failure Transparency, Fault Tolerance, Resilience, Recoverability, Orthogonality, Degradability
- Fidelity, Responsiveness, Seamlessness
- Growth, Flexibility, Modifiability, Scalability, Upgradability, Evolvability, Extensibility
- Interchangeability, Compatibility, Reusability, Interoperability, Ubiquity
- Maintainability, Modularity, Installability, Serviceability, Debugability
- Manageability, Operability, Learnability, Administrability, Auditability, Understandability, Usability
- Mobility, Portability
- Predictability, Repeatability, Reproducibility, Determinability
- Relevance, Timeliness
- Robustness, Stability, Survivability, Safety, Securability
- Self Sufficiency, Self Sustainability, Sustainability
- Standards Compliance, Testability, Provability, Traceability

9.14.8.2 Quality Assurance - Design in Quality

Quality Assurance is the prevention of defects. Quality cannot be inspected or tested into a product or system. Quality needs to be designed and built into the product to minimize defects. The ideal goal is to have zero defects at the end of design and implementation. Evidence of high quality includes:

- Small tolerances and extreme accuracy such as narrow compartment lid seams, perfect spacing between adjoining areas, straight lines, no burs or surfaces that can cut
- Sensitivity to maintainability such as color coded or stripped wires, hoses, pipes, modularity, ease of access
- HMI that is easy to use, complete, consistent, properly uses colors, text size, field of view, controls, alerts, indicators, tactile feedback
- Ergonomics that uses proper sizes, weights, reach, and adjustments
- Ability to not only handle design peak load but above design peak load with no loss of function, performance, or damage to system
- Excellent finishes and coatings with uniform application, no drips, thin areas, blotches, changes in reflection, immune to scratching and rub off
- Ability to do everything well without degradation, attention to ALL the details no matter how far hidden from users

9.14.8.2.1 Quality Assurance - Design

The first step to take when designing in quality is to realize that a quality stakeholder should be involved at the earliest stages of a project. They should be part of the architecture team and follow the project as the system unfolds. That quality stakeholder needs to pull in other quality and quality related stakeholders as needed. The quality information, which will influence the architecture and system evolution, is as follows:

- Identify disasters from similar systems
- Identify catastrophic failures from similar systems
- Echo the concerns of the stakeholders
- Identify classes of problems that may be encountered
- List the top 10 problems from similar systems
- Identify the potential showstoppers in this system

Every system can be killed. These are the system showstoppers. Use the history of previous systems to identify the current system showstoppers. The system approach should mitigate these quality issues. There should be documented evidence of this mitigation, especially the showstoppers. At some point systems practices such as Failure Mode Equipment Analysis (FMEA) are used as part of an integrated quality management system[188] for quality assurance.

Some designs are inherently more prone towards higher quality. For example, some approaches have fewer parts, interfaces, and process steps. Elegantly simple designs and low complexity lead to inherently higher quality approaches. When a tradeoff is performed, use the quality-criterion as a tradeoff criterion and consider the past history and the design complexity when rating the approach.

Adopting the systems approach for a project will significantly enhance quality. Many elements associated with quality are normal systems practices:

- Understand past quality problems - history is critical
- Do FMEA early and regularly update - start simple then expand
- Quality function deployment (QFD)189 - design the right system
- Use multi-functional teamwork - basic to systems engineering
- Begin with the concept or architecture - start as early as possible
- Simplify the design - less interface, parts, complexity
- Use high quality parts - pay me now pay me later
- Design with fewest parts - less things to break
- Use highest quality automated tools - intuitively obvious
- Raise and resolve issues early - so others learn from you
- Identify critical dimensions, tolerances, and precision parts
- Reuse proven designs - learn from others
- Document thoroughly and completely - no finger pointing or blame games
- When designing always address quality - make statements

9.14.8.2.2 Quality Assurance - Implementation

Quality assurance practices during implementation overlap the quality assurance practices during design. The concepts are the same, but the environment might be the manufacturing floor, the computer software development environment, or job sites for buildings, roads, bridges, etc. They are:

Understand past quality problems	Use highest quality automated tools
Continue the FMEA	Raise and resolve issues early
Use multi-functional teamwork	Screen critical parts
Simplify the process	Reuse proven processes
Use high quality parts	Document thoroughly and completely

---

[188] ISO 9000 an example of standards for a quality management system.

[189] System engineering is about capturing the stakeholder needs so that the correct system can be developed. QFD and capturing the voice of the customer is a restatement of basic System Engineering.

9.14.8.3 Quality Control

Quality control emphasizes testing of products to uncover defects. In a system intensive setting quality personnel do not produce test procedures and execute tests. Instead they witness the testing and stamp off the test documentation to indicate that the procedure was executed as written or as modified by relines developed and documented on the physical test procedure.

In many small commercial organization's quality is given the task of testing a product. There may or may not have been systems analysts involved in conceiving, documenting, and specifying the product requirements. So, the quality representative may actually need to develop tests without any requirement documentation. In this setting there is no traceability. This is a challenge and it is not representative of a system practice driven organization. However, it may make perfect sense and the products may be wonderful but not necessarily important. For example, no one's life is in danger, no industry is dependent on the products performance, no significant financial investment is involved.

In more significant commercial and industrial companies, and government settings, test is a complex subject. It requires specialists able to understand the requirements and develop tests that fully verify that the system behaves as specified in the requirement specifications. Quality representatives are used to ensure that the tests are executed as written with no deviations unless approved by the test director and clearly documented on the actual test procedure information product.

As tests are executed, defects may surface. The defects are recorded in a defect tracking mechanism usually embedded within the change request mechanism for the project. Quality attends the meetings associated with defect tracking and eventually witnesses the tests associated with the corrective actions.

The concept of monitoring and control is broadened even further in the significant organization. All critical processes are monitored and controlled by quality. For example, they monitor and signoff on all deliverable documents. In this case they review documents and other information products for defects such as inconsistencies, omissions, and content. This is typically performed via spot checking which challenges the other reviewers (authors of the information product) who are not part of quality. If there is a trend suggesting reviews are not being adequately performed, quality can withhold approval and prevent delivery.

Table 42 Classifying Defects For Quality Control

Priority	Applies if a problem could
1 Grave	a. Prevent accomplishment of an operational or mission essential capability b. Jeopardize safety, security, or other requirement designated critical c. Result in loss of life or health
2 Catastrophic	a. Adversely affect the accomplishment of an operational or mission essential capability and no work-around solution is known b. Adversely affect technical, cost, or schedule risks to the project or to life

Table 42 Classifying Defects For Quality Control

Priority	Applies if a problem could
	cycle support of the system, and no work-around solution is known
3 Critical	a. Adversely affect the accomplishment of an operational or mission essential capability, but a work-around solution is known b. Adversely affect technical, cost, or schedule risks to the project or to life cycle support of the system, but a work-around solution is known
4 Marginal	a. Result in user operator inconvenience or annoyance but does not affect a required operational or mission essential capability b. Result in inconvenience or annoyance for development or support personnel, but does not prevent the accomplishment of those responsibilities
5 Negligible	Any other effect

Whenever a defect is detected as much information about the defect should be gathered and documented. This should include an initial assessment of the defect[190].

There is a severe quality downward spiral that easily surfaces with defect tracking. The danger is that the team finds defects and fixes them in isolation. There is no desire to spot trends or worse no desire to fix a collection of defects even if the defects are located in the same area. In these settings it is not uncommon to see teams touch a single element such as a software file dozens of times rather than touch it once and fix all the defects at once. The excuses are usually cost and schedule. Meanwhile most of the cost is in the touching of the element not in the individual fixes. An approach to recover from this downward quality spiral is to create a single defect whose sole purpose is to improve quality and let the personnel work in a level of effort mode to increase the quality. Hundreds or thousands of elements cannot be micro-managed, but a focused team could address. This is easy for software and problematic when physical elements are involved.

9.14.8.4 Organizational Alternatives

There are different organizational alternatives for Quality. Depending on the organizational structure there are different checks and balances and organization efficiencies. Ideally Quality would never be compromised regardless of organization, However, as systems practitioners we know organization behavior is a function of organizational structure. This is not any different than any system we might conceive. The organization alternatives are:

- Quality reports directly to the CEO
- Quality reports to Engineering

[190] MIL-STD-498 Appendix C Category And Priority Classifications For Problem Reporting. There is an overlap with the FMEA categories found in MIL-STD-1629A.

- Embed within the Test Organization and reports to CEO
- Embed within the Test Organization and reports to Engineering

9.14.8.5 Quality Improvement

There is an axiom that states you cannot inspect in quality. Its corollary is that you cannot fix in quality. However, there is an approach to systematically improve the quality of a system. The approach is to build upon and expand the Failure Reporting, Analysis and Corrective Action System (FRACAS) that is part of the reliability program. So, the FRACAS not only tracks failure, incidents such as safety, but also elements related to poor quality. The sources of the poor-quality reports include:

- Field feedback from user, customers, maintainers, managers
- Internal development and support staff
- Marketing and sales staff
- Independent analysis of FRACAS reliability and incident reports

Quality staff uses this database and engages in the same process as described in the FRACAS reliability section of this text. Their goals are to improve quality rather than reliability. Reliability may be related to quality, but it is not the whole set that represents quality.

Typically, high quality products, systems, services do everything well. Poor quality is usually perceived when one aspect is done well while the other aspects are ignored, usually because of cost, and so they are of poor quality. For example, an automobile can have great acceleration, but corner poorly, stop poorly, be uncomfortable, etc. However, the acceleration is great. This is opposed to another automobile, which executes everything very well and matches or exceeds the acceleration of the fast but poor-quality automobile. So, high quality encompasses functionality, performance, and perception.

Poor quality also can manifest from disrespect of the system users or customers. This is usually present in a monopoly, oligopoly, or unregulated utility situation. Money is not even the issue; it is just a poor attitude on the part of the managers of the system or product developers. Improving quality in this setting is not possible without using antitrust laws or severe regulation and penalties.

9.14.8.6 Root Cause Analysis

Root cause analysis is based on the concept of causality or cause and effect. A result is the final detected consequence of a chain of events. Root cause analysis attempts to find the first cause in the cause and effect chain. The reality is that it is usually difficult to pin down a single cause that leads to a problem. Usually multiple root causes surface.

The best way to view root cause analysis is as a backward chain of events analysis. For the observable event a cause is postulated. That cause is then treated as an event so that its cause can be postulated.

Obviously finding the root cause is secondary to preventing the same problem from resurfacing. The following steps are suggested:

- Define the problem
- Gather data and evidence
- Create a cause and effect chain
- Identify solutions that address the root cause
- Implement the recommendations
- Observe the fix for effectiveness
- Investigate to see if this root cause applies elsewhere
- Share the findings (e.g. Internet web page)

Assume an automobile fails its annual emissions inspection. The cause and effect chain can be represented as: A <= B <= C <= D

A: Car fails emission inspection
B: Electric air pump has failed
C: No airflow clogs the air injection valves
D: Car not maintained

In this case the root cause analysis points to a car not being properly maintained. However, if we dig deeper into the analysis of why the electronic air pump failed, we see: A <= B <= C <= D

A: Car fails emission inspection
B: Electric air pump has failed
C: Water sucked into air pump
D: Poor air pump intake design

In this case we see that the design is at fault. The air pump is sucking road water during normal driving conditions. This is almost impossible to detect because water has evaporated long before the pump is removed and examined. It is only after the pump is disassembled that it is detected that the pump is frozen because the bearing is covered with calcium deposits. When the pump installation is physically inspected it is clear the air intake can easily suck water in heavy rain and minor flood conditions.

In this case the root cause analysis points to two separate root causes. The first is poor design and the second is poor maintenance, which leads to air injection valve failure[191]. When the new air pump and air injection valves are installed the air pump intake should be moved to prevent future water contamination.

---

[191] This is an actual root cause analysis of the authors' daughters 1997 automobile.

There are different broad lists of root causes depending on industry. The following are some common root causes.

- **The 8 Ms used in manufacturing:** Machine or technology, Method or process, Material, Manpower, Measurement, Milieu or Environment, Management, Maintenance
- **The 8 Ps used in service industry:** Product or Service, Price, Place, Promotion, People, Process, Physical Evidence, Productivity and Quality
- **The 4 Ss used in service industry:** Surroundings, Suppliers, Systems, Skills
- **The Ishikawa Diagram:** is a fishbone diagram[192] that suggests the root causes can be categorized into: Equipment and Materials, Process and Environment, People and Management

All problems are traceable to Bad Process. However, all processes can be subverted. This is the dilemma of humanity and soft elements surface such as personal integrity, confidence, and motivation that influence quality. In the absence of the soft elements the second root cause is Management. It is management's responsibility to make sure the processes work, the technology and tools are current, and the financial box defined by cost and schedule is sufficient for a successful high-quality project.

9.14.8.7 Parts Tracking

When part tracking is mentioned most people think in terms of initial manufacturing of a device. The parts tracking mechanism is established to meet some level of quality in the manufactured item. A system may start out as a high-quality system, However, as time progresses its quality may start to drop. This is usually because of increasing failures due to age, wear, or abuse. There is also the possibility that functionality may disappear because of neglected maintenance and decreased performance because of inferior parts being used in maintenance. A parts tracking mechanism is an approach to minimize quality degradation from the introduction of poor-quality parts.

9.14.9 Certification

Certification applies to systems that must be safe and secure under all conditions including in the presence of multiple failures. This is typically accomplished with inherent system safety and security and with significant levels of fault detection, fault tolerance, and fail-safe mechanisms. Trying to certify a system without fault detection, fault tolerance, and fail-safe mechanisms is usually a sign of a severely compromised organization. It is rare when a system can be certified with just

[192] Kaoru Ishikawa proposed Ishikawa diagrams in the 1960s.

inherent safety and or security in the architecture and the resulting implementation.

Certification is given by the organization best positioned to make the judgment that the system is acceptable. The organization may be the operational user or client, program office or sponsor, or a third-party entity such as a government agency, depending upon the purposes intended.

Certification includes analysis of the process and the solution. It can involve proof like elements. The developers need to show that there was a consistent process that was followed to design and implement the system. Deviation from the process raises concern because it may represent compromises in system. The solution needs to be documented and show strong traceability, especially to the tests. Without the traceability there is concern because once again it may represent compromises in the system.

In many ways the ultimate systems approach needs to be strongly followed with very high levels of accuracy, precision, rigor, and methodical behavior.

During certification all information products (plans, analysis, specifications, design artifacts, tests, manuals, etc.) are examined and a confidence level is achieved so that the system can be certified.

A separate body of people based on the certification evidence approves accreditation. This is the certification board. The certification board consists of representatives from: Engineering, Test, Quality, Production, Users, Maintenance, Support, Logistics, Training, Deployment, Users. Since most systems use machines and significant technology the greatest weight is carried by the Engineers and Testers. The other organization will typically approve the system because their concerns are easiest to address. Engineering on the other hand looks inside the system and has an enormous responsibility to ensure nothing was missed. Next comes test who provide the test results. The issue with test is similar to engineering to ensure in this case that no tests were missed or incorrectly performed.

The certification process starts with the architecture. If the architecture is flawed the system cannot be certified[193]. It continues with the design, implementation, and if applicable production. At any point the certification can be rejected. This suggests that certification begins with the start of the project. Information products are developed and offered to the certification board. The information products in sequence are:

- Plans
- Process Description
- Analysis Results
- Architecture Description

---

[193] For example, the B737 MAX Maneuvering Characteristics Augmentation System (MCAS) architecture was completely flawed because it was not a fault tolerant architecture with fail-safe mechanisms. No certification board with reasonable engineering background would allow the system to move forward. Certification would be instantly stopped.

- Design Artifacts
- Production Plans
- Deployment Plans
- Integrated Logistics Support (ILS) Plans[194]
- Test Results

As the system unfolds the information products are updated and provided to the certification board. This ensures that the board is not overwhelmed with data and the board can check the system to see if there may be certification problems moving forward. Most automation-based system developers run at risk and continue with system development and do not wait for the board to provide comments. This is contrary to physical systems like an office building where activity stops or slows significantly until there is an official signal from the certification authority to continue.

Most people equate diagnostics with maintenance and trying to isolate a fault so that it can be repaired. However, diagnostics are also used to certify that a system is ready to be used. Well check or certification diagnostics are used to surface faults in an operational system. The idea is that the diagnostics stimulate all the critical points in the system that normal operations may not immediately stimulate.

The diagnostics can be manual or automated. Most people think in terms of automated diagnostics especially in computer-based systems. However, manual diagnostics are just as important. A manual diagnostic might be a visual inspection using an approved or certified checklist. For example, those who fly small personal airplanes check the airplane using an approved checklist prior to starting the engine and proceeding to taxi. The checklist includes visual inspection of the tires, landing gear, rudder, tail, ailerons, wings, flaps, propeller, fuselage, etc. When the automobile was new it was not uncommon for people to check the belts, tires, fluids, brakes, lights, and filters prior to a long trip[195].

9.14.10 Non-Deterministic and Artificial Intelligence Systems

Many have attempted to define Artificial Intelligence (AI) and determine if it has been achieved. Most point to the Turing Test[196] as an approach to determine if something is intelligent. This test suggests that if a machine can converse with a human and the human is unable to detect if it is a machine then there is intelligence. We now know that is a narrow view of the situation.

For most of history humanity relied on special purpose machines. They were designed to perform a predefined set of functions for very narrow needs. The

[194] ILS includes Maintenance, Support, Logistics, Training

[195] I still tell my kids to check their automobile prior to a long trip.

[196] The Turing test was developed by Alan Turing in 1950 and is a test of a machine's ability to exhibit intelligent behavior equivalent to or indistinguishable from that of a human.

mechanical engineering age during the early industrial revolution exemplifies these machines. The goal has been to find a way to build a general-purpose machine that could be easily modified to support unanticipated needs and functions. This became the general-purpose computer that came with the computer automation age in the last half of the 20th century.

Both the special purpose machine and general-purpose computer relied on one or more algorithms to implant functionality that satisfies some needs. An algorithm uses math and logic. It also provides the same output for the same input. One can trace through the operations within the machine to see how the answer is found and then check via testing if there are errors. This is a deterministic machine or system.

A non-deterministic machine or system will provide different outputs when the same input is provided. The source of the non-deterministic mechanism can be the conscious introduction of randomness or the nature of the machine.

A machine can be built using what we think is the physical structure and observations of a biological brain. It can have neurons tied together in a neural network[197]. This can be physically implemented using special purpose hardware that mimics neurons or implemented in a general-purpose computer as software that mimics neurons. The neural network can be subjected to learning and used to then detect patterns once learning is complete. Self-learning machines use self-learning algorithms. However, the machine is non-deterministic, and one cannot trace and find out how the machine came to its answer. No one knows how the machine works except that it follows certain rules about neuron interaction and machine learning algorithms. Yet it provides an answer.

The Melpar Mouse had 10 neurons in 1962. The mouse began its first pass through a maze with no special instructions or tendencies to follow. It found its way through by a process of trial and error, bumping into blind alleys, retracing its path, and beginning repeatedly. Each time the mouse began the maze again it learned something and got through in less time. Finally, it made its way through the maze with no errors in seconds.

This is the challenge for this new century. Self-learning algorithms and machines have been available for decades but now because of the extreme low cost of computer hardware they can be made available to anyone.

The dangers of such machines have been known since the start of the computer age. The COBOL language was modified to remove its ability to perform self-modifying code. The requirements for complex systems like air traffic control had requirements that the system could not contain self-modifying code and must be deterministic.

Many see the Internet as a marvel but currently it is based on algorithms. The search engines which many may view as AI or an Expert System are nothing more than regular expression processing implanted on very fast computers. What the

[197] Self-Synthesizing Machine R. J. Lee, Patent number: 3327291, Filing date: Sep 14, 1961 Issue date: Jun 1967.

Internet does have is a planetary storehouse of data and information that can be connected to one or more self-learning machines. The question is what will emerge when that happens.

Observation 19 Non-Deterministic and Artificial Intelligence Systems

Privatization Comment: What does this have to do with privatization? Everything because the high technology industry leaders are looking to experts in government for guidance and rational policy. Because of privatization and the closely associated deregulation policies there is none. In fact, the government policy makers have taken the position to do nothing and let the technology take us wherever it may go using the magic hand of the market.

9.15 System Design Theory Philosophies and Art

Is there a theory of system design? How does system design relate to philosophy and art? These are interesting topics and worth considering when trying to understand how we develop systems engineering designs.

We know that as part of our formal and informal education we are introduced to many different topics. These topics tend to fall into the liberal arts and the sciences. As very young children before we start school we are introduced to colors, shapes, texture, size via coloring books, blocks, clay, and finished toys of all forms and function. During all our years we are exposed to film, music, writings, art, theatre, etc. which expose us to more liberal arts and sciences as part of informal education.

When we enter school, our formal education begins. In liberal arts we study literature, history, the mechanics of language and writing, music, painting, drawing, and even sculpting with clay and papier Mache. In the sciences we study the earth, our solar system, biology, chemistry, physics, and mathematics. Many who may be interested in engineering take mechanical drawing, drafting, software programming, and other engineering related classes before university.

Everyone engages in building and modifying various things long before they enter the university to study engineering and or design. Some build structures to play in while others may create paintings. Some may draw, others may write. Still others may modify home machines like lawn mowers, televisions, stereos, automobiles, etc. Others may cook and develop new eating delights, and some modify or write software, websites, or music.

So long before we enter the system engineering space, we have a broad foundation that allows us to design even though we may not view it as design. The reality is that to design is human. We just do what comes naturally when we have the freedom and time to express ourselves. So, when we discuss design theory philosophies and art we are just trying to explain some part of our universe.

9.15.1 Art

Art exists everywhere you look. Art takes a medium like paint and canvas and transforms those fundamental building elements into a finished item, a work of art. This is design - from nothing comes something. In order to bring this design into being knowledge is needed of the medium and its limitations. For example, working with paint and canvas will not result in sound. It is a visual image. This seems obvious but if the artist is trying to express a vision and have it become a final design with physical attributes that vision may require a different medium, such as stone which has texture and is 3 dimensional. So, perhaps the vision may be implemented with paint, canvas and stone in motion.

In art the final vision is always modified by the medium. There is only so much you can do with paint and canvas when trying to express colors, brightness, contrast, shape, and perspective. So, perhaps the artist needs to distort one element of the artwork so that another element of the artwork or design becomes prominent.

Many tend to equate beautiful buildings as works of art rather than works of engineering. Also, some may view the architecture of the building as a subset of art. These are excellent examples of the medium affecting the vision and the medium being understood via the engineering discipline.

When an artist produces multiple copies of the same item there are always differences. When multiple artists produce the same item there are differences. For example, when multiple software programmers write code to solve the same problem, the solution is always different except in the rarest and most simple cases. The same is true of system designers. Multiple teams will rarely develop the exact same system design. However, when a work of art or design is subjected to a manufacturing process those differences become significantly smaller. Depending on the manufacturing process even machines may be unable to detect the differences between multiple copies.

In art just like any discipline one can study art or one can do art. The study can include history, mediums, techniques, artists and what they did and or do, etc. Art can be a tiny logo or very large as in the case of the layout of an entire city. This small treatment of art may not do justice to artists but the key elements for designers are visible. They are:

- The medium needs to be selected
- The medium modifies the designers' visions
- The designer must respect and use the medium for maximum effectiveness
- There may be unexpected wonderful emergence as the designer works with the medium, this might be called great art

Hand eye coordination is a critical skill that is developed in early childhood education. It is at that time when children engage in their art projects that make their way to the kitchen refrigerator. Many unfamiliar with the basics of child development do not know or understand the importance of a simple crayon drawing or strange shape formed from papier Mache or clay. They don't realize some may be getting nurtured and matured to one day become great designers.

With the rise of computer technology many are missing the chance to develop important hand eye coordination skills. The simple act of being able to write letters clearly on a straight-line help to build spatial relations, printing and cursive writing are just as important as drawing and sculpting. Today we are at a crossroads where a generation that had the opportunity to develop these skills and use computers is disappearing. There is a fundamental question we need to address - how is the computer medium with its software helping or hindering our ability to capture our visions. There has been a large trend in reuse across disciplines. Could that be because it is difficult to capture original visions on a computer? What does this mean? It may suggest that all great design organizations should include artists who are capable of expressing visions without using the computer. This could be via drawings, sketches, graphics, line art, cartoons, physical mockups, physical model structures, animations, etc.

Conversely the computer is a new medium and as such should be able to lead to new designs if we believe that the medium impacts the designers' vision. This suggests that the computer needs to be effectively applied and not used to compromise the design in the name of expediency and or cost. The computer has also allowed the user to perform tasks not possible in the past without other resources. For example:

- It is easy to develop and print a book with hundreds of pages
- It is possible to produce interesting animations without an art department and slow turnaround time medium like film
- It is possible to quickly author and preview music including compositions with an entire orchestra

We just need to ensure we don't use the computer to destroy our art when computers cannot meet the challenge of capturing the vision.

9.15.2 Designers and Medium

When designers work, they need to work with the available "medium". The term Medium is a broad reference to the materials, tools, practices, and technologies. This suggests the designers are not only familiar with the medium but also understand the ramifications of their use under various conditions. Materials is also a broad term that includes fundamental physical material such as wood, stone, metals to abstract materials such as software. Material also can include what we view as an aggregation such as a subsystem. So, when we are designing an automobile at one abstraction level the mechanical engineer designing the engine may focus on different metals, ceramics, and composites to use for the engine components. At a different abstraction level, the system designer may be focusing on the types of engines, such as gas, electric, or diesel to use in the design of the automobile.

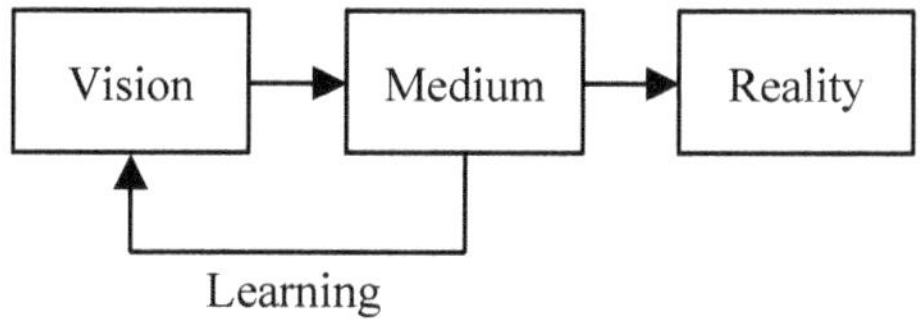

Figure 85 Designers and Medium

In all cases the materials, tools, practices, and technologies need to be fully understood so that appropriate design choices can be selected. For example, an electric engine may be desired However, technology may need to be matured in one or more areas before the electric engine can be considered for the particular automobile application.

A block diagram can illustrate this concept. The block diagram is a visualization and just like any other medium it has limitations that will impact the final reality.

9.15.3 Critical Thinking

Educators take great pride in being able to produce critical thinkers. But what is critical thinking and why is it important to systems engineering design? The following are some definitions of critical thinking:

- Disciplined thinking that is clear, rational, open-minded, and informed by evidence
- Mental process of actively and skillfully conceptualizing, applying, analyzing, synthesizing, and evaluating information to reach an answer or conclusion

Critical thinking is a situation where someone is able to filter out all the irrelevant elements and get to the heart of a situation very quickly and explain their thought process so that everyone understands the conclusion, its lineage, and it is the correct conclusion with no bias or agenda. This requires a well-trained and disciplined mind that is challenged to engage in critical thinking throughout their formal education from first grade through to the university, work, and life experiences. The idea is that practice makes perfect.

Critical thinking is extremely important in the liberal arts and is constantly addressed. That is why some with liberal arts backgrounds can enter the high technology systems arena. Their ability to think critically and get a team off a dead end or stalled position is invaluable. They can challenge accepted doctrines from the technologists and defend their positions because of the clarity of their thinking possible because of their critical thinking skills. It is a given that technical team members also must be able to think critically. However, they have the luxury of falling back on quantitative aspects of a situation using math and logic. The interesting scenario is when qualitative elements are all that are available. This is a scenario where again liberal arts inspired team members using their critical thinking skills can move the situation forward. Some of the key elements of critical thinking and its results are:

- Clarifies goals, examines assumptions, discerns and articulates the relevant from the irrelevant, offers evidence through observation, evaluates evidence, assesses conclusions
- Enters into the logic of problems and issues to see them for what they are without egocentric, social, financial, organizational, personal, or other bias
- Does not shift context to deflect into wrong or useless thinking leading to wrong conclusions or abandonment of finding a solution
- Uses logic and criteria such as clarity, credibility, accuracy, precision, relevance, depth, breadth, significance, and fairness
- Fair-minded, intellectual humility, empathy, integrity, perseverance, courage, and autonomy - without these key traits the results may be clever, but manipulative and often unethical
- Enables analysis, evaluation, explanation, and restructuring of thinking to prevent adopting, acting on, or thinking with a false belief
- Identifies prejudice, bias, propaganda, deception, self-deception, distortion, misinformation

Some of the attributes of critical thinkers are:

- Wants to engage problems and decisions using critical thinking skills
- Raises important questions and problems
- Formulates questions and problems clearly and precisely
- Recognizes problems, wants to find solutions to those problems
- Understands prioritization and order of precedence in problem solving
- Gathers, assesses, and offers relevant information
- Interprets information effectively
- Recognizes unstated assumptions and values
- Comprehends and uses language with accuracy, clarity, and discernment
- Interprets data, to appraise evidence and evaluate arguments
- Recognizes existence or non-existence of logical relationships
- Thinks open-mindedly within alternative systems of thought, recognizing and assessing, assumptions, implications, and practical consequences
- Draws warranted conclusions and generalizations

- Comes to well-reasoned conclusions, solutions, and generalizations
- Tests conclusions, solutions and generalizations using relevant criteria
- Renders accurate judgments
- Reconstructs beliefs on basis of wider experience

From a systems engineering design perspective the team members must always ask themselves if they are engaged in critical thinking as they discuss and address their respective design areas.

Some suggest that individuals can have intellectual skills without critical thinking skills. I disagree. It may be a matter of context but being able to execute a math problem without being able to critically think about the nature of the problem and its elements is in my view being devoid of intellectual skill. Computers have that luxury people do not have that luxury. We all must embrace and enhance our critical thinking skills especially when engaged in systems, which by their very nature have large impacts and many consequences.

Those who come from a biased position will attempt to shut down or discredit critical thinking and its activities. A common method to compromise critical thinking is to de-scope the problem or change the context so that the problem goes away. In this manner a naïve manager may believe they have successfully managed the situation and closed out the activity. Many times, this leads to terrible consequences and injustices. An example is a jury that is instructed to disregard physical evidence or events, which are the only items that matter for the final obvious conclusion. We can become victims to rules that really do not need to be followed but are set by those interested in their exclusive agenda. Thus, critical thinking is attacked and shut down. This can and should never be tolerated, including in systems engineering design.

Observation 20 Critical Thinking

Privatization Comments: It is unclear how privatization could be making such inroads into the culture unless there is a departure from critical thinking in the society. This is not a good sign moving forward.

9.15.4 Scientific Method

For students to be accepted to a university engineering program typically they must be exposed to science course material in high school. Why is there this emphasis on science courses? Let's step back and examine the scientific method.

Many people do not understand that engineering requires significant education including the liberal arts, science, and mathematics. This is especially true of people who have less formal education or come from cultures where these foundations are not known, understood, and appreciated.

The scientific method is used for acquiring knowledge and investigating phenomena. We soon learn there are basic steps in the scientific method:

- Define a question
- Gather information
- Form a hypothesis
- Develop a reproducible experiment to test the hypothesis
- Collect the data
- Analyze the data
- Interpret the data
- Draw conclusions that prove or disprove the hypothesis
- Publish the results
- Have others duplicate the experiment
- Proven hypothesis then becomes a theory

Within the scientific method are certain key elements. Scientists think in terms of cause and effect. The cause and effect is framed in terms of data. The data is usually quantitative to avoid misinterpretation of results. The data analysis uses mathematics and logic to understand the results. This can be presented in graphical format using charts and table formats. The hypothesis selected tends to follow Occam's razor[198] where the simplest explanation is usually the correct one. This can be viewed as succinctness, fewest assumptions, and economy. The conclusion also tends to follow Occam's razor. This is especially important when the conclusion shows the hypothesis is incorrect.

Contrary to what many who refused to take science classes, disproving a hypothesis is just as important as proving a hypothesis. This is especially important if the failed hypothesis is a significant surprise.

So, the scientific method transfers to systems engineering and design. Our initial system design starts out as hypothetical design. As we perform analysis, especially systems engineering analysis, the design quickly starts to fall apart and so we move into a space of multiple system alternatives. The systems just like the scientific method hypothesis and conclusion tend to follow Occam's razor. The simplest most elegant system designs[199] tend to survive the analysis findings. The analysis tends to be rooted in quantitative data using mathematics and logic. The analysis itself is like a reproducible experiment where the system design is tested by the analysis.

The structure of the experiment in the scientific method has several important elements. It needs to be easily and consistently[200] reproducible. It should be as

---

[198] William of Ockham (1287 – 1347) was an English Franciscan friar and scholastic philosopher and theologian.

[199] This is also known as the KISS principle - Keep it Simple Stupid. One of the measures of elegance in a design is simplicity.

[200] Reproducible suggests consistency. Some claim one reproduction is all that is needed and that is incorrect. In the scientific method the experiment always must be reproducible or

simple as possible without compromising the experiment. It should have the following fundamental steps:

1. Tester names and date
2. Hypothesis statement
3. Purpose of experiment (prove or disprove hypothesis)
4. Expected results
5. Materials
6. Test Steps
7. Observations
8. Data collected
9. Data analysis
10. Conclusions and next steps

When our system designs are implemented and produced, they are subjected to tests. The design tests follow the basic principles in a scientific method experiment:

1. Purpose of test
2. Test materials
3. Test steps
4. Data collected
5. Tester and witness names and date

We then prepare a test report, it includes:

1. Observations
2. Data collected
3. Data analysis
4. Conclusions and next steps

As we engage in systems engineering design, we should appreciate the scientific method and what it brings to the party.

Observation 21 Scientific Method

Privatization Comments: It is unclear how privatization could be making such inroads into the culture unless there is a departure from the scientific method in the society. This is not a good sign moving forward.

9.15.5 Deductive and Inductive Reasoning

Deductive reasoning or thinking is a top down approach. The starting point is to

---

the error in the experiment must be detected and corrected.

find the broadest level general statement or facts about a situation and logically proceed to lower levels until they reach a logical conclusion. This suggests:

- There are no errors in the logic
- No statements are flawed or missing
- The full set of statements or facts are known
- All statements are precise and accurate

The problem is that there are always assumptions mixed in with the givens that form the set of statements. There is also the issue of introducing invalid assumptions and or givens. A formal system engineering design analysis practice that uses deductive reasoning is Fault Tree Analysis (FTA).

Inductive reasoning or thinking is a bottom up approach where very specific statements are aggregated to form a conclusion. Although inductive reasoning descriptions typically use examples to lead to general propositions with limited or no assumptions, there is always reality where assumptions enter into the inductive conclusion. Just like in deductive reasoning, the assumptions, givens, examples and the resulting propositions can be flawed, missing, or not available thus leading to a wrong conclusion. A formal system engineering design analysis practice that uses inductive reasoning is Failure Mode Effects Analysis (FMEA).

In the scientific method inductive reasoning is used to develop the hypothesis and deductive reasoning is used to develop the experiment and conclusion. In this scenario the inductive reasoning hypothesis is tested by the deductive reasoning experiment / conclusion while the deductive reasoning experiment / conclusion is tested by the inductive reasoning hypothesis. The goal is to prove or disprove the hypothesis in the scientific method. In systems engineering design analysis when FTA and FEMA is performed on the same aspect of the system they complement and check each other to add more confidence to the proposed system.

Deductive reasoning is much easier to practice. The biggest issue is ensuring all the facts and assumptions are known, then a logical path to a conclusion can be traced. Inductive reasoning is difficult because all the detailed facts and assumptions can be known but the pattern is not detected. Part of this is actually being able to find the relevant detailed set of facts and assumptions, but the connections are not made, or the wrong connections are made resulting in a flawed conclusion. When teaching inductive reasoning simple examples are offered of a few statements. In practice there are dozens or even thousands of items to consider, such as when FMEA is used or a major go no go decision is needed for a new technology, product, or system.

9.15.6 Socratic Method

The Socratic Method is a form of dialog between individuals based on asking and answering questions. It can be used in the design process. For example, you propose this system design. I ask a question and a response is provided by you or others on the team. This prompts the next question and response sequence. This continues until the questions and responses are exhausted.

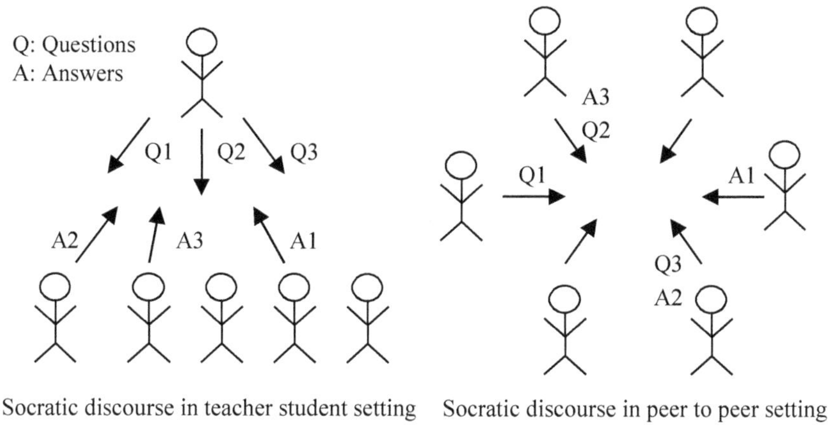

Figure 86 Socratic Discourse Alternatives

The Socratic Method is used to stimulate critical thinking and further development of ideas. Typically, the discussion involves defense of a point of view. One participant asking a series of questions may lead another into contradiction thus weakening the point of view being defended and strengthening an alternative point of view. This should result in a modification of the compromised point of view so that it is strengthened. As questions are asked failure is detected and modification occurs - the modification then strengthens the idea, point of view, or in our case a system design.

This method also tends to surface important elements of different points of views that not only become key discriminators between the different points of views, but also become the key strengths of each point of view. Once applied to design, alternative system designs also start to rise and fall with key discriminators and strengths surfacing as the questions are being asked.

Many who engage in the Socratic method tend to work in a real time mode, such as a classroom setting where a teacher is engaging their students. In these settings the questions and responses happen on the spot, there is no time delay. The same can be done when addressing system design, where the technical director questions the team and the team questions itself. However, in the system design setting there comes a point in the dialog where a break needs to happen, and the participants go to their respective work settings to perform research, investigation, and reflection to address outstanding unanswered questions. The dialog break can be a few hours, days, weeks, months, and perhaps years.

In many ways engineering processes based on design reviews, such as

Preliminary Design Review (PDR) and Critical Design Review (CDR) are based on the Socratic method as they have expectations that translate into key questions that must be answered at the design reviews. If the questions cannot be adequately answered, then the designers must go back to the drawing board and mature and or correct the system designs. Designers can pull the standard questions asked at PDR, CDR[201], and other reviews and start to ask them on the first day of the system design activity. These standard questions can form the basis of their unique questions associated with their unique need and the unique system designs trying to fulfill the unique need.

Socratic questioning is used to explore complex ideas, find truth, surface issues and problems, find assumptions, explore concepts, and determine known from unknown elements. Some believe the questions need to be systematic, disciplined, and deep However, that tends to create an intimidating environment where the most important question may never be asked. Some also believe the questions should focus on fundamental concepts, principals, theories, issues, or problems. However, a detailed question that most initially view as noise may push the discourse into a new level and result in a major breakthrough.

I always make a point of asking questions or moving the conversation into left field. Most participants view this as a distraction. Some get angry and naive management wants to stop the activity. However, as the discourse continues and the redirection is followed, massive creativity is unleashed. It's at this point that innovation takes place and new technologies, approaches, systems, products, etc. are born. I was first exposed to this design technique at Hughes Aircraft[202]. Few follow this path and that is why few organizations can truly innovate.

There have been attempts to identify general categories of questions to consider while engaged in the Socratic method. When reviewing the following list think in terms of questions that the root word suggests.

Table 43 Socratic Method General Questions

- **Purpose:** forces the team members to define the task
- **Information:** what is the source and quality of the information
- **Interpretation:** examine how the team members organize and give meaning to the information, consider alternative meanings
- **Assumptions:** what is being taken for granted, what is being missed
- **Implications:** force team members to follow where the thinking is going

[201] MIL-STD-1521, Technical Reviews and Audits, June 1995, lists a standard set of topics, which are easily interpreted as questions that can be asked at PDR, CDR, and other systems engineering design major milestones.

[202] Improving R&D Productivity A Study Program and Its Applications, Robert M Ranftl, National Conference on Productivity and Effectiveness in Educational Research and Development, December 1977.

Table 43 Socratic Method General Questions

- **Point of View:** state the point of view then consider other points of views as offered by other team members
- **Relevance:** what matters and what is noise
- **Accuracy:** force team to test for correctness
- **Precision:** force team to provide details and be specific
- **Consistency:** look for contradictions
- **Logic:** challenging team to put it all together, make sense, make reasonable
- **Clarification:** close areas open to significant interpretation
- **Evidence:** request examples, analogies, data, information
- **Consequence:** challenge team to address where current logic path is going
- **Questions:** the most important question is questions about the questions, have they all been asked and addressed

The answers are irrelevant. It is all about the questions. Are all the questions being asked? As the right questions surface the answers become self-evident. If someone is suppressing the asking of questions they must be removed from the mix, they are anti-civilization. A good technical director will practice the Socratic Method with the team and good management will allow, encourage, and facilitate this process.

9.15.7 Rational and Action Centric Design Models

Software engineering is a relatively new discipline. Many tend to forget the struggle of first understanding different computing architecture possibilities, different operating systems, and different languages. These three items alone can consume a career. Yet it has been acknowledged that software engineering must exist and mature as a discipline. This has yielded many new discussions, which many traditional engineers find to be spins on existing engineering concepts and ideas. For example, agile methods are easily equated to maturing prototypes from initial research to a fielded implementation. We see that software has this luxury because it is easily changed while the implementation of an office building is difficult if not impossible to change. You cannot argue that after the first floor is built you will learn more about the challenge and then build a better second floor.

Yet there are system design ideas that should be discussed. Because software is easy to change, its design process is both positively and negatively impacted. It is much more accepting of the art concept where the medium shapes the final solution. There tends to be a rejection of what some might suggest hard core engineering. This is engineering driven by rational principles, or a rational centric model. This contrasts with an action centric model where an action is taken and then an observation is made. This is like striking the chisel on a stone sculpture or making a brush stroke on a painting.

The action centric model is influenced by empiricism, where knowledge comes from sensory experience. This is analogous to science, which is based on evidence discovered in experiments. In the scientific method all hypotheses and theories must be tested against observations rather than relying solely on a priori reasoning, intuition, or revelation. The process of science can find its application in the design process. This is a way to view the action centric model.

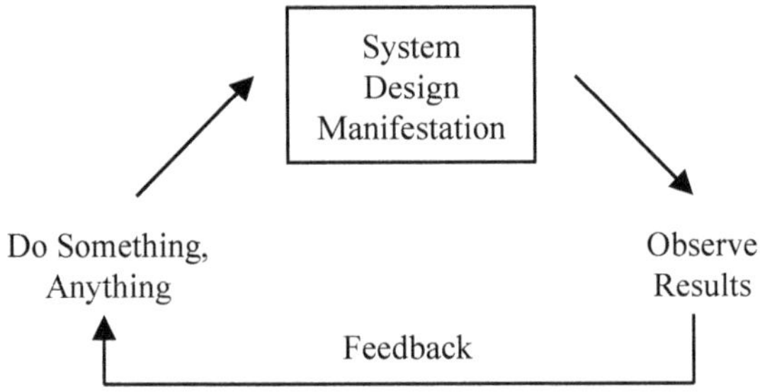

Figure 87 Action Centric Model

Proponents of the action centric model point to extremely high-quality software as viewed as by users. This software is developed with the user closely connected to the design process. Using software, it is easy to develop user interactions and immediately get feedback that then results in appropriate changes.

However, even though this software design may be viewed as spectacular in terms of effectiveness, which includes use and stability, internally it may be a design nightmare. The internal design may be such that no one knows how it works, changes may be impossible, changes may have massive negative ripple effects, or a latent design defect may be present that can cause significant harm when surfaced months or years later.

Yet the action centric model does have significant merits if it is acknowledged that a production ready system needs to be developed from the prototype, even if the prototype is already in field operations. This is the advantage of software; the next release is always possible.

If we examine the system design process closely, we see the action centric model is not only relegated to software. All system design starts at the concept stage. The artifacts in the form of documents, presentations, and models are all relatively easy to change. All engineering engages in the action centric model early in the effort. There are always questions asked, elements proposed, and observations made. The observations may be formal or informal analysis. They can be on the spot during a technical interchange or somewhat delayed via an action item response. The point is that elements of a system design are offered and then observed by the system design team. Based on those observations, the system design elements are modified and matured.

This brings the discussion back to the Socratic method of discourse. When a question is asked a response is anticipated. The question and response modify the solution space. The question or questions can be in the form of words, a spin through a software increment with immediate user feedback, outputs from models, mockups, prototypes, etc.

The rational and action centric models exist in a design activity. If the team is free to express themselves during design, these models will naturally emerge. They then need to be recognized for their strengths and effectively managed.

9.15.8 Linear and Nonlinear Thinking

Linear thinking is an approach where a starting point is selected and then using logic a selected path is followed to a conclusion. The starting point is critical. Nonlinear thinking is contrasted by changing the starting point and departing from the context or even logic to the next point in the thought process.

Linear thinking is easily seen and practiced when solving simple problems such as might be presented in mathematics. When complex problems are encountered people get stuck and they are unable to proceed to the next step of a particular thread of reason. So, they jump to a related area in the problem space, back track to find a different logical path or even change the starting point.

When solving complex problems, jumping to a different aspect of a problem when stuck and unable to make progress can be viewed as following the path of least resistance. As the focus changes to an area where the path and its logic are easily seen and addressed, there is time for the mind to internalize the other aspects of the problem. No problem or aspect of a complex problem is solved before its time. In this way progress is always made.

Some people fear nonlinear thinking especially if they come from simple management settings. This is viewed by some as chaotic with no end in sight. If managers have no background in this area, new system design can quickly be shutdown. So, it is important to understand when nonlinear thinking surfaces in a team and to allow for its natural progression.

Linear and nonlinear thinking are not labels applied to people. Instead they are practices that anyone can apply individually or in a team setting. They each have their advantages and should be respected when they naturally emerge as complex problems are being addressed.

The STOP[203] approach is ideal for capturing design concepts because it easily fits into non-linear thinking. Even though STOP requires that the design be mature before writing begins, it can be used to capture the design as it unfolds. First in storyboard format and then in finished white papers that represent key topics and issues associated with the designs.

---

[203] Sequential Thematic Organization of Publications (STOP), Hughes Aircraft Fullerton, 1963.

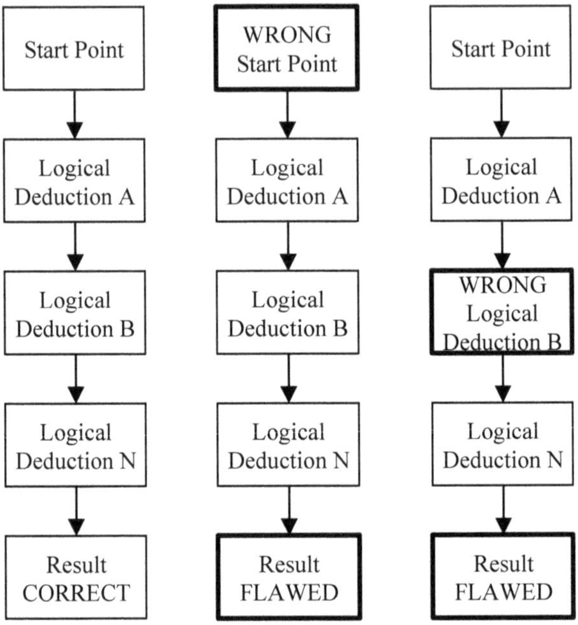

Figure 88 Linear Thinking

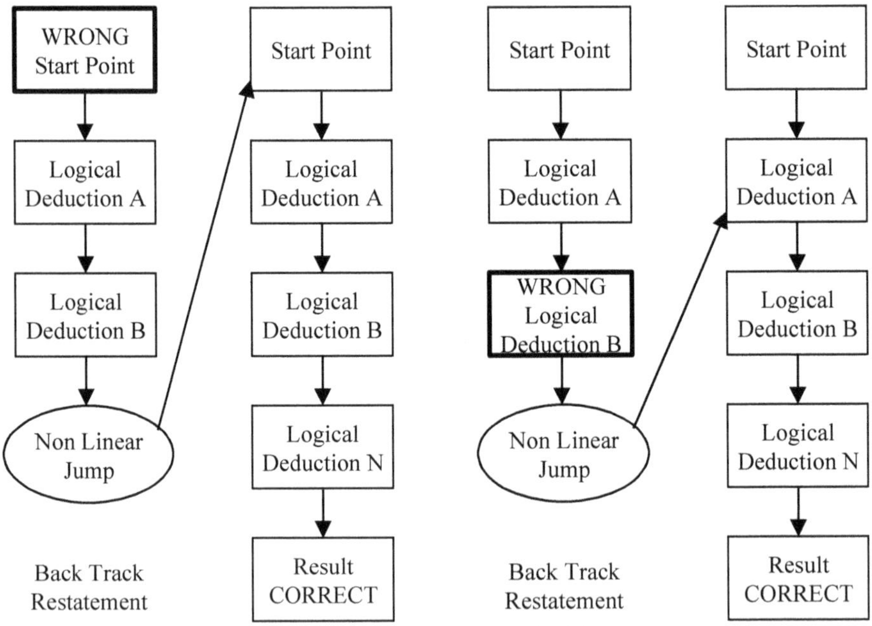

Figure 89 Nonlinear Thinking

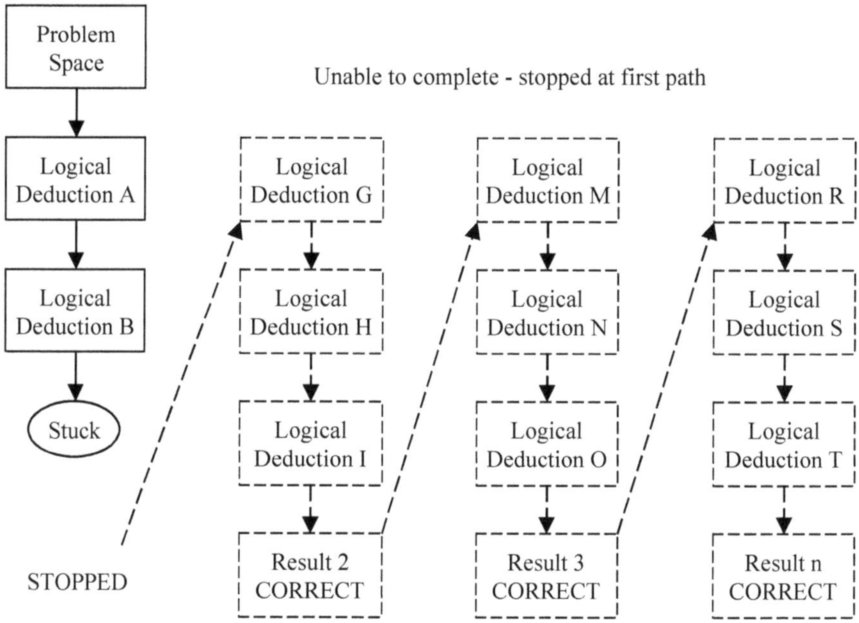

Figure 90 Linear Thinking Complex Problem

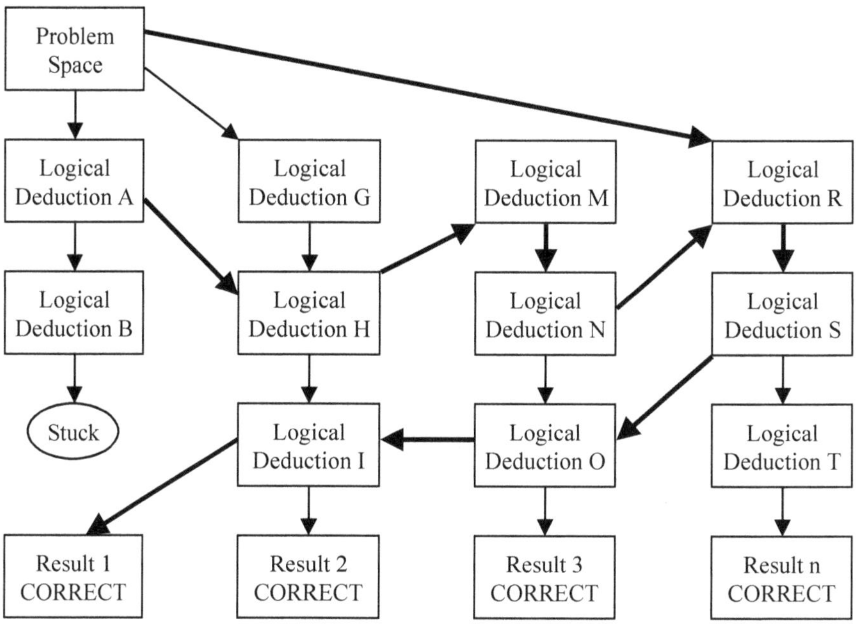

Figure 91 Nonlinear Thinking Complex Problem

9.15.9 Systems Thinking

Systems' thinking is the opposite of reductionism. Systems' thinking views the system as a whole within the context of its environment. Systems' thinking is in contrast with other forms of thinking. These other approaches frame the arguments and set the starting points in their favor. This is why practicing nonlinear thinking is important to the systems thinking process. Examples of other forms of thinking that drive enterprises and solutions are:

- **Financial:** Driven by finance and accounting with little or no knowledge in what the enterprise or system is doing.
- **Marketing:** This goes beyond the traditional marketing boundary and has marketing dictating all system decisions as they see it at this instant in time, including day to day operations. There is also little or no knowledge in how the enterprise or system is executed other than through organizational titles.
- **Product:** All problems are modified so that all solutions match the in house or pre-selected product or products.
- **Technology:** All problems are modified so that all solutions match the in house or pre-selected technology or technologies.

Not all engineers are systems oriented. Many prefer to specialize. Others are new to the profession and may not have a full appreciation for the systems view. However, as time progresses most engineers move into the systems space and become very valuable to their organizations. The paths are varied but include exposure to other engineering disciplines on large projects via design reviews and technical interaction. There is also movement into proposal and marketing areas. At some point, leadership roles surface where the systems perspective is critical for success. If engineers work their respective areas with no consideration to the rest of the system, the risk is:

- Each engineering area optimizes their solution from their point
- Each area may compromise the solutions of the other engineering areas
- With one or more engineering areas unknowingly compromised the system may not work

9.15.10 Systems Theory Thoughts

Many engineering students are introduced to systems in classes associated with control theory[204]. A black box is drawn, inputs and outputs are labeled and then the question is asked: what happens at the output as the input passes through the

[204] Modern Control Systems, Richard C. Dorf, Addison-Wesley Publishing Company, 1967, 1974, Library of Congress CCN 67-15660, ISBN 0201016060.

system, how is the input transformed into an output. The term transfer function is used to describe how the input is processed to yield the output. The system is characterized by its transfer function. This is an important concept as we move the discussion away from quantitative into qualitative analysis.

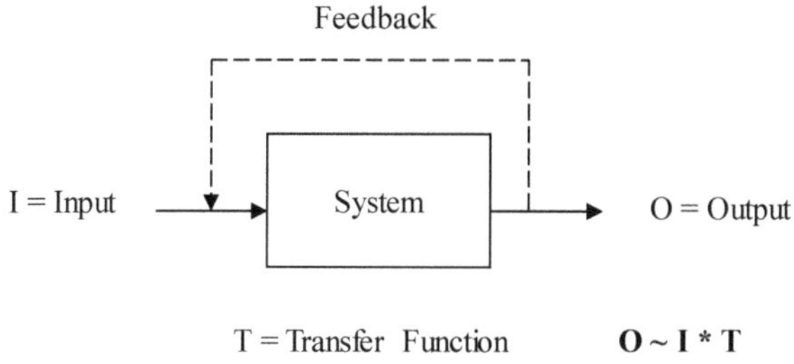

Figure 92 System Transfer Function with Feedback

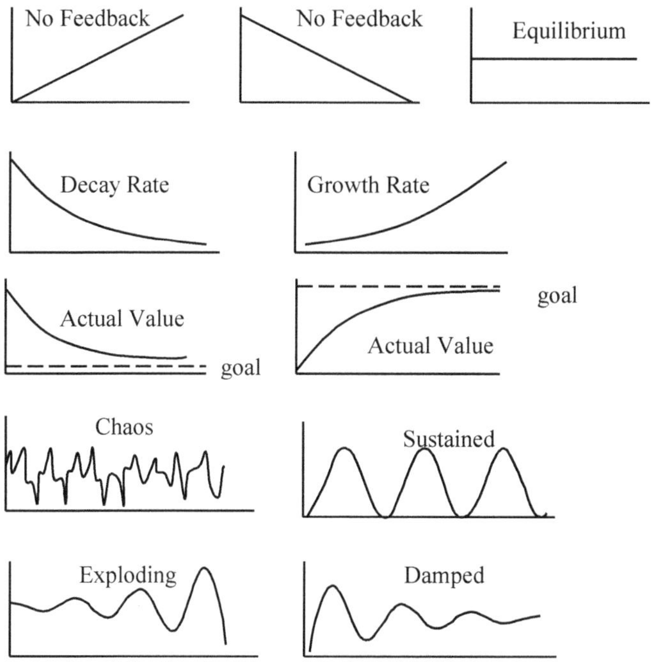

Figure 93 Potential System Outputs

The transfer function is determined using science with experimentation then mathematics to characterize a device. For example, an inductor or capacitor that behave in certain ways as a function of input and time can be measured. The behavior is easily duplicated. The behavior can be mathematically characterized. The process of characterizing a device and capturing its transfer function allows us to build passive filters. The filters can be different (high pass, low pass, band pass, notch, and complex) with different characteristics (frequency cutoff and drop off).

A more complex system is associated with what is termed a valve. A valve can be implemented as a tube or transistor. This is an active device that also can be characterized in a lab setting and then modeled using mathematical equations. In this way different amplifiers can be designed in terms of the desired output and the devices' transfer function.

These systems have feedback. The feedback tends to introduce non-linearity and unexpected results in the system output. The system output is tracked over time. An unstable system is characterized by an exploding output that may eventually lead to a chaotic system. The idea system is one that is in equilibrium or moving towards a desired goal.

For example, history shows war or revolution breaks out when there a shift in the balance of power. The shift in the balance of power shows itself as a chaotic condition. Until equilibrium is achieved with a return to the balance of power, the threat of war or revolution is significant.

This concept of feedback and different system outputs was recognized in electrical engineering when trying to understand an amplifier. The term system surfaces when the amplifier or active device is represented in an ideal form. This is called an operational amplifier (op amp). This device has infinite gain and bandwidth with zero noise.

Using the op amp, it is possible to study the effects of feedback. We quickly see that positive feedback leads to system instability and negative feedback leads to reduced gain and bandwidth. If the system is not ideal and there is noise, we also see that positive feedback leads to more noise and negative feedback leads to less noise.

Using math and the models of idealized components the performance of an analog electrical system can be understood in terms of gain, power output, frequency response, and noise. This begs the question: can any system be understood in terms of its inputs and transfer function if the inputs and transfer function could be found and understood?

A complex system is more than a single input and single output with a transfer function. A system has many inputs, many interacting transfer functions, and many outputs. A system is also more than just one view of a black box with its input, output, and transfer function. A system is a collection of black boxes that need to be understood on their own terms and how they might interact with each other. For example, in the amplifier case:

- There may be a single transfer function that can capture the frequency response, gain, power output, and noise.
- However, the amplifier has weight, physical size, generates heat, has reliability characteristics and an expected life. These can be quantitatively calculated.

- There are multiple sustainability performance characteristics that can be calculated such as energy to produce, transport, use, dispose and then waste to production, transport, use, dispose.
- There are multiple qualitative elements associated with the amplifier such as safety, maintenance, training, human factors, testability, etc. which can be understood using logic and quantitative elements.

Single Input Single Output

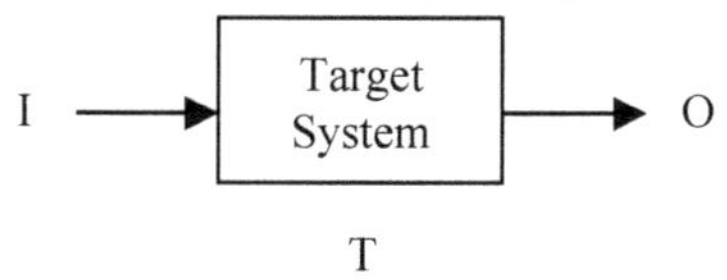

$O = I * T$

$O \sim f, g, p, n$
$T \sim f, g, p, n$

f = Frequency Response — $T_f = O_f / I_f$
g = Gain — $T_g = O_g / I_g$
p = Power — $T_p = O_p / I_p$
n = Noise — $T_n = O_f / I_n$

Figure 94 Single Input Single Output System

Multiple Input Multiple Output

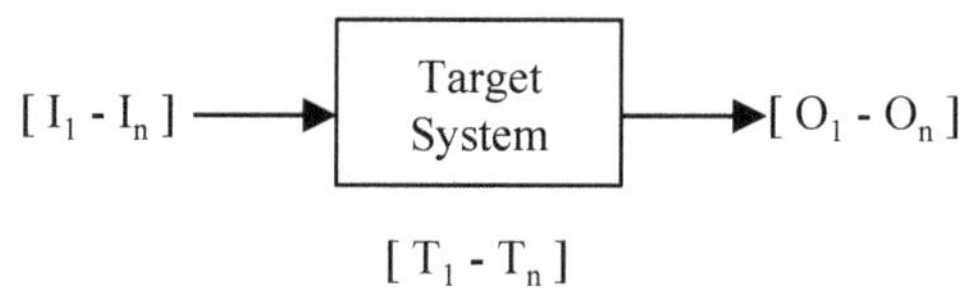

Quantitative Analysis

Generic Performance
Physical Size
Weight
Heat
Reliability, Availability Maintenance Time
Expected Life

Sustainability
Energy to produce, transport, use
Waste to produce, transport, dispose
Waste half life

Human Performance
Number of staff to operate, manage, maintain

Qualitative Analysis - Complex

Sophisticated Practices
Tools: management, maintenance, training
Staff skill levels
Complexity
(# of interfaces, components, functions, etc)
Behavior across unexpected events
Safety
Security
Human Factors
Maintenance
Training
Support
Quality

Figure 95 Multiple Input Multiple Output Complex Systems

These are sophisticated practices usually applied to more complex systems, but they still need to be addressed in even the simplest systems.

The transfer function for complex systems is captured both in quantitative and qualitative analysis. One analysis may impact another analysis and the impact may not be known in the accepted literature and reduced to a universally known equation representing a model.

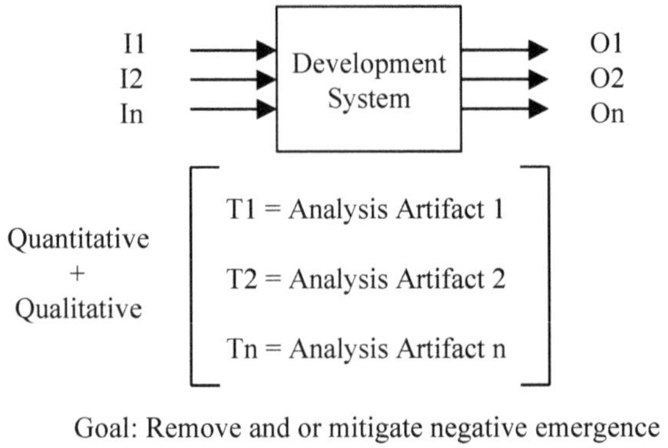

Figure 96 System Development as a System

For a system that is used to develop a system (the process) this suggests that the transfer function is distributed into the humans engaged in the system development. The transfer function of the target system is captured in the body of artifacts that represent the system analysis. The artifacts are the result of a system that was used to develop the target system. This is the development system. It too has a transfer function that includes process, tools, artifacts, and management.

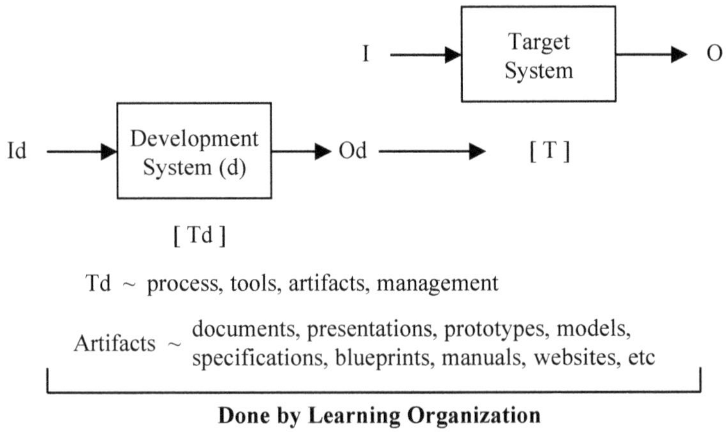

Figure 97 System Solution

This suggests that a learning organization is engaged in the system design activity because the target system is a function of the development system suggesting the development system is modified or tuned by the target system solution. The relationship between the target system and development system suggests that there might be generic practices that can apply to any system. The variable might be system complexity where less complex systems may not need the breadth and depth of the systems practices that are needed for complex system.

The development system tools include engineering and management tools. They are varied and a function of the domain. These management tools also include what many may consider analysis.

Table 44 System Management Tools

Requirements	Requests for Information	Certifications
Specifications	Requests for Proposal	Artifacts Evidence
Databases	Proposals	Decisions Analysis
Blueprints Drawings	Statements of Work	Tradeoffs
Traceability	Business Plans	Analytical Hierarchy
Plans	Goals	Process
Milestones	Schedules	Life Cycle Cost
Technical Meetings	PERT Charts	Design to Cost
Working Groups	Earned Value Management	Return on Investment
Reviews and Audits	Verifications Validations	Measure of Effectiveness

Continuing down the transfer function path, there are many additional items that apply to the development system. They also are varied and a function of the domain.

Table 45 What Applies to All Systems

System Boundaries	Physical Structure	Certifications
Stakeholders	Human Factors	Training
Architecture Descriptions	Safety	Installations
Key Performance	Security	Switch on
Key Functions	Reliability Availability	Sustainment
Requirements	Maintenance	Shutdown
Specifications	Design	Decommissioning
Complexity Analysis	Implementation	Disposal
Technologies	Production	Internal Sustainability
Allocations	Verifications	External Sustainability
Interface Analysis	Validations	Operations

The goal of the development system or process is to surface all the emergent properties of the system. That means all views and analysis practices should be considered until a point of diminishing returns is reached.

At some point placing more people on an effort, doing more analysis, doing different analysis yields no more insights about the system. This can and should be measured. When that point is discovered, it is the point of diminishing returns and the system has its lowest risk of unexpected negative emergence.

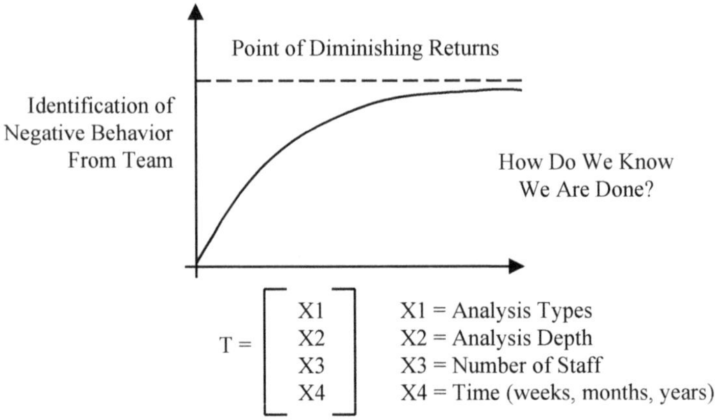

Figure 98 Mitigating Negative Emergence

It's not just the parts. It's not just the interfaces. It's about the infinite possibilities when the parts and interfaces come together. This begs the question of how emergent properties can be detected. Is the human brain (neural network performing math, logic, plus magic) the infinite pattern matcher that can detect emergent properties of a system? What prepares the human, with their brain to become a wondrous detector of emergent properties?

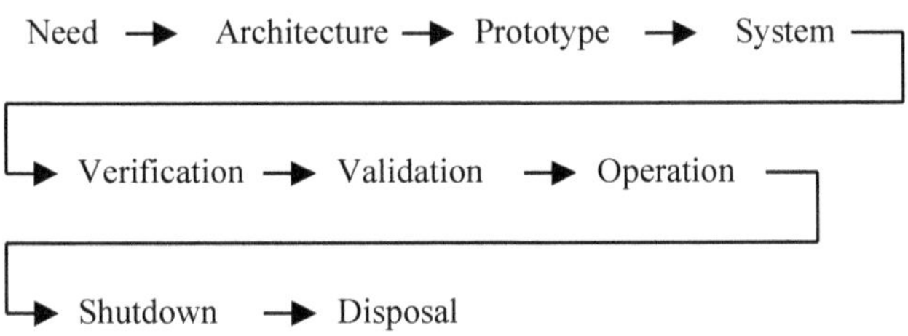

Figure 99 System Evolution

A system starts with a need and then moves through various phases of development, operation, and eventual shutdown. It is this characteristic that makes a system theory complex. In many ways it might be a collection of theories that connect in a way that eventually leads to a unifying theory.

Putting together the black box control theory of input, transfer function that then yields an output with the desire to find emergent properties of the system offers some insight into a possible design process. For example, what can be said about architecture, prototype, or system validation if we apply these ideas?

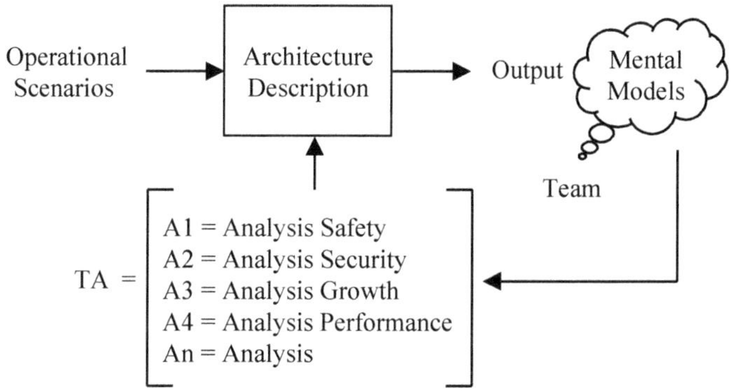

Figure 100 Architecture Validation

Using the same control theory concepts of inputs, outputs, and complex transfer function [TA] an architecture or design might be validated. The validation includes various operational scenarios with a transfer function of various analyses that feeds architecture descriptions that are then compared against various mental models. As this system for the design of architecture is permitted to unfold mental models from the team check the various approaches and issues surface. These issues are then used to iterate the analysis and architecture descriptions of the various alternatives until the preferred architecture design surfaces.

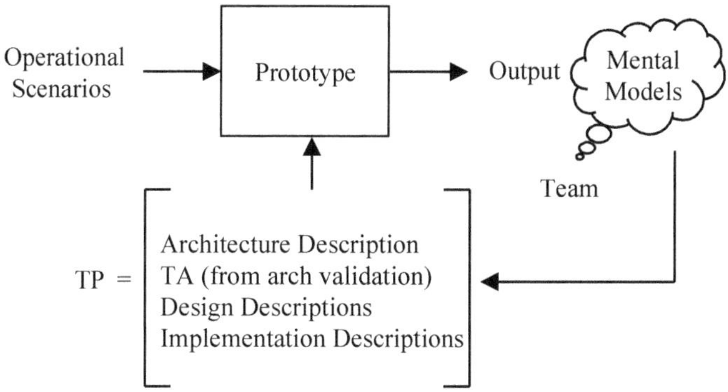

Figure 101 Prototype Validation

Prototype validation might follow the same approach as architecture validation. However, the information products will be different. The TA from the architecture validation might be part of the TP for the prototype validation.

System validation might follow the same approach as architecture and prototype validation. However, the information products will be different. The TA from the architecture validation and TP from the prototype validation might be part of the TS for the system validation.

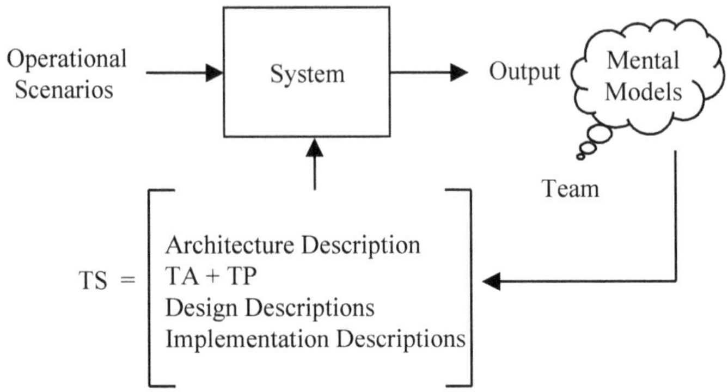

Figure 102 System Validation

The transfer function coupled with the system boundary can be used to understand a system from a qualitative point of view. For example, assume we are looking at a company as a system. The transfer function can include the parameters of profit, tax rate, tax deductions, and antitrust legislation.

The following discussion is an example of two metal models associated with a system that uses tax rates to stimulate the economy.

Mental Model A

If the tax rate is very high such as 90% and the tax law allows for deductions for the cost of doing business, a company can either pay the 90% tax on profits or use the profits to invest. The investment can be in tools, personnel, and material, for existing or future operations and or research and development.

If suddenly the tax rate is lowered to 15% or eliminated the company can decide to accumulate cash that then can be used to buy out their competition. Eventually this will allow a company to enjoy monopoly or oligopoly status unless antitrust legislation exists and is enforced. Once all the reasonable companies are bought then there is cash sitting on the sidelines. If the condition also exists in the transfer function that executive bonuses are also based on earnings per share the executives can purchase company stock, reducing the number of shares, increasing their bonuses and maintaining the stock price in a changing environment[205]. The investment in the future is delayed or not funded at the same level if the tax rate were extremely high.

In this scenario the people are not bad; it is just that the system has a transfer function that will result in a certain output under certain input conditions. The issue with complex systems is that the transfer function is always complex. For example, what if the executives were not driven by immediate self-interest? What if they

---

[205] Personal author experience. This practice was well established in the 1980s shortly after the US corporate tax rates were changed and continues as of the writing of this book.

were driven by trying to benefit all stakeholders so that everyone wins[206]?

In the absence of relying on higher ideals of the system participants and accepting self-interest as a driver, the system transfer function could change. For example, the tax rate could change to 90% or antitrust laws, could be enforced, or both. This was the situation for most of the post WW II time frame up until the 1980s. The question is why was the system changed in the 1980s and allowed to exist even though many realized its flaws and resulting damages?

Mental Model B

If the system has a tax rate that is too high on company profits, then companies will relocate their operations to other areas including outside the country. Since there are many locations where the tax rates are very low the ideal situation is to not have any taxes levied on profits. Further the proceeds used to pay taxes can be used by companies to invest in their operations and that would be a better use of the money than wasting it on inefficient government.

These are two interesting mental models. We now have data from decades of operations using Mental Model A and B. Many do not realize that the same system may change behavior over time because it is extremely complex with many elements. So it is possible that the ideal system may be based on Mental Model A, it may then exhibit unintended consequences and the ideal system then might be Mental Model B, and then it may exhibit unintended consequences so then the ideal system might be based once again on Mental Model A. The idea system might be one that moves between A and B as needed with changing times.

Observation 22 Systems Theory Thoughts

Privatization Comments: One of the fundamental questions that must be asked is how privatization became such a powerful force. One of the possibilities is the change in tax law that allowed the accumulations of vast wealth into the hands of the few. This led to incredible power including the power to subvert Democracy. The next question is why anyone would want to subvert Democracy. One possible answer is that to continue expansion of the wealth of the few, new markets needed to be tapped. The largest and most obvious market to tap was and continues to be the taxpayers. This is an example of cause and effect and modifying the system transfer functions to benefit the few.

One of the reasons why there is no unified systems theory is because transfer functions are both quantitative and qualitative. Also, the quantitative transfer functions are stove piped unable to easily cross connect across boundaries of analysis. For example, what are the training impacts on the frequency response of a

---

[206] Many movies in the 1980's were made where this was the main struggle. The movies as most art were a reflection of society, in this case the results of lowering corporate tax rates.

reel to reel tape recorder. This is not easy to see or quantitatively address. The frequency response can be quantitatively measured over time. However, if it degrades there needs to be an understanding of when and why it degrades. This translates into a maintenance activity where the tape heads are cleaned and demagnetized to ensure that the maximum frequency response is offered by the tape recorder. This analysis is obvious now, but extremely complex when first performed. It falls into the category of preventative maintenance to ensure peak system performance.

Qualitative elements are based on logic and set theory, but the considered elements and parameters vary between people. That is why assumptions are so important when addressing qualitative aspects of the system analysis. Two people will design and implement the same system differently regardless of the level of detail offered in the analysis, specifications, and design. So, verification and validation are critical process elements and are used because people will implement the same system differently.

The systems theory needs to lead to a practical representation of the systems engineering design process. This system engineering design process is usually captured and described in the Systems Engineering Management Plan (SEMP).

In the absence of a unified system theory we have previous experience, knowledge, and some techniques or practices requested in the SEMP. We engage in these practices to surface, develop, maintain, and dispose of our systems.

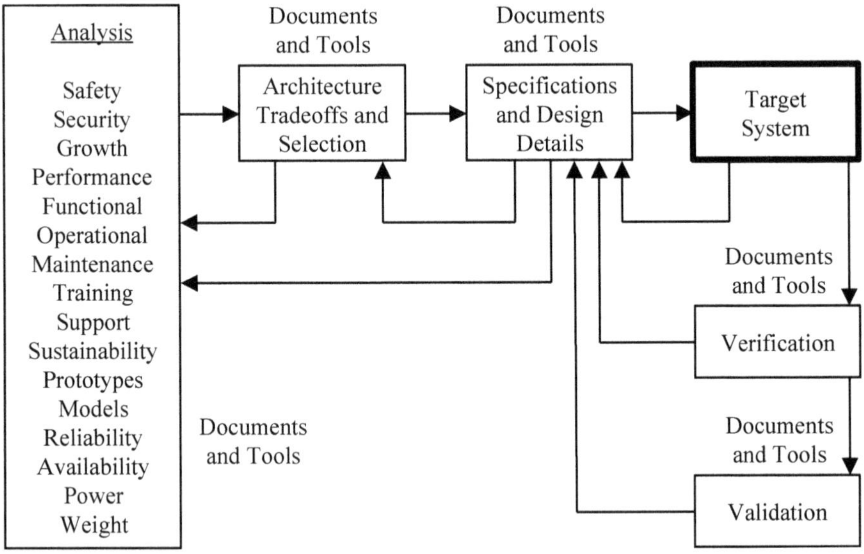

Figure 103 Potential SEMP Diagram

9.16 Social Architecture Observations

Centralized and fully distributed architectures[207] are easily extrapolated to the architecture of social systems such as a company, government, industry, or an entire economy. In the case of a government based on a monarchy or dictatorship the architecture is centralized. As we move into a Democracy the government architecture is distributed. In the case of an economy based on monopolies the architecture is centralized. In a free market economy, the architecture is distributed. Left unchecked a free market economy that starts out as a distributed system will always transition to a centralized system based on monopolies. This is common sense and shown in history. The free market economy as a distributed architecture needs to interact with a government architecture in the absence of any other mechanism to prevent its transition to a centralized system[208].

Table 46 Social Architecture Types and Characteristics

Centralized Architecture	Distributed Architecture
Dictatorship	Democracy
Monopoly	Utility[210] or non-profit with oversight
Unchecked Free Market	Checked Free Market[211]
Privatized Government	Democratic Government
Absolute Power corrupts absolutely	Distributed Power is not absolute
No checks and balances	Checks and balances
No transparency	Transparency
Rule by whim	Rule by law
No accepted system of rules	Accepted system of rules
Easily compromised	Difficult to compromise
Difficult to change and grow with times	Easier to change and grow with times
Very bad cause and effect history[209]	Better cause and effect history

Each of the architecture choices exhibit the same characteristics. The centralized architecture has the least overhead and is the easiest to control because no coordination is needed with other elements. It is the easiest to maintain because status monitoring and control is in one place. However, if the central element fails then the architecture fails and the whole system goes down. The centralized

---

[207] See section 9.8.7 Architecture Types.

[208] This is the purpose of antitrust legislation.

[209] See section 9.2.6 Cause and Effect and Balance of Power.

[210] A Utility is a natural monopoly, stakeholder needs can't be met in a free market. It is subjected to government oversight. For example, community trash collection services.

[211] A free market cannot exist without laws to protect the free market participants from toxic predators. Once the toxic predators form a cartel or monopoly the system no longer serves the stakeholder needs.

architecture also does not gracefully accept growth and technology insertion. This is because of the status quo and the inability to deal with displacement technologies and knowledge. A distributed system is not locked into a single status quo or concept. This allows for more graceful acceptance of displacement technology or new knowledge and lets the system evolve into an unpredictable future.

Many people equate failure with breakage. However, failure includes system compromise. When the system is compromised it no longer performs some or any of its functions, the performance level is unacceptable, or new functions are introduced that harm the system stakeholders.

When we move into government or economy settings, we know that the system can be easily compromised from many sources and for many reasons. The most fundamental observation is that absolute power corrupts absolutely. To mitigate this terrible system failure the power in the system from the start needs to be distributed. Then we know that checks and balances in a distributed system are critical. Finally, we know transparency is critical to check the system and ensure that it has not been compromised. In a democracy this exits. In a true free market setting this exists. In a dictatorship this does not exist. In a monopoly this does not exist. In a privatized setting this does not exist, but it is worse because stakeholders must live with the system and there is no way to correct the system when it gets compromised.

Observation 23 Social Architecture Observations

Privatization Comments: When a government privatizes some function, the result is always a monopoly. This is because of the massive size of the resulting system. This system previously would have been part of a distributed architecture within a Democratic government but once it moves out to the newly created monopoly it is a centralized system.

9.17 Systems Perspective Comments

The Space Act of 1958 included the forces of defense, control with ownership, and the elusive "for all mankind" idea. I remember the space race like yesterday. Many people believed in the "for all mankind" part of the equation. People were very excited about the early space walks and the first moon landing; but as time passed people started to believe that this was easy. Meanwhile we had enormous problems of war and hunger on Earth. So, many people started asking the fundamental question of why we were spending so much energy and resources on space when there were needs here on Earth.

Going into space required enormous intellect, will power, resources, etc. Few realized that shutting it down would be a huge act of hubris. Today few realize that if you shutdown something you never may be able to recreate it regardless of our desires. This is emergence at its most significant level.

There is no question that the military used space funding to further their needs.

There is also no question that those who think they have a right to own everything furthered their needs. The problem is where does the "for all mankind" fit into the equation and what does it really mean.

Today when we point to hunger, want, and other ills we immediately shift to the idea that this is all rooted in our politics. We think our technologies and systems are mature enough to feed and provide for everyone. However, what if that is not the case. What if we use politics as an excuse and instead, we are engaged in an act of extreme hubris? What if we really are lacking the technologies, know how, and systems to beat the elements and live well on Earth.

In the spring of 2011, we witnessed the earthquake and tsunami in Japan with the resulting nuclear disaster. Not only were we not able to gracefully deal with the earthquake and tsunami but the nuclear disaster was beyond our control. This occurred even though the Japanese earthquake preparedness was state-of-the-art and an example to the rest of the world. This is a classic case of being humbled by Mother Nature and our best technologies failing.

10 Supporting Information

This section contains primarily government documents. Typically, this is found at the end of a document or book but because this section is so large, I moved it to the point just before I provide my closing thoughts. I wanted to offer a system that allows those who jump to the end of a book to find the end of the book.

At this point you are welcomed to skip this section and go to section 11 Privatization System Conclusions and then return to this section. Each section is large. You can jump past any section and then go back and revisit it in the future. You can also jump around in this section and review the topics that are of initial interest. Eventually you should go through all the sections so that you are fully immersed in the supporting information and have a greater appreciation for the privatization content of this book.

If you decide to jump in, start by reading the executive orders and then scan the other supporting information. The FAA history is fascinating, and you may want to read those supporting information sections next. The final step would be to read the remaining information.

10.1 Government Policy 1987 to Present

This section contains the actions taken by the US government that set policy from approximately 1987 to the present.

10.1.1 EO-12607 President's Commission on Privatization

President Ronald Reagan
Wednesday, September 2, 1987

By the authority vested in me as President by the Constitution and laws of the United States of America, and in order to establish, in accordance with the Federal Advisory Committee Act, as amended (5 U.S.C. App. I), a Commission to review the appropriate division of responsibilities between the Federal government and the private sector, it is hereby ordered as follows:

Section 1. Establishment.

(a) There is established the President's Commission on Privatization. The Commission shall be composed of not more than 13 members appointed or designated by the President. The members shall be drawn from among a bipartisan cross-section of distinguished leaders.

(b) The President shall designate a Chairman from among the members of the Commission.

Sec. 2. Functions.

(a) The Commission shall study and evaluate:

(1) Past and current privatization efforts by the Federal government, State and local governments, and foreign governments, including asset sales by the Federal government;

(2) Literature and writing on privatization; and

(3) The environment for additional privatization efforts by the Federal government.

(b) The Commission shall review the current activities of the Federal government, including asset holdings, and identify those functions that:

(1) Are not properly the responsibility of the Federal government and should be divested or transferred to the private sector, with no residual involvement by the Federal government; or

(2) Require continuing oversight by an Executive Branch agency but can be performed more efficiently by a private entity, including the use of vouchers as an alternative to direct service.

(c) The Commission shall develop the framework for a privatization program, identifying:

(1) Privatization opportunities, including those identified in (b) above, listed in

order of priority;

(2) Legislative and administrative actions necessary to effect the privatization initiatives or remove existing privatization restrictions;

(3) Needed improvements to personnel and administrative policy to create an environment conducive to privatization;

(4) Organizational and resource requirements necessary to implement successfully the privatization program; and

(5) Actions necessary to create broadbased support for privatization efforts.

(d) The Commission shall submit its findings and recommendations to the President and the Director of the Office of Management and Budget by March 1, 1988. Interim recommendations shall be transmitted to the Director for consideration in the formulation of the President's FY 1989 budget.

Sec. 3. Administration.

(a) The heads of Executive departments, agencies, and independent instrumentalities shall, to the extent permitted by law, provide the Commission, upon request, with such information as it may require for purposes of carrying out its functions.

(b) Members of the Commission shall serve without compensation for their work on the Commission. While engaged in the work of the Commission, members appointed from among private citizens of the United States may be allowed travel expenses, including per diem in lieu of subsistence, as authorized by law for persons serving intermittently in the government service (5 U.S.C. 5701-5707).

(c) To the extent provided by law and subject to the availability of appropriations, the Director of the Office of Management and Budget shall provide the Commission with such administrative services, funds, facilities, staff, and other support services as may be necessary for the performance of its functions.

Sec. 4. General Provision.

(a) Notwithstanding the provisions of any other Executive Order, the functions of the President under the Federal Advisory Committee Act that are applicable to the Commission, except that of reporting annually to the Congress, shall be performed by the Director of the Office of Management and Budget, in accordance with guidelines and procedures established by the Administrator of General Services; and

(b) The Commission shall terminate 30 days after submitting its final report to the President.

Signature of Ronald Reagan

Ronald Reagan, The White House, September 2, 1987. Filed with the Office of the Federal Register, 11:57 a. m., September 8, 1987. The Executive order was released by the Office of the Press Secretary on September 3, 1987.

10.1.2 Report of the President's Commission on Privatization

This section is a summary of the report that was the result of Executive Order 12607 - President's Commission on Privatization issued on September 2, 1987 by President Reagan. This is a key document because it clearly outlines the plan to privatized major portions of the US Federal Government. As of 2018 we clearly see a major portion of this plan has been executed. However, in that time frame they were sensitive to the needs of employees.

What is not stated in the report is that at that time it was important to ensure that second class workers were not created with lower salaries and benefits. This was part of the perception that the Federal Government, as the largest employer in the US, should set an example and not facilitate downward spirals. Ensuring and encouraging commerce and upward economic growth and mobility were part of the social fabric when this report was produced.

10.1.2.1 Letter of Transmittal

Dear Mr. President

I am pleased to transmit to you the report of the President's Commission on Privatization, PRIVATIZATION Toward More Effective Government. Created by your Executive Order No. 12607 on the Commission has devoted the past several months to examining the appropriate division of responsibilities between the federal government and the private sector.

During the conduct of our examination, we reviewed extensive literature on privatization, considered the testimony of 140 witnesses, and analyzed information and data provided by the pertinent federal agencies in each of the subject areas addressed in this report.

In our deliberations, we considered first and most critically the needs of the American consumer and how those needs can best be satisfied. In this report we recommend alternative approaches for administering many government programs and services, when we determined that they could be better managed at less cost by involving the private sector and/or providing for individual consumer's choice.

It is our belief and hope that this report of findings and recommendations, if adopted, would serve as the linchpin in the identification and transfer of federal activities that can be performed more effectively by the private sector.

For all of us, participation in the work of the Commission has been a challenging and stimulating opportunity to serve our nation. We appreciate having had this privilege.

Sincerely, David F. Linowes Chairman

A copy of the letter was also sent to James C. Miller, III the Director of Office of Management and Budget.

10.1.2.2 Executive Summary Extract

The following is an extract of the executive summary. The executive summary provides additional details on how to deal with each of the targeted agencies and government functions.

<u>Executive Summary</u>

The President's Commission on Privatization was established on September 2, 1987 "to review the appropriate division of responsibilities between the federal government and the private sector," and to identify those government programs that are not properly the responsibility of the federal government or that can be performed more efficiently by the private sector.

The Commission reviewed a broad spectrum of government activities

- Low-Income Housing
- Housing Finance
- Federal Loan Programs
- Air Traffic Control and other FAA Functions
- Educational Choice
- Postal Service
- Contracting Out Military Commissaries; Prisons
- Federal Asset Sales Amtrak; Naval Petroleum Reserves
- Other Programs Medicare; International Development Programs; Urban Mass Transit

In all these representative areas, the Commission found potential for improved efficiency, quality of service, or both, to be derived from increased private sector participation in the provision of services. In some areas, such as the Naval Petroleum Reserves, the Commission found that the public would be best served by complete government divestiture. In other areas, such as Housing, Education, and Medicare, the Commission found that the continued need for public sector support could be served by means of vouchers, which act as vehicles for private sector participation, and hence, competition. In yet other areas, such as Air Traffic Control, Postal Service, and Urban Mass Transit, the Commission found that a combination of private sector initiatives, from contracting out to asset sales, may best serve the public interest. However, federal workers should be assured that normally any staff reductions resulting from the implementation of Commission recommendations should be handled through attrition. **In addition, any recommendation supporting increased contracting out should be implemented only after full consideration has been given to employee interests.**

10.1.3 EO-12803 Infrastructure Privatization

President George Herbert Walker Bush
Thursday, April 30, 1992

By the authority vested in me as President by the Constitution and the laws of the United States of America, and in order to ensure that the United States achieves the most beneficial economic use of its resources, it is hereby ordered as follows:

Section 1. Definitions.

For purposes of this order:

(a) "Privatization" means the disposition or transfer of an infrastructure asset, such as by sale or by long-term lease, from a State or local government to a private party.

(b) "Infrastructure asset" means any asset financed in whole or in part by the Federal Government and needed for the functioning of the economy. Examples of such assets include, but are not limited to roads, tunnels, bridges, electricity supply facilities, mass transit, rail transportation, airports, ports, waterways, water supply facilities, recycling and wastewater treatment facilities, solid waste disposal facilities, housing, schools, prisons, and hospitals.

(c) "Originally authorized purposes" means the general objectives of the original grant program; however, the term is not intended to include every condition required for a grantee to have obtained the original grant.

(d) "Transfer price" means:

(i) the amount paid or to be paid by a private party for an infrastructure asset, if the asset is transferred as a result of competitive bidding; or

(ii) the appraised value of an infrastructure asset, as determined by the head of the executive department or agency and the Director of the Office of Management and Budget, if the asset is not transferred as a result of competitive bidding.

(e) "State and local governments" means the government of any State of the United States, the District of Columbia, any commonwealth, territory, or possession of the United States, and any county, municipality, city, town, township, local public authority, school district, special district, intrastate district, regional or interstate governmental entity, council of governments, and any agency or instrumentality of a local government, and any federally recognized Indian Tribe.

Sec. 2. Fundamental Principles.

Executive departments and agencies shall be guided by the following objectives and principles:

(a) Adequate and well maintained infrastructure is critical to economic growth. Consistent with the principles of federalism enumerated in Executive Order No. 12612, and in order to allow the private sector to provide for infrastructure modernization and expansion, State and local governments should have greater freedom to privatize infrastructure assets.

(b) Private enterprise and competitively driven improvements are the foundation of our Nation's economy and economic growth. Federal financing of infrastructure assets should not act as a barrier to the achievement of economic efficiencies through additional private market financing or competitive practices, or both.

(c) State and local governments are in the best position to assess and respond to local needs. State and local governments should, subject to assuring continued compliance with Federal requirements that public use be on reasonable and nondiscriminatory terms, have maximum possible freedom to make decisions concerning the maintenance and disposition of their federally financed infrastructure assets.

(d) User fees are generally more efficient than general taxes as a means to support infrastructure assets. Privatization transactions should be structured so as not to result in unreasonable increases in charges to users.

Sec. 3. Privatization Initiative.

To the extent permitted by law, the head of each executive department and agency shall undertake the following actions:

(a) Review those procedures affecting the management and disposition of federally financed infrastructure assets owned by State and local governments and modify those procedures to encourage appropriate privatization of such assets consistent with this order;

(b) Assist State and local governments in their efforts to advance the objectives of this order; and

(c) Approve State and local governments' requests to privatize infrastructure assets, consistent with the criteria in section 4 of this order and, where necessary, grant exceptions to the disposition requirements of the "Uniform Administrative Requirements for Grants and Cooperative Agreements to State and Local Governments" common rule, or other relevant rules or regulations, for infrastructure assets; provided that the transfer price shall be distributed, as paid, in the following manner:

(i) State and local governments shall first recoup in full the unadjusted dollar amount of their portion of total project costs (including any transaction and fix-up costs they incur) associated with the infrastructure asset involved;

(ii) if proceeds remain, then the Federal Government shall recoup in full the amount of Federal grant awards associated with the infrastructure asset, less the applicable share of accumulated depreciation on such asset (calculated using the Internal Revenue Service accelerated depreciation schedule for the categories of assets in question); and

(iii) finally, the State and local governments shall keep any remaining proceeds.

Sec. 4. Criteria.

To the extent permitted by law, the head of an executive department or agency shall approve a request in accordance with section 3(c) of this order only if the grantee:

(a) Agrees to use the proceeds described in section 3 (c) (iii) of this order only for investment in additional infrastructure assets (after public notice of the proposed investment), or for debt or tax reduction; and

(b) Demonstrates that a market mechanism, legally enforceable agreement, or regulatory mechanism will ensure that:

> (i) the infrastructure asset or assets will continue to be used for their originally authorized purposes, as long as needed for those purposes, even if the purchaser becomes insolvent or is otherwise hindered from fulfilling the originally authorized purposes; and
>
> (ii) user charges will be consistent with any current Federal conditions that protect users and the public by limiting the charges.

Sec. 5. Government-wide, Coordination and Review.

In implementing Executive Order Nos. 12291 and 12498 and OMB Circular No. A-19, the Office of Management and Budget, to the extent permitted by law and consistent with the provisions of those authorities, shall take action to ensure that the policies of the executive departments and agencies are consistent with the principles, criteria, and requirements of this order. The Office of Management and Budget shall review the results of implementing this order and report thereon to the President 1 year after the date of this order.

Sec. 6. Preservation of Existing Authority.

Nothing in this order is in any way intended to limit any existing authority of the heads of executive departments and agencies to approve privatization proposals that are otherwise consistent with law.

Sec. 7. Judicial Review.

This order is intended only to improve the internal management of the executive-branch, and is not intended to create any right or benefit, substantive or procedural, enforceable by a party against the United States, its agencies or instrumentalities, its officers or employees, or any other persons.

Signature of George H.W. Bush

George Bush The White House, April 30, 1992.

10.1.4 Federal Activities Inventory Reform Act of 1998

It was not until the Federal Activities Inventory Reform Act of 1998 Public Law 105–270 that serious action was taken towards privatizing the federal government. The law required that the head of each executive agency submit to the Director of the Office of Management and Budget a list of activities performed by the Federal Government that in the judgment of the head of the executive agency are not inherently governmental functions.

It includes a provision for realistic and fair cost comparisons when considering contracting in the private sector. This includes the costs of quality assurance, technical monitoring of the performance of the function, liability insurance, and employee retirement and disability benefits, and all other overhead costs. The all other overhead costs provision is significant because it has huge impacts in the presence of a government shutdown event.

Federal Activities Inventory Reform Act of 1998

Public Law 105–270

112 STAT. 2382 PUBLIC LAW 105–270 OCT. 19, 1998

Public Law 105–270 105th Congress

An Act

To provide a process for identifying the functions of the Federal Government that are not inherently governmental functions, and for other purposes.

Be it enacted by the Senate and House of Representatives of the United States of America in Congress assembled,

SECTION 1. SHORT TITLE.

This Act may be cited as the ''Federal Activities Inventory Reform Act of 1998''.

SEC. 2. ANNUAL LISTS OF GOVERNMENT ACTIVITIES NOT INHERENTLY GOVERNMENTAL IN NATURE.

(a) LISTS REQUIRED. Not later than the end of the third quarter of each fiscal year, the head of each executive agency shall submit to the Director of the Office of Management and Budget a list of activities performed by Federal Government sources for the executive agency that, in the judgment of the head of the executive agency, are not inherently governmental functions. The entry for an activity on the list shall include the following

(1) The fiscal year for which the activity first appeared on a list prepared under this section.

(2) The number of full-time employees (or its equivalent) that are necessary for the performance of the activity by a Federal Government source.

(3) The name of a Federal Government employee responsible for the activity from whom additional information about the activity may be obtained.

(b) OMB REVIEW AND CONSULTATION. The Director of the Office of Management and Budget shall review the executive agency's list for a fiscal year and consult with the head of the executive agency regarding the content of the final list for that fiscal year.

(c) PUBLIC AVAILABILITY OF LISTS.

(1) PUBLICATION. Upon the completion of the review and consultation regarding a list of an executive agency

(A) the head of the executive agency shall promptly transmit a copy of the list to Congress and make the list available to the public; and

(B) the Director of the Office of Management and Budget shall promptly publish in the Federal Register a notice that the list is available to the public.

(2) CHANGES. If the list changes after the publication of the notice as a result of the resolution of a challenge under section 3, the head of the executive agency shall promptly

(A) make each such change available to the public and transmit a copy of the change to Congress; and Federal Register,

(B) publish in the Federal Register a notice that the change is available to the public.

(d) COMPETITION REQUIRED. Within a reasonable time after the date on which a notice of the public availability of a list is published under subsection (c), the head of the executive agency concerned shall review the activities on the list. Each time that the head of the executive agency considers contracting with a private sector source for the performance of such an activity, the head of the executive agency shall use a competitive process to select the source (except as may otherwise be provided in a law other than this Act, an Executive order, regulations, or any executive branch circular setting forth requirements or guidance that is issued by competent executive authority). The Director of the Office of Management and Budget shall issue guidance for the administration of this subsection.

(e) REALISTIC AND FAIR COST COMPARISONS. For the purpose of determining whether to contract with a source in the private sector for the performance of an executive agency activity on the list on the basis of a comparison of the costs of procuring services from such a source with the costs of performing that activity by the executive agency, the head of the executive agency shall ensure that all costs (including the costs of quality assurance, technical monitoring of the performance of such function, liability insurance, employee retirement and disability benefits, and all other overhead costs) are considered and that the costs considered are realistic and fair.

SEC. 3. CHALLENGES TO THE LIST.

(a) CHALLENGE AUTHORIZED. An interested party may submit to an executive agency a challenge of an omission of a particular activity from, or an inclusion of a particular activity on, a list for which a notice of public availability has been published under section 2.

(b) INTERESTED PARTY DEFINED. For the purposes of this section, the term ''interested party'', with respect to an activity referred to in subsection (a), means the following

(1) A private sector source that

(A) is an actual or prospective offeror for any contract, or other form of agreement, to perform the activity; and

(B) has a direct economic interest in performing the activity that would be adversely affected by a determination not to procure the performance of the activity from a private sector source.

(2) A representative of any business or professional association that includes within its membership private sector sources referred to in paragraph (1).

(3) An officer or employee of an organization within an executive agency that is an actual or prospective offeror to perform the activity.

(4) The head of any labor organization referred to in section 7103 (a) (4) of title 5, United States Code, that includes within its membership officers or employees of an organization referred to in paragraph (3).

(c) TIME FOR SUBMISSION. A challenge to a list shall be submitted to the executive agency concerned within 30 days after the publication of the notice of the public availability of the list under section 2.

(d) INITIAL DECISION. Within 28 days after an executive agency receives a challenge, an official designated by the head of the executive agency shall

(1) decide the challenge; and

(2) transmit to the party submitting the challenge a written notification of the decision together with a discussion of the rationale for the decision and an explanation of the party's right to appeal under subsection (e).

(e) APPEAL.

(1) AUTHORIZATION OF APPEAL. An interested party may appeal an adverse decision of the official to the head of the executive agency within 10 days after receiving a notification of the decision under subsection (d).

(2) DECISION ON APPEAL. Within 10 days after the head of an executive agency receives an appeal of a decision under paragraph (1), the head of the executive agency shall decide the appeal and transmit to the party submitting the appeal a written notification of the decision together with a discussion of the rationale for the decision.

SEC. 4. APPLICABILITY.

(a) EXECUTIVE AGENCIES COVERED. Except as provided in subsection (b), this Act applies to the following executive agencies

(1) EXECUTIVE DEPARTMENT. An executive department named in section 101 of title 5, United States Code.

(2) MILITARY DEPARTMENT. A military department named in section 102 of title 5, United States Code.

(3) INDEPENDENT ESTABLISHMENT. An independent establishment, as defined in section 104 of title 5, United States Code.

(b) EXCEPTIONS. This Act does not apply to or with respect to the following

(1) GENERAL ACCOUNTING OFFICE. The General Accounting Office.

(2) GOVERNMENT CORPORATION. A Government corporation or a Government controlled corporation, as those terms are defined in section 103 of title 5, United States Code.

(3) NONAPPROPRIATED FUNDS INSTRUMENTALITY. A part of a department or agency if all of the employees of that part of the department or agency are employees referred to in section 2105 (c) of title 5, United States Code.

(4) CERTAIN DEPOT-LEVEL MAINTENANCE AND REPAIR. Depot-level maintenance and repair of the Department of Defense (as defined in section 2460 of title 10, United States Code).

SEC. 5. DEFINITIONS.

In this Act

(1) FEDERAL GOVERNMENT SOURCE. The term ''Federal Government source'', with respect to performance of an activity, means any organization within an executive agency that uses Federal Government employees to perform the activity.

(2) INHERENTLY GOVERNMENTAL FUNCTION.

(A) DEFINITION. The term ''inherently governmental function'' means a function that is so intimately related to the public interest as to require performance by Federal Government employees.

(B) FUNCTIONS INCLUDED. The term includes activities that require either the exercise of discretion in applying Federal Government authority or the making of value judgments in making decisions for the Federal Government, including judgments relating to monetary transactions and entitlements. An inherently governmental function involves, among other things, the interpretation and execution of the laws of the United States so as

(i) to bind the United States to take or not to take some action by contract, policy, regulation, authorization, order, or otherwise;

(ii) to determine, protect, and advance United States economic, political, territorial, property, or other interests by military or diplomatic action, civil or criminal judicial proceedings, contract management, or otherwise;

(iii) to significantly affect the life, liberty, or property of private persons;

(iv) to commission, appoint, direct, or control officers or employees of the United States; or

(v) to exert ultimate control over the acquisition, use, or disposition of the property, real or personal, tangible or intangible, of the United States, including the collection, control, or disbursement of appropriated and other Federal funds.

(C) FUNCTIONS EXCLUDED. The term does not normally include

(i) gathering information for or providing advice, opinions, recommendations, or ideas to Federal Government officials; or

(ii) any function that is primarily ministerial and internal in nature (such as building security, mail operations, operation of cafeterias, housekeeping, facilities operations and maintenance, warehouse operations, motor vehicle fleet management operations, or other routine electrical or mechanical services).

SEC. 6. EFFECTIVE DATE.

This Act shall take effect on October 1, 1998.

Approved October 19, 1998.

10.1.5 Circular A-76 Performance of Commercial Activities

This Circular establishes Federal policy regarding the performance of commercial activities and implements the statutory requirements of the Federal Activities Inventory Reform Act of 1998, Public Law 105-270. It is an important policy document because it establishes that the Government should not compete with the commercial industrial base. This suggests what a commercial entity looks like – it engages in commercial business.

Unfortunately as a result of the privatization efforts over the past few decades the Government has established a new entity that has no commercial activity and yet is considered a company that offers privatized contract services exclusively to the Government. This is a violation of the policy. The policy states that the business needs to be a commercial business, not one artificially created by the Government.

EXECUTIVE OFFICE OF THE PRESIDENT
OFFICE OF MANAGEMENT AND BUDGET
WASHINGTON. D.C. 20503

August 4, 1983 (REVISED 1999) CIRCULAR NO. A-76 TO THE HEADS OF EXECUTIVE DEPARTMENTS AND ESTABLISHMENTS

SUBJECT Performance of Commercial Activities

1. Purpose. This Circular establishes Federal policy regarding the performance of commercial activities and implements the statutory requirements of the Federal Activities Inventory Reform Act of 1998, Public Law 105-270. The Supplement to this Circular sets forth the procedures for determining whether commercial activities should be performed under contract with commercial sources or in-house using Government facilities and personnel.

2. Rescission. OMB Circular No. A-76 (Revised), dated March 29, 1979; and Transmittal Memoranda 1 through 14 and 16 through 18.

3. Authority. The Budget and Accounting Act of 1921 (31 U.S.C. 1 et seq.), The Office of Federal Procurement Policy Act Amendments of 1979. (41 U.S.C. 401 et seq.), and The Federal Activities Inventory Reform Act of 1998. (P. L. 105-270).

4. Background.

a. In the process of governing, the Government should not compete with its citizens. The competitive enterprise system, characterized by individual freedom and initiative, is the primary source of national economic strength. In recognition of this principle, it has been and continues to be the general policy of the Government to rely on commercial sources to supply the products and services the Government needs.

b. This national policy was promulgated through Bureau of the Budget Bulletins issued in 1955, 1957 and 1960. OMB Circular No. A-76 was issued in 1966. The Circular was previously revised in 1967, 1979, and 1983. The Supplement (Revised Supplemental Handbook) was previously revised in March 1996 (Transmittal

Memorandum 15).

5. Policy. It is the policy of the United States Government to:

a. Achieve Economy and Enhance Productivity. Competition enhances quality, economy, and productivity. Whenever commercial sector performance of a Government operated commercial activity is permissible, in accordance with this Circular and its Supplement, comparison of the cost of contracting and the cost of in-house performance shall be performed to determine who will do the work. When conducting cost comparisons, agencies must ensure that all costs are considered and that these costs are realistic and fair.

b. Retain Governmental Functions In-House. Certain functions are inherently Governmental in nature, being so intimately related to the public interest as to mandate performance only by Federal employees. These functions are not in competition with the commercial sector. Therefore, these functions shall be performed by Government employees.

c. Rely on the Commercial Sector. The Federal Government shall rely on commercially available sources to provide commercial products and services. In accordance with the provisions of this Circular and its Supplement, the Government shall not start or carry on any activity to provide a commercial product or service if the product or service can be procured more economically from a commercial source.

6. Definitions. For purposes of this Circular:

a. A commercial activity is one which is operated by a Federal executive agency and which provides a product or service that could be obtained from a commercial source. Activities that meet the definition of an inherently Governmental function provided below are not commercial activities. A representative list of commercial activities is provided in Attachment A. A commercial activity also may be part of an organization or a type of work that is separable from other functions or activities and is suitable for performance by contract.

b. A conversion to contract is the changeover of an activity from Government performance to performance under contract by a commercial source.

c. A conversion to in-house is the changeover of an activity from performance under contract to Government performance.

d. A commercial source is a business or other non-Federal activity located in the United States, its territories and possessions, the District of Columbia or the Commonwealth of Puerto Rico, which provides a commercial product or service.

e. An inherently Governmental function is a function which is so intimately related to the public interest as to mandate performance by Government employees. Consistent with the definitions provided in the Federal Activities Inventory Reform Act of 1998 and OFPP Policy Letter 92-1, these functions include those activities which require either the exercise of discretion in applying Government authority or the use of value judgment in making decisions for the Government. Services or products in support of inherently Governmental functions, such as those listed in

Attachment A, are commercial activities and are normally subject to this Circular. Inherently Governmental functions normally fall into two categories:

(1) The act of governing; i.e., the discretionary exercise of Government authority. Examples include criminal investigations, prosecutions and other judicial functions; management of Government programs requiring value judgments, as in direction of the national defense; management and direction of the Armed Services; activities performed exclusively by military personnel who are subject to deployment in a combat, combat support or combat service support role; conduct of foreign relations; selection of program priorities; direction of Federal employees; regulation of the use of space, oceans, navigable rivers and other natural resources; direction of intelligence and counter-intelligence operations; and regulation of industry and commerce, including food and drugs.

(2) Monetary transactions and entitlements, such as tax collection and revenue disbursements; control of the Treasury accounts and money supply; and the administration of public trusts.

f. A cost comparison is the process of developing an estimate of the cost of Government performance of a commercial activity and comparing it, in accordance with the requirements of the Supplement, to the cost to the Government for contract performance of the activity.

g. Directly affected parties are Federal employees and their representative organizations and bidders or offerors on the instant solicitation.

h. Interested parties for purposes of challenging the contents of an agency's Commercial Activities Inventory under the Federal Activities Inventory Reform Act of 1998 are:

(1) A private sector source that (A) is an actual or prospective offeror for any contract or other form of agreement to perform the activity; and (B) has a direct economic interest in performing the activity that would be adversely affected by a determination not to procure the performance of the activity from a private sector source.

(2) A representative of any business or professional association that includes within its membership private sector sources referred to in (1) above.

(3) An officer or employee of an organization within an executive agency that is an actual or prospective offeror to perform the activity.

(4) The head of any labor organization referred to in section 7103(a) (4) of Title 5, United States Code that includes within its membership officers or employees of an organization referred to in (3) above.

7. Scope.

a. Unless otherwise provided by law, this Circular and its Supplement shall apply to all executive agencies and shall provide administrative direction to heads of agencies.

b. This Circular and its Supplement apply to printing and binding only in those agencies or departments which are exempted by law from the provisions of Title 44 of the U.S. Code.

c. This Circular and its Supplement shall not:

(1) Be applicable when contrary to law, Executive Orders, or any treaty or international agreement;

(2) Apply to inherently Governmental functions as defined in paragraph 6.e.;

(3) Apply to the Department of Defense in times of a declared war or military mobilization;

(4) Provide authority to enter into contracts;

(5) Authorize contracts which establish an employer-employee relationship between the Government and contractor employees. An employer-employee relationship involves close, continual supervision of individual contractor employees by Government employees, as distinguished from general oversight of contractor operations. However, limited and necessary interaction between Government employees and contractor employees, particularly during the transition period of conversion to contract, does not establish an employer-employee relationship.

(6) Be used to justify conversion to contract solely to avoid personnel ceilings or salary limitations;

(7) Apply to the conduct of research and development. However, severable in-house commercial activities in support of research and development, such as those listed in Attachment A, are normally subject to this Circular and its Supplement; or

(8) Establish and shall not be construed to create any substantive or procedural basis for anyone to challenge any agency action or inaction on the basis that such action or inaction was not in accordance with this Circular, except as specifically set forth in Part 1, Chapter 3, paragraph K of the Supplement, " Appeals of Cost Comparison Decisions" and as set forth in Appendix 2, Paragraph G, consistent with Section 3 of the Federal Activities Inventory Reform Act of 1998.

d. The requirements of the Federal Activities Inventory Reform Act of 1998 apply to the following executive agencies:

(1) an executive department named in 5 USC 101,

(2) a military department named in 5 USC 102, and

(3) an independent establishment as defined in 5 USC 104.

e. The requirements of the Federal Activities Inventory Reform Act of 1998 do not apply to the following entities or activities:

(1) the General Accounting Office,

(2) a Government corporation or a Government controlled corporation as defined in 5 USC 103,

(3) a non-appropriated funds instrumentality if all of its employees are referred to in 5 USC 2105(c), or

(4) Depot-level maintenance and repair of the Department of Defense as defined in 10 USC 2460.

8. Government Performance of a Commercial Activity. Government

performance of a commercial activity is authorized under any of the following conditions:

a. No Satisfactory Commercial Source Available. Either no commercial source is capable of providing the needed product or service, or use of such a source would cause unacceptable delay or disruption of an essential program. Findings shall be supported as follows:

(1) If the finding is that no commercial source is capable of providing the needed product or service, the efforts made to find commercial sources must be documented and made available to the public upon request. These efforts shall include, in addition to consideration of preferential procurement programs (see Part I, Chapter 1, paragraph C of the Supplement) at least three notices describing the requirement in the Commerce Business Daily over a 90-day period or, in cases of bona fide urgency, two notices over a 30-day period. Specifications and requirements in the solicitation shall not be unduly restrictive and shall not exceed those required of in-house Government personnel or operations.

(2) If the finding is that a commercial source would cause unacceptable delay or disruption of an agency program, a written explanation, approved by the assistant secretary or designee in paragraph 9.a. of the Circular, must show the specific impact on an agency mission in terms of cost and performance. Urgency alone is not adequate reason to continue in-house operation of a commercial activity. Temporary disruption resulting from conversion to contract is not sufficient support for such a finding, nor is the possibility of a strike by contract employees. If the commercial activity has ever been performed by contract, an explanation of how the instant circumstances differ must be documented. These decisions must be made available to the public upon request.

(3) Activities may not be justified for in-house performance solely on the basis that the activity involves or supports a classified program or the activity is required to perform an agency's basic mission.

b. National Defense.

(1) The Secretary of Defense shall establish criteria for determining when Government performance of a commercial activity is required for national defense reasons. Such criteria shall be furnished to OMB, upon request.

(2) Only the Secretary of Defense or his designee has the authority to exempt commercial activities for national defense reasons.

c. Patient Care. Commercial activities performed at hospitals operated by the Government shall be retained in-house if the agency head, in consultation with the agency's chief medical director, determines that in-house performance would be in the best interests of direct patient care.

d. Lower cost. Government performance of a commercial activity is authorized if a cost comparison prepared in accordance with the Supplement demonstrates that the Government is operating or can operate the activity on an ongoing basis at an estimated lower cost than a qualified commercial source.

9. Action Requirements. To ensure that the provisions of this Circular and its Supplement are followed, each agency head shall:

a. Designate an official at the assistant secretary or equivalent level and officials at a comparable level in major component organizations to have responsibility for implementation of this Circular and its Supplement within the agency.

b. Establish one or more offices as central points of contact to carry out implementation. These offices shall have access to all documents and data pertinent to actions taken under the Circular and its Supplement and will respond in a timely manner to all requests concerning inventories, schedules, reviews, results of cost comparisons and cost comparison data.

c. Be guided by Federal Acquisition Regulation (FAR) Subpart 24.2 (Freedom of Information Act) in considering requests for information.

d. Implement this Circular and its Supplement with a minimum of internal instructions. Cost comparisons shall not be delayed pending issuance of such instructions.

e. Ensure the reviews of all existing in-house commercial activities are completed within a reasonable time in accordance with the Federal Activities Inventory Reform Act of 1998 and the Supplement.

10. Annual Reporting Requirement. As required by the Federal Activities Inventory Reform Act of 1998 and Appendix 2 of the Supplement, no later than June 30 of each year, agencies shall submit to OMB a Commercial Activities Inventory and any supplemental information requested by OMB. After review and consultation by OMB, agencies will transmit a copy of the Commercial Activities Inventory to Congress and make the contents of the Inventory available to the public. Agencies will follow the process provided in the Supplement for interested parties to challenge (and appeal) the contents of the inventory.

11. OMB Responsibility and Contact Point. All questions or inquiries should be submitted to the Office of Management and Budget, Room 6002 NEOB, Washington, DC 20503. Telephone number (202) 395-6104, FAX (202) 395-7230.

12. Effective Date. This Circular and the changes to its Supplement are effective immediately.

EXAMPLES OF COMMERCIAL ACTIVITIES

Attachment A OMB Circular No. A-76

Audiovisual Products and Services

- Photography (still, movie, aerial, etc.)
- Photographic processing (developing, printing, enlarging, etc.)
- Film and videotape production (script writing, direction, animation, editing, acting, etc.)
- Microfilming and other microforms
- Art and graphics services
- Distribution of audiovisual materials

- Reproduction and duplication of audiovisual products
- Audiovisual facility management and operation
- Maintenance of audiovisual equipment

Automatic Data Processing

- ADP services - batch processing, time-sharing, facility management, etc.
- Programming and systems analysis, design, development, and simulation
- Key punching, data entry, transmission, and teleprocessing services
- Systems engineering and installation
- Equipment installation, operation, and maintenance

Food Services

- Operation of cafeterias, mess halls, kitchens, bakeries, dairies, and commissaries
- Vending machines Ice and water

Health Services

- Surgical, medical, dental, and psychiatric care
- Hospitalization, outpatient, and nursing care
- Physical examinations
- Eye and hearing examinations and manufacturing and fitting glasses and hearing aids
- Medical and dental laboratories
- Dispensaries
- Preventive medicine
- Dietary services
- Veterinary services

Industrial Shops and Services

- Machine, carpentry, electrical, plumbing, painting, and other shops
- Industrial gas production and recharging
- Equipment and instrument fabrication, repair and calibration
- Plumbing, heating, electrical, and air conditioning services, including repair
- Fire protection and prevention services
- Custodial and janitorial services
- Refuse collection and processing

Maintenance, Overhaul, Repair, and Testing

- Aircraft and aircraft components
- Ships, boats, and components
- Motor vehicles
- Combat vehicles

- Railway systems
- Electronic equipment and systems
- Weapons and weapon systems
- Medical and dental equipment
- Office furniture and equipment
- Industrial plant equipment
- Photographic equipment
- Space systems

Management Support Services

- Advertising and public relations services
- Financial and payroll services
- Debt collection

Manufacturing, Fabrication, Processing, Testing, and Packaging

- Ordnance equipment
- Clothing and fabric products
- Liquid, gaseous, and chemical products
- Lumber products
- Communications and electronics equipment
- Rubber and plastic products
- Optical and related products
- Sheet metal and foundry products
- Machined products
- Construction materials
- Test and instrumentation equipment

Office and Administrative Services

- Library operations
- Stenographic recording and transcribing
- Word processing/data entry/typing services
- Mail/messenger
- Translation
- Management information systems, products and distribution
- Financial auditing and services
- Compliance auditing
- Court reporting
- Material management
- Supply services

Other Services

- Laundry and dry cleaning

- Mapping and charting
- Architect and engineer services
- Geological surveys
- Cataloging
- Training -- academic, technical, vocational, and specialized
- Operation of utility systems (power, gas, water steam, and sewage)
- Laboratory testing services

Printing and Reproduction

- Facility management and operation
- Printing and binding -- where the agency or department is exempted from the provisions of Title 44 of the U.S. Code
- Reproduction, copying, and duplication
- Blueprinting

Real Property

- Design, engineering, construction, modification, repair, and maintenance of buildings and structures; building mechanical and electrical equipment and systems; elevators; escalators moving walks
- Construction, alteration, repair, and maintenance of roads and other surfaced areas
- Landscaping, drainage, mowing and care of grounds
- Dredging of waterways

Security

- Guard and protective services
- Systems engineering, installation, and maintenance of security systems and individual privacy systems Forensic laboratories

Special Studies and Analyses

- Cost benefit analyses
- Statistical analyses
- Scientific data studies
- Regulatory studies
- Defense, education, energy studies
- Legal/litigation studies
- Management studies

Systems Engineering, Installation, Operation, Maintenance, and Testing

- Communications systems - voice, message, data, radio, wire, microwave, and satellite
- Missile ranges
- Satellite tracking and data acquisition

- Radar detection and tracking
- Television systems - studio and transmission equipment, distribution systems, receivers, antennas, etc.
- Recreational areas Bulk storage facilities

Transportation

- Operation of motor pools
- Bus service
- Vehicle operation and maintenance
- Air, water, and land transportation of people and things
- Trucking and hauling

10.1.6 The Trap What Happened to Our Dream of Freedom

The Trap What Happened to Our Dream of Freedom[212] is a BBC television documentary by Adam Curtis. It aired in the United Kingdom in March 2007 on the BBC. The series consists of three 60-minute programs that explore the concepts and definition of freedom in the late 1990s.

- Episode 1 F**k You Buddy
- Episode 2 The Lonely Robot
- Episode 3 We Will Force You to Be Free

The series describes how a model of human beings performing as self-seeking robotic creatures resulted in major policy changes. This led to a flawed idea of freedom and the unintended negative consequences that are now serious problems moving forward in this new century. Although the documentary is not about privatization, it offers information on how privatization may have taken root. The following descriptions are key elements from the documentary and my views of the presented content and how it may have impacted privatization.

Episode 1 Fk You Buddy**

Episode one examines the rise of game theory during the Cold War and the way in which its mathematical models of human behavior filtered into economic thought. It describes the development of game theory and the work of John Nash. He believed that all humans are suspicious and selfish creatures that strategize constantly. Building on this theory he developed mathematically verifiable models and won the Nobel Prize in Economics because of this work.

Nash invented system games that reflected his beliefs about human behavior, including one he called 'Fuck You Buddy' (later published as "So Long Sucker"), in which the only way to win was to betray the playing partner. These games only

---

[212] 1. The Trap What Happened to Our Dream of Freedom, BBC Documentary, Adam Curtis, March 2007.

worked correctly if the players obeyed the ground rules to behave selfishly and try to outwit their opponents.

When RAND Corporation tried the games on their own secretaries, they were surprised to find that instead of betraying each other, the secretaries cooperated every time. This did not discredit the models in the eyes of the analysts. From their perspective it suggested that the secretaries were unfit subjects.

Comment: System verification and operational validation is critical to ensuring that the system works. The analysts were obviously bad.

Comment: The episode did not try to determine how a false set of assumptions in the model would lead to the wrong conclusion. This is a serious problem in settings that are driven by ideology rather than science, engineering, and systems thinking. For example, what would happen when one or both players in the game determined that they were deceived. How would the game really end?

Comment: Though not relevant, at the time when doing this work Nash was suffering from paranoid schizophrenia. As a result, he was deeply suspicious of everyone around him including his colleagues and was convinced that many were involved in conspiracies against him. It was this mistaken belief that led to his view of people that formed the basis of his theories. Footage of an older and wiser Nash was shown in which he acknowledged that his paranoid views of other people were false. The reason why his illness was irrelevant is because his work was not properly reviewed and vetted.

Comment: It was clear that the model and proof was gamed to result in the desired outcome to match the mental model that Nash accepted. Once a system input and output are known it is easy to determine the transfer function. That is systems theory 101. It is obvious that others with different mental models of the situation would have communicated their findings, including the flawed set of assumptions and a system boundary that never considered the repercussions beyond the first event of the deception. The example of the test with the secretaries should have sounded the alarm bells that something was seriously wrong with the Nash model and proof.

The episode shows how game theory was used to create the US nuclear strategy during the Cold War. Because no nuclear war occurred, it was concluded that game theory was correct. The Soviet Union did not attack the US with its nuclear weapons, so it must have worked.

Comment: The episode did not examine if anyone thought that the game theory driven policy decisions were irrelevant and that perhaps there were other reasons why there was no attack from the Soviet Union.

The episode goes on to examine work in psychiatry by R.D. Laing that led him to model family interactions using game theory. His conclusion was that humans are inherently selfish and shrewd and generate strategy during everyday interactions. Laing's theories became more developed when he concluded that some forms of mental illness were merely artificial labels used by the state to suppress individual suffering. This belief became a part of the counterculture in the 1960s.

An experiment run by one of Laing's students, David Rosenhan, presented normal and genuine patients at several American psychiatric institutions. Normal patients were falsely diagnosed as having mental disorders and genuine patients were identified as imposters. The results of the experiment were a disaster for American psychiatry because it showed that psychiatrists were not able to diagnose, and therefore treat, mental illness.

The Rosenhan experiment inspired a mental health model implemented in a computer program as a diagnostic tool. Input to the computer program consisted of answers to a questionnaire issued to hundreds of thousands of randomly selected Americans. The diagnostic program identified over 50% of the ordinary people tested as suffering from a mental disorder. According to Dr. Jerome Wakefield, the results found were viewed as a general conclusion that there is a hidden epidemic.

Comment: The leaders in the psychiatric field never addressed whether the computer model was tested or validated. Instead they used the model to justify increasing the population they were treating.

In an interview, economist James M. Buchanan criticized the concept of public interest, asking what it is and suggested that it consists purely of self-interest of the governing bureaucrats. Buchanan also proposed that organizations should employ managers who are motivated only by money. He described those who are motivated by other factors, such as job satisfaction or a sense of public duty as zealots.

Comment: The program did not explore or challenge this extreme view. For example, Maslow's Hierarchy of Needs as proposed by Abraham Maslow in a paper A Theory of Human Motivation, 1945 was common knowledge at the time. The theory was fully described in the book Motivation and Personality, 1954[213]. The theory suggests that once lower level needs are satisfied then ones' full potential can be achieved. Full potential suggests greatest productivity in society. This is counter to pushing humanity down so that their only concern is money for survival. To suggest that people try to reach their highest potential are zealots is extreme and attacks the messengers rather than the message. It is a form of propaganda to push

---

[213] Motivation and Personality, Abraham Harold Maslow, HarperCollins Publishers, 1954, 3d Sub edition January 1987, ISBN 0060419873.

an agenda. This is an important disclosure because this is what played out in the workforce at the time. Yes, people were labeled as zealots, jobs were lost, and careers destroyed. They were replaced with greedy self-serving zealots.

The episode suggests that at the start of the 1970s, the theories of Laing and the models of Nash began to converge, leading to a popular belief that the state, a surrogate family, was a mechanism of social control which kept power out of the hands of the public. The episode suggested that it was this belief which allowed the theories of Hayek to look credible, and underpinned the free-market beliefs of Margaret Thatcher, who believed that by dismantling as much of the British state as possible and placing former nationalized institutions into the hands of public shareholders a form of social equilibrium could be reached. This was a return to Nash's work, in which he proved mathematically that if everyone pursued their own interests, a stable, yet perpetually dynamic, society would result.

Comment: Challenges in the UK were completely different than in the US. The US had a massive commercial and industrial base. While privatization in the UK would expand its commercial and industrial base, privatization in the US would compromise its Democracy. The US did not have government owned commercial and industrial operations.

Comment: The NASH work and proof was incorrect and based on flawed science, mathematics, reason, and logic and most importantly no one caught this serious error.

The episode ends with the suggestion that this mathematically modeled society is run on data such as performance targets, quotas, statistics and these figures, combined with the exaggerated belief in human selfishness, have created "a cage" for Western humans. The cage is discussed in Episode two.

Episode 2 The Lonely Robot

Episode two develops the theme that drugs such as Prozac and lists of psychological symptoms which might indicate anxiety or depression were being used to normalize behavior and make humans behave more predictably, like machines. This was not presented as a conspiracy theory, but as a logical outcome of market-driven self-diagnosis by checklist based on symptoms, not actual causes, as discussed in part one.

People with standard mood fluctuations diagnosed themselves as abnormal. They arrived at psychiatrist's offices, fulfilled the diagnostic criteria without offering personal histories, and were medicated. The result is that vast numbers of Western people had their behavior and mental activity modified by Selective Serotonin Reuptake Inhibitors (SSRIs) without medical necessity.

Footage of Richard Dawkins describing his gene-centered view of evolution is shown. This brings Curtis back to the economic models of Hayek and the game theories of the Cold War. Curtis explains how, with the "robotic" description of mankind apparently validated by geneticists, the game theory systems gained even more acceptance.

The Trap describes how the Clinton administration gave in to market theorists in the US and how New Labor in the UK decided to measure everything it could by introducing arbitrary and not measurable targets such as Reduction of hunger in Sub-Saharan Africa by 48% and Reduction of global conflict by 6%. It introduced a rural community vibrancy index in order to gauge the quality of life in Britain's villages and a birdsong index to measure the apparent decline of wildlife.

In industry and public services, this led to targets, quotas, and plans. It was meant to set workers free to achieve these targets in any way they decided. What policy makers did not realize was that the players, faced with impossible demands, would cheat. In order to meet impossible arbitrary targets, the cheating included:

- Lothian and Borders Police reclassified dozens of criminal offences as "suspicious occurrences" in order to keep them out of crime figures.
- Some NHS hospital trusts created the unofficial post of "The Hello Nurse," whose sole task it was to greet new arrivals in order to claim for statistical purposes that the patient had been "seen", even though no treatment or examination took place during the encounter.
- NHS managers took the wheels off trolleys and reclassified them as beds, while simultaneously reclassifying corridors as wards, in order to falsify Accident & Emergency waiting time statistics.

A section called 'The Death of Social Mobility' describes how the theory of the free market was applied to education. In the UK, the introduction of school performance league tables was intended to give individual schools more power and autonomy, to enable them to compete for pupils, the theory that it would motivate the poorly performing schools to improve. It was an attempt to move away from the rigid state control that had offered little choice to parents while failing to improve educational standards, and towards a culture of free choice and incentives, without going as far as privatizing the schools.

Following publication of the school league tables, wealthier parents moved into the areas of the best schools, causing house prices in those areas to rise dramatically ensuring that poor children were left with the poorly performing schools. This is just one aspect of a more rigidly stratified society where the incomes of working class Americans have actually fallen in real terms since the 1970s, while the incomes of the middle class have increased slightly, and those of the highest one percent of earners (the upper class) have quadrupled. Babies in the poorest areas in the UK are twice as likely to die in their first year as children from prosperous areas.

The episode ends with the observation that game theory and the free market model is now being questioned by economists who suspect a more irrational model of behavior is appropriate and useful. In formal experiments the only people who behaved exactly according to the mathematical models created by game theory are economists themselves, and psychopaths.

Comments: All of this is a symptom of the loss of the systems perspective and systems thinking. This may be because of the massive rise of specialization that surfaced in the last half of the last century.

Part 3 We Will Force You to Be Free

The final episode focuses on the concepts of positive and negative liberty introduced in the 1950s by Isaiah Berlin. Negative liberty is defined as freedom from coercion and Positive liberty as the opportunity to strive to fulfill one's potential. Berlin's opinion was that negative liberty was the safer of the two concepts because it lacked coercion. The episode explains how many political groups that sought their vision of freedom ended up using violence to achieve it. For example, the French revolutionaries wanted to overthrow a monarchical system which they viewed as preventing freedom, but in doing so they ended up with the Reign of Terror. The Bolshevik revolutionaries in Russia, who wanted to overthrow the established order and replace it with a society where everyone is equal, ended up creating a totalitarian regime that used violence to achieve its objectives.

This episode also explores how economic freedom had been used in Russia and the problems this introduced. A set of policies known as "shock therapy" (also described in the 2007 book The Shock Doctrine by Naomi Klein) were brought in mainly by outsiders, which had the effect of destroying the social safety net that existed in Russia. The sudden removal of the subsidies for basic goods caused their prices to rise, making them hardly affordable for ordinary people. An economic crisis escalated during the 1990s and some people were paid in goods rather than money. Then President Boris Yeltsin was accused by his parliament of economic genocide because of the large numbers of people too poor to eat. Yeltsin responded by removing parliament's power and becoming more autocratic.

At the same time, many formerly state-owned industries were sold to private entities, often at a fraction of their real value. Ordinary people, often in financial difficulties, would sell shares, which to them were worthless, for cash. This culminated with the rise of the, Oligarchs, super rich businessmen who attributed their rise to the sell offs of the 1990s. It resulted in a polarization of society into the poor and ultra-rich, and indirectly led to a more autocratic style of government under Vladimir Putin. While less free it promised to give people dignity and basic living requirements.

10.2 Government Policy 1945 – 1981

This section is a summary of the request and report on Science the Endless Frontier. On November 17, 1944 President Franklin D. Roosevelt requested a report from the Office of Scientific Research and Development on what can be done after the War using the lessons learned during the World War II. The request resulted in the report Science the Endless Frontier, July 1945. This report set the policy and tone of the United States up until 1987 when it was abandoned, and the President's Commission on Privatization set the policy and tone of the United States.

10.2.1 Science the Endless Frontier

A Report to the President by Vannevar Bush, Director of the Office of Scientific Research and Development, July 1945. (United States Government Printing Office, Washington 1945)

10.2.1.1 Letter Of Transmittal

OFFICE OF SCIENTIFIC RESEARCH AND DEVELOPMENT
1530 P Street, NW. Washington 25, D.C. JULY 25, 1945

DEAR MR. PRESIDENT:

In a letter dated November 17, 1944, President Roosevelt requested my recommendations on the following points

(1) What can be done, consistent with military security, and with the prior approval of the military authorities, to make known to the world as soon as possible the contributions which have been made during our war effort to scientific knowledge?

(2) With particular reference to the war of science against disease, what can be done now to organize a program for continuing in the future the work which has been done in medicine and related sciences?

(3) What can the Government do now and in the future to aid research activities by public and private organizations?

(4) Can an effective program be proposed for discovering and developing scientific talent in American youth so that the continuing future of scientific research in this country may be assured on a level comparable to what has been done during the war?

It is clear from President Roosevelt's letter that in speaking of science that he had in mind the natural sciences, including biology and medicine, and I have so interpreted his questions. Progress in other fields, such as the social sciences and the humanities, is likewise important; but the program for science presented in my report warrants immediate attention.

In seeking answers to President Roosevelt's questions I have had the assistance of distinguished committees specially qualified to advise in respect to these subjects. The committees have given these matters the serious attention they deserve; indeed, they have regarded this as an opportunity to participate in shaping the policy of the country with reference to scientific research. They have had many meetings and have submitted formal reports. I have been in close touch with the work of the committees and with their members throughout. I have examined all of the data they assembled and the suggestions they submitted on the points raised in President Roosevelt's letter.

Although the report which I submit herewith is my own, the facts, conclusions, and recommendations are based on the findings of the committees which have studied these questions. Since my report is necessarily brief, I am including as appendices the full reports of the committees.

A single mechanism for implementing the recommendations of the several committees is essential. In proposing such a mechanism, I have departed somewhat from the specific recommendations of the committees, but I have since been assured that the plan I am proposing is fully acceptable to the committee members.

The pioneer spirit is still vigorous within this nation. Science offers a largely unexplored hinterland for the pioneer who has the tools for his task. The rewards of such exploration both for the Nation and the individual are great. Scientific progress is one essential key to our security as a nation, to our better health, to more jobs, to a higher standard of living, and to our cultural progress.

Respectfully yours,
V. Bush, Director

10.2.1.2 President Roosevelt's Letter

THE WHITE HOUSE, Washington, D. C., November 17, 1944

DEAR DR. BUSH

The Office of Scientific Research and Development, of which you are the Director, represents a unique experiment of teamwork and cooperation in coordinating scientific research and in applying existing scientific knowledge to the solution of the technical problems paramount in war. Its work has been conducted in the utmost secrecy and carried on without public recognition of any kind; but its tangible results can be found in the communiques coming in from the battlefronts all over the world. Some day the full story of its achievements can be told.

There is, however, no reason why the lessons to be found in this experiment cannot be profitably employed in times of peace. The information, the techniques, and the research experience developed by the Office of Scientific Research and

Development and by the thousands of scientists in the universities and in private industry, should be used in the days of peace ahead for the improvement of the national health, the creation of new enterprises bringing new jobs, and the betterment of the national standard of living.

It is with that objective in mind that I would like to have your recommendations on the following four major points

First What can be done, consistent with military security, and with the prior approval of the military authorities, to make known to the world as soon as possible the contributions which have been made during our war effort to scientific knowledge?

The diffusion of such knowledge should help us stimulate new enterprises, provide jobs four our returning servicemen and other workers, and make possible great strides for the improvement of the national well-being.

Second With particular reference to the war of science against disease, what can be done now to organize a program for continuing in the future the work which has been done in medicine and related sciences?

The fact that the annual deaths in this country from one or two diseases alone are far in excess of the total number of lives lost by us in battle during this war should make us conscious of the duty we owe future generations.

Third What can the Government do now and in the future to aid research activities by public and private organizations? The proper roles of public and of private research, and their interrelation, should be carefully considered.

Fourth Can an effective program be proposed for discovering and developing scientific talent in American youth so that the continuing future of scientific research in this country may be assured on a level comparable to what has been done during the war?

New frontiers of the mind are before us, and if they are pioneered with the same vision, boldness, and drive with which we have waged this war we can create a fuller and more fruitful employment and a fuller and more fruitful life.

I hope that, after such consultation as you may deem advisable with your associates and others, you can let me have your considered judgment on these matters as soon as convenient - reporting on each when you are ready, rather than waiting for completion of your studies in all.

Very sincerely yours,
FRANKLIN D. ROOSEVELT

****

Dr. VANNEVAR BUSH,
Office of Scientific Research and Development,
Washington, D. C.

Science - The Endless Frontier

"New frontiers of the mind are before us, and if they are pioneered with the same vision, boldness, and drive with which we have waged this war we can create a fuller and more fruitful employment and a fuller and more fruitful life."

FRANKLIN D. ROOSEVELT
November 17, 1944.

10.2.1.3 SUMMARY OF THE REPORT

10.2.1.3.1 SCIENTIFIC PROGRESS IS ESSENTIAL

Progress in the war against disease depends upon a flow of new scientific knowledge. New products, new industries, and more jobs require continuous additions to knowledge of the laws of nature, and the application of that knowledge to practical purposes. Similarly, our defense against aggression demands new knowledge so that we can develop new and improved weapons. This essential, new knowledge can be obtained only through basic scientific research.

Science can be effective in the national welfare only as a member of a team, whether the conditions be peace or war. But without scientific progress no amount of achievement in other directions can insure our health, prosperity, and security as a nation in the modern world.

10.2.1.3.2 For the War Against Disease

We have taken great strides in the war against disease. The death rate for all diseases in the Army, including overseas forces, has been reduced from 14.1 per thousand in the last war to 0.6 per thousand in this war. In the last 40 years life expectancy has increased from 49 to 65 years, largely as a consequence of the reduction in the death rates of infants and children. But we are far from the goal. The annual deaths from one or two diseases far exceed the total number of American lives lost in battle during this war. A large fraction of these deaths in our civilian population cut short the useful lives of our citizens. Approximately 7,000,000 persons in the United States are mentally ill and their care costs the public over $175,000,000 a year. Clearly much illness remains for which adequate means of prevention and cure are not yet known.

The responsibility for basic research in medicine and the underlying sciences, so essential to progress in the war against disease, falls primarily upon the medical schools and universities. Yet we find that the traditional sources of support for medical research in the medical schools and universities, largely endowment income, foundation grants, and private donations, are diminishing and there is no immediate prospect of a change in this trend. Meanwhile, the cost of medical research has been rising. If we are to maintain the progress in medicine which has marked the last 25 years, the Government should extend financial support to basic medical research in the medical schools and in universities.

10.2.1.3.3 For Our National Security

The bitter and dangerous battle against the U-boat was a battle of scientific techniques - and our margin of success was dangerously small. The new eyes which radar has supplied can sometimes be blinded by new scientific developments. V-2 was countered only by capture of the launching sites.

We cannot again rely on our allies to hold off the enemy while we struggle to catch up. There must be more - and more adequate - military research in peacetime. It is essential that the civilian scientists continue in peacetime some portion of those contributions to national security which they have made so effectively during the war. This can best be done through a civilian-controlled organization with close liaison with the Army and Navy, but with funds direct from Congress, and the clear power to initiate military research which will supplement and strengthen that carried on directly under the control of the Army and Navy.

10.2.1.3.4 And for the Public Welfare

One of our hopes is that after the war there will be full employment. To reach that goal the full creative and productive energies of the American people must be released. To create more jobs we must make new and better and cheaper products. We want plenty of new, vigorous enterprises. But new products and processes are not born full-grown. They are founded on new principles and new conceptions which in turn result from basic scientific research. Basic scientific research is scientific capital. Moreover, we cannot any longer depend upon Europe as a major source of this scientific capital. Clearly, more and better scientific research is one essential to the achievement of our goal of full employment.

How do we increase this scientific capital? First, we must have plenty of men and women trained in science, for upon them depends both the creation of new knowledge and its application to practical purposes. Second, we must strengthen the centers of basic research which are principally the colleges, universities, and research institutes. These institutions provide the environment which is most conducive to the creation of new scientific knowledge and least under pressure for immediate, tangible results. With some notable exceptions, most research in industry and Government involves application of existing scientific knowledge to practical problems. It is only the colleges, universities, and a few research institutes that devote most of their research efforts to expanding the frontiers of knowledge.

Expenditures for scientific research by industry and Government increased from \$140,000,000 in 1930 to \$309,000,000 in 1940. Those for the colleges and universities increased from \$20,000,000 to \$31,000,000, while those for the research institutes declined from $5,200,000 to $4,500,000 during the same period. If the colleges, universities, and research institutes are to meet the rapidly increasing demands of industry and Government for new scientific knowledge, their basic research should be strengthened by use of public funds.

For science to serve as a powerful factor in our national welfare, applied research both in Government and in industry must be vigorous. To improve the quality of scientific research within the Government, steps should be taken to modify the procedures for recruiting, classifying, and compensating scientific personnel in order to reduce the present handicap of governmental scientific bureaus in competing with industry and the universities for top-grade scientific talent. To provide coordination of the common scientific activities of these governmental agencies as to policies and budgets, a permanent Science Advisory Board should be created to advise the executive and legislative branches of Government on these matters.

The most important ways in which the Government can promote industrial research are to increase the flow of new scientific knowledge through support of basic research, and to aid in the development of scientific talent. In addition, the Government should provide suitable incentives to industry to conduct research, (a) by clarification of present uncertainties in the Internal Revenue Code in regard to the deductibility of research and development expenditures as current charges against net income, and (b) by strengthening the patent system so as to eliminate uncertainties which now bear heavily on small industries and so as to prevent abuses which reflect discredit upon a basically sound system. In addition, ways should be found to cause the benefits of basic research to reach industries which do not now utilize new scientific knowledge.

10.2.1.3.5 We Must Renew Our Scientific Talent

The responsibility for the creation of new scientific knowledge - and for most of its application - rests on that small body of men and women who understand the fundamental laws of nature and are skilled in the techniques of scientific research. We shall have rapid or slow advance on any scientific frontier depending on the number of highly qualified and trained scientists exploring it.

The deficit of science and technology students who, but for the war, would have received bachelor's degrees is about 150,000. It is estimated that the deficit of those obtaining advanced degrees in these fields will amount in 1955 to about 17,000 - for it takes at least 6 years from college entry to achieve a doctor's degree or its equivalent in science or engineering. The real ceiling on our productivity of new scientific knowledge and its application in the war against disease, and the development of new products and new industries, is the number of trained scientists available.

The training of a scientist is a long and expensive process. Studies clearly show that there are talented individuals in every part of the population, but with few exceptions, those without the means of buying higher education go without it. If ability, and not the circumstance of family fortune, determines who shall receive higher education in science, then we shall be assured of constantly improving quality at every level of scientific activity. The Government should provide a reasonable number of undergraduate scholarships and graduate fellowships in order to develop scientific talent in American youth. The plans should be designed to attract into science only that proportion of youthful talent appropriate to the needs of science in relation to the other needs of the nation for high abilities.

10.2.1.3.6 Including Those in Uniform

The most immediate prospect of making up the deficit in scientific personnel is to develop the scientific talent in the generation now in uniform. Even if we should start now to train the current crop of high-school graduates none would complete graduate studies before 1951. The Armed Services should comb their records for men who, prior to or during the war, have given evidence of talent for science, and make prompt arrangements, consistent with current discharge plans, for ordering those who remain in uniform, as soon as militarily possible, to duty at institutions here and overseas where they can continue their scientific education. Moreover, the Services should see that those who study overseas have the benefit of the latest scientific information resulting from research during the war.

10.2.1.3.7 The Lid Must Be Lifted

While most of the war research has involved the application of existing scientific knowledge to the problems of war, rather than basic research, there has been accumulated a vast amount of information relating to the application of science to particular problems. Much of this can be used by industry. It is also needed for teaching in the colleges and universities here and in the Armed Forces Institutes overseas. Some of this information must remain secret, but most of it should be made public as soon as there is ground for belief that the enemy will not be able to turn it against us in this war. To select that portion which should be made public, to coordinate its release, and definitely to encourage its publication, a Board composed of Army, Navy, and civilian scientific members should be promptly established.

10.2.1.3.8 A Program For Action

The Government should accept new responsibilities for promoting the flow of new scientific knowledge and the development of scientific talent in our youth. These responsibilities are the proper concern of the Government, for they vitally affect our health, our jobs, and our national security. It is in keeping also with basic United States policy that the Government should foster the opening of new frontiers and this is the modern way to do it. For many years the Government has wisely supported research in the agricultural colleges and the benefits have been great. The time has come when such support should be extended to other fields.

The effective discharge of these new responsibilities will require the full attention of some over-all agency devoted to that purpose. There is not now in the permanent Governmental structure receiving its funds from Congress an agency adapted to supplementing the support of basic research in the colleges, universities, and research institutes, both in medicine and the natural sciences, adapted to supporting research on new weapons for both Services, or adapted to administering a program of science scholarships and fellowships.

Therefore I recommend that a new agency for these purposes be established. Such an agency should be composed of persons of broad interest and experience, having an understanding of the peculiarities of scientific research and scientific education. It should have stability of funds so that long-range programs may be undertaken. It should recognize that freedom of inquiry must be preserved and should leave internal control of policy, personnel, and the method and scope of research to the institutions in which it is carried on. It should be fully responsible to the President and through him to the Congress for its program.

Early action on these recommendations is imperative if this nation is to meet the challenge of science in the crucial years ahead. On the wisdom with which we bring science to bear in the war against disease, in the creation of new industries, and in the strengthening of our Armed Forces depends in large measure our future as a nation.

10.2.1.4 Chapter 1 INTRODUCTION

10.2.1.4.1 Scientific Progress is Essential

We all know how much the new drug, penicillin, has meant to our grievously wounded men on the grim battlefronts of this war - the countless lives it has saved - the incalculable suffering which its use has prevented. Science and the great practical genius of this nation made this achievement possible.

Some of us know the vital role which radar has played in bringing the United Nations to victory over Nazi Germany and in driving the Japanese steadily back from their island bastions. Again it was painstaking scientific research over many years that made radar possible.

What we often forget are the millions of pay envelopes on a peacetime Saturday night which are filled because new products and new industries have provided jobs for countless Americans. Science made that possible, too.

In 1939 millions of people were employed in industries which did not even exist at the close of the last war - radio, air conditioning, rayon and other synthetic fibers, and plastics are examples of the products of these industries. But these things do not mark the end of progress - they are but the beginning if we make full use of our scientific resources. New manufacturing industries can be started and many older industries greatly strengthened and expanded if we continue to study nature's laws and apply new knowledge to practical purposes.

Great advances in agriculture are also based upon scientific research. Plants which are more resistant to disease and are adapted to short growing season, the prevention and cure of livestock diseases, the control of our insect enemies, better fertilizers, and improved agricultural practices, all stem from painstaking scientific research.

Advances in science when put to practical use mean more jobs, higher wages, shorter hours, more abundant crops, more leisure for recreation, for study, for learning how to live without the deadening drudgery which has been the burden of the common man for ages past. Advances in science will also bring higher standards of living, will lead to the prevention or cure of diseases, will promote conservation of our limited national resources, and will assure means of defense against aggression. But to achieve these objectives - to secure a high level of employment, to maintain a position of world leadership - the flow of new scientific knowledge must be both continuous and substantial.

Our population increased from 75 million to 130 million between 1900 and 1940. In some countries comparable increases have been accompanied by famine. In this country the increase has been accompanied by more abundant food supply, better living, more leisure, longer life, and better health. This is, largely, the product of three factors - the free play of initiative of a vigorous people under democracy, the heritage of great national wealth, and the advance of science and its application.

Science, by itself, provides no panacea for individual, social, and economic ills. It can be effective in the national welfare only as a member of a team, whether the conditions be peace or war. But without scientific progress no amount of achievement in other directions can insure our health, prosperity, and security as a nation in the modern world.

10.2.1.4.2 Science Is a Proper Concern of Government

It has been basic United States policy that Government should foster the opening of new frontiers. It opened the seas to clipper ships and furnished land for pioneers. Although these frontiers have more or less disappeared, the frontier of science remains. It is in keeping with the American tradition - one which has made the United States great - that new frontiers shall be made accessible for development by all American citizens.

Moreover, since health, well-being, and security are proper concerns of Government, scientific progress is, and must be, of vital interest to Government. Without scientific progress the national health would deteriorate; without scientific progress we could not hope for improvement in our standard of living or for an increased number of jobs for our citizens; and without scientific progress we could not have maintained our liberties against tyranny.

10.2.1.4.3 Government Relations to Science - Past and Future

From early days the Government has taken an active interest in scientific matters. During the nineteenth century the Coast and Geodetic Survey, the Naval Observatory, the Department of Agriculture, and the Geological Survey were established. Through the Land Grant College acts the Government has supported research in state institutions for more than 80 years on a gradually increasing scale. Since 1900 a large number of scientific agencies have been established within the Federal Government, until in 1939 they numbered more than 40.

Much of the scientific research done by Government agencies is intermediate in character between the two types of work commonly referred to as basic and applied research. Almost all Government scientific work has ultimate practical objectives but, in many fields of broad national concern, it commonly involves long-term investigation of a fundamental nature. Generally speaking, the scientific agencies of Government are not so concerned with immediate practical objectives as are the laboratories of industry nor, on the other hand, are they as free to explore any natural phenomena without regard to possible economic applications as are the educational and private research institutions. Government scientific agencies have splendid records of achievement, but they are limited in function.

We have no national policy for science. The Government has only begun to utilize science in the nation's welfare. There is no body within the Government charged with formulating or executing a national science policy. There are no standing committees of the Congress devoted to this important subject. Science has been in the wings. It should be brought to the center of the stage - for in it lies much of our hope for the future.

There are areas of science in which the public interest is acute but which are likely to be cultivated inadequately if left without more support than will come from private sources. These areas - such as research on military problems, agriculture, housing, public health, certain medical research, and research involving expensive capital facilities beyond the capacity of private institutions - should be advanced by active Government support. To date, with the exception of the intensive war research conducted by the Office of Scientific Research and Development, such support has been meager and intermittent.

For reasons presented in this report we are entering a period when science needs and deserves increased support from public funds.

10.2.1.4.4 Freedom of Inquiry Must Be Preserved

The publicly and privately supported colleges, universities, and research institutes are the centers of basic research. They are the wellsprings of knowledge and understanding. As long as they are vigorous and healthy and their scientists are free to pursue the truth wherever it may lead, there will be a flow of new scientific knowledge to those who can apply it to practical problems in Government, in industry, or elsewhere.

Many of the lessons learned in the war-time application of science under Government can be profitably applied in peace. The Government is peculiarly fitted to perform certain functions, such as the coordination and support of broad programs on problems of great national importance. But we must proceed with caution in carrying over the methods which work in wartime to the very different conditions of peace. We must remove the rigid controls which we have had to impose, and recover freedom of inquiry and that healthy competitive scientific spirit so necessary for expansion of the frontiers of scientific knowledge.

Scientific progress on a broad front results from the free play of free intellects, working on subjects of their own choice, in the manner dictated by their curiosity for exploration of the unknown. Freedom of inquiry must be preserved under any plan for Government support of science in accordance with the Five Fundamentals listed on page 26.

The study of the momentous questions presented in President Roosevelt's letter has been made by able committees working diligently. This report presents conclusions and recommendations based upon the studies of these committees which appear in full as the appendices. Only in the creation of one over-all mechanism rather than several does this report depart from the specific recommendations of the committees. The members of the committees have reviewed the recommendations in regard to the single mechanism and have found this plan thoroughly acceptable.

10.2.1.5 Chapter 2 THE WAR AGAINST DISEASE

10.2.1.5.1 In War

The death rate for all diseases in the Army, including the overseas forces, has been reduced from 14.1 per thousand in the last war to 0.6 per thousand in this war.

Such ravaging diseases as yellow fever, dysentery, typhus, tetanus, pneumonia, and meningitis have been all but conquered by penicillin and the sulfa drugs, the insecticide DDT, better vaccines, and improved hygenic measures. Malaria has been controlled. There has been dramatic progress in surgery.

The striking advances in medicine during the war have been possible only because we had a large backlog of scientific data accumulated through basic research in many scientific fields in the years before the war.

10.2.1.5.2 In Peace

In the last 40 years life expectancy in the United States has increased from 49 to 65 years largely as a consequence of the reduction in the death rates of infants and children; in the last 20 years the death rate from the diseases of childhood has been reduced 87 percent.

Diabetes has been brought under control by insulin, pernicious anemia by liver extracts; and the once widespread deficiency diseases have been much reduced, even in the lowest income groups, by accessory food factors and improvement of diet. Notable advances have been made in the early diagnosis of cancer, and in the surgical and radiation treatment of the disease.

These results have been achieved through a great amount of basic research in medicine and the preclinical sciences, and by the dissemination of this new scientific knowledge through the physicians and medical services and public health agencies of the country. In this cooperative endeavour the pharmaceutical industry has played an important role, especially during the war. All of the medical and public health groups share credit for these achievements; they form interdependent members of a team.

Progress in combating disease depends upon an expanding body of new scientific knowledge.

10.2.1.5.3 Unsolved Problems

As President Roosevelt observed, the annual deaths from one or two diseases are far in excess of the total number of American lives lost in battle during this war. A large fraction of these deaths in our civilian population cut short the useful lives of our citizens. This is our present position despite the fact that in the last three decades notable progress has been made in civilian medicine. The reduction in death rate from diseases of childhood has shifted the emphasis to the middle and old age groups, particularly to the malignant diseases and the degenerative processes prominent in later life. Cardiovascular disease, including chronic disease of the kidneys, arteriosclerosis, and cerebral hemorrhage, now account for 45 percent of the deaths in the United States. Second are the infectious diseases, and third is cancer. Added to these are many maladies (for example, the common cold, arthritis, asthma and hay fever, peptic ulcer) which, through infrequently fatal, cause incalculable disability.

Another aspect of the changing emphasis is the increase of mental diseases. Approximately 7 million persons in the United States are mentally ill; more than one-third of the hospital beds are occupied by such persons, at a cost of $175 million a year. Each year 125,000 new mental cases are hospitalized.

Notwithstanding great progress in prolonging the span of life and relief of suffering, much illness remains for which adequate means of prevention and cure are not yet known. While additional physicians, hospitals, and health programs are needed, their full usefulness cannot be attained unless we enlarge our knowledge of the human organism and the nature of disease. Any extension of medical facilities must be accompanied by an expanded program of medical training and research.

10.2.1.5.4 Broad and Basic Studies Needed

Discoveries pertinent to medical progress have often come from remote and unexpected sources, and it is certain that this will be true in the future. It is wholly probable that progress in the treatment of cardiovascular disease, renal disease, cancer, and similar refractory diseases will be made as the result of fundamental discoveries in subjects unrelated to those diseases, and perhaps entirely unexpected by the investigator. Further progress requires that the entire front of medicine and the underlying sciences of chemistry, physics, anatomy, biochemistry, physiology, pharmacology, bacteriology, pathology, parasitology, etc., be broadly developed.

Progress in the war against disease results from discoveries in remote and unexpected fields of medicine and the underlying sciences.

10.2.1.5.5 Coordinated Attack on Special Problems

Penicillin reached our troops in time to save countless lives because the Government coordinated and supported the program of research and development on the drug. The development moved from the early laboratory stage to large scale production and use in a fraction of the time it would have taken without such leadership. The search for better anti-malarials, which proceeded at a moderate tempo for many years, has been accelerated enormously by Government support during the war. Other examples can be cited in which medical progress has been similarly advanced. In achieving these results, the Government has provided over-all coordination and support; it has not dictated how the work should be done within any cooperating institution.

Discovery of new therapeutic agents and methods usually results from basic studies in medicine and the underlying sciences. The development of such materials and methods to the point at which they become available to medical practitioners requires teamwork involving the medical schools, the science departments of universities, Government and the pharmaceutical industry. Government initiative, support, and coordination can be very effective in this development phase.

Government initiative and support for the development of newly discovered therapeutic materials and methods can reduce the time required to bring the benefits to the public.

10.2.1.5.6 Action is Necessary

The primary place for medical research is in the medical schools and universities. In some cases coordinated direct attack on special problems may be made by teams of investigators, supplementing similar attacks carried on by the Army, Navy, Public Health Service, and other organizations. Apart from teaching, however, the primary obligation of the medical schools and universities is to continue the traditional function of such institutions, namely, to provide the individual worker with an opportunity for free, untrammeled study of nature, in the directions and by the methods suggested by his interests, curiosity, and imagination. The history of medical science teaches clearly the supreme importance of affording the prepared mind complete freedom for the exercise of initiative. It is the special province of the medical schools and universities to foster medical research in this way - a duty which cannot be shifted to government agencies, industrial organizations, or to any other institutions.

Where clinical investigations of the human body are required, the medical schools are in a unique position, because of their close relationship to teaching hospitals, to integrate such investigations with the work of the departments of preclinical science, and to impart new knowledge to physicians in training. At the same time, the teaching hospitals are especially well qualified to carry on medical research because of their close connection with the medical schools, on which they depend for staff and supervision.

Between World War I and World War II the United States overtook all other nations in medical research and assumed a position of world leadership. To a considerable extent this progress reflected the liberal financial support from university endowment income, gifts from individuals, and foundation grants in the 20's. The growth of research departments in medical schools ahs been very uneven, however, and in consequence most of the important work has been done in a few large schools. This should be corrected by building up the weaker institutions, especially in regions which now have no strong medical research activities.

The traditional sources of support for medical research, largely endowment income, foundation grants, and private donations, are diminishing, and there is no immediate prospect of a change in this trend. Meanwhile, research costs have steadily risen. More elaborate and expensive equipment is required, supplies are more costly, and the wages of assistants are higher. Industry is only to a limited extent a source of funds for basic medical research.

It is clear that if we are to maintain the progress in medicine which has marked the last 25 years, the Government should extend financial support to basic medical research in the medical schools and in the universities, through grants both for research and for fellowships. The amount which can be effectively spent in the first year should not exceed 5 million dollars. After a program is under way perhaps 20 million dollars a year can be spent effectively.

10.2.1.6 Chapter 3 SCIENCE AND THE PUBLIC WELFARE

10.2.1.6.1 Relation to National Security

In this war it has become clear beyond all doubt that scientific research is absolutely essential to national security. The bitter and dangerous battle against the U-boat was a battle of scientific techniques - and our margin of success was dangerously small. The new eyes which radar supplied to our fighting forces quickly evoked the development of scientific countermeasures which could often blind them. This again represents the ever continuing battle of techniques. The V-1 attack on London was finally defeated by three devices developed during this war and used superbly in the field. V-2 was countered only by the capture of the launching sites.

The Secretaries of War and Navy recently stated in a joint letter to the National Academy of Sciences

This war emphasizes three facts of supreme importance to national security (1) Powerful new tactics of defense and offense are developed around new weapons created by scientific and engineering research; (2) the competitive time element in developing those weapons and tactics may be decisive; (3) war is increasingly total war, in which the armed services must be supplemented by active participation of every element of civilian population.

To insure continued preparedness along farsighted technical lines, the research scientists of the country must be called upon to continue in peacetime some substantial portion of those types of contribution to national security which they have made so effectively during the stress of the present war * * *.

There must be more - and more adequate - military research during peacetime. We cannot again rely on our allies to hold off the enemy while we struggle to catch up. Further, it is clear that only the Government can undertake military research; for it must be carried on in secret, much of it has no commercial value, and it is expensive. The obligation of Government to support research on military problems is inescapable.

Modern war requires the use of the most advanced scientific techniques. Many of the leaders in the development of radar are scientists who before the war had been exploring the nucleus of the atom. While there must be increased emphasis on science in the future training of officers for both the Army and Navy, such men cannot be expected to be specialists in scientific research. Therefore a professional partnership between the officers in the Services and civilian scientists is needed.

The Army and Navy should continue to carry on research and development on the improvement of current weapons. For many years the National Advisory Committee for Aeronautics has supplemented the work of the Army and Navy by conducting basic research on the problems of flight. There should now be permanent civilian activity to supplement the research work of the Services in other scientific fields so as to carry on in time of peace some part of the activities of the emergency war-time Office of Scientific Research and Development.

Military preparedness requires a permanent independent, civilian-controlled organization, having close liaison with the Army and Navy, but with funds directly from Congress and with the clear power to initiate military research which will supplement and strengthen that carried on directly under the control of the Army and Navy.

Military preparedness requires a permanent independent, civilian-controlled organization, having close liaison with the Army and Navy, but with funds directly from Congress and with the clear power to initiate military research which will supplement and strengthen that carried on directly under the control of the Army and Navy.

10.2.1.6.2 Science and Jobs

One of our hopes is that after the war there will be full employment, and that the production of goods and services will serve to raise our standard of living. We do not know yet how we shall reach that goal, but it is certain that it can be achieved only by releasing the full creative and productive energies of the American people.

Surely we will not get there by standing still, merely by making the same things we made before and selling them at the same or higher prices. We will not get ahead in international trade unless we offer new and more attractive and cheaper products.

Where will these new products come from? How will we find ways to make better products at lower cost? The answer is clear. There must be a stream of new scientific knowledge to turn the wheels of private and public enterprise. There must be plenty of men and women trained in science and technology for upon them depend both the creation of new knowledge and its application to practical purposes.

More and better scientific research is essential to the achievement of our goal of full employment.

10.2.1.6.3 The Importance of Basic Research

Basic research is performed without thought of practical ends. It results in general knowledge and an understanding of nature and its laws. This general knowledge provides the means of answering a large number of important practical problems, though it may not give a complete specific answer to any one of them. The function of applied research is to provide such complete answers. The scientist doing basic research may not be at all interested in the practical applications of his work, yet the further progress of industrial development would eventually stagnate if basic scientific research were long neglected.

One of the peculiarities of basic science is the variety of paths which lead to productive advance. Many of the most important discoveries have come as a result of experiments undertaken with very different purposes in mind. Statistically it is certain that important and highly useful discoveries will result from some fraction of the undertakings in basic science; but the results of any one particular investigation cannot be predicted with accuracy.

Basic research leads to new knowledge. It provides scientific capital. It creates the fund from which the practical applications of knowledge must be drawn. New products and new processes do not appear full-grown. They are founded on new principles and new conceptions, which in turn are painstakingly developed by research in the purest realms of science.

Today, it is truer than ever that basic research is the pacemaker of technological progress. In the nineteenth century, Yankee mechanical ingenuity, building largely upon the basic discoveries of European scientists, could greatly advance the technical arts. Now the situation is different.

A nation which depends upon others for its new basic scientific knowledge will be slow in its industrial progress and weak in its competitive position in world trade, regardless of its mechanical skill.

10.2.1.6.4 Centers of Basic Research

Publicly and privately supported colleges and universities and the endowed research institutes must furnish both the new scientific knowledge and the trained research workers. These institutions are uniquely qualified by tradition and by their special characteristics to carry on basic research. They are charged with the responsibility of conserving the knowledge accumulated by the past, imparting that knowledge to students, and contributing new knowledge of all kinds. It is chiefly in these institutions that scientists may work in an atmosphere which is relatively free from the adverse pressure of convention, prejudice, or commercial necessity. At their best they provide the scientific worker with a strong sense of solidarity and security, as well as a substantial degree of personal intellectual freedom. All of these factors are of great importance in the development of new knowledge, since much of new knowledge is certain to arouse opposition because of its tendency to challenge current beliefs or practice.

Industry is generally inhibited by preconceived goals, by its own clearly defined standards, and by the constant pressure of commercial necessity. Satisfactory progress in basic science seldom occurs under conditions prevailing in the normal industrial laboratory. There are some notable exceptions, it is true, but even in such cases it is rarely possible to match the universities in respect to the freedom which is so important to scientific discovery.

To serve effectively as the centers of basic research these institutions must be strong and healthy. They must attract our best scientists as teachers and investigators. They must offer research opportunities and sufficient compensation to enable them to compete with industry and government for the cream of scientific talent.

During the past 25 years there has been a great increase in industrial research involving the application of scientific knowledge to a multitude of practical purposes - thus providing new products, new industries, new investment opportunities, and millions of jobs. During the same period research within Government - again largely applied research - has also been greatly expanded. In the decade from 1930 to 1940 expenditures for industrial research increased from $116,000,000 to $240,000,000 and those for scientific research in Government rose from $24,000,000 to $69,000,000. During the same period expenditures for scientific research in the colleges and universities increased from $20,000,000 to $31,000,000, while those in the endowed research institutes declined from $5,200,000 to $4,500,000. These are the best estimates available. The figures have been taken from a variety of sources and arbitrary definitions have necessarily been applied, but it is believed that they may be accepted as indicating the following trends

(a) Expenditures for scientific research by industry and Government - almost entirely applied research - have more than doubled between 1930 and 1940. Whereas in 1930 they were six times as large as the research expenditures of the colleges, universities, and research institutes, by 1940 they were nearly ten times as large.

(b) While expenditures for scientific research in the colleges and universities increased by one-half during this period, those for the endowed research institutes have slowly declined.

If the colleges, universities, and research institutes are to meet the rapidly increasing demands of industry and Government for new scientific knowledge, their basic research should be strengthened by use of public funds.

10.2.1.6.5 Research Within the Government

Although there are some notable exceptions, most research conducted within governmental laboratories is of an applied nature. This has always been true and is likely to remain so. Hence Government, like industry, is dependent on the colleges, universities, and research institutes to expand the basic scientific frontiers and to furnish trained scientific investigators.

Research within the Government represents an important part of our total research activity and needs to be strengthened and expanded after the war. Such expansion should be directed to fields of inquiry and service which are of public importance and are not adequately carried on by private organizations.

The most important single factor in scientific and technical work is the quality of the personnel employed. The procedures currently followed within the Government for recruiting, classifying and compensating such personnel place the Government under a severe handicap in competing with industry and the universities for first-class scientific talent. Steps should be taken to reduce that handicap.

In the Government the arrangement whereby the numerous scientific agencies form parts of larger departments has both advantages and disadvantages. but the present pattern is firmly established and there is much to be said for it. There is, however, a very real need for some measure of coordination of the common scientific activities of these agencies, both as to policies and budgets, and at present no such means exist.

A permanent Science Advisory Board should be created to consult with these scientific bureaus and to advise the executive and legislative branches of Government as to the policies and budgets of Government agencies engaged in scientific research.

This board should be composed of disinterested scientists who have no connection with the affairs of any Government agency.

10.2.1.6.6 Industrial Research

The simplest and most effective way in which the Government can strengthen industrial research is to support basic research and to develop scientific talent.

The benefits of basic research do not reach all industries equally or at the same speed. Some small enterprises never receive any of the benefits. It has been suggested that the benefits might be better utilized if "research clinics" for such enterprises were to be established. Businessmen would thus be able to make more use of research than they now do. This proposal is certainly worthy of further study.

One of the most important factors affecting the amount of industrial research is the income-tax law. Government action in respect to this subject will affect the rate of technical progress in industry. Uncertainties as to the attitude of the Bureau of Internal Revenue regarding the deduction of research and development expenses are a deterrent to research expenditure. These uncertainties arise from lack of clarity of the tax law as to the proper treatment of such costs.

The Internal Revenue Code should be amended to remove present uncertainties in regard to the deductibility of research and development expenditures as current charges against net income.

Research is also affected by the patent laws. They stimulate new invention and they make it possible for new industries to be built around new devices or new processes. These industries generate new jobs and new products, all of which contribute to the welfare and the strength of the country.

Yet, uncertainties in the operation of the patent laws have impaired the ability of small industries to translate new ideas into processes and products of value to the nation. These uncertainties are, in part, attributable to the difficulties and expense incident to the operation of the patent system as it presently exists. These uncertainties are also attributable to the existence of certain abuses, which have appeared in the use of patents. The abuses should be corrected. They have led to extravagantly critical attacks which tend to discredit a basically sound system.

It is important that the patent system continue to serve the country in the manner intended by the Constitution, for it has been a vital element in the industrial vigor which has distinguished this nation.

The National Patent Planning Commission has reported on this subject. In addition, a detailed study, with recommendations concerning the extent to which modifications should be made in our patent laws is currently being made under the leadership of the Secretary of Commerce. It is recommended, therefore, that specific action with regard to the patent laws be withheld pending the submission of the report devoted exclusively to that subject.

International Exchange of Scientific Information

International exchange of scientific information is of growing importance.

Increasing specialization of science will make it more important than ever that scientists in this country keep continually ahead of developments abroad. In addition a flow of scientific information constitutes one facet of general international accord which should be cultivated.

The Government can accomplish significant results in several ways by aiding in the arrangement of international science congresses, in the official accrediting of American scientists to such gatherings, in the official reception of foreign scientists of standing in this country, in making possible a rapid flow of technical information, including translation service, and possibly in the provision of international fellowships. Private foundations and other groups partially fulfill some of these functions at present, but their scope is incomplete and inadequate.

The Government should take an active role in promoting the international flow of scientific information.

10.2.1.6.7 The Special Need for Federal Support

We can no longer count on ravaged Europe as a source of fundamental knowledge. In the past we have devoted much of our best efforts to the application of such knowledge which has been discovered abroad. In the future we must pay increased attention to discovering this knowledge for ourselves particularly since the scientific applications of the future will be more than ever dependent upon such basic knowledge.

New impetus must be given to research in our country. Such impetus can come promptly only from the Government. Expenditures for research in the colleges, universities, and research institutes will otherwise not be able to meet the additional demands of increased public need for research.

Further, we cannot expect industry adequately to fill the gap. Industry will fully rise to the challenge of applying new knowledge to new products. The commercial incentive can be relied upon for that. But basic research is essentially noncommercial in nature. It will not receive the attention it requires if left to industry.

For many years the Government has wisely supported research in the agricultural colleges and the benefits have been great. The time has come when such support should be extended to other fields.

In providing government support, however, we must endeavor to preserve as far as possible the private support of research both in industry and in the colleges, universities, and research institutes. These private sources should continue to carry their share of the financial burden.

10.2.1.6.8 The Cost of a Program

It is estimated that an adequate program for Federal support of basic research in the colleges, universities, and research institutes and for financing important applied research in the public interest, will cost about 10 million dollars at the outset and may rise to about 50 million dollars annually when fully underway at the end of perhaps 5 years.

10.2.1.7 Chapter 4 RENEWAL OF OUR SCIENTIFIC TALENT

10.2.1.7.1 Nature of the Problem

The responsibility for the creation of new scientific knowledge rests on that small body of men and women who understand the fundamental laws of nature and are skilled in the techniques of scientific research. While there will always be the rare individual who will rise to the top without benefit of formal education and training, he is the exception and even he might make a more notable contribution if he had the benefit of the best education we have to offer. I cannot improve on President Conant's statement that "in every section of the entire area where the word science may properly be applied, the limiting factor is a human one. We shall have rapid or slow advance in this direction or in that depending on the number of really first-class men who are engaged in the work in question. So in the last analysis, the future of science in this country will be determined by our basic educational policy."

10.2.1.7.2 A Note of Warning

It would be folly to set up a program under which research in the natural sciences and medicine was expanded at the cost of the social sciences, humanities, and other studies so essential to national well-being. This point has been well stated by the Moe Committee as follows

"As citizens, as good citizens, we therefore think that we must have in mind while examining the question before us - the discovery and development of scientific talent - the needs of the whole national welfare. We could not suggest to you a program which would syphon into science and technology a disproportionately large share of the nation's highest abilities, without doing harm to the nation, nor, indeed, without crippling science. Science cannot live by and unto itself alone."

"The uses to which high ability in youth can be put are various and, to a large extent, are determined by social pressures and rewards. When aided by selective devices for picking out scientifically talented youth, it is clear that large sums of money for scholarships and fellowships and monetary and other rewards in disproportionate amounts might draw into science too large a percentage of the nation's high ability, with a result highly detrimental to the nation and to science. Plans for the discovery and development of scientific talent must be related to the other needs of society for high ability. There is never enough ability at high levels to satisfy all the needs of the nation; we would not seek to draw into science any more of it than science's proportionate share."

10.2.1.7.3 The Wartime Deficit

Among the young men and women qualified to take up scientific work, since 1940 there have been few students over 18, except some in medicine and engineering in Army and Navy programs and a few 4-F's, who have followed an integrated scientific course of studies. Neither our allies nor, so far as we know, our enemies have done anything so radical as thus to suspend almost completely their educational activities in scientific pursuits during the war period.

Two great principles have guided us in this country as we have turned our full efforts to war. First, the sound democratic principle that there should be no favored classes or special privilege in a time of peril, that all should be ready to sacrifice equally; second, the tenet that every man should serve in the capacity in which his talents and experience can best be applied for the prosecution of the war effort. In general we have held these principles well in balance.

In my opinion, however, we have drawn too heavily for nonscientific purposes upon the great natural resource which resides in our trained young scientists and engineers. For the general good of the country too many such men have gone into uniform, and their talents have not always been fully utilized. With the exception of those men engaged in war research, all physically fit students at graduate level have been taken into the armed forces. Those ready for college training in the sciences have not been permitted to enter upon that training.

There is thus an accumulating deficit of trained research personnel which will continue for many years. The deficit of science and technology students who, but for the war, would have received bachelor's degrees is about 150,000. The deficit of those holding advanced degrees - that is, young scholars trained to the point where they are capable of carrying on original work - has been estimated as amounting to about 17,000 by 1955 in chemistry, engineering, geology, mathematics, physics, psychology, and the biological sciences.

With mounting demands for scientists both for teaching and for research, we will enter the post-war period with a serious deficit in our trained scientific personnel.

10.2.1.7.4 Improve the Quality

Confronted with these deficits, we are compelled to look to the use of our basic human resources and formulate a program which will assure their conservation and effective development. The committee advising me on scientific personnel has stated the following principle which should guide our planning

"If we were all-knowing and all-wise we might, but we think probably not, write you a plan whereby there might be selected for training, which they otherwise would not get, those who, 20 years hence, would be scientific leaders, and we might not bother about any lesser manifestations of scientific ability. But in the present state of knowledge a plan cannot be made which will select, and assist, only those young men and women who will give the top future leadership to science. To get top leadership there must be a relatively large base of high ability selected for development and then successive skimmings of the cream of ability at successive times and at higher levels. No one can select from the bottom those who will be the leaders at the top because unmeasured and unknown factors enter into scientific, or any, leadership. There are brains and character, strength and health, happiness and spiritual vitality, interest and motivation, and no one knows what else, that must needs enter into this supra-mathematical calculus.

"We think we probably would not, even if we were all-wise and all-knowing, write you a plan whereby you would be assured of scientific leadership at one stroke. We think as we think because we are not interested in setting up an elect. We think it much the best plan, in this constitutional Republic, that opportunity be held out to all kinds and conditions of men whereby they can better themselves. This is the American way; this is the way the United States has become what it is. We think it very important that circumstances be such that there be no ceilings, other than ability itself, to intellectual ambition. We think it very important that every boy and girl shall know that, if he shows that he has what it takes, the sky is the limit. Even if it be shown subsequently that he has not what it takes to go to the top, he will go further than he would otherwise go if there had been a ceiling beyond which he always knew he could not aspire.

"By proceeding from point to point and taking stock on the way, by giving further opportunity to those who show themselves worthy of further opportunity, by giving the most opportunity to those who show themselves continually developing - this is the way we propose. This is the American way a man work for what he gets."

10.2.1.7.5 Remove the Barriers

Higher education in this country is largely for those who have the means. If those who have the means coincided entirely with those persons who have the talent we should not be squandering a part of our higher education on those undeserving of it, nor neglecting great talent among those who fail to attend college for economic reasons. There are talented individuals in every segment of the population, but with few exceptions those without the means of buying higher education go without it. Here is a tremendous waste of the greatest resource of a nation - the intelligence of its citizens.

If ability, and not the circumstance of family fortune, is made to determine who shall receive higher education in science, then we shall be assured of constantly improving quality at every level of scientific activity.

10.2.1.7.6 The Generation in Uniform Must Not Be Lost

We have a serious deficit in scientific personnel partly because the men who would have studied science in the colleges and universities have been serving in the Armed Forces. Many had begun their studies before they went to war. Others with capacity for scientific education went to war after finishing high school. The most immediate prospect of making up some of the deficit in scientific personnel is by salvaging scientific talent from the generation in uniform. For even if we should start now to train the current crop of high school graduates, it would be 1951 before they would complete graduate studies and be prepared for effective scientific research. This fact underlines the necessity of salvaging potential scientists in uniform.

The Armed Services should comb their records for men who, prior to or during the war, have given evidence of talent for science, and make prompt arrangements, consistent with current discharge plans, for ordering those who remain in uniform as soon as militarily possible to duty at institutions here and overseas where they can continue their scientific education. Moreover, they should see that those who study overseas have the benefit of the latest scientific developments.

10.2.1.7.7 A Program

The country may be proud of the fact that 95 percent of boys and girls of the fifth grade age are enrolled in school, but the drop in enrollment after the fifth grade is less satisfying. For every 1,000 students in the fifth grade, 600 are lost to education before the end of high school, and all but 72 have ceased formal education before completion of college. While we are concerned primarily with methods of selecting and educating high school graduates at the college and higher levels, we cannot be complacent about the loss of potential talent which is inherent in the present situation.

Students drop out of school, college, and graduate school, or do not get that far, for a variety of reasons they cannot afford to go on; schools and colleges providing courses equal to their capacity are not available locally; business and industry recruit many of the most promising before they have finished the training of which they are capable. These reasons apply with particular force to science the road is long and expensive; it extends at least 6 years beyond high school; the percentage of science students who can obtain first-rate training in institutions near home is small.

Improvement in the teaching of science is imperative; for students of latent scientific ability are particularly vulnerable to high school teaching which fails to awaken interest or to provide adequate instruction. To enlarge the group of specially qualified men and women it is necessary to increase the number who go to college. This involves improved high school instruction, provision for helping individual talented students to finish high school (primarily the responsibility of the local communities), and opportunities for more capable, promising high school students to go to college. Anything short of this means serious waste of higher education and neglect of human resources.

To encourage and enable a larger number of young men and women of ability to take up science as a career, and in order gradually to reduce the deficit of trained scientific personnel, it is recommended that provision be made for a reasonable number of (a) undergraduate scholarships and graduate fellowships and (b) fellowships for advanced training and fundamental research. The details should be worked out with reference to the interests of the several States and of the universities and colleges; and care should be taken not to impair the freedom of the institutions and individuals concerned.

The program proposed by the Moe Committee in Appendix 4 would provide 24,000 undergraduate scholarships and 900 graduate fellowships and would cost about $30,000,000 annually when in full operation. Each year under this program 6,000 undergraduate scholarships would be made available to high school graduates, and 300 graduate fellowships would be offered to college graduates. Approximately the scale of allowances provided for under the educational program for returning veterans has been used in estimating the cost of this program.

The plan is, further, that all those who receive such scholarships or fellowships in science should be enrolled in a National Science Reserve and be liable to call into the service of the Government, in connection with scientific or technical work in time of war or other national emergency declared by Congress or proclaimed by the President. Thus, in addition to the general benefits to the nation by reason of the addition to its trained ranks of such a corps of scientific workers, there would be a definite benefit to the nation in having these scientific workers on call in national emergencies. The Government would be well advised to invest the money involved in this plan even if the benefits to the nation were thought of solely - which they are not - in terms of national preparedness.

10.2.1.8 Chapter 5 A PROBLEM OF SCIENTIFIC RECONVERSION

10.2.1.8.1 Effects of Mobilization of Science for War

We have been living on our fat. For more than 5 years many of our scientists have been fighting the war in the laboratories, in the factories and shops, and at the front. We have been directing the energies of our scientists to the development of weapons and materials and methods, on a large number of relatively narrow projects initiated and controlled by the Office of Scientific Research and Development and other Government agencies. Like troops, the scientists have been mobilized, and thrown into action to serve their country in time of emergency. But they have been diverted to a greater extent than is generally appreciated from the search for answers to the fundamental problems - from the search on which human welfare and progress depends. This is not a complaint - it is a fact. The mobilization of science behind the lines is aiding the fighting men at the front to win the war and to shorten it; and it has resulted incidentally in the accumulation of a vast amount of experience and knowledge of the application of science to particular problems, much of which can be put to use when the war is over. Fortunately, this country had the scientists - and the time - to make this contribution and thus to advance the date of victory.

10.2.1.8.2 Security Restrictions Should Be Lifted Promptly

Much of the information and experience acquired during the war is confined to the agencies that gathered it. Except to the extent that military security dictates otherwise, such knowledge should be spread upon the record for the benefit of the general public.

Thanks to the wise provision of the Secretary of War and the Secretary of the Navy, most of the results of war-time medical research have been published. Several hundred articles have appeared in the professional journals; many are in process of publication. The material still subject to security classification should be released as soon as possible.

It is my view that most of the remainder of the classified scientific material should be released as soon as there is ground for belief that the enemy will not be able to turn it against us in this war. Most of the information needed by industry and in education can be released without disclosing its embodiments in actual military material and devices. Basically there is no reason to believe that scientists of other countries will not in time rediscover everything we now know which is held in secrecy. A broad dissemination of scientific information upon which further advances can readily be made furnishes a sounder foundation for our national security than a policy of restriction which would impede our own progress although imposed in the hope that possible enemies would not catch up with us.

During the war it has been necessary for selected groups of scientists to work on specialized problems, with relatively little information as to what other groups were doing and had done. Working against time, the Office of Scientific Research and Development has been obliged to enforce this practice during the war, although it was realized by all concerned that it was an emergency measure which prevented the continuous cross-fertilization so essential to fruitful scientific effort.

Our ability to overcome possible future enemies depends upon scientific advances which will proceed more rapidly with diffusion of knowledge than under a policy of continued restriction of knowledge now in our possession.

10.2.1.8.3 Need for Coordination

In planning the release of scientific data and experience collected in connection with the war, we must not overlook the fact that research has gone forward under many auspices - the Army, the Navy, the Office of Scientific Research and Development, the National Advisory Committee for Aeronautics, other departments and agencies of the Government, educational institutions, and many industrial organizations. There have been numerous cases of independent discovery of the same truth in different places. To permit the release of information by one agency and to continue to restrict it elsewhere would be unfair in its effect and would tend to impair the morale and efficiency of scientists who have submerged individual interests in the controls and restrictions of war.

A part of the information now classified which should be released is possessed jointly by our allies and ourselves. Plans for release of such information should be coordinated with our allies to minimize danger of international friction which would result from sporadic uncontrolled release.

10.2.1.8.4 A Board to Control Release

The agency responsible for recommending the release of information from military classification should be an Army, Navy, civilian body, well grounded in science and technology. It should be competent to advise the Secretary of War and the Secretary of the Navy. It should, moreover, have sufficient recognition to secure prompt and practical decisions.

To satisfy these considerations I recommend the establishment of a Board, made up equally of scientists and military men, whose function would be to pass upon the declassification and to control the release for publication of scientific information which is now classified.

10.2.1.8.5 Publication Should Be Encouraged

The release of information from security regulations is but one phase of the problem. The other is to provide for preparation of the material and its publication in a form and at a price which will facilitate dissemination and use. In the case of the Office of Scientific Research and Development, arrangements have been made for the preparation of manuscripts, while the staffs under our control are still assembled and in possession of the records, as soon as the pressure for production of results for this war has begun to relax.

We should get this scientific material to scientists everywhere with great promptness, and at as low a price as is consistent with suitable format. We should also get it to the men studying overseas so that they will know what has happened in their absence.

It is recommended that measures which will encourage and facilitate the preparation and publication of reports be adopted forthwith by all agencies, governmental and private, possessing scientific information released from security control.

10.2.1.9 Chapter 6 THE MEANS TO THE END

10.2.1.9.1 New Responsibilities for Government

One lesson is clear from the reports of the several committees attached as appendices. The Federal Government should accept new responsibilities for promoting the creation of new scientific knowledge and the development of scientific talent in our youth.

The extent and nature of these new responsibilities are set forth in detail in the reports of the committees whose recommendations in this regard are fully endorsed.

In discharging these responsibilities Federal funds should be made available. We have given much thought to the question of how plans for the use of Federal funds may be arranged so that such funds will not drive out of the picture funds from local governments, foundations, and private donors. We believe that our proposals will minimize that effect, but we do not think that it can be completely avoided. We submit, however, that the nation's need for more and better scientific research is such that the risk must be accepted.

It is also clear that the effective discharge of these responsibilities will require the full attention of some over-all agency devoted to that purpose. There should be a focal point within the Government for a concerted program of assisting scientific research conducted outside of Government. Such an agency should furnish the funds needed to support basic research in the colleges and universities, should coordinate where possible research programs on matters of utmost importance to the national welfare, should formulate a national policy for the Government toward science, should sponsor the interchange of scientific information among scientists and laboratories both in this country and abroad, and should ensure that the incentives to research in industry and the universities are maintained. All of the committees advising on these matters agree on the necessity for such an agency.

10.2.1.9.2 The Mechanism

There are within Government departments many groups whose interests are primarily those of scientific research. Notable examples are found within the Departments of Agriculture, Commerce, Interior, and the Federal Security Agency. These groups are concerned with science as collateral and peripheral to the major problems of those Departments. These groups should remain where they are, and continue to perform their present functions, including the support of agricultural research by grants to the Land Grant Colleges and Experiment Stations, since their largest contribution lies in applying fundamental knowledge to the special problems of the Departments within which they are established.

By the same token these groups cannot be made the repository of the new and large responsibilities in science which belong to the Government and which the Government should accept. The recommendations in this report which relate to research within the Government, to the release of scientific information, to clarification of the tax laws, and to the recovery and development of our scientific talent now in uniform can be implemented by action within the existing structure of the Government. But nowhere in the Governmental structure receiving its funds from Congress is there an agency adapted to supplementing the support of basic research in the universities, both in medicine and the natural sciences; adapted to supporting research on new weapons for both Services; or adapted to administering a program of science scholarships and fellowships.

A new agency should be established, therefore, by the Congress for the purpose. Such an agency, moreover, should be an independent agency devoted to the support of scientific research and advanced scientific education alone. Industry learned many years ago that basic research cannot often be fruitfully conducted as an adjunct to or a subdivision of an operating agency or department. Operating agencies have immediate operating goals and are under constant pressure to produce in a tangible way, for that is the test of their value. None of these conditions is favorable to basic research. research is the exploration of the unknown and is necessarily speculative. It is inhibited by conventional approaches, traditions, and standards. It cannot be satisfactorily conducted in an atmosphere where it is gauged and tested by operating or production standards. Basic scientific research should not, therefore, be placed under an operating agency whose paramount concern is anything other than research. Research will always suffer when put in competition with operations. The decision that there should be a new and independent agency was reached by each of the committees advising in these matters.

I am convinced that these new functions should be centered in one agency. Science is fundamentally a unitary thing. The number of independent agencies should be kept to a minimum. Much medical progress, for example, will come from fundamental advances in chemistry. Separation of the sciences in tight compartments, as would occur if more than one agency were involved, would retard and not advance scientific knowledge as a whole.

10.2.1.9.3 Five Fundamentals

There are certain basic principles which must underlie the program of Government support for scientific research and education if such support is to be effective and if it is to avoid impairing the very things we seek to foster. These principles are as follows

(1) Whatever the extent of support may be, there must be stability of funds over a period of years so that long-range programs may be undertaken. (2) The agency to administer such funds should be composed of citizens selected only on the basis of their interest in and capacity to promote the work of the agency. They should be persons of broad interest in and understanding of the peculiarities of scientific research and education. (3) The agency should promote research through contracts or grants to organizations outside the Federal Government. It should not operate any laboratories of its own. (4) Support of basic research in the public and private colleges, universities, and research institutes must leave the internal control of policy, personnel, and the method and scope of the research to the institutions themselves. This is of the utmost importance. (5) While assuring complete independence and freedom for the nature, scope, and methodology of research

carried on in the institutions receiving public funds, and while retaining discretion in the allocation of funds among such institutions, the Foundation proposed herein must be responsible to the President and the Congress. Only through such responsibility can we maintain the proper relationship between science and other aspects of a democratic system. The usual controls of audits, reports, budgeting, and the like, should, of course, apply to the administrative and fiscal operations of the Foundation, subject, however, to such adjustments in procedure as are necessary to meet the special requirements of research.

Basic research is a long-term process - it ceases to be basic if immediate results are expected on short-term support. Methods should therefore be found which will permit the agency to make commitments of funds from current appropriations for programs of five years duration or longer. Continuity and stability of the program and its support may be expected (a) from the growing realization by the Congress of the benefits to the public from scientific research, and (b) from the conviction which will grow among those who conduct research under the auspices of the agency that good quality work will be followed by continuing support.

10.2.1.9.4 Military Research

As stated earlier in this report, military preparedness requires a permanent, independent, civilian-controlled organization, having close liaison with the Army and Navy, but with funds direct from Congress and the clear power to initiate military research which will supplement and strengthen that carried on directly under the control of the Army and Navy. As a temporary measure the National Academy of Sciences has established the Research Board for National Security at the request of the Secretary of War and the Secretary of the Navy. This is highly desirable in order that there may be no interruption in the relations between scientists and military men after the emergency wartime Office of Scientific Research and Development goes out of existence. The Congress is now considering legislation to provide funds for this Board by direct appropriation.

I believe that, as a permanent measure, it would be appropriate to add to the agency needed to perform the other functions recommended in this report the responsibilities for civilian-initiated and civilian-controlled military research. The function of such a civilian group would be primarily to conduct long-range scientific research on military problems - leaving to the Services research on the improvement of existing weapons.

Some research on military problems should be conducted, in time of peace as well as in war, by civilians independently of the military establishment. It is the primary responsibility of the Army and Navy to train the men, make available the weapons, and employ the strategy that will bring victory in combat. The Armed Services cannot be expected to be experts in all of the complicated fields which make it possible for a great nation to fight successfully in total war. There are certain kinds of research - such as research on the improvement of existing weapons - which can best be done within the military establishment. However, the job of long-range research involving application of the newest scientific discoveries to military needs should be the responsibility of those civilian scientists in the universities and in industry who are best trained to discharge it thoroughly and successfully. It is essential that both kinds of research go forward and that there be the closest liaison between the two groups.

Placing the civilian military research function in the proposed agency would bring it into close relationship with a broad program of basic research in both the natural sciences and medicine. A balance between military and other research could thus readily be maintained.

The establishment of the new agency, including a civilian military research group, should not be delayed by the existence of the Research Board for National Security, which is a temporary measure. Nor should the creation of the new agency be delayed by uncertainties in regard to the postwar organization of our military departments themselves. Clearly, the new agency, including a civilian military research group within it, can remain sufficiently flexible to adapt its operations to whatever may be the final organization of the military departments.

10.2.1.9.5 National Research Foundation

It is my judgment that the national interest in scientific research and scientific education can best be promoted by the creation of a National Research Foundation.

I. Purposes. - The National Research Foundation should develop and promote a national policy for scientific research and scientific education, should support basic research in nonprofit organizations, should develop scientific talent in American youth by means of scholarships and fellowships, and should by contract and otherwise support long-range research on military matters.

II. Members. - 1. Responsibility to the people, through the President and Congress, should be placed in the hands of, say nine Members, who should be persons not otherwise connected with the Government and not representative of any special interest, who should be known as National Research Foundation Members, selected by the President on the basis of their interest in and capacity to promote the purposes of the Foundation.

2. The terms of the Members should be, say, 4 years, and no Member should be eligible for immediate reappointment provided he has served a full 4-year term. It should be arranged that the Members first appointed serve terms of such length that at least two Members are appointed each succeeding year.

3. The Members should serve without compensation but should be entitled to their expenses incurred in the performance of their duties.

4. The Members should elect their own chairman annually.

5. The chief executive officer of the Foundation should be a director appointed by the Members. Subject to the direction and supervision of the Foundation

Members (acting as a board), the director should discharge all the fiscal, legal, and administrative functions of the Foundation. The director should receive a salary that is fully adequate to attract an outstanding man to the post.

6. There should be an administrative office responsible to the director to handle in one place the fiscal, legal, personnel, and other similar administrative functions necessary to the accomplishment of the purposes of the Foundation.

7. With the exception of the director, the division members, and one executive officer appointed by the director to administer the affairs of each division, all employees of the Foundation should be appointed under Civil Service regulations.

```
==================================================================
    Proposed Organization of National Research Foundation
                      ===============================
                      | National Research Foundation |
                      |------------------------------|
                      |           Members            |
                      ===============================
                                   |
                          ----------------------
                          |     Director       |
                          ----------------------
                                   |
                                   |--------------------
                                   |                   |
                                   |          ---------------------------
                                   |          | Staff offices           |
                                   |          | General Counsel         |
                                   |          | Finance Officer         |
                                   |          | Administrative planning |
                                   |          | Personnel               |
                                   |          ---------------------------
                                   |
                                   |
------------------------------------------------------------------
Div of       Div of         Div of       Div of       Div of
Medical      Scientific     Natural      National     Publications
Research     Personnel &    Sciences     Defense      & Scientific
             Education                                Collaboration
--------     --------       --------     --------     --------
Members      Members        Members      Members      Members
--------     --------       --------     --------     --------
Exec. Off.   Exec. Off.     Exec. Off.   Exec. Off.   Exec. Off.
--------     --------       --------     --------     --------
==================================================================
```

III. Organization. - 1. In order to accomplish the purposes of the Foundation the Members should establish several professional Divisions to be responsible to the Members. At the outset these Divisions should be

a. Division of Medical Research. - The function of this Division should be to support medical research.

b. Division of Natural Sciences. - The function of this Division should be to support research in the physical and natural sciences.

c. Division of National Defense. - It should be the function of this Division to support long-range scientific research on military matters.

d. Division of Scientific Personnel and Education. - It should be the function of this Division to support and to supervise the grant of scholarships and fellowships in science.

e. Division of Publications and Scientific Collaboration. - This Division should be charged with encouraging the publication of scientific knowledge and promoting international exchange of scientific information.

2. Each Division of the Foundation should be made up of at least five members, appointed by the Members of the Foundation. In making such appointments the Members should request and consider recommendations from the National Academy of Sciences which should be asked to establish a new National Research Foundation nominating committee in order to bring together the recommendations of scientists in all organizations. The chairman of each Division should be appointed by the Members of the Foundation.

3. The division Members should be appointed for such terms as the Members of the Foundation may determine, and may be reappointed at the discretion of the Members. They should receive their expenses and compensation for their services at a per diem rate of, say, $50 while engaged on business of the Foundation, but no division member should receive more than, say, $10,000 compensation per year.

4. Membership of the Division of National Defense should include, in addition to, say, five civilian members, one representative designated by the Secretary of War, and one representative of the Secretary of the Navy, who should serve without additional compensation for this duty.

IV. Functions. - 1. The Members of the Foundation should have the following functions, powers, and duties

a. To formulate over-all policies of the Foundation.

b. To establish and maintain such offices within the United States, its territories and possessions, as they may deem necessary.

c. To meet and function at any place within the United States, its territories and possessions.

d. To obtain and utilize the services of other Government agencies to the extent that such agencies are prepared to render such services.

e. To adopt, promulgate, amend, and rescind rules and regulations to carry out the provisions of the legislation and the policies and practices of the Foundation.

f. To review and balance the financial requirements of the several Divisions and to propose to the President the annual estimate for the funds required by each Division. Appropriations should be earmarked for the purposes of specific Divisions, but the Foundation should be left discretion with respect to the expenditure of each Division's funds.

g. To make contracts or grants for the conduct of research by negotiation without advertising for bids.

And with the advice of the National Research Foundation Divisions concerned -

h. To create such advisory and cooperating agencies and councils, state, regional, or national, as in their judgment will aid in effectuating the purposes of the legislation, and to pay the expenses thereof.

i. To enter into contracts with or make grants to educational and nonprofit research institutions for support of scientific research.

j. To initiate and finance in appropriate agencies, institutions, or organizations, research on problems related to the national defense.

k. To initiate and finance in appropriate organizations research projects for which existing facilities are unavailable or inadequate.

l. To establish scholarships and fellowships in the natural sciences including biology and medicine.

m. To promote the dissemination of scientific and technical information and to further its international exchange.

n. To support international cooperation in science by providing financial aid for international meetings, associations of scientific societies, and scientific research programs organized on an international basis.

o. To devise and promote the use of methods of improving the transition between research and its practical application in industry.

2. The Divisions should be responsible to the Members of the Foundation for -

a. Formulation of programs and policy within the scope of the particular Divisions.

b. Recommendations regarding the allocation of research programs among research organizations.

c. Recommendation of appropriate arrangements between the Foundation and the organizations selected to carry on the program.

d. Recommendation of arrangements with State and local authorities in regard to cooperation in a program of science scholarships and fellowships.

e. Periodic review of the quality of research being conducted under the auspices of the particular Division and revision of the program of support of research.

f. Presentation of budgets of financial needs for the work of the Division.

g. Maintaining liaison with other scientific research agencies, both governmental and private, concerned with the work of the Division.

V. Patent Policy. - The success of the National Research Foundation in promoting scientific research in this country will depend to a very large degree upon the cooperation of organizations outside the Government. In making contracts with or grants to such organizations the Foundation should protect the public interest adequately and at the same time leave the cooperating organization with adequate freedom and incentive to conduct scientific research. The public interest will normally be adequately protected if the Government receives a royalty-free license for governmental purposes under any patents resulting from work financed by the Foundation. There should be no obligation on the research institution to patent discoveries made as a result of support from the Foundation. There should certainly not be any absolute requirement that all rights in such discoveries be assigned to the Government, but it should be left to the discretion of the director and the interested Division whether in special cases the public interest requires such an assignment. Legislation on this point should leave to the Members of the Foundation discretion as to its patent policy in order that patent arrangements may be adjusted as circumstances and the public interest require.

VI. Special Authority. - In order to insure that men of great competence and experience may be designated as Members of the Foundation and as members of the several professional Divisions, the legislation creating the Foundation should contain specific authorization so that the Members of the Foundation and the Members of the Divisions may also engage in private and gainful employment, notwithstanding the provisions of any other laws provided, however, that no compensation for such employment is received in any form from any profit-making institution which receives funds under contract, or otherwise, from the Division or Divisions of the Foundation with which the individual is concerned. In normal times, in view of the restrictive statutory prohibitions against dual interests on the part of Government officials, it would be virtually impossible to persuade persons having private employment of any kind to serve the Government in an official capacity. In order, however, to secure the part-time services of the most competent men as Members of the Foundation and the Divisions, these stringent prohibitions should be relaxed to the extent indicated.

Since research is unlike the procurement of standardized items, which are susceptible to competitive bidding on fixed specifications, the legislation creating the National Research Foundation should free the Foundation from the obligation to place its contracts for research through advertising for bids. This is particularly so since the measure of a successful research contract lies not in the dollar cost but in the qualitative and quantitative contribution which is made to our knowledge. The extent of this contribution in turn depends on the creative spirit and talent which can be brought to bear within a research laboratory. The National Research Foundation must, therefore, be free to place its research contracts or grants not only with those institutions which have a demonstrated research capacity but also with other institutions whose latent talent or creative atmosphere affords promise of research success.

As in the case of the research sponsored during the war by the Office of Scientific Research and Development, the research sponsored by the National Research Foundation should be conducted, in general, on an actual cost basis without profit to the institution receiving the research contract or grant.

There is one other matter which requires special mention. Since research does not fall within the category of normal commercial or procurement operations which are easily covered by the usual contractual relations, it is essential that certain statutory and regulatory fiscal requirements be waived in the case of research contractors. For example, the National Research Foundation should be authorized by legislation to make, modify, or amend contracts of all kinds with or without legal consideration, and without performance bonds. Similarly, advance payments should be allowed in the discretion of the Director of the Foundation when required. Finally, the normal vouchering requirements of the General Accounting Office with respect to detailed itemization or substantiation of vouchers submitted under cost contracts should be relaxed for research contractors. Adherence to the usual procedures in the case of research contracts will impair the efficiency of research operations and will needlessly increase the cost of the work of the Government. Without the broad authority along these lines which was contained in the First War Powers Act and its implementing Executive Orders, together with the special relaxation of vouchering requirements granted by the General Accounting Office, the Office of Scientific Research and Development would have been gravely handicapped in carrying on research on military matters during this war. Colleges and universities in which research will be conducted principally under contract with the Foundation are, unlike commercial institutions, not equipped to handle the detailed vouchering procedures and auditing technicalities which are required of the usual Government contractors.

Activity	Millions of dollars	
	First year	5th yr
Division of Medical Research	5.0	20.0
Division of Natural Sciences	10.0	50.0
Division of National Defense	10.0	20.0
Div of Scientific Personnel and Education	7.0	29.0
Div of Pubs & Scientific Collaboration	.5	1.0
Administration	1.0	2.5

VII. Budget. - Studies by the several committees provide a partial basis for making an estimate of the order of magnitude of the funds required to implement the proposed program. Clearly the program should grow in a healthy manner from modest beginnings. The following very rough estimates are given for the first year of operation after the Foundation is organized and operating, and for the fifth year of operation when it is expected that the operations would have reached a fairly stable level

10.2.1.9.6 Action by Congress

The National Research Foundation herein proposed meets the urgent need of the days ahead. The form of the organization suggested is the result of considerable deliberation. The form is important. The very successful pattern of organization of the National Advisory Committee for Aeronautics, which has promoted basic research on problems of flight during the past thirty years, has been carefully considered in proposing the method of appointment of Members of the Foundation and in defining their responsibilities. Moreover, whatever program is established it is vitally important that it satisfy the Five Fundamentals.

The Foundation here proposed has been described only in outline. The excellent reports of the committees which studied these matters are attached as appendices. They will be of aid in furnishing detailed suggestions.

Legislation is necessary. It should be drafted with great care. Early action is imperative, however, if this nation is to meet the challenge of science and fully utilize the potentialities of science. On the wisdom with which we bring science to bear against the problems of the coming years depends in large measure our future as a nation.

10.2.2 Social Gospel Movement and President Johnson

Biographer Randall Woods writes that President Lyndon B. Johnsons early childhood exposure to Social Gospel themes explains his longtime commitment to social justice, as exemplified by the Great Society and commitment to racial equality. Social Gospel also inspired President Johnson's foreign policy approach of Christian internationalism and nation building.

The Protestant Social Gospel movement applied Christian ethics to social problems such as social justice as economic inequality, poverty, alcoholism, crime, racial tensions, slums, unclean environment, child labor, inadequate labor unions, poor schools, and the danger of war. It was most prominent in the United States and Canada during the early 20th century.

The movement started during the second half of the nineteenth century. They argued that people must help other people especially the needy and that purpose of wealth was not to hoard it but to share it with less fortunate people. They attacked the concept of Social Darwinism.

In the late 19th century, many were disgusted by the poverty level and the low quality of living in the slums. The Social Gospel movement addressed public health, education, and labor reforms, such as abolishing child labor and regulating the hours of work by mothers. By 1920 they were crusading against the 12-hour day for workers at US Steel. One of their most important contributions was the establishment of settlement houses that provided opportunities for less fortunate people to access to education, free or low-cost health care, free or low-cost housing, and other benefits.

The movement peaked in the early 20th century with some suggesting that the destruction and trauma caused by World War I left many disillusioned. Others suggest the war stimulated Social Gospel reform efforts and influenced the New Deal prior to and after WW II. Many of its ideas reappeared in the Civil Rights Movement of the 1960s.

10.3 FAA NAS Plan 1989

The FAA in the past acknowledged and used systems engineering to support its planning. Much of this work impacted the National Airspace System Plan (NAS Plan) starting in 1981 and ending approximately 1989. The NAS Plan Chapter II – Demand on the System had key performance data associated with the system. The following is an extract from the NAS Plan 1989. It is fascinating to see the FAA try to shave minutes off of a flight. This is in contrast today where the system adds hours to a traveler's time without a second thought and then adds massive overhead to the people with what was once a simple act of booking a flight.

Today the FAA should track and publish in easy to read and search format the flight destinations for each airport in the USA. As destinations are eliminated the FAA should clearly track and communicate the lost services. The data should go back to pre-deregulation days and consistently track to the present to gain an understating of system effectiveness. *** Start excerpt ***

Chapter II – Demand on the System

The United States National Airspace System is the busiest and most complex in the world. The airspace accommodates over 240,000 active civil and military aircraft. Performance characteristics of these air- craft vary widely and the missions flown have differing impacts on the system. The overall trend is toward the production of more sophisticated aircraft which make greater use of controlled airspace and the services which FAA provides.

The continuing growth in aircraft operations, diversity of operations, number of aircraft, and sophistication of aircraft will place unprecedented demands on the National Airspace System from now through the turn of the century. In addition, the full effects of the Deregulation Act of 1978 and the resulting increase in competitive scheduling, lower prices, new airline entries, and airport hubbing will continue to place extra demands on the system. The safe and efficient operation of the National Airspace System will require improved services, new facilities for system expansion, orderly replacement of aging facilities, and provision of adequate airport capacity.

Despite its high level of safety, the National Airspace System is not without difficulties. Problems of expanding capacity at congested airports, the provision of more direct routings, and the accommodation of greater numbers of sophisticated aircraft must be dealt with effectively.

GENERAL SYSTEM DEMAND

Forecasts indicate that demand in terms of aviation activity will increase substantially in the next two decades. Table I depicts the growth anticipated in aviation demand for the years 1990, 1995, and 2000.

OPERATIONS AND ENPLANEMENTS

Aircraft operations, including takeoffs and landings at all towered and non-towered airports in the National Airport System Plan (NASP) (the forerunner to the National Plan of Integrated Airport Systems (NPIAS)), were anticipated to grow by 45 percent between 1982 and 2000, with itinerant operations increasing 64 percent. Itinerant operations refer to those aircraft departing to or arriving from an area outside an airport's local operating area. A breakdown of aircraft operations for the different types of civil airports can also be found in Tables II and III. Table IV provides information concerning military-owned and operated airports Instrument operations represent a separation service provided to aircraft while conducting flight in accordance with instrument flight rules (IFR). In the terminal area, IFR separation services are provided either by the air route traffic control center (ARTCC) or terminal approach facility, and are expected to increase by 92 percent. Enroute service into and from terminal areas is provided by the ARTCC and is expected to increase by 71 percent. Flight service station (FSS) operations, including pilot briefings, flight plan origination, and aircraft contacted, will deer ease by 23 percent. Domestic enplanements include all enplanements for the activity indicated, regardless of airport type. Air carrier domestic enplanements are expected to increase by 155 percent and commuter enplanements by 269 percent.

AIRCRAFT HOURS, FLEET, AND PILOTS

Air carrier hours flown are forecast to increase 120 percent, general aviation hours flown to increase 2 percent, and military hours flown to increase 13 percent. The number of air carrier aircraft will increase by 92 percent, commuter aircraft by 50 per- cent, general aviation by 3.7 percent, and the helicopter fleet by 47 percent (see Table I.)

The mix of the general aviation fleet will be altered dramatically during this period. The single-engine piston fleet, which normally operates visual flight rules (VFR) below 12,000 feet, will decrease from 172,000 to 162,000 aircraft. The more sophisticated twin-engine and turbine- powered aircraft will comprise the fastest growing segment of the fixed- wing fleet, increasing from 34,500 to 39,000 aircraft. The number of pilots will increase by 3 percent, but those with instrument ratings will grow by 22 percent.

MILITARY AVIATION REQUIREMENT

Response to military requirements places special demands on the National Airspace System, particularly in the en route airspace. The F'AA also provides approach control services for over half of the 233 military airfields in the United States. This service is in addition to over 50 approach control facilities and 180 control towers that are operated by the military. The Department of Defense operates over 20,000 aircraft within the National Airspace System, flying approximately 6 million hours a year. Over 90 percent of this flying is dedicated to training missions. These training missions include high- speed maneuvering flight in all altitude bands, with increasing need for very low-level operations.

Increased air refueling activity, air drop missions, and frequent large-scale joint exercises require close coordination with civil traffic flows. The increased speed, range, and capabilities of military flight operations also indicate that a higher level of demand will be placed on the National Airspace System for training and testing, even though the total number of military aircraft will remain relatively constant. A relatively small amount of airspace is reserved exclusively for military use. Therefore, there will be a need for continued coordination and improved navigation and air traffic control service as growing civil aviation and military aviation requirements must be accommodated within common airspace.

TABLE I. TOTAL NATIONAL AIRSPACE SYSTEM ACTIVITY – 1985 report

	1982	1985	1990	1995	2000	Percent Growth 1982-2000
PIAS Airports *	3195	3219	3472	3600	3750	17.4
Airport Operations (millions)						
Aircraft Operations	127.6	143.0	146.1	160.iJ	185.1	45.1
Itinerant Operations	68.0	78.8	86.0	98.9	111.6	64.1
Instrument Operations	31.7	38.7	47.7	55.1	61.0	92.4
Towered Airport Operations	50.6	57.9	64.0	72.5	80.2	58.5
ARTCC Operations (millions)						
IFR Aircraft Handled	27.9	32.7	38.2	43.5	47.8	71.3
ACF Approach Control Operations **					61.0	
FSS Service (millions)	62.4	52.9	44.2	46.4	48.2	(22.8)
Hours Flown (millions)						
Air Carrier	6.1	7.4	10.6	12.0	13.4	119.7
General Aviation	37.7	36.2	34.4	36.7	38.6	2.4
Military	6.2	5.9	6.0	7.0	7.0	12.9
Domestic Enplanements (Revenue Passenger) (millions)						
Air Carrier	272.8	350.4	447.8	570.4	695.8	155.1
Commuter	17.8	24.4	35.4	49.6	65.6	268.5
Aircraft Fleet (thousands)						
Air Carrier	2.5	2.9	4.1	4.4	4.8	92.0
Commuter ***	1.4	1.5	1.8	2.0	2.1	50.0
Total General Aviation	213.3	220.9	216.7	217.8	221.1	3.7
Civil Helicopter ***	7.0	7.1	7.1	8.7	10.3	47.1
Total Military	21.7	19.9	21.1	21.9	21.9	0.9
Military Helicopter ***	9.7	7.3	8.9	9.2	9.2	(5.2)

Pilots (thousands)						
Instrument Rated	252.5	256.6	275.8	295.4	308.0	22.0
Total Pilots	764.2	722.4	715.8	756.8	787.8	3.1

* Aircraft operations forecasts are based on the existing airports included in the National Plan of Integrated Airport Systems (NPIAS).

* * Approach control operations conducted for area control facilities equal the number of instrument operations conducted by towers.

*** Civil Helicopter and Commuter Fleets are included in the Total General Aviation Fleet. Military Helicopter Fleet is included in Total Military Fleet.

TABLE II. COMMERCIAL SERVICE AIRPORT ACTIVITY – 1985 report

	1982	1985	1990	1995	2000	Percent Growth 1982-2000
Large Hub Commercial Service •						
Airports	24	28	29	31	32	33.3
Operations (millions)	8.2	11.1	12.4	14.6	16.1	96.3
Enplanements ** (millions)	196.3	280.3	352.3	453.0	538.8	174.5
Based Aircraft (thousands)	2.4	3.5	3.1	3.2	3.6	50.0
Other Commercial Service ***						
Airports	521	518	534	537	556	6.7
Operations (millions)	53.8	40.0	48.7	57.5	66.5	23.6
Enplanements ** (millions)	112.7	125.2	182.8	220.7	264.1	134.3
Based Aircraft (thousands)	61.0	60.3	57.8	58.3	60.4	(1.0)

* Airports at which over 1 percent of total U.S. passengers are enplaned.

** Includes scheduled and nonscheduled traffic by domestic and foreign flag carriers, commuters, and air taxis.

* * * Airports receiving regularly scheduled service when 2,500 or more passengers are enplaned annually (excludes large hub commercial airports).

TABLE III. GENERAL AVIATION AIRPORT ACTIVITY – 1985 report

	1982	1 985	1 990	1995	2000	Percent Growth 1982-2000
Reliever Airports						
Airports	202	227	275	320	340	68.3
Operations (millions)	20.0	26.6	31.0	37.5	43.5	117.5
Based Aircraft (thousands)	44.3	55.5	63.6	74.0	78.6	77.4
General Aviation Airports						
Airports	2424	2440	2634	2712	2822	16.4

Operations (millions)	45.6	65.3	54.0	56.0	59.0	29.4
Based Aircraft (thousands)	67.9	79.4	84.4	73.8	69.3	2.1

TABLE IV. MILITARY AIRPORTS – 1985 report

	1982	1 985	1990	1995	2000	Percent Growth 1982-2000
Airports	233	233	233	233	233	00.0
Operations (millions)	24.7	26.7	28.6	29.6	30.5	23.5
Military	21.7	23.1	24.3	24.9	25.5	17.5
Civil	3.0	3.5	4.3	4.5	4.6	53.3

There are about 17,200 landing areas in the United States, of which over 5,700 are open to the public. Currently the nation's most important civil airports are included in the National Plan of Integrated Airport Systems (NPIAS) prepared biannually by the Federal Aviation Administration, consistent with the Airport and Airway Improvement Act of 1982, as amended by the Airport and Airway Safety and Capacity Improvement Act of 1987. The plan includes the type and estimated costs of eligible airport development work in coordination with the National Airspace System Plan necessary to provide a safe, efficient system of public-use airports.

OPERATIONS

Today, civil airports handle about 143 million aircraft operations and enplane over 450 million passengers. They accommodate over 240,000 aircraft.

Airport development is largely the responsibility of state and local governments. The Federal Government participates in development at the request of state and local governments through its airport grant program and encourages airport planning and development to enhance safety, reduce congestion, and protect the environment.

Airport activity will increase substantially by the year 2000. Accommodating this additional demand will be more difficult in the future than it has been in the past. Although most of the nation's airports will have adequate airside capacity through the turn of the century, many of our key metropolitan areas are now congested and many more are expected to become congested before the turn of the century. In many metropolitan areas, there is little or no reserve capacity and the potential for airside expansion is limited. Though only a relatively small percentage of airports are involved, they handle a disproportionately high percentage of scheduled passengers. Today, the 28 largest commercial airports enplane approximately 68 percent of all passengers. In non-metropolitan areas, needed capacity may usually be obtained through conventional construction of runways and associated taxiways.

The basic methods for adding airport capacity in congested areas are:

- High speed turnoffs.
- Short commuter runways.
- New or improved pavement at existing airports.
- Procedural changes such as reduction in longitudinal (in-trail) and lateral (e.g., separation between centerlines of parallel runways) separation standards.
- Terminal area flow optimization.
- New airports.

Some increases in airport capacity will result from FAA's broad efforts to modernize the National Airspace System which include improved techniques for metering and controlling traffic flow and the implementation of the microwave landing system. Further increases in capacity and reductions in delay may potentially be realized through the use of converging instrument approaches, development of short parallel runways for smaller aircraft, reduced spacing between runways for independent instrument flight rules (IFR) operations, and triple parallel instrument approaches.

Together with emphasis on safety, these measures will provide an important share, but not all, of the required increase in airport system capacity. Construction of new airports and new or improved pavements at existing airports provide the largest incremental gains to capacity. To the extent possible, FAA is encouraging use of airport planning and development grants for capacity-related projects at airports that are now congested or are expected to be congested within the next decade.

In some communities it will not be feasible to expand existing airports to accommodate forecast demand. Therefore, local and state governments must consider the construction of new major airports. The FAA will play an active role, as anticipated at Denver, in supporting such studies and providing local officials with appropriate aid to alleviate adverse environmental impact and overcome financial obstacles. There are major obstacles to new airport construction in metropolitan areas, but there are also substantial gains to be achieved when new procedures or airport improvements are made.

Establishing new major airports involves large financial, environmental, and land-use commitments. When the new proposed airports replace existing airports, large economic dislocations may result. It is for these reasons that metropolitan areas, when faced with overcrowded airports, seek alternatives to new construction. These alternatives can be broadly grouped as:

- Increasing the capacity and efficiency of existing airports through technical changes, scheduling changes and/or possibly peak pricing.
- Encouraging the use of aircraft with greater seating capacity.

- Increasing the use of existing secondary airports within the hub.

Further increases in the capacity of existing airports are possible through conventional construction (such as new runways) when feasible, incorporation of new and improved technology into the air traffic control system and related areas, and use of improved and innovative air traffic control procedures. Delays at individual airports may also be reduced by local authorities through spreading and/or meeting peak- hour traffic through regulatory or economic devices and encouraging the restructuring of airline service patterns so that connecting flights are not concentrated at a few large cities.

The second area for achieving increased capacity by employing large aircraft has been a key factor in accommodating growth for the past 20 years. The average seating capacity of large commercial aircraft has grown from less than 50 in 1950 to about 152 today. A significant part of projected passenger growth will continue to be absorbed through the use of larger aircraft. Adding more seats to existing aircraft and higher load factors will also contribute. Table II indicates that, at large airports, rate of passenger growth is about twice the growth of aircraft operations.

The severe aircraft delays experienced at certain major hub airports illustrate the need for increased airport capacity. Some increases in capacity can be achieved through greater use of secondary airports. To do this will require improving some reliever airports and constructing new ones, as well as more intensive use of existing second or third airports for scheduled service. The following chart depicts the number of airports that are presently congested through the turn of the century, if additional capacity is not provided through new construction or implementation of capacity-enhancing programs.

Alleviation of congestion through demand reduction by either economic or regulatory means is not reflected. Priority will be given to research and facilities projects which show promise of reducing congestion at airports. Priority will also be given under the airport grant program to projects which may alleviate congestion.

The Airport and Airway Improvement Act of 1982 as amended includes a restructured airport grant program which provides an expanded program focus on airport capacity enhancement as well as safety improvements. Through a significantly enlarged discretionary fund, incorporating a capacity set-aside, the grant program will provide more funds for projects which enhance system capacity. Airport noise and reliever airport projects which expand system capacity will also be eligible for these discretionary funds. While enhanced airport safety is the primary thrust of the annual airport grant program proposal, the emphasis on airport system capacity will allow gains in airspace capacity through implementation of the NAS Plan to be matched by gains in airport capacity. *** End excerpt ***

10.4 FAA Taxpayer Investment

This is the FAA budget by year and the adjusted budget based on 2017 dollars using inflation adjustments. The budget came from the FAA and represents the actual or proposed budget. There are years in the 2000s where the numbers were not available, so previous years or future years numbers were used. The FAA budget is much higher after privatization than before privatization.

Year	Inflation CPI	Inflation Factor	FAA Budget	2017 dollars
2017	2.50%	1	$16,280,724,000	$16,280,724,000
2016	1.37%	1.0137	$15,717,450,000	$15,932,779,065
2015	-0.09%	1.012788	$15,864,030,000	$16,066,893,981
2014	1.58%	1.02879	$15,519,953,000	$15,966,768,027
2013	1.59%	1.045147	$15,902,353,000	$16,620,304,031
2012	2.93%	1.07577	$15,902,353,000	$17,107,278,939
2011	1.63%	1.093305	$15,956,000,000	$17,444,780,138
2010	2.63%	1.122059	$14,077,349,000	$15,795,620,069
2009	0.03%	1.122396	$14,077,349,000	$15,800,358,755
2008	4.28%	1.170434	$13,724,000,000	$16,063,042,271
2007	2.08%	1.194779	$13,866,860,000	$16,567,839,746
2006	3.99%	1.242451	$13,972,000,000	$17,359,527,869
2005	2.97%	1.279352	$13,873,000,000	$17,748,450,001
2004	1.93%	1.304043	$13,506,000,000	$17,612,411,131
2003	2.60%	1.337949	$13,506,000,000	$18,070,333,821
2002	1.14%	1.353201	$13,506,000,000	$18,276,335,626
2001	3.73%	1.403676	$13,506,000,000	$18,958,042,945
2000	2.74%	1.442136	$8,549,000,000	$12,328,823,516
1999	1.67%	1.46622	$8,549,000,000	$12,534,714,869
1998	1.57%	1.48924	$8,549,000,000	$12,731,509,892
1997	3.04%	1.534513	$8,196,000,000	$12,576,864,863
1996	2.73%	1.576405	$8,322,000,000	$13,118,840,271
1995	2.80%	1.620544	$8,644,000,000	$14,007,982,991
1994	2.52%	1.661382	$8,862,000,000	$14,723,165,392
1993	3.26%	1.715543	$8,887,000,000	$15,246,029,155
1992	2.60%	1.760147	$7,937,700,000	$13,971,518,416
1991	5.65%	1.859595	$7,366,600,000	$13,698,894,360

Year	Inflation CPI	Inflation Factor	FAA Budget	2017 dollars
1990	5.20%	1.956294	$6,589,500,000	$12,891,000,643
1989	4.67%	2.047653	$6,169,000,000	$12,631,972,227
1988	4.05%	2.130583	$4,946,100,000	$10,538,077,038
1987	1.46%	2.16169	$4,869,300,000	$10,525,915,201
1986	3.89%	2.245779	$5,355,800,000	$12,027,944,947
1985	3.53%	2.325055	$4,642,700,000	$10,794,534,439
1984	4.19%	2.422475	$4,167,700,000	$10,096,149,730
1983	3.71%	2.512349	$3,156,600,000	$7,930,480,821
1982	8.39%	2.723135	$3,412,500,000	$9,292,698,427
1981	11.83%	3.045282	$3,273,900,000	$9,969,948,573
1980	13.91%	3.468881	$3,150,300,000	$10,928,014,768
1979	9.28%	3.790793	$2,792,500,000	$10,585,788,877
1978	6.84%	4.050083	$2,599,150,000	$10,526,773,284
1977	5.22%	4.261497	$2,816,679,000	$12,003,270,108
1976	6.72%	4.54787	$2,078,259,750	$9,451,655,122
1975	11.80%	5.084519	$1,934,837,000	$9,837,714,781
1974	9.39%	5.561955	$1,851,753,000	$10,299,366,735
1973	3.65%	5.764966	$1,901,174,000	$10,960,204,020
1972	3.27%	5.953481	$1,786,829,000	$10,637,851,942
1971	5.29%	6.26842	$1,287,977,000	$8,073,580,548
1970	6.18%	6.655808	$902,174,000	$6,004,697,071
1969	4.40%	6.948664	$915,650,000	$6,362,543,934
1968	3.65%	7.20229	$993,026,500	$7,152,064,776
1967	3.46%	7.451489	$0	$0
1966	1.92%	7.594558	$549,980,750	$4,176,860,578
1965	0.97%	7.668225	$567,995,000	$4,355,513,447
1964	1.64%	7.793984	$707,424,000	$5,513,651,244
1963	1.33%	7.897644	$799,800,000	$6,316,535,555
1962	0.67%	7.950558	$775,881,600	$6,168,691,715
1961	1.71%	8.086513	$833,341,500	$6,738,826,549
1960	1.03%	8.169804	$733,792,000	$5,994,936,590
1959	1.40%	8.284181	$866,910,500	$7,181,643,443
1958	3.62%	8.584068	$0	$0

Year	Inflation CPI	Inflation Factor	FAA Budget	2017 dollars
1957	2.99%	8.840732	$406,100,000	$3,590,221,239
1956	0.37%	8.873443	$278,400,000	$2,470,366,432
1955	-0.74%	8.807779	$197,300,000	$1,737,774,830
1954	1.13%	8.907307	$131,400,000	$1,170,420,149
1953	0.38%	8.941155	$115,900,000	$1,036,279,846
1952	4.33%	9.328307	$136,400,000	$1,272,381,053
1951	8.09%	10.08297	$138,900,000	$1,400,524,098
1950	-2.08%	9.873241	$151,900,000	$1,499,745,332
1949	1.27%	9.998631	$187,100,000	$1,870,743,920
1948	10.23%	11.02149	$100,470,000	$1,107,329,231
1947	18.13%	13.01969	$119,314,334	$1,553,435,364
1946	2.25%	13.31263	$121,537,720	$1,617,986,776
1945	2.30%	13.61882	$51,090,000	$695,785,573
1944	2.96%	14.02194	$35,781,478	$501,725,675
1943	7.64%	15.09321	$31,653,000	$477,745,514
1942	11.35%	16.80629	$38,237,775	$642,635,295
1941	1.44%	17.0483	$224,772,687	$3,831,993,280
1940	-0.71%	16.92726	$103,390,537	$1,750,118,692
1939	-1.41%	16.68859	$0	$0
1938	0.71%	16.80708	$25,768,000	$433,084,745
1937	2.17%	17.17179	$14,351,480	$246,440,600
1936	1.47%	17.42422	$0	$0
1935	3.03%	17.95217	$10,878,500	$195,292,671
1934	2.33%	18.37045	$6,850,000	$125,837,614
1933	-9.79%	16.57199	$5,909,800	$97,937,129
1932	-10.06%	14.90485	$5,511,800	$82,152,526
1931	-7.02%	13.85853	$0	$0
1930	0.00%	13.85853	$7,660,780	$106,167,111
1929	-1.16%	13.69777	$9,053,500	$124,012,726
1928	-1.14%	13.54161	$10,362,300	$140,322,242
1927	-2.23%	13.23963	$92,048,303	$1,218,685,811
			Total	**$729,575,886,746**

10.5 FAA History

The following sections contain FAA history. They were developed using a mining tool, General document Analysis (GDA), that was applied to FAA documents that each contain thousands of history events.

The mining tool was developed by this author in 2005. The tool works much like an Internet search engine, but it is applied to a single document. Also, the search is much more sophisticated and based on the user's ability to add dozens of simultaneous search items each with their own unique reporting categories using color and other visualization technique. For these sections the color has been removed but the highlighting of the search criteria was preserved. Also, the number of the mined item is preserved and shown as GDA. In the webpage report GDA is a link that takes the user to the point of the mined event so that context is offered.

10.5.1 SAGE History

The SAGE system was developed after World War II to defend against the new nuclear threat. It was the first computer-based system for tracking and intercepting enemy bomber aircraft. The engineering effort was huge, and it gave birth to our modern computers. Prior to this time computers were viewed only as calculators. SAGE introduced the concept of situational awareness and presented alphanumeric data and graphics to operators sitting at display consoles.

1. **GDA-561** Apr 10, 1953 The U.S. Air Force decided to proceed with the production of **SAGE** (Semiautomatic Ground Environment), an electronic defense system developed by MIT's Lincoln Laboratory. (See Jul 10, 1956.).
2. **GDA-615** Jul 10, 1956 CAA announced the establishment in the Boston area of a Military Integration Branch of the Technical Development Center. The new office was created to provide closer coordination with military development programs, such as the **SAGE** Air Defense System, at Lexington and Deer Island, Mass. (See Apr 10, 1953, and Sep 21, 1959.).
3. **GDA-708** Sep 21, 1959 FAA announced that its representatives and those of DOD and the Air Force had signed an agreement to establish nine FAA air route traffic control centers at Air Force **SAGE** supercombat centers. The supercombat centers were part of the **SAGE** (semiautomatic ground environment) system for radar surveillance and identification of air traffic for air defense. (See Jul 10, 1956, and Apr 12, 1960.) Sep 29, 1959 A Braniff Lockheed Electra lost a wing and exploded in flight over Buffalo, Tex., with the loss of all 34 persons aboard. (See Mar 17, 1960.).
4. **GDA-735** Apr 12, 1960 FAA announced the start of a live test of the **SAGE** air defense system as a means of improving high-altitude air traffic control services. A part of a joint FAA-USAF project called Trailsmoke, the flight advisory service test (FAST) aimed essentially at evaluating the capability of the **SAGE** system to provide civil and military radar advisory information on

potential air traffic conflicts. Specific operating positions would be occupied by FAA controllers at two **SAGE** direction centers of an Air Defense Division monitoring air activity in the Midwest section of the nation. (See Sep 21, 1959, and Apr 17, 1960.).

5. **GDA-737** Apr 17, 1960 FAA announced a contract award totaling nearly $6 million to the MITRE Corporation, Lexington, Mass., for advanced experimentation on automated air traffic control. Work to be performed under the contract included research and experimentation on joint use of military **SAGE** equipment and facilities for air traffic control, as well as for air defense purposes. FAA and the Air Force would share the cost of the project. (See Apr 12, 1960, and Sep 11, 1961.).
6. **GDA-814** Sep 11, 1961 The Project Beacon task force on Air Traffic Control (see Mar 8, 1961) submitted its report to the FAA Administrator. While finding that the air traffic control system was "being expertly operated by a highly skilled organization," the report concluded that substantial improvements were needed to meet the future challenge of aviation's projected growth. FAA urgently needed an overall systems plan. In effect, the recommended improvement involved a major reorientation of the modernization effort that had been launched in 1957 following the Curtis report. Keyed to the use of an air traffic control radar beacon system (ATCRBS) as a primary means of providing controllers with aircraft position information, the new concept found little promise in ground-based altitude measuring devices such as the 3-D radar under test as part of the earlier program (see Apr 7, 1961, and Dec 27, 1963). The report also urged expanded use of general purpose computers rather than special computer systems formerly under development for air traffic control. Rejecting the idea of fully merging air traffic control with the **SAGE** air defense system, the report urged that only radar elements of **SAGE** be used for the air traffic control system (see Apr 17, 1960, Feb 21, 1962, and Dec 1, 1963). The task force also urged a variety of changes involving airports, the segregation of controlled traffic, navigation and all-weather landing systems, a new category of flight known as controlled visual rules (CVR), and the extension of positive control and weather information. On Nov 7, having reviewed the Project Beacon report, President Kennedy directed FAA Administrator Halaby to begin carrying out the report's recommendations. With respect to unresolved differences of opinion between FAA and DOD concerning integrating the **SAGE** air defense and air traffic control systems--a matter which had delayed release of the report by some two months--Kennedy asked Halaby "to consult with the Secretary of Defense and the President's Scientific Advisor, Dr. [Jerome B.] Wiesner, so that the optimum application of all resources of the Government in the safe and economical use of the airspace may be assured." .
7. **GDA-833** Feb 21, 1962 The U.S. Senate confirmed Major General Harold W. Grant, USAF, as FAA's Deputy Administrator, succeeding James T. Pyle (see

Dec 31, 1958). A specialist in communications, General Grant was Commander of the Air Force Communications Service when the President selected him, on Feb 1, for the FAA position. Born in Louisville, Ky., General Grant received a bachelor of science degree from Northwestern University in 1928, and was commissioned in the Army Air Corps the following year. In World War II, he served as U.S. Air Signal Planner for Combined Operations in the European Theater and as Deputy Signal Officer in Chief of the Southeast Asia Command in India. During the Korean conflict, he was Vice Commander of the Japan Air Defense Force. After other assignments of high responsibility in the Far East and the United States, he became, in mid-1958, director of communications and electronics in the Office of the Deputy Chief of Staff for Operations, U.S. Air Force Headquarters. From this position he was assigned in July 1961 to the command from which he came to FAA. His decorations include the Legion of Merit with two clusters and the Order of the British Empire. (See Jul 1, 1965.) During the two years after his appointment, Grant helped to work out a series of agreements with military commands that provided close integration of communication systems and joint use of facilities, espcially radar. Under an agreement with the Continental Air Defense Command, FAA handled the ATC operations of interceptor flights going to and returning from a target. These agreements reduced the chances of civil-military midair collisions and provided better defense readiness. The improved coordination of military and FAA activities helped to ease tensions that had developed over the FAA decision to make only limited use the military's **SAGE** system in the national ATC system (see Sep 11, 1961, and Dec 1, 1963). .

8. **GDA-899** Dec 1, 1963 FAA's air route traffic control center at Great Falls, Mont., began joint use with the Air Force of facilities originally installed to serve the latter's **SAGE** direction center at Malmstrom Air Force Base, Great Falls. Under this arrangement the same facilities served the dual purpose of air traffic control and air defense. This marked the first use of **SAGE** data for air traffic control by an FAA facility. (See Sep 11, 1961.)

10.5.2 Replacing the Manual System

10.5.2.1 Project Beacon

1. **GDA-814** Sep 11, 1961 The Project Beacon task force on Air Traffic Control (see Mar 8, 1961) submitted its report to the FAA Administrator. While finding that the air traffic control system was "being expertly operated by a highly skilled organization," the report concluded that substantial improvements were needed to meet the future challenge of aviation's projected growth. FAA urgently needed an overall systems plan. In effect, the recommended improvement involved a major reorientation of the modernization effort that had been launched in 1957 following the Curtis report. Keyed to the use of an

air traffic control radar beacon system (**ATCRBS**) as a primary means of providing controllers with aircraft position information, the new concept found little promise in ground-based altitude measuring devices such as the 3-D radar under test as part of the earlier program (see Apr 7, 1961, and Dec 27, 1963). The report also urged expanded use of general purpose computers rather than special computer systems formerly under development for air traffic control. Rejecting the idea of fully merging air traffic control with the SAGE air defense system, the report urged that only radar elements of SAGE be used for the air traffic control system (see Apr 17, 1960, Feb 21, 1962, and Dec 1, 1963). The task force also urged a variety of changes involving airports, the segregation of controlled traffic, navigation and all-weather landing systems, a new category of flight known as controlled visual rules (CVR), and the extension of positive control and weather information. On Nov 7, having reviewed the Project Beacon report, President Kennedy directed FAA Administrator Halaby to begin carrying out the report's recommendations. With respect to unresolved differences of opinion between FAA and DOD concerning integrating the SAGE air defense and air traffic control systems--a matter which had delayed release of the report by some two months--Kennedy asked Halaby "to consult with the Secretary of Defense and the President's Scientific Advisor, Dr. [Jerome B.] Wiesner, so that the optimum application of all resources of the Government in the safe and economical use of the airspace may be assured." .

2. **GDA-903** Dec 27, 1963 The civil-military common system of air navigation and air traffic control moved forward a step with a final action on FAA-DOD agreements defining the use, technical standards, and equipment characteristics of a key component--the air traffic control radar beacon system (**ATCRBS**). (See Sep 11, 1961, and Mar 4, 1976.).

10.5.2.2 NAS Stage A and Project Beacon Evolution

3. **GDA-932** Sep 26, 1964 The Bureau of Budget released the first significant amount of hardware-procurement funds for modernizing the National Airspace System (NAS). These funds were specifically designated for installing the first complete NAS En Route **Stage A** configuration (FAA's semiautomated system for en route air traffic control) at the ARTCC at Jacksonville, Fla. (See Feb 1, 1967.) Modernization of both the en route and terminal air traffic control subsystems of NAS had been recommended in 1961 by the Project Beacon task force (see Sep 11, 1961). The modernization was a long-range program that would require a decade or longer to fully implement. The air traffic control system targeted for replacement was essentially a **manually operated** system employing radar, general purpose computers, radio communications, and air traffic controllers. Only five ARTCCs (New York, Boston, Washington, Cleveland, and Indianapolis) had computers capable of processing flight data, calculating flight progress, checking for errors, and distributing flight data to

control sectors. The old system had a two-dimensional radar display, which permitted controllers to view only an aircraft's range and bearing. Vital information such as altitude and identity was obtained through voice contact with the pilot or from the flight plan. To retain the correct identity of an aircraft target, controllers were required to tag the targets with plastic markers (known as "shrimp boats") and move the markers by hand across the radar display. The planned semiautomated system would perform these functions automatically, faster, and more accurately than the controller. Properly equipped aircraft would report their altitude, identity, and other flight data automatically at any given time. The computer processed messages would appear on a radar display next to the aircraft they identified, in the form of alphanumeric symbols which would make the radar display three-dimensional in effect. (See Oct 6, 1964, May 24, 1965, and Dec 30, 1968.).

4. **GDA-1082** Feb 1, 1967 FAA awarded a contract to the Raytheon Company for the purchase of computer display channels for NAS En Route **Stage A**, the agency's automation program for its air route traffic control centers (ARTCC's). The computer display channel comprised about a third of the equipment in an automated ARTCC and was the final link in the process of providing the air traffic controllers with three- dimensional information on their radar display. The contract was the largest awarded to that date for air traffic control equipment. (See Sep 2, 1964.).
5. **GDA-1184** Dec 30, 1968 The data-processing capability of the NAS En Route **Stage A** system at the Jacksonville (Fla.) ARTCC went into operation on a part-time basis. The system's new computer complex processed and automatically updated flight plans filed by pilots with the Jacksonville ARTCC area. (See May 24, 1965, and Feb 18, 1970.).
6. **GDA-1214** Jun 1, 1969 The shifting of the New York common IFR room from a **manual radar** system to a computerized alphanumeric radar system further enhanced the traffic-handling capabilities of the New York terminal area. The semiautomated system permitted an aircraft equipped with a beacon transponder to provide the terminal controller automatically with information on its identity, altitude, range, and bearing. Under the old system, the controller could obtain an aircraft's altitude and identity only through voice contact with the aircraft's pilot. (See Jul 15, 1968.).
7. **GDA-1250** Dec, 1969 The Air Traffic Control Advisory Committee (see Jul 17, 1968) submitted its report to the Secretary of Transportation. The committee saw a continued rise in the demand for air traffic control services during the decades ahead, and stated that if FAA expected to accommodate the anticipated growth in aviation traffic, three critical problems required solutions the shortage of terminal capacity; the need for new means of assuring separation; and the limited capacity and increasing cost of air traffic control. The committee believed that major improvements in airport capacity could be achieved through the use of parallel runways, high speed turnoffs, advanced

terminal automation, and reduced longitudinal separation between aircraft on final approach for landing. For the safe separation of aircraft, the report recommended further efforts to upgrade radar beacon transponders for tracking aircraft on radar. The committee believed that the midair collision problem could be overcome in airspace under radar surveillance by automating and making more precise the air traffic control advisory service. The report also noted that a higher level of automation would enable the system to handle perhaps two or three times the 1969 traffic with the same controller work force. This higher automation might be achieved by expanding NAS En Route **Stage A** and ARTS III version of the Automated Radar Terminal System to include spacing, sequencing, and conflict prediction/resolution, and by adding data link. The committee's report, which was made public in May 1970, also recommended rapid development of the Microwave Landing System (see Jun 19, 1970). .

8. **GDA-1258** Jan 19, 1970 FAA established the Facility Installation Service under the Associate Administrator for Operations. This service assumed the management of FAA's facilities establishment program from the Logistics Service. It also assumed from the Systems Research and Development Service the responsibility for preparing procurement specifications for production equipment and for prescribing technical instructions and standards for its installation. The new service's mission included the facilities establishment programs for air navigation, air traffic control, aeronautical communications, and visual ground marking; however, it did not include facilities establishment for NAS En Route **Stage A** and the various terminal automation programs. (See Dec 22, 1967, and Oct 1, 1971.) Jan 20, 1970 FAA and the Department of Health, Education, and Welfare reached an agreement with 31 scheduled and charter airlines on the retrofit of Pratt & Whitney JT8D engines with smoke-reducing combustors. Under the retrofit plan, the airlines voluntarily agreed to install combustors on approximately 1,000 Boeing 727s, Boeing 737s, and Douglas DC-9s by Dec 31, 1972. The combustors reduced the level of visible pollutants emitted by jet engines, but had no effect on invisible pollutants. (See Dec 31, 1970.).
9. **GDA-1263** Feb 18, 1970 FAA's first IBM 9020 computer and its associated software program became operational at the Los Angeles ARTCC (see Jun 30, 1967). The new computer system was at the heart of the new semiautomated airway air traffic control system--NAS En Route **Stage A**. This equipment reduced controller workload by automatically handling incoming flight information messages, performing necessary calculations, and distributing flight data strips, as needed, to controller positions. The agency planned to install similar equipment at all of the centers, and with the new automated nationwide system each center would have the capability to collect and distribute information about each aircraft's course and altitude to all the sector controllers along its flight path. The new computers also had the ability to

record and distribute any changes registered in aircraft flight plans en route. (See Dec 30, 1968, and Feb 13, 1973.).

10. **GDA-1410** Feb 10, 1972 FAA consolidated the National Airspace System Program Office (NASPO) with the Systems Research and Development Service. On Jul 26 FAA abolished NASPO, established in 1966 (see Apr 25, 1966). As the installation of NAS En Route **Stage A** at FAA's ARTCCs was proceeding satisfactorily, there was no further need for a separate office to manage this program. Also, effective Jul 26, FAA transferred NASPO's facilities systems and ARTCC building program functions to the Airway Facilities Service. .
11. **GDA-1455** Feb 13, 1973 Ceremonies at the Memphis Air Traffic Control Center celebrated the center's switch over to computer processing of flight-plan data, completing Phase One of the NAS En Route **Stage A**, FAA's decade-long program to automate and computerize the nation's en route air traffic control system (see Sep 26, 1964). With the new computer installation at Memphis, all twenty ARTCCs in the contiguous 48 states gained an automatic capability to collect and distribute information about each aircraft's course and altitude to all the sector controllers along its flight path. Pilots still had to file flight plans at flight service stations and military operations offices, but now computers would handle the centers' "bookkeeping functions" of assigning and printing out controller flight strips. The new computers also had the ability to record and distribute any changes registered in aircraft flight plans en route. The system eventually tied in with the Automated Radar Terminal System (ARTS III) units then being installed at major airports (see Oct 4, 1971 and Feb 15, 1973). Phase Two of the en route automation program was still under way; it would provide controllers at the twenty centers with new radar displays that would show such vital flight information as altitude and speed directly on the screen. (See Feb 18, 1970 and Jun 14, 1973.).
12. **GDA-1562** Aug 26, 1975 The commissioning of the computerized radar data processing system (RDP) at the Miami Air Route Traffic Control Center marked the end of the final phase of the completion of NAS En Route **Stage A**, FAA's program of automating and computerizing the nation's en route air traffic control system, an effort covering more than a decade (see Feb 13, 1973). Miami was the last of the 20 ARTCCs to receive RDP capability. The RDP system consisted of three key elements radar digitizers located at long-range radar sites that converted raw radar data and aircraft transponder beacon signals into computer-readable signals transmitted to the centers' computers; computer complexes in each center able to relay this information to the controllers' screens; and new screens that displayed the information to the controllers in alphanumeric characters. .
13. **GDA-1569** Jan 9, 1976 As of this date, FAA implemented a conflict alert system, capable of warning air traffic controllers of less-than-standard separation between aircraft under their control, at all 20 air route traffic control

centers in the contiguous U.S. FAA added the new conflict alert capability to the radar data processing system of the NAS En Route **Stage A** center computers (see Aug 26, 1975). The new system projected the flight paths of all aircraft on the controllers' radar sector for two minutes ahead, and flashed the relevant aircraft data tags if the projection showed the paths approaching closer than the required horizontal and vertical minimums. The controller could then radio appropriate orders to the aircraft to avoid a collision. The conflict alert system initially operated only above 18,000 feet, but by Dec 1978 all 20 centers had implemented it from the ground up. FAA later installed a similar capability in the Automated Radar Terminal System (ARTS) computers (see Jan 10, 1978). .

14. **GDA-1576** Mar 4, 1976 FAA announced a contract for the development of three engineering model Discrete Address Beacon System (**DABS**) ground sensors and 30 compatible transponders. This new advanced radar beacon system was designed to eventually replace **ATCRBS**, the existing air traffic control radar beacon system (see Dec 27, 1963). The chief advantage of **DABS** was its ability to interrogate and receive a transponder reply from a specific aircraft rather than from all aircraft in the zone of coverage. This would help eliminate the problem of overlapping and garbling of transponder replies from aircraft flying in close proximity to one another. Since **DABS** would address aircraft on an individual basis, it would also provide a vehicle for automatic communications between aircraft and the ground. This data link capability was seen as the basis for future implementation of a ground-based collision avoidance system called Intermittent Positive Control (IPC), later designated the Automatic Traffic Advisory and Resolution System (ATARS). (See Mar 1976.).
15. **GDA-1636** Sep 15, 1977 The dynamic simulation radar controller training laboratory (DYSIM) became operational at the Denver Air Route Traffic Control Center, the last of the 20 centers to be so equipped. FAA had determined that it was better to train new center controllers on a simulator than on an operational ATC sector, and began a program in 1975 to provide the centers with training equipment that duplicated all the conditions experienced on operational NAS En Route **Stage A** display equipment. .
16. **GDA-1681** Dec 27, 1978 FAA Administrator Bond and Secretary of Transportation Brock Adams announced a regulatory program to reduce the risk of midair collisions by 80 percent. Formulated in response to criticism of FAA after the San Diego midair collision (see Sep 25, 1978), and submitted as a notice of proposed rulemaking, the program included * Establishing new voluntary Terminal Radar Service Areas (TRSAs) at 80 air carrier airports (see Dec 22, 1983), and establishing new Terminal Control Areas (TCAs) at 44 additional airports. * Lowering the floor of positive area control from 18,000 feet to 10,000 feet over the States east of the Mississippi and much of California, and to 12,000 feet over the rest of the contiguous 48 States. *

Establishing a new flight category, controlled visual flight rules, for positive airspace below 18,000 feet, which would allow non-instrument rated pilots to use the airspace above 10,000 feet with radar separation provided by air traffic controllers. * Requiring all aircraft operating in TRSAs and TCAs to have altitude-reporting transponders installed by Jul 1981. All transponders installed after Jul 1982 would have to incorporate the new Discrete Area Beacon Systems (**DABS**), which would provide an automatic data link with a ground-based collision avoidance system (see Mar 4, 1976 and Jun 23, 1981). * Requiring all airliners and air taxi aircraft to carry an airborne "active" Beacon Collision Avoidance System (BCAS) by Jan 1985. A proposed national standard for such systems had been issued earlier in December. (See Jun 23, 1981.) These proposals elicited a massive negative public response, much of it orchestrated by the Aircraft Owners and Pilots Association (AOPA). On Sep 7, 1979, Administrator Bond announced he had withdrawn all the en route proposals. Although the general plan to increase the number of TCAs temporarily remained in effect, FAA gradually withdrew most of the proposed new TCAs. (See May 15, 1980.).

17. **GDA-1769** Jun 23, 1981 Administrator Helms announced FAA's decision to adopt the Threat Alert and Collision Avoidance System, soon renamed the Traffic Alert and Collision Avoidance System (TCAS). The TCAS system was an evolutionary improvement of the Beacon Collision Avoidance System (BCAS) that the agency had been developing (see Mar 1976). Like BCAS, TCAS would work in conjunction with the Air Traffic Control Radar Beacon System (**ATCRBS**) transponder already in wide use. It would also be compatible with the next-generation transponder, originally designated the Discrete Address Beacon System (**DABS**) and later known as Mode S (see Dec 27, 1978, and Oct 5, 1984). Two types of the new collision avoidance system were planned. TCAS I, intended for general aviation use, would in its basic form simply alert the pilot to the proximity of another aircraft carrying TCAS I or a conventional **ATCRBS** transponder. More expensive TCAS I versions would have some ability to provide certain data on the altitude and/or "o'clock" position of threat aircraft. TCAS II would provide more sophisticated advisories, including data on range and bearing of transponder-equipped aircraft. When the transponder aboard the threat aircraft had altitude-reporting capability, TCAS II's advisories would also include altitude data. In the case of two aircraft equipped with TCAS II, coordinated advisories would be provided. TCAS II would suggest vertical escape manuevers. If feasible, the system might be enhanced to include both vertical and horizontal escape manuevers, a version later designated TCAS III. TCAS was expected to overcome a fundamental limitation of BCAS by its ability to operate effectively even in the highest air traffic densities. This modified the need for a new ground-based collision avoidance system, and led to discontinuance of the Automatic Traffic Advisory and Resolution System (ATARS) project, originally known as

Intermittent Positive Control (see Mar 4, 1976). On Nov 13, 1981, FAA announced a contract with Bendix Corporation to provide two TCAS II engineering models to be tested and then enhanced to advise pilots of horizontal escape manuevers. (See Mar 18, 1987.).

18. **GDA-1816** Aug 30, 1982 FAA established an Advanced Automation Program Office, which reported directly to the Administrator. The office had responsibility for the Advanced Automation Program, that element of National Airspace System modernization concerned with developing a replacement for NAS En Route **Stage A** and ARTS air traffic control systems. (See Jan 28, 1982 and Jul 25, 1983.).
19. **GDA-1870** Mar 1984 Sperry Corporation received a contract to upgrade the En Route Automated Radar Tracking System (EARTS) at the Anchorage, Honolulu, and San Juan Centers, as well as at Nellis Air Force Base (see Aug 4, 1980). The contractor would provide radar mosaic to allow EARTS controllers to view the best data from multiple radars on a single screen, a capability similar to that available at Centers with NAS En Route **Stage A** systems. In Apr 1985, Sperry received another contract to enhance the EARTS facilities by providing conflict alert (see Jan 9, 1976) and minimum safe altitude warning (MSAW) capabilities (see Nov 5, 1976). FAA accepted delivery of the combined conflict alert/MSAW software package in Aug 1987. By fiscal year 1991, all the upgraded operational EARTS had been commissioned. .
20. **GDA-1887** Oct 1984 FAA awarded a contract for design of the Oceanic Display and Planning System (ODAPS) with features that would include visual displays of oceanic air traffic. ODAPS would automatically provide controllers with flight data for aircraft flying in oceanic sectors, thus eliminating time-consuming procedures involving use of flight strips and repeated voice communications. A planned second phase of the contract would include delivery of ODAPS equipment to FAA's Technical Center and two air route traffic control centers. (See Dec 14, 1989.) Oct 5, 1984 FAA announced a contract for ground stations for the new Mode S radar beacon system, a secondary radar system employing advanced ground sensors and radar beacon transponders aboard aircraft. Two corporations participated in the joint contract to produce 78 of the stations, with an option for another 59 units. The Mode S system was designed to replace the existing air traffic control radar beacon system, known as **ATCRBS** (see Jun 23, 1981). The discrete address capability of the new system would enable controllers to interrogate aircraft individually and selectively to determine their position, identity, and altitude, without having to use voice communications. This would eliminate the overlapping and garbled signals that were sometimes a problem in busy terminal areas. Mode S would also make possible the development of a capability for controllers to transmit data to properly equipped aircraft directly without using voice communications. (See Jan 29, 1987, and May 9, 1993.).

10.5.2.3 Advanced Automation System and NAS Stage A Evolution

21. **GDA-1916** Jul 26, 1985 FAA announced the award of a contract for replacement of the IBM 9020 computers at the nation's 20 air route traffic control centers (ARTCCs) as part of the agency's Advanced Automation Program. IBM won the replacement contract in a competition with Sperry Corp. under a pair of contracts that had been announced on Sept 22, 1983. The new installations were designated the "Host" Computer Systems (HCSs) because of their ability to run the existing 9020 software package with minimum modifications. Using the IBM 3083-BX1 computer as its key element, the Host system would provide greater speed, reliability, and storage capacity. Each installation would consist of two units, one serving as the primary processor and the other providing support and backup. (See Mar 22, 1983, and May 29, 1987.) In addition to installing the Host systems at the ARTCCs, IBM agreed to supply the systems to teams working on the other major element of the Advanced Automation Program, the Advanced Automation System (**AAS**). Under a pair of contracts announced on Aug 16, 1984, IBM and Hughes Aircraft Co. were engaged in a competition to produce the best **AAS** design (see Jul 26, 1988). Among the key elements of **AAS** were controller work stations, called "sector suites," that would incorporate new display, communications and processing capabilities. **AAS** would also include new computer hardware and software to bring the air traffic control system to higher levels of automation. Once the full **AAS** system was operational, FAA planned to begin the integration of en route and terminal radar control services at the ARTCCs, which would be renamed Area Control Facilities (ACFs) and expanded to handle the new functions (see Apr 19, 1993). Among the planned future enhancements to **AAS** was Automated En Route Air Traffic Control (**AERA**), which would automatically examine aircraft flight plans to detect and resolve potential conflicts.
22. **GDA-1980** Jan 29, 1987 FAA issued a rule establishing requirements pertaining to the use, installation, inspection, and testing of transponders in U.S.-registered civil aircraft. The rule continued the requirement that aircraft be equipped with a transponder for operation in Terminal Control Areas (TCAs) and in the airspace of the 48 contiguous states above 12,500 feet above ground level (see Nov 1, 1985). The requirement for automatic pressure altitude reporting (Mode C) equipment, currently mandatory in all of the above airspace except Group II TCAs, was extended to include Group II TCAs, effective Dec 1, 1987 (see Jun 21, 1988). The rule also contained provisions intended to provide for transition from Air Traffic Control Radar Beacon System (**ATCRBS**) transponders to Mode S transponders (see Oct 5, 1984). All transponders newly installed in U.S.-registered aircraft were required to be

Mode S transponders after Jan 1, 1992, a deadline that was subsequently extended to Jul 1, 1992. (See Jul 30, 1992.).

23. **GDA-2044** Jul 26, 1988 FAA announced it had awarded IBM a $3.55 billion contract to develop, deploy, and service the Advanced Automation System (**AAS**). The announcement ended almost four years of competition between IBM and Hughes Aircraft Corp. (See Jul 26, 1985, and Oct 1, 1991.).
24. **GDA-2256** Nov 30, 1992 FAA gave a "cure notice" to IBM concerning its development of the Initial Sector Suite System (ISSS), a part of the Advanced Automation System (**AAS**). The agency stated that unless the company provided a plan to remedy deficiencies within 10 calendar days, the government would withhold progress payments under the contract. Earlier in November, IBM had stated that, because of software difficulties and other problems, the ISSS would not be ready for FAA acceptance until Sep 1994, thus adding another 14 months to an already delayed timetable. Following the cure notice, IBM submitted to FAA an initial and later a final cure plan. FAA's own steps to remedy the situation included changes in the project's management structure and an Apr 1 ban on further changes in user requirements for the ISSS. (See Oct 1, 1991, and Dec 13, 1993.).
25. **GDA**-2290 Dec 13, 1993 FAA Administrator David Hinson ordered an extensive review of the Advanced Automation System (AAS), a multi-billion dollar program designed to help modernize the nation's air traffic control system. The contractor, IBM, was far behind schedule and had major cost overruns (see Nov 30, 1992). Hinson's recommended review included conferring with IBM to determine the impact the company's plan to sell its unit in charge of the **AAS** contract to Loral Corp., a sale subsequently concluded. On Mar 3, 1994, FAA announced initial actions as a result of the review that included a new **AAS** management team and suspension of the portion of the program designated the Area Control Computer Complex (ACCC). Subsequently, on Jun 3, 1994, FAA announced a major overhaul of the **AAS** program. The agency terminated ACCC. FAA also cancelled another **AAS** element, the Terminal Advanced Automation System (T**AAS**), stating that it would substitute a new procurement for modernization of terminal radar approach control facilities (see Sep 16, 1996). The agency reduced the number of towers planned to receive the Tower Control Computer Complex (TCCC). In addition, the agency planned to review the software for the Initial Sector Suite System (ISSS), a program to provide new workstations for en route controllers. On Sep 30, 1994, FAA announced that it would seek a proposal from Loral that would permit the company to move forward with this work under a new program, the Display System Replacement (DSR), which would replace ISSS. (See Apr 27, 1995.).

10.5.3 ADIZ

The Air Defense Identification Zone (ADIZ) on the surface may not appear to fit in this discussion. However, the ADIZ is only one aspect of airspace management. For example, there is controlled and restricted airspace in the history record. All of this is conceptually similar to our roads on the ground. You can't drive on the sidewalk or through lawns or front yards. Also driving through a house or a business would be a serious crime like flying through the ADIZ or restricted airspace, it can happen only under certain conditions. Depending on the nature of the situation the military might need to get involved and rather quickly.

1. **GDA-513** Dec 20, 1950 Executive Order No. 10197, prepared and issued this date at the request of the Department of Defense, directed the Secretary of Commerce to exercise security control over aircraft in flight. Subsequent regulations promulgated by the CAA Administrator under delegation from the Secretary of Commerce made mandatory the filing of flight plans for aircraft entering or flying within designated air defense identification zones (**ADIZ**s) over and adjoining the continental United States. A system for voluntary filing of plans for flights within **ADIZ**s had been in effect previously. (See Sep 9, 1950, and Jun 1952.).
2. **GDA-546** Jun 1952 The U.S. Air Force and the Civil Aeronautics Administration worked out an agreement under which 11 CAA air route traffic control centers would furnish appropriate air defense units with flight movement data on aircraft penetrating or operating within air defense identification zones (**ADIZ**s). This agreement followed tests conducted by experimental aircraft movement identification sections (AMIS) established at the Boston and Seattle ARTCC centers. (See Dec 20, 1950, and Dec 1, 1955.).
3. **GDA-599** Dec 1, 1955 Major changes in the structure of the U.S. air defense identification zones (**ADIZ**s) became effective, superseding substantial changes already established on Jan 15, 1953. Increased military capability made it possible to revise the structure in such a way as to exempt a substantial volume of flying from **ADIZ** requirements. Rules governing the security of air traffic were eased further on Jan 1, 1957. (See Jun 1952 and Apr 1, 1959.).
4. **GDA-688** Apr 1, 1959 Three air defense identification zones (**ADIZ**s) were eliminated and flight requirements within the remaining zones were relaxed effective this date. Elimination of the Western, Eastern, and Presque Isle Identification Zones became possible by the complete encirclement of the United States following establishment of an **ADIZ** in the Gulf of Mexico on Feb l. (See Dec 1, 1955.).
5. **GDA-1804** Apr 22, 1982 Tighter rules for aircraft entering the south Florida area through off-shore Air Defense Identification Zones (**ADIZ**s) became effective. Previously, aircraft flying at less than 180 knots had not been required to file flight plans and make regular position reports in any **ADIZ** off the coast of the continental U.S. Now all aircraft entering an **ADIZ** south of the 30th parallel and east of the 86th meridian had to comply with these requirements, regardless of their airspeed. In addition, FAA now required pilots

flying into any **ADIZ** to report if their aircraft carried a transponder--and if so, what kind. The agency mandated changes in response to increased flights by drug smugglers. (See Sep 1, 1987.).

6. **GDA-2008** Sep 1, 1987 AN FAA rule issued this date required that 12-inch high nationality and registration marks be displayed on all aircraft that penetrate and Air Defense Identification Zone (**ADIZ**) or Defense Early Warning Identification Zone (DEWIZ); that an identification data plate be displayed on the exterior of each U.S.-registered civil aircraft; and that operators of aircraft modified to carry fuel tanks within the passenger or baggage compartment keep a copy of the form authorizing that modification on board. A related rule, issued Oct 5, 1988, required transponder-equipped aircraft to have their transponders turned on during flights into or out of the United States penetrating an **ADIZ**. The rule also established flight plan and position report requirements for operations penetrating the **ADIZ** around the contiguous 48 states. Both rules were a response to concerns raised by the U.S. Customs Service in 1985, and FAA stated that they were actions to combat hazards resulting from airborne drug smuggling. (See Apr 22, 1982, and Mar 6, 1990.).
7. **GDA-2116** Mar 5, 1990 FAA's Administrator Busey announced a new policy on fostering compliance with FAA regulations by private pilots. He described a series of changes emphasizing communication and education rather than sanctions. Also in March, and as part of that program, Busey revoked the enforcement bulletin implementing a 60-day suspension of the certificate of any pilot who violated a Terminal Control Area (see Oct 10, 1986). Instead, inspectors were allowed to recommend lesser penalities and remedial training for the infraction. Mar 6, 1990 FAA issued a rule requiring private aircraft flying into or out of the country through an Air Defense Identification Zone (**ADIZ**) to be equipped with altitude-reporting (Mode C) transponders by Dec 30. (See Sep 1, 1987.).

10.5.4 Hijack and Terrorists

1. **GDA-786** May 1, 1961 The first series of aircraft **hijackings** in the U.S. began when a passenger on a flight to Key West, Fla., forced the pilot to fly to Cuba. Four other "skyjacking" incidents took place before the end of Aug. In concert with other agencies, FAA actively supported congressional efforts to remedy a lack of criminal laws applicable to these and other threats to air safety. On Sep 5, President Kennedy signed Public Law 87-197, an amendment to the Federal Aviation Act of 1958. The law prescribed death or imprisonment for not less than 20 years for interference with aircrew members or flight attendants in the performance of their duties. Pertinent parts of the U.S. Code were made applicable to certain other crimes aboard aircraft in flight. To help enforce the act, a special corps of FAA safety inspectors were trained for duty aboard airline flights (see Aug 10, 1961). .

2. **GDA-891** Sep 14, 1963 The Convention on Offenses and Certain Other Acts Committed on Board Aircraft (known as the Tokyo Convention) was opened for signature at a diplomatic conference held under the auspices of the International Civil Aviation Organization (ICAO). AN FAA official representing President Kennedy signed the document on behalf of the United States. The Legal Committee of ICAO had spent many years drafting the convention, which clarified certain jurisdictional issues concerning **hijacked** aircraft, and recognized the authority of aircraft commanders to use reasonable force to preserve law and order aboard their aircraft. The agreement also obligated signatory nations in which a **hijacked** aircraft might land to restore that aircraft to its lawful commander and to permit passengers and crew to continue their journey as soon as possible. The convention was to become effective 90 days after the twelfth signatory state deposited its instrument of ratification. (See Dec 4, 1969.).
3. **GDA-1138** Feb 21, 1968 A sustained wave of U.S. air carrier **hijackings** began when a fugitive aboard a Delta Air Lines DC-8 forced the pilot to divert to Havana. By Jul 17, four more U.S. airliners had been diverted to the same destination. On Jul 19, FAA announced that specially trained FAA safety inspectors ("sky marshals") had begun boarding Florida-bound airline flights (see Aug 10, 1961, and Oct 28, 1970). The inspectors, sworn in as deputy U.S. marshals after being trained at the U.S. Border Patrol Academy, were generally assigned to flights on a random, unannounced basis. **Hijackings** continued, however, and a total of twelve airliners and six general aviation aircraft were diverted to Cuba during 1968. (See Jan 1969.).
4. **GDA-1195** Jan, 1969 Eight U.S. airliners were **hijacked** to Cuba during the month (see Feb 21, 1968). In February, FAA created an eight-man Task Force on the Deterrence of Air Piracy that combined a broad spectrum of expertise under the leadership of the Deputy Federal Air Surgeon (see Aug 3, 1970). Systematic study by the Task Force revealed that a **hijacker** "profile" could be constructed from behavioral characteristics shared by past perpetrators. When used in conjunction with a magnetometer weapons-screening device developed by the agency, the profile system offered a promising method of preventing potential **hijackers** from boarding aircraft. On Oct 15, FAA announced that Eastern Air Lines was using the system at several key locations. By Jun 15, 1970, four U.S. air carriers were employing the system. (See Jul 17, 1970.) Feb 4, 1969 The XB-70 supersonic research aircraft made its final flight, from Edwards AFB, Calif., to Wright-Patterson AFB, Ohio, where it was placed on exhibit in the Air Force Museum. (See Mar 25, 1967.).
5. **GDA-1231** Aug 29, 1969 In the first **hijacking** of a U.S. aircraft outside of the Western Hemisphere, two Arabs seized control of a TWA 707 bound for Israel and diverted it to Syria, where they deplaned the occupants and then threw hand grenades into the cockpit area (see Calendar Year 1969). .

6. **GDA-1238** Oct 31, 1969 Rafael Minichiello, a U.S. Marine absent without leave, commandeered a TWA 707 bound for San Francisco and embarked on a 17-hour journey that ended in Rome, Italy. The first **hijacker** to force a crew to land and refuel repeatedly, Minichiello received worldwide publicity that included some sympathetic coverage (see Calendar Year 1969). .
7. **GDA-1244** Dec 4, 1969 Dulles International Airport banned student pilot operations because of the rising traffic volume at the airport. Dec 4, 1969 The Convention on Offences and Certain Other Acts Committed on Board Aircraft, popularly known as the Tokyo Convention, went into force among ratifying countries. The United States had ratified the agreement on Sep 5, 1969, completing the 12 ratifications required to bring it into force 90 days later. Though ineffectual against the **hijacking** of aircraft to nonsignatory or nonratifying countries, the convention was a forward step in its clarifying of jurisdiction over crimes aboard aircraft anywhere in the world. It afforded a useful framework within which an international or diplomatic solution to aircraft piracy could be pursued. Denmark, the Republic of China, Italy, Norway, the Philippines, Portugal, Sweden, the United Kingdom, the Republic of Upper Volta, Mexico, and Niger ratified the convention before the United States. A dozen more countries ratified the convention soon after the United States and over 130 eventually became party to it. (See Sep 14, 1963, and Oct 14, 1970.).
8. **GDA-1245** Dec 5, 1969 The Legal Committee of the United Nations General Assembly voted a resolution urging governments to prosecute aircraft **hijackers,** and urged member states without laws against aircraft piracy to enact such legislation. .
9. **GDA-1252** Calendar year, 1969 Worldwide concern focused on **hijacking** as the number of aircraft involved in such incidents during the year totaled 87, as compared to 37 for 1968. The number of U.S. aircraft involved was 40, as compared to 47 foreign aircraft. (In 1968, 22 out of a total of 35 incidents involved U.S. aircraft.) Cuba remained the most popular destination for **hijackers** during 1969 31 U.S. and 25 foreign air carrier aircraft, as well as one foreign general aviation aircraft, were forced to land there. But the year also saw a break in the diversion-to-Cuba pattern when 11 foreign and 2 U.S. air carrier aircraft were forced to land in other countries. (See Aug 29 and Oct 31, 1969.) For U.S. aircraft, the only previous **hijacking** completed to a destination other than Cuba had been an Aug 31, 1965, incident in which an airliner was forced to return to Honolulu shortly after takeoff. 1960s The number of U.S. civil aircraft possessing current airworthiness certificates increased 89 percent during the decade, from 70,747 on Dec 31, 1959, to 133,814 on Dec 31, 1969. The general aviation fleet increased 90 percent (from 68,727 to 130,806), while air carrier aircraft increased 49 percent (from 2,020 to 3,008). .
10. **GDA-1270** Mar 17, 1970 The first death in a domestic U.S. aircraft **hijacking** incident occurred when a **hijacker** shot and killed the copilot on an Eastern Air

Lines shuttle (Newark-Boston). Although fatally wounded, the copilot still managed to shoot and severely wound the **hijacker** with the latter's gun. The aircraft's captain, himself wounded in both arms, landed his DC-9 safely in Boston. .

11. **GDA-1310** Jul 17, 1970 New Orleans' Moisant International Airport became the first U.S. airport to subject all passengers to the FAA-developed anti**hijacking** screening system. (See Jan 1969.) The system was based on a behavioral profile used in conjunction with weapons detection by magnatometer. If a person identified by the system as a possible risk did not satisfactorily resolve the question with airline personnel, he was further investigated by a U.S. marshal or deputy marshal. Previously, individual airlines had used the system only on selected flights. (See Feb 2, 1972.).
12. **GDA-1311** Jul 31, 1970 FAA issued to Pan American World Airways the first aviation war risk insurance premium policy under a new coverage plan. Previously, FAA's only war risk insurance for which a premium was charged was a standby plan that would make coverage available in the event of war between major powers (see Jun 14, 1951). The new plan was offered in response to the entry into airline service of the Boeing 747. Because of the high cost of this aircraft (some $24 million), commercial insurers would cover only about 60 percent of its value. FAA's new policy covered war risks for the commercially uninsurable portion of Boeing 747s flying international routes, and was later expanded to cover the aircraft's whole value. On Feb 4, 1971, FAA transferred the responsibility for administering the aviation war risk insurance program from its General Counsel to the Assistant Administrator for International Aviation Affairs. In Nov 1977, Public Law 95-163 expanded the scope of insurable risks to allow the FAA Administrator broad discretionary authority in extraordinary circumstances to insure air services deemed in the national interest. On Feb 4, 1984, the aviation insurance program was transferred from the Office of International Aviation to the Office of Aviation Policy and Plans. In 1992, legislation further expanded the scope of the program by allowing coverage for some domestic flight segments and certain services in direct support of flight operations. In addition to the 747 coverage mentioned above, examples of uses of the aviation insurance program have included both premium and non-premium coverage of flights in the Vietnam area during 1967-75; Middle East flights during the 1990-91 Operation Desert Shield/Storm; and flights to Somalia in support of Operation Restore Hope in 1992-93. Aug 2, 1970 The first **hijacking** of a wide-bodied airliner occurred as a Pan American 747 bound from New York to San Juan with 388 passengers was diverted to Havana. .
13. **GDA-1312** Aug 3, 1970 FAA renamed its Office of Investigations and Security the Office of Air Transportation Security. At the same time, the agency established an Air Operations Security Division within the new office and gave it responsibility for dealing with **hijacking** security, bomb threats, aircraft and

cargo security, and for developing and implementing deterrent systems for the prevention of criminal acts against air transportation. (See Nov 18, 1969 and Jun 11, 1974.) On Jun 15, 1970, the Secretary of Transportation had announced that the nine-member Task Force on the Deterrence of Air Piracy would be replaced by a permanent organizational component staffed with full-time specialists to deal not only with aircraft piracy, but also with sabotage and all other air transportation security problems (see Jan 1969). .

14. **GDA-1319** Sep 6-9, 1970 Members of the Popular Front for the Liberation of Palestine **hijacked** four airliners over Europe, blew them up, and held many passengers hostage. The **hijackers** originally planned to seize two Israeli, one Swiss, and one U.S. aircraft, and take the planes to a level stretch of Jordanian desert dubbed "Revolution Airstrip." The plan failed insofar as the Israeli aircraft were concerned. Front members were refused admittance to one of them, whereupon they **hijacked** a U.S. flight. When they learned that the wide-body jet was too large to land at Revolution Airstrip, they ordered it to Cairo, where they blew it up after deplaning its occupants. Front members succeeded in boarding the other Israeli airliner, but their **hijacking** attempt was foiled in flight. One **hijacker** was killed and another arrested by British authorities when the plane landed in London. The part of the original plan involving U.S. and Swiss airliners succeeded, and on Sep 6 these aircraft landed at Revolution Airstrip with all passengers. To gain bargaining power for the release of their member arrested in London, the Front **hijacked** a British airliner and forced it to land at Revolution Airstrip on Sep 9. The Front blew up the three empty airliners on Sep 12. All hostages except six were freed on Sep 27. Those six were freed two days later, in return for the release of the **hijacker** under arrest in London and six other Front members held by the Swiss and West Germans. .
15. **GDA-1321** Sep 11, 1970 President Nixon announced a comprehensive anti**hijacking** program that called for * The U.S. government to place specially trained, armed guards on American commercial airline flights. * Extending, under DOT auspices, the use of electronic and other surveillance techniques by U.S. flag carriers to all gateway airports in the U.S., and in other countries wherever possible. * Accelerated efforts by Federal agencies to develop security measures, including new methods for detecting weapons and explosives devices. * The State Department and other appropriate agencies to consult foreign governments and foreign carriers on anti**hijacking** techniques. * All countries to accept the multilateral convention (to be considered at a conference held under the auspices of the International Civil Aviation Organization) providing for extradition or punishment of **hijackers.** .
16. **GDA-1322** In addition, the President called on the international community to suspend airline service to countries refusing to extradite or punish **hijackers** involved in international blackmail. He stated that it was U.S. policy to hold nations in which a **hijacked** plane landed responsible for appropriate steps to

protect the lives and property of U.S. citizens. (See Sep 21, 1970, Oct 28, 1970, and Sep 23, 1971.).

17. **GDA-1323** Sep 21, 1970 The Department of Transportation announced the appointment of Lt. Gen. Benjamin O. Davis, Jr. (USAF-Ret), as Director of Civil Aviation Security for DOT. Davis advised the Secretary of Transportation on the Department's anti**hijacking** program and coordinated the functions of the airport and airborne security force, composed of components from the Departments of Defense, Justice, Transportation, and Treasury, and other government agencies. (See Sep 11, 1970.).
18. **GDA-1324** Sep 25, 1970 The Departments of Justice and Transportation signed a memorandum of understanding dividing responsibilities for responding to **hijackings.** The FBI had jurisdiction when an aircraft was neither airborne nor moving on the runway for purposes of takeoff or landing. The pilot retained command at other times, and FAA's recommendations to him had precedence. A further agreement in Dec 1971 assigned the pilot the responsibility of signaling whether the aircraft should be disabled or stormed. On Feb 26, 1975, FAA and the FBI signed a new memorandum of understanding governing responsibilities during a **hijacking.** Following guidelines provided by the Anti-**Hijacking** Act of Aug 5, 1974 (see that date), the new agreement extended FAA jurisdiction to include the period from the closing of all external doors following embarkation until the opening of one such door for disembarkation. Both the FAA and the FBI agreed to fully consider each other's views, as well as the views of the airline and the pilot in command, before initiating law enforcement action. .
19. **GDA-1337** Dec 16, 1970 The U.S. and 49 other nations signed the Convention for the Suppression of Unlawful Seizure of Aircraft (known as The Hague or **Hijacking** Convention) at a diplomatic conference held under the auspices of the International Civil Aviation Organization. The U.S. was an active participant in developing the convention, which declared the **hijacking** of civil aircraft to be an offense punishable by severe penalties. The convention obligated contracting states to extradite **hijackers** or to submit their cases to prosecutorial authorities. The U.S. Senate approved ratification on Sep 8, 1971, and the U.S. deposited its instruments of ratification on Sep 14. This completed the 10 ratifications needed to bring the convention into force among ratifying states 30 days later, and it became effective on Oct 14, 1971. Signatories to the convention depositing instruments of ratification before the U.S. were Japan, Bulgaria, Sweden, Costa Rica, Gabon, Hungary, Israel, Norway, and Switzerland. .
20. **GDA-1366** May 14, 1971 In United States v. Lopez, the United States District Court for the Eastern District of New York declared FAA's anti**hijacking** profile system constitutional (see Jul 17, 1970). The court found that the system had provided the "reasonable suspicion" required to justify a personal search. On another key point, that of the characteristics contained in the profile for

identifying potential **hijackers,** the Court said that careful adherence to the absolute objectivity and neutrality of the system as designed would avoid discrimination on the basis of religion, origin, race, or political views. The case arose when two men preparing to board a New York-San Juan flight were arrested and charged with concealing a packet of narcotics. Charges against one of the men were dropped. The other man--the defendant in this case--was acquitted on a motion to suppress the evidence, which the court found had been gathered outside the government's system to deter and apprehend **hijackers.** .

21. **GDA-1371** Jun 12, 1971 The first passenger death in a domestic **hijacking** incident occurred on a TWA aircraft bound from Albuquerque to New York. The **hijacker** had forced his way aboard the Boeing 727 aircraft during a scheduled stop at Chicago's O'Hare International Airport, seized a stewardess, and demanded to be flown to Vietnam. The passenger was killed attempting to aid the stewardess. When the medium-range aircraft landed at New York's Kennedy International Airport for substitution of a long-range aircraft, the **hijacker** was wounded and arrested. (See Mar 17, 1970.).
22. **GDA-1396** Nov 24, 1971 The first in a series of **hijackings** involving extortion occurred when a passenger on a flight from Portland to Seattle successfully demanded $200,000 and four parachutes, then parachuted from the rear stairway of the Boeing 727. The **hijacker--who** used the name Dan Cooper, but became known as D.B. Cooper in the press--was never found. (In Feb 1980, however, tattered bills from his loot were discovered along the Columbia River in Washington.) Another incident involving a demand for ransom and parachutes occurred on Dec 24, 1971, and 17 more extortion attempts on U.S. air carriers were made during the next 6 months. (See Mar 7-9, 1972.).
23. **GDA-1408** Feb 2, 1972 FAA published a rule requiring scheduled air carriers and certain commercial operators of large aircraft to implement a passenger and baggage screening system acceptable to the Administrator before Feb 6, 1972 (see Jul 17, 1970, and Mar 7-9, 1972). The agency stated its opinion that the "simple and inexpensive" system used by some carriers would have prevented the majority of recent **hijackings** if used to the fullest extent possible (see Jan 1969). On the same day, at FAA request, the Federal Communications Commission issued a notice which informed broadcasters and FCC licensees that the Communications Act of 1934 prohibited unauthorized broadcast of FAA air-to-ground communications. This action followed instances in which FAA's communications were monitored and rebroadcast, seriously hampering FAA's efforts to control aerial piracy. .
24. **GDA-1413** Mar 7-9, 1972 Sabotage incidents prompted new security measures. On Mar 7, a bomb planted as part of an extortion plot against Trans World Airlines was discovered and defused aboard an airliner at New York's Kennedy Airport. On Mar 9, another bomb damaged a TWA airliner parked at Las Vegas, and a third was found aboard a United Air Lines jet at Seattle. That same day, President Nixon ordered into immediate effect an FAA rule

published on Mar 7 that had required scheduled air carriers and certain commercial operators of large aircraft to submit written security programs no later than Jun 5, 1972. The President's directive required the airlines to implement their programs immediately, and to submit them for formal approval by May 8. The programs were to prevent or deter unauthorized persons, baggage, or cargo from entering the carrier's aircraft, and were to include the procedures the carrier intended to use in the mandatory passenger screening system (see Feb 2, 1972). The rule also specified certain procedures to be followed in the event of a bomb or air piracy threat. On Mar 9, the President also ordered that new security rules for airport operators be expedited. On Mar 18, 1972, FAA published a rule applicable to operators of airports regularly served by air carriers using large aircraft. Such operators were required to take prescribed actions to prevent or deter unauthorized access to designated air operations areas, and to submit written security programs for FAA approval by Jun 16, 1972. (See Jan 3, 1989.) On Mar 15, a cabinet-level task force formed by President Nixon and chaired by Transportation Secretary Volpe approved the following steps * Increased personnel for FAA's Security Task Force. * Deployment of sky marshals from airborne duty to posts at major airports. * Increased research and development funding for weapons and explosives detection systems. * Use of trained dogs for detection of explosives at major airports and the training of additional dogs. * Expedited prosecution of extortion and **hijacking** suspects. .

25. **GDA-1422** Jun 19, 1972 A 24-hour worldwide stoppage of airline traffic declared by the International Federation of Air Line Pilots Associations took place. This action, intended to dramatize the need for sterner measures against **hijackers,** brought to a standstill domestic and international airline operations in more than 30 countries. The strike officially began at 2:00 a.m. (EST) and was supported by more than 40 of the Federation's 64 units in 62 countries; in the United States, however, following a Federal restraining order on Jun 18, only 10 percent of the Air Line Pilots Association's members joined in the job action. In addition, pilots in Australia, Japan, the Philippines, and most Arab and Communist countries refused to participate in the protest. .
26. **GDA-1433** Sep 15, 1972 A 17-nation anti-**hijacking** conference sponsored by the Legal Subcommittee of the International Civil Aviation Organization was concluded. The conference, convened in response to the persisting high incidence of aircraft **hijackings** during 1972, had attempted to draw up a treaty imposing economic sanctions against those nations that provided havens to aircraft **hijackers** and saboteurs. The failure to agree on a draft resolution cosponsored by the U.S. and Canada, however, brought the meeting to an end. .
27. **GDA-1439** Oct 29, 1972 Four fugitives killed a ticket agent and **hijacked** an Eastern Air Lines Boeing 727 at Houston, Tex., and forced it to fly to Cuba. This was followed by an even more sensational incident on Nov 10-12 when three wanted criminals **hijacked** a Southern Airways DC-9 at Birmingham,

Ala. During the following 29 hours, they flew to Jackson, Miss.; Cleveland, Ohio; Toronto, Ont.; Lexington, Ky.; Chattanooga, Tenn.; Havana, Cuba; Key West, Fla.; and Orlando, Fla. In a desperate attempt to keep the DC-9 on the ground at Orlando, FBI agents shot out its tires. The **hijackers** responded by seriously wounding the copilot and ordering a takeoff. The pilot succeeded in clearing the runway and making a second and final landing in Havana. The four **hijackers** were initially imprisoned in Cuba, but were released. U.S. officials subsequently arrested all four, the last being sentenced in 1994. This incident contributed directly to issuance of an anti-**hijacking** rule (see Dec 5, 1972), and to negotiation of a **hijacking** agreement between the Nixon Administration and Cuba (see Feb 15, 1973). .

28. **GDA-1442** Dec 5, 1972 A landmark FAA anti**hijacking** emergency rule issued this date required U.S. air carriers, beginning on Jan 5, 1973, to inspect all carry-on baggage for weapons or other dangerous objects and scan each passenger with a metal detector (magnetometer) before boarding or, if a detector was not available, conduct a physical search, or pat down. (See Aug 5, 1974.) If a passenger refused to consent to a search, he or she would not be permitted to board. The rule further required, beginning on Feb 5, 1973, that the nation's 531 air carrier airports have a law enforcement officer in the boarding area during the screening and boarding process. The critical difference between this rule and previous anti**hijacking** measures was the universality of the new regulation. Previously, FAA had required air carriers to conduct a weapons scan of only those passengers who fitted a **hijacker** profile--about one percent of the 500,000 passengers boarding airliners daily. (See Oct 29, 1972.).
29. **GDA-1456** Feb 15, 1973 The United States and Cuba signed an anti-**hijacking** agreement calling for the two nations to extradite or punish any person "who seizes, removes, appropriates or diverts from its normal route or activities an aircraft or vessel" of one country and takes it to the other. The pact was to run for five years, but Cuba abrogated it on Oct 15, 1976, on grounds of alleged American involvement in the explosion of a Cuban airliner. (See Oct 29, 1972.).
30. **GDA-1490** Dec 17, 1973 Arab **terrorists** used incendiaries to kill 30 passengers aboard a Pan American airliner at Rome's Leonardo Da Vinci Airport. They then killed a guard, **hijacked** a Lufthansa jet, murdered a passenger in Greece, and eventually surrendered in Kuwait. .
31. **GDA-1493** Calendar year, 1973 Not a single airliner was **hijacked** in the U.S. in 1973, a record traceable at least in part to the stringent airport security measures implemented early in the year. (See Dec 5, 1972.).
32. **GDA-1512** Aug 5, 1974 President Nixon signed the Anti-**Hijacking** Act of 1974 into law. Under its provisions, the act * authorized the President to suspend air transportation between the United States and nations that aided **terrorist groups** who used the illegal seizure of aircraft as an instrument of policy. * empowered the Secretary of Transportation, with the approval of the

Secretary of State, to impose sanctions against the carriers of nations that failed to maintain minimum security standards in the transportation of persons, property, and mail, as required by the Convention on International Civil Aviation. * required air carriers to refuse to carry persons unwilling to submit to personal search, and any article that a passenger did not allow to be inspected. * required FAA to continue in effect passenger and baggage screening procedures (see Dec 5, 1972). * allowed FAA to use, for as long as needed, Federal personnel, including FAA personnel, to supplement state, local, and private law enforcement officers in airport security programs. (In anticipation of this responsibility, FAA had established a new unit, the Civil Aviation Security Service, out of what had been the anti-**hijacking** and cargo security section of the Office of Air Transportation Security see Jun 11, 1974.) The passenger screening program and other precautionary measures continued to be effective in combating the **hijacking** menace. For the second consecutive year (see Calendar year 1973) not one successful **hijacking** occurred on a scheduled U.S. air carrier aircraft. .

33. **GDA-1577** Mar 21, 1976 Effective this date, FAA required foreign air carriers operating large aircraft to and from the United States in scheduled passenger operations to maintain security programs which would insure that all passengers and property carried aboard their aircraft were subject to effective weapons screening procedures prior to boarding; that there was no unauthorized access to their aircraft; that no unauthorized weapons, bombs, or incendiary devices were carried aboard; that appropriate baggage security measures were in place; and that they were in compliance with the FARs in dealing with bomb threats and threats of **hijacking.** In addition, each foreign carrier was to provide the FAA Administrator upon his request information on the status of its screening program. In addition, as of Aug 23, 1976, the FAA also required foreign carriers to deny boarding to passengers refusing to permit their persons or property to be screened for weapons; ensure that their x-ray equipment in use at U.S. airports met minimum U.S. safety and effectiveness standards; and provided that the prohibition against carrying weapons aboard a foreign aircraft would not apply if the weapons, after inspection by the carrier, were in checked baggage and inaccessible to the passenger. .
34. **GDA-1597** Sep 10, 1976 The first successful **hijacking** of a scheduled American air carrier aircraft since comprehensive security measures were instituted on Dec 5, 1972, occurred when five Croatian nationalists commandeered a TWA jetliner en route from New York's La Guardia Airport to Chicago. The **hijackers** seized the plane by threatening to blow it up with realistic-looking "bombs" they had assembled in a lavatory from an assortment of innocuous objects brought aboard on their persons and in their carry-on luggage. To bolster their deception, they revealed the location of a real bomb in a New York subway locker. That device exploded after removal to a disposal area, killing one policeman. The **hijackers** demanded that newspapers publish

a pro-Croatian manifesto and that aircraft drop leaflets over cities in the U.S., Canada, England, and France. This was complied with, and the **hijackers** eventually surrendered in France. .

35. **GDA-1665** Jul 17, 1978 At an economic summit conference in Bonn, the leaders of United States, West Germany, France, Great Britain, Japan, Canada, and Italy announced a joint resolution to isolate from international air traffic all countries harboring air **hijackers.** In the resolution, they stated their intent to stop all flights to any country that refused to extradite or prosecute those who have **hijacked** an aircraft and/or failed to return such an aircraft. The resolution also called for a ban on incoming flights from an offending nation, as well as a ban on any traffic to it by airlines of participating countries. The conferees informally agreed to make no exceptions, not even for persons escaping from totalitarian governments. Diplomatic efforts were begun to gain the agreement of as many other countries as possible. The Bonn Resolution followed the doubling of **hijacking** attempts throughout the world in 1977 -- the death toll in **hijackings** for that year was 129 persons. In Dec, a Malaysian Airlines Boeing 737 crashed after being **hijacked,** killing all 100 persons aboard. The most spectacular incident of 1977, however, was the five-day odyssey of a Lufthansa B-737 **hijacked** in Oct over the Mediterranean and flown to various places in the Near East. The **hijackers** murdered the pilot, and later, in Somalia, threatened to massacre the other 86 people on board. Just 90 minutes before their deadline, West German commandos stormed the aircraft and rescued all the hostages. After this episode, the International Federation of Air Line Pilots threatened a two-day international pilots' strike unless the United Nations took immediate action on air piracy. In Dec, the Flight Engineers International Association urged extradition or prosecution of **hijackers** held in four countries. .
36. **GDA-1666** Jul 25, 1978 A new FAA regulation extended to both domestic and international charter operations security screening procedures long in effect for scheduled airlines. Although no charter aircraft operating from American airports had ever been **hijacked,** FAA took this action in response to two recent developments the worldwide increase in **hijacking** attempts (see Jul 17, 1978), and rulings of CAB that relaxed many of the regulations that governed charter operations. The old requirement that only "affinity" groups could qualify for reduced charter fares had heretofore been regarded as a protection against **hijackers,** but that was among the rules no longer applied by CAB. .
37. **GDA-1683** Calendar year, 1978 Aircraft of U.S. registry experienced eight **hijacking** attempts during 1978--the highest level since the screening of passengers and carry-on luggage was instituted in early 1973. None of the **hijackers,** however, had been able to slip firearms or explosives through airport screening points. Their claims to have a gun or bomb in their possession proved to be false in every case. The eight **hijacking** attempts were the most since 1972, when 27 attempts were made, eight of them successful. In the six years

since beginning mandatory screening, **hijackers** had attempted to commandeer U.S. airlines on 25 separate occasions. None involved the smuggling of weapons through a screening point, and only one was successful. .

38. **GDA-1717** Jan 25, 1980 Armed with a pistol and pretending to have a bomb, a **hijacker** who identified himself as a Black Muslim diverted a Delta Airlines L-1011 to Cuba. He demanded to be flown to Iran, but eventually surrendered to Cuban authorities. This was the first U.S. air carrier **hijacking** in which real weapons or high explosives passed through the passenger screening system since the implementation of strict new airport security measures on Dec 5, 1972 (see that date and Jul 22, 1980). .
39. **GDA-1734** Jul 22, 1980 Holding what was reported to be a small handgun to the back of a flight attendant, a man diverted a Delta Air Lines L-1011 to Cuba, beginning a series of **hijackings** by Cuban refugees who had arrived in the U.S. during the boat lift from the port of Mariel that began in Apr 1980 (see Jan 25, 1980). Mariel refugees returned to their homeland in 10 **hijackings** between Aug 10 and Sep 17. During the last quarter of 1980, however, no successful "Marielista" **hijackings** occurred. Factors in this improvement were special FAA security measures, coupled with the immediate return of two **hijackers** by the Cuban government. The phenomenon continued, however, and one successful Marielista **hijacking** took place in 1981. During 1982, three airliners were diverted to Cuba by Spanish-speaking men (at least one of whom was a Marielista) using flammable liquid as their weapon. The threat to ignite real or alleged flammable liquid had been used in every successful **hijacking** to Cuba since Aug 13, 1980. (See May 1, 1983.).
40. **GDA-1755** Jan 30, 1981 FAA announced the adoption of new security rules making commuter aircraft with a seating capacity of 60 or more passengers subject to the same anti-**hijacking** programs as the aircraft of larger airlines. .
41. **GDA-1837** May 1, 1983 A **hijacker** succeeded in reaching Havana by locking himself in a lavatory during an airline flight and issuing notes threatening to blow up the aircraft. The incident began a renewed upsurge of **hijackings** to Cuba, many perpetuated by Mariel boat lift refugees (see Jul 22, 1980). By Sep 22, **hijackers** had diverted 10 additional airliners to Cuba, prompting FAA to increase security measures at airports in selected areas. **Hijackings** to Cuba began to decline in the last quarter of 1983, although three such diversions took place in 1984. No **hijackers** succeeded in reaching Cuba from the U.S. during 1985 or 1986. .
42. **GDA-1892** Dec 4, 1984 Four Arab **hijackers** diverted a Kuwait Air A-310 to Iran, where they murdered two American passengers and committed other brutalities while demanding the release of prisoners held in Kuwait. The **hijackers** released 153 of their hostages in several groups, and Iranian forces freed the remainder when they stormed the aircraft on Dec 9. The **hijacking** was part of an increase in **terrorist seizures** of foreign airliners that began in Jun 1984. .

43. **GDA-1912** Jun 14, 1985 Two Lebanese Shiite Moslems **hijacked** a TWA 727 departing Athens and diverted it to Beirut, where additional **hijackers** joined them. During a two-week confrontation, they demanded the release of Shiite prisoners held by Israel. The **hijackers** murdered one passenger, a U.S. Navy diver. They released the other 155 hostages (including 39 Americans) in stages, the last being freed on Jun 30. Lebanese authorities held the aircraft in Beirut until Aug 16. The TWA **hijacking** and an upsurge in Middle East terrorism prompted a series of U.S. actions. Events included * On Jun 18, President Reagan warned travelers of inadequate security measures at Athens airport. This advisory was lifted on Jul 22, after an FAA inspection found improvements. * On Jun 23, an Air India jet crashed under mysterious circumstances (see entry for this date below). * On Jun 27, Transportation Secretary Dole urged the International Civil Aviation Organization (ICAO) to act immediately to enhance airport security. The ICAO Council met on an accelerated schedule, and on Dec 19 adopted amendments strengthening international security standards and recommended practices. * On Jul 1, the President suspended airline travel between U.S. and Lebanon. * During July, FAA issued an emergency regulatory amendment requiring airlines to carry Federal Air Marshals on certain flights. Eight days later, the agency issued another emergency rule that required airlines to expand security training for crew members and to provide a ground security coordinator and an in-flight security coordinator for every flight. * Between mid-Aug and early Nov, FAA personnel assisted by law enforcement officers from other agencies inspected U.S. air carrier security procedures at 79 foreign airports. * FAA also issued a number of emergency amendments to the agency-approved security programs of both airlines and airport operators. On Aug 8, the President signed the International Security and Development Cooperation Act of 1985. The Act authorized the use of $5 million from the Airport and Airway Trust Fund for research on and development of airport security devices and explosives detection techniques. It also mandated a system for conducting security assessments at foreign airports, and authorized Federal Air Marshals as a permanent FAA workforce. The agency began hiring additional security inspectors and training them to serve as Air Marshals. FAA also reorganized its Office of Civil Aviation Security to reflect its expanded responsibilities under the Act, creating an International Civil Aviation Security Division and an Intelligence Division. (See Aug 5, 1986.).
44. **GDA-1932** Nov 23, 1985 An unusually bloody **hijacking** began when three men seized control of an Egyptair 737 with 98 persons aboard shortly after takeoff from Athens. In a midair gunfight, one **hijacker** was killed and an Egyptian security guard and two flight attendants were wounded. The **hijackers** demanded to fly to Libya or Tunisia, but agreed to refuel at Malta. In an attempt to force Maltese authorities to supply the fuel, the **hijackers** shot five hostages, killing two of them, including an American woman. After 22

hours of negotiation, an Egyptian military force stormed the plane. During the rescue action, 57 persons were killed and about 30 others injured. .

45. **GDA-1936** Dec 27, 1985 Near-simultaneous Arab **terrorist attacks** on airports in Rome and Vienna caused the death of 20 persons, including four of the **terrorists,** and injured approximately 120. Five of the victims killed were U.S. citizens. The attacks centered on the check-in counters of the Israeli airline El Al. Libyan leader Muammar Qaddafi praised the **terrorists,** thus contributing to tensions between his nation and the United States. (See Feb 11, 1986.).
46. **GDA-1967** Sep 5, 1986 At Karachi, Pakistan, four men dressed as security guards stormed a Pan American 747. The flight crew escaped, but the four **terrorists** demanded a crew to fly them to Cyprus. They killed an American passenger during the ensuing 17 hour negotiations. When the lights aboard the aircraft failed, the **terrorists** began a massacre, killing 22 persons and injuring 125 before being arrested. .
47. **GDA-2144** Oct 16, 1990 The Department of State announced that it had raised to $4 million the maximum reward for information helping to catch **terrorists,** due to $1 million donations from both the Air Transport Association and the Air Line Pilots Association. The rewards program had begun in 1984 with a maximum payment of $500,000, but Congress increased that limit to $2 million after the bombing of Pan American Flight 103 (see Dec 21, 1988). Jan 4, 1991 In the first of a series of telecommunications failures which created air traffic control problems during this year, the AT&T company's maintenance workers accidentally cut a fiber-optic telephone cable in New Jersey, disrupting communications between air traffic control sites and delaying air travel for several hours in the New York area. Other significant delays occurred on May 4, when a farmer cut a fiber cable, limiting operations at four air route traffic control centers; on Sep 17, when an AT&T equipment failure in New York City cut controller communications and disrupted airline travel in the Northeast; and on Nov 5, when AT&T maintenance errors disrupted New England long distance telephone service, delaying flight operations at Boston Logan airport. (See May 8, 1988.).
48. **GDA-2763** September 11, 2001 Nineteen radical Islamic extremists with the group al Qaeda penetrated security at three major airports, seized four U.S. domestic airliners, and turned them into missiles that destroyed the **World Trade Center** in New York City, and damaged the Pentagon in Arlington, Virginia, killing thousands. Passengers on one of the planes fought the **hijackers** causing the plane to crash in a Pennsylvania field, killing all on board. For the first time in history, FAA put a ground stop on all U.S. air traffic. Related details follow .
49. **GDA-2765** . 8:38 a.m. FAA notifies the North American Aerospace Defense Command's (NORAD) Northeast Air Defense Sector about the suspected **hijacking** of American Flight 11. .

50. **GDA-2769** . 9:15 a.m. FAA (New York Center) notifies NORAD's Northeast Air Defense Sector that United Airlines 175 was the second aircraft that crashed into the World Trade Center. .
51. **GDA-2909** October 15, 2003 The White House commission established to investigate the September 11, 2001, **terrorist attacks** issued a subpoena to obtain needed documents from FAA. In May, the commission had requested all documents relating to FAA's tracking of the **hijacked** airliners and communications with the North American Aerospace Defense Command. FAA had provided 40 boxes containing 150,000 pages of information in September, but during subsequent interviews, the commission had learned that some materials had not been included. FAA officials responded that their failure to turn over all documents had been caused in part by internal procedures used to search for material. (See July 22, 2004.).
52. **GDA-3854** May 9, 2014 FAA issued a special security NOTAM advising that due to **terrorist activities** and civil unrest in Yemen, there was a significant risk to civil flight operations in that country. FAA warned that "**terrorists** and insurgents in the region possess man- portable air defense systems (manpads) and indirect fire weapons, and have threatened and targeted both international civil aviation and airports in country, most notably, Sanaa International airport (OYSN). U.S. operators planning to fly in the territory and airspace of Yemen at or below Fl240 must obtain current threat information, comply with all applicable FAA regulations and directives, and provide advance notice to FAA" with specific flight details.

10.5.5 Super Sonic Transport (SST)

The SST reference was found at random while mining the FAA history. It was interesting to see when and how it started. I remember the debates and eventual shutdown of the SST. Even as a child my perception was that they were very serious, long, and very public.

Do we enjoy the offshoots of this program in the form of the large jets that are common in our time? I wonder what air travel would look like today if the SST continued? Do people today realize that air travel is still heavily subsidized and could not exist in its current form without the taxpayer regardless of if the funds come from DOD or the FAA?

It is nice to have a restaurant in the suburbs but unless someone pays for the roads to allow people to come visit the restaurant, the restaurant is not a viable business. Such a simple concept but unless it is clearly stated no one will know about it until the roads breakdown and the restaurant goes out of business.

1. **GDA-741** Jun 30, 1960 The House Committee on Science and Astronautics recommended that Congress support a Federal program for the development of a commercial **supersonic transport** (**SST**). The committee report called for completion of the B-70 bomber program, which it considered justified on

defense grounds and which was expected to blaze a technological trail for the **SST**. The report also recommended that NASA assume leadership in devising a program for **SST** development. (See Jan 9, 1961.).

2. **GDA-765** Jan 9, 1961 The Federal Aviation Agency released a report on the commercial **supersonic transport** (**SST**), prepared by FAA with the assistance of DOD and NASA. The report concluded that a Mach 3 (2,000 mph.) transport could and should be built by U.S. industry, with governmental financial support limited to demonstrated needs. Although he had been unable to persuade the outgoing Eisenhower Administration to request funds for **SST** development, Administrator Quesada recommended prompt and careful consideration of the immediate establishment of such a program. (See Jun 30, 1960, and Jul 24, 1961.).
3. **GDA-805** Jul 24, 1961 A joint FAA-DOD-NASA Commercial **Supersonic Transport** Aircraft Report was issued. Based on a review of information gathered from industry and Federal government sources, the report concluded that development of a commercial transport aircraft to fly three times the speed of sound (Mach 3) was feasible and could be done by 1970-71. During August, Congress made its first appropriation for FAA research on the **Supersonic Transport** (**SST**). (See Jan 9 and Sep 25, 1961.).
4. **GDA-818** Sep 25, 1961 FAA, NASA, and the Defense Department agreed on a plan for the research and study phase of the commercial **supersonic transport** (**SST**) program. Assigning FAA responsibility for overall program leadership and management direction, the plan provided for a **Supersonic Transport** Steering Group--headed by the FAA Administrator and including the Assistant Secretary of the Air Force for Materiel and NASA's Director of Advanced Research Programs--to formulate broad policy and give overall guidance for the Federal role in the program. The Steering Group would be supported on the working level by the **SST** task group, which had been in operation for some time. Comprised of designated FAA-DOD-NASA representatives, the task group was to continue coordinating the **SST** activities of the three agencies. (See Jul 24 and Dec 11, 1961.).
5. **GDA-824** Dec 11, 1961 A **Supersonic Transport** Advisory Group established in November held its first formal meeting with the joint **Supersonic Transport** Steering Group. The new group was headed by General Orval R. Cook (USAF Ret.) and included aviation industry leaders. Its major tasks were to assess basic technical background material of the **supersonic transport** (**SST**); to define Federal-industry roles in program management; to consider the impact on U.S. and world markets if a European Mach 2 **SST** flew before the American **SST**; to develop a plan for financing development; to prepare a blueprint for development, production, and entry into airline service; and to consider methods for airline financing of **SST** purchases. (See Sep 25, 1961, and Jan 16, 1963.).
6. **GDA-865** Jan 16, 1963 The Federal Aviation Agency's **Supersonic Transport** Advisory Group recommended U.S. development of a commercial

supersonic transport (**SST**) as a top-priority Federal-industry program in a report made public this date. In acknowledging the report, Administrator Halaby said that it made a "powerful" case for proceeding with **SST** development, but he asked for additional conclusions and recommendations in the following areas cost of development and testing up to the preproduction stage for each airplane; unit cost which should be charged to the air carriers by manufacturers after the production stage was reached, "assuming production of some 200 aircraft"; direct operating costs; and management organization for development of an **SST**. The group submitted this supplementary report in May 1963 before dissolving in July. At the end May 1963, a Cabinet-level committee headed by Vice President Lyndon B. Johnson submitted recommendations to President Kennedy that were favorable to the program. (See Dec 11, 1961, and Jun 5, 1963.).

7. **GDA-880** Jun 5, 1963 President Kennedy announced his decision to proceed with the development of a U.S. **supersonic transport** (**SST**) in an address at the Air Force Academy's commencement exercises. In a Jun 14 letter to Congress, Kennedy wrote that the national interest required a U.S. **SST** superior to any comparable transport, and he formally recommended a program to develop such an aircraft. He suggested that private industry bear 25 percent of the development costs, with the Federal government paying the remaining 75 percent. To provide this Federal share, the President on Jun 24 requested Congress to appropriate $60 million. The money was subsequently included in FAA's appropriation for fiscal 1964. (See Jan 16, 1963, and Jul 29, 1963.) Jun 5, 1963 Administrator Halaby announced the establishment of an aviation mechanic safety awards program, to be administered by FAA in conjunction with the Flight Safety Foundation of New York City. Under the program, annual awards would honor airline and general aviation mechanics at state, regional, and national levels on the basis of their suggestions for improving either maintenance procedures or the mechanical reliability of aircraft and component systems. State aviation officials and representatives of FAA and industry would select the winners at the state and regional levels. FAA, the Flight Safety Foundation, and a committee of prominent members of the aviation community would select national winners. .

8. **GDA-886** Jul 29, 1963 FAA Administrator Halaby announced the appointment of Gordon M. Bain to the new position of Deputy Administrator for **Supersonic Transport** Development. Bain was to head the organization within the FAA charged with overall responsibility for the Federal-industry program to develop a commercial **supersonic transport** (**SST**) aircraft. A division-level organization had previously handled the agency's role in the feasibility and research phase of the program, which was conducted jointly with NASA and the Defense Department. (See Jun 5, 1963, Aug 15, 1963, and Sep 15, 1965.).

9. **GDA-888** Aug 15, 1963 FAA issued a request for proposals (RFP) that established performance objectives for the United States **supersonic transport** (**SST**), providing the basis for design competition among airframe and engine

manufacturers. The program timetable called for initial submission of manufacturers' designs based on this RFP by Jan 15, 1964. By Sep 10, 1963, three major airframe manufacturers and three major engine builders had notified FAA of their intention to submit proposals. (See Jul 29, 1963, and Nov 19, 1963.).

10. **GDA-896** Nov 19, 1963 Responding to requests from U.S. and foreign carriers for priority deliveries of the U.S. **supersonic transport** (**SST**) when it became available, FAA established a delivery priorities system for the first 70 airliners to come off the production line. The agency stated it was acting as intermediary for the airlines pending final selection of a manufacturer to make the **SST** available at an early time to the broadest possible market, while maintaining a reasonable balance of distribution been U.S. and foreign carriers. (See Aug 15, 1963, and Jan 15, 1964.).
11. **GDA-908** Jan 15, 1964 Six companies submitted **supersonic transport** (**SST**) design proposals to FAA in response to the agency's Aug 1963 request for such proposals. The companies included three airframe manufacturers (Boeing, Lockheed, and North American Aviation) and three engine manufacturers (General Electric, Pratt & Whitney, and Curtiss-Wright). (See Nov 19, 1963, and Apr 1, 1964.).
12. **GDA-911** Feb 3, 1964 A series of sonic boom studies began as FAA launched a six-month project to test public reaction to the phenomenon in Oklahoma City, using regularly scheduled overflights by Air Force supersonic jets. On Aug 5, the National Academy of Sciences announced the establishment of a committee to study effects of sonic boom as related to the development of the **supersonic transport**. On Nov 18, FAA launched a three-month study of the effects of sonic boom on typical structures in White Sands, N.M. (See Jan 27, 1965.).
13. **GDA-915** Apr 1, 1964 Executive Order 11149 established the President's Advisory Committee on **Supersonic Transport** (**SST**) to advise President Lyndon B. Johnson on "all aspects of the **supersonic transport** program." The committee's original membership included Defense Secretary Robert S. McNamara (chairman), Treasury Secretary C. Douglas Dillon, Commerce Secretary Luther H. Hodges, NASA Administrator James E. Webb, FAA Administrator N. E. Halaby, CIA Director John A. McCone, and two private citizens Eugene R. Black, former president of the World Bank, and Stanley de J. Osborne, Chairman of the Board of Olin Mathieson. The committee remained in existence until Sep 5, 1968, when it was terminated by the President. Also on Apr 1, 1964, FAA's Deputy Administrator for **SST** Development Gordon Bain reported on the results of a evaluation made in Phase I of the **SST** design competition. A 210-person Federal team gave the highest competitive scores to the Boeing variable-sweep wing airframe design and the General Electric after-burning turbojet engine design. In transmitting these results to Administrator Halaby, Bain recommended that the two

companies be selected to go into a one-year noncompetitive detailed-design phase. (See Jan 15 and May 20, 1964.).

14. **GDA-921** May 20, 1964 President Johnson gave his approval for the U.S. **supersonic transport** (**SST**) development program to proceed into Phase IIA--a six-month design competition between two airframe manufacturers (Boeing and Lockheed) and two engine manufacturers (General Electric and Pratt & Whitney). The President based his decision on the recommendations of the President's Advisory Committee on **Supersonic Transport** made on May 15, 1964. On Jun 1, the four competitors signed the six- month Phase IIA contracts. The contracts authorized each air frame manufacturer to spend at the rate of $1 million per month during the contract period and each engine manufacturer at a rate of $835,000 per month. All four manufacturers agreed to bear 25 percent of the contract costs. The design competition was subsequently extended for an additional six month period designated Phase IIB. (See Apr 1, 1964, and Jul 1, 1965.) Jun 1, 1964 La Guardia Airport opened to scheduled air carrier jet operations. Jet air carriers had begun operating at John F. Kennedy International Airport on Oct 4, 1958, and at Newark Airport on Sep 11, 1961. (See Apr 24, 1966.).
15. **GDA-922** Jun 1, 1964 The French-Anglo-United States **Supersonic Transport** (FAUSST) group opened its first meeting. The group was established to exchange information on airworthiness and environmental matters in **SST** development, certification, and operation. FAA represented the United States in the group. .
16. **GDA-931** Sep 21, 1964 The Air Force XB-70A supersonic aircraft made its first flight. Subsequent flights of this steel-bodied airplane, which had been conceived as a bomber but recast as a research aircraft, provided the FAA-managed U.S. **supersonic transport** development program with useful technical data. (See Jun 8, 1966.).
17. **GDA-958** Jan 27, 1965 The National Academy of Sciences' Committee on **Supersonic Transport** Sonic Boom concluded that prototype development of a **supersonic transport** (**SST**) was "clearly warranted" by evidence from research, tests, and studies of sonic boom phenomena (see Jul 1, 1965). This finding was largely based on data collected by FAA in the Oklahoma City area (see Feb 3, 1964). On Apr 25, 1965, FAA made public a summary of its Oklahoma City sonic boom study, in which U.S. Air Force jets had subjected residents to 1,253 booms during daylight hours. Most boom intensities ranged between 1.0 and 2.0 pounds of overpressure per square foot, but adverse atmospheric influences caused approximately 11 percent to exceed the intended limit of 2.0 pounds of overpressure. FAA also released an interim report on the related test at White Sands, N.M., in which Air Force jets subjected 16 representative structures to 1,494 booms varying in intensity from 2.0 to 20.0 pounds of overpressure. The findings of the two tests included * Sonic booms of less than 5 pounds of overpressure caused no discernible damage to structurally sound buildings; however, booms of this intensity probably triggered cracks in faultily constructed walls, breaks in cracked

windows, and other damage in structurally unsound buildings. * Booms of the order of those expected to be generated by the U.S. **supersonic transport** (**SST**) had no measurable physiological effect on humans. * The subjective reaction of individuals to sonic boom would be the area of greatest concern for the U.S. **SST** program. * Fully 27 percent of the people polled in the Oklahoma City area during the closing weeks of testing declared they could not live with sonic boom; additionally, 40 percent of those polled were unconvinced that booms did not cause damage to buildings. .

18. **GDA-959** In releasing the information, Administrator Halaby stated his conclusion that a **supersonic transport** could be designed in terms of configuration, operating attitude, and flight paths so as to achieve public acceptance in the early 1970s. On Mar 8, 1969, the Federal government lost its appeal in a class action suit involving claims for property damage allegedly caused by the Oklahoma City tests. (See Apr 27, 1973.).

19. **GDA-968** Apr 6, 1965 The British government disclosed it had abandoned the TSR-2 tactical-strike- reconnaissance jet program. The Ministry of Defence stated that the program's cost "was out of all proportion to the aircraft's military value." The loss of technical experience resulting from this decision was perceived as a setback for development of the **supersonic transport** Concorde (see Dec 11, 1967). .

20. **GDA-994** Jul 1, 1965 General William F. McKee (USAF, Ret.) became the third FAA Administrator, succeeding Najeeb E. Halaby (see Mar 3, 1961). President Johnson had announced his selection of McKee on Apr 27, but did not submit his name for Senate confirmation until Congress passed special legislation exempting the general from a provision of the Federal Aviation Act that required the Administrator to be a civilian. This legislation cleared Congress on Jun 22, after prolonged debate. Johnson formally nominated McKee on Jun 23, and the Senate confirmed the nomination on Jun 30. Born in Chilhowie, Va., in 1906, "Bozo" McKee graduated from West Point in 1929. He began his career with the U.S. Army Coast Artillery Corps, but transferred in 1942 to the Army Air Forces. McKee received his first star in 1945. The following year, he was appointed Chief of Staff of the Air Transport Command. In 1947, when the Air Force became a separate service, McKee became Assistant Vice Chief of Staff, Air Force, a position held for six years. He was serving as Commander of the Air Force Logistics Command when selected for the Vice Chief of Staff post, the second highest military position in the Air Force. At the time he received his fourth star, he was the only Air Force officer to have attained that rank without holding an aeronautical rating. Upon his retirement from the military in 1964, he joined the National Aeronautics and Space Administration as Assistant Administrator for Management Development. The selection of McKee to head FAA was linked to the need for an experienced executive to oversee the development of the U.S. **supersonic transport** (see Jul 1, 1965, entry on this topic, below). He served as Administrator for three years and one month (see Jul 31, 1968). .

21. **GDA-996** Jul 1, 1965 President Johnson announced that the **supersonic transport** (**SST**) development program would move into Phase IIC, an 18-month detailed design phase costing approximately $220 million. The President's decision, which was made known during General William F. McKee's swearing-in as FAA Administrator, was based on the recommendations of the President's Advisory Committee on **Supersonic Transport**. The decision postponed prototype development and fabrication for at least 18 months, prolonging the program's competitive phase by retaining the two airframe competitors (Boeing and Lockheed) and the two engine competitors (General Electric and Pratt & Whitney) selected in 1964. Unlike the previous design phases, however, Phase IIC was not purely a "paper" competition. The airframe manufacturers would construct full-scale mock-ups, and the engine manufacturers would build and test full-scale demonstrator engines. The President enumerated four primary objectives of the new competitive design phase (1) to provide a sound foundation for realistic estimates of operating performance and production costs; (2) to take advantage of the flight experience of the SR-71, the XB-70, and the variable swept-wing F-111; (3) to reduce developmental risks and developmental costs, while retaining the capacity to accelerate the program in its later phases; (4) and to provide a better basis for judgment as to the manner in which the program should proceed after the 18-month period. The President asked Congress for $140 million to initiate the 18-month program. (See May 20, 1964, and Dec 31, 1966.).
22. **GDA-1009** Sep 15, 1965 Deputy Administrator for **Supersonic Transport** Development Gordon Bain resigned from FAA effective this date. Brig. Gen. Jewell C. Maxwell (USAF) was assigned to replace Bain with the new title Director of **Supersonic Transport** Development. The new designation entailed no change in responsibilities or organizational relationship. (See Jul 29, 1963, and Apr 6, 1970.).
23. **GDA-1075** Dec 31, 1966 FAA declared the Boeing Company and the General Electric Company winners of the **supersonic transport** (**SST**) development program competitive design and study phase (Phase IIC). The agency selected Boeing's variable-sweep-wing airframe design over the Lockheed Corporation's double-delta-wing design and General Electric's after-burning turbojet engine over the Pratt & Whitney ductburning turbofan engine. The selections were based on an intensive two-month evaluation conducted by a 240-person team of aeronautical experts from the Defense Department, NASA, CAB, and FAA. In addition, 10 U.S. and foreign airlines independently evaluated the proposals and submitted individual recommendations. (See Jul 1, 1965, and Feb 6, 1967.).
24. **GDA-1084** Feb 6, 1967 FAA asked U.S. air carriers to help finance the **supersonic transport** (**SST**) prototype program by contributing $1 million in risk capital for each **SST** delivery position held (see Nov 19, 1963). The agency took the step at the direction of President Johnson, who considered it a way in which the airlines could demonstrate to the Congress and the public

their faith in the **SST** program. Under the proposal, contributions would in no way affect the established places of contributing and noncontributing carriers on the reservation schedule. The money would go directly to the Boeing Company to be used in the development program in lieu of Federal funds. The airlines would recover their investment--up to a maximum of $1.5 million for each $1 million contributed--through aircraft royalty payments. Ten U.S. air carriers holding a total of 52 delivery positions agreed to put up risk capital. Details of the participation agreement could not be worked out before April, however, and this became a factor in delaying the President's announcement of his decision to take the **SST** program into prototype development. (See Dec 31, 1966, and Apr 29, 1967.).

25. **GDA-1088** Mar 25, 1967 The management of the XB-70 supersonic aircraft research program was transferred from the U.S. Air Force to the National Aeronautics and Space Administration's Flight Research Center. The program, much of which was devoted to the study of supersonic flight in support of the U.S. **supersonic transport** development program, continued as a joint NASA-USAF effort. (See Sep 21, 1964, Jun 8, 1966, and Feb 4, 1969.).
26. **GDA-1097** Apr 29, 1967 President Johnson announced that the U.S. **supersonic transport** (**SST**) development program would proceed into the prototype development phase (Phase III). Johnson based his decision on the recommendations of the President's Advisory Committee on **Supersonic Transport**. On May 1, 1967, the date of the President's formal approval, FAA, Boeing, and General Electric signed the Phase III contracts retroactive to Jan 1, 1967, which called for the construction of two identical variable, sweep-wing **SST** prototypes. (See Feb 6 and Jun 5, 1967.).
27. **GDA-1100** Jun 5, 1967 The Boeing Company assumed from FAA responsibility for allocating **supersonic transport** (**SST**) delivery positions to purchasers (see Nov 19, 1963). At the same time, FAA raised the cost of reserving future positions from $200,000 to $750,000. The $750,000 deposit would be made directly to Boeing, would be in the form of risk capital, and would bear no interest. It would be used by Boeing in lieu of Federal funds to help finance the prototype program. Boeing agreed to honor the 113 delivery positions already allocated by FAA among 26 airlines. (See Apr 29, 1967, and Jan 15, 1968.).
28. **GDA-1131** Dec 11, 1967 Sud Aviation and the British Aircraft Corporation unveiled a prototype of the British- French Concorde, the West's first **supersonic transport**, in Toulouse, France. On Mar 2, 1969, the Concorde made its first flight. Almost ten years later, on Sep 21, 1979, after meeting in London, aviation officials of France and the United Kingdom agreed to end the unprofitable Concorde production program. Unsold Concordes were allocated to the flag carriers of the two countries--Air France and British Airways. Only sixteen of the supersonic jet transports had been built. .
29. **GDA-1136** Jan 15, 1968 AN FAA technical team began a review of modifications made by Boeing to its **supersonic transport** (**SST**) prototype

design (variable-sweep-wing model 2707-200). The team found that these changes, by increasing the aircraft's weight, had resulted in a poor weight-payload ratio. This overweight factor limited range and payload to such an extent that the prototype's calculated performance fell well below the specifications for the Phase III contract. (With a full payload, the 2707-200 had a range of only 2,775 statute miles.) An amendment to the Phase III contract, dated Mar 29, 1968, required Boeing to submit to FAA by Jan 15, 1969, a fully substantiated design capable of meeting the Phase III contract criteria for the prototype airplane. (See Jun 5, 1967, and Oct 21, 1968.).

30. **GDA-1174** Oct 21, 1968 The Boeing Company formally announced it had abandoned its variable-sweep-wing design for the U.S. **supersonic transport** (**SST**) in favor of a conventional fixed-wing. The company's engineers had never been able to overcome the weight penalties imposed by the variable-sweep wing design. Boeing would submit the new design to FAA for approval in Jan 1969. (See Jan 15, 1968, and Jan 15, 1969.).

31. **GDA-1185** Dec 31, 1968 The Soviet Union's Tupolev TU-144 prototype became the world's first **supersonic transport** to make its maiden flight. (See entry for Dec 11, 1967.).

32. **GDA-1191** Jan 15, 1969 The Boeing Company submitted to FAA for evaluation a new **supersonic transport** (**SST**) configuration, a delta-wing design with a horizontal tail. A 100-person review team drawn from FAA, NASA, and the Defense Department found that Boeing had adequately integrated the new design. In February, President Nixon appointed an interdepartmental committee headed by Under Secretary of Transportation James M. Beggs to review the **SST** program. The committee's report, submitted in early April, contained mixed views on the program's future. Secretary of Transportation Volpe, however, continued to advise in favor of the program. On Sep 23, 1969, Nixon announced that the **SST** development program would be continued because the project was essential to maintaining U.S. leadership in world air transport. The President requested Congress to appropriate $96 million during fiscal year 1970 ($662 million over a five- year period, fiscal 1970 through fiscal 1974) to pursue the program. (See Oct 21, 1968, and Apr 6, 1970.).

33. **GDA-1276** Apr 6, 1970 Management responsibility for the **supersonic transport** (**SST**) development program was transferred from the FAA to the Office of the Secretary, Department of Transportation. The Director of **Supersonic Transport** Development would henceforth take guidance and direction from the Under Secretary of Transportation, while FAA would continue to provide a variety of support functions for the program. In announcing the transfer a few days earlier, Secretary Volpe had explained that it would increase his oversight of the program. In addition, the change would ensure that FAA, the agency responsible for certificating the aircraft, would not be responsible for its development. Volpe had also announced the appointment of William M. Magruder as Director of the program, succeeding

Brig. Gen. Jewell C. Maxwell, who had resigned during the previous summer. (See Jan 15, 1969, and Apr 22, 1970.).

34. **GDA-1279** Apr 22, 1970 The first annual Earth Day observance throughout the United States included protests indicating environmentalists' rising opposition to the **supersonic transport** (**SST**) program. Concerns about the **SST** included such issues as sonic booms (see Jan 27, 1965) and the aircraft's effect on the ozone layer of the earth's upper atmosphere. (See Apr 6 and Dec 30, 1970.).

35. **GDA-1334** Dec 3, 1970 The **supersonic transport** (**SST**) program suffered a reverse in Congress as the Senate adopted an amendment to delete from the Department of Transportation fiscal 1971 appropriations bill an administration request for $290 million to continue **SST** prototype development. Subsequently, House- Senate conferees restored $210 million of the administration's request to the bill. But the Senate balked again, and the House refused to take part in another conference. Accordingly, the two chambers passed a joint resolution continuing appropriations for the Department (including the **SST** project) through Mar 30, 1971, at the fiscal 1970 level; at the same time, they agreed to vote on the **SST** appropriation separately from the rest of the DOT appropriation early in the 92d Congress. (See Apr 22, 1970, and Mar 24, 1971.).

36. **GDA-1353** Mar 15, 1971 FAA adopted a marking and lighting standard for identifying transmission lines and their support structures that could constitute a potential hazard to air navigation. The standard called for three sequentially flashing white lights of high intensity to be installed on transmission line support structures. Each light would flash 60 times per minute. These lights replaced unlighted spherical markers on transmission lines, which provided little or no help to pilots at night or in bad weather. Mar 24, 1971 The Senate in effect terminated the U.S. civil **supersonic transport** (**SST**) program when it voted against the appropriation of $289 million to continue **SST** prototype development. The House of Representatives had voted down the **SST** appropriation on Mar 18, 1971. Later, in May 1971, pro-**SST** forces in the House seeking to revive the program succeeded by a vote of 201-197 in amending a Department of Transportation supplemental appropriations bill to include $85.3 million for **SST** development; however, the Senate struck out the amendment by a vote of 58-37. (See Dec 3, 1970, and Oct 12, 1971.).

37. **GDA-1391** Oct 12, 1971 FAA abolished the Office of **Supersonic Transport** Development and established the **Supersonic Transport** Office under the Associate Administrator for Engineering and Development to continue **SST** engineering and research activities. The agency also established a **SST** Contracts Branch in the Logistics Service to perform the contracting and procurement functions for the negotiation, administration, and termination of **SST** contracts. (See Mar 24, 1971.).

38. **GDA-1461** Apr 27, 1973 AN FAA rule imposing a virtual ban on civilian supersonic flights over the United States went into effect. The rule, first

proposed on Apr 10, 1970, prohibited any operator of a civil aircraft from exceeding the speed of sound (Mach 1) when flying over the land mass or territorial waters of the United States, except when such operations would not cause a "measurable sonic boom overpressure to reach the surface." This wording left room for certain authorized operations at the lower end of the supersonic speed range. The rule was not seen as a bar to planned operations of the Anglo-French **supersonic transport** Concorde, which was expected to fly subsonic over U.S. territorial waters and mainland. (See Feb 4, 1976.).

39. **GDA-1467** Jun 3, 1973 The crash of a Tupolev TU-144 during a demonstration flight at the Paris Air Show dealt a serious blow to the Soviet **supersonic transport** program. (See Dec 31, 1968, and Dec 26, 1975.).

40. **GDA-1539** Jan 21, 1975 FAA announced that it would study the effects of high-altitude flight on the earth's atmosphere, building upon DOT's recently-ended Climatic Impact Assessment Program, which had begun in 1971 in response to concern about environmental consequences of the fleets of **supersonic transport**s then anticipated. FAA's study, the High Altitude Pollution Program (HAPP), ended in 1982. Its final report, published in Jan 1984, concluded that the effects of civilian aircraft on ozone depletion and climactic change were not a cause of immediate concern at that time. .

41. **GDA-1570** Jan 21, 1976 British Airways and Air France began the world's first scheduled supersonic passenger service (see Dec 26, 1975) with simultaneous takeoffs of Anglo-French Concorde **SST** aircraft from London and Paris for flights to Bahrain and Rio de Janeiro. The London-Bahrain flight, normally 6 hours 30 minutes by subsonic jet, took 4 hours 10 minutes. The Paris-Rio flight, scheduled to take 7 hours 5 minutes (compared with a subsonic time of 11 hours 10 minutes), arrived 40 minutes late. (See Feb 4, 1976.).

42. **GDA-1571** Feb 4, 1976 Secretary of Transportation William T. Coleman, Jr., announced his decision to permit the Anglo-French **supersonic transport** Concorde to land in the U.S. on a temporary, restricted basis. Air France and British Airways had made application in Jan 1975 to conduct limited commercial operations with the **SST** into New York Kennedy and Washington Dulles airports, proposing a maximum of four flights daily into Kennedy and two daily into Dulles. In an environmental impact statement issued in draft in Mar 1975 and in final on this date, FAA recommended granting the application on the grounds that the limited operations could not significantly harm the environment. Secretary Coleman authorized the proposed service for a trial period not to exceed 16 months. Working with the National Aeronautics and Space Administration, the Environmental Protection Agency, and the Office of the Secretary, FAA developed plans for noise, sonic boom, and low altitude pollution monitoring of the Concorde to determine its environmental impact during the trial period. Devices to monitor noise and emissions were installed at Washington Dulles and surrounding communities, and most were in operation when Concorde service to Dulles began on May 24, 1976. Intense opposition from environmental and citizen groups in the New York area and a

ban by the Port Authority of New York and New Jersey delayed Concorde service at Kennedy. (See Apr 27, 1973, Sep 23, 1977, and Oct 17, 1977).

43. **GDA-1582** May 5, 1976 The United States, France, and the United Kingdom concluded an agreement providing for the monitoring of ozone levels in the stratosphere and cooperation to ensure that the ozone layer was not degraded by emissions from **supersonic transports**. (See Feb 4, 1976, and Sep 23, 1977.).

44. **GDA-1639** Sep 23, 1977 At the end of the 16-month trial of the Anglo-French Concorde **supersonic transport** at Dulles International Airport (see Feb 4, 1976), Secretary of Transportation Brock Adams announced proposed permanent rules for civil **supersonic transport (SST)** operations in the United States. Most of these related to the new noise restrictions adopted in 1977. Secretary Adams proposed to exempt the 16 Concordes manufactured before Jan 1, 1980, from retrofit requirements for older jet transports (see Dec 23, 1976), while requiring future SST's to meet all noise standards for newer subsonic aircraft (see Mar 3, 1977). In view of the exceptional loudness of the Concorde, however, the ban on Concorde operations between 10 p.m. and 7 a.m. was retained, as was the absolute prohibition on supersonic flight over land. In addition, the Concorde was granted permission to land at Washington, New York, and 11 other American cities. These proposed regulations became final on Jul 31, 1978, after several more public hearings on the subject. At that time, FAA justified its "grandfather clause" for the first 16 Concordes by noting that they constituted the entire production run of the aircraft. (Because of its high fuel costs and limited payload, the Concorde had been purchased only by the state airlines of France and Britain.) FAA felt that modifications that would bring these aircraft into compliance with subsonic noise standards were neither technologically practicable nor economically reasonable. On the other hand, some restrictions on the Concorde were justified by thorough analysis of FAA test results on the plane's loudness, which showed that the perceived noise generated by a Concorde on its takeoff path was double that of a Boeing 707, four times that of a Boeing 747, and eight times that of a DC-10. FAA also reviewed a number of environmental concerns that had been expressed about SSTs, the most important of which was the fear that emission from **SST** engines might damage the ozone layer of the earth's atmosphere (see May 5, 1976). Citing a number of recent research studies, including one submitted by the National Academy of Sciences, FAA concluded that the possibility of such damage from the Concordes was too small to be an immediate concern. .

45. **GDA-1643** Oct 17, 1977 A U.S. Supreme Court decision ended the long dispute over landing rights for the Anglo-French Concorde **supersonic transport** at New York Kennedy airport. In 1976, Secretary of Transportation William T. Coleman had allowed a 16-month trial of the Concorde at Washington and New York (see Feb 4, 1976); however, the Port Authority of New York and New Jersey, operator of Kennedy airport, had banned the Concorde pending further study of its environmental impact. During the spring

of 1977, citizens concerned about the Concorde's potential noise conducted demonstrations that included the deliberate snarling of automobile traffic by driving cars very slowly down Kennedy's access roads. Meanwhile, on May 11, 1977, a Federal District Court ruled that the Port Authority's landing ban was illegal because it was in "irreconcilable conflict" with Federal prerogatives. A month later, on Jun 14, the U.S. Court of Appeals for the Second Circuit modified this ruling, holding that the Port Authority had the right to establish "fair, reasonable, and nondiscriminatory" noise standards. The Court of appeals sent the case back to the District Court to determine whether the Port Authority's actions met the "fair, reasonable, and nondiscriminatory" test. On Aug 17, the District Court ruled that the Port Authority's long delay in formulating noise standards constituted unreasonable and discriminatory treatment of the Concorde. It was this decision that the Supreme Court upheld. Concorde passenger service from New York to London and Paris began on Nov 22, 1977.

10.5.6 Startup Shutdown

1. **GDA-6** May 20, 1926 President Calvin Coolidge signed the Air Commerce Act of 1926 into law. The act instructed the Secretary of Commerce to foster air commerce; designate and establish airways; establish, operate, and maintain aids to air navigation (but not airports); arrange for research and development to improve such aids; license pilots; issue airworthiness certificates for aircraft and major aircraft components; and investigate accidents. (See Introduction.).
2. **GDA-244** Aug 22, 1938 The Civil Aeronautics Act of 1938 became operative (see Jun 23, 1938). To implement the act, the Bureau of Air Commerce was transferred from the Department of Commerce, and the Bureau of Air Mail from the Interstate Commerce Commission to the Civil Aeronautics Authority.

.

3. **GDA-658** May 21, 1958 Senator A. S. Mike Monroney (D-Okla.) introduced S. 3880, a bill "to create an independent Federal Aviation Agency, to provide for the safe and efficient use of the airspace by both civil and military operations and to provide for the regulation and promotion of civil aviation in such a manner as to best foster its development and safety." By the next day 33 Senators were listed as cosponsors of the bill, and Representative Oren Harris (D-Ark.) introduced the same bill as H.R. 12616. On Jun 13, President Eisenhower, in a message to Congress, recommended early enactment of such legislation to consolidate "all the essential management functions necessary to support the common needs of our civil and military aviation." (See Aug 23, 1958.).
4. **GDA-665** Aug 23, 1958 President Eisenhower signed the Federal Aviation Act of 1958 (P.L. 85-726) into law. Treating comprehensively the Federal role in fostering and regulating civil aeronautics and air commerce, the new statute repealed the Air Commerce Act of 1926, the Civil Aeronautics Act of 1938, the Airways Modernization Act of 1957, and those portions of the various

Presidential reorganization plans dealing with civil aviation. The act assigned the functions exercised under these repealed laws, which had been dispersed within the Federal structure, to two independent agencies--the Federal Aviation Agency (FAA), which was created by the act, and the Civil Aeronautics Board (CAB), which was freed of its administrative ties with the Department of Commerce. FAA came into existence with the signing of the Act, but assumed its functions in stages. Pursuant to the legislation, it also took over the responsibilities and personnel of the Airways Modernization Board, which were transferred to it by Executive Order 10786, on November l. FAA inherited as a nucleus the organization and functions of CAA on Dec 31, 1958. Later (on August 11, 1960), Executive Order 10883 terminated the Air Coordinating Committee, transferring its functions to FAA. Section 103 of the act concisely stated the Administrator's major powers and responsibilities as follows "(a) The regulation of air commerce in such manner as to best promote its development and safety and fulfill the requirements of national defense; "(b) The promotion, encouragement, and development of civil aeronautics; "(c) The control of the use of the navigable airspace of the United States and the regulation of both civil and military operations in such airspace in the interest of the safety and efficiency of both; "(d) The consolidation of research and development with respect to air navigation facilities, as well as the installation and operation thereof; "(e) The development and operation of a common system of air traffic control and navigation for both military and civil aircraft." CAB, though retaining responsibility for economic regulation of the air carriers and for accident investigation, lost under the act most of its former authority in the safety regulation and enforcement field to FAA. The law provided, however, that any FAA order involving suspension or revocation of a certificate might be appealed to CAB for hearing, after which CAB could affirm, amend, modify, or reverse the FAA order. Provision was made for FAA participation in accident investigation, but determination of probable cause was to be the function of CAB alone. When the FAA assumed full operational status on Dec 31, 1958, it absorbed certain CAB personnel associated with the safety rulemaking function. (See Nov 1 and Dec 31, 1958.).

5. **GDA-667** Oct 1, 1958 The National Aeronautics and Space Administration (NASA) was established under the National Aeronautics and Space Act of 1958. Passage of the Space Act (signed into law by President Eisenhower on Jul 29, 1958) settled the question of whether space exploration should be under civilian or military control. The National Advisory Committee for Aeronautics (NACA), which had been in existence since 1915, was absorbed by and formed the nucleus for the new civilian space agency. .
6. **GDA-915** Apr 1, 1964 Executive Order 11149 established the President's Advisory Committee on Supersonic Transport (SST) to advise President Lyndon B. Johnson on "all aspects of the supersonic transport program." The committee's original membership included Defense Secretary Robert S.

McNamara (chairman), Treasury Secretary C. Douglas Dillon, Commerce Secretary Luther H. Hodges, NASA Administrator James E. Webb, FAA Administrator N. E. Halaby, CIA Director John A. McCone, and two private citizens Eugene R. Black, former president of the World Bank, and Stanley de J. Osborne, Chairman of the Board of Olin Mathieson. The committee remained in existence until Sep 5, 1968, when it was terminated by the President. Also on Apr 1, 1964, FAA's Deputy Administrator for SST Development Gordon Bain reported on the results of a evaluation made in Phase I of the SST design competition. A 210-person Federal team gave the highest competitive scores to the Boeing variable-sweep wing airframe design and the General Electric after-burning turbojet engine design. In transmitting these results to Administrator Halaby, Bain recommended that the two companies be selected to go into a one-year noncompetitive detailed-design phase. (See Jan 15 and May 20, 1964.).

7. **GDA-921** May 20, 1964 President Johnson gave his approval for the U.S. supersonic transport (SST) development program to proceed into Phase IIA--a six-month design competition between two airframe manufacturers (Boeing and Lockheed) and two engine manufacturers (General Electric and Pratt & Whitney). The President based his decision on the recommendations of the President's Advisory Committee on Supersonic Transport made on May 15, 1964. On Jun 1, the four competitors signed the six- month Phase IIA contracts. The contracts authorized each air frame manufacturer to spend at the rate of $1 million per month during the contract period and each engine manufacturer at a rate of $835,000 per month. All four manufacturers agreed to bear 25 percent of the contract costs. The design competition was subsequently extended for an additional six month period designated Phase IIB. (See Apr 1, 1964, and Jul 1, 1965.) Jun 1, 1964 La Guardia Airport opened to scheduled air carrier jet operations. Jet air carriers had begun operating at John F. Kennedy International Airport on Oct 4, 1958, and at Newark Airport on Sep 11, 1961. (See Apr 24, 1966.).
8. **GDA-925** Jul 7, 1964 President Johnson issued Executive Order 11161 directing FAA and the Department of Defense (DOD) to plan on the basis of the probability that in time of war FAA would become an adjunct of DOD. Under the guiding concept, FAA would remain organizationally intact and the Administrator would retain responsibility for his statutory functions, "subject to the authority, direction, and control of the Secretary of Defense to the extent deemed by the Secretary to be necessary for the discharge of his responsibilities . . . ." The Secretary of Defense was explicitly authorized to direct the Administrator to place operational elements of FAA under the direct control of military commanders. The order also required the Secretary and the Administrator to assure that during any national emergency short of war the functions of FAA would be performed in a manner satisfying essential national defense requirements. As a step in executing the order, FAA and DOD agreed

on a memorandum of understanding on Apr 13, 1966. The understanding covered the relationship between the two agencies in the event that FAA became an adjunct of DOD, and provided for planning for this eventuality and for lesser emergencies. .

9. **GDA-2227** Apr 30, 1992 President Bush signed an order directing Federal agencies to modify their procedures in order to facilitate the **privatization** of airports and other public assets built with Federal assistance. .
10. **GDA-2432** January 14, 1997 In a conference sponsored by the White House Commission on Aviation Safety and Security and held in Washington, DC, at George Washington University, airline executives called upon the Clinton Administration to **privatize** key functions of FAA and to install a nonprofit, airline-organized cooperative that would manage security issues. Participants recommended funding these changes with user fees instead of the, then-current, ticket tax. (See July 17, 1996; February 12, 1997.).
11. **GDA-2463** April 22, 1997 FAA published a proposal to accept applications, beginning December 1, for participation in an airport **privatization** pilot program established by the Federal Aviation Reauthorization Act of 1996 (Public Law 104-264). .
12. **GDA-2479** May 28, 1997 The National Civil Aviation Review Commission, lead by Norman Mineta, held the first of two public hearings regarding the financing of certain FAA services. Seventeen organizations testified. September 25, the commission made its "Preliminary Finance Report" available to the public. October 28, a second, and final, public hearing was held. December 11, Mineta issued the commission's final report, "Avoiding Aviation Gridlock and Reducing the Accident Rate A Consensus for Change," which noted that airline passengers were doomed to massive airport congestion and more dangerous skies unless FAA received a radical overhaul. The 21-member panel called on lawmakers and the White House to improve FAA management and finances. It urged a partial **privatization** of the agency and steps to shield aviation regulation from partisan budget battles. The proposed reforms would let the FAA beef up funding for the air traffic control system and airports to accommodate a rise in air traffic. (See September 30, 1996.).
13. **GDA-3677** February 22, 2013 Secretary of Transportation Ray LaHood issued a statement which said that as a result of mandatory **sequestration**, the majority of the FAA's nearly 47,000 employees would be furloughed for approximately one day per pay period until the end of the fiscal year. (See July 23, 2011; March 22, 2013.).
14. **GDA-3680** March 22, 2013 FAA announced that 149 federal contract towers would close beginning on April 7 as part of the agency's **sequestration** implementation plan. The agency made the decision to keep 24 federal contract towers open that it had previously proposed for closure because of national interest considerations. An additional 16 federal contract towers under the "cost share" program would remain open because Congressional statute set aside

funds every fiscal year for those towers. FAA planned to begin a four-week phased closure of the 149 federal contract towers beginning on April 7. (See February 22, 2013; April 5, 2013.).

15. **GDA-3683** April 5, 2013 FAA announced it would delay the closure of all 149 federal contract air traffic control towers until June 15. The previous month, FAA had announced it would eliminate funding for these towers as part of the agency's required $637 million budget cuts under **sequestration**. This additional time would allow the agency to attempt to resolve multiple legal challenges to the closure decisions. As part of the tower closure implementation process, the agency continued to consult with airports and operators and reviewed appropriate risk mitigations. (See March 22, 2013; April 23, 2013.).
16. **GDA-3687** April 23, 2013 As a result of employee furloughs due to **sequestration**, which began on April 21, FAA began implementing traffic management initiatives at airports and facilities around the country. FAA announced that travelers could expect to see a wide range of delays that would change throughout the day depending on staffing and weather- related issues. For example, the FAA experienced staffing challenges at the New York and Los Angeles En Route Centers and at the Dallas-Ft. Worth and Las Vegas TRACONs. Controllers spaced planes farther apart so they could manage traffic with smaller staffs. This led to delays at airports including Dallas, Las Vegas and Los Angeles. The FAA also expected delays at Newark and LaGuardia because of weather and winds. On April 21, FAA attributed more than 1,200 delays in the system to staffing reductions resulting from the furlough. 1,400 additional delays resulted from weather and other factors. (See April 5, 2013 April 24, 2013.).
17. **GDA-3688** April 24, 2013 FAA announced that due to employee furloughs as a result of **sequestration**, on April 23 the furlough caused more than 1,025 delays in the system. Weather and other delays caused more than 975 additional delays. The following day, FAA announced that on April 25, furlough-related staffing reductions at the New York, Washington, Cleveland, Jacksonville, and Los Angeles En Route Centers, the Potomac, Dallas and Southern California TRACONs and Detroit Tower contributed to more than 863 delays, and weather and other factors caused more than 1,269 additional delays. (See April 23, 2013; April 27, 2013.).
18. **GDA-3695** May 9, 2013 FAA announced it no longer planned to close 72 medium-sized air traffic control facilities overnight because of **sequestration**. The following day, on May 10, Transportation Secretary Ray LaHood announced that the recently enacted Reducing Flight Delays Act of 2013 would allow the FAA to transfer sufficient funds to end employee furloughs and keep the 149 low activity contract towers originally slated for closure in June open for the remainder of fiscal year 2013. The FAA also planned to put $10 million towards reducing cuts and delays in core NextGen programs and allocated approximately $11 million to partially restore infrastructure support in the

national airspace system. (See September 28, 2012; April 27, 2013; May 20, 2013; August 14, 2013.).

19. **GDA-3702** May 29, 2013 The Office of Management and Budget told federal agencies to prepare their fiscal 2015 budget requests with three levels of spending in mind, including 5% and 10% cuts from the projection laid down in April with the 2014 request. The budget- crafting guidance represented the first formal recognition of the long-term effects of the 2011 Budget Control Act, whose first round of widespread, automatic **sequestration** rescissions took effect in March 2013. .
20. **GDA-3964** June 15, 2015 Chairman of the House transportation and Infrastructure Committee, Bill Shuster (R-PA), announced he was drafting legislation to create a federally chartered, but independent, not-for-profit corporation to operate and modernize the U.S. air traffic control system. Some airlines, industry officials, and lawmakers expressed support for **privatization** proposals, and Secretary of Transportation Anthony Foxx responded to Shuster's announcement, saying, "This country deserves a serious conversation about the future of our transportation system." .
21. **GDA-4043** February 3, 2016 Republican leaders in the House Transportation and Infrastructure Committee introduced a $69 billion funding bill, the Aviation Innovation, Reform, and Reauthorization Act, that would move air traffic control operations from the FAA to a not-for-profit corporation. Bill Shuster (R-PA) sponsored the bill. The National Air Traffic Controllers Association and Airlines for America, a trade group for most major airlines, backed the legislation. The committee held hearings on the bill on February 11, and approved the bill the following day. The bill did not go to the full House for a vote. (See June 15, 2015.).

10.5.7 Advanced Automation System

Excerpt from a textbook on systems engineering[214]:

In the late 1970's the FAA had a number of technologies that were ready to move from the laboratory into operational settings. They were associated with the ground and cockpit environment:

- *Discrete Address Beacon System (DABS)*
- *Electronic Tabular Display System (ETABS)*
- *Color Stroker Plan View Displays*

All three technologies were rejected as a new program called the Advanced Automation System (AAS) was created. AAS was supposed to incorporate the ETABS and color display work. The problem is AAS failed and with it the introduction of color displays and electronic tabular display of information was

---

[214] Systems Practices as Common Sense by Walter Sobkiw, CassBeth Publishing, 2011. Sorry for the self-reference.

delayed by years. The DABS program eventually resurfaced as Mode-s and was eventually fielded.

So the big questions are why the delay in introducing these new technologies into Air Traffic Control (ATC) and what impact did these delays have? The simple answer is the user community was able to keep the current system operational within a reasonable performance envelope. The old system just continued to work. The more complex answer is politics, money, and entrenched interests.

New technologies are very disruptive to the status quo. That was true in this case but the status quo were in a better position to influence decisions in Washington D.C. than the smaller companies closer to the new technologies. As long as the current system was not leading to a visible crisis, there was no need to change as perceived by the non-technologist stakeholders.

If we believe that technology is not a commodity that can be created at any time, then the delay of introducing these technologies to the ATC community probably caused irreparable harm. There was a technology growth path that was naturally evolving and it was disrupted and stopped for the air traffic control application.

However, something interesting happened with the AAS program. The FAA is one of three government organizations in the U.S. that have taken the time to develop technology readiness levels. Research and development is part of the FAA as stated in the Federal Aviation Act of 1958..

Some have suggested AAS was a failure because it was never fielded in the U.S. They suggest that AAS was a pure technology effort when technology was not the current need. However, Hughes Aircraft fielded AAS derivatives in Canada, the Pacific Rim, and other countries outside the US. AAS also pioneered many of the technologies we take for granted in our world today. They are:

- *Local Area Networks*
- *Distributed Computing and Workstations*
- *Graphic User Interface (GUI) Windows Based Displays*
- *UNIX which hosted the first Internet Web Servers*

It's unclear what level of funding is attributed to AAS for maturing these technologies that were adopted around the world, but there is no question AAS was stimulating these areas. It's possible that without AAS the Internet may have been delayed by several years as other funding sources would have been needed to help mature these technologies.

So other countries received ATC systems with newer technology than the US and the entire computing world benefited from the spin-offs of AAS[215]*. Interesting turn of events.*

At the time of AAS the Office of Technology Assessment performed an

[215] Hughes Aircraft viewed themselves as a technology company rather than a product company. They worked with industry to mature technology as needed. Their air defense and ATC systems were worldwide. These systems benefited from knowledge gained on AAS. This included the new workstation display, distributed processing, and LAN capabilities.

assessment of the NAS Plan. The following is an excerpt from the same textbook in a section addressing Sustainability and Progress.

In the early 1980's the FAA had concluded that the current Air Traffic Control (ATC) System would start to saturate; reach capacity limits in certain parts of the country that would then affect all flights. The National Air Space (NAS) Plan or Brown Book was developed in response to this future projection of capacity limits. The Office of Technology Assessment (OTA)[216] *performed a review of the NAS plan in 1982 and concluded that it was primarily technology driven and emphasized Enroute ATC*[217]*. According to the OTA "The national air space system is a three-legged stool made up of airports, the ATC system, and procedures for using the airspace".*

The original FAA intent was to significantly raise the automation level of the Enroute systems while the planes were within Enroute airspace. Effectively the planes would be metered and spaced so that the airport peak loads could be spread out in time[218]*. It was a continuation of the flow control concepts at the national level that were found to be very effective.*

It did not matter that the OTA may not have fully understood the impact of the planned automation. It was reasonable to add the other two legs of the ATC system (Airports and Procedures) to the NAS plan. A revised plan was issued the following year in 1983. Many years ago I concluded there are only a few ways to increase capacity of an ATC system.

- ***<u>Cities</u>*** *The first is to build new cities away from existing cities with new airports some distances away from existing cities. The FAA has no control over how and where cities should be built. This is a bigger issue and may actually be the source of the ATC capacity problem and other problems. So, the only answer might be to start to think broader and bigger and realize new cities are needed.*
- ***<u>Bigger Planes</u>*** *The second is to build bigger airplanes and make sure they are filled to capacity. The FAA could encourage the airlines to buy bigger airplanes and increase seating capacity. However, some airports may be unable to handle the bigger airplanes and huge numbers of people arriving and departing. History suggests that is what may have actually happened as the casual traveler compares air travel of the 1970's and early 1980's with air travel today.*
- ***<u>Procedures</u>*** *The third is to change the procedures. The procedures could be*

[216] The OTA was established with The Technology Assessment Act of 1972. It was de-funded in 1995 as part of the 104th Congress "Contract with America".

[217] Review of the FAA 1982 National Airspace System Plan, August 1982, NTIS order #PB83-102772. Library of Congress Catalog Card Number 82-600595, U.S. Government Printing Office, Washington, D.C.

[218] In the early 1970's the FAA established a Central Flow Control Facility to prevent clusters of congestion from disrupting the nationwide air traffic flow.

modified. Approach departure routes could abandon sound abatement rules and subject ground neighborhoods to the stresses of loud noise and possible fear of airplane accidents. Some might even suggest changes to reduce minimum separation standards. Others might suggest removing airplanes from standard air routes[219] *to significantly improve capacity. However, removing airplanes from air routes would require new navigational aids like Global Positioning System (GPS)*[220] *and a new control system. Basic things like Flight Plan Aided Tracking, Fix Posting Determination, etc all embedded within the existing automated system would need changes.*

- ***Automation*** *The fourth is to increase automation to allow more airplanes to be pumped through the system. The reality is the system was very automated circa 1980. Many of the manual activities had been addressed with the introduction of the computer. Also automation is most effective where the airplanes have time to respond and maneuver.*

The job at the tower is to basically watch the airplane on the taxiway and get it safely and quickly to and from the runway via the taxiways. Some airports can be expanded with additional runways, more taxiways, and larger physical terminals. However, many airports that mattered reached their capacity limits.

The Terminal RADAR Approach Control Facility (TRACON) also has little options to increase capacity. The airplanes fly fast and 30 miles away from an airport does not leave much time for metering or other techniques to increase capacity.

If the airport peak loads could be spread out where there was time to respond, such as when the airplane is Enroute, then the system capacity could increase. So, the automation was most appropriate for the Enroute centers.

The problem is the automation of the Enroute centers was captured within the Advanced Automation System Program (AAS) and the Automated En Route ATC (AERA) system concept. From the beginning, the GAO report found the AERA concept was flawed. So, the ambitious goal of automation failed as AAS was restructured to just replace the existing hardware and software with new technology while essentially staying within the same levels of automation. Portions of the GAO report findings are included in this text and summarized with author comments as

---

[219] Air routes are like railroad tracks in the sky. It makes sense given that railroads existed before airplanes. It is easy to see how people from the previous century would adopt this approach for order, efficiency, and safety. Flying from visual point to visual point or navigation beacon to navigation beacon made perfect sense.

[220] First experimental Block-I GPS satellite was launched in 1978. In 1996, U.S. President Bill Clinton issued a policy directive declaring GPS to be a dual-use system. The policy presents a vision for management and use of GPS for military, civil, commercial, and scientific interests, both national and international where the Department of Defense, Department of Transportation, and Department of State manage it as a national asset.

follows[221].

From Executive Summary

- *"Growth. —FAA's traffic forecasts have been too high in the past and there are questions about the methodologies and assumptions underlying the projections on which the NAS Plan is based. Overestimation may have led FAA to foreclose technological options and accelerate the implementation schedule unnecessarily. It may also have led FAA to overestimate the user-fee revenues that will be available to pay for the proposed improvements."*

Author Comment *Growth is an interesting concept. It is unclear how aviation may have changed if the original AAS program were permitted to evolve. Everyone in the community at the time knew that the introduction of the computer into air traffic control was sold as a labor saving device. However, what really happened is the system was transformed to a new level allowing more people to fly while at the same time increasing the labor force as new kinds of activities surfaced. This not only happened in air traffic control but also in every segment of the world that adopted computer technology. What would have happened if AAS as originally envisioned emerged? We may never know.*

- *"En Route Computer Replacement. —FAA's option analysis issued in January 1982 supports upgrading the 10 en route computers that face capacity problems.*[222] *The NAS Plan, released at about the same time, calls instead for replacing the computer hardware (called rehosting the software) in all 20 centers as a part of a long-term plan to increase productivity and reliability as well as capacity. OTA does not find persuasive the reasons advanced by FAA for rejecting the previously preferred option of upgrading only selected en route centers. In addition, the choice of a host computer now may limit the options available to the contractor for the sector suite and software. OTA conferees were sharply divided in their views on this question. Some felt that the choice of a host computer now might limit future ability to benefit from a distributed computer architecture, local area networking, and new techniques in software development. Others believed that, if the host is chosen judiciously, the transition to a new system embodying these advanced and desirable features could be made without difficulty."*

Author Comment *The proposed Hughes architecture was highly distributed in anticipation of the coming automation. Hughes was concerned that the cost of the*

---

[221] Review of the FAA 1982 National Airspace System Plan, August 1982, NTIS order #PB83-102772. Library of Congress Catalog Card Number 82-600595, U.S. Government Printing Office, Washington, D.C.

[222] Federal Aviation Administration, "Response to Congressional Recommendations Regarding the FM's En Route Air Traffic Control Computer System, " report to the Senate and House Appropriations Committees pursuant to Senate report 96-932, DOT/FAA/ AAP-823, January 1982.

rehost program would eventually stop AAS and the full-scale automation envisioned with AERA. In hindsight they were probably correct.

- *"Automation. —While the NAS Plan envisions substantial cost savings due to extensive automation, supporting analysis is not provided in the plan. This analysis is probably still in progress and may take some time to complete, but it would be useful for the interim results to be made available to assist in congressional review of the automation portions of the overall plan. In addition, there is concern on the part of some experts about the ability of human operators to participate effectively in such a highly automated system and to intervene in the event of system error or failure."*

Author Comment *Hughes was very aware of the role of automation in air defense systems. It was common knowledge that moving from a manual system to an automated system significantly reduced fighter intercept time and could mean the difference between winning and losing a battle. Everyone was also aware of the manual air defense and air traffic control system prior to RADAR and its effect on aircraft separation. So, the practitioners in the business did not need to be sold on the concept of AERA. It was intuitively obvious that using machines to find ideal trajectories was significantly safer and faster than using humans. This was all lost in the politics of the day, as air traffic controllers feared losing their jobs and existing companies feared losing their contracts.*

- *"Satellites. —Satellite technology has significant potential applications for communication, and eventually for surveillance and navigation. FAA does not see a role for satellites in the period covered by the NAS Plan. FAA's decision against satellites appears to have been driven by timing and present cost effectiveness, rather than technology readiness or long-term system advantages."*

Author Comment *Satellites were interesting and exciting. However, no one at the time could figure out how satellites could allow more aircraft to be pumped through the system. The USA fortunately spent the money to provide RADAR coverage down to the ground level using gap filler RADARs where they were needed. Hughes had more satellite experience than anyone, but they were unable to see an application to address the ATC capacity problem. Hughes was extremely technology driven, with no real interest in products, so rather than trying to sell unneeded satellites, which they easily could have, the team continued to work the AAS program. While some were concerned about machines failing when offering advanced automation no one seemed concerned about satellite failure.*

- *"User Effects. —A great many of the proposed ATC system improvements are directed to the needs of traffic operating under the instrument flight rules (IFR), particularly while en route at cruise altitude. These improvements will benefit FAA itself by automating functions and reducing labor costs. The principal beneficiaries among users will be air carriers and larger business aircraft. Personal general aviation (GA) users could receive improved weather information, an important benefit; but in order to obtain this benefit and other operational advantages of the new system, more avionics will be required, and there would be restrictions on access to airspace by aircraft not so equipped. The Department of Defense (DOD) too, is concerned about the cost of new ATC avionics and feels that the new plan must be carefully coordinated with the military services to ensure that their mission needs and responsibilities for administration of the airspace are integrated with those of FAA."*

Author Comment *The problem was system capacity. Some radicals were even suggesting taking GA out of the equation entirely so that the system could be sustainable in the future. The cost of avionics for DOD was a red hearing. The DOD budget at the time was at least 10 times more than the FAA budget. This cost would have been trivial compared to the cost of a typical DOD aircraft.*

- *"Cost and Funding. —Implementing the improvements proposed in the 1982 NAS Plan would more than double FAA's facilities and equipment budget through 1987, compared to the last 10 years. FAA has not yet released cost estimates for completing the proposed programs, but it seems likely that expenditures of like magnitude will be needed in the years beyond 1987. FAA proposes to recover 85 percent of its total budget through user fee revenues and a drawdown of the uncommitted Trust Fund balance. The user fee schedule would perpetuate the existing crosssubsidy from airline passengers and shippers of air cargo to GA. Business aviation would benefit particularly because of the extensive use these aircraft make of the IFR system. In addition, higher user fees may dampen the growth of aviation, thereby reducing the revenues expected to pay for the proposed improvements."*

Author Comment *Many organizations were after the FAA trust fund coming from the gate fees in the 1980's and 1990's. For years there were movements to privatize the FAA while shifting all the indirect costs to the taxpayers via various privatization schemes. The reality is air travel is very high technology with huge indirect costs paid for by the taxpayer. From research for new aircraft via DOD to RADAR and other such systems that have no commercial equivalents that business can justify as investment.*

From Technologies

- *"Rand's principal conclusion is that the goal of full automation sought under AERA is a questionable research and development strategy that may present serious problems with regard to safety, efficiency, and increased productivity. An ATC system in which computers make most of the time-critical decisions in controlling aircraft, while the human operator serves in a managerial and back-up role, implies a needlessly complete and irrevocable commitment to automation. Rand argues for an alternative approach, called "shared control, " that would construct the future ATC system as a series of independently operable, serially deployable modules that would aid—not replace— the human controller and keep him routinely involved in the minute-to-minute operation of the system."*

Author Comment *This killed the automation program. Placing the human in the minute-to-minute operation of the system would have been like placing people on the ground with binoculars to radio in positions (like they did at one time) rather than use RADAR. It would have been like not digitizing RADAR and using a computer to generate tracks, instead just staying with the proven broad band system and letting everyone use grease pencils and shrimp boats (like they did at one time).*

AERA is represented as a phased implementation of progressively more elaborate automation and is structured as AERA I, II, and III.

The AERA I goal is to access the flight plan database and use it to perform flight plan conflict probes prior to providing a clearance that would need an update to a flight plan. This automation is of a strategic nature because the database is slowly updated, on the order of minutes. The automation includes graphical projections of the trajectories of the aircraft.

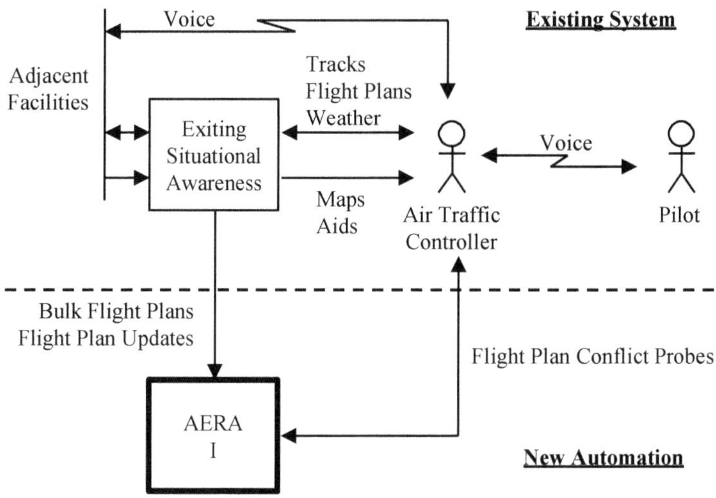

Figure 104 AERA I

In AERA II the goal is to access the tactical database populated by tracks (from RADAR) and winds aloft data to work with the flight plan database and offer a list of suggested clearances. The graphical projections of the trajectories of the aircraft now include the tactical information associated with the tracks. With this real time information a list of possible clearances is offered to a controller.

In AERA III additional automation is added to offer a best clearance suggestion from the list of clearances. It is the choice of the controller to use or not use the information provided by the automation system. If the system could actually achieve this level of automation then the clearances could be data linked directly to the pilot with the air traffic controller becoming more of a system monitor rather than an active decision maker in the system.

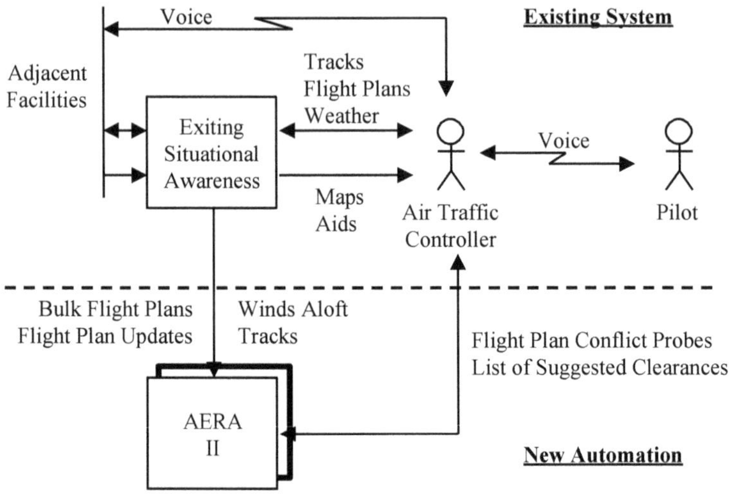

Figure 105 AERA II

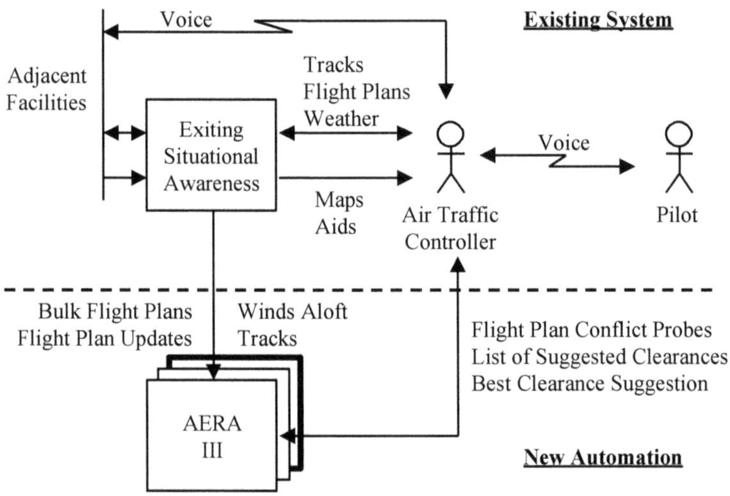

Figure 106 AERA III

Author Comment *It is obviously very easy to draw the AERA pictures. However, turning these pictures into reality is much more difficult. The AAS program was supposed to provide the foundation for AERA. But AAS failed, in part because of the complexities of not only replacing an existing system that evolved over decades, but also because of the technical challenges of AERA, and the political challenges of its suggested levels of automation.*

Today air travel is not a pleasant experience. All flights are booked to maximum capacity. There are no open seats as existed in the 1980's. Even the galleys have been removed to add more seating. Delays were common in the past but today we see delays of hours on the Tarmac. This was unheard of in the past. The bottom line is the system has reached its limits. The question now is will there be restrictions to reduce the number of passengers (airplanes in the sky) or will there be a new system[223]*? The following is a summary of the SE2020 solicitation:*

> *"December 4, 2009. The FAA is soliciting bids from companies interested in competing for NextGen support contracts with an approximate combined value of $7 billion, the largest award in the agency's history. Under the umbrella awards, called System Engineering 2020 (SE2020), the FAA will award as many as five separate contracts for research and development and systems engineering work that will help the agency deliver NextGen.*
>
> *The SE2020 contracts will be awarded to teams of companies, up to three of which will perform research and development work and two of which will perform systems engineering work. This work will complement and enhance major NextGen initiatives already under way, such as Automatic Dependent Surveillance - Broadcast, System Wide Information Management and Data Communications. Contract teams will focus on a series of operational capabilities, including Trajectory Based Operations, Collaborative Air Traffic Management and Reduced Weather Impact. The goal is to achieve early NextGen successes to improve safety and bring greater efficiencies to the nation's airspace system."*

The following is a summary description of the NextGen program:

> *"NextGen is an umbrella term for the ongoing, wide-ranging transformation of the National Airspace System (NAS). At its most basic level, NextGen represents an evolution from a ground-based system of air traffic control to a satellite-based system of air traffic management. This evolution is vital to meeting future demand, and to avoiding gridlock in the sky and at our nation's airports.*
>
> > *NextGen will open America's skies to continued growth and increased safety while reducing aviation's environmental impact.*
> >
> > *We will realize these goals through the development of aviation-specific applications for existing, widely-used technologies, such as the Global Positioning System (GPS) and technological innovation in areas such as weather forecasting, data networking and digital communications. Hand in hand with state-of-the-art technology will be new airport infrastructure and new procedures, including the shift of certain decision-making responsibility from the ground to the cockpit.*
> >
> > *When fully implemented, NextGen will allow more aircraft to safely fly*

---

[223] SE2020 and NextGen are the programs to build a new air traffic control system.

> *closer together on more direct routes, reducing delays and providing unprecedented benefits for the environment and the economy through reductions in carbon emissions, fuel consumption and noise."*

Hindsight is always 20/20. That was a common saying in the ATC community circa 1980. However, the GAO report, which rejected the AERA concept because it was too risky, was the wrong answer. It is interesting they did not give a history of air traffic control and reference the SAGE system. Without that context no one would realize that air traffic control advances were always driven with new and innovative technologies. Certainly satellites were new and innovative and GAO pointed out that the FAA ignored satellites in the plans. However, GAO and others failed to identify how satellites could translate to increased capacity[224]*.*

Perhaps the most significant failure of the GAO report was to realize that air traffic control is a classic control loop with the human in the feedback loop. There were many automated control loops in everyday practice by 1982. For example, radios used automatic frequency and gain control circuits so that they would not drift off frequency and the sound not vary in loudness. Television used these same closed loop control mechanisms to make sure the picture maintained correct brightness, contrast, and color. A simple example of removing any of these automated control systems and placing the human in the loop to control and balance the sound or video by turning knobs would have clearly demonstrated how the current air traffic control system was limited by the human. The poor air traffic controller continuously turns knobs to provide safe and efficient separation services.

The real tragedy is the option offered was an all or nothing option for AERA. Rather than allowing the AERA technology to continue to evolve with limited operational tests, it was abandoned. Hughes with their air defense intercept algorithms could have substantially moved the AERA concept forward. A simple approach of awarding production to IBM for the status quo and a new research and development activity associated with AERA concepts would have been interesting.

Few are aware that at that time there were proponents of moving the entire air traffic control function into the airplane cockpit. The idea was to provide full situational awareness in the cockpit and let the pilots negotiate the airspace.

The AERA technology was the next logical step in automation. It did not propose moving the function into the cockpit. It is unclear how AERA compared to the SAGE system, which introduced the computer into the system with incredible levels of automation and communications networking. It is unclear how it compared with the manned space program and the mission to the moon.

What is clear is that with the removal of AERA from the system goals many

---

[224] Satellites were great for countries with no infrastructure, hostile environments, or spread out over vast bodies of water. It is like cellular phone communications; the infrastructure can be quickly and easily established.

challenges disappeared. It is possible that with AERA many of the computer companies that went out of business in the late 1980's could have remained and perhaps new forms of computing could have surfaced. Perhaps the Internet could have arrived 10 years earlier. So, the impact of this decision had far ranging consequences that no one can really identify except to say that progress certainly stopped and the current system internal sustainability is now in question.

The following is then offered to close out the subject.

AAS is a very important lesson for all sustainability practitioners. In this case the institutions were in place, they were very effective, the money was there, and everyone had the best of intentions. Yet the big goal was never achieved and the system stagnated.

What happened was the age-old battle of the status quo and the new. Eventually the status quo won and the new was abandoned. There were actually camps that formed. IBM and the air traffic controllers represented the status quo. IBM was awarded the AAS production contract. Hughes and many engineers represented the new. Hughes lost the AAS production contract and moved on to field air traffic control systems in Canada and the Pacific Rim. The Pacific Rim shortly followed by Canada were the first to embrace satellites both for data link and position keeping.

So the status quo is extremely powerful and at times dangerous. In the 1980's it was not uncommon for older people to always refer to status quo and the bureaucracy. The bureaucracy was a thing to be avoided. However, that is easier said than done.

In the 1980's there was a huge gap between technologists and everyone else in society. Today that gap is significantly smaller partly because the engineers have abandoned much of their high tech views with downsizing and partly because everyone else has become more technically literate with the Personal Computer, Cell Phones, and the Internet. Most are now familiar with their version of SAGE. The sad part is the system that everyone thought was high risk, developed by extremely high tech people, was dwarfed by what was to come and is now common in this century. The following points summarize the whole sad situation:

- *In the early 80's they were asked to create a new architecture that would not fail and support growth and technology insertion into the next century.*
- *The solution was a highly distributed system with over 300 computers per facility with 30 facilities across the USA.*
- *Never did they visualize hundreds of millions of computers connected together into a single machine, the Internet.*

10.6 B737 MAX JATR Findings

The following is an \extract of the Joint Authorities Technical Review (JATR) report in response to the B737 MAX disaster. The team consisted of technical representatives from the FAA, National Aeronautics and Space Administration (NASA), and civil aviation authorities from Australia, Brazil, Canada, China, Europe, Indonesia, Japan, Singapore, and the United Arab Emirates.[225]

NOTE: The original report included footnotes. The footnote numbers were preserved using a manual footnote approach. These footnotes are in the body of the text and marked as [#].

10.6.1 Mining Results

The JATR was subjected to document mining to try and find key insights that may not be initially apparent[226]. The tool uses rules that the user creates and modifies based on a set of starting rules. The rules themselves eventually become key insights about the document. The mining surfaced the following rules or key insights about the JATR:

- Missing Fault Tolerance
- Compromised Engineering
- Inadequate Systems Engineering
- Inadequate Human Factors Engineering
- B737 is a System
- FAA should
- FAA should Not
- Inadequate Test
- Inadequate FAA and Boeing
- Lost FAA and Boeing Capability
- Compromised Hazard & Safety Analysis
- Compromised Failure Analysis

The following search criteria was used for each rule:

---

[225] Joint Authorities Technical Review Observations, Findings, and Recommendations, Submitted to the Associate Administrator for Aviation Safety, U.S. Federal Aviation Administration October 11, 2019.

[226] Like GDA, SAT is a mining tool developed by this author in 2005. The tool works like an Internet search engine, but it is applied to a single document. The search is based on the user's ability to add dozens of simultaneous search items each with their own unique reporting categories using color and other visualization technique. For these sections the color has been removed but the highlighting of the search criteria was preserved.

<table>
<tr><td>Missing Fault Tolerance</td><td>fault.toler\w+|redundant|faul\w+|fail-safe</td></tr>
<tr><td>Compromised Engineering</td><td>engineer\w+</td></tr>
<tr><td>Inadequate Systems Engineering</td><td>syste\w+ engin\w+|holistic|top-down approach|unintended consequences</td></tr>
<tr><td>Inadequate Human Factors Engineering</td><td>alarm\w+|cognative|overload|human \w+</td></tr>
<tr><td>B737 is a System</td><td>syste\w+</td></tr>
<tr><td>FAA should</td><td>FAA should \w+ \w+ \w+ \w+ \w+</td></tr>
<tr><td>FAA should Not Color</td><td>FAA should not \w+ \w+ \w+ \w+ \w+</td></tr>
<tr><td>Certification Color</td><td>\stest.*cert\w+</td></tr>
<tr><td>Inadequate Test Color</td><td>scenari\w+| tes\w+|worst-case|not adequate</td></tr>
<tr><td>Inadequate FAA and Boeing Color</td><td>not adequat\w+|inadequat\w+|compromis\w+| limited experience and knowledge|experiencelknowledge</td></tr>
<tr><td>Lost FAA and Boeing Capability</td><td>Capability|capable|incapable|no criteria|FAA should develop|Boeing should</td></tr>
<tr><td>Compromised Hazard & Safety Analysis</td><td>hazar\w+|unsafe|safe\w+ analysis|safe\w+ critical|safe\w+ assess\w+|fault|failure analysis</td></tr>
<tr><td>Compromised Failure Analysis</td><td>Failure Analysis|cascading|runaway|catastrophic|worst.case|failur\w+|fail-safe|single failur\w+|cascading|multiple failur\w+|impact of failure</td></tr>
</table>

10.6.2 Background

In March 2017, the Federal Aviation Administration (FAA) issued an amended type certificate to The Boeing Company (Boeing) for the Boeing 737-8 MAX (B737-8 MAX), which was based on the type certificate for the Boeing 737 Next Generation (B737 NG). [1] In February 2018, the FAA approved the Boeing 737-9 MAX (B737-9 MAX). The B737-8 MAX and B737-9 MAX are hereinafter collectively referred to as the B737 MAX.

---

[1] The B737 MAX aircraft series is the fourth generation of the B737 (i.e., a "derivative" or "related" aircraft), succeeding the B737 NG. Boeing applied for certification of the B737-8 MAX (the first in the series) on June 30, 2012, and the FAA certified the aircraft on March 8, 2017. See Type Certificate Data Sheet No. A16WE.

The B737 MAX incorporated a number of design changes from the B737 NG. These changes included, but were not limited to, the incorporation of CFM LEAP-1B Series turbofan engines, structural changes to accommodate the new engines, advanced technology winglets, aft body aerodynamic improvements, fly-by-wire spoilers, and a Maneuvering Characteristics Augmentation System (MCAS) function. Collectively, the changes incorporated into the B737 MAX design resulted in increased fuel efficiency, increased range, and a reduced noise profile compared to its predecessor, the B737 NG.

On October 29, 2018, Lion AIR Flight JT610 (JT610), a B737-8 MAX, crashed shortly after takeoff in Jakarta, Indonesia. On November 7, 2018, the FAA issued Emergency Airworthiness Directive (AD) 2018-23-51 to require revising certificate limitations and operating procedures of the Airplane Flight Manual (AFM) for the B737 MAX to provide the flight crew with runaway horizontal stabilizer trim procedures to follow under certain conditions.

On March 10, 2019, Ethiopian Airlines Flight 302 (ET302), also a B737-8 MAX, crashed shortly after takeoff in Addis Ababa, Ethiopia. On March 13, 2019, the FAA issued an emergency order prohibiting operation of the B737 MAX in the United States.

Because of apparent similarities in factors that may have contributed to these accidents, the FAA Associate Administrator for Aviation Safety established a Joint Authorities Technical Review (JATR) to review the type certification of the flight control **system** on the B737 MAX.

The JATR was chaired by Mr. Christopher Hart, an independent aviation safety professional and former Chairman of the National Transportation Safety Board (NTSB). The remainder of the JATR team was comprised of 28 members from the FAA, [2] the National Aeronautics and Space Administration (NASA), and nine civil aviation authorities (CAAs) representing:

- Australia
- Brazil
- Canada
- China
- European Union
- Indonesia
- Japan
- Singapore
- United Arab Emirates

[2] The FAA participants selected for the JATR team did not participate in certification of the B737 MAX.

The FAA chartered the JATR to review the work conducted during the B737 MAX certification program, to assess whether compliance was shown with the required applicable airworthiness standards related to the flight control **system** and its interfaces, and to recommend improvements to the certification process if warranted. Of particular concern to the FAA in chartering the JATR was the function, evaluation, and certification of the MCAS function on the B737 MAX. [3] The JATR team's review also focused on flight crew training and operational suitability of the design. The JATR team considered whether the appropriate regulations and policy were applied, as well as how applicable regulations and policy material could be improved to enhance **safety**.

The FAA did not charter the JATR to review the entire certification process for all aspects of the aircraft, nor did it task the team to review details related to returning the B737 MAX to service. The FAA made clear that it did not create the JATR to inform its decision on returning the B737 MAX to service.

---

[3] The MCAS function resides in the aircraft's flight control computer.

The JATR team conducted its review from approximately May through September 2019. The team met in person three times during this period for a total of four weeks and exchanged information electronically between meetings. The team received briefings from FAA and Boeing personnel **knowledgeable** of the B737 MAX program, and the team conducted an intensive two- week review of certification compliance documentation and related data held by Boeing. The JATR team also reviewed applicable FAA regulations and guidance. The team's findings and compilation of members' recommendations are commensurate with the information made available to the team and with the time constraints inherent in such a review.

The charter did not require consensus recommendations; the recommendations provided in this submittal are a compilation of team members' recommendations. Also in accordance with the charter, the JATR team produced observations and findings but did not prepare a report. The team endeavored to provide sufficient context through the background information included with each of the 12 main recommendations below and through the detailed supporting observations, findings, and recommendations that follow this Executive Summary.

NOTE: The following sections are from the body of the report. There was also an executive summary that tracked each of these sections. The additional text was added from the executive summary to the following text.

10.6.3 Observations, Findings, and Recommendations

The following observations, findings, and recommendations are based on the data and information that was made accessible to the JATR team. The team's access to some information was limited by factors such as U.S. export controls and the obligations that participants in accident investigations conducted by another State have under International Civil Aviation Organization (ICAO) Annex 13 not to divulge certain information.

Some of the JATR team members' recommendations for the FAA are specifically related to Boeing and/or the B737 MAX, and these recommendations are clearly stated as such. Because the JATR team was also chartered to identify potential enhancements to the certification process, many of the team members' recommendations are general in nature. These general recommendations should not necessarily be construed as a reflection on Boeing or the B737 MAX specifically, but rather as opportunities identified by the JATR team members for the FAA to improve the certification process.

The FAA, European Aviation Safety Agency (EASA), and Transport Canada Civil Aviation previously conducted B737 MAX development assurance certification/validation reviews. The JATR team's findings below are not intended to invalidate the results of those reviews but rather to supplement them with a more focused, event-driven review.

The order of the observations, findings, and recommendations does not imply any level of importance or priority.

10.6.4 The Certification Process

10.6.4.1 Changed Product Rule

Executive Summary

The FAA continually amends aircraft design regulations to improve **safety**. New aircraft designs are required to meet the latest amendments to the regulations, but in some circumstances, changes to previously approved designs can be certified under previous regulatory amendments. The process for determining the applicable amendments is governed by Section 21.101 of Title 14 of the Code of Federal Regulations (CFR), known as the Changed Product Rule. [4] The design regulations for the B737 MAX included a combination of the following:

- Regulatory amendments in effect when the B737 was originally certified in 1967.
- Regulatory amendments in effect when Boeing applied for certification of the B737 MAX project.
- Regulatory amendments in effect during the time between original certification in 1967 and application for certification of the B737 MAX.
- Certain regulatory amendments that became effective after Boeing's application date that the company elected to comply with. [5]
- Special conditions, exemptions, and equivalent level of **safety** findings (typical of similar certification projects).
- Additional design requirements and conditions (ADRCs).

---

[4] The certification procedures for aircraft are in 14 CFR part 21. Subparts A through E specify certain regulations and the applicable airworthiness standards for type certification of new and changed products. Airworthiness standards for transport category aircraft are in 14 CFR parts 25 and 26. The term "changed

product" includes changes that are made through an amended type certificate (ATC), a supplemental type certificate (STC), or an amended STC. Guidance for complying with the Changed Product Rule (14 CFR 21.101) is found in Advisory Circular 21.101-1B, Establishing the Certification Basis of Changed Aeronautical Products, and FAA Order 8110.48A, How to Establish the Certification Basis for Changed Aeronautical Products.

---

[5] An applicant for a change to a type certificate must show that the change and areas affected by the change comply with the applicable airworthiness requirements in effect on the date of the application for the change (i.e., the latest amendment of the regulation), unless the applicant shows that the change meets the criteria for an exception set out in § 21.101(b) or (c). Under § 21.101(b), an applicant may propose a certification basis using an airworthiness requirement in effect before the date of application (but not earlier than the existing certification basis) if the earlier amendment is considered adequate and meets one of the criteria in § 21.101(b) – i.e., the change is not significant (§ 21.101(b)(1)); the area, ***system****, component, equipment, or appliance is not affected by the change (§ 21.101(b)(2)); or compliance with latest amendment would not contribute materially to the level of* ***safety*** *of the product or would be impractical (§ 21.101(b)(3)). Even if an exception is available under § 21.101(b), an applicant may still elect to comply with the latest amendment.*

The Changed Product Rule requires changed areas of the design and areas affected by the change to be assessed for compliance, but allows unaffected areas of the aircraft not to be reassessed.

The JATR team reviewed how the Changed Product Rule process was applied to the certification of the flight control **system** of the B737 MAX. The JATR team determined that the Changed Product Rule process was followed and that the process was effective for addressing discrete changes. However, the team determined that the process did **not adequately** address cumulative effects, **system** integration, and **human factors** issues. The Changed Product Rule process allows the applicant [6] to only address in a limited way changed aspects (and areas affected by the change) and does not require analysis of all interactions at the aircraft level.

The current Changed Product Rule process lacks an adequate assessment of how proposed design changes integrate with existing **systems** and the associated impact of this interaction at the aircraft level. A more fulsome assessment process would apply to establishing the certification basis as well as to finding compliance throughout the certification process.

---

[6] The term "applicants" as used in this document refers to persons applying for a type certificate (TC), a supplemental type certificate (STC), or an amendment

to either a TC or STC. This includes both aircraft manufacturers (often referred to as original equipment manufacturers) and, in the case of STCs and amended STCs, aircraft modifiers as well.

Recommendation R1

Based on the JATR team's observations and findings related to the application of the Changed Product Rule to the certification of the flight control ***system*** *of the B737 MAX, JATR team members recommend that the FAA work with other civil aviation authorities to revise the harmonized approach to the certification of changed products. Changed Product Rules (e.g., 14 CFR §§ 21.19 & 21.101) and associated guidance (e.g., Advisory Circular 21.101-1B and FAA Orders 8110.4C and 8110.48A) should be revised to require a* ***top-down approach*** *whereby every change is evaluated from an integrated whole aircraft* ***system*** *perspective. These revisions should include criteria for determining when core attributes of an existing transport category aircraft design make it* ***incapable*** *of supporting the* ***safety*** *advancements introduced by the latest regulations and should drive a design change or a need for a new type certificate. The aircraft* ***system*** *includes the aircraft itself with all its subsystems, the flight crew, and the maintenance crew.*

These Changed Product Rule revisions should take into consideration the following key principles:

- *A comprehensive integrated* ***system****-level analysis recognizing that in this complex interactive* ***system****, every change could interact with other parts of the* ***system****.*
- *The assessment of proposed design changes on existing* ***systems*** *at the aircraft level includes using development assurance principles,* ***system safety*** *principles, and validation & verification techniques. The level of assessment should be proportional to the impact of the change at the aircraft level.*
- *The consideration of training and qualification of flight and maintenance personnel, as well as detailed explicit procedures for the* ***safe*** *operation of the aircraft.*

Recommendation R1 is based on the following observations, findings, and supporting recommendations related to the JATR team's review of how the Changed Product Rule process was applied to the certification of the B737 MAX. In achieving R1, JATR team members advise the FAA to take actions that include, but are not necessarily limited to, the supporting recommendations below.

- Recommendation R1.1: The FAA, in collaboration with other CAAs, should:

  (a) Revise the harmonized approach to certifying changed products to achieve the expectations of a **top-down approach** intended by 14 CFR 21.101, where every change is evaluated from an integrated, whole aircraft/**human system engineering** perspective and where the whole aircraft is assumed affected by the change(s) until substantiated otherwise. This approach should focus on a **safe** design that as a by- product leads to compliance with regulatory requirements.

(b) Develop criteria for determining when core attributes of an existing design make it **incapable** of supporting the **safety** advancements introduced by the latest regulations and therefore warrant consideration of a design change and/or certification under a new type certificate.

(c) Expand the guidance as to what constitutes a substantial change and what can be considered as only a significant change to address such aspects as changes in software, changes in the roles and responsibilities of the flight crew, and changes to maintenance practices.

- Finding F1.1-A: Although many aspects of the B737 design have been required to meet updated certification requirements each time the type certificate has been amended over the years, some elements of the design and certification remain rooted in the original 1967 certification of the B737-100. The basic federated architecture of the B737 has remained largely unchanged from its original conception and drove many design decisions more than 50 years after it was originally designed [10] In the intervening 50 years, significant advancements have been made in design methodologies and tools and in analysis and analytical tools, which have led to significant improvements in the **safety** of air transportation. While some of these advancements and associated design concepts have been incorporated into the B737 MAX, others have been determined to be impractical for incorporation into the B737 MAX design or certification requirements using current regulations and policies.
- Observation O1.1-A: There are **no criteria** for determining when the core attributes of an existing design make it fundamentally **incapable** of supporting the **safety** advancements introduced by the latest amendments to airworthiness standards.

[10] "Federated architecture" refers to a style of avionics architecture in which each digital flight control function (e.g., autopilot, autothrottle, flight management) has its own ***fault-tolerant*** *computer* ***system****, which is only loosely coupled to the computer* ***systems*** *of other functions.*

- Finding F1.1-B: The guidance given in AC 21.101-1B, *Establishing the Certification Basis of Changed Aeronautical Products*, as to what constitutes a substantial change that requires a new type certificate is insufficient. This guidance is focused on large-scale structural changes and does not consider changes in software or changes in the roles of either the flight crew or the maintenance crew to be "substantial changes."
- Observation O1.1-B: Section 21.101 was designed to lead to a **top-down approach** to the certification of changed products whereby the whole aircraft is assumed to be affected by changes, and compliance with current amendments must be found at the level of the aircraft, unless otherwise noted.
- Finding F1.1-C: Boeing's compliance submissions to the FAA followed a bottom- up approach whereby each change and areas affected by a change were presented separately, showing compliance at the level of the specific regulation and its application to a given change.
- Finding F1.1-D: Several risk and **failure** analyses were mostly done at the level of the change and subsystem and not at an integrated aircraft level.
- Finding F1.1-E: Some of the Boeing **engineers** the JATR team spoke with described the Boeing process in a manner that reflected an emphasis on meeting individual certification requirements, without necessarily having an appreciation for the overall **safety**-based reasons for those requirements.

- Recommendation R1.2: The FAA, in collaboration with other CAAs, should expand the certification process to include "change, areas affected by the change, and ***areas affecting a change***." This expansion should allow for the identification of interactions such as the one between the angle of attack (AOA) **system** and MCAS in the case of the B737 MAX.
  - Observation O1.2-A: The certification process of a derivative aircraft is focused on "change and areas affected by the change." The AOA sensing **system** of the B737 MAX was not changed from the B737 NG and was not affected by any of the changes, including the MCAS.
  - Observation O1.2-B: Based on preliminary accident information, both B737-8 MAX accidents appear to have involved an interaction between the AOA **system** and MCAS.
- Recommendation R1.3: The **FAA should** implement mandatory aircraft-level reviews along the certification process. These reviews should require

risk and **failure** analyses at the integrated aircraft **system**-level including the flight crew.

- Finding F1.3-A: The certification process is focused on a large number of small details which may minimize the opportunity for a "big picture" view.

- Recommendation R1.4: The **FAA should** provide clear definitions of key terms in its guidance for 14 CFR §§ 21.19 and 21.101.
  - Finding F1.4-A: The FAA and Boeing adhered to the applicable regulations, policy, and guidance that existed at the time of application for determining whether a new type certificate (versus amended type certificate) would be required, and for determining the certification basis for the B737 MAX.
  - Finding F1.4-B: During the certification process of the B737 MAX, FAA personnel had no doubt about its suitability to qualify as a derivative aircraft which does not require a new type certificate.
  - Finding F1.4-C: The existing rules and guidance governing the certification process leave much room for interpretation. Key terms such as "substantial" as in "substantially complete investigation" in § 21.19, as well as "affect" as in "areas affected by the change" and "material" as in "contribute materially to the level of **safety**" in § 21.101, are not clearly defined.
- Recommendation R1.5: The **FAA should** define and clearly describe the intent and expected use of an ADRC in available guidance. In addition, the **FAA should** elaborate on the application of ADRCs in future developments (e.g., future applicant modification and supplemental type certificates (STCs)). The **FAA should** identify the legal standing that ensures the adherence to ADRCs for future changes.
  - Observation O1.5-A: ADRCs are identified in the certification basis for the B737 MAX, but the term is not defined in FAA directives or guidance. The term also appears in other aircraft type certificate data sheets (TCDSs).
- Recommendation R1.6: The **FAA should develop** processes for identifying perceptions of vagueness and ambiguity in its guidance and strive to clarify all certification guidance that is deemed vague or incomplete.
  - Observation O1.6-A: Different FAA officials the JATR team spoke with demonstrated differences in opinions about how to apply the Changed Product Rule.
  - Observation O1.6-B: Some FAA officials the JATR team spoke with complained about vague and partial guidance for the

implementation of the Changed Product Rule.

- Recommendation R1.7: The FAA and applicants should develop, validate, and implement analytical tools appropriate for the analysis of complex **systems**.
    - Finding F1.7-A: The requirements of an amended type certificate certification process to focus only on "change and areas affected by the change" may fail to recognize that the whole aircraft **system** (including the flight crew) could be affected by seemingly small changes.
    - Observation O1.7-A: A complicated **system** is characterized by a linear relationship between cause and effect, whereas a complex **system** is characterized by a non-linear relationship between cause and effect, such that small causes could lead to very large effects.
    - Finding F1.7-B: Although the aircraft itself may only be a complicated **system**, the aircraft **system** including the flight crew is a complex **system**.
    - Finding F1.7-C: Analytical tools designed for complicated **systems** may not be sufficient for the analysis of complex **systems**.
- Recommendation R1.8: The **FAA should** ensure that the TCDS for the B737 MAX (TCDS No. A16WE) clearly states which part of 14 CFR 25.1322 (Flightcrew Alerting), and at which amendment level, the B737 MAX complies to.
    - F1.8-A: The A16WE TCDS does not clearly state the applicable amendment level that the B737 MAX complies with for § 25.1322. Significant review and background **knowledge** is required to determine that the B737 MAX is compliant with the following:
        - Amdt 131: (a), (b)(1), (c)(1), (e), and (f).
        - Amdt 38: none, even though this is the certification basis of the B737 NG.
        - Amdt NA: none, § 25.1322 not present in initial part 25 regulation.
        - ADRC: (b)(2), which is technically equivalent to Amdt 38 para (b), and (c)(3).
- Recommendation R1.9: The **FAA should** ensure that TCDSs accurately reflect when compliance is found at the stated amendment level and when compliance is limited to a subset of the aircraft (such as a change).
    - Finding F1.9-A: Compliance with regulatory requirements and

the certification process as a whole are the results of a negotiation process between the applicant and the FAA. The TCDS contains the certification basis for the aircraft, which is the output of the Changed Product Rule process. In some cases, For example, where compliance is limited to a change rather than to the whole aircraft, this negotiated agreement between the applicant and the FAA is not consistently documented. For example, the certification basis for the B737 MAX documented exceptions to the application of some amendments, but not others. Exceptions are listed for 14 CFR 25.607 (typical of about 40 regulations that had exceptions), and not for 14 CFR 25.1302. This indicates that § 25.1302 applies to the entire aircraft; yet, § 25.1302 was only partially applied on the B737 MAX.

- Finding F1.9-B: Because the aircraft alerting **system** is not designed to comply with all aspects of the latest amendment of § 25.1322 (Amendment 131), § 25.1302 cannot be fully applicable. These rules depend on each other, and this is further indication that § 25.1302 was not applied to the entire aircraft despite the TCDS indicating that it was.

10.6.4.2 Development and Use Of Up-To-Date Requirements And Practices

Executive Summary

The JATR team reviewed the regulations, policy, and compliance methods applied to the B737 MAX. The JATR team determined that some regulations, policies, and compliance methods that address **safety** issues related to **system** integration and **human factors** and that were available at the time of the B737 MAX certification process were not applied to the B737 MAX or were only partially applied in a way that failed to achieve the full **safety** benefit. In some cases, this **failure** to achieve the full **safety** benefit associated with the application of the latest compliance methods was because the FAA regulations and guidance were out of date. Another area the JATR team determined is in need of an update is the guidance concerning pilot recognition time and pilot reaction time to **failures**. Additionally, the JATR team determined that new and novel application of specific design features was **not adequately** considered.

Recommendation R2

Based on the JATR team's observations and findings related to the regulations, policy, and compliance methods applied to the B737 MAX, JATR team members recommend that the FAA update regulations and guidance that are out of date and update certification procedures to ensure that the applied requirements, issue papers, means of compliance, and policies fully address the ***safety*** *issues related to state-of-the-art designs employed on new projects. JATR team members also recommend that the FAA review its processes to ensure that regulations and guidance materials are kept up to date.*

Recommendation R2 is based on the following observations, findings, and supporting recommendations related to the JATR team's review of the regulations, policy, and compliance methods applied to the certification of the B737 MAX. In achieving R2, JATR team members advise the FAA to take actions that include, but are not necessarily limited to, the supporting recommendations below.

- Recommendation R2.1: The **FAA should** review the scope of 14 CFR 25.1302 (Installed Systems and Equipment for Use by the Flightcrew) applicability and clearly define in the TCDS the approach taken for certification.
    - Observation O2.1-A: MCAS, although a significant functional change, was never highlighted as an area requiring additional scrutiny from a **human factors** perspective. As a result, no **human factors test** cases were designed to investigate the adequacy of the design.
- Recommendation R2.2: The **FAA should** update AC 25.1302-1, *Installed Systems and Equipment for Use by the Flightcrew*, to clarify the acceptability (or not) of using 14 CFR 25.1302 in changed areas.

o Observation O2.2-A: The application of § 25.1302 to areas of change is not explicitly described in its associated guidance material, AC 25.1302-1. The intent of § 25.1302 is stated as follows in its introductory paragraph:

> This section applies to installed **systems** and equipment intended for flightcrew members' use in operating the airplane from their normally seated positions on the flight deck. The applicant must show that these **systems** and installed equipment, individually and in combination with other such **systems** and equipment, are designed so that qualified flightcrew members trained in their use can **safely** perform all of the tasks associated with the **systems**' and equipment's intended functions.

o Finding F2.2-A: The JATR team's assessment is that the design and evaluation aspects should be considered for the whole of the cockpit environment, and not to components in isolation.

- Recommendation R2.3: The **FAA should** expedite a rule change to 14 CFR 25.1309 (Equipment, Systems, and Installations) and its associated means of compliance in order to implement the recommendations stemming from the Aviation Rulemaking Advisory Committee (ARAC) Systems Design and Analysis Harmonization Working Group (SDAHWG) (2001). This action is necessary to minimize the possibility of applicants using old guidance that is not fully effective for the **system** development and for conducting SSA in the context of increased **system** complexity and interactions.

  - Finding F2.3-A: Although the certification basis for § 25.1309 was updated for the latest amendment per Changed Product Rule analysis, delayed FAA rulemaking for updating § 25.1309 and related guidance according to the recommendations of the ARAC SDAHWG allows applicants to use geriatric guidance for **safety** assessment demonstration.

- Recommendation R2.4: The **FAA should** evaluate applicants' procedures for determining the need of any sub**system** and any change to show compliance with a regulatory requirement. Special attention should be paid to compliance with new requirements.
  - Observation O2.4-A: Boeing did not identify MCAS as requiring compliance with § 25.1302, and MCAS was not assessed for such compliance.
- Recommendation R2.5: Sufficient time and resources should be allocated for the proper treatment of issue papers to avoid inconsistencies and errors.
  - Observation O2.5-A: Issue papers document the negotiation process between the applicant and the FAA to determine the certification basis of a product, establish means of compliance, and resolve other issues.
  - Observation O2.5-B: All issue papers must be closed prior to granting certification.
  - Finding F2.5-A: Some closed B737-8 MAX issue papers contain inconsistencies. For instance, in Issue Paper O-1, MDR and ODR stand for different definitions between Boeing's position and the FAA's response.
  - Finding F2.5-B: Some B737-8 MAX issue papers contain typographical and grammatical errors which could indicate a hurried process.
- Recommendation R2.6: The **FAA should** review its internal procedures to emphasize the need for issue papers when the applicant proposes means of compliance that deviates from advisory circulars.
  - Observation O2.6-A: A combination of ACs was used for demonstrating compliance with **system safety** requirements; no AC/acceptable means of compliance (AMC) was followed in its entirety. The detailed use of the referenced ACs and an

  indication of which sections are applicable was not formally recorded in any certification document that the JATR team reviewed.
  - Finding F2.6-A: The use of a combination of partial ACs as means of compliance should have led the FAA to formalize the agreement with this strategy, possibly by means of an AMC issue paper.
- Recommendation R2.7: If any flight control surface is used in a novel manner, the **FAA should** be directly involved. The **FAA should** assess the need for an issue paper for development of acceptable means of compliance with existing regulations, or develop special conditions if the regulations do not contain adequate or appropriate **safety** standards.
  - Finding F2.7-A: The FAA was not completely unaware of MCAS; however, because the information and discussions about MCAS were so fragmented and were delivered to disconnected groups within the process, it was difficult to recognize the impacts and implications of this **system**. If the FAA technical staff had been fully aware of the details of the MCAS function, the JATR team believes the agency likely would have required an issue paper for using the stabilizer in a way that it had not previously been used. MCAS used the stabilizer to change the column force feel, not trim the aircraft. This is a case of using the control surface in a new way that the regulations never accounted for and should have required an issue paper for further analysis by the FAA. If an issue paper had been required, the JATR team believes it likely would have identified the potential for the stabilizer to overpower the elevator.
- Recommendation R2.8: The **FAA should** establish appropriate pilot recognition times and reaction times, based on substantive scientific studies which take into account the operational environment, the circumstances under which malfunctions may occur, and the effect of surprise.
  - Observation O2.8-A: FAA guidance for **test** flights in AC 25-7D, *Flight Test Guide for Certification of Transport Category Airplanes*, and AC 25.1329-1C, *Approval of Flight Guidance Systems*, require **test** pilots to delay initiation of response to flight control or flight guidance malfunctions to account for pilot recognition time and pilot reaction time. Often, recognition time is assumed to be 1 second, and reaction time is assumed to be 3 seconds. Thus, **test** pilots are told that "Recovery action should not be initiated until 3 seconds after the recognition point" (AC 25.1329-1C).

- Observation O2.8-B: The current guidance recognizes that pilot recognition time may depend on various factors including the nature of the **failure**, but applicants are only required to prepare specific justification of their assumed recognition time if it is less than 1 second.
- Observation O2.8-C: Although the above guidance is aimed at **test** pilots conducting **test** flights, applicants seem to use this guidance as a design assumption that the pilot will be able to respond correctly within 4 seconds of the occurrence of a malfunction. For example, in the case of the B737 MAX, it was assumed that, since MCAS activation rate is 0.27 degrees of horizontal stabilizer movement per second, during the 4 seconds that it would take a pilot to respond to an erroneous activation, the stabilizer will only move a little over 1 degree, which should not create a problem for the pilot to overcome.
- Observation O2.8-D: No studies were found that substantiate the FAA guidance concerning pilot recognition time and pilot reaction time.
- Observation O2.8-E: Several FAA studies with general aviation pilots demonstrate that these general aviation pilots may take many seconds, and in some cases many minutes, to recognize and respond to malfunctions (e.g., DOT/FAA/AM-97/24; DOT/FAA/AM-02/19; DOT/FAA/AM-05/23).
- Observation O2.8-F: A NASA study of abnormal flight events with qualified, current, and active airline pilots also found substantially longer recognition times and reactions times, even in the case of expected events, than the times given in AC 25-7D and AC 25.1329-1C. [11]

---

[11] Casner, S.M., R.W. Geven, and K.T. Williams (2013). The Effectiveness of Airline Pilot Training for Abnormal Events, Human Factors, 55, 477-485.

- Observation O2.8-G: Analysis of aviation accidents demonstrates that pilots may take a significantly longer time to recognize a malfunction and respond to it than the **test** flight guidance suggests. For example, the NTSB states: "When a flight crew is confronted with a sudden, abnormal event, responses are more likely to be delayed or inappropriate." (NTSB/AAR-14/01)
- Observation O2.8-H: Modern aircraft can have subtle **failure** modes that may take substantial amounts of time to be recognized. Furthermore, automation can mask some **failures**

and significantly delay the possibility for the pilot to recognize the malfunction.

- Finding F2.8-A: It is not clear on what the FAA guidance concerning pilot recognition time and pilot reaction time is based.
- Finding F2.8-B: Pilot recognition time and reaction time to a malfunction may depend on the particular nature of the malfunction, the circumstances under which it occurs, the corrective action required, and the individual pilot.
- Finding F2.8-C: There is a substantial difference between the situation of a **test** pilot who is **testing** a particular malfunction with precise fore**knowledge** of the malfunction to be **tested** and the proper response to be initiated, and the situation of a line pilot on a routine revenue flight who is not expecting any malfunction. Thus, guidance that is relevant to **test** flights may not be appropriate for routine revenue flights.
- Finding F2.8-D: The 3-second reaction time assumption dates back decades, to where the performance of the autopilot was constantly monitored by the crew in flight (e.g., guidance given in AC 25.1329-1A, *Automatic Pilot Systems Approval*, dated July 8, 1968). However, with increasing reliability and advances in flight deck alerting and displays, it may no longer be appropriate to assume that the pilot flying will be monitoring the automation as closely as in the past.
- Finding F2.8-E: The FAA's guidance concerning pilot reaction time of 3 seconds may not be appropriate given current aircraft technology and the current operational environment.
- Finding F2.8-F: Although current guidance seems to recognize potential variability in pilot recognition time, it is not clear that applicants are following the spirit of that guidance, because only recognition times of less than 1 second must be formally justified.

- Recommendation R2.9: The **FAA should** require applicants to provide validated and justified pilot recognition and reaction times for any given **failure**, with consideration of all associated flight deck effects within the expected operational environment.
    - This recommendation is based on Observations O2.8-A through O2.8-H and Findings F2.8-A through F2.8-F, above.
- Recommendation R2.10: The **FAA should** provide guidance to **test** pilots to initiate recovery action only once the combined recognition time and reaction time validated for the given **failure** being **tested** have elapsed.

- This recommendation is based on Observations O2.8-A through O2.8-H and Findings F2.8-A through F2.8-F, above.

10.6.4.3 Consistent Interpretation and Application of Requirements

Executive Summary

The JATR team reviewed the certification of the Boeing B737 MAX flight control **system** and related interfaces to assess whether compliance was shown to the applicable design standards and requirements. The JATR team identified concerns with the consistent application and interpretation of regulatory guidance pertaining to the **system safety** assessment (SSA), handling qualities rating method (HQRM), and conformity requirements for **engineering** simulators and devices. The application of 14 CFR § 25.1329 (Flight Guidance System) and § 25.1581 (Airplane Flight Manual - General) and the supporting data and techniques used for § 25.201 (Stall Demonstration) were questioned.

Recommendation R3

Based on the JATR team's observations and findings related to the certification of the B737 MAX flight control ***system*** *and related interfaces, JATR team members recommend that the FAA review the B737 MAX compliance to 14 CFR §§ 25.1329 (Flight Guidance System), 25.1581 (Airplane Flight Manual – General), and 25.201 (Stall Demonstration) and ensure the consistent application and interpretation of regulatory guidance material for the* ***system safety*** *assessment, handling qualities rating method, and conformity requirements for* ***engineering*** *simulators and devices. Should there be a non-compliance, the root cause should be identified and measures implemented to prevent recurrence.*

Recommendation R3 is based on the following observations, findings, and supporting recommendations related to the JATR team's review of the certification of the B737 MAX flight control **system** and related interfaces. In achieving R3, JATR team members advise the FAA to take actions that include, but are not necessarily limited to, the supporting recommendations below.

- Recommendation R3.1: The **FAA should** ensure early involvement by applicants and the FAA in the establishment of the detailed means of compliance for SSA demonstration (e.g., 14 CFR §§ 25.1309 (Equipment, Systems, and Installations) and 25.671 (Control Systems – General)), especially in case any deviations from standard guidance are planned, or if additional guidance not originally intended for §§ 25.1309 and 25.671 is expected to be part of the compliance demonstration.

  - This recommendation is based on Observation O2.6-A and Finding F2.6-A, above.
- Recommendation R3.2: The **FAA should** issue a policy statement on the need for caution and early negotiation with the certification authority when an applicant proposes using additional guidance not originally intended for showing compliance to **system safety** requirements.
  - Observation O3.2-A: The JATR team observed that the SSA takes credit for the probability that the aircraft will be flying in certain portions of the flight envelope, as documented in AC 25-7C. A probability of 1E-3 for the aircraft in the operational flight envelope (OFE) was used in combination with the probability of the **system failure** to achieve the 1E-7 minimum probability required for the "**hazardous**" MCAS **failure** condition. Use of AC 25-7C is not a standard industry approach for § 25.1309 compliance. The JATR team's view of the intent of the probability of 1E-3 for the OFE in the HQRM is to select flight **test** cases for handling qualities evaluation, not to support the quantitative aspects of §§ 25.1309 or 25.672(c) compliance.

- Recommendation R3.3: The **FAA should** implement policy that emphasizes compliance with "safe and reliable" guidance (e.g., AC 25-22, *Certification of Transport Airplane Mechanical Systems*) for establishing minimum reliability requirements for **system** functions used for flight requirements demonstration in addition to the minimum reliability **safety** requirements defined by the FHA process.
  - Observation O3.3-A: The JATR team observed that the minimum required probability for the loss of MCAS is 1E-3 as recorded in the internal **safety** requirements, i.e., consistent with the "minor" classification in the FHA. "Safe and reliable" guidance for **system** functions used for compliance with 14 CFR part 25, subpart B requirements was not considered during development, nor required by the FAA. Because quantitative analysis for "minor" **failure** conditions is not required, it is unclear if the MCAS design would be considered **safe** and reliable to be used as an augmentation function for compliance with flight requirements under 14 CFR part 25, subpart B.
- Recommendation R3.4: The **FAA should** review the natural (bare airframe) stalling characteristics of the B737 MAX to determine if **unsafe** characteristics exist. If **unsafe** characteristics exist, the design of the speed trim **system** (STS)/MCAS/elevator feel shift (EFS) should be reviewed for acceptability.

  - Observation O3.4-A: The original implementation of MCAS was driven primarily by its ability to provide the B737 MAX with FAA-compliant flight characteristics at high speed. An unaugmented design would have been at risk of not meeting 14 CFR part 25 maneuvering characteristics requirements due to aerodynamics.
  - Observation O3.4-B: Extension of MCAS to the low-speed and 1g environment during the flight program was due to unacceptable stall characteristics with STS only. The possibility of a pitch-up tendency during approach to stall was identified for the flaps-up configuration prior to the implementation of MCAS.
  - Finding F3.4-A: The acceptability of the natural stalling characteristics of the aircraft should form the basis for the design and certification of augmentation functions such as EFS and STS (including MCAS) that are used in support of meeting 14 CFR part 25, subpart B requirements.
- Recommendation R3.5: The **FAA should** review 14 CFR 25.201 (Stall Demonstration) compliance for the B737 MAX and determine if the flight control augmentation functions provided by STS/MCAS/EFS constitute a stall identification **system**.
  - Finding F3.5-A: The nose-down pitch identified during Boeing flight **tests** for stall appears to the JATR team to be the product of **system** augmentation with flaps and gear up, and is likely due to stabilizer motion from the MCAS function.
  - Finding F3.5-B: The FAA-accepted Boeing flight **test** technique of freezing column deflection at the onset of EFS was perceived by the JATR team as possibly not meeting the requirements of § 25.201 for natural stall identification from nose-down pitch, not readily arrested. Column/elevator deflection data indicates that there may be an insufficient column input to attempt to arrest the nose-down pitch created by **system** augmentation.
  - Finding F3.5-C: The JATR team considers that the STS/MCAS and EFS functions could be considered as stall identification **systems** or stall protection **systems**, depending on the natural (unaugmented) stall characteristics of the aircraft. From its data review, the JATR team was unable to completely rule out the possibility that these augmentation **systems** function as a stall protection **system**.
- Recommendation R3.6: The **FAA should** review the use of non-standard flight **test** techniques, such as freezing column position at EFS actuation, when showing compliance with 14 CFR 25.201 (Stall Demonstration). The use of non-standard flight **test** techniques may not meet the

associated regulatory requirements.

  - This recommendation is based on Findings F3.5-A, F3.5-B, and F3.5-C, above.

- Recommendation R3.7: The **FAA should** review how compliance was shown for the stall identification **system** on the B737 MAX with respect to inadvertent operation due to **single failures**.
  - Finding F3.7-A: The JATR team considers that **system** features on the B737 MAX might constitute a stall identification **system**. This **system** is vulnerable to inadvertent actuation due to a **single failure**, which would not meet the accepted guidance contained within AC 25-7C, Chapter 8, Section 228.
- Recommendation R3.8: The **FAA should** review the prescriptive use of 3 seconds under 14 CFR 25.255 (Out-of-Trim Characteristics) for the evaluation of mis-trim conditions, especially for automatic trim **systems** where pilot recognition is relied upon to detect and arrest **runaway failures**. The rate of trim used by these automatic **systems** should also be considered in showing compliance to § 25.255.
  - Observation O3.8-A: Out-of-trim characteristics, per the requirements of § 25.255, were found acceptable for a 0.6 unit nose-down out-of-trim condition. This out-of-trim value was determined by 3 seconds of trim input at the flaps-up main electric stabilizer trim rate of 0.2 degrees per second, which is greater than the autopilot trim rate.
  - Observation O3.8-B: The higher MCAS trim rate of 0.27 degrees per second was not selected for the demonstration of compliance with § 25.255, even though **failures** could result in un-commanded stabilizer trim movement at this rate.
  - Finding F3.8-A: Section 25.255 applies to jet upset events and uses a prescriptive 3 seconds as the amount of out-of-trim that could occur before pilot reaction. For automatic trim **systems**, the 3-second reaction time may not be appropriate, depending on the cockpit alerting philosophy and trim **system** architecture and controls.
- Recommendation R3.9: The **FAA should** review the AFM procedure for stabilizer **runaway** and ensure that adequate emphasis is placed on the importance of using main electric stabilizer trim to return to a trimmed state. Crew error should be considered in the event that aisle stand stabilizer cutout switches are used before returning to trim conditions.
  - Finding F3.9-A: Certain stabilizer **runaway failures** may generate significant out- of-trim conditions. Main electric stabilizer trim is considered the primary means to stop **runaway**

stabilizer in Boeing's assumptions and validation **tests**. The degree of stabilizer mis-trim and resulting transient from steady-state flight may result in **hazardous** or even **catastrophic failure** conditions.

- Recommendation R3.10: The **FAA should** review the Boeing assumption of a 4-second pilot reaction time to stabilizer **runaway failures** to ensure that a conservative value is used, since pilot action is required to counter these **failures**.
  - Finding F3.10-A: Manual stabilizer trim wheel forces increase with increased speed and degree of out-of-trim condition. The degree of out-of-trim condition is dependent on pilot recognition and reaction technique and time. Manual stabilizer trim wheel forces could become significant when assumed pilot reaction times are reasonably exceeded, especially for high-speed conditions. During stabilizer **runaway** conditions where main electric stabilizer trim is not available, either due to **system failures** or the erroneous selection of stabilizer cutout switches prior to returning to trim, the crew must use the manual stabilizer trim wheel to return to a trimmed condition.
- Recommendation R3.11: For **failure** of the STS, the **FAA should** consider the requirement to alert flight crews to the reduction in **safety** margins due to the absence of the stability augmentation function provided by the **system**. Consideration should be given to AFM flight envelope limitations or warning/caution statements, if required.
  - Observation O3.11-A: STS inoperative wind-up turns were completed to 1.6g as part of the B737 MAX certification. STS inoperative stalls were completed to stick shaker + 1 second (approach to stall). The JATR team's assessment is that the limited envelope for evaluation of characteristics for this **failure** condition does not support the absence of an envelope limitation in the associated non- normal procedure.
  - Observation O3.11-B: STS inoperative wind-up turns, flown by Boeing during the course of the JATR, did not show any **unsafe** characteristics to approximately 2g.
  - Finding F3.11-A: HQRM guidance from AC 25-7C was applied for the evaluation of control **systems** malfunctions. The application of the probabilistic aspects of this guidance was appropriate to the determination of the required handling qualities, but may not be suitable for evaluation of the **failure** condition per AC 25.1309-1A, *System Design and Analysis*, and AC 25-7C.
  - Finding F3.11-B: For § 25.1309 compliance, the criticality of

the **failure** condition should account for intensifying conditions, such as crew workload or multiple cockpit indications, and effects and interrelationship of **failures** with the flight envelopes.

- Finding F3.11-C: Boeing's application of HQRM allowed for a reduced envelope in the evaluation of SPEED TRIM FAIL, which may not meet the intent of guidance within AC 25-7C and AC 25-1309-1A.

- Recommendation R3.12: Because the guidance provided by the HQRM in AC 25-7D is not harmonized, the **FAA should** determine if continued application of HQRM is appropriate for the evaluation of **failure** conditions and revise the AC accordingly.
  - This recommendation is based on Observations O3.11-A and O3.11-B and Findings F3.11-A, F3.11-B, and F3.11-C, above.
- Recommendation R3.13: The **FAA should** ensure that simulation devices that are used for certification credit have the required level of fidelity for the associated **test**.
  - Observation O3.13-A: During evaluation in the Boeing **engineering** simulator (E- Cab), the JATR team observed that the device does not incorporate control loading on the manual stabilizer trim wheel. As a result, control forces on the manual stabilizer trim wheel are not representative of the aircraft.
- Recommendation R3.14: The **FAA should** review the B737 MAX's compliance to 14 CFR 25.1581 (Airplane Flight Manual – General) and address the inconsistency between AC 25.1581-1 and 14 CFR §§ 25.1581 thru 25.1587, which outline the required information to be included in the AFM and approved under § 25.1581.
  - Finding F3.14-A: Part 25 regulations require that the AFM be approved by the FAA and contain information necessary to **safely** operate the aircraft, including all the normal, non-normal, and emergency operating procedures. Contradictory guidance in AC 25.1581-1 has allowed Boeing AFMs to minimize the content of operating procedures that are subject to FAA scrutiny and approval. The result is that the FCOM/Quick Reference Handbook includes most of the operating procedures, in accordance with FAA guidance (AC 25.1581-1), and has become the master document for procedures to ensure **safe** operation. The FCOM, which is not approved by the FAA, includes **systems** information that is not included in the AFM. Subsequent changes to these procedures can therefore occur without certification oversight. As a result, there is a question

about whether compliance to § 25.1581 in accordance with AC 25.1581-1 for the B737 MAX meets the intent of § 25.1581.

- Recommendation R3.15: The **FAA should** exercise careful oversight and scrutiny of AFM procedures for Boeing aircraft.
  - This recommendation is based on Finding F3.14-A, above.
- Recommendation R3.16: The **FAA should** review the certification of the B737 MAX to Amendment 119 for 14 CFR 25.1329 (Flight Guidance System). If necessary, **system** changes should be introduced to ensure compliance and **safe** operations.
  - Observation O3.16-A: The B737 MAX TCDS shows that the B737 MAX complies with Amendment 119 for § 25.1329 at the whole aircraft level with no exceptions.
  - Observation O3.16-B: The B737 MAX autopilot does not automatically disconnect upon stick shaker activation. The JATR team was unable to determine how compliance was shown to Amendment 119 for § 25.1329.
- Recommendation R3.17: The **FAA should** review the compliance details of the optional head-up display (HUD) approved under STC on the B737 MAX and determine if its alerting meets regulatory requirements.
  - Finding F3.17-A: The JATR team was unable to determine that the third-party HUD installed at the factory follows FAA guidance in AC 25-11B, *Electronic Flight Displays*, because the team could not conclusively determine whether the HUD includes the IAS DISAGREE, ALT DISAGREE, and AOA DISAGREE alerts. Further, the HUD displays an AOA gauge but the head-down display does not display an AOA gauge unless the customer requested this option to be enabled. The alerting presented to the pilot who is using the HUD will be different from the alerting presented to the pilot who is using the head-down display.

10.6.4.4 Additional Observations

<u>**Executive Summary**</u>

No text in executive summary.

The JATR team makes the following additional observations:

- Observation O3.18-A: The high-speed MCAS function was reviewed, and for normal operation (not considering **failure** cases) no concerns were noted.

- Observation O3.18-B: Within the limited scope of the E-Cab session conducted by the JATR team, no **unsafe** conditions were noted with MCAS inoperative for high-speed wind-up turns.
- Observation O3.18-C: The certification of the fly-by-wire spoiler **system**, from a 14 CFR part 25, subpart B perspective, appeared to meet all related requirements.
- Observation O3.18-D: The certification of the B737 MAX for flight in icing was reviewed and judged acceptable with respect to 14 CFR part 25, subpart B requirements.

10.6.4.5 Changes During the Certification Process

Executive Summary

The JATR team reviewed the type certification process (per FAA Order 8110.4C, Type Certification, and related guidance) to determine whether the process includes sufficient feedback paths to accommodate changes in aircraft design and methods of compliance during the lengthy span (e.g., five years) of a typical major aircraft certification program such as the B737 MAX. The JATR team identified specific areas related to the evolution of the design of the MCAS where the certification deliverables were not updated during the certification program to reflect the changes to this function within the flight control **system**. In addition, the design assumptions were **not adequately** reviewed, updated, or validated; possible flight deck effects were not evaluated; the SSA and functional **hazard** assessment (FHA) were not consistently updated; and potential crew workload effects resulting from MCAS design changes were not identified.

Recommendation R4

Based on the JATR team's observations and findings related to the FAA type certification process, JATR team members recommend that the FAA review and update the regulatory guidance pertaining to the type certification process with particular emphasis on early FAA involvement to ensure the FAA is aware of all design assumptions, the aircraft design, and all changes to the design in cases where a changed product process is used. The ***FAA should*** *consider adding feedback paths in the process to ensure that compliance,* ***system safety****, and flight deck/****human factors*** *aspects are considered for the aircraft design throughout its development and certification.*

Recommendation R4 is based on the following observations, findings, and supporting recommendations related to the JATR team's review of the FAA type certification process. In achieving R4, JATR team members advise the FAA to take actions that include, but are not necessarily limited to, the supporting recommendations below.

- Recommendation R4.1: The **FAA should** consider defining objective criteria for FAA familiarization with design details and FAA involvement in compliance findings, to be applied initially and all along the certification process, when development and certification prompt design or compliance method revision.
    - Finding F4.1-A: The JATR team finds it unclear how items to be presented to the FAA BASOO staff are selected. Other authorities have published guidelines in the matter, which typically require items to be presented to the authority based upon critically, novelty, or past **experience**. [Note: In the context of the B737 MAX, the JATR team's assessment is that MCAS should have been considered a novelty (and therefore clearly highlighted to the FAA technical staff) owing to the important differences in function and implementation it has on the B737 MAX compared with the previous MCAS installed on the B767-C2 (tanker).]
    - Finding F4.1-B: Although some FAA personnel may have been briefed on the MCAS function, the JATR team did not have access to the contents of such briefings to evaluate the level of information provided to the FAA. In addition, based on its review, the JATR team concluded that the content of certification deliverables would not have provided FAA technical staff with awareness of key details of the MCAS function on the B737 MAX, including architecture, signal inputs, and limits of authority.
    - Finding F4.1-C: The JATR team found that the certification plans and some certification deliverables (e.g., the preliminary **system safety** assessment (PSSA)) were not updated to describe the expansion of the MCAS function for the low Mach portion of the flight envelope and for compliance with stall-related requirements.
- Recommendation R4.2: The **FAA should** consider developing policy or standards to be followed by applicants on proper visibility, clarity, and consistency of key design and compliance information that is submitted for certification, particularly with new design features.
    - Finding F4.2-A: As an amended type certificate under the Changed Product Rule (§ 21.101), many B737 MAX certification deliverables consisted of revisions to B737 NG certification documents. As a result, the MCAS description,

including architecture, interfaces, logics, etc., is fragmented among several documents.
  - Finding F4.2-B: Although MCAS may have been briefed to some FAA personnel, key aspects of the MCAS function such as intended function description, its interfaces, and architecture, were not directly visible to the FAA in a straightforward manner through the certification deliverable documents.
- Recommendation R4.3: The **FAA should** implement policy or further guidance that emphasizes the need for early coordination with the certification authority for the FHA validation and PSSA review to ensure the proposed **system** architecture can reasonably meet the FHA **safety** requirements. In addition, the **FAA should** emphasize that early involvement with the certification authority is recommended for design changes.
  - Finding F4.3-A: The FAA certification process resulted in FHA/ PSSA information being submitted much too late (at type inspection authorization) for the FAA to have any influence on the proposed MCAS design for the purpose of demonstrating compliance. The FHA information that is delivered to the FAA is the FHA summary. Therefore, the FAA does not have the details of the analysis, which are documented in Boeing's internal coordination sheets (including important FHA assumptions). FAA's visibility into important **system safety** information was therefore incomplete and fragmented.
- Recommendation R4.4: The **FAA should** refuse to accept function descriptions that are fragmented among several documents.
  - This recommendation is based on Finding F4.2-A, above.
- Recommendation R4.5: The **FAA should** require applicants to highlight and properly describe any functional change at the earliest stage possible in the certification process regardless of the preliminary functional **hazard** classification.
  - This recommendation is based on Findings F4.1-A, F4.1-B, and F4.1-C, above.
- Recommendation R4.6: The **FAA should** ensure applicants maintain records of interactions with certification authorities, especially if those interactions lead to agreements affecting documentation and certification deliverables.
  - Observation O4.6-A: Regarding aircraft-level **safety** analyses, the aircraft functional **hazard** assessment was included as a certification deliverable to the FAA in the "Airplane Level FHA and Development Assurance process Certification Plan" (13449

Revision F), but the aircraft **safety** assessment was not. The JATR team was informed that there was an agreement with the certification authorities not to include the aircraft **safety** assessment in the certification plan, but the team could not find the recording of such agreement outside of the agreement inherent in the acceptance of the certification plan.

10.6.4.6 Delegation of certification authority

Executive Summary

Under the FAA's Organization Designation Authorization (ODA) program, the FAA granted Boeing designee authority over parts of the certification project. [7] FAA oversight of the certification process was performed by the FAA's Boeing Aviation Safety Oversight Office (BASOO). [8]

---

7 Under 49 U.S.C. 44702(d), the FAA may delegate to a qualified private person a matter related to issuing certificates or related to the examination, **testing**, and inspection necessary to issue a certificate.

8 FAA's Transport Aircraft Seattle Aircraft Evaluation Group coordinated and assisted in the certification process. FAA also formed a Flight Standardization Board to evaluate and validate Boeing's (as the applicant) proposed training program for the B737 MAX.

The act of delegating, i.e., designating industry as representatives of a CAA, is well established and is common practice by the majority of CAAs around the world. Delegation provides CAAs with a pool of expertise to exercise approvals and findings of compliance within the scope of delegated authority. However, the ongoing oversight of designees and ODAs by the CAA is critically important to provide assurance to the CAA that **safety** and certification work is being carried out satisfactorily.

The BASOO is required to perform a certification function, including making findings of compliance of retained (non-delegated) requirements, while also performing the oversight function of the Boeing ODA. The BASOO must have the resources to carry out these two primary functions without **compromise**. The JATR team concluded that FAA resource shortfalls in the BASOO (and other allocated resources) may have contributed to an **inadequate** number of FAA specialists being involved in the B737 MAX certification program. In some cases, BASOO **engineers** had **limited experience and knowledge** of key technical aspects of the B737 MAX program.

The BASOO delegated a high percentage of approvals and findings of compliance to the Boeing ODA for the B737 MAX program. With adequate FAA engagement and oversight, the extent of delegation does not in itself **compromise safety**. However, in the B737 MAX program, the FAA had **inadequate** awareness of the MCAS function which, coupled with limited involvement, resulted in an inability of the FAA to provide an independent assessment of the adequacy of the Boeing proposed certification activities associated with MCAS. In addition, signs were reported of undue pressures on Boeing ODA **engineering** unit members (E-UMs) performing certification activities on the B737 MAX program, which further erodes the level of assurance in this **system** of delegation.

Recommendation R5

Based on the JATR team's observations and findings related to FAA's oversight by the Boeing Aviation Safety Oversight Office (BASOO), JATR team members recommend that the FAA conduct a workforce review of the BASOO ***engineer*** *staffing level to ensure there is a sufficient number of* ***experience****d specialists to adequately perform certification and oversight duties, commensurate with the extent of work being performed by Boeing. The workforce levels should be such that decisions to retain responsibility for finding compliance are not constrained by a lack of* ***experienced engineers****.*

The ***FAA should*** *review the Boeing Organization Designation Authorization (ODA) work environment and ODA manual to ensure the Boeing ODA* ***engineering*** *unit members (E-UMs) are working without any undue pressure when they are making decisions on behalf of the FAA. This review should include ensuring the E-UMs have open lines of communication to FAA certification* ***engineers*** *without fear of punitive action or process violation.*

Recommendation R5 is based on the following observations, findings, and supporting recommendations related to the JATR team's review of the FAA's oversight of the Boeing ODA. In achieving R5, JATR team members advise the FAA to take actions that include, but are not necessarily limited to, the supporting recommendations below.

- Recommendation R5.1: The **FAA should** identify and implement procedures for increased direct FAA involvement in **safety** critical areas of ODA certification projects. Safety critical areas may include certain regulations, reports, inspections, **tests**, or other critical items. Direct involvement may include the FAA retaining approvals, conducting real-time oversight, or implementing other procedures.
    - Observation O5.1-A: The FAA initially delegated acceptance of approximately 40% of the B737 MAX project's certification plans to the Boeing ODA. Additional certification plans that were originally retained for acceptance by the FAA were later delegated to the Boeing ODA as the certification project

progressed. While the JATR team did not conduct an exhaustive review of other ODAs, the team observed that delegating the acceptance of certification plans does not appear to be a widespread practice for the FAA.

- Finding F5.1-A: The FAA extensively delegated compliance findings on the B737-8 MAX project to the Boeing ODA. Safety critical areas, including **system safety** documents related to MCAS, were initially retained by the FAA and then delegated to the Boeing ODA. (See also Findings F4.1-A, F4.1-B, and F4.1-C.)

o Finding F5.1-B: The JATR team's belief is that FAA involvement in the certification of MCAS would likely have resulted in design changes that would have improved **safety**.

- Recommendation R5.2: The **FAA should** conduct a workforce review of the BASOO **engineer** staffing level to ensure sufficient personnel to adequately perform all assigned duties (including but not limited to: certification document approval, findings of compliance, and ODA oversight).
    - Observation O5.2-A: The certification process of the B737-8 MAX was extensive and produced a large number of large documents.
    - Observation O5.2-B: The Boeing ODA organization is staffed by approximately 1,500 people, whereas the FAA's BASOO is staffed by 45 people.
    - Finding F5.2-A: There may be a lack of capacity and depth of **experience** of BASOO **engineering** members to approve and make findings of compliance for retained items.
        a) Out of 45 BASOO personnel, there are 18 working-level **engineers** and 6 senior **engineers** (24 **engineers** total). The JATR team was unable to conclusively determine the levels of **experience** of the working-level **engineers** and understands at least some of them may be entry-level **engineers**. Depending on the number of entry-level **engineers** in the BASOO, there could be an imbalance of working-level **engineers** in relation to the number of senior **engineers** reasonably expected to be required given the complexity of work by Boeing.
        b) Depending on the number of working-level **engineers** who are entry-level, there could be a training burden that may further impact the capacity of senior **engineers** and program managers.
    - Finding F5.2-B: The allocated staffing levels of 24 BASOO

engineers may not be sufficient to carry out the work associated with retained items and with the conduct of oversight duties.

a) BASOO **engineers** are required to review and find compliance for retained items as well as conduct on-site and desk audits of the Boeing ODA.

b) The BASOO may not be sufficiently staffed to review all the Boeing programs (737, 747, 767, 777, and 787). There are two technical staff assigned per Boeing program. Some of the technical staff are new **engineers** with limited airworthiness **experience**.

- Finding F5.2-C: BASOO **engineers** may not have had the technical insight, due to lack of involvement, to assess compliance.

- Recommendation R5.3: The **FAA should** review the Boeing work environment for E- UMs to ensure the FAA requirements for undue pressure are being complied with such that E-UMs have an acceptable environment to perform certification work on behalf of the FAA.
    - Observation O5.3-A: FAA Order 8100.15B, *Organization Designation Authorization Procedures*, paragraph 3-6, calls on ODAs to administer duties for the FAA without undue pressure or influences from other organizational segments or individuals.
    - Finding F5.3-A: There are signs of undue pressure on E-UMs performing delegated functions, which may be attributed to conflicting priorities and an environment that does not support FAA requirements.
    - Observation O5.3-B: The BASOO conducted oversight interviews of the E-UMs, resulting in a finding and associated corrective action pertaining to undue pressure.
- Recommendation R5.4: The **FAA should** review ODA procedures in order to remove undue burdens and barriers between the Boeing ODA and the FAA and promote cultural changes at both organizations.
    - Observation O5.4-A: The FAA is responsible for establishing the certification basis for new and changed products, including guidance to be followed. Boeing, as the applicant, was ultimately responsible for the design, compliance with the defined certification basis, and delivery of a **safe** product. The FAA is not able to properly perform its reviews if the technical staff is missing an adequate level of information on the proposed change.
    - Observation O5.4-B: In its review of Boeing's ODA manual and related Boeing Process Instructions, the JATR team observed

that Boeing's procedures could be improved to facilitate a culture where Boeing and the FAA work together toward the common goal of **safety** and certification.

- Recommendation R5.5: The **FAA should** emphasize that the ODA **system** should allow for direct contact between the E-UMs and the FAA technical experts without fear of reprisal for the ODA E-UMs. The **FAA should** also reinforce the need for the ODA to protect the E-UMs from reprisal so that the communication is as direct and as open as possible with the FAA technical staff.
    - Finding F5.5-A: There are a number of Boeing internal procedural layers that hinder the E-UMs from directly communicating with the BASOO/FAA **engineers**. If an E-UM has questions or has difficulties with a subject, the E-UM is required to first try to solve the issue within the ODA instead of directly involving the BASOO experts. Although Boeing's internal guidelines documented in D6- 85963, *Guidelines for Communicating Certification Related Issues*, allow E-UMs to directly contact the FAA, this contact is for technical-only communication and only to better understand a documented FAA method of compliance. Even though the communication is allowed between the E-UM and FAA, the E-UM would have to submit a summary of the conversation to the ODA. These procedural layers may prevent "free" communication of issues/concerns to the FAA.
- Recommendation R5.6: The **FAA should** review all oversight corrective actions and survey results (open and closed) raised by the BASOO to identify any **system**ic trends in non-compliances and ensure all open findings are being actioned in the appropriate timeframe.
    - Observation O5.6-A: There have been many Boeing ODA corrective actions initiated and verified by the BASOO since 2009. These corrective actions provide 10 years of oversight findings on the Boeing ODA and are a valuable source of data to analyze and review the performance of the Boeing ODA, including any themes of recurring findings or longstanding open corrective actions.
- Recommendation R5.7: The **FAA should** require Boeing to submit compliance data recommending FAA approval for FAA flight **test** activities. Compliance data submissions should include FAA Form 8100-9, *Statement of Compliance with Airworthiness Standards*, signed by the appropriate E-UM recommending approval of the data.
    - Observation O5.7-A: For FAA flight **test** activities, the Boeing

ODA manual specifically excludes E-UMs' use of "Recommend Approval" using FAA Form 8100-9 for FAA-retained flight **test** reports. This practice of the Boeing ODA not recommending approval of flight **test** data is inconsistent with other ODAs. The Boeing ODA manual states that Boeing will assist and submit the compliance data for approval; however, compliance data submitted by **Boeing should** be accompanied by FAA Form 8100-9(s) signed by the appropriate E-UM(s) recommending approval of these data.

- Finding F5.7-A: The Boeing ODA manual refers to internal procedures documents, which the JATR team believes creates an additional and unnecessary level of complexity. This practice of referring to internal procedures is inconsistent with other ODAs, which have a single manual (standalone document) that contains all necessary information.

10.6.5 Integrated Approach to Development and Certification

10.6.5.1 Holistic, Integrated Aircraft-Level Approach

Executive Summary

The JATR team reviewed the design process of the flight control **system** and the related SSAs for the B737 MAX to assess whether the flight control **system** complies with applicable **system** design and **safety** requirements and standards. The JATR team found that the MCAS was not evaluated as a complete and integrated function in the certification documents that were submitted to the FAA. The lack of a unified top-down development and evaluation of the **system** function and its **safety** analyses, combined with the extensive and fragmented documentation, made it difficult to assess whether compliance was fully demonstrated. The MCAS design was based on data, architecture, and assumptions that were reused from a previous aircraft configuration without sufficient detailed aircraft-level evaluation of the appropriateness of such reuse, and without additional **safety** margins and features to address conditions, omissions, or errors not foreseen in the analyses.

Recommendation R6

*Based on the JATR team's observations and findings related to the design process of the flight control **system** and the related **system safety** assessments for the B737 MAX, JATR team members recommend that the FAA promote a **safety** culture that drives a primary focus on the creation of **safe** products, which in turn* *comply with certification requirements. Aircraft functions should be assessed, not in an incremental and fragmented manner, but* ***holistic****ally at the aircraft level. System function and performance, including the effects of* ***failures****, should be demonstrated and associated assumptions should be challenged to ensure robust designs are realized. The* ***safety*** *analysis process should be integrated with the aircraft development assurance process to ensure all* ***safety*** *requirements and associated assumptions are correct, complete, and verified. The* ***FAA should*** *encourage applicants to have a* ***system safety*** *function that is independent from the design organization, with the authority to impartially assess aircraft* ***safety*** *and influence the aircraft/****system*** *design details. Adoption of a* ***safety*** *management* ***system*** *is one way this can be achieved.*

Recommendation R6 is based on the following observations, findings, and supporting recommendations related to the JATR team's review of the design process of the flight control **system** and the related SSAs for the B737 MAX. In achieving R6, JATR team members advise the FAA to take actions that include, but are not necessarily limited to, the supporting recommendations below.

- Recommendation R6.1: The **FAA should** ensure applicants improve adherence to fail- **safe** design concept principles when designing or modifying **systems**. The **FAA should** encourage applicants not to design only for compliance, but also to follow basic principles to design for **safety** when developing or changing **system** functions. This should include elimination of **hazards** and use of design features, warnings, and procedures.
    - Observation O6.1-A: Proper flight crew action was considered an adequate mitigation to risks such as erroneous activation of MCAS.
    - Finding F6.1-A: The JATR team identified that the design process was not sufficient to identify all the potential MCAS **hazards**. As part of the single- channel speed trim **system**, the MCAS function did not include **fault tolerant** features, such as sensors voting or limits of authority, to limit **failure** effects consistent with the **hazard** classification.
    - Finding F6.1-B: The use of pilot action as a primary mitigation means for MCAS **hazards**, before considering eliminating such **hazards** or providing design features or warnings to mitigate them, is not in accordance with Boeing's process instructions for **safe** design in the conception of MCAS for the B737 MAX.
    - Finding F6.1-C: The JATR team found that there was a missed opportunity to further improve the **system** design through the use of available **fail-safe** design principles and techniques presented in AC 25.1309-1A and in EASA AMC 25.1309 in the

MCAS design.

- Recommendation R6.2: As part of the certification process for transport category airplanes, the **FAA should** examine all "major **hazards**" where a key mitigation is flight crew action to see if they are potentially **catastrophic**. The **FAA should** evaluate the impact of the **hazard** and its mitigations at the aircraft level, including the impact on the crew and cockpit environment, to determine if additional mitigating design features are required.
    - This recommendation is based on Findings F6.1-A, F6.1-B, and F6.1-C, above.
- Recommendation R6.3: The **FAA should** implement policies and further guidance to reinforce that all **system** functions that are used in flight critical functions should implement means for increased **fault tolerance**, such as signal health monitoring, voting means, and **failure** annunciation. Increased **system fault tolerance** should be sought to the extent practicable to accommodate unforeseen **scenarios** or unconfirmed assumptions during **system** operation.
    - This recommendation is based on Findings F6.1-A, F6.1-B, and F6.1-C, above.
- Recommendation R6.4: The **FAA should** implement policies and further guidance to reinforce that workload evaluations should not be limited to the areas affected by the design changes alone. Workload evaluation should be performed with the complete flight deck effects of the **failure** conditions, including associated procedures.
    - Finding F6.4-A: When all flight deck effects are considered, the introduction of the MCAS function invalidated aircraft-level assumptions for flight crew responses related to erroneous AOA **failures** under certain conditions. A complete workload assessment was not performed for validation of the erroneous AOA effects with the added MCAS functionality. The same assumptions for flight crew responses to erroneous AOA were carried over from previous programs without formal validation.
- Recommendation R6.5: The **FAA should** emphasize the need to perform a functional SSA. The complete **system** function, including interfaces and unchanged parts of the implementation, should be assessed. When adding new functions, a complete top-down **safety** assessment process from the aircraft level should be performed. Special emphasis should be given on exercising care for reuse of **safety** assessment analysis information.
    - Finding F6.5-A: An integrated SSA to investigate the MCAS as a complete function was not performed. The **safety** analyses were fragmented among several documents, and parts of the

SSA from the B737 NG were reused in the B737 MAX without sufficient evaluation. ARP4754A section 6, for example, has guidance that should have been used, given Boeing's election to follow ARP4754A as means of compliance.

 - Observation O6.5-A: While the JATR team would not expect applicants to prepare a specific SSA for a flight control law, **safety** analyses should be conducted from a functional perspective. Applicants may document the **safety** analyses in multiple documents provided the documents are well organized and clearly record the results of the **safety** analyses conducted from a functional perspective.

- Recommendation R6.6: The **FAA should** ensure that when new functions are introduced, the applicants develop a new FHA specific to that function that is used to develop design mitigations for identified **hazards**.
  - Finding F6.6-A: There is a perception that the FHA reports are not used to drive the design; rather, they are used to document the design as already defined. The STS and flight control computer (FCC) FHAs were updated reports from the B737 NG, and in the JATR team's assessment, they did not appear to be used as tools to identify new **hazards** related to MCAS and drive design mitigations. As an example, in the hierarchy of **safety** solutions, mitigation by design should be prioritized over warnings and training/procedures. By documenting the as-is configuration, Boeing concluded that pilot training and procedures were sufficient to ensure **safety**.
- Recommendation R6.7: The **FAA should** encourage applicants to have a **system safety** function that is independent from the design organization in order to independently assess aircraft **safety**, and that has the authority to influence the aircraft/**system** design details. Such **system safety** function should ensure that comprehensive and integrated risk, **failure**, and **safety** analyses are performed any time a design change is made that could affect the **safe** operation of the aircraft. Adoption of a **safety** management **system** is one way this can be achieved.
  - Observation O6.7-A: The JATR team could not identify whether Boeing has an independent **safety** group coordinating the **systems safety** analysis and their role within a development program. Each **system** team conducts both the design and related **safety** assessments. It was also noted that flight **test** pilots, including the chief pilot, are often used to validate key design decisions. This is not a problem, as long as the **engineers** have robust information, which might be an issue, considering that the **system** description and SSA documentation are

fragmented.

- Finding F6.7-A: The Boeing analysis of erroneous MCAS activation did **not adequately** take into account what else might be happening at the same time, such as the possibility of an AOA **failure** with all its associated flight deck effects potentially distracting the crew from recognizing the trim action.

- Recommendation R6.8: Given the importance of the single & multiple **failure** (S&MF) analysis or equivalent in the development assurance process, the **FAA should** require the S&MF analysis or equivalent as a certification deliverable to demonstrate **system**-level integration and the effects of **cascading hazards** at the aircraft level.
  - Observation O6.8-A: The aircraft-level S&MF analysis was developed and used by Boeing as an internal document and not as a certification deliverable. The JATR team expects the S&MF analysis to have been a compliance artifact and provided to the FAA to demonstrate **system**-level integration. This was already an EASA recommendation in its certification review item CRI-F6 for the B737-8 MAX.
- Recommendation R6.9: The **FAA should not** accept analysis of a single "**worst-case scenario**" as covering all possible **failure** modes of the related **systems**. The **FAA should** require applicants to analyze each function to identify **failure** modes for each signal input considering all foreseeable **scenarios** and the multiple possible outcomes for each flight phase in their **cascading** effects analysis.
  - Observation O6.9-A: As far as AOA **failures** are concerned, the JATR team observed that the S&MF analysis was limited to a single **worst-case scenario**: loss of AOA on one side plus erroneous AOA on the other side. Other AOA **failures** were not evaluated because the **worst-case failure** modes were analyzed and the **hazard** analyses in the S&MF was limited to only those combined **worst-case failures**. Because this **worst-case scenario** was already considered **catastrophic**, the S&MF analysis was not updated after introduction of MCAS.
  - Finding F6.9-A: Evaluating **worst-case scenario** for the AOA **failures** was **not adequate** to identify the **hazardous** effects (including complete flight deck effects) of the single AOA **failures**.
  - Observation O6.9-B: Boeing **engineers** did not see MCAS as "new or novel," partly because it was already operational on the military tanker version of the B767.
  - Observation O6.9-C: Boeing conducted an S&MF analysis on

Revision C of the STS requirements for MCAS software, which only included high-speed values in its lookup table (as was used in the military tanker version of the B767).

- Observation O6.9-D: During Boeing flight **tests**, the company added low-speed values to the MCAS lookup table in its Revision D of the STS requirements for MCAS.
- Observation O6.9-E: The B737-8 MAX was certified with Revision E of the STS requirements for MCAS software.
- Observation O6.9-F: The SSA was not updated beyond Revision C of the STS requirements for MCAS. The JATR team observed no documented risk, **failure**, or **safety** analyses conducted on the MCAS software beyond Revision C.
- Observation O6.9-G: Boeing determined the high-speed regime to be the critical aspect of MCAS, and thus no revision to the SSA was necessary when the low speeds were added to the software's lookup table.
- Observation O6.9-H: Boeing concluded that multiple erroneous MCAS activations were not worse than a single erroneous activation, based on the assumption that the crew would return the aircraft to a trimmed state (consistent with AC 25-7C guidance) following each activation.

- Recommendation R6.10: The **FAA should not** accept a mitigation for the single "worst- case **scenario**" as mitigating all possible **scenarios**. The **FAA should** ensure that mitigations are developed as appropriate for the multiple outcomes identified in the **cascading** effects analysis.
  - This recommendation is based on Observation O6.9-A and Finding F6.9-A, above.
- Recommendation R6.11: The **FAA should** require applicants to develop an SSA process description to be followed by each **system** for consistency of methodology, use of guidance, and assumptions.
  - Observation O6.11-A: The JATR team was unable to identify a Boeing document that provides a consistent process and methodology for the SSA process to be followed across each **system**. Report templates are provided, but templates are not sufficient to ensure uniformity of analysis.
- Recommendation R6.12: The **FAA should develop** a practice of questioning the validity of assumptions made by the applicant and require substantive support for all such assumptions.
  - Finding F6.12-A: The JATR observed in Issue Paper G-1 that Boeing's rationale for exceptions from current amendments for the B737 MAX was focused on similarity with the B737 NG model and the risk of confusing the pilots by introducing

differences between the two models (e.g., exceptions for § 25.1322). These approaches were driven by Boeing's assumptions that the MAX is a replacement for the NG and that MAX pilots will be **experience**d NG pilots. These assumptions were not warranted, as demonstrated by airlines for which the MAX was the first B737 model to be purchased (e.g., Air Canada), and by new pilots entering service directly to the MAX (e.g., the First Officer on ET302).

- Finding F6.12-B: Basic assumptions about trained and qualified flight crew response to malfunctions used in the design and certification of the B737-8 MAX did not appear to hold in the two accident cases, based on preliminary information.

10.6.5.2 Human Factors

Executive Summary

Humans design, build, maintain, and operate every part of the global aviation **system**. The enviable **safety** record of the aviation **system** is a direct result of **human capabilities**. At the same time, all aviation accidents are the result of **human limitations**. This is not to say that all accidents are the result of **human error**, but of **human limitations**, such as limitations to people's imagination and their ability to foresee, predict, and anticipate possible situations. As the technology becomes more advanced, and as the operational environment becomes more complex, understanding the scope and nature of the interactions between the technology, the human, and the environment becomes more critical to aviation **safety**. This criticality of **human factors** to aviation **safety** has been recognized and has been codified in various rules such as 14 CFR §§ 25.1302 (Installed Systems and Equipment for Use by the Flightcrew), 25.1309 (Equipment, Systems, and Installations), and 25.1322 (Flightcrew Alerting). While issues in human-machine interaction are at the core of all recent aviation accidents and are implicated in the two B737 MAX accidents, the FAA has very few **human factors** and **human system** integration experts on its certification staff. The JATR team identified multiple **human factors**- related issues in the certification process. Because **human factors** is a cross-cutting aspect, related recommendations are made under several of the different areas identified in this summary.

Recommendation R7

Based on the JATR team's observations and findings related to ***human factors****-related issues in the certification process, JATR team members recommend that the*

*FAA integrate and emphasize **human factors** and **human system** integration throughout its certification process. Human factors-relevant policies and guidance should be expanded and clarified, and compliance with such regulatory requirements as 14 CFR §§ 25.1302 (Installed Systems and Equipment for Use by the Flightcrew), 25.1309 (Equipment, Systems, and Installations), and 25.1322 (Flightcrew Alerting) should be thoroughly verified and documented. To enable the thorough analysis and verification of compliance, the **FAA should** expand its aircraft certification resources in **human factors** and in **human system** integration.*

Recommendation R7 is based on the JATR team's identification of **human factors**-related issues in the certification process. These issues are reflected in multiple recommendations throughout the JATR's submittal, including but not limited to Recommendations R1.3, R1.9, R2.1, R2.2, R2.4, R2.8, R2.9, R2.10, R3.8, R3.9, R3.10, R3.11, R3.13, R3.14, R3.15, R3.17, R6.2, R6.4, R9.1, R9.6, R9.7, and R11.2. In achieving R7, JATR team members advise the FAA to also take actions that include, but are not necessarily limited to, the additional supporting recommendation below.

- Recommendation R7.1: The **FAA should** expand its aircraft certification resources in **human factors** and in **human system** integration to enable the thorough analysis and verification of compliance with such regulatory requirements as 14 CFR §§ 25.1302 (Installed Systems and Equipment for Use by the Flightcrew) and 25.1322 (Flightcrew Alerting).
    - Observation O7.1-A: There are very few **human factors** specialists in the FAA's nationwide Aircraft Certification Organization.
    - Observation O7.1-B: The FAA has extremely limited **human factors** and **human system** integration resources in an era where most **safety failures** are linked to human-machine interaction.

- Recommendation R7.2: The **FAA should** review existing guidance material and update as necessary to emphasize the importance of **human factors** and **human system** integration throughout the certification process.
    - Observation O7.2-A: Existing **human factors** guidance material (e.g., AC 25- 1302-1) may be insufficient to emphasize the importance of **human factors** and **human system** integration throughout the certification process. (See also Observations O2.1-A and O2.2-A and Findings F2.2-A and F6.4-A)

10.6.5.3 Development Assurance

Executive Summary

Development assurance is a methodology applied to aircraft and aircraft **systems** to ensure **safe** and compliant designs in increasingly complex and integrated aircraft **systems**. Design and analysis techniques traditionally applied to deterministic risks or to conventional, non-complex **systems** may not provide adequate **safety** coverage for complex **systems**. As evidenced in the B737 MAX, integrated aircraft-level functions, such as the MCAS, present a risk of development error (requirements determination and design errors) and undesirable, unintended effects.

The **system**atic use of development assurance techniques increases confidence that errors in requirements or design, and integration or interaction effects, have been adequately identified and corrected by the applicant.

Boeing elected to meet the objectives of SAE International's Aerospace Recommended Practice 4754A, Guidelines for Development of Civil Aircraft and Systems, (ARP4754A) for development assurance of the B737 MAX. Issue Paper SA-1 documented the methods and means that Boeing used to show that the processes used for B737 MAX **systems** development were, when appropriate, in accordance with the objectives of ARP4754A and were an acceptable means of addressing requirement, design, and implementation errors. The use of ARP4754A is consistent with the guidance contained in FAA Advisory Circular (AC) 20-174, Development of Civil Aircraft and Systems. The JATR team identified areas where the Boeing processes can be improved to more robustly meet the development assurance objectives of ARP4754A.

Recommendation R8

Based on the JATR team's observations and findings related to the development assurance process applied to the design of the flight control ***system*** *of the B737 MAX, JATR team members recommend that the FAA ensure applicants apply industry best practice for development assurance, including requirements management, visibility of assumptions, process assurance activities, and configuration management. The* ***FAA should*** *ensure achievement of the close coupling that is required between the applicant* ***safety*** *analysis process and the development assurance process to classify* ***failure*** *conditions and derive the level of rigor of design development and verification. A current example of industry best practice is SAE International's Aerospace Recommended Practice 4754 (ARP4754).*

The ***FAA should*** *review and amend Advisory Circular 20-174 to clearly articulate the principles of ARP4754A, promoting industry best practice for development assurance of aircraft and aircraft* ***systems*** *to address applicants' design trend of increasing integration between aircraft functions and* ***systems****.*

Recommendation R8 is based on the following observations, findings, and supporting recommendations related to the JATR team's review of the Boeing development assurance process applied to the design of the flight control **system** of the B737 MAX. In achieving R8, JATR team members advise the FAA to take actions that include, but are not necessarily limited to, the supporting recommendations below.

- Recommendation R8.1: The FAA, as part of the BASOO oversight activities, should review the Boeing development assurance process to ensure industry best practice for development assurance is being followed for an integrated approach to design changes at the aircraft, **system**, sub**system** and item levels. Developing internal procedures to more robustly meet the objectives of ARP4754A and the adoption of Dynamic Object-Oriented Requirements System (DOORS) to manage all requirements is one way to achieve this integrated approach.
    - Observation O8.1-A: The Boeing development assurance process was agreed to by the FAA via Issue Paper SA-1; however, the process was not aligned to industry best practice for integrated **systems**.
        - a) Section 3 of the B737 MAX Development Assurance Compliance Plan D925A003-01 states that the development assurance process meets the objectives of ARP4754A; however, the JATR found numerous instances where the development assurance process does not satisfy the objectives of ARP4754A for an integrated approach to design.
        - b) Not all requirements are traceable, and assumptions are managed independent of requirements.
        - c) Boeing attempted to apply ARP4754A methodology to the B737 MAX, However, the benefits could not be fully realized as the application was limited to changed areas. The retirement of older design provides opportunities to use more fulsome assurance methods.
    - Observation O8.1-B: The JATR team's assessment is that Boeing's integration of the design and **safety** analysis is heavily reliant on the use of the chief pilot or **test** pilot to perform development assurance integration functions at the aircraft level.
        - a) It is not clear to the JATR team how pilot verification and validation activities are captured within an integrated approach to design development.
        - b) It is not clear to the JATR team how discipline specialists are identified for assessment of a design change after regression **testing** has been completed, or

how these specialists provide assistance to an aircraft-level integrated assessment.

- o Finding F8.1-A: The Boeing development assurance process, as applied to the B737 MAX, can be improved to more robustly meet the objectives of ARP4754A for an integrated approach to design – specifically, the integration of more complex **systems** and software into legacy aircraft.

- Recommendation R8.2: The FAA, as part of the BASOO oversight activities, should review the Boeing **safety** analysis process, including how candidate items are identified for the S&MF analysis, to ensure **hazards** are assessed in an integrated manner across **systems** and sub**systems**, and all credible **hazards** are identified for assessment at the aircraft level.
  - o Observation O8.2-A: The Boeing **safety** analysis process is not fully aligned with the development assurance process.
    - a) Documenting identified risks and mitigating only the "**worst-case scenario**" does not necessarily identify all critical **failure** modes, particularly when the interaction between related **systems** is not considered.
    - b) Requirements-based **testing** and intended-function **testing** may **not adequately** capture **cascading failure** conditions if the S&MF candidate item list does **not adequately** document a complete set of **hazards**.
  - o Finding F8.2-A: The Boeing **safety** analysis process, as applied to the B737 MAX, can be improved to be more integrated with the development assurance process at the aircraft, **system**, sub**system**, and item levels.

- Recommendation R8.3: The FAA, as part of the BASOO oversight activities, should review the Boeing **safety** analysis process and ensure it is aligned with the Boeing development assurance process to meet the objectives of ARP4754A. A more robust alignment between these two processes will ensure completeness of **hazard** identification in the S&MF candidate list, identification of all critical **failure** modes, and incorporation of the mitigations into the design.
  - o This recommendation is based on Observation O8.2-A and Finding F8.2-A, above.

- Recommendation R8.4: The FAA, as part of the BASOO oversight activities, should review the Boeing process for managing assumptions to ensure assumptions are visible throughout the development assurance and **safety** analysis processes. Increased visibility includes the integrated reassessment of assumptions to ensure that associated **hazards** are appropriately identified and remain valid and that the design complies with functional and **safety** requirements derived from assumptions.

- Observation O8.4-A: The JATR team's assessment is that the approach taken to record assumptions in coordination sheets (and not DOORS) results in a loss of visibility of assumptions through the development assurance process. The assumptions listed in the coordination sheet are not directly visible to **system**-level requirements, and there is no obvious feedback loop to ensure these assumptions remain valid throughout the development process.

- Recommendation R8.5: The FAA, as part of the BASOO oversight activities, should ensure Boeing implements a more iterative approach to verify and validate requirement functional dependencies and assess the interaction between **hazards** identified at the **system** level and the aircraft level. Such an approach would increase the involvement of **system safety** specialists, **human factors** specialists, and pilots to perform independent reviews of potential **hazard** impacts at the aircraft level. This independent review would supplement and inform the aircraft-level development assurance integration activities carried out by the Boeing chief pilot/test pilot.
  - Finding F8.5-A: An opportunity exists for Boeing to adopt an integrated approach for requirements management though use of requirements management tools like DOORS for all requirements. This will improve the robustness of requirements management and verification and validation activities.
    - a) While the JATR team observed that Boeing had managed requirements through a number of different processes, this does not meet the objectives of ARP4754A for an integrated approach to requirements management.
    - b) The process assurance checklist for requirements identified as "Alternate MoC" and "Alternate MoC Plus" may not be sufficient to address the integration effects of the design change.
    - c) Adopting an integrated approach using a requirements management tool like DOORS will allow airworthiness authorities and delegated persons/designees to easily and independently review findings of compliance and understand the interrelationships between **systems** to ensure completeness of certification activities.
  - Finding F8.5-B: Establishing requirements baselines at **system** and sub**system** levels will assist configuration management of requirements throughout the development assurance process.

a) The process to establish a requirements baseline should be aligned to the configuration management process.

b) At a minimum, the establishment of baselines for requirements identified as "safety" will facilitate increased control of these requirements throughout the development assurance process.

- o Observation O8.5-A: DOORS information notes observed by the JATR team read like requirements and were reportedly identified in the coordination sheet but were not identified in DOORS as a requirement to be verified.

- Recommendation R8.6: The FAA, as part of the BASOO oversight activities, should ensure Boeing improves the **system** architecture used for requirements management. This includes expanding the use of a requirements management tool, such as DOORS, to manage all requirements to improve the integration of **system**- and item- level requirements to other **systems** and items and also to parent aircraft-level requirements.
  - o This recommendation is based on Observation O8.5-A and Findings F8.5-A and F8.5-B, above.
- Recommendation R8.7: To the extent applicants rely on original aircraft- and **system**- level assumptions, the **FAA should** ensure the applicants perform a thorough review of **system** design changes to ensure they are not inconsistent with those assumptions.
  - o This recommendation is based on Finding F6.4-A, above.
- Recommendation R8.8: The **FAA should** emphasize in guidance that, besides requirements-based **testing**, the applicant should perform robustness **test** cases for identifying and investigating unexpected **system** effects and flight crew responses. For example, the process should account for evaluation of cases where pilots do not follow the assumptions (e.g., not trimming out the **failure**).
  - o This recommendation is based on Finding F6.4-A, above.
- Recommendation R8.9: The **FAA should develop**, validate, and implement design and analysis models, methodologies, and approaches **capable** of identifying interactions among **systems** such as the **catastrophic** interaction between the AOA **system** and MCAS.
  - o Observation O8.9-A: FAA Order 8110.48A, *How to Establish the Certification Basis for Changed Aeronautical Products*, provides the following guidance in paragraph 2-1: "Essentially, a substantial design change is an alteration to a product that is so extensive that the design models, methodologies, and approaches used to demonstrate a previous compliance finding

cannot be used."

- o Finding F8.9-A: The B737-8 MAX accident **scenarios** were not identified during the **testing** and certification process. This is an indication that the "design models, methodologies, and approaches" used to demonstrate compliance need improvement to identify interactions among **systems**.

- Recommendation R8.10: The **FAA should** review AC 20-174 to ensure that expectations for a **holistic** aircraft-level design assurance practice for transport category aircraft is achieved which includes consideration of all **systems** (including **safety**) requirements and assumptions. In particular, the AC should address how credit can be given for traditional techniques for simple deterministic **systems** within a structured methodology.
  - o Finding F8.10-A: AC 20-174 does not provide clear and unambiguous guidance for the application of ARP4754A to Part 25 Aircraft.
  - o Observation O8.10-A: AC 20-174 provides for limited application of the development assurance process "where traditional techniques have been shown to be acceptable for more traditional **systems** designs."
    - a) Not requiring the more structured techniques be applied as indicated in AC 20-174 may result in misinterpretation that the structured methodology would not be required. This is not the expectation of the ARP4754A.
    - b) There is no definition provided within AC 20-174 to identify what constitutes a "traditional **systems** design" or "traditional techniques."
    - c) Previous design practice considered as "traditional" did not include the design assurance processes rigor provided by ARP4754A. The process is expected to identify, validate, and verify all **system** requirements including **safety** requirements and would include identification and disposition of all assumptions.

- Recommendation R8.11: The **FAA should** ensure applicants provide a full list of all aircraft proposed changes (no matter how trivial), complete with a **system** description and all interfaces associated with each proposed change, such that an informed assessment can be made using established criteria prior to agreeing on the **systems** which will be subject to limited application of a development assurance process.
  - o Finding F8.11-A: The practice of applying a limited application of a development assurance process for modifications to aircraft or **systems** can be improved – specifically, the criteria used to assess each proposed modification and the requirement to satisfy

safety assessment objectives.

- Observation O8.11-A: The limited application of a development assurance process agreed between the FAA and Boeing did **not adequately** establish the criteria for determining which new or modified **systems** require certification compliance findings relative to development assurance.
  a) Each candidate **system** should be critically assessed against a robust set of criteria.
  b) Criteria should be informed by the objectives and requirements of ARP4754A.
  c) The **FAA should** be provided with sufficient insight into the modifications to make an informed assessment of each proposed modification against the established criteria.
  d) The rationale and decisions resulting from this assessment should be documented.

- Recommendation R8.12: The **FAA should** ensure that agreement of any limited application of a development assurance process includes the requirement for the applicant's **safety** analysis processes to satisfy the ARP 4754A **safety** assessment objectives.
  - Observation O8.12-A: The limited application of a development assurance process agreed between the FAA and Boeing did **not adequately** consider the applicant's **safety** analysis process and how that integrates with the tailored development assurance process for complex and integrated **systems**.
    a) The FAA's participation in **system** reviews did not result in ensuring Boeing's process was equivalent to ARP4754A.
    b) The expectation that **safety** requirements be considered within the design assurance process was not realized.
    c) ARP4754A Section 6 provides the necessary guidance for modifications to aircraft or **systems**.
    d) ARP4754A Section 5.1 details the objectives of the **safety** assessment process regarding analysis of functional interactions and interdependencies.

10.6.6 Impact of Design Changes on Operations and Training

10.6.6.1 Impact of Product Design Changes on Operations

Executive Summary

A review of preliminary accident reports KNKT.18.10.35.04 (for Lion AIR Flight JT610) and AI-0/19 (for Ethiopian Airlines Flight 302) indicates that the complex operational environment that faced the flight crews during the events leading up to the accidents and the associated flight crew workload may not have been anticipated in the certification process. Applicants make various assumptions during the requirements definition phase which can influence the design and how that design is certified. Boeing made several assumptions for the B737 MAX which directly influenced the design and certification of MCAS. The evaluation of an applicant's operational design assumptions concerning crew response is under the purview of the FAA Aircraft Evaluation Group (AEG).

FAA Order 8110.4C articulates the need for AEG's early involvement in the certification process, starting at the requirements definition phase. Test pilots working in the certification process may not have complete **knowledge** of operational issues, while pilots working in the operational evaluation process may not have complete **knowledge** of certification issues. This gap may contribute to limited communication between the two processes, creating the potential for a lack of operational insight into the certification process.

Recommendation R9

Based on the JATR team's findings and observations related to the operational design assumptions of crew response applied during the certification process for the flight control ***system*** *of the B737 MAX, JATR team members recommend that the FAA require the integration of certification and operational functions during the certification process. The* ***FAA should*** *be provided all* ***system*** *differences between related aircraft in order to adequately evaluate operational impact,* ***systems*** *integration, and* ***human performance****.*

Recommendation R9 is based on the following observations, findings, and supporting recommendations related to the JATR team's review of the operational design assumptions of crew response that Boeing applied during the certification process for the B737 MAX. In achieving R9, JATR team members advise the FAA to take actions that include, but are not necessarily limited to, the supporting recommendations below.

- Recommendation R9.1: The **FAA should** revise AC 120-53B and FAA Order 8900.1 Volume 8, Chapter 2 to include an assessment of the cumulative effects of changed products, such as differences in aircraft **systems**, displays, flight characteristics, and procedures.
    - Observation O9.1-A: AC 120-53B does not require the cumulative effects on **system** changes to be considered.
    - Observation O9.1-B: Boeing submitted to the FAA's AEG a list of features of the B7378 MAX cockpit which were changed

from the base model B737-800. In Issue Paper O-1, *Type Rating Determination and 14 CFR Training Requirements*, the FAA raised concerns about cumulative effects of **system** changes from the B737 NG to the B737 MAX that may cause greater than level B differences training. Boeing's response to this concern was that there was no precedent in prior Boeing amended type certification projects and that AC 120-53B did not require the cumulative effects on **system** changes to be considered. The FAA accepted Boeing's response on 26 January 2016.

- Recommendation R9.2: The **FAA should** review and if necessary revise AC 120-53B to ensure that the AEG and FSB are provided with all the **system** differences between related aircraft irrespective of **engineering** determination of the **safety** significance.
  - Observation O9.2-A: Issue Paper O-6 and FAA Order 8110.4C articulate AEG's responsibility, among other things, to address Flight Standards considerations such as contribution of operational perspective to **engineering** activities during the type certification process. The Order specifically requires AEG's early involvement in the certification process starting at the requirements definition phase of the **system**'s life-cycle.
  - Finding F9.2-A: The limited information provided to the FSB limited their ability to assess the operational impacts of **failures** of **systems** associated with MCAS and the subsequent requirements for flight crew training. With the information AEG was provided, it is reasonable to conclude that the FSB would not know the full impact of the changed design and thus would be unaware that they had been provided insufficient information to adequately comply with the requirements in FAA Order 8110.4C.
- Recommendation R9.3: Where the assessment of the effectiveness of differences training is not conducted in an aircraft, the **FAA should** require the AEG to use operational flight crew complements (e.g., line captains and line first officers), with a range of flight **experience**, as part of the assessment.
  - Observation O9.3-A: To be consistent with §§ 25.671 and 25.672, and to comply with the guidance in AC 25-7C, Boeing utilized four fundamental assumptions on crew actions in the flight control FHA for the B737 MAX and other Boeing models. The third assumption, taken from AC 25-7C, stated: "The pilot will take immediate action to reduce or eliminate high control forces by re-trimming or changing configuration or flight

conditions."

- Finding F9.3-A: Based on the JATR team's review of preliminary accident information, in both aircraft accidents the flight crew did not appear to meet the "immediate action" assumption. This assumption makes no allowance for differing training and certification requirements for flight crew operating under other CAAs. The FAA requires an air transport license with 1,500 hours **experience** before being employed by a Part 121 operator. Other CAAs have no such requirement, with co-pilots required only to have a commercial pilot's license.

- Recommendation R9.4: The AEG should have deeper involvement during the certification process and collaborate closely with FAA's Aircraft Certification Service (AIR) to ensure they have the proper **knowledge** to make informed decisions about operational suitability issues that may be affected by certification details.
  - Observation O9.4-A: Pilots working in the certification process may not have complete **knowledge** of operational issues, while pilots working in the operational evaluation process may not have complete **knowledge** of certification issues. This may contribute to a lack of communication between the two processes.
  - Finding F9.4-A: Communication of MCAS functionality between certification and AEG was not sufficiently robust for AEG to fully understand MCAS implications in an operational environment.
- Recommendation R9.5: The **FAA should** conduct a study to determine the value of AEG pilots receiving familiarization training to enhance their understanding of certification flight **tests**.
  - This recommendation is based on Observation O9.4-A and Finding F9.4-A, above.
- Recommendation R9.6: The **FAA should** review and if necessary revise AC 25.1302-1, *Installed Systems and Equipment for Use by the Flightcrew,* to ensure that **failures** of related **systems** are assessed taking into account **human performance** and the operational environment utilizing an AEG operational specialist.
  - Observation O9.6-A: A review of preliminary accident reports KNKT.18.10.35.04 and AI-0/19 indicates that the complex operational environment that faced the flight crews and the associated workload may not have been anticipated in the certification process.
  - Finding F9.6-A: AC 25.1302-1 does **not adequately** address the operational aspect of an aircraft's design.

  - Finding F9.6-B: AC 25.1302-1, paragraph 1-2(a), Applicability, lists a number of certification roles that the guidance is directed toward, and the list does not include an operational pilot specialist such as an aviation **safety** inspector from the AEG.
- Recommendation R9.7: The **FAA should** review and if necessary revise guidance material to ensure that operational considerations associated with the design change are adequately risk-assessed to minimise the potential for flight crew error.
  - This recommendation is based on Observation O9.6-A and Findings F9.6-A and F9.6-B, above.

10.6.6.2 Impact of Product Design Changes on Flight Crew Training

Executive Summary

A review of preliminary accident reports KNKT.18.10.35.04 and AI-0/19 indicates that both flights suffered an extreme mis-trim event which involved the activation of the MCAS function. During the certification process, a decision was made to remove information relating to MCAS functionality from the draft Flight Crew Operating Manual (FCOM). This decision meant that the FAA Flight Standardization Board (FSB) was not fully aware of the MCAS function and was not in a position to adequately assess training needs.

The Boeing AFM does not include all the normal, non-normal, and emergency operating procedures as required by regulations. Boeing has included most of the operating procedures in the FCOM in accordance with FAA guidance (AC 25.1581-1, Airplane Flight Manual). This difference between the rule and the guidance enabled Boeing to make changes to aircraft operating procedures (via the FCOM) without requiring FAA approval for such changes. This can result in situations where the FAA is unaware of changes to normal, non-normal, and emergency operating procedures. Systems information is often included in the FCOM and may not be required to be included in the FAA-approved AFM. However, technology, even if it functions without pilot involvement, may be integrated with other aircraft **systems**, such that one **system** or functional **failure** could impact other **systems** and require pilot intervention. When such technologies, **systems**, or possible malfunctions are not included in the FCOM or in the Flight Crew Training Manual (FCTM), the pilot is unlikely to be aware of them and may fail to recognize a malfunction when it occurs or may not know how to respond appropriately.

To be compliant with FAA regulations and guidance material, Boeing utilized four fundamental assumptions on crew actions in the flight control functional **hazard** assessment (FHA) for the B737 MAX and other Boeing models. The third assumption, taken from AC 25-7C, stated: "The pilot will take immediate action to reduce or eliminate high control forces by re-trimming or changing configuration or flight conditions." [9] It is evident from the accident flights that the flight crews' actions were not consistent with Boeing's third operational design assumption.

---

[9] Some of the FAA advisory circulars (ACs) referenced in this document are referred to at different revision levels depending on the context. Where the JATR team made an observation or finding about an AC as applied to the certification of the B737 MAX, the revision of the AC in effect at the time of certification was the version reviewed by the JATR team and is referenced accordingly. If such an AC has since been revised, the later revision of the AC is referred to in observations or findings about current content and in recommendations for improvements to FAA guidance. For example, several references are made to AC 25-7C, which was current at the time of the B737 MAX certification program and was used as compliance guidance. Other references are made to AC 25-7D, which is the current version of the AC and is therefore referred to in observations and findings about current content and in the JATR team's recommendations for future enhancements to the AC.

<u>Recommendation R10</u>

*Based on the JATR team's findings and observations related to flight crew training, JATR team members recommend that the FAA require a documented process to determine what information will be included in the Airplane Flight Manual, the Flight Crew Operating Manual, and the Flight Crew Training Manual. The **FAA should** review training programs to ensure flight crews are competent in the handling of mis-trim events.*

Recommendation R10 is based on the following observations, findings, and supporting recommendations related to the JATR team's review of the FCOM, FCTM, and AFM developed during the certification process for the B7378 MAX. In achieving R10, JATR team members advise the FAA to take actions that include, but are not necessarily limited to, the supporting recommendations below.

- Recommendation R10.1: The **FAA should** include in the FSB report the flight **experience** level and qualification of the flight crew used to assess the effectiveness of the differences training.
    - Finding F10.1-A: Boeing's **test** pilots are not a representative sample of the operators' pilot population.
    - Finding F10.1-B: The AEG pilots are not a representative sample of the operators' pilot population.
    - Finding F10.1-C: A validation flight conducted under AC 120.53B is conducted with an **experience**d line captain in the

left seat, and includes an **experience**d flight **test** pilot in the right seat as a **safety** pilot.

  - Finding F10.1-D: The AEG's evaluation flights do not evaluate crew performance and do not represent operators' pilots' **experience** level or operation.
  - This recommendation is also based on Observation O9.3-A and Finding F9.3-A, above.

- Recommendation R10.2: The **FAA should** review the B737 MAX type rating training program to include training in the operation of the manual stabilizer trim wheel throughout the speed range.
  - Observation O10.2-A: A review of preliminary accident reports KNKT.18.10.35.04 and AI-0/19 indicates both flights suffered an extreme mis- trim event which involved the activation of the MCAS function.
  - Finding F10.2-A: A review of the B737 MAX type rating training syllabus indicates that, although exercises are conducted in the flight simulator to address a STAB TRIM **runaway**, the syllabus does not specifically address awareness of airspeed versus the forces required to manually trim the aircraft and to recognize and correct a mis-trim state.
- Recommendation R10.3: The **FAA should** require operators of the B737 to include operation of the manual stabilizer trim wheel throughout the speed range in their recurrent training programs.
  - This recommendation is based on Observation O10.2-A and Finding F10.2-A, above.
- Recommendation R10.4: The **FAA should** add a special emphasis training item to the B737 FSB Report to include training in the operation of the main electric stabilizer trim and the manual stabilizer trim wheel and recovery from a mis-trim state throughout the speed range.
  - This recommendation is based on Observation O10.2-A and Finding F10.2-A, above.
- Recommendation R10.5: The **FAA should develop** a documented process to determine what information will be included in the AFM, FCOM, and FCTM. The process must include agreement from all disciplines (e.g., certification, operations, maintenance, **human factors**) for the **system** or function descriptions to be removed.
  - Observation O10.5-A: Information related to the MCAS functionality within the FCC originally was in the draft FCOM and was subsequently removed (around the time of MCAS Revision D, in early 2016), but without a formal process in place to ensure agreement from all disciplines on the removal of that

information. Technology, even if it functions without pilot involvement, may be integrated with other aircraft **systems**. One **system** or functional **failure** could impact other **systems** requiring pilot involvement.

- Finding F10.5-A: Information related to MCAS functionality and **failure scenarios** is critical for pilot **knowledge** and understanding of the **system** as it interfaces with the aircraft's trim **system** and AOA inputs.

- R10 is also supported by Recommendation R3.14 and accompanying Finding F3.14-A, and by Recommendation R9.2 and accompanying Observation O9.2-A and Finding F9.2- A, above.

10.6.6.3 Impact of Product Design Changes on Maintenance Training

Executive Summary

A review of preliminary accident reports KNKT.18.10.35.04 (for Lion AIR Flight JT610) and AI-0/19 (for Ethiopian Airlines Flight 302) indicates that the complex operational environment that faced the flight crews during the events leading up to the accidents and the associated flight crew workload may not have been anticipated in the certification process. Applicants make various assumptions during the requirements definition phase which can influence the design and how that design is certified. Boeing made several assumptions for the B737 MAX which directly influenced the design and certification of MCAS. The evaluation of an applicant's operational design assumptions concerning crew response is under the purview of the FAA Aircraft Evaluation Group (AEG).

FAA Order 8110.4C articulates the need for AEG's early involvement in the certification process, starting at the requirements definition phase. Test pilots working in the certification process may not have complete **knowledge** of operational issues, while pilots working in the operational evaluation process may not have complete **knowledge** of certification issues. This gap may contribute to limited communication between the two processes, creating the potential for a lack of operational insight into the certification process.

Recommendation R11

JATR team members recommend that the FAA conduct a study to determine the adequacy of policy, guidance, and assumptions related to maintenance and ground handling training requirements.

In furtherance of R11, JATR team members advise the FAA to take actions that include, but are not necessarily limited to, the supporting recommendations below.

- Recommendation R11.1: The **FAA should** conduct a study to focus on adequacy of maintenance and ground handling differences training requirements for transport category aircraft.
  - Observation O11.1-A: JATR tasking included assessing the adequacy of policy/guidance and assumptions related to training of mechanics and ground handlers for new and related aircraft. The B737 MAX Maintenance Review Board Chairman briefed the JATR team. The JATR team solicited an AEG maintenance specialist that was not associated with the B737 MAX certification activities for discussion.
  - Finding F11.1-A: The JATR team was unable to make a determination of the adequacy of policy/guidance and assumptions related to training of mechanics and ground handlers for new/related aircraft.
- Recommendation R11.2: The **FAA should develop** regulatory requirements to consider and mitigate potential errors by maintenance technicians and by ground handling personnel as part of the certification process of a product.
  - Observation O11.2-A: Section 25.1302 requires applicants to consider and mitigate potential flight crew errors.
  - Observation O11.2-B: There are no aircraft-level regulatory requirements, equivalent to § 25.1302, to consider and mitigate potential errors by maintenance technicians or by ground handling personnel.
  - Observation O11.2-C: Maintenance and ground handling errors have contributed to several accidents and multiple incidents, and maintenance issues might also be relevant to the Lion Air B737 MAX accident based on the preliminary report.

10.6.7 Post-Certification Activities

10.6.7.1 Post-Certification Corrective Actions and Data Sharing

Executive Summary

In accordance with its charter, the JATR team focused on reviewing the flight controls work conducted by Boeing and the FAA leading up to certification of the B737 MAX. The team did not conduct an in-depth review of post-certification activities, as this was beyond the initial scope of the JATR. However, during the course of its review, the team became aware of some aspects of post-certification activities. As a result, the team took advantage of the provision in the charter for expanding the JATR's scope at the discretion of the Chair and Co-chair in order to identify additional observations and recommendations that have the potential for further enhancing aviation **safety**.

Recommendation R12

*JATR team members recommend that the FAA review its policies for analyzing **safety** risk and implementing interim airworthiness directive action following a fatal transport aircraft accident. The **FAA should** ensure that it shares post-accident **safety** information with the international community to the maximum extent possible.*

Recommendation R12 is based on the following observations, findings, and supporting recommendations. In achieving R12, JATR team members advise the FAA to take actions that include, but are not necessarily limited to, the supporting recommendations below.

- Recommendation R12.1: The **FAA should** review FAA Order 8110.107A, *Monitor Safety/Analyze Data*, and consider reducing the control program risk guideline for post- accident corrective action if a **catastrophic** fatal accident of a transport category aircraft has occurred. For example, the allowable FAA Monitor Safety/Analyze Data (MSAD) guidelines for control program fleet risk for the related corrective action could be reduced to between 10% and 25% of their normal values.
    - Observation O12.1-A: The FAA uses the MSAD process, Order 8110.107A, to manage potential **safety** issues. If an **unsafe** condition is discovered, the FAA uses the MSAD process to assess the adequacy of the timeline to implement a corrective action (the airworthiness directive (AD) compliance time) using quantitative risk analysis. The FAA compares the calculated control program fleet and individual risk to an allowable risk guideline.
    - Observation O12.1-B: Most of the **safety** issues assessed and managed using the MSAD process are triggered by in-service data, production escapes, or **engineering** discoveries. Actions taken in response to these precursors, through use of the MSAD process, generally proactively prevent a fatal accident from occurring.
    - Finding F12.1-A: It is evident that the impact of a second fatal transport aircraft accident due to the same cause far exceeds the impact of the first. When the MSAD process is initiated due to a

fatal transport accident, there should be lower risk tolerance for a second accident and the control program fleet risk guideline should be reduced.

- Recommendation R12.2: The FAA, in harmonization with other CAAs, should review the airworthiness directive processes to determine the need and proper intervals for a flight crew pre-flight briefing when an interim action AD mandates an existing AFM procedure or mandates a revision to the AFM to address a major contributing factor to a **catastrophic** fatal accident of a transport category aircraft.
    - Observation O12.2-A: After a **catastrophic** fatal accident, an interim corrective action is often issued to prevent a second accident. Sometimes flight crew procedural changes are used, and the interim action AD requires a revision to the AFM.
    - Finding F12.2-A: Flight crew procedural changes can be ineffective. After the Helios Airways Flight 522 accident in 2005, the FAA issued AD 2006-13-13 that required a flight crew recall item: if the altitude warning horn sounds, don the oxygen masks. After issuance of the AD, an FAA inspector was performing an enroute inspection of a major U.S. airline B737 flight crew when the altitude warning horn sounded. Despite the AFM revision, the crew did not don their masks as required. [12]
    - Finding F12.2-B: A method to increase the effectiveness of a flight crew procedural change is to require that the AFM revision be part of a pre-flight briefing. Having briefed a procedure, the crew is more likely to remember and perform the procedure correctly if the need arises during flight. This briefing could be performed less frequently than every flight, For example, before the first flight of the day or other suitable interval.
- Recommendation R12.3: Where the FAA assigns responsibility for continued operational **safety** oversight of a product to a different FAA office than the one that conducted oversight of the type certification, the agency should ensure that it has sufficient mechanisms in place for the transfer of requisite technical **knowledge** about the design to the responsible office.
    - Observation O12.3-A: The FAA BASOO is responsible for overseeing the Boeing ODA and certification of Boeing products, while the Seattle Aircraft Certification Office (SACO) is responsible for overseeing continued operational **safety** management of Boeing products once they are certificated. This transfer of responsibility after the product is certificated was not

a review area of the JATR team, but the team assumes the transfer may involve familiarizing and/or briefing SACO staff on design details.

---

12 After the FAA issued AD 2006-13-13, it received continuing reports of in-service events involving ***failure*** *of the flight crew to recognize and react properly to valid cabin altitude warning horns. Therefore, the FAA issued AD 2008-23-07 that required a new flight crew briefing before the first flight of the day and following any change in flight crewmembers, in addition to the existing AFM procedures.*

- Observation O12.3-B: Some details, such as the **system safety** analyses related to the MCAS function, were fragmented among several documents for the B737 MAX. This could hinder the successful transfer of information to the SACO for the purpose of overseeing the continued operational **safety** management of the product.

- Recommendation R12.4: The **FAA should** review its **safety** information sharing policy to ensure that it shares technical **safety** information with other CAAs to the maximum extent possible. Maximum sharing of such information would enhance **safety** and minimize incorrect speculation by parties that are not participants in an ongoing accident investigation.
  - Observation O12.4-A: As a participant in an accident investigation conducted by another State, the FAA is obligated under International Civil Aviation Organization (ICAO) Annex 13, *Aircraft Accident and Incident Investigation*, not to divulge information on the progress and the findings of the investigation without the express consent of the State conducting the investigation.
  - Observation O12.4-B: A benefit of participating in an accident investigation as the State of Design is that it allows risks to be addressed by the State of Design as quickly as possible. [13] Unfortunately, due to constraints on the flow of information from the design state and other CAAs, the third-party CAAs are reliant on the State of Design to act in their interest. The State of Design will apply their own risk processes as influenced by their regulatory and cultural environment. Delays or absence of authoritative and consistent communication results in the outside party's speculation.
  - Observation O12.4-C: ICAO Annex 13 also recommends that, "States should promote the establishment of **safety** information sharing networks among all users of the aviation **system** and should facilitate the free exchange of information on actual and

potential **safety** deficiencies."

- Finding F12.4-A: Restrictions on the flow of **safety** information impacted the capacity and efficiency of the JATR under the umbrella of, "the accidents are still under investigation."

Part 21 defines "State of Design" as "the country or jurisdiction having regulatory authority over the organization responsible for the design and continued airworthiness of a civil aeronautical product or article." 14 CFR 21.1(b)(8).

10.7 Jet Airliners

Table 47 Aircraft Currently in Production (2019)

Type	Country	Engines	First Flight	Airline service entry	Number Built	In Service (2018 / 19)
Embraer ERJ 135 ERJ 140 ERJ 145	Brazil	2	1995	1996	1,213 (Oct 2017)	505
Embraer E-170/E-175/E-190/E-195	Brazil	2	2002	2004	1,414 (Mar 2018)	1346
Airbus A220	Canada	2	2013	2016	49 (Dec 2018)	39
Bombardier CRJ700 CRJ705 CRJ900 CRJ1000	Canada	2	1999	2001	822 (Dec 2017)	777
Comac ARJ21 Xiangfeng	China	2	2008	2015	6	5
Comac C919	China	2	2017	2021 (planned)	1	-
Airbus A319 A320 A321	France	2	1986	1987	9,086 (Oct 2019)	7465
Airbus A330	France	2	1992	1994	1,479 (Oct 2019)	1265
Airbus A350 XWB	France	2	2013	2014	320 (Oct 2019)	185
Airbus A380	France	4	2005	2007	239 (Oct 2019)	223
Mitsubishi Regional Jet	Japan	2	2015	2020 (planned)	5 (2017)	-
Irkut MC-21	Russia	2	2017	2020 (planned)	4	-
Sukhoi Superjet SSJ100	Russia	2	2008	2011	169 (Jul. 2018)	114
Antonov An-148 An-158	Ukraine	2	2004	2009	35	7
Boeing 737	USA	2	1967	1968	10,162 (Jul 2018)	7310
Boeing 737 MAX grounded in 2018 may fly in 2020	USA	2	2015	2019	**387 Orders: 4930**	**0 (2019)**
Boeing 747	USA	4	1969	1970	1,546 (Jul 2018)	462
Boeing 767	USA	2	1981	1982	1,116 (Jul 2018)	742
Boeing 777	USA	2	1994	1995	1,559	1416

Table 47 Aircraft Currently in Production (2019)

Type	Country	Engines	First Flight	Airline service entry	Number Built	In Service (2018 / 19)
					(Jul 2018)	
Boeing 787 Dreamliner	USA	2	2009	2011	716 (Jul 2018)	675
Ilyushin Il-96	USSR	4	1988	1992	30	16
Tupolev Tu-204 Tu-214	USSR	2	1989	1996	85 (Dec 2017)	17

Table 48 Out of Production (2019)

Type	Country	Engines	First Flight	Service entry	End of Production	Number Built	In Service (2018)
Bombardier CRJ100 CRJ200/CRJ440	Canada	2	1991	1992	2006	1,021	498
Airbus A300	France	2	1972	1974	2007	561	212
Airbus A310	France	2	1982	1983	1998	255	31
Airbus A318	France	2	2002	2003	2013	80 (Nov 2015)	41
Airbus A340	France	4	1991	1993	2011	377	159
Fairchild-Dornier 328JET	Germany	2	1998	1999	2002	110	11
Fokker F28 Fellowship	Netherlands	2	1967	1969	1987	241	1
Fokker 70	Netherlands	2	1993	1994	1997	48	23
Fokker 100	Netherlands	2	1986	1988	1997	283	109
British Aerospace BAe146/Avro RJ	UK	4	1981	1983	2001	387	118
McDonnell Douglas DC-9	USA	2	1965	1965	1982	976	30
McDonnell Douglas DC-9 Super 80/MD-80	USA	2	1979	1980	1999	1,191	298
McDonnell Douglas DC-10/MD-10	USA	3	1970	1971	1988	386	39
McDonnell Douglas MD-11	USA	3	1990	1990	2000	200	121
McDonnell Douglas MD-90	USA	2	1993	1995	2000	116	53
Douglas DC-8	USA	4	1958	1959	1972	556	1
Boeing 757	USA	2	1982	1983	2004	1,050	666
Boeing 717	USA	2	1997	1999	2006	156	148

Table 48 Out of Production (2019)

Type	Country	Engines	First Flight	Service entry	End of Production	Number Built	In Service (2018)
Boeing 727	USA	3	1963	1964	1984	1,832	44
Yakovlev Yak-40	USSR	3	1966	1968	1981	1,011	22
Yakovlev Yak-42	USSR	3	1975	1980	2003	185 (Jan 1995)	23
Tupolev Tu-134	USSR	2	1963	1967	1984	854	6
Tupolev Tu-154	USSR	3	1968	1972	2013	1,026	10
Ilyushin Il-62	USSR	4	1963	1967	1995	292	6

Table 49 Historical Aircraft (2019)

Type	Country	Engines	First Flight	Airline service entry	End of Production	Number Built
Avro Canada C102 Jetliner	Canada	4	1949	cancelled	1949	1
Shanghai Y-10	China	4	1980	cancelled	1980	3
Baade 152	East Germany	4	1958	cancelled	1961	3
Sud Aviation SE-210 Caravelle	France	2	1955	1959	1973	282
Dassault Mercure 100	France	2	1971	1974	1975	12
Aérospatiale-BAC Concorde	France/UK	4	1969	1976	1979	20
VFW-Fokker 614	Germany	2	1971	1975	1978	19
Rombac 1-11	Romania [k]	2	1982	1983	1993	9
Tupolev Tu-334	Russia	2	1999	cancelled	2009	2
Vickers VC10	UK	4	1962	1964	1970	54
Hawker Siddeley HS121 Trident	UK	3	1962	1964	1978	117
de Havilland DH 106 Comet	UK	4	1949	1952	1964	112
BAC One-Eleven	UK	2	1963	1965	1989	244
Lockheed L-1011 TriStar	USA	3	1970	1972	1984	250
Convair 880	USA	4	1959	1960	1962	65
Convair 990 Coronado	USA	4	1961	1962	1963	37
Boeing 720	USA	4	1959	1960	1967	154
Boeing 707	USA	4	1957	1958	1979	1,010
Tupolev Tu-104	USSR	2	1955	1956	1960	201
Tupolev Tu-110	USSR	4	1957	cancelled	1957	4
Tupolev Tu-124	USSR	2	1960	1962	1965	164
Tupolev Tu-144	USSR	4	1968	1977	1983	16
Ilyushin Il-86	USSR	4	1976	1980	1995	106

Commercial short-haul civilian passenger regional airliners seat fewer than 100 passengers. They support the short-hop routes in the hub and spoke model of passenger and cargo distribution as well as taking the point-to-point routes. They can fly up to 810 miles.

Table 50 Regional Airliners

Model	Country	Type	Seats	Seats/Row	Intro.	Prod. end	Built	In Service (orders)
GAF Nomad	Australia	Utility	12	2	1975	1985	172	2
Embraer E-Jet E2 family	Brazil	Jet	80-146	4	2018	in prod.	8	3 (153)
Embraer E-Jet family	Brazil	Jet	66-124	4	2004	in prod.	1414	1346 (133)
Embraer ERJ family	Brazil	Jet	37–50	3	1997	in prod.	1213	505 (0)
Embraer EMB 110 Bandeirante	Brazil	Utility	15-21	3	1973	1990	501	39
Embraer EMB 120 Brasilia	Brazil	Turboprop	30	3	1985	2001	354	98
Airbus A220	Canada	Jet	108-160	5	2016	in prod.	52	39 (282)
Bombardier CRJ700/900/1000	Canada	Jet	66-104	4	2001	in prod.	822	777 (54)
De Havilland Canada Dash 8	Canada	Turboprop	37-90	4	1984	in prod.	1244	844 (55)
DHC-6 Twin Otter (Viking - 400)	Canada	Utility	19	3	2010	in prod.	123	40 (14)
Bombardier CRJ100/200	Canada	Jet	50	4	1992	2006	1021	498
de Havilland Canada Dash 7	Canada	Turboprop	50	4	1978	1988	113	11
DHC-6 Twin Otter (-100/-200/-300)	Canada	Utility	19-20	3	1966	1988	844	230
Comac ARJ21	China	Jet	78-105	5	2016	in prod.	9	5 (103)
Harbin Y-12	China	Utility	17	3	1985	in prod.	105 (?)	
Xian Y-7 / MA60 / MA600	China	Turboprop	52–62	4	1984	in prod.	231	41 (46)

Table 50 Regional Airliners

Model	Country	Type	Seats	Seats/Row	Intro.	Prod. end	Built	In Service (orders)
Let L-410 Turbolet	Czech Republic	Utility	19	3	1970	in prod.	1200	178 (3)
Aérospatiale N 262	France	Utility	23-29	3	1964	1976	110	
ATR 42	France & Italy	Turboprop	40-52	4	1985	in prod.	470	220 (19)
ATR 72	France & Italy	Turboprop	68-74	4	1989	in prod.	1000	745 (202)
Dornier Do 228/Do 228NG	Germany	Utility	19	2	1982	in prod.	370	57 (2)
Dornier 328	Germany	Turboprop	30-33	3	1993	2000	217	24
Fairchild-Dornier 328JET	Germany	Jet	30-33	3	1999	2004	110	11
VFW-Fokker 614	Germany	Jet	40-44	4	1975	1977	19	
IAI Arava	Israel	Utility	20-24	4	1972	1988	80	
Mitsubishi MRJ	Japan	Jet	69-92	4	2020 (est)	in prod.	4	0 (203)
NAMC YS-11	Japan	Turboprop	64	4	1965	1974	182	1
Mitsubishi MU-2	Japan	Utility	4-12	2	1963	1986	704	
Fokker 100	Netherlands	Jet	97-122	5	1988	1997	283	109
Fokker 50	Netherlands	Turboprop	58	4	1987	1997	213	88
Fokker 70	Netherlands	Jet	72-85	5	1994	1997	48	23
Fokker F27 Friendship	Netherlands	Turboprop	48-56	4	1958	1987	586	10
Fokker F28 Fellowship	Netherlands	Jet	55-70	5	1969	1987	241	1
PZL M28 Skytruck	Poland	Utility	18	3	1993	in prod.	39	
Ilyushin Il-114	Russia	Turboprop	52–64	4	1998	in prod.	20	
Sukhoi Superjet 100	Russia	Jet	87-108	5	2011	in prod.	159	114
Yakovlev Yak-40	Russia	Jet	32	4	1968	1981	1011	22
CASA C-212	Spain	Utility	26	3	1974	in	583	

Table 50 Regional Airliners

Model	Country	Type	Seats	Seats/Row	Intro.	Prod. end	Built	In Service (orders)
Aviocar						prod.		
CASA IPTN CN-235	Spain & Indonesia	Turboprop	51	4	1988	in prod.	341	
Saab 2000	Sweden	Turboprop	50-58	3	1994	1999	63	24
Saab 340	Sweden	Turboprop	34	3	1984	1999	459	210
Saab 90 Scandia	Sweden	Utility	24-32	3	1950	1954	18	
Britten-Norman Islander	UK	Utility	9	2	1967	in prod.	1280	
BAe 146 Avro RJ	UK	Jet	70-112	5	1983	2001	387	118
BAe ATP	UK	Turboprop	64	4	1988	1996	64	17
BAe Jetstream	UK	Utility	19	3	1982	1993	386	91
BAe Jetstream 41	UK	Turboprop	29-30	3	1992	1997	100	51
Britten-Norman Trislander	UK	Utility	16-17	2	1971	1982	72	4
Hawker Siddeley HS 748	UK	Turboprop	40-58	4	1962	1988	380	12
Airspeed Ambassador	UK	Utility	60	5	1951	1953	23	
de Havilland Dove	UK	Utility	8	2	1946	1967	542	
de Havilland Heron	UK	Utility	14	2	1950	1963	150	
Handley Page Dart Herald	UK	Turboprop	47-56	4	1961	1968	50	
Handley Page Jetstream	UK	Utility	16	3	1969	1975	66	
Short 330	UK	Turboprop	30	3	1976	1992	125	
Short 360	UK	Turboprop	36	3	1982	1991	165	
Short SC.7 Skyvan	UK	Utility	19	3	1963	1986	153	
Antonov An-140	Ukraine	Turboprop	52	4	2002	in prod.	35	
Antonov An-148	Ukraine	Jet	68–99	5	2009	in prod.	42	7

Table 50 Regional Airliners

Model	Country	Type	Seats	Seats/Row	Intro.	Prod. end	Built	In Service (orders)
Antonov An-24	Ukraine	Turboprop	40-50	4	1962	2012	1264	86
Antonov An-28	Ukraine	Utility	18	3	1986	1993	191	
Cessna 208	USA	Utility	13	3	1984	in prod.	2,500	
Beechcraft 1900	USA	Utility	19	2	1984	2002	695	306
Beechcraft Model 99	USA	Turboprop	15	2	1968	1987	700	105
Boeing 717	USA	Jet	106-117	5	1999	2006	156	148
Fairchild Swearingen Metroliner	USA	Turboprop	19	2	1972	2001	600+	213
Yakovlev Yak-42	USSR / Russia	Jet	104-120	6	1980	2003	185	23

10.8 Government Constitutions

In 1776 a new system of government started that would eventually sweep across the planet. The new system of government is based on democracy and the system of government is codified in what is easily seen as a system specification for the system of government.

Although I had history classes in elementary school, junior high school and then all 4 years of high school, I was unaware of this connection with systems. I was told over and over again we have a system of government, but it did not click. I did not fully make the connection to the concept of a systems perspective and the US government. I had suspicions when I would take lunch walks along the Camden NJ waterfront with collogues working at the former RCA facility. It was at that time that someone stated that one of the first groups of systems engineers were the founders of the USA. That was a major revelation.

It was not until I developed the Constitutional Analysis Tool (CAT) that this hit me like a wet dish rag in the face. I found constitutions from across the planet and used CAT to try and understand what was happening. Essentially CAT allows a user to analyze Constitutions and make quantitative consistent comparisons of different struggles across our planet, both today and throughout our history.

There is an old saying, "actions speak louder than words". And so, it goes with written and spoken words of all types. Across time and cultures people on earth have attempted to act reasonably with one another and at some point, written the words to represent these actions. These are great words, Constitutions, usually born from great struggles. We use them in important works such as framing our roles in nations to providing us guidelines in simple activities such as student organizations and technical societies.

As one reads these words many questions arise. Such as, were these words created in reaction to great injustices or were these words created in hopes of preserving a way of life? Do these words still apply or are they lost in history? Should we now have new words, and will it matter? Who is CAT for and what does it do for us?

- CAT is for every teacher and student in every country on earth. If you are able to use an Internet search engine you are able to use CAT. So, children can use it in their history and social studies classes that we provide.
- CAT is for every professor and advanced student in every country on earth. It allows the serious academic to ruthlessly slice through text and provide quantitative results of our studies. It helps to remove the bias of our cultural and educational past.
- CAT is for every government representative on earth. As we ponder our actions and seal our role in history. As we create legislation and serve the forces we decide to serve.

- CAT is for every human on earth. To help us understand our history and the history of our fellow humans on earth. To help remind us of the struggles and great dreams or nightmares of our ancestors as we engage in our lives.
- CAT is for every new organization, technical society, student club forming under the rules of a constitution or collection of by-laws. Though not as critical as nation state constitutions, they are just as important in their educational value and remind us of our civic responsibilities.

CAT mines constitutions starting with a default set of rules. The users expand on the rules as new insights surface. The default rules include:

- Government Type: Monarchy, Democracy, Republic, Socialist, Communist, Fascist, Capitalist, Revolutionary
- Inalienable Rights: Government Power, People Natural Rights, Prohibitions
- Separation of Powers: Executive, Legislative, Judicial, State, People Corporate
- Roles: Religion, Defense, Money, Wealth, Education
- Agriculture, Health, State, People, Labor
- Representatives: Elections, Officials, Removal
- Current Challenges: Challenges 1900, Challenges 2000

So why did I provide this product description in this book? Simple, no one is using CAT or a tool like CAT even though the technology is now available to have a tool like CAT. Perhaps this is another negative unintended consequence of privatization. A bigger question is, has privatization led to the bypassing of the Bill of Rights and the Constitution?

10.8.1 Declaration of Independence

From a systems perspective the Declaration of Independence is an operational concept for the establishment of a new system for governance. It contains the stakeholder needs and suggests goals and requirements for the new system.

The following text is a transcription of the Stone Engraving of the parchment Declaration of Independence. There are some spelling and punctuation changes. The document is on display in the Rotunda at the National Archives Museum. The PUIs were added to support the requirements analysis in this book.

PUI	Declaration of Independence Text
GN-1	In Congress, July 4, 1776.
GN-2	The unanimous Declaration of the thirteen united States of America, When in the Course of human events, it becomes necessary for one people to dissolve the political bands which have connected them with another, and to assume among the

PUI	Declaration of Independence Text
	powers of the earth, the separate and equal station to which the Laws of Nature and of Nature's God entitle them, a decent respect to the opinions of mankind requires that they should declare the causes which impel them to the separation.
GN-3	We hold these truths to be self-evident, that all men are created equal, that they are endowed by their Creator with certain unalienable Rights, that among these are Life, Liberty and the pursuit of Happiness.--That to secure these rights, Governments are instituted among Men, deriving their just powers from the consent of the governed, --That whenever any Form of Government becomes destructive of these ends, it is the Right of the People to alter or to abolish it, and to institute new Government, laying its foundation on such principles and organizing its powers in such form, as to them shall seem most likely to effect their Safety and Happiness. Prudence, indeed, will dictate that Governments long established should not be changed for light and transient causes; and accordingly all experience hath shewn, that mankind are more disposed to suffer, while evils are sufferable, than to right themselves by abolishing the forms to which they are accustomed. But when a long train of abuses and usurpations, pursuing invariably the same Object evinces a design to reduce them under absolute Despotism, it is their right, it is their duty, to throw off such Government, and to provide new Guards for their future security.--Such has been the patient sufferance of these Colonies; and such is now the necessity which constrains them to alter their former Systems of Government. The history of the present King of Great Britain is a history of repeated injuries and usurpations, all having in direct object the establishment of an absolute Tyranny over these States. To prove this, let Facts be submitted to a candid world.
GN-4	-
GN-5	He has refused his Assent to Laws, the most wholesome and necessary for the public good.
GN-6	He has forbidden his Governors to pass Laws of immediate and pressing importance, unless suspended in their operation till his Assent should be obtained; and when so suspended, he has utterly neglected to attend to them.
GN-7	He has refused to pass other Laws for the accommodation of large districts of people, unless those people would relinquish the right of Representation in the Legislature, a right inestimable to them and formidable to tyrants only.
GN-8	He has called together legislative bodies at places unusual, uncomfortable, and distant from the depository of their public Records, for the sole purpose of fatiguing them into compliance with his measures.
GN-9	He has dissolved Representative Houses repeatedly, for opposing with manly firmness his invasions on the rights of the people.
GN-10	He has refused for a long time, after such dissolutions, to cause others to be elected; whereby the Legislative powers, incapable of Annihilation, have returned to the People at large for their exercise; the State remaining in the mean time exposed to all the dangers of invasion from without, and convulsions within.
GN-11	He has endeavoured to prevent the population of these States; for that purpose obstructing the Laws for Naturalization of Foreigners; refusing to pass others to

PUI	Declaration of Independence Text
	encourage their migrations hither, and raising the conditions of new Appropriations of Lands.
GN-12	He has obstructed the Administration of Justice, by refusing his Assent to Laws for establishing Judiciary powers.
GN-13	He has made Judges dependent on his Will alone, for the tenure of their offices, and the amount and payment of their salaries.
GN-14	He has erected a multitude of New Offices, and sent hither swarms of Officers to harrass our people, and eat out their substance.
GN-15	He has kept among us, in times of peace, Standing Armies without the Consent of our legislatures.
GN-16	He has affected to render the Military independent of and superior to the Civil power.
GN-17	NOTE: punctuation changes from colon to a period.
GN-18	-
GN-19	He has combined with others to subject us to a jurisdiction foreign to our constitution, and unacknowledged by our laws; giving his Assent to their Acts of pretended Legislation.
GN-20	For Quartering large bodies of armed troops among us.
GN-21	For protecting them, by a mock Trial, from punishment for any Murders which they should commit on the Inhabitants of these States.
GN-22	For cutting off our Trade with all parts of the world.
GN-23	For imposing Taxes on us without our Consent.
GN-24	For depriving us in many cases, of the benefits of Trial by Jury.
GN-25	For transporting us beyond Seas to be tried for pretended offences.
GN-26	For abolishing the free System of English Laws in a neighbouring Province, establishing therein an Arbitrary government, and enlarging its Boundaries so as to render it at once an example and fit instrument for introducing the same absolute rule into these Colonies.
GN-27	For taking away our Charters, abolishing our most valuable Laws, and altering fundamentally the Forms of our Governments.
GN-28	For suspending our own Legislatures, and declaring themselves invested with power to legislate for us in all cases whatsoever.
GN-29	He has abdicated Government here, by declaring us out of his Protection and waging War against us.
GN-30	He has plundered our seas, ravaged our Coasts, burnt our towns, and destroyed the lives of our people.
GN-31	He is at this time transporting large Armies of foreign Mercenaries to compleat the works of death, desolation and tyranny, already begun with circumstances of Cruelty & perfidy scarcely paralleled in the most barbarous ages, and totally unworthy the Head of a civilized nation.

PUI	Declaration of Independence Text
GN-32	He has constrained our fellow Citizens taken Captive on the high Seas to bear Arms against their Country, to become the executioners of their friends and Brethren, or to fall themselves by their Hands.
GN-33	He has excited domestic insurrections amongst us, and has endeavoured to bring on the inhabitants of our frontiers, the merciless Indian Savages, whose known rule of warfare, is an undistinguished destruction of all ages, sexes and conditions.
GN-34	-
GN-35	In every stage of these Oppressions We have Petitioned for Redress in the most humble terms: Our repeated Petitions have been answered only by repeated injury. A Prince whose character is thus marked by every act which may define a Tyrant, is unfit to be the ruler of a free people.
GN-36	Nor have We been wanting in attentions to our Brittish brethren. We have warned them from time to time of attempts by their legislature to extend an unwarrantable jurisdiction over us. We have reminded them of the circumstances of our emigration and settlement here. We have appealed to their native justice and magnanimity, and we have conjured them by the ties of our common kindred to disavow these usurpations, which, would inevitably interrupt our connections and correspondence. They too have been deaf to the voice of justice and of consanguinity. We must, therefore, acquiesce in the necessity, which denounces our Separation, and hold them, as we hold the rest of mankind, Enemies in War, in Peace Friends.
GN-37	We, therefore, the Representatives of the united States of America, in General Congress, Assembled, appealing to the Supreme Judge of the world for the rectitude of our intentions, do, in the Name, and by Authority of the good People of these Colonies, solemnly publish and declare, That these United Colonies are, and of Right ought to be Free and Independent States; that they are Absolved from all Allegiance to the British Crown, and that all political connection between them and the State of Great Britain, is and ought to be totally dissolved; and that as Free and Independent States, they have full Power to levy War, conclude Peace, contract Alliances, establish Commerce, and to do all other Acts and Things which Independent States may of right do. And for the support of this Declaration, with a firm reliance on the protection of divine Providence, we mutually pledge to each other our Lives, our Fortunes and our sacred Honor.

10.8.2 Constitution and Amendments

The US constitution and amendments is a system level specification for a new system that will perform governance in the new country.

PUI	Constitution Text
C-1	**Constitution for the United States of America**
C-2	We the People of the United States, in Order to form a more perfect Union, establish Justice, insure domestic Tranquility, provide for the common defence, promote the

PUI	Constitution Text
	general Welfare, and secure the Blessings of Liberty to ourselves and our Posterity, do ordain and establish this Constitution for the United States of America.
C-3	**Article. I.**
C-4	**Section. 1.** All legislative Powers herein granted shall be vested in a Congress of the United States, which shall consist of a Senate and House of Representatives.
C-5	**Section. 2.** The House of Representatives shall be composed of Members chosen every second Year by the People of the several States, and the Electors in each State shall have the Qualifications requisite for Electors of the most numerous Branch of the State Legislature.
C-6	No Person shall be a Representative who shall not have attained to the Age of twenty five Years, and been seven Years a Citizen of the United States, and who shall not, when elected, be an Inhabitant of that State in which he shall be chosen.
C-7	Representatives and direct Taxes shall be apportioned among the several States which may be included within this Union, according to their respective Numbers, which shall be determined by adding to the whole Number of free Persons, including those bound to Service for a Term of Years, and excluding Indians not taxed, three fifths of all other Persons [Modified by Amendment XIV]. The actual Enumeration shall be made within three Years after the first Meeting of the Congress of the United States, and within every subsequent Term of ten Years, in such Manner as they shall by Law direct. The Number of Representatives shall not exceed one for every thirty Thousand, but each State shall have at Least one Representative; and until such enumeration shall be made, the State of New Hampshire shall be entitled to chuse three, Massachusetts eight, Rhode-Island and Providence Plantations one, Connecticut five, New-York six, New Jersey four, Pennsylvania eight, Delaware one, Maryland six, Virginia ten, North Carolina five, South Carolina five, and Georgia three.
C-8	When vacancies happen in the Representation from any State, the Executive Authority thereof shall issue Writs of Election to fill such Vacancies.
C-9	The House of Representatives shall chuse their Speaker and other Officers; and shall have the sole Power of Impeachment.
C-10	**Section. 3.** The Senate of the United States shall be composed of two Senators from each State, chosen by the Legislature thereof [Modified by Amendment XVII], for six Years; and each Senator shall have one Vote.
C-11	Immediately after they shall be assembled in Consequence of the first Election, they shall be divided as equally as may be into three Classes. The Seats of the Senators of the first Class shall be vacated at the Expiration of the second Year, of the second Class at the Expiration of the fourth Year, and of the third Class at the Expiration of the sixth Year, so that one third may be chosen every second Year; and if Vacancies happen by Resignation, or otherwise, during the Recess of the Legislature of any State, the Executive thereof may make temporary Appointments until the next Meeting of the Legislature, which shall then fill such Vacancies [Modified by Amendment XVII].
C-12	No Person shall be a Senator who shall not have attained to the Age of thirty Years, and been nine Years a Citizen of the United States, and who shall not, when elected, be an Inhabitant of that State for which he shall be chosen.

PUI	Constitution Text
C-13	The Vice President of the United States shall be President of the Senate, but shall have no Vote, unless they be equally divided.
C-14	The Senate shall chuse their other Officers, and also a President pro tempore, in the Absence of the Vice President, or when he shall exercise the Office of President of the United States.
C-15	The Senate shall have the sole Power to try all Impeachments. When sitting for that Purpose, they shall be on Oath or Affirmation. When the President of the United States is tried, the Chief Justice shall preside: And no Person shall be convicted without the Concurrence of two thirds of the Members present.
C-16	Judgment in Cases of Impeachment shall not extend further than to removal from Office, and disqualification to hold and enjoy any Office of honor, Trust or Profit under the United States: but the Party convicted shall nevertheless be liable and subject to Indictment, Trial, Judgment and Punishment, according to Law.
C-17	**Section. 4.** The Times, Places and Manner of holding Elections for Senators and Representatives, shall be prescribed in each State by the Legislature thereof; but the Congress may at any time by Law make or alter such Regulations, except as to the Places of chusing Senators.
C-18	The Congress shall assemble at least once in every Year, and such Meeting shall be on the first Monday in December [Modified by Amendment XX], unless they shall by Law appoint a different Day.
C-19	**Section. 5.** Each House shall be the Judge of the Elections, Returns and Qualifications of its own Members, and a Majority of each shall constitute a Quorum to do Business; but a smaller Number may adjourn from day to day, and may be authorized to compel the Attendance of absent Members, in such Manner, and under such Penalties as each House may provide.
C-20	Each House may determine the Rules of its Proceedings, punish its Members for disorderly Behaviour, and, with the Concurrence of two thirds, expel a Member.
C-21	Each House shall keep a Journal of its Proceedings, and from time to time publish the same, excepting such Parts as may in their Judgment require Secrecy; and the Yeas and Nays of the Members of either House on any question shall, at the Desire of one fifth of those Present, be entered on the Journal.
C-22	Neither House, during the Session of Congress, shall, without the Consent of the other, adjourn for more than three days, nor to any other Place than that in which the two Houses shall be sitting.
C-23	**Section. 6.** The Senators and Representatives shall receive a Compensation for their Services, to be ascertained by Law, and paid out of the Treasury of the United States. They shall in all Cases, except Treason, Felony and Breach of the Peace, be privileged from Arrest during their Attendance at the Session of their respective Houses, and in going to and returning from the same; and for any Speech or Debate in either House, they shall not be questioned in any other Place.
C-24	No Senator or Representative shall, during the Time for which he was elected, be appointed to any civil Office under the Authority of the United States, which shall have been created, or the Emoluments whereof shall have been encreased during such time; and no Person holding any Office under the United States, shall be a Member of either House during his Continuance in Office.

PUI	Constitution Text
C-25	**Section. 7.** All Bills for raising Revenue shall originate in the House of Representatives; but the Senate may propose or concur with Amendments as on other Bills.
C-26	Every Bill which shall have passed the House of Representatives and the Senate, shall, before it become a Law, be presented to the President of the United States; If he approve he shall sign it, but if not he shall return it, with his Objections to that House in which it shall have originated, who shall enter the Objections at large on their Journal, and proceed to reconsider it. If after such Reconsideration two thirds of that House shall agree to pass the Bill, it shall be sent, together with the Objections, to the other House, by which it shall likewise be reconsidered, and if approved by two thirds of that House, it shall become a Law. But in all such Cases the Votes of both Houses shall be determined by yeas and Nays, and the Names of the Persons voting for and against the Bill shall be entered on the Journal of each House respectively. If any Bill shall not be returned by the President within ten Days (Sundays excepted) after it shall have been presented to him, the Same shall be a Law, in like Manner as if he had signed it, unless the Congress by their Adjournment prevent its Return, in which Case it shall not be a Law.
C-27	Every Order, Resolution, or Vote to which the Concurrence of the Senate and House of Representatives may be necessary (except on a question of Adjournment) shall be presented to the President of the United States; and before the Same shall take Effect, shall be approved by him, or being disapproved by him, shall be repassed by two thirds of the Senate and House of Representatives, according to the Rules and Limitations prescribed in the Case of a Bill.
C-28	**Section. 8.** The Congress shall have Power To lay and collect Taxes, Duties, Imposts and Excises, to pay the Debts and provide for the common Defence and general Welfare of the United States; but all Duties, Imposts and Excises shall be uniform throughout the United States;
C-29	To borrow Money on the credit of the United States;
C-30	To regulate Commerce with foreign Nations, and among the several States, and with the Indian Tribes;
C-31	To establish an uniform Rule of Naturalization, and uniform Laws on the subject of Bankruptcies throughout the United States;
C-32	To coin Money, regulate the Value thereof, and of foreign Coin, and fix the Standard of Weights and Measures;
C-33	To provide for the Punishment of counterfeiting the Securities and current Coin of the United States;
C-34	To establish Post Offices and post Roads;
C-35	To promote the Progress of Science and useful Arts, by securing for limited Times to Authors and Inventors the exclusive Right to their respective Writings and Discoveries;
C-36	To constitute Tribunals inferior to the supreme Court;
C-37	To define and punish Piracies and Felonies committed on the high Seas, and Offences against the Law of Nations;

PUI	Constitution Text
C-38	To declare War, grant Letters of Marque and Reprisal, and make Rules concerning Captures on Land and Water;
C-39	To raise and support Armies, but no Appropriation of Money to that Use shall be for a longer Term than two Years;
C-40	To provide and maintain a Navy;
C-41	To make Rules for the Government and Regulation of the land and naval Forces;
C-42	To provide for calling forth the Militia to execute the Laws of the Union, suppress Insurrections and repel Invasions;
C-43	To provide for organizing, arming, and disciplining, the Militia, and for governing such Part of them as may be employed in the Service of the United States, reserving to the States respectively, the Appointment of the Officers, and the Authority of training the Militia according to the discipline prescribed by Congress;
C-44	To exercise exclusive Legislation in all Cases whatsoever, over such District (not exceeding ten Miles square) as may, by Cession of particular States, and the Acceptance of Congress, become the Seat of the Government of the United States, and to exercise like Authority over all Places purchased by the Consent of the Legislature of the State in which the Same shall be, for the Erection of Forts, Magazines, Arsenals, dock-Yards, and other needful Buildings; — And
C-45	To make all Laws which shall be necessary and proper for carrying into Execution the foregoing Powers, and all other Powers vested by this Constitution in the Government of the United States, or in any Department or Officer thereof.
C-46	**Section. 9.** The Migration or Importation of such Persons as any of the States now existing shall think proper to admit, shall not be prohibited by the Congress prior to the Year one thousand eight hundred and eight, but a Tax or duty may be imposed on such Importation, not exceeding ten dollars for each Person.
C-47	The Privilege of the Writ of Habeas Corpus shall not be suspended, unless when in Cases of Rebellion or Invasion the public Safety may require it.
C-48	No Bill of Attainder or ex post facto Law shall be passed.
C-49	No Capitation, or other direct, Tax shall be laid, unless in Proportion to the Census or Enumeration herein before directed to be taken.
C-50	No Tax or Duty shall be laid on Articles exported from any State.
C-51	No Preference shall be given by any Regulation of Commerce or Revenue to the Ports of one State over those of another; nor shall Vessels bound to, or from, one State, be obliged to enter, clear, or pay Duties in another.
C-52	No Money shall be drawn from the Treasury, but in Consequence of Appropriations made by Law; and a regular Statement and Account of the Receipts and Expenditures of all public Money shall be published from time to time.
C-53	No Title of Nobility shall be granted by the United States: And no Person holding any Office of Profit or Trust under them, shall, without the Consent of the Congress, accept of any present, Emolument, Office, or Title, of any kind whatever, from any King, Prince, or foreign State.

PUI	Constitution Text
C-54	**Section. 10.** No State shall enter into any Treaty, Alliance, or Confederation; grant Letters of Marque and Reprisal; coin Money; emit Bills of Credit; make any Thing but gold and silver Coin a Tender in Payment of Debts; pass any Bill of Attainder, ex post facto Law, or Law impairing the Obligation of Contracts, or grant any Title of Nobility.
C-55	No State shall, without the Consent of the Congress, lay any Imposts or Duties on Imports or Exports, except what may be absolutely necessary for executing it's inspection Laws; and the net Produce of all Duties and Imposts, laid by any State on Imports or Exports, shall be for the Use of the Treasury of the United States; and all such Laws shall be subject to the Revision and Controul of the Congress.
C-56	No State shall, without the Consent of Congress, lay any Duty of Tonnage, keep Troops, or Ships of War in time of Peace, enter into any Agreement or Compact with another State, or with a foreign Power, or engage in War, unless actually invaded, or in such imminent Danger as will not admit of delay.
C-57	**Article. II.**
C-58	**Section. 1.** The executive Power shall be vested in a President of the United States of America. He shall hold his Office during the Term of four Years, and, together with the Vice President, chosen for the same Term, be elected, as follows:
C-59	Each State shall appoint, in such Manner as the Legislature thereof may direct, a Number of Electors, equal to the whole Number of Senators and Representatives to which the State may be entitled in the Congress: but no Senator or Representative, or Person holding an Office of Trust or Profit under the United States, shall be appointed an Elector.
C-60	The Electors shall meet in their respective States, and vote by Ballot for two Persons, of whom one at least shall not be an Inhabitant of the same State with themselves. And they shall make a List of all the Persons voted for, and of the Number of Votes for each; which List they shall sign and certify, and transmit sealed to the Seat of the Government of the United States, directed to the President of the Senate. The President of the Senate shall, in the Presence of the Senate and House of Representatives, open all the Certificates, and the Votes shall then be counted. The Person having the greatest Number of Votes shall be the President, if such Number be a Majority of the whole Number of Electors appointed; and if there be more than one who have such Majority, and have an equal Number of Votes, then the House of Representatives shall immediately chuse by Ballot one of them for President; and if no Person have a Majority, then from the five highest on the List the said House shall in like Manner chuse the President. But in chusing the President, the Votes shall be taken by States, the Representation from each State having one Vote; a quorum for this Purpose shall consist of a Member or Members from two thirds of the States, and a Majority of all the States shall be necessary to a Choice. In every Case, after the Choice of the President, the Person having the greatest Number of Votes of the Electors shall be the Vice President. But if there should remain two or more who have equal Votes, the Senate shall chuse from them by Ballot the Vice President [Modified by Amendment XII].
C-61	The Congress may determine the Time of chusing the Electors, and the Day on which they shall give their Votes; which Day shall be the same throughout the

PUI	Constitution Text
	United States.
C-62	No Person except a natural born Citizen, or a Citizen of the United States, at the time of the Adoption of this Constitution, shall be eligible to the Office of President; neither shall any Person be eligible to that Office who shall not have attained to the Age of thirty five Years, and been fourteen Years a Resident within the United States.
C-63	In Case of the Removal of the President from Office, or of his Death, Resignation, or Inability to discharge the Powers and Duties of the said Office, the Same shall devolve on the Vice President, and the Congress may by Law provide for the Case of Removal, Death, Resignation or Inability, both of the President and Vice President, declaring what Officer shall then act as President, and such Officer shall act accordingly, until the Disability be removed, or a President shall be elected [Modified by Amendment XXV].
C-64	The President shall, at stated Times, receive for his Services, a Compensation, which shall neither be increased nor diminished during the Period for which he shall have been elected, and he shall not receive within that Period any other Emolument from the United States, or any of them.
C-65	Before he enter on the Execution of his Office, he shall take the following Oath or Affirmation: — "I do solemnly swear (or affirm) that I will faithfully execute the Office of President of the United States, and will to the best of my Ability, preserve, protect and defend the Constitution of the United States."
C-66	**Section. 2.** The President shall be Commander in Chief of the Army and Navy of the United States, and of the Militia of the several States, when called into the actual Service of the United States; he may require the Opinion, in writing, of the principal Officer in each of the executive Departments, upon any Subject relating to the Duties of their respective Offices, and he shall have Power to grant Reprieves and Pardons for Offences against the United States, except in Cases of Impeachment.
C-67	He shall have Power, by and with the Advice and Consent of the Senate, to make Treaties, provided two thirds of the Senators present concur; and he shall nominate, and by and with the Advice and Consent of the Senate, shall appoint Ambassadors, other public Ministers and Consuls, Judges of the supreme Court, and all other Officers of the United States, whose Appointments are not herein otherwise provided for, and which shall be established by Law: but the Congress may by Law vest the Appointment of such inferior Officers, as they think proper, in the President alone, in the Courts of Law, or in the Heads of Departments.
C-68	The President shall have Power to fill up all Vacancies that may happen during the Recess of the Senate, by granting Commissions which shall expire at the End of their next Session.
C-69	**Section. 3.** He shall from time to time give to the Congress Information of the State of the Union, and recommend to their Consideration such Measures as he shall judge necessary and expedient; he may, on extraordinary Occasions, convene both Houses, or either of them, and in Case of Disagreement between them, with Respect to the Time of Adjournment, he may adjourn them to such Time as he shall think proper; he shall receive Ambassadors and other public Ministers; he shall take Care that the Laws be faithfully executed, and shall Commission all the Officers of the United

PUI	Constitution Text
	States.
C-70	**Section. 4.** The President, Vice President and all civil Officers of the United States, shall be removed from Office on Impeachment for, and Conviction of, Treason, Bribery, or other high Crimes and Misdemeanors.
C-71	**Article. III.**
C-72	**Section. 1.** The judicial Power of the United States shall be vested in one supreme Court, and in such inferior Courts as the Congress may from time to time ordain and establish. The Judges, both of the supreme and inferior Courts, shall hold their Offices during good Behaviour, and shall, at stated Times, receive for their Services a Compensation, which shall not be diminished during their Continuance in Office.
C-73	**Section. 2.** The judicial Power shall extend to all Cases, in Law and Equity, arising under this Constitution, the Laws of the United States, and Treaties made, or which shall be made, under their Authority; — to all Cases affecting Ambassadors, other public Ministers and Consuls; — to all Cases of admiralty and maritime Jurisdiction; — to Controversies to which the United States shall be a Party; — to Controversies between two or more States; — between a State and Citizens of another State [Modified by Amendment XI]; — between Citizens of different States; — between Citizens of the same State claiming Lands under Grants of different States, and between a State, or the Citizens thereof, and foreign States, Citizens or Subjects.
C-74	In all Cases affecting Ambassadors, other public Ministers and Consuls, and those in which a State shall be Party, the supreme Court shall have original Jurisdiction. In all the other Cases before mentioned, the supreme Court shall have appellate Jurisdiction, both as to Law and Fact, with such Exceptions, and under such Regulations as the Congress shall make.
C-75	The Trial of all Crimes, except in Cases of Impeachment, shall be by Jury; and such Trial shall be held in the State where the said Crimes shall have been committed; but when not committed within any State, the Trial shall be at such Place or Places as the Congress may by Law have directed.
C-76	**Section. 3.** Treason against the United States shall consist only in levying War against them, or in adhering to their Enemies, giving them Aid and Comfort. No Person shall be convicted of Treason unless on the Testimony of two Witnesses to the same overt Act, or on Confession in open Court.
C-77	The Congress shall have Power to declare the Punishment of Treason, but no Attainder of Treason shall work Corruption of Blood, or Forfeiture except during the Life of the Person attainted.
C-78	**Article. IV.**
C-79	**Section. 1.** Full Faith and Credit shall be given in each State to the public Acts, Records, and judicial Proceedings of every other State. And the Congress may by general Laws prescribe the Manner in which such Acts, Records and Proceedings shall be proved, and the Effect thereof.
C-80	**Section. 2.** The Citizens of each State shall be entitled to all Privileges and Immunities of Citizens in the several States.
C-81	A Person charged in any State with Treason, Felony, or other Crime, who shall flee from Justice, and be found in another State, shall on Demand of the executive

PUI	Constitution Text
	Authority of the State from which he fled, be delivered up, to be removed to the State having Jurisdiction of the Crime.
C-82	No Person held to Service or Labour in one State, under the Laws thereof, escaping into another, shall, in Consequence of any Law or Regulation therein, be discharged from such Service or Labour, but shall be delivered up on Claim of the Party to whom such Service or Labour may be due [Modified by Amendment XIII].
C-83	**Section. 3.** New States may be admitted by the Congress into this Union; but no new State shall be formed or erected within the Jurisdiction of any other State; nor any State be formed by the Junction of two or more States, or Parts of States, without the Consent of the Legislatures of the States concerned as well as of the Congress.
C-84	The Congress shall have Power to dispose of and make all needful Rules and Regulations respecting the Territory or other Property belonging to the United States; and nothing in this Constitution shall be so construed as to Prejudice any Claims of the United States, or of any particular State.
C-85	**Section. 4.** The United States shall guarantee to every State in this Union a Republican Form of Government, and shall protect each of them against Invasion; and on Application of the Legislature, or of the Executive (when the Legislature cannot be convened), against domestic Violence.
C-86	**Article. V.**
C-87	The Congress, whenever two thirds of both Houses shall deem it necessary, shall propose Amendments to this Constitution, or, on the Application of the Legislatures of two thirds of the several States, shall call a Convention for proposing Amendments, which, in either Case, shall be valid to all Intents and Purposes, as Part of this Constitution, when ratified by the Legislatures of three fourths of the several States, or by Conventions in three fourths thereof, as the one or the other Mode of Ratification may be proposed by the Congress; Provided that no Amendment which may be made prior to the Year One thousand eight hundred and eight shall in any Manner affect the first and fourth Clauses in the Ninth Section of the first Article; and that no State, without its Consent, shall be deprived of its equal Suffrage in the Senate.
C-88	**Article. VI.**
C-89	All Debts contracted and Engagements entered into, before the Adoption of this Constitution, shall be as valid against the United States under this Constitution, as under the Confederation.
C-90	This Constitution, and the Laws of the United States which shall be made in Pursuance thereof; and all Treaties made, or which shall be made, under the Authority of the United States, shall be the supreme Law of the Land; and the Judges in every State shall be bound thereby, any Thing in the Constitution or Laws of any State to the Contrary notwithstanding.
C-91	The Senators and Representatives before mentioned, and the Members of the several State Legislatures, and all executive and judicial Officers, both of the United States and of the several States, shall be bound by Oath or Affirmation, to support this Constitution; but no religious Test shall ever be required as a Qualification to any

PUI	Constitution Text
	Office or public Trust under the United States.
C-92	**Article. VII.**
C-93	The Ratification of the Conventions of nine States, shall be sufficient for the Establishment of this Constitution between the States so ratifying the Same.
C-94	The Word, "the," being interlined between the seventh and eighth Lines of the first Page, The Word "Thirty" being partly written on an Erazure in the fifteenth Line of the first Page, The Words "is tried" being interlined between the thirty second and thirty third Lines of the first Page and the Word "the" being interlined between the forty third and forty fourth Lines of the second Page.
C-95	Attest William Jackson
C-96	Secretary
C-97	done in Convention by the Unanimous Consent of the States present the Seventeenth Day of September in the Year of our Lord one thousand seven hundred and Eighty seven and of the Independence of the United States of America the Twelfth In witness whereof We have hereunto subscribed our Names,
C-98	Go. WASHINGTON
C-99	Presidt. and deputy from Virginia
C-100	New Hampshire
C-101	JOHN LANGDON, NICHOLAS GILMAN
C-102	Massachusetts
C-103	NATHANIEL GORHAM, RUFUS KING
C-104	Connecticut
C-105	WM. SAML. JOHNSON, ROGER SHERMAN
C-106	New York
C-107	ALEXANDER HAMILTON
C-108	New Jersey
C-109	WIL LIVINGSTON, DAVID BREARLEY, WM. PATERSON, JONA DAYTON
C-110	Pennsylvania
C-111	B FRANKLIN, THOMAS MIFFLIN, ROBT MORRIS, GEO. CLYMER, THOS. FITZ SIMONS, JARED INGERSOLL, JAMES WILSON, GOUV MORRIS
C-112	Delaware
C-113	GEO: READ, GUNNING BEDFORD jun, JOHN DICKINSON, RICHARD BASSETT, JACO: BROOM

PUI	Constitution Text
C-114	Maryland
C-115	JAMES MCHENRY, DAN OF ST THOS. JENIFER, DANL CARROLL
C-116	Virginia
C-117	JOHN BLAIR, JAMES MADISON
C-118	North Carolina
C-119	WM. BLOUNT, RICHD. DOBBS SPAIGHT, HU WILLIAMSON
C-120	South Carolina
C-121	J. RUTLEDGE, CHARLES COTESWORTH PINCKNEY, CHARLES PINCKNEY, PIERCE BUTLER
C-122	Georgia
C-123	WILLIAM FEW, ABR BALDWIN
C-124	In Convention Monday, September 17th, 1787.
C-125	Present
C-126	The States of
C-127	New Hampshire, Massachusetts, Connecticut, MR. Hamilton from New York, New Jersey, Pennsylvania, Delaware, Maryland, Virginia, North Carolina, South Carolina and Georgia.
C-128	Resolved,
C-129	That the preceeding Constitution be laid before the United States in Congress assembled, and that it is the Opinion of this Convention, that it should afterwards be submitted to a Convention of Delegates, chosen in each State by the People thereof, under the Recommendation of its Legislature, for their Assent and Ratification; and that each Convention assenting to, and ratifying the Same, should give Notice thereof to the United States in Congress assembled. Resolved, That it is the Opinion of this Convention, that as soon as the Conventions of nine States shall have ratified this Constitution, the United States in Congress assembled should fix a Day on which Electors should be appointed by the States which have ratified the same, and a Day on which the Electors should assemble to vote for the President, and the Time and Place for commencing Proceedings under this Constitution. That after such Publication the Electors should be appointed, and the Senators and Representatives elected: That the Electors should meet on the Day fixed for the Election of the President, and should transmit their Votes certified, signed, sealed and directed, as the Constitution requires, to the Secretary of the United States in Congress assembled, that the Senators and Representatives should convene at the Time and Place assigned; that the Senators should appoint a President of the Senate, for the sole purpose of receiving, opening and counting the Votes for President; and, that

PUI	Constitution Text
	after he shall be chosen, the Congress, together with the President, should, without Delay, proceed to execute this Constitution.
C-130	By the Unanimous Order of the Convention
C-131	Go. WASHINGTON — Presidt.
C-132	W. JACKSON Secretary.

PUI	Bill of Rights Text
R-1	**Bill of Rights**
R-2	The conventions of a number of the States having at the time of their adopting the Constitution, expressed a desire, in order to prevent misconstruction or abuse of its powers, that further declaratory and restrictive clauses should be added.
R-3	**Article the first [Not Ratified]**
R-4	After the first enumeration required by the first article of the Constitution, there shall be one Representative for every thirty thousand, until the number shall amount to one hundred, after which the proportion shall be so regulated by Congress, that there shall be not less than one hundred Representatives, nor less than one Representative for every forty thousand persons, until the number of Representatives shall amount to two hundred; after which the proportion shall be so regulated by Congress, that there shall not be less than two hundred Representatives, nor more than one Representative for every fifty thousand persons.
R-5	**Article the second [Amendment XXVII - Ratified 1992]**
R-6	No law, varying the compensation for the services of the Senators and Representatives, shall take effect, until an election of Representatives shall have intervened.
R-7	**Article the third [Amendment I]**
R-8	Congress shall make no law respecting an establishment of religion, or prohibiting the free exercise thereof; or abridging the freedom of speech, or of the press; or the right of the people peaceably to assemble, and to petition the Government for a redress of grievances.
R-9	**Article the fourth [Amendment II] [4]**
R-10	A well regulated Militia, being necessary to the security of a free State, the right of the people to keep and bear Arms, shall not be infringed.
R-11	**Article the fifth [Amendment III]**
R-12	No Soldier shall, in time of peace be quartered in any house, without the consent of the Owner, nor in time of war, but in a manner to be prescribed by law.
R-13	**Article the sixth [Amendment IV]**

PUI	Bill of Rights Text
R-14	The right of the people to be secure in their persons, houses, papers, and effects, against unreasonable searches and seizures, shall not be violated, and no Warrants shall issue, but upon probable cause, supported by Oath or affirmation, and particularly describing the place to be searched, and the persons or things to be seized.
R-15	**Article the seventh [Amendment V]**
R-16	No person shall be held to answer for a capital, or otherwise infamous crime, unless on a presentment or indictment of a Grand Jury, except in cases arising in the land or naval forces, or in the Militia, when in actual service in time of War or public danger; nor shall any person be subject for the same offence to be twice put in jeopardy of life or limb; nor shall be compelled in any criminal case to be a witness against himself, nor be deprived of life, liberty, or property, without due process of law; nor shall private property be taken for public use, without just compensation.
R-17	**Article the eighth [Amendment VI]**
R-18	In all criminal prosecutions, the accused shall enjoy the right to a speedy and public trial, by an impartial jury of the State and district wherein the crime shall have been committed, which district shall have been previously ascertained by law, and to be informed of the nature and cause of the accusation; to be confronted with the witnesses against him; to have compulsory process for obtaining witnesses in his favor, and to have the Assistance of Counsel for his defence.
R-19	**Article the ninth [Amendment VII]**
R-20	In Suits at common law, where the value in controversy shall exceed twenty dollars, the right of trial by jury shall be preserved, and no fact tried by a jury, shall be otherwise re-examined in any Court of the United States, than according to the rules of the common law.
R-21	**Article the tenth [Amendment VIII]**
R-22	Excessive bail shall not be required, nor excessive fines imposed, nor cruel and unusual punishments inflicted.
R-23	**Article the eleventh [Amendment IX]**
R-24	The enumeration in the Constitution, of certain rights, shall not be construed to deny or disparage others retained by the people.
R-25	**Article the twelfth [Amendment X]**
R-26	The powers not delegated to the United States by the Constitution, nor prohibited by it to the States, are reserved to the States respectively, or to the people.
R-27	**Additional Amendments to the Constitution**
R-28	ARTICLES in addition to, and Amendment of, the Constitution of the United States of America, proposed by Congress, and ratified by the Legislatures of the several States, pursuant to the fifth Article of the original Constitution
R-29	**[Article. XI.]**

PUI	Bill of Rights Text
R-30	**[Proposed 1794; Ratified 1798]**
R-31	The Judicial power of the United States shall not be construed to extend to any suit in law or equity, commenced or prosecuted against one of the United States by Citizens of another State, or by Citizens or Subjects of any Foreign State.
R-32	**[Article. XII.]**
R-33	**[Proposed 1803; Ratified 1804]**
R-34	The Electors shall meet in their respective states, and vote by ballot for President and Vice-President, one of whom, at least, shall not be an inhabitant of the same state with themselves; they shall name in their ballots the person voted for as President, and in distinct ballots the person voted for as Vice-President, and they shall make distinct lists of all persons voted for as President, and of all persons voted for as Vice-President, and of the number of votes for each, which lists they shall sign and certify, and transmit sealed to the seat of the government of the United States, directed to the President of the Senate; — The President of the Senate shall, in the presence of the Senate and House of Representatives, open all the certificates and the votes shall then be counted; — The person having the greatest number of votes for President, shall be the President, if such number be a majority of the whole number of Electors appointed; and if no person have such majority, then from the persons having the highest numbers not exceeding three on the list of those voted for as President, the House of Representatives shall choose immediately, by ballot, the President. But in choosing the President, the votes shall be taken by states, the representation from each state having one vote; a quorum for this purpose shall consist of a member or members from two-thirds of the states, and a majority of all the states shall be necessary to a choice. And if the House of Representatives shall not choose a President whenever the right of choice shall devolve upon them, before the fourth day of March next following, then the Vice-President shall act as President, as in the case of the death or other constitutional disability of the President. — The person having the greatest number of votes as Vice-President, shall be the Vice-President, if such number be a majority of the whole number of Electors appointed, and if no person have a majority, then from the two highest numbers on the list, the Senate shall choose the Vice-President; a quorum for the purpose shall consist of two-thirds of the whole number of Senators, and a majority of the whole number shall be necessary to a choice. But no person constitutionally ineligible to the office of President shall be eligible to that of Vice-President of the United States.
R-35	**[Contested Article.]**
R-36	**[Proposed 1810; Probably Ratified 1819]**
R-37	If any Citizen of the United States shall accept, claim, receive or retain any Title of Nobility or Honour, or shall, without the Consent of Congress, accept and retain any present, Pension, Office or Emolument of any kind whatever, from any Emperor, King, Prince or foreign Power, such Person shall cease to be a Citizen of the United States, and shall be incapable of holding any Office of Trust or Profit under them, or

PUI	Bill of Rights Text
	either of them.
R-38	**[Unratified Article.]**
R-39	**[Proposed 1861; Signed by President Lincoln; Unratified]**
R-40	Article Thirteen.
R-41	No amendment shall be made to the Constitution which will authorize or give to Congress the power to abolish or interfere, within any State, with the domestic institutions thereof, including that of persons held to labor or service by the laws of said State.
R-42	**Article. XIII.**
R-43	**[Proposed 1865; Ratified 1865]**
R-44	Section. 1. Neither slavery nor involuntary servitude, except as a punishment for crime whereof the party shall have been duly convicted, shall exist within the United States, or any place subject to their jurisdiction.
R-45	Section. 2. Congress shall have power to enforce this article by appropriate legislation.
R-46	**Article. XIV.**
R-47	**[Proposed 1866; Ratified Under Duress 1868]**
R-48	Section. 1. All persons born or naturalized in the United States, and subject to the jurisdiction thereof, are citizens of the United States and of the State wherein they reside. No State shall make or enforce any law which shall abridge the privileges or immunities of citizens of the United States; nor shall any State deprive any person of life, liberty, or property, without due process of law; nor deny to any person within its jurisdiction the equal protection of the laws.
R-49	Section. 2. Representatives shall be apportioned among the several States according to their respective numbers, counting the whole number of persons in each State, excluding Indians not taxed. But when the right to vote at any election for the choice of electors for President and Vice President of the United States, Representatives in Congress, the Executive and Judicial officers of a State, or the members of the Legislature thereof, is denied to any of the male inhabitants of such State, being twenty-one years of age, and citizens of the United States, or in any way abridged, except for participation in rebellion, or other crime, the basis of representation therein shall be reduced in the proportion which the number of such male citizens shall bear to the whole number of male citizens twenty-one years of age in such State.
R-50	Section. 3. No person shall be a Senator or Representative in Congress, or elector of President and Vice President, or hold any office, civil or military, under the United States, or under any State, who, having previously taken an oath, as a member of Congress, or as an officer of the United States, or as a member of any State legislature, or as an executive or judicial officer of any State, to support the Constitution of the United States, shall have engaged in insurrection or rebellion

PUI	Bill of Rights Text
	against the same, or given aid or comfort to the enemies thereof. But Congress may by a vote of two-thirds of each House, remove such disability.
R-51	Section. 4. The validity of the public debt of the United States, authorized by law, including debts incurred for payment of pensions and bounties for services in suppressing insurrection or rebellion, shall not be questioned. But neither the United States nor any State shall assume or pay any debt or obligation incurred in aid of insurrection or rebellion against the United States, or any claim for the loss or emancipation of any slave; but all such debts, obligations and claims shall be held illegal and void.
R-52	Section. 5. The Congress shall have power to enforce, by appropriate legislation, the provisions of this article.
R-53	**Article. XV.**
R-54	**[Proposed 1869; Ratified 1870]**
R-55	Section. 1. The right of citizens of the United States to vote shall not be denied or abridged by the United States or by any State on account of race, color, or previous condition of servitude.
R-56	Section. 2. The Congress shall have power to enforce this article by appropriate legislation.
R-57	**Article. XVI.**
R-58	**[Proposed 1909; Questionably Ratified 1913]**
R-59	The Congress shall have power to lay and collect taxes on incomes, from whatever source derived, without apportionment among the several States, and without regard to any census or enumeration.
R-60	**[Article. XVII.]**
R-61	**[Proposed 1912; Ratified 1913; Possibly Unconstitutional (See Article V, Clause 3 of the Constitution)]**
R-62	The Senate of the United States shall be composed of two Senators from each State, elected by the people thereof, for six years; and each Senator shall have one vote. The electors in each State shall have the qualifications requisite for electors of the most numerous branch of the State legislatures.
R-63	When vacancies happen in the representation of any State in the Senate, the executive authority of such State shall issue writs of election to fill such vacancies: Provided, That the legislature of any State may empower the executive thereof to make temporary appointments until the people fill the vacancies by election as the legislature may direct.
R-64	This amendment shall not be so construed as to affect the election or term of any Senator chosen before it becomes valid as part of the Constitution.
R-65	**Article. [XVIII.]**
R-66	**[Proposed 1917; Ratified 1919; Repealed 1933 (See Amendment XXI, Section 1]**
R-67	Section. 1. After one year from the ratification of this article the manufacture, sale,

PUI	Bill of Rights Text
	or transportation of intoxicating liquors within, the importation thereof into, or the exportation thereof from the United States and all territory subject to the jurisdiction thereof for beverage purposes is hereby prohibited.
R-68	Section. 2. The Congress and the several States shall have concurrent power to enforce this article by appropriate legislation.
R-69	Section. 3. This article shall be inoperative unless it shall have been ratified as an amendment to the Constitution by the legislatures of the several States, as provided in the Constitution, within seven years from the date of the submission hereof to the States by the Congress.
R-70	**Article. [XIX.]**
R-71	**[Proposed 1919; Ratified 1920]**
R-72	The right of citizens of the United States to vote shall not be denied or abridged by the United States or by any State on account of sex.
R-73	Congress shall have power to enforce this article by appropriate legislation.
R-74	[Unratified Article.]
R-75	[Proposed 1926; Unratified]
R-76	Article —
R-77	Section. 1. The Congress shall have power to limit, regulate, and prohibit the labor of persons under eighteen years of age.
R-78	Section. 2. The power of the several States is unimpaired by this article except that the operation of State laws shall be suspended to the extent necessary to give effect to legislation enacted by the Congress.
R-79	**Article. [XX.]**
R-80	**[Proposed 1932; Ratified 1933]**
R-81	Section. 1. The terms of the President and Vice President shall end at noon on the 20th day of January, and the terms of Senators and Representatives at noon on the 3d day of January, of the years in which such terms would have ended if this article had not been ratified; and the terms of their successors shall then begin.
R-82	Section. 2. The Congress shall assemble at least once in every year, and such meeting shall begin at noon on the 3d day of January, unless they shall by law appoint a different day.
R-83	Section. 3. If, at the time fixed for the beginning of the term of the President, the President elect shall have died, the Vice President elect shall become President. If a President shall not have been chosen before the time fixed for the beginning of his term, or if the President elect shall have failed to qualify, then the Vice President elect shall act as President until a President shall have qualified; and the Congress may by law provide for the case wherein neither a President elect nor a Vice President elect shall have qualified, declaring who shall then act as President, or the manner in which one who is to act shall be selected, and such person shall act

PUI	Bill of Rights Text
	accordingly until a President or Vice President shall have qualified.
R-84	Section. 4. The Congress may by law provide for the case of the death of any of the persons from whom the House of Representatives may choose a President whenever the right of choice shall have devolved upon them, and for the case of the death of any of the persons from whom the Senate may choose a Vice President whenever the right of choice shall have devolved upon them.
R-85	Section. 5. Sections 1 and 2 shall take effect on the 15th day of October following the ratification of this article.
R-86	Section. 6. This article shall be inoperative unless it shall have been ratified as an amendment to the Constitution by the legislatures of three-fourths of the several States within seven years from the date of its submission.
R-87	**Article. [XXI.]**
R-88	**[Proposed 1933; Ratified 1933]**
R-89	Section. 1. The eighteenth article of amendment to the Constitution of the United States is hereby repealed.
R-90	Section. 2. The transportation or importation into any State, Territory, or possession of the United States for delivery or use therein of intoxicating liquors, in violation of the laws thereof, is hereby prohibited.
R-91	Section. 3. This article shall be inoperative unless it shall have been ratified as an amendment to the Constitution by conventions in the several States, as provided in the Constitution, within seven years from the date of the submission hereof to the States by the Congress.
R-92	**Article. [XXII.]**
R-93	**[Proposed 1947; Ratified 1951]**
R-94	Section. 1. No person shall be elected to the office of the President more than twice, and no person who has held the office of President, or acted as President, for more than two years of a term to which some other person was elected President shall be elected to the office of the President more than once. But this Article shall not apply to any person holding the office of President when this Article was proposed by the Congress, and shall not prevent any person who may be holding the office of President, or acting as President, during the term within which this Article becomes operative from holding the office of President or acting as President during the remainder of such term.
R-95	Section. 2. This article shall be inoperative unless it shall have been ratified as an amendment to the Constitution by the legislatures of three-fourths of the several States within seven years from the date of its submission to the States by the Congress.
R-96	**Article. [XXIII.]**
R-97	**[Proposed 1960; Ratified 1961]**
R-98	Section. 1. The District constituting the seat of Government of the United States shall appoint in such manner as the Congress may direct:

PUI	Bill of Rights Text
R-99	A number of electors of President and Vice President equal to the whole number of Senators and Representatives in Congress to which the District would be entitled if it were a State, but in no event more than the least populous State; they shall be in addition to those appointed by the States, but they shall be considered, for the purposes of the election of President and Vice President, to be electors appointed by a State; and they shall meet in the District and perform such duties as provided by the twelfth article of amendment.
R-100	Section. 2. The Congress shall have power to enforce this article by appropriate legislation.
R-101	**Article. [XXIV.]**
R-102	**[Proposed 1962; Ratified 1964]**
R-103	Section. 1. The right of citizens of the United States to vote in any primary or other election for President or Vice President, for electors for President or Vice President, or for Senator or Representative in Congress, shall not be denied or abridged by the United States or any State by reason of failure to pay any poll tax or other tax.
R-104	Section. 2. The Congress shall have power to enforce this article by appropriate legislation.
R-105	**Article. [XXV.]**
R-106	**[Proposed 1965; Ratified 1967]**
R-107	Section. 1. In case of the removal of the President from office or of his death or resignation, the Vice President shall become President.
R-108	Section. 2. Whenever there is a vacancy in the office of the Vice President, the President shall nominate a Vice President who shall take office upon confirmation by a majority vote of both Houses of Congress.
R-109	Section. 3. Whenever the President transmits to the President pro tempore of the Senate and the Speaker of the House of Representatives his written declaration that he is unable to discharge the powers and duties of his office, and until he transmits to them a written declaration to the contrary, such powers and duties shall be discharged by the Vice President as Acting President.
R-110	Section. 4. Whenever the Vice President and a majority of either the principal officers of the executive departments or of such other body as Congress may by law provide, transmit to the President pro tempore of the Senate and the Speaker of the House of Representatives their written declaration that the President is unable to discharge the powers and duties of his office, the Vice President shall immediately assume the powers and duties of the office as Acting President.
R-111	Thereafter, when the President transmits to the President pro tempore of the Senate and the Speaker of the House of Representatives his written declaration that no inability exists, he shall resume the powers and duties of his office unless the Vice President and a majority of either the principal officers of the executive department or of such other body as Congress may by law provide, transmit within four days to the President pro tempore of the Senate and the Speaker of the House of Representatives their written declaration that the President is unable to discharge the

PUI	Bill of Rights Text
	powers and duties of his office. Thereupon Congress shall decide the issue, assembling within forty-eight hours for that purpose if not in session. If the Congress, within twenty-one days after receipt of the latter written declaration, or, if Congress is not in session, within twenty-one days after Congress is required to assemble, determines by two-thirds vote of both Houses that the President is unable to discharge the powers and duties of his office, the Vice President shall continue to discharge the same as Acting President; otherwise, the President shall resume the powers and duties of his office.
R-112	**Article. [XXVI.]**
R-113	**[Proposed 1971; Ratified 1971]**
R-114	Section. 1. The right of citizens of the United States, who are eighteen years of age or older, to vote shall not be denied or abridged by the United States or by any State on account of age.
R-115	Section. 2. The Congress shall have power to enforce this article by appropriate legislation.
R-116	**[Inoperative Article.]**
R-117	**[Proposed 1972; Expired Unratified 1982]**
R-118	Article —
R-119	Section. 1. Equality of rights under the law shall not be denied or abridged by the United States or by any State on account of sex.
R-120	Section. 2. The Congress shall have the power to enforce, by appropriate legislation, the provisions of this article.
R-121	Section. 3. This amendment shall take effect two years after the date of ratification.
R-122	**[Inoperative Article.]**
R-123	**[Proposed 1978; Expired Unratified 1985]**
R-124	Article —
R-125	Section. 1. For purposes of representation in the Congress, election of the President and Vice President, and article V of this Constitution, the District constituting the seat of government of the United States shall be treated as though it were a State.
R-126	Section. 2. The exercise of the rights and powers conferred under this article shall be by the people of the District constituting the seat of government, and as shall be provided by the Congress.
R-127	Section. 3. The twenty-third article of amendment to the Constitution of the United States is hereby repealed.
R-128	Section. 4. This article shall be inoperative, unless it shall have been ratified as an amendment to the Constitution by the legislatures of three-fourths of the several States within seven years from the date of its submission.
R-129	**Article. [XXVII.]**

PUI	Bill of Rights Text
R-130	**[Proposed 1789; Ratified 1992; Second of twelve Articles comprising the Bill of Rights]**
R-131	No law, varying the compensation for the services of the Senators and Representatives, shall take effect, until an election of Representatives shall have intervened.

10.9 Presidential Impeachment

10.9.1 Impeachment Inquiry Report

The Trump-Ukraine Impeachment Inquiry Report, Report of the House Permanent Select Committee on Intelligence, Pursuant to H. Res. 660 in Consultation with the House Committee on Oversight and Reform and the House Committee on Foreign Affairs, December 2019 was produced by the House Permanent Select Committee on Intelligence. The following is the table of contents from the 300-page report, the preface and the executive summary.

PREFACE

This report reflects the evidence gathered thus far by the House Permanent Select Committee on Intelligence, in coordination with the Committee on Oversight and Reform and the Committee on Foreign Affairs, as part of the House of Representatives' impeachment inquiry into Donald J. Trump, the 45th President of the United States.

The report is the culmination of an investigation that began in September 2019 and intensified over the past three months as new revelations and evidence of the President's misconduct towards Ukraine emerged. The Committees pursued the truth vigorously, but fairly, ensuring the full participation of both parties throughout the probe.

Sustained by the tireless work of more than three dozen dedicated staff across the three Committees, we issued dozens of subpoenas for documents and testimony and took more than 100 hours of deposition testimony from 17 witnesses. To provide the American people the opportunity to learn and evaluate the facts themselves, the Intelligence Committee held seven public hearings with 12 witnesses—including three requested by the Republican Minority—that totaled more than 30 hours.

At the outset, I want to recognize my late friend and colleague Elijah E. Cummings, whose grace and commitment to justice served as our North Star throughout this investigation. I would also like to thank my colleagues Eliot L. Engel and Carolyn B. Maloney, chairs respectively of the Foreign Affairs and Oversight and Reform Committees, as well as the Members of those Committees, many of whom provided invaluable contributions. Members of the Intelligence Committee, as well, worked selflessly and collaboratively throughout this investigation. Finally, I am grateful to Speaker Nancy Pelosi for the trust she placed in our Committees to conduct this work and for her wise counsel throughout.

I also want to thank the dedicated professional staff of the Intelligence Committee, who worked ceaselessly and with remarkable poise and ability. My deepest gratitude goes to Daniel Goldman, Rheanne Wirkkala, Maher Bitar, Timothy Bergreen, Patrick Boland, Daniel Noble, Nicolas Mitchell, Sean Misko, Patrick Fallon, Diana Pilipenko, William Evans, Ariana Rowberry, Wells Bennett, and William Wu. Additional Intelligence Committee staff members also assured that the important oversight work of the Committee continued, even as we were required to take on the additional responsibility of conducting a key part of the

House impeachment inquiry. Finally, I would like to thank the devoted and outstanding staff of the Committee on Oversight and Reform, including but not limited to Dave Rapallo, Susanne Sachsman Grooms, Peter Kenny, Krista Boyd, and Janet Kim, as well as Laura Carey from the Committee on Foreign Affairs.

* * *

In his farewell address, President George Washington warned of a moment when "cunning, ambitious, and unprincipled men will be enabled to subvert the power of the people and to usurp for themselves the reins of government, destroying afterwards the very engines which have lifted them to unjust dominion."

The Framers of the Constitution well understood that an individual could one day occupy the Office of the President who would place his personal or political interests above those of the nation. Having just won hard-fought independence from a King with unbridled authority, they were attuned to the dangers of an executive who lacked fealty to the law and the Constitution.

In response, the Framers adopted a tool used by the British Parliament for several hundred years to constrain the Crown—the power of impeachment. Unlike in Britain, where impeachment was typically reserved for inferior officers but not the King himself, impeachment in our untested democracy was specifically intended to serve as the ultimate form of accountability for a duly-elected President. Rather than a mechanism to overturn an election, impeachment was explicitly contemplated as a remedy of last resort for a president who fails to faithfully execute his oath of office "to preserve, protect and defend the Constitution of the United States."

Accordingly, the Constitution confers the power to impeach the president on Congress, stating that the president shall be removed from office upon conviction for "Treason, Bribery, or other high Crimes and Misdemeanors." While the Constitutional standard for removal from office is justly a high one, it is nonetheless an essential check and balance on the authority of the occupant of the Office of the President, particularly when that occupant represents a continuing threat to our fundamental democratic norms, values, and laws.

Alexander Hamilton explained that impeachment was not designed to cover only criminal violations, but also crimes against the American people. "The subjects of its jurisdiction," Hamilton wrote, "are those offenses which proceed from the misconduct of public men, or, in other words, from the abuse or violation of some public trust. They are of a nature which may with peculiar propriety be denominated political, as they relate chiefly to injuries done immediately to the society itself."

Similarly, future Associate Justice of the United States Supreme Court James Wilson, a delegate from Pennsylvania at the Constitutional Convention, distinguished impeachable offenses from those that reside "within the sphere of ordinary jurisprudence." As he noted, "impeachments are confined to political characters, to political crimes and misdemeanors, and to political punishments."

* * *

As this report details, the impeachment inquiry has found that President Trump, personally and acting through agents within and outside of the U.S. government, solicited the interference of a foreign government, Ukraine, to benefit his reelection. In furtherance of this scheme, President Trump conditioned official acts on a public announcement by the new Ukrainian President, Volodymyr Zelensky, of politically-motivated investigations, including one into President Trump's domestic political opponent. In pressuring President Zelensky to carry out his demand, President Trump withheld a White House meeting desperately sought by the Ukrainian President, and critical U.S. military assistance to fight Russian aggression in eastern Ukraine.

The President engaged in this course of conduct for the benefit of his own presidential reelection, to harm the election prospects of a political rival, and to influence our nation's upcoming presidential election to his advantage. In doing so, the President placed his own personal and political interests above the national interests of the United States, sought to undermine the integrity of the U.S. presidential election process, and endangered U.S. national security.

At the center of this investigation is the memorandum prepared following President Trump's July 25, 2019, phone call with Ukraine's President, which the White House declassified and released under significant public pressure. The call record alone is stark evidence of misconduct; a demonstration of the President's prioritization of his personal political benefit over the national interest. In response to President Zelensky's appreciation for vital U.S. military assistance, which President Trump froze without explanation, President Trump asked for "a favor though": two specific investigations designed to assist his reelection efforts.

Our investigation determined that this telephone call was neither the start nor the end of President Trump's efforts to bend U.S. foreign policy for his personal gain. Rather, it was a dramatic crescendo within a months-long campaign driven by President Trump in which senior U.S. officials, including the Vice President, the Secretary of State, the Acting Chief of Staff, the Secretary of Energy, and others were either knowledgeable of or active participants in an effort to extract from a foreign nation the personal political benefits sought by the President.

The investigation revealed the nature and extent of the President's misconduct, notwithstanding an unprecedented campaign of obstruction by the President and his Administration to prevent the Committees from obtaining documentary evidence and testimony. A dozen witnesses followed President Trump's orders, defying voluntary requests and lawful subpoenas, and refusing to testify. The White House, Department of State, Department of Defense, Office of Management and Budget, and Department of Energy refused to produce a single document in response to our subpoenas.

Ultimately, this sweeping effort to stonewall the House of Representatives' "sole Power of Impeachment" under the Constitution failed because witnesses courageously came forward and testified in response to lawful process. The report that follows was only possible because of their sense of duty and devotion to their country and its Constitution.

Nevertheless, there remain unanswered questions, and our investigation must continue, even as we transmit our report to the Judiciary Committee. Given the proximate threat of further presidential attempts to solicit foreign interference in our next election, we cannot wait to make a referral until our efforts to obtain additional testimony and documents wind their way through the courts. The evidence of the President's misconduct is overwhelming, and so too is the evidence of his obstruction of Congress. Indeed, it would be hard to imagine a stronger or more complete case of obstruction than that demonstrated by the President since the inquiry began.

The damage the President has done to our relationship with a key strategic partner will be remedied over time, and Ukraine continues to enjoy strong bipartisan support in Congress. But the damage to our system of checks and balances, and to the balance of power within our three branches of government, will be long-lasting and potentially irrevocable if the President's ability to stonewall Congress goes unchecked. Any future President will feel empowered to resist an investigation into their own wrongdoing, malfeasance, or corruption, and the result will be a nation at far greater risk of all three.

* * *

The decision to move forward with an impeachment inquiry is not one we took lightly. Under the best of circumstances, impeachment is a wrenching process for the nation. I resisted calls to undertake an impeachment investigation for many months on that basis, notwithstanding the existence of presidential misconduct that I believed to be deeply unethical and damaging to our democracy. The alarming events and actions detailed in this report, however, left us with no choice but to proceed.

In making the decision to move forward, we were struck by the fact that the President's misconduct was not an isolated occurrence, nor was it the product of a naïve president. Instead, the efforts to involve Ukraine in our 2020 presidential election were undertaken by a President who himself was elected in 2016 with the benefit of an unprecedented and sweeping campaign of election interference undertaken by Russia in his favor, and which the President welcomed and utilized.

Having witnessed the degree to which interference by a foreign power in 2016 harmed our democracy, President Trump cannot credibly claim ignorance to its pernicious effects. Even more pointedly, the President's July call with Ukrainian President Zelensky, in which he solicited an investigation to damage his most feared 2020 opponent, came the day after Special Counsel Robert Mueller testified to Congress about Russia's efforts to damage his 2016 opponent and his urgent warning of the dangers of further foreign interference in the next election. With this backdrop, the solicitation of new foreign intervention was the act of a president unbound, not one chastened by experience. It was the act of a president who viewed himself as unaccountable and determined to use his vast official powers to secure his reelection.

This repeated and pervasive threat to our democratic electoral process added urgency to our work. On October 3, 2019, even as our Committee was engaged in this inquiry, President Trump publicly declared anew that other countries should open investigations into his chief political rival, saying, "China should start an investigation into the Bidens," and that "President Zelensky, if it were me, I would recommend that they start an investigation into the Bidens." When a reporter asked the President what he hoped Ukraine's President would do following the July 25 call, President Trump, seeking to dispel any doubt as to his continuing intention, responded: "Well, I would think that, if they were honest about it, they'd start a major investigation into the Bidens. It's a very simple answer."

By doubling down on his misconduct and declaring that his July 25 call with President Zelensky was "perfect," President Trump has shown a continued willingness to use the power of his office to seek foreign intervention in our next election. His Acting Chief of Staff, Mick Mulvaney, in the course of admitting that the President had linked security assistance to Ukraine to the announcement of one of his desired investigations, told the American people to "get over it." In these statements and actions, the President became the author of his own impeachment inquiry. The question presented by the set of facts enumerated in this report may be as simple as that posed by the President and his chief of staff's brazenness: is the remedy of impeachment warranted for a president who would use the power of his office to coerce foreign interference in a U.S. election, or is that now a mere perk of the office that Americans must simply "get over"?

* * *

Those watching the impeachment hearings might have been struck by how little discrepancy there was between the witnesses called by the Majority and Minority. Indeed, most of the facts presented in the pages that follow are uncontested. The broad outlines as well as many of the details of the President's scheme have been presented by the witnesses with remarkable consistency. There will always be some variation in the testimony of multiple people witnessing the same events, but few of the differences here go to the heart of the matter. And so, it may have been all the more surprising to the public to see very disparate reactions to the testimony by the Members of Congress from each party.

If there was one ill the Founding Founders feared as much as that of an unfit president, it may have been that of excessive factionalism. Although the Framers viewed parties as necessary, they also endeavored to structure the new government in such a way as to minimize the "violence of faction." As George Washington warned in his farewell address, "the common and continual mischiefs of the spirit of party are sufficient to make it the interest and duty of a wise people to discourage and restrain it."

Today, we may be witnessing a collision between the power of a remedy meant to curb presidential misconduct and the power of faction determined to defend against the use of that remedy on a president of the same party. But perhaps even more corrosive to our democratic system of governance, the President and his allies are making a comprehensive attack on the very idea of fact and truth. How can a democracy survive without acceptance of a common set of experiences?

America remains the beacon of democracy and opportunity for freedom-loving people around the world. From their homes and their jail cells, from their public squares and their refugee camps, from their waking hours until their last breath, individuals fighting human rights abuses, journalists uncovering and exposing corruption, persecuted minorities struggling to survive and preserve their faith, and countless others around the globe just hoping for a better life look to America. What we do will determine what they see, and whether America remains a nation committed to the rule of law.

As Benjamin Franklin departed the Constitutional Convention, he was asked, "what have we got? A Republic or a Monarchy?" He responded simply: "A Republic, if you can keep it."

Adam B. Schiff
Chairman, House Permanent Select Committee on Intelligence

EXECUTIVE SUMMARY

The impeachment inquiry into Donald J. Trump, the 45th President of the United States, uncovered a months-long effort by President Trump to use the powers of his office to solicit foreign interference on his behalf in the 2020 election. As described in this executive summary and the report that follows, President Trump's scheme subverted U.S. foreign policy toward Ukraine and undermined our national security in favor of two politically motivated investigations that would help his presidential reelection campaign. The President demanded that the newly-elected Ukrainian president, Volodymyr Zelensky, publicly announce investigations into a political rival that he apparently feared the most, former Vice President Joe Biden, and into a discredited theory that it was Ukraine, not Russia, that interfered in the 2016 presidential election. To compel the Ukrainian President to do his political bidding, President Trump conditioned two official acts on the public announcement of the investigations: a coveted White House visit and critical U.S. military assistance Ukraine needed to fight its Russian adversary.

During a July 25, 2019, call between President Trump and President Zelensky, President Zelensky expressed gratitude for U.S. military assistance. President Trump immediately responded by asking President Zelensky to "do us a favor though" and openly pressed for Ukraine to investigate former Vice President Biden and the 2016 conspiracy theory. In turn, President Zelensky assured President Trump that he would pursue the investigation and reiterated his interest in the White

House meeting. Although President Trump's scheme intentionally bypassed many career personnel, it was undertaken with the knowledge and approval of senior Administration officials, including the President's Acting Chief of Staff Mick Mulvaney, Secretary of State Mike Pompeo, and Secretary of Energy Rick Perry. In fact, at a press conference weeks after public revelations about the scheme, Mr. Mulvaney publicly acknowledged that the President directly tied the hold on military aid to his desire to get Ukraine to conduct a political investigation, telling Americans to "get over it."

President Trump and his senior officials may see nothing wrong with using the power of the Office of the President to pressure a foreign country to help the President's reelection campaign. Indeed, President Trump continues to encourage Ukraine and other foreign countries to engage in the same kind of election interference today. However, the Founding Fathers prescribed a remedy for a chief executive who places his personal interests above those of the country: impeachment. Accordingly, as part of the House of Representatives' impeachment inquiry, the Permanent Select Committee on Intelligence, in coordination with the Committees on Oversight and Reform and Foreign Affairs, were compelled to undertake a serious, sober, and expeditious investigation into whether the President's misconduct warrants that remedy.

In response, President Trump engaged in an unprecedented campaign of obstruction of this impeachment inquiry. Nevertheless, due in large measure to patriotic and courageous public servants who provided the Committees with direct evidence of the President's actions, the Committees uncovered significant misconduct on the part of the President of the United States. As required under House Resolution 660, the Intelligence Committee, in consultation with the Committees on Oversight and Reform and Foreign Affairs, has prepared this report to detail the evidence uncovered to date, which will now be transmitted to the Judiciary Committee for its consideration.

10.9.2 H.R.755 Articles of Impeachment

116th CONGRESS, 1st Session, H. RES. 755, December 10, 2019. Impeaching Donald John Trump, President of the United States, for high crimes and misdemeanors.

IN THE HOUSE OF REPRESENTATIVES

Mr. Nadler submitted the following resolution; which was referred to the Committee on the Judiciary

RESOLUTION

Impeaching Donald John Trump, President of the United States, for high crimes and misdemeanors.

Resolved, That Donald J. Trump, President of the United States, is impeached for high crimes and misdemeanors and that the following articles of impeachment be exhibited to the United States Senate:

Articles of impeachment exhibited by the House of Representatives of the United States of America in the name of itself and of the people of the United States of America, against Donald J. Trump, President of the United States of America, in maintenance and support of its impeachment against him for high crimes and misdemeanors.

ARTICLE I: ABUSE OF POWER

The Constitution provides that the House of Representatives "shall have the sole Power of Impeachment" and that the President "shall be removed from Office on Impeachment for, and Conviction of, Treason, Bribery, or other high Crimes and Misdemeanors". In his conduct of the office of President of the United States—and in violation of his constitutional oath faithfully to execute the office of President of the United States and, to the best of his ability, preserve, protect, and defend the Constitution of the United States, and in violation of his constitutional duty to take care that the laws be faithfully executed—Donald J. Trump has abused the powers of the Presidency, in that:

Using the powers of his high office, President Trump solicited the interference of a foreign government, Ukraine, in the 2020 United States Presidential election. He did so through a scheme or course of conduct that included soliciting the Government of Ukraine to publicly announce investigations that would benefit his reelection, harm the election prospects of a political opponent, and influence the 2020 United States Presidential election to his advantage. President Trump also sought to pressure the Government of Ukraine to take these steps by conditioning official United States Government acts of significant value to Ukraine on its public announcement of the investigations. President Trump engaged in this scheme or course of conduct for corrupt purposes in pursuit of personal political benefit. In so doing, President Trump used the powers of the Presidency in a manner that compromised the national security of the United States and undermined the integrity of the United States democratic process. He thus ignored and injured the interests of the Nation.

President Trump engaged in this scheme or course of conduct through the following means:

(1) President Trump—acting both directly and through his agents within and outside the United States Government—corruptly solicited the Government of Ukraine to publicly announce investigations into—

(A) a political opponent, former Vice President Joseph R. Biden, Jr.; and

(B) a discredited theory promoted by Russia alleging that Ukraine—rather than Russia—interfered in the 2016 United States Presidential election.

(2) With the same corrupt motives, President Trump—acting both directly and through his agents within and outside the United States Government—conditioned

two official acts on the public announcements that he had requested—

(A) the release of $391 million of United States taxpayer funds that Congress had appropriated on a bipartisan basis for the purpose of providing vital military and security assistance to Ukraine to oppose Russian aggression and which President Trump had ordered suspended; and

(B) a head of state meeting at the White House, which the President of Ukraine sought to demonstrate continued United States support for the Government of Ukraine in the face of Russian aggression.

(3) Faced with the public revelation of his actions, President Trump ultimately released the military and security assistance to the Government of Ukraine, but has persisted in openly and corruptly urging and soliciting Ukraine to undertake investigations for his personal political benefit.

These actions were consistent with President Trump's previous invitations of foreign interference in United States elections.

In all of this, President Trump abused the powers of the Presidency by ignoring and injuring national security and other vital national interests to obtain an improper personal political benefit. He has also betrayed the Nation by abusing his high office to enlist a foreign power in corrupting democratic elections.

Wherefore President Trump, by such conduct, has demonstrated that he will remain a threat to national security and the Constitution if allowed to remain in office, and has acted in a manner grossly incompatible with self-governance and the rule of law. President Trump thus warrants impeachment and trial, removal from office, and disqualification to hold and enjoy any office of honor, trust, or profit under the United States.

ARTICLE II: OBSTRUCTION OF CONGRESS

The Constitution provides that the House of Representatives "shall have the sole Power of Impeachment" and that the President "shall be removed from Office on Impeachment for, and Conviction of, Treason, Bribery, or other high Crimes and Misdemeanors". In his conduct of the office of President of the United States—and in violation of his constitutional oath faithfully to execute the office of President of the United States and, to the best of his ability, preserve, protect, and defend the Constitution of the United States, and in violation of his constitutional duty to take care that the laws be faithfully executed—Donald J. Trump has directed the unprecedented, categorical, and indiscriminate defiance of subpoenas issued by the House of Representatives pursuant to its "sole Power of Impeachment". President Trump has abused the powers of the Presidency in a manner offensive to, and subversive of, the Constitution, in that:

The House of Representatives has engaged in an impeachment inquiry focused on President Trump's corrupt solicitation of the Government of Ukraine to interfere in the 2020 United States Presidential election. As part of this impeachment inquiry, the Committees undertaking the investigation served subpoenas seeking documents and testimony deemed vital to the inquiry from various Executive Branch agencies and offices, and current and former officials.

In response, without lawful cause or excuse, President Trump directed Executive Branch agencies, offices, and officials not to comply with those subpoenas. President Trump thus interposed the powers of the Presidency against the lawful subpoenas of the House of Representatives, and assumed to himself functions and judgments necessary to the exercise of the "sole Power of Impeachment" vested by the Constitution in the House of Representatives.

President Trump abused the powers of his high office through the following means:

(1) Directing the White House to defy a lawful subpoena by withholding the production of documents sought therein by the Committees.

(2) Directing other Executive Branch agencies and offices to defy lawful subpoenas and withhold the production of documents and records from the Committees—in response to which the Department of State, Office of Management and Budget, Department of Energy, and Department of Defense refused to produce a single document or record.

(3) Directing current and former Executive Branch officials not to cooperate with the Committees—in response to which nine Administration officials defied subpoenas for testimony, namely John Michael "Mick" Mulvaney, Robert B. Blair, John A. Eisenberg, Michael Ellis, Preston Wells Griffith, Russell T. Vought, Michael Duffey, Brian McCormack, and T. Ulrich Brechbuhl.

These actions were consistent with President Trump's previous efforts to undermine United States Government investigations into foreign interference in United States elections.

Through these actions, President Trump sought to arrogate to himself the right to determine the propriety, scope, and nature of an impeachment inquiry into his own conduct, as well as the unilateral prerogative to deny any and all information to the House of Representatives in the exercise of its "sole Power of Impeachment". In the history of the Republic, no President has ever ordered the complete defiance of an impeachment inquiry or sought to obstruct and impede so comprehensively the ability of the House of Representatives to investigate "high Crimes and Misdemeanors". This abuse of office served to cover up the President's own repeated misconduct and to seize and control the power of impeachment—and thus to nullify a vital constitutional safeguard vested solely in the House of Representatives.

In all of this, President Trump has acted in a manner contrary to his trust as President and subversive of constitutional government, to the great prejudice of the cause of law and justice, and to the manifest injury of the people of the United States.

Wherefore, President Trump, by such conduct, has demonstrated that he will remain a threat to the Constitution if allowed to remain in office, and has acted in a manner grossly incompatible with self-governance and the rule of law. President Trump thus warrants impeachment and trial, removal from office, and disqualification to hold and enjoy any office of honor, trust, or profit under the United States.

10.9.3 Doomsday Clock

The Doomsday Clock was started in 1947 and is a symbol that represents the likelihood of a nuclear catastrophe. The clock uses midnight to represent global catastrophe and the number of minutes before midnight to represent how close we are to global catastrophe. The sacrifice of Ukraine had no impact on the clock.

Doomsday Clock

Year	Minutes to Mid-night	Change (min)	Reason
1947	7	NA	The initial setting of the Doomsday Clock.
1949	3	−4	The Soviet Union tests its first atomic bomb officially starting the nuclear arms race.
1953	2	−1	The United States tests its first thermonuclear device in November 1952 as part of Operation Ivy, before the Soviet Union follows suit in August.
1960	7	+5	In response to a perception of increased scientific cooperation and public understanding of the dangers of nuclear weapons, the United States and Soviet Union cooperate and avoid direct confrontation in regional conflicts such as the 1956 Suez Crisis. Scientists from various countries help establish the International Geophysical Year, a series of coordinated, worldwide scientific observations between nations allied with both the United States and the Soviet Union, and the Pugwash Conferences on Science and World Affairs, which allow Soviet and American scientists to interact.
1963	12	+5	The United States and the Soviet Union sign the Partial Test Ban Treaty, limiting atmospheric nuclear testing.
1968	7	−5	The involvement of the United States in the Vietnam War intensifies, the Indo-Pakistani War of 1965 takes place, and the Six-Day War occurs in 1967. France and China, two nations which have not signed the Partial Test Ban Treaty, acquire and test nuclear weapons to assert themselves as global players in the nuclear arms race.
1969	10	+3	Every nation in the world, with the notable exceptions of

Doomsday Clock

Year	Minutes to Mid-night	Change (min)	Reason
			India, Israel, and Pakistan, signs the Nuclear Non-Proliferation Treaty.
1972	12	+2	The United States and the Soviet Union sign the first Strategic Arms Limitation Treaty (SALT I) and the Anti-Ballistic Missile (ABM) Treaty.
1974	9	−3	India tests a nuclear device and SALT II talks stall. Both the United States and the Soviet Union modernize multiple independently targetable reentry vehicles (MIRVs).
1980	7	−2	Unforeseeable end to deadlock in American–Soviet talks as the Soviet–Afghan War begins. As a result of the war, the US Senate refuses to ratify the SALT II agreement.
1981	4	−3	The Soviet war in Afghanistan toughens the US nuclear posture. President Jimmy Carter withdraws the United States from the 1980 Summer Olympic Games in Moscow. The Carter administration considers ways in which the United States could win a nuclear war. Ronald Reagan becomes President of the United States, scraps further arms reduction talks with the Soviet Union, and argues that the only way to end the Cold War is to win it. Tensions between the United States and the Soviet Union contribute to the danger of the nuclear annihilation.
1984	3	−1	Further escalation of the tensions between the United States and the Soviet Union, with the ongoing Soviet–Afghan War intensifying the Cold War. US Pershing II medium-range ballistic missile and cruise missiles are deployed in Western Europe. Ronald Reagan pushes to win the Cold War by intensifying the arms race between the superpowers. The Soviet Union and its allies (except Romania) boycott the 1984 Olympic Games in Los Angeles, as a response to the US led boycott in 1980.
1987	6	+3	The Clock is moved back three minutes as the United States and the Soviet Union sign the Intermediate-Range Nuclear Forces Treaty, to eliminate intermediate-range nuclear missiles, and their relations improve.
1990	10	+4	The Fall of the Berlin Wall and the Iron Curtain, along with the reunification of Germany, suggest that the Cold War is ending.
1991	17	+7	The United States and Soviet Union sign the first Strategic Arms Reduction Treaty (START I), and the Soviet Union dissolves on December 26. This is the farthest from midnight the Clock has been since its inception.

Doomsday Clock

Year	Minutes to Mid-night	Change (min)	Reason
1994	**17**	**0**	**The Budapest Memorandum on Security Assurances was signed on 5 December 1994 and as a result, between 1994 and 1996, Ukraine, Belarus, and Kazakhstan gave up their nuclear weapons. Their sacrifice and trust in humanity did not move the clock.**
1995	14	−3	Global military spending continues at Cold War levels amid concerns about post-Soviet nuclear proliferation of weapons and nuclear staff.
1998	9	−5	Both India and Pakistan test nuclear weapons in a tit-for-tat show of aggression; the United States and Russia run into difficulties in further reducing stockpiles.
2002	7	−2	Little progress on global nuclear disarmament. United States rejects a series of arms control treaties and announces its intentions to withdraw from the Anti-Ballistic Missile Treaty, amid concerns about the possibility of a nuclear terrorist attack due to the amount of weapon-grade nuclear materials that are unsecured and unaccounted for worldwide.
Starting in 2007 the clock includes climate change, new life sciences developments, and unchecked scientific and technology advances that could inflict irrevocable harm to humanity including inducing nuclear war.			
2007	5	−2	North Korea tests a nuclear weapon on October 2006, Iran's nuclear ambitions, a renewed American emphasis on the military utility of nuclear weapons, the failure to adequately secure nuclear materials, and the continued presence of some 26,000 nuclear weapons in the United States and Russia. After assessing the dangers posed to civilization, climate change was added to the prospect of nuclear annihilation as the greatest threats to humankind.
2010	6	+1	Worldwide cooperation to reduce nuclear arsenals and limit effect of climate change. New START agreement is ratified by both the United States and Russia, and more negotiations for further reductions in the American and Russian nuclear arsenal are already planned. The 2009 United Nations Climate Change Conference in Copenhagen results in the developing and industrialized countries agreeing to take responsibility for carbon emissions and to limit global temperature rise to 2 degrees Celsius.
2012	5	−1	Lack of global political action to address global climate change, nuclear weapons stockpiles, the potential for regional

Doomsday Clock

Year	Minutes to Mid-night	Change (min)	Reason
			nuclear conflict, and nuclear power safety.
2015	3	−2	Concerns amid continued lack of global political action to address global climate change, the modernization of nuclear weapons in the United States and Russia, and the problem of nuclear waste.
2017	2 1⁄2	−1⁄2	United States President Donald Trump's comments over nuclear weapons, the threat of a renewed arms race between the US and Russia, and the expressed disbelief in the scientific consensus over climate change by the Trump Administration. This is the first use of a fraction in the time.
2018	2	−1⁄2	The failure of world leaders to deal with looming threats of nuclear war and climate change. This is the clock's closest approach to midnight, matching that of 1953. In 2019, the Bulletin reaffirmed the two minutes to midnight time, citing continuing climate change and Trump administration's abandonment of US efforts to lead the world toward decarbonization; US withdrawal from Joint Comprehensive Plan of Action and Intermediate-Range Nuclear Forces Treaty; US and Russian nuclear modernization efforts; information warfare threats and other dangers from disruptive technologies such as synthetic biology, artificial intelligence, and cyberwarfare. **It appears that everyone forgot about the Budapest Memorandum on Security Assurances agreement and the enormous sacrifice and trust in humanity made by Ukraine, Belarus, and Kazakhstan when they gave up their nuclear weapons.**

11 Privatization System Conclusions

If only some of the systems perspectives were considered in the privatization policy making decisions, the direction since 1987 would have been radically different. Back in 1980 when all of this started no one could have imagined that such disregard for the past and the fundamental way in which the country operates would have been so compromised.

The magic hand of the market and ignoring fundamental system checks like controlling monopolies moved the country away from basic logic and reason to belief in magic and Bullshit[227] as vested interests captured the money from taxpayers and used it for their own interests. Using tax money to prop up the new privatized services companies that cannot survive in a free market economy was a clear indication that the system had become completely compromised by external forces and totally broken.

This book focused on the Air Transportation System, FAA and a few other systems. This text did not address how privatization may have negatively impacted other areas. However, the evidence in the popular media and daily life shows that the entire Federal Government is faced with the same types of scenarios and unintended consequences with the same level of breakdown for the same reasons. The following is a partial list of other impacted areas:

- Border Security
- Prisons
- Primary and Secondary Education
- Consumer Protection
- Other Federal Government Organizations (FCC FTC FDA DOD etc.)
- State and Local Governments
- etc.

11.1 Systems Perspectives

This text provided discussions of some systems perspectives. Each of the negatively impacted areas ignored some aspect of most of the systems perspectives. The following table shows the most egregiously ignored system perspectives.

---

[227] On Bullshit, Harry G. Frankfurt, Princeton University Press, January 2005, ISBN 9780691122946.

Table 51 Egregiously Ignored System Perspectives

Key Requirements	Automation levels and Safety
Stakeholder Needs	Systems Theory Thoughts
System Boundary	Socratic Method
Function Allocation and Performance	Critical Thinking
Good and Bad systems	Scientific Method
Mental Models	Cause and Effect
Architecture Measure of Effectiveness	Momentum
Economics 101	Hysteresis
Supply and Demand	Timing and Sizing
Cost Shifting and Life Cycle Cost	Mission Critical Systems
Value Systems	Security & Security Abuse
Human Factors	Safety Analysis
Ergonomics	Protecting Humans from Themselves
Cognitive Overload	Fault Tolerance & Fail-Safe
Technology Readiness Levels	Certification Tests
Misuse of Technology	Certification
Quality	Maslow's Hierarchy of Needs
Root Cause Analysis	Ethics
Tests Verifications and Validations	Organizational Capabilities
Safety Tests	Previous Century Systems

This text has suggested that privatization has negatively impacted various systems. The following is a list of systems discussed and the most ignored systems perspectives:

Table 52 Privatization Most Ignored Systems Perspectives

Privatized Areas	**Most Ignored Systems Perspectives**
Industrial Base	Organizational capabilities, stakeholder needs, ethics, cost shifting, key requirements, system boundary, function allocation and performance, good and bad systems,
Universities and Colleges	Stakeholder needs, ethics, key requirements, systems theory thoughts Socratic method, critical thinking.
Air Transportation	Stakeholder needs, ergonomics, cost shifting, ethics, key requirements, good and bad systems, architecture measure of effectiveness, value systems, human factors, misuse of technology, security abuse.
Federal Aviation Administration	Certification, stakeholder needs, organizational capabilities, pervious century systems, root cause analysis, good and bad systems, safety, ethics, scientific method.
Privatized Workers	Organizational capabilities, stakeholder needs, ethics, cost shifting, key requirements, system boundary, function allocation and performance, good and bad systems, architecture measure of effectiveness, life cycle cost, value systems, mental models, cause and effect, Maslow's

Table 52 Privatization Most Ignored Systems Perspectives

Privatized Areas	Most Ignored Systems Perspectives
	hierarchy of needs.
Federal Government	Key requirements and specifications, , function allocation and performance, organizational capabilities, stakeholder needs, ethics, cost shifting, root cause analysis, good and bad systems, certification
Other Areas	**Within the FAA discussion the following were negatively impacted**
Small & Medium Sized Cities	Key requirements, stakeholder needs, mental models, cause and effect, ethics, good and bad systems, timing and sizing, economics 101, supply and demand.
Aviation Industry	Organizational capabilities, good and bad systems, ethics, economics 101, supply and demand, systems theory thoughts, Socratic method, critical thinking.
Boeing and B737 MAX	Certification, organizational capabilities, good and bad systems, mission critical systems, safety analysis, levels of automation and safety, fault tolerance & fail-safe, quality, root cause analysis, safety tests, certification tests, ethics.
Airlines	Organizational capabilities, good and bad systems, ethics, economics 101, supply and demand, cost shifting, ergonomics, safety.

11.2 The Big Picture System

In this text we saw an analysis of the industrial base and the government as related to privatization. The analysis was performed in isolation. However, there is the big picture of the total system that includes both. When the big picture system is examined there are new insights that surface.

The big picture system has inputs and like all systems it has outputs based on a transfer function[228]. The transfer function is based on laws, regulations, international agreements, enforcement, and available natural resources. As the transfer function changes, the outcomes change. This is a massive system so any changes in the transfer function have a large hysteresis[229]. Most of the transfer function changes manifest themselves in the outcomes over years or decades. We also know that this is a complex system with massive internal dependencies, and it is difficult to predict the outcomes when there are changes. In most instances all we can really do is observe the outcomes. If the outcomes are bad, we can tweak the system in some direction until the outcomes move away from a bad condition[230]. If the outcomes are good, we can still tweak the system to get even better outcomes.

The outcomes can be identified and tracked using quantitative and or qualitative data. The ultimate check comes with the citizens who control the system by votes and participation in the system.

---

[228] See section 9.15.10 Systems Theory Thoughts.

[229] See section 9.2.3 Hysteresis.

[230] See section 9.2.1 Good and Bad Systems.

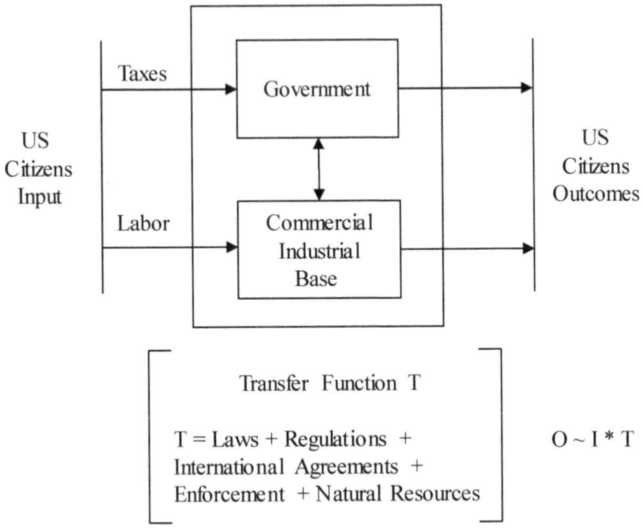

Figure 107 The Big Picture System

The system should respond to the outcomes in a causal loop, but it does not in all instances. If the outcomes are ignored for a very long period and the population suffers long enough the system self corrects with a revolution[231]. The big issue is the outcome levels between an ideal system and a poor system. The citizens may suffer but not enough to move into a revolutionary state[232].

The transfer function in the system might be reasonable or even the same as in other high-performance systems but the system outcomes may be very poor. In this case the system is compromised and the transfer functions while written down and institutionalized may not be used by the actual system. Instead hidden stakeholders have implemented hidden transfer functions to game the system in their favor at the expense of everyone else[233]. This is a compromised system.

The following table is a mental model that lists the possible outcomes and rates each outcome for the pre and post privatization time frames.

Table 53 Pre and Post Privatization System Outcomes

Outcomes	**Pre-Privatization 1945-1987**	**Post Privatization 1987-2019**
Consumer protections	Improved	**Worse**
Education level	Improved	**Worse**
Health level	Improved	**Worse**

231 See section 9.2.6 Cause and Effect and Balance of Power.

232 See section 9.2.9 Maslow's Hierarchy of Needs.

233 See section 9.2.10 Ethics.

Table 53 Pre and Post Privatization System Outcomes

Outcomes	**Pre-Privatization 1945-1987**	**Post Privatization 1987-2019**
Nutrition level	Improved	**Worse**
Leisure time during high school	Improved	**Worse**
Leisure time during university	Improved	**Worse**
Leisure time during working years	Improved	**Worse**
Leisure time during retirement	Improved	**Worse**
Earlier retirement age	Improved	**Worse**
Retirement income level	Improved	**Worse**
Vacation time	Improved	**Worse**
Consumer products	Improved	Same
Luxury products	Improved	Same
Life expectancy	Improved	**Worse**
Quality of life	Improved	**Worse**
Access to potable water	Improved	Same
Sanitation level	Improved	Same
Access to air transportation	Improved	**Way Worse**
Quality of air transportation	Improved	**Way Worse**
Access to personal transportation	Improved	Same
Quality of personal transportation	Improved	Improved
Access to public transportation	**Worse**	Same
Quality of public transportation	**Worse**	Improved
Infrastructure new	Improved	**Worse**
Infrastructure maintenance	Improved	**Way Worse**
Access to higher education	Improved	**Worse**
Quality of libraries	Improved	**Worse**
Number of press outlets	Improved	**Worse**
Number of journalists	Improved	**Worse**
Number of media outlets	Improved	**Worse**
Number of media conglomerates	Neutral	**Worse**
Amount of time to conclude wars	**Worse**	**Way Worse**
Intrusive intimidating security	Improved	**Way Worse**
Confidence in government	**Worse**	**Way Worse**
Confidence in companies	Improved	**Worse**
Confidence in institutions	Improved	**Way Worse**
Number of monopolies	Improved	**Way Worse**
Trade Imbalance	**Worse**	**Way Worse**
Exports	Improved	**Worse**
Production capacity	Improved	**Worse**
Diverse Food production	Improved	**Worse**
Water capacity	Improved	Same
Energy production	Improved	Same
Industrial capacity	Improved	**Worse**

Table 53 Pre and Post Privatization System Outcomes

Outcomes	Pre-Privatization 1945-1987	Post Privatization 1987-2019
Fundamental R&D institutions	Improved	Same
Applied R&D institutions	Improved	**Worse**
Companies with internal R&D	Improved	**Way Worse**

If you gather a group of people in a room and ask them to fill in the above table there will be differences. However, it is unlikely that the differences will show a different trend. Something is happening that may be attributed to privatization. The following is a list of some key events that led to the introduction of this table:

- FAA B737 Max certification failure and crashed grounded aircraft[234]
- Air Transportation cities lose access and horrible consumer experience[235]
- Rise of security state with very dangerous privacy precedents being set[236]
- Retirement is not happening with 5 generations in the workforce[237]
- Poor health outcomes with highest costs[238]
- Declining life expectancy
- Massive higher education debt[239]
- Young adult leisure time is very low or none
- Family leisure time is very low or none
- Retirement leisure time is very low or nonexistent
- FDA constant stream of lawsuits[240]
- DOD Afghanistan the longest war in US history[241]

11.3 Recommendations

Each section has detailed recommendations for moving forward. They fall into the category of legislation and education to try and fix the existing system of privatization. Waiting for the magic hand of the market to fix things is not an option. There were decades since 1987 for magic to appear and it did not appear. These are broad recommendations that apply to each of the systems examined:

---

[234] See section 6.4.7 B737 MAX.

[235] See section 5 Air Transportation.

[236] See section 5.8 System Recommendations, TSA Effects.

[237] See section 3 Industrial Base.

[238] See section 6.4.8 It's Not Just The FAA.

[239] See section 4 Universities and Colleges.

[240] See section 6.4.8 It's Not Just The FAA.

[241] See section 8.4 DOD and Defense Companies.

- **Anti-Trust Legislation:** It is critical to start to enforce the existing antitrust laws and remove laws that conflict with the antitrust laws. These laws allowed special interests to evade the critical checks in the system. The monopolies and oligopolies that surfaced in the past 30 years are gaming the system. Including more competition in the mix will not lead to a pure market setting but will add more players with divergent needs that will force alternative legislation in the system.
- **Primary and Secondary Education:** The purpose of education is to prepare the next generation of citizens to engage in our Democracy. The US is a Democracy implemented as a Republic. The representatives are supposed to represent the people not a few confused people with lots of money. Education is not about training workers for the unique needs of a select few companies. That is the responsibility of the companies, to provide training for their workforce. It was always known that when the next generation arrives the companies and the training needed will be gone – out of business with totally new technologies to master. Time is never waisted on even the most basic elements of training. It always was and will be about education not training.
- **It's Not Just The FAA:** As described in the section on the FAA, it's not just the FAA. Every government organization needs to be examined to determine the extent of damages due to privatization. Corrective actions based on the recommendations offered in this text need to be applied to all the other impacted government organizations.

The following is a composite list of the recommendations that were offered in the previous sections. The key is that responsible people need to act with legislation. You may be wondering why I duplicated these recommendations at the end of this book. This is systems thinking and engineering at work. Information is gathered, placed in information products, and duplicated to offer different perspectives. It is about viewing the situation from different perspectives. In this case the first set of perspectives offered were small isolated analysis. The analysis started to show a pattern and the system corrections needed started out as relatively small in isolation. In total, in this perspective, we now see that the recommendations are massive. There is a huge amount of work that needs to be done to correct the broken privatized system in this new century.

This is the full list of recommendations. Any duplicate recommendations will be marked as 2x, 3x, etc. indicating the number of duplicates.

<u>**Industrial Base**</u>

1. The new service companies must engage in new product and or technology development related to the work performed.
2. The new service companies must provide a semiannual report on product and or technology development. It is recognized that most will be failures.

Previous history suggests a 10% success rate, but companies must not be penalized for failures.

3. All services contracts must allocate reasonable funding to support product and technology development that starts at a minimum of 3% of the contract value. (2x)
4. The government must maintain a database of the products and or technologies developed so that they can move into the broader industrial base as part of a market clearing house.
5. In no instance shall these overhead items be used to discriminate between different vendor cost proposals. (2x)
6. The government must maintain a database on the number of privatized workers and number of privatized services companies by year beginning in 1980 and make this data easily accessible by the people.
7. Science the Endless Frontier set the policy and tone of the United States from 1945 to 1981. This document needs to be reviewed by everyone that is in a position charting a course for the future. The US is a system of government based on fundamental scientific principles. We need to rediscover that simple fact.
8. Industrial policy is tightly coupled to basic engineering principles. The Engineers especially the Systems Engineers need to be at the front of the table during future policy discussions and decisions. Locking them out of the conversation has been devastating to the industrial base. The product and systems oriented industrial base have been and will continue to be Engineering based.
9. There was a huge shift away from basic systems thinking as focus was placed entirely on finance and self-interest where the belief surfaced that the greatest profits and self-interest would lead to the greatest good. We once again know that is a fantasy and a path that eventually leads to disaster. (2x)
10. When President Johnson was interviewed by Walter Cronkite during the Apollo 11 Moon Landing Walter Cronkite specifically asked President Johnson his thoughts on the new Management Techniques and Systems Engineering that were developed and how they might be applied broader to industry. Having lived through that time I know that they were adopted and used across the spectrum of industry up until approximately the mid 1990's when they were replaced by the new MBA generation ideas and techniques. Systems engineering and the new management techniques that are now old need to be reinvigorated. There are systems engineering programs growing at the University level but once again government policy is needed to ensure that this investment is not lost. (2x)
11. It is critical that the government not accept practices of faster better cheaper for the sole purpose of hiding the true costs of systems development, maintenance, and operations. This can only happen if the government relies on the foundation of education coming from engineering and science-based

Universities and companies. The age of snake oil salespeople selling a quick fix tool and or process never goes away and the government must always be vigilant and ensure that those seeds never sprout. At the same time the government should encourage innovation. This is difficult with so much of the industrial base centered on services contract staff with no connection to product development, manufacturing, or technology development. Somehow service staff employees need to be bought back into the reality loop via effective government policy mechanisms. (2x)

12. All service contracts need to include requirements to encourage and reward service contract employees that contribute to and or develop new products and or technology.
13. All product and or technology developed during the execution of a services contract is jointly owned by the originating employee or employees and the company. The ownership split is determined by the service contract requirements. It is recognized that no one will participate unless the split is in the favor of the originators. The company can reduce their split, if they desire, as it competes for talent.
14. The product, products, technology, technologies may be sold or licensed to other entities and markets outside the government. This translates to government investment that is then spun off to the non-government commercial industrial base and economy.
15. Having thousands of service contracts that are constantly expiring is a great employment mechanism for contract administrators but a complete disaster for employees and companies that want to produce products and technologies. Unfortunately, significant organizational knowledge has been lost on how to avoid this grossly inefficient system on the way to privatization. There needs to be research into the past to determine how government previously operated especially in civilian high technology areas such as the FAA, NASA, etc.
16. The Federal Government must stop the practice of lowest bidder to justify lowest costs at the cost of the worker. Money must be put back into the Overhead items. Yes, the costs will be higher than the costs of a civil service organization because there is management overhead associated with administration and control on both ends and there is a fee (profit) that must be paid. However, we now have to fix the damage and move forward with a new system.
17. There should be no large service companies deriving more than 50% of their revenues from government services. They need to figure it out - merge, invest, do something to engage in the economy and grow it. No one will do this voluntarily so legislation may be needed for companies to wean themselves off government funds. Legislation must be passed so that after 5 years no entity can derive more than 50% of its earnings from the

government unless it is less than 200 employees where 50% are highly experienced or end of career workers or 100% employee owned.

18. Money and compensation are much simpler to manage today than 30 years ago when entities were conceived where their only purpose was to print pay checks. The Government must establish a mechanism that cannot be compromised where people can directly bill the government for services they provide. The system must ensure that nepotism and conflicts of interest are detected and properly addressed.
19. The US Government needs to be De-Privatized. President Reagan called for smaller and less intrusive government. Instead it has been privatized with trillions of taxpayer dollars wasted as vested interests just enabled the flow of money into a select few with little regard for any serious investments in the economy. As a result, the industrial base has been severely damaged with symptoms throughout the population of economic hardships.
20. The last time the government was reorganized was in the late 1950's and early 1960's. As the path to De-Privatization is set the government needs to be reorganized to meet the needs of the 21st century. This will not happen overnight and will take time to correct the path that took decades to get us to this point of severe dysfunction and lost opportunities.
21. As the economy has struggled and new threats have surfaced a new security state apparatus has surfaced that is privatized. History teaches that such trends are very dangerous as accountability gets lost and freedoms disappear in the name of security but actually driven by revenues and profits. The security apparatus should be the first to be De-Privatized. The responsibility for protecting citizens clearly rests with the government and not private companies with no other revenue streams other than taxpayer dollars.
22. NASA was able to send humans to the Moon in 1969. To accomplish this 400,000 people worked on the program and 20,000 companies were involved in the effort. This effort involved developing new technologies and engineering systems that transformed our world using new materials, machines, management techniques, new systems and space age products. This was an example of a balance between government, industry, and academia – a magic mixture. That mixture does not exist today because of the privatization efforts of the past few decades. When examining the De-Privatization of the government, this history needs to be studied to find a reasonable path forward. (3x)

Universities and Colleges

23. All services contracts must allocate reasonable funding to support education reimbursement. (2x)

24. The reimbursement level must be such that a student can complete a degree in the minimum amount of time and not be limited because of funding constraints.
25. Life is complex and even more complex when employees work and go to school. All service contracts must allocate reasonable funding to support an effective employee assistance program.
26. In no instance shall these overhead items be used to discriminate between different vendor cost proposals. (2x)
27. There was a huge shift away from basic systems thinking as focus was placed entirely on finance and self-interest where the belief surfaced that the greatest profits and self-interest would lead to the greatest good. We once again know that is a fantasy and a path that eventually leads to disaster. (2x)
28. It has been acknowledged within many academic circles that the huge movement of MBA staff into board rooms as a result of the massive number of MBA degrees in the 1980's has caused serious damage. While MBA staffs are great at executing business activities, they have no vision. The vision comes from the engineers and they need to return back to the board rooms. As a result, many Universities have introduced entrepreneur programs specifically to get engineers into the board rooms of major companies. However, they are acting alone, and it is unclear how this can happen without major policy from the government. The government needs to investigate how to help shift away from the previous model to the new model the universities have adopted.
29. It is critical that the government not accept practices of faster better cheaper for the sole purpose of hiding the true costs of systems development, maintenance, and operations. This can only happen if the government relies on the foundation of education coming from engineering and science-based Universities and companies. The age of snake oil salespeople selling a quick fix tool and or process never goes away and the government must always be vigilant and ensure that those seeds never sprout. At the same time the government should encourage innovation. This is difficult with so much of the industrial base centered on services contract staff with no connection to product development, manufacturing, or technology development. Somehow service staff employees need to be bought back into the reality loop via effective government policy mechanisms. (2x)
30. Everyone needs to understand that there is a huge difference between a Government Organization and a Private Company. Basic civics education needs to be made part of all levels of the educational system from elementary school to the college and university levels. It is outrageous to have adults with significant educational backgrounds not know and understand the difference between government and industry or know that government can accomplish certain things that are impossible for industry

to accomplish alone and that industry should not even be given those burdens. (2x)

31. NASA was able to send humans to the Moon in 1969. To accomplish this 400,000 people worked on the program and 20,000 companies were involved in the effort. This effort involved developing new technologies and engineering systems that transformed our world using new materials, machines, management techniques, new systems and space age products. This was an example of a balance between government, industry, and academia – a magic mixture. That mixture does not exist today because of the privatization efforts of the past few decades. When examining the De-Privatization of the government, this history needs to be studied to find a reasonable path forward. (3x)

Air Transportation

32. The first recommendation is to provide an air transportation system that serves the entire USA from commerce and citizen needs perspectives.
33. The second recommendation is to ensure not only safe but comfortable transportation in the passenger cabin.
34. The third recommendation is to address the negative effects of TSA on the traveling public and the airport infrastructure.
35. The fourth recommendation is to start doing some real systems engineering to maximize the performance of the system.
36. The FAA role must be expanded to include some old functions performed by the defunct CAB and some new functions to deal with the unintended consequences of deregulation and recent security challenges:
    a) Regulate air transportation routes and ensure reasonable prices for unprofitable routes.
    b) Ensure community requested routes are provided to all commercial airports.
    c) Prohibit unequal pricing based on gambling concepts (random unequal pricing).
    d) Prohibit hidden fees that are part of normal travel (baggage, cancelations, changes, etc.).
    e) Require mutual aid agreements between all air carriers.
    f) Remove antitrust immunity on all air carriers.
    g) Encourage establishment of new airlines.
    h) Always expedite processing of various requests.
    i) Ensure passenger cabin safety and comfort.
    j) Provide guidelines to TSA to re-establish normal airport operations.
    k) Remove prison camp mentality re-establish architectural travel wonders of our airports.

l) Assume a new role of Systems Engineering for the Air Travel Transportation system.

FAA

37. Fix the FAA R&D program so that the FAA can do what it needs to do for NextGen and long after NextGen - all the future programs in the next 100 years.
38. Provide proper FAA R&D funds normally associated with such organizations.
39. Provide proper funds to rebuild the FAA certification capability. This includes hiring career industry international resources with proper education and experience backgrounds.
40. Fix the human resources organization by removing elements that attempted to allow for FAA privatization that instead severely damaged the workforce and industrial base.
41. Retitle all employees directly paid by the government to remove any business implications such as COO, Vice Presidents, etc. This is not a company; it is a nation state government organization.
42. Fix the systems engineering elements within the FAA with a proper education and training program.
43. Refocus the FAA away from just operations and safety to also ensuring a proper high-quality Air Traffic Control system, Industrial Base, and Air Transportation system, it's about commerce.
44. To deal with any future attempts to harm the FAA with privatization schemes the next budget cycle legislation should include the following:
    a. If the FAA is privatized, the trust fund tax ceases immediately and its balance transfers to the taxpayer.
    b. If the FAA is privatized, the taxpayers are reimbursed for all tangible and intangible assets as identified in the analysis in this text.
    c. If the FAA is privatized, the taxpayers are reimbursed for all costs since 1926. Reimburse the trillion dollars to the taxpayer, period.

Privatized Workers

45. All future legislation that allows civil servants to be compensated after a shutdown must include their privatized counterparts who work side by side everyday as part of the United States of America government functions. The reasons include breach of contract, unequal treatment under the law, preserve the rule of law by not violating precedent set by Ruth Bader Ginsburg in Charles E. Morito vs IRS care giver deduction 10th Circuit 1972 and it is the right thing to do.

46. An investigation of previous shutdowns must be performed to determine how previous shutdowns affected the privatized workforce and if needed they must be compensated for their lost income and harm since 1988.
47. Legislation must be provided to ensure that such gross injustice does not occur in the future.
48. This must happen immediately. It's not that complex. Essentially each contract for privatized workers is automatically updated to include a new payment associated with the shutdown.
49. Automatically reimbursing privatized workers after a government shutdown should be added to the body of law for future shutdowns.
50. As we pursued the path of privatization beginning in 1987 no one really bothered to investigate the role of government and industry. Basic civics class 101 was never considered. This analysis needs to happen, and future policy needs to be established to correct this serious problem that leads to constant budget standoffs and government shutdowns that penalize one group of workers while preserving another group of workers.

Federal Government

51. The recommendations for fixing the government include the same recommendations suggested for fixing the Industrial Base, Colleges and Universities, Air Transportation and the FAA.
52. The most fundamental recommendation is to pass legislation so that no entity can receive more than 50% of their earnings from government unless they are a nonprofit or less than 200 employees.
53. It is critical that the process of De-Privatization start immediately. The new privatized companies need to merge with viable consumer and or industrial companies responding to real market needs.
54. The citizens need to be told that privatization has been pushed into the government without their full knowledge and that they need to decide what to do moving forward.
55. The congress needs to stop doing what hidden interests want especially because of campaign contributions. This is a democracy where all the people must be represented, or it will collapse. The democracy is key because when someone claims that this is a republic that immediately justifies the actions of hidden interests. This is a form of bribery and tyranny. It is taxation without representation.
56. Everyone needs to understand that there is a huge difference between a Government Organization and a Private Company. Basic civics education needs to be made part of all levels of the educational system from elementary school to the college and university levels. It is outrageous to have adults with significant educational backgrounds not know and understand the difference between government and industry or know that

government can accomplish certain things that are impossible for industry to accomplish alone and that industry should not even be given those burdens. (2x)

57. A massive education effort needs to show everyone how and why US government was founded, how it operates, the responsibility of the citizens, and the dangers of hidden interests that want to destroy the system of government that is this Democracy implemented as a Republic.
58. NASA was able to send humans to the Moon in 1969. To accomplish this 400,000 people worked on the program and 20,000 companies were involved in the effort. This effort involved developing new technologies and engineering systems that transformed our world using new materials, machines, management techniques, new systems and space age products. This was an example of a balance between government, industry, and academia – a magic mixture. That mixture does not exist today because of the privatization efforts of the past few decades. When examining the De-Privatization of the government, this history needs to be studied to find a reasonable path forward. (3x)

I know that there was repetition in the above list. That repetition suggests the deep scars in the system that must be healed for this new century.

11.4 Conclusion

Not everyone may agree with the findings and recommendations offered in this text. However, we all should agree that the broad policy decision of privatization should be closely reexamined. We also should agree that having a systems perspective on all major decisions especially policy decisions may help to make and maintain a brighter future in this new century.

History will not look favorably on the system that is privatization nor will it treat the leaders and policy makers during this time favorably. Evidence existed that the system was bad and needed fixing almost from the start and yet the people were forced to live with this terrible system. We examined the following:

1. **Privatization Recent History.** There are two presidential executive orders and a report that allowed for the privatization of a large portion of the federal civil service. This system change began in 1987. The electorate was never informed of this agenda which came from the political libertarian movement and used by companies unable to perform in the free market to tap into tax dollars for their benefit.
2. **Industrial Base.** There is now evidence to show that privatization has led to damage to the industrial base. There is serious damage to the workers with five generations in the workforce for the first time in history. There is loss of creativity and innovation with the loss of ability to perform research, development, and establish new products as taxpayer funds were syphoned off

to the new services companies. We also may be losing systems from the broad industrial base that we may regret in the future.

3. **Universities and Colleges.** There is now evidence to show that privatization has led to damage to colleges and universities because the pool of available master's and undergraduate degree students has been reduced. The new privatized companies do not have those overhead funds. This has led to loss of financial commitment from the broader social fabric for educating the next generation to the highest levels possible.
4. **Air Transportation.** The current state of US Air Travel is not good. Everyone knows this yet nothing is happening to correct the situation. The decline in quality of air travel services has taken decades but now we have reached a point where the system is in serious trouble. This is a direct result of shutting down the CAB and not moving the functions into another government organization but instead moving it out as part of privatization to the airlines.
5. **FAA Privatization.** The effort to fully privatize the FAA is a decade's long battle that traces back to the Air Traffic Controllers strike in 1981. The FAA mission is huge and complex. It has been compromised by privatization and it needs to be fixed. The Boeing B737 MAX has been grounded for a very long time and it is a direct result of privatization.
6. **Privatized Workers.** In 2018-2019 the United States Government had another shutdown due to budget issues directly related to the role of government. A key stakeholder was left out of the entire shutdown and recovery activities, the new privatized workforce. The impacts of the shutdowns on the existing privatized workforce are huge. This issue has been fully ignored by all parties and our laws have not been enforced.
7. **Federal Government.** There is now evidence to show that privatization has led to serious harm to US Citizens. This includes systemic government shutdowns, chaos in the defense industry, privatized security clearance investigations that failed and gravely compromised citizens, a presidential impeachment, and a privatized military that is now engaged in the longest war in US history.

This book offered different systems perspectives on privatization and some potential fixes. It offered how we may have arrived here. However, there is a bigger picture that ties all this together and it is the root cause of the systemic breakdown.

Privatization as a system cannot be decoupled from deregulation as a system. Deregulation was not discussed in this book, but it is the undercurrent flowing throughout the text. Both are the result of the Reagan revolution of trying to deal with the perceived problems of the 1970's. It was a reaction to the threats that seemed to surface from nowhere. The reality is these threats did not come from a dark hole; they were natural as the world finally started to dig itself out of the WWII disaster. Japan was selling the US great automobiles, televisions, and stereos. Other countries were also having an impact on the US industrial base[242].

The policy approach, born from panic and misunderstanding of the systemic changes across the planet, was to move everything in the US to standalone profit centers with the thought that maximizing profits would maximize efficiency and provide for the best products and services. The words that were used were "The magic hand of the market" would make everything work.

This was a very naïve view and rejected the US tradition of common sense and systems thinking as embodied in everything starting with the highest level, the US government as a system of governance. Magic and faith have a role in human affairs but not at the expense of working systems. This policy broke working systems found in the new high-tech industries and empowered the failed old rust belt industry systems[243].

The original Reagan Revolution as a system vision was gamed and failed.

- **Government did not get smaller it was privatized.** It is bigger than ever and now government and corporations have become one. This is taxation without representation.
- **Individuals were not empowered.** Empowerment of the individual has gone in the opposite direction. People have less power today across the board to influence decisions and their lives. Examples include franchising of small family businesses to removal of budget authority from working staff everywhere. Go ahead, try to get information from the government that is now in the hands of a privatized contractor.
- **We don't have less management.** Management is seen as the magic bullet somehow directing the most educated, engaged, self-actuated generation in history. All that exists is intimidation, employee non-disclosure agreements, employee non-compete agreements, damage control, and talking points.
- **We don't have common sense and systems thinking.** Abandoned are common sense and systems thinking in all areas of industry as the system was gammed to maximize executive compensation.[244]
- **Tax revenues were not reduced.** The tax revenues were targeted as a new market and were opened to an exclusive club of new services companies that know how to manipulate the system for their advantage.

The price has been enormous, and it is the loss of creativity, innovation and invention in every aspect of society but mostly from the high-tech industries. We have converted our traditional high-tech beacons of leadership into rust belt feeble

---

[242] I lived through this time. This is my personal experience.

[243] Sustainable development Possible with Creative Systems Engineering, Walter Sobkiw, 2008. Sorry for the self-reference.

[244] This is now clearly stated in the popular media of 2019.

attempts to make money, now, and for me, not you. The promise of the Internet is gone as massive monopolies have surfaced and control the entire system.

Once again, the question is how did we get here?

By 1987 it was clear that deregulation was showing signs of failure. The popular media via movies, newspapers, magazines, and books had story after story showing people rigging the system so that they could amass vast amounts of money. But there was no incentive to revisit deregulation. Instead politicians engaged in more and more Bullshit[245] to further the agenda of a new rising elite with serious money to get what they wanted which was more deregulation.

Unfortunately, as the battle raged between deregulation and doing something else, privatization became a major policy. Privatization was not visible to the general population in the same way as deregulation so there was little popular media coverage and even less citizen engagement on privatization. So, here we sit. Those who are protecting a broken system and those who are trying to save the system from itself before it is too late.

There is a broad systemic breakdown as a result of privatization. Extremely negative unintended system consequences surfaced, and they must be addressed. This will not be an easy fix and what took decades to unfold will take years to fix, but the systems must be fixed if we are to move forward in this new century.

There is always a system. The system may be good or bad. The problem is when people must live with a bad system because there is no ability to modify or change it for the better. The previous generations changed their systems. The current generation must learn that again and change the failed privatization system.

The previous generations did not have the luxury of computers, systems practices like modeling and even the luxury of people to think about things from systems engineering perspectives. They had to live through it and then make changes along the way. The current generation has these tools and should never have to live through systemic blunders. They must learn to modify their systems at the first sign that there are negative unintended consequences.

Before you get too depressed remember that Hope Springs Eternal. However, hope is not a plan and resulting action. It's bad but fixable and that is the challenge for this new generation. Remember to have fun each day and don't let the bad get you down.

---

[245] On Bullshit, Harry G. Frankfurt, Princeton University Press, January 2005, ISBN 9780691122946.

Bibliography

Privatization

1. Boeing 737 MAX Flight Control System Joint Authorities Technical Review Observations, Findings, and Recommendations (JATR), Submitted to the Associate Administrator for Aviation Safety, U.S. Federal Aviation Administration Oct 11, 2019.
2. Circular A-76 Performance of Commercial Activities, Implements Public Law 105-270, US Government, Executive Office of The President Office of Management and Budget, August 4, 1983, Revised 1999.
3. Executive Order No. 12607 President's Commission on Privatization, US Government, President Ronald Reagan, September 2, 1987.
4. Executive Order No. 12803 Infrastructure Privatization, US Government, President George Herbert Walker Bush, April 30, 1992.
5. FAA Historical Chronology 1926-1996, Civil Aviation and Federal Government, Federal Aviation Administration, 1996.
6. FAA Historical Chronology 1997-2016, Civil Aviation and Federal Government, Federal Aviation Administration, 1997.
7. PRIVATIZATION: Toward More Effective Government, Response to Executive Order No. 12607, President's Commission on Privatization, March 18, 1988.
8. Public Law 105-270, Federal Activities Inventory Reform (FAIR) Act of 1998, US Government, 105th Congress, October 19, 1998.
9. Report to the Chairman, Committee on National Security, House of Representatives, April 1997 Cooperative Threat Reduction, Status of Defense Conversion Efforts in the Former Soviet Union, GAO/NSIAD-97-101.
10. Reshaping an Industry: Lockheed Martin's Survival Story, Norman R. Augustine, Harvard Business Review, May–June 1997 Issue.
11. The Trump-Ukraine Impeachment Inquiry Report, House Committee on Foreign Affairs, December 2019.
12. Transforming Government Through Privatization, Annual Privatization Report 2006, 20th Anniversary Edition, Reason Foundation.

Popular Media

13. A tiny pharmacy is identifying big problems with common drugs, including Zantac, The Washington Post, Carolyn Y. Johnson, November 8, 2019.
14. Al Gore Reinventions Created USIS's Outsourced Vettings, Bloomberg, Nick Taborek,
15. Boeing Had Too Much Sway in Vetting Own Jets, FAA Was Told, Bloomberg, Peter Robison, and Alan Levin, March 17, 2019.
16. Boeing's 737 Max Software Outsourced to $9-an-Hour Engineers, Bloomberg, Peter Robison, June 28, 2019.
17. Boeing's fix tames the 'tiger' in the 737 MAX flight controls, say experts and critics, Dominic Gates, Seattle Times, Nov. 17, 2019.
18. FAA misled Congress on inspector training for Boeing 737 Max, investigators say, Washington Post, Michael Laris, September 23, 2019.

19. FAA's Lax Oversight Played Part in Boeing 737 Max Crashes, But Agency Is Pushing To Become More Industry-Friendly, Washington Post, Michael Laris, Ian Duncan Lori Aratani, Oct. 28, 2019.
20. Firm that did background check on Snowden is under investigation, The Washington Post, Joe Davidson, June 20, 2013.
21. Flawed analysis, failed oversight: How Boeing, FAA certified the suspect 737 MAX flight control system, Seattle Times, Dominic Gates aerospace reporter, March 17, 2019.
22. Flying the Boeing 737 Max 8: A pilot's view from inside the cockpit, Washington Post, Todd C. Frankel, March 17, 2019.
23. How the Boeing 737 Max safety system differs from others, USA TODAY, George Petras, March 11, 2019.
24. How the FAA Allows Jetmakers To Self Certify That Planes Meet U.S. Safety Requirements, Washington Post, Aaron C. Davis, Marina Lopes, March 15, 2019.
25. June 24, 2013.
26. Justice Department says USIS submitted 665,000 incomplete background checks, The Washington Post, Tom Hamburger and Debbi Wilgoren, January 23, 2014.
27. Major DHS contractor hit by cyberattack, The Hill, Julian Hattem, August 6, 2014.
28. Millennials, Gen Xers to baby boomers: Can you retire so I can get a job promotion, Paul Davidson, USA TODAY, November 7, 2019.
29. Must Reads: How a 50-year-old design came back to haunt Boeing with its troubled 737 Max jet, Los Angeles Times, Ralph Vartabedian, March 15, 2019.
30. Not Expecting Back Pay, Government Contractors Collect Unemployment, Dip into Savings, NPR, January 7, 2019.
31. NSA leaker Snowden's clearance had 'problems'; firm that vetted him under probe, The Washington Times, Shaun Waterman, June 21, 2013.
32. Same firm checked background of Navy Yard shooter, Snowden, Reuters, Tabassum Zakaria, September 19, 2013.
33. The Trap What Happened to Our Dream of Freedom, BBC Documentary, Adam Curtis, March 2007.
34. The whistleblower who exposed U.S.'s flawed security clearance system finally gets his reward, The Washington Post, Christian Davenport, December 18, 2015.
35. U.S. Homeland Security contractor reports computer breach, Reuters, Eric Walsh, August 6, 2014.
36. United Airlines CEO: By the time you sit on our planes, 'you're just pissed at the world' David Oliver, USA TODAY Published 9:18 a.m. ET April 25, 2019.
37. Washington Monthly, Terminal Sickness, by Phillip Longman and Lina Khan, March / April 2012.
38. Watchdog faults background check of NSA leaker, Associated Press, Richard Lardner and Kimberly Dozier, June 20, 2013.

Legislation

39. H.R.2997 - 21st Century Aviation Innovation, Reform, and Reauthorization Act or 21st Century AIRR Act, 115th Congress (2017-2018).
40. H.R.339 - Low-Wage Federal Contractor Employee Back Pay Act of 2019, 116th Congress (2019-2020).
41. H.R.4441 - Aviation Innovation, Reform, and Reauthorization Act of 2016, 114th Congress (2015-2016).

42. H.R.755 Articles of Impeachment, 116th CONGRESS, 1st Session, Dec 10, 2019.
43. H.R.824 - Fairness for Federal Contractors Act of 2019, 116th Congress (2019-2020).
44. S.162 - Fair Compensation for Low-Wage Contractor Employees Act of 2019, 116th Congress (2019-2020).
45. S.24 - Government Employee Fair Treatment Act of 2019, 116th Congress (2019-2020).

Systems Perspectives

46. A Theory of Human Motivation, Psychological Review 50(4), A.H. Maslow, 1943.
47. Department of Transportation, Human Factors Coordinating Committee, Research and Special Programs Administration, July 2003.
48. Earth Days, Documentary Film, December 2009.
49. Federal Aviation Administration, "Response to Congressional Recommendations Regarding the FM's En Route Air Traffic Control Computer System", report to the Senate and House Appropriations Committees pursuant to Senate report 96-932, DOT/FAA/ AAP-823, January 1982.
50. Federal-Aid Highway Act of 1956 also known as National Interstate and Defense Highways Act of 1956.
51. Fundamentals of Physics, David Halliday and Robert Resnick, John Wiley & Sons Inc; Revised edition (January 1, 1974), ISBN: 0471344311
52. Generic TRL descriptions found in NPR 7123.1, NASA Systems Engineering Processes and Requirements, Table G-19.
53. Harvard University by Charles Czeisler, M.D., Ph.D. and associates. William J. Cromie, Human Biological Clock Set Back an Hour, The Harvard University Gazzette, 1999.
54. How I Became a Quant: Insights from 25 of Wall Street's Elite, Richard R. Lindsey, Wiley, 2009 ISBN 0470452579.
55. Human Engineering Design Criteria, DOD, MIL-STD-1472C May 1981, MIL-STD-1472D March 1989, MIL-STD-1472E October 1996, MIL-STD-1472F August 1999.
56. Human Information Processing, Peter H. Lindsay, Donald A. Norman, Academic Press, 1977.
57. Improving R&D Productivity A Study Program and Its Applications, Robert M Ranftl, National Conference on Productivity and Effectiveness in Educational Research and Development, December 1977.
58. Mackay, Charles (1841), Memoirs of Extraordinary Popular Delusions and the Madness of Crowds
59. Military Standard Procedures For Performing A Failure Mode, Effects And Criticality Analysis, MIL-STD-1629a, 24 November 1980,.
60. Modern Control Systems, Richard C. Dorf, Addison-Wesley Publishing Company, 1967, 1974, Library of Congress CCN 67-15660, ISBN 0201016060.
61. Motivation and Personality, Abraham Harold Maslow, HarperCollins Publishers, 1954, 3d Sub edition January 1987, ISBN 0060419873.
62. My Life as a Quant: Reflections on Physics and Finance, Emanuel Derman, Wiley, 2007, SBN 0470192739.
63. NASA Systems Engineering Handbook, NASA/SP-2007-6105 Rev1, National Aeronautics and Space Administration NASA Headquarters Washington, D.C. 20546, December 2007.
64. On Bullshit, Harry G. Frankfurt, Princeton University Press, January 2005, ISBN 9780691122946.

65. Our Common Future, also known as Brundtland Report, Brundtland Commission, United Nations, 1987.
66. Physical and Quantum Electronics Series, Demetrius T. Paris, F. Kenneth Hard, McGraw-Hill Book Company, 1969, Library of Congress CCN 68-8775, ISBN 070484708.
67. R&D Productivity Second Edition; Hughes Aircraft, June 1978, AD Number A075387, Ranftl, R.M., Carver City, CA Hughes Aircraft Co., Second Edition, 1978, OCLC Number 4224641 or 16945892. ASIN B000716B96.
68. Review of the FAA 1982 National Airspace System Plan, August 1982, NTIS order #PB83-102772. Library of Congress Catalog Card Number 82-600595, U.S. Government Printing Office, Washington, D.C.
69. Review of the FAA 1982 National Airspace System Plan, August 1982, NTIS order #PB83-102772. Library of Congress Catalog Card Number 82-600595, U.S. Government Printing Office, Washington, D.C.
70. Science The Endless Frontier, A Report to the President by Vannevar Bush, Director of the Office of Scientific Research and Development, July 1945.
71. Sequential Thematic Organization of Publications (STOP), Hughes Aircraft Fullerton, 1963.
72. Software Development And Documentation, MIL-STD-498, Military Standard, 5 December 1994.
73. Strategic Management: A stakeholder approach, Freeman, R. Edward, Pitman Publishing, 1984, ISBN 0273019139.
74. System Safety, DOD Standard Practice, MIL-STD-882E, 11 May 2012.
75. Technical Reviews And Audits Systems Equipments And Computer Software, MIL-STD-1521A June 1976, MIL-STD-1521B June 1995.
76. Technology Readiness Levels (TRLs), NPR 7120.8, NASA Procedural Requirements, NASA Research and Technology Program and Project Management Requirements, February 05, 2008.
77. The Electrical World, A weekly Review of Current Progress in Electricity and Its Practical Applications, Volume 29, WJJC (The W.J. Johnston Company), Library of Princeton University, January 2 to June 26, 1897.
78. The impaired judgement, decision-making, and flying abilities of the captain and flightcrew due to the effects of fatigue: Guantanamo Bay, Cuba involving a DC-8, NTSB report probable cause, NTSB, August 18, 1993.
79. The Organism, Kurt Goldstein, 1934.
80. The Quants: How a New Breed of Math Whizzes Conquered Wall Street and Nearly Destroyed It, Scott Patterson, Crown Business, 2010, ISBN 0307453375
81. The Rural Electrification Act of 1936, May 20, 1936, S. 3483, Public, No. 605.
82. The Theory of the Leisure Class, An Economic Study of Institutions, Thorstein Bunde Veblen, London Macmillan Publishers, 1899.

Index

www.ingramcontent.com/pod-product-compliance
Ingram Content Group UK Ltd.
Pitfield, Milton Keynes, MK11 3LW, UK
UKHW020223290926
15470UKWH00001B/343

9 780983 25306